E-Business Models, Services, and Communications

In Lee
Western Illinois University, USA

INFORMATION SCIENCE REFERENCE

Hershey · New York

Acquisitions Editor: Kristin Klinger
Development Editor: Kristin Roth
Senior Managing Editor: Jennifer Neidig
Managing Editor: Sara Reed
Copy Editor: Larissa Vinci
Typesetter: Jamie Snavely
Cover Design: Lisa Tosheff
Printed at: Yurchak Printing Inc.

Published in the United States of America by
Information Science Reference (an imprint of IGI Global)
701 E. Chocolate Avenue, Suite 200
Hershey PA 17033
Tel: 717-533-8845
Fax: 717-533-8661
E-mail: cust@igi-pub.com
Web site: http://www.igi-global.com/reference

and in the United Kingdom by
Information Science Reference (an imprint of IGI Global)
3 Henrietta Street
Covent Garden
London WC2E 8LU
Tel: 44 20 7240 0856
Fax: 44 20 7379 0609
Web site: http://www.eurospanonline.com

Library of Congress Cataloging-in-Publication Data

E-business models, services and communications / In Lee, editor.

p. cm.

Summary: "This book provides researchers and practitioners with valuable information on recent advances and developments in emerging e-business models and technologies. It covers a variety of topics such as e-business models, telecommunication network utilization, online consumer behavior, electronic communication adoption and service provider strategies, and privacy policies and implementation issues"—Provided by publisher.

Includes bibliographical references and index.

ISBN-13: 978-1-59904-831-4 (hardcover)

ISBN-13: 978-1-59904-833-8 (ebook)

1. Electronic commerce. I. Lee, In, 1958-

HF5548.32.E17752 2008

658.8'72—dc22

2007024946

British Cataloguing in Publication Data
A Cataloguing in Publication record for this book is available from the British Library.

E-Business Models, Services, and Communications is part of the IGI Global series named *Advances in E-Business Research Series (AEBR)* (ISSN: 1935-2700).

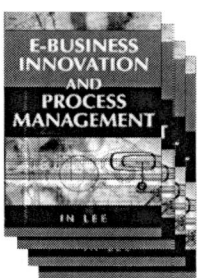

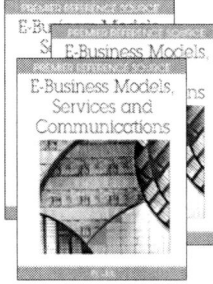

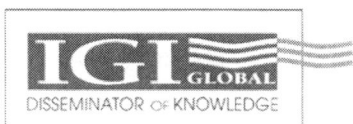

Table of Contents

Detailed Table of Contents

The decreasing cost of IT has encouraged organizations to seek new ways of cooperating with members of the supply chain and other key strategic partners. This increased cooperation is giving rise to a new type of interorganizational system (IOS). Before the advent of the Internet, IS integration required significant investments on the part of organizations participating in an IOS. Such heavy investments, in turn, necessitated close strategic cooperation in the non-IS domain as well. Thus, IS integration went hand-in-hand with non-IS (relational) integration in the pre-Internet era. However, advances in Internet technology have commoditized IS integration to a significant extent, thereby allowing the uncoupling of IS integration and relational integration. It is now possible for organizations to have IS integration without developing strong non-IS linkages. We propose a framework to account for this recent shift and present a typology for classifying interorganizational systems based on the segregation of IS and relational integration. We also verify the typology in case studies of four large firms.

Despite the significant progress made by research into e-business models, the issue of how public sector organisations can successfully make the transition from traditional approaches to e-business by taking advantage of e-technologies has received little attention. This chapter draws on qualitative, longitudinal case-study research carried out between 2001 and 2005 in Britain's national mapping agency to reveal the processes of strategic and organisational transformation engendered by e-business in an organisation evolving from the classical, bureaucratic, and centralised "public sector model" toward a new organisational form through embracing e-business as a corporate philosophy. The study also explores the key components of the new e-business model implemented by the organisation and the contextual factors that impacted on the effectiveness of e-strategy implementation in order to draw a list of best practices for the implementation of e-business in a public sector context.

Most of existing mobile services were designed based on the client/server architecture. Those mobile services neither paid much attention to mobile users' interactions with their environments nor considered the collective efforts between the mobile users in a dynamic peer group. In this chapter, the notion of ambient e-service is so defined as to identify a new scope of mobile e-service, which address dynamic collective efforts between mobile users (enabled by mobile peer-to-peer technology), dynamic interactions with ambient environments (envisioned by location-based service), the moment of value (empowered by wireless technologies), and low cost service provision. The notable features of ambient e-services are the exhilarated linkage based on social context and significantly rapid growth of connections. We also present an ambient e-service framework that characterizes ambient e-services with three dimensions (value stack, environment stack, and technology stack), followed by several exemplars of ambient e-service applications. Moreover, we present the ambient e-service embracing model (ASEM) that addresses the integrated consideration of trust, reputation, and privacy required for fostering the growth of ambient e-services and steers the directions of future fruitful relevant research. The embracing model can also guide the government or service providers to implement the ambient e-service applications that satisfy customers' unique needs under various circumstances.

Network effect indicates that the value of connecting to a network is positively associated with the current number of customers connected to that network. Network effect strengthens the strong firms, weakens the weak firms, and may lead to a winner-take-all market. Thus, managing customer perceived value is crucial in markets with network effects. This chapter models customer perceived value, presents ways to improve the value, and discusses the relationship between customer perceived value and network size. Implications for e-business practitioners are discussed.

Pure Play and Bricks-and-Clicks represent today's two major retailing models. The current study answers four questions comparing the two models in terms of the e-commerce benefits achieved and information systems management practices used to achieve them. It applies a Web-based survey to compare 69 Pure

Plays to 348 Bricks-and-Clicks retailers in terms of the market expansion, customer service, back-end efficiency, inventory management, and cost reduction benefits reaped as well as in terms of the benchmarking, process redesign, and planning practices used. It found market expansion as the top benefit for both types of retailers. Pure plays exceed Bricks-and-Clicks at achieving back-end efficiency, inventory management, and cost reduction benefits. Pure play retailers apply benchmarking to reap their benefits while Bricks-and-Clicks retailers use process redesign and planning to reap theirs. Pure play retailers are better able to utilize benchmarking to realize market expansion and customer service benefits. On the other hand, Bricks-and-Clicks retailers are better able to utilize process redesign to realize inventory management and cost reduction benefits. The findings suggest potential directions for future research as well as electronic retail practice.

The rapid rise of e-business has brought profound impact on, as well as significant challenges to, businesses of all sizes. The lack of anticipated engagement in e-business by small- and medium-sized enterprises (SMEs) is still a concern to the UK government. Findings from the literature appear to have revealed a contradictory picture of SMEs' engagement in e-business. There is limited systematic research into how companies, especially small companies, are adopting the Internet technologies. This book chapter reviews current research on SMEs' e-business adoption by following various adoption models. The chapter examines the driving forces and inhibitors that effect the adoption of e-business technology in SMEs. Through interviews with 40 owner managers in the electronic components industry, the chapter reveals that most of the small firms in this industry are at the lower level of the "e-adoption ladder"—predominantly using the Internet for searching information and e-mail. SMEs in this industry have not yet widely engaged in online transactions. The current level of adoption is driven by both internal and external factors, including operational benefits, industry common practice, and peer pressure. External forces such as a lack of push from suppliers and customers and a lack of strategic vision of using advanced e-business technology for competitive advantages have determinant effects on the level and scale of e-adoption in SME sector.

The Internet has changed the way many companies do business, but has also tended to increase the disparity between firms in developed countries and those in developing countries. As the digital divide seems to grow, the question becomes how will developing countries catch up? We examine two large developing countries, China and India, in an attempt to understand their approaches to developing e-business. While both countries had access to the technology at about the same time, each has taken a different path to utilizing it. These approaches are based on a number of factors, including government initiatives and focus, infrastructure building, experience and understanding of business operations, and culture, among others. China appears to be ahead of India in the mechanics and infrastructure, but India is ahead in e-readiness. Both countries are poised for rapidly increasing e-business, however, they have huge problems of poverty and inequality between urban and rural connectivity that must be resolved to take advantage of e-business.

This research explores inter-organizational collaboration in business-to-business e-commerce and the factors that influence its development in a unique Australian environment. Using a qualitative case study approach, seven informants from four Tasmanian organisations were interviewed. The data confirmed trust was an important prerequisite for the establishment and development of both electronic and traditional inter-organisational relationships. Collaborative relations such as communication and repeated interactions facilitated the development of trading partner trust. Interestingly, trading partner size did not influence trading partner trust, although "volume of business conducted" between trading partners was an influencing factor. Other factors included trading partner reputation and length of pre-existing relationship. Perceived benefits of trading partner trust included general business efficiencies, business growth, faster payment, increased information sharing and confidence, improved business relations, delivery, and reliability. The results enhance organisational awareness of similarities and differences between traditional and electronic business-to-business trading relationships, and contribute to the growing body of knowledge on inter-organisational trust and business-to-business e-commerce. The influence of the unique Tasmanian environment was acknowledged and discussed as a mediating variable in considering the findings.

There are a multitude of benefits and challenges that can be derived from the convergence of two major current technologies: (a) Web services (WS)—technology that allows application development and integration using the service-oriented computing paradigm; and (b) E-business systems—using the Internet as the basis for interacting with customers, suppliers, and other business partners. This combination called WS-based e-business systems promises to provide a dynamic e-business environment. We investigate the existing deployment barriers for such an environment from the perspectives of the three WS stakeholders, namely the service providers, service consumers, and the WS standards organizations and presents a challenges framework that organizes and interrelates these barriers in an easily understandable manner to help study further the factors that impact the deployment and use of WS within e-business.

Using this framework, we analyze WS incorporation challenges for small- and medium-sized enterprises (SMEs) since they are a vital engine driving the world economy, and are realizing significant benefits from adoption and implementation of Internet-based business solutions. WS-based e-business system applications promise to do even more for them.

Chapter X
Modelling in Clinical Practice with Web Services and BPEL /
Iain Morrison, Bryn Lewis, and Sony Nugrahanto 209

The aim of increasing the quality of healthcare has led to the development of a number of "guideline" systems whereby clinicians receive assistance in decision making in a given care context—for example in areas such as prescribing or therapeutics. These guidelines range in complexity and functionality from simple textual references through to executable modules, which can subsume some of the clinical decision making process. In the latter case, ensuring consistent and interoperable engagement between the guideline engine, clinical information system, and patient record can become problematic. Critical areas include vocabulary and terminology (in differing use contexts) and the interfaces and interaction between different sub-systems where traditional approaches have been focused on tightly coupling of sub-systems and in the generation of special purpose "glue" languages and logic. In this chapter, we briefly describe an approach to clinical, information, and service modelling. This approach uses tools and techniques gaining increasing acceptance in the e-commerce domain, which shares many of the technical and interoperability problems present in e-health.

Chapter XI
Assessing the Potential Impact of Web Services on Business Processes /
Jan-Hendrik Sewing, Michael Rosemann, Marlon Dumas, and Marcello La Rosa 222

Though Web services offer unique opportunities for the design of new business processes, the assessment of the potential impact of Web services on existing business information systems is often reduced to technical aspects. This chapter proposes a four-phase methodology, which facilitates the evaluation of the potential use of Web services on business information systems both from a technical and from a strategic viewpoint. It is based on business process models, which are used to frame the adoption and deployment of Web services and to assess their impact on existing business processes. The application of this methodology is described using a procurement scenario.

Chapter XII
Web Service Orchestration and Choreography: Enabling Business Processes on the Web /
Florian Daniel and Barbara Pernici 251

The Web service domain is a fast growing and fast changing environment. From a business perspective, the trend over the last few years in the Web services area firmly points toward seamless business logic integration and inter-enterprise collaboration. However, in order to accomplish such goals, both technological and conceptual advances are required. Some already have proven their viability; others still have to be made. Among them, Web service orchestration and choreography are of crucial importance, but still lack a widely agreed on development framework comprising both technological and conceptual aspects.In this chapter, we try to provide a critical snapshot of current standards for Web service development and particularly we focus on Web service orchestration and choreography. We discuss problems and solutions from a conceptual point of view, exemplify the illustrated ideas by means of real-world technologies and standards, and highlight the mutual dependencies that exist among orchestration and choreography of Web services.

Chapter XIII
Metering and Accounting for Service-Oriented Computing /
Arun Kumar, Vikas Agarwal, and Neeran Karnik 275

Distributed systems of today have evolved from tightly coupled architectures such as CORBA and DCOM to loosely coupled service-oriented architectures such as Web services. The success of such architectures depends upon availability of supporting functions such as security, systems management, service level agreements, and development environments with associated tooling. An important management component of such an infrastructure is the metering and accounting for service usage which is essential for successful deployments in commercial environments. This chapter explores the problem space and presents an architecture that addresses this need. We start by defining taxonomy of services from the perspective of usage metering, charging, and business models. We discuss how service usage can be measured, aggregated, and communicated in a uniform way. Finally, we report on a prototype design and implementation.

Section IV
Online Consumer Behavior

Chapter XIV
Effects of Web-Based Customer Relationship Management on Customer Satisfaction:
A Structual Equation Modeling Analysis /
Wen-Jang Jih, Su-Fang Lee, Yuan-Cheng Tsai, and Shyh-Rong Fang 306

This study addresses the effect of e-customer relationship management (e-CRM) practices on online customers' satisfaction with their experience in interacting with the company Web sites. Recognizing the importance of maintaining a healthy relationship with customers, companies are actively seeking ways to enhance the customer value of their offerings through relationship marketing. Since effective managing of customer relationship essentially involves managing customer information flow, Internet technologies have become an important element of a firm's e-CRM program. The company Web site is functioning as the focal point of contact for interacting with existing and prospective customers. An important concern is how the company Website affects customers' overall perception of the Web site. Using the concepts of Internet-mediated market orientation in marketing and user satisfaction in information systems, this study analyzes causal as well as correlation relationships between e-CRM practices and online customer Web site satisfaction. Based on the primary data collected in Taiwan, the study found that e-CRM practices positively impact online customers' Web site satisfaction through their perception of the Web site's customer orientation.

Chapter XV
The Formation of Online Trust / *Anol Bhattacherjee* 325

This study outlines three trust-building processes (relational, calculative, and institutional) that shape individual trust in online firms and describes how these processes change over time as users gain experience with the online firms. It hypothesizes three alternative belief structures resulting from the previous processes as determinants of trust, theorizes the temporal nature of their effects on trust as users observe and learn from the firm's actual behavior, and then empirically tests the hypothesized associations using data collected from a field survey of online banking users. The results indicate that relational, calculative, and institutional beliefs are indeed significant drivers of trust. However, calculative and institutional beliefs have stronger initial effects than relational beliefs for new consumers of online firms. The effect of calculative belief on trust decreases with time, while that of relational beliefs increases and that of institutional beliefs remains relatively unchanged. Research and practical implications of these findings are discussed.

Chapter XVI
The Influence of Familiarity and Security on Decision Making Processes in E-Commerce:
The Role of User Experience / *Fahim Akhter and Wendy Hui* 344

E-commerce can enhance its acceptance among users through fostering online trust, which is vital for decision-making process. The perception and computation of trust is crucial for vendors and users for the success of e-commerce. The calculation and measurement of trust antecedent involves complex aspect such as presence of security controls and familiarity within the Web site. Most companies are acquiring "security technology" because everybody else is doing the same, but not because there has been a proper assessment of its association with trust. The purpose of this paper is to analyze the role of trust antecedents such as security, and familiarity when they are used collectively to do online transactions. Trust, in general, is an important factor in conducting e-transaction, which revolve around uncertainty and ambiguity. The fuzzy logic approach provides a means for coping with this uncertainty and vagueness that are present in e-commerce. Therefore, the fuzzy logic approach is been deployed to develop scales to measure the effects of users' familiarity and perception of security in an online business-to-consumer (B2C) context. This research provides guidelines to vendors on how they could ascertain the trust level of their business and ways of mitigate the negative impact on the trust level.

Section V
Online Intermediaries

Chapter XVII
The Roles of Online Intermediaries in Collective Memory-Supported Electronic Negotiation /
Nongkran Lertpittayapoom and Souren Paul 355

Following the emergence of the Internet, electronic negotiation has become an alternative to face-to-face negotiation. The rise of Web sites such as electronic marketplaces or electronic brokerages also fueled the popularity of electronic negotiation. The current forms of negotiation support systems (NSS)

used to support many electronic negotiations offer very little support for historical negotiation data. In order to address this issue, the idea of a collective memory support in negotiations has been proposed in recent years. This paper highlights the use of an online intermediary as an effective location from which collective memory support can be offered. The paper proposes that an intermediary based collective memory support will increase confidence in negotiation, reduce overall negotiation time, and strengthen trust between negotiators.

The case study showcases "morethailand.com," an e-intermediary in the tourism industry. Based out of Thailand, the firm is in the process of finding a niche for itself through innovative online and offline marketing strategies with the constraint of limited resources. The case study attempts to focus on the e-business challenges in the travel and tourism sector especially in a developing country like Thailand. It specifically highlights the clash between the traditional and modern form of intermediaries in the travel and tourism sector and how it is bound to evolve in the future. A comparison between different approaches to search engine marketing offers an interesting perspective to the literature pertaining to online e-commerce. An economic view on the case is also presented.

Preface

The last few years have seen a phenomenal growth and dramatic changes in the field of e-business technologies and practices. Business organizations have begun to explore the use of emerging technologies such as grid computing, mobile computing, Web services, and Web 2.0. While these new technologies have opened an array of new market and business opportunities, many organizations face numerous technical, managerial, and organizational challenges and still lack reference sources for the e-business development and management. As e-business evolution continues with the emerging technologies and business models, an in-depth understanding of e-business models, services, and consumer behavior proves more valuable than ever before for the successful e-business development and management. *E-Business Models, Services, and Communication (Advances in E-Business Research, Vol. 2)* provides researchers, professionals, and educators with the newest research on e-business trends, technologies, and practices. Forty-six noted researchers from 14 countries have conferred their expertise to this publication. The book consists of eighteen chapters and is divided into five segments: Section I discusses various e-business models and organizations; Section II addresses e-business strategies; Section III evaluates Web services; Section IV investigates online consumer behavior; and Section IV discusses online intermediaries.

Section I: E-Business Models and Organizations consists of four chapters. Chapter I, *Markets, Hierarchies, and the Evolving Nature of Interorganizational Cooperation* by Wonyoung Lee, Praveen Aggarwal, Hyonkil Shin, Taihoon Cha, and Seunghan Kim, proposes a framework to account for a recent shift in IS integration and presents a typology for classifying interorganizational systems based on the segregation of IS and relational integration. The resulting 2x2 matrix provides a fuller array of interorganizational relationships that are emerging in the post-Internet era. This study verifies the typology in case studies of four large firms. The study also found evidence that a single organization can engage in different hierarchical relationships with different vendors.

Chapter II, *Implementing E-Business Models in the Public Services: Challenges, Constraints, and Successful Elements* by Francesca Andreescu, draws on qualitative, longitudinal research carried out between 2001 and 2005 in Britain's National Mapping Agency to reveal the processes of strategic and organisational transformation engendered by e-business in an organisation evolving from the classical, bureaucratic, and centralised "public sector model" toward a new organisational form through embracing e-business as a corporate philosophy. This study also explores the key components of the new e-business model implemented by the organisation and the contextual factors that impacted on the effectiveness of e-strategy implementation in order to draw a list of best practices for the implementation of e-business in a public sector context.

Chapter III, *Ambient E-Service: Applications and Embracing Model* by Yuan-Chu Hwang and Soe-Tsyr Yuan, presents an ambient e-service framework that characterizes ambient e-service with three dimensions, followed by several exemplars of ambient e-service applications. In this chapter, the notion of ambient e-service is so defined as to identify a new scope of mobile e-service, which address dynamic collective efforts between mobile users (enabled by mobile peer-to-peer technology), dynamic interactions with ambient environments (envisioned by location-based service), the moment of value (empowered by wireless technologies), and low cost service provision. The notable features of ambient e-services are the exhilarated linkage based on social context and significantly rapid growth of connections. The ambient e-service embracing model (ASEM) is also proposed to address the integrated consideration of trust, reputation, and privacy required for fostering the growth of ambient e-service.

Chapter IV, *Superior Customer Value and Network Size in Markets Characterized by Network Effects* by Fan-Chen Tseng, Ching-I Teng, and David M. Chiang, models customer perceived value, presents ways to improve the value, and discusses the relationship between customer's perceived value and network size. This study showed that firms can adopt two approaches: increasing customer value and reducing customer costs to delivering superior customer value. This study provides significant insights to firms regarding how to improve customer perceived value.

Section II: E-Business Strategies consists of four chapters. Chapter V, *Pure Play vs. Bricks-and-Clicks: A Study of Their Benefits and Practices* by Youlong Zhuang and Albert L. Lederer, compares Pure Play and Bricks-and-Clicks, two major retailing models, in terms of the e-commerce benefits achieved and information systems management practices used to achieve them. The study found Pure Play retailers apply benchmarking to reap their benefits while Bricks-and-Clicks retailers use process redesign and planning to reap theirs. Pure play retailers are better able to utilize benchmarking to realize market expansion and customer service benefits. On the other hand, Bricks-and-Clicks retailers are better able to utilize process redesign to realize inventory management and cost reduction benefits.

Chapter VI, *Engaging SMEs in E-Business: Insights from an Empirical Study* by Mark Xu, Ravni Rohatgi, and Yanqing Duan, reviews various e-business adoption models and the influential factors affecting the adoption in SMEs. This study empirically examined the adoption level of e-business in a specific industry in the UK, and identified the driving forces and the barriers that push SME up or down the adoption ladder. The current level of adoption is driven by both internal and external factors, including operational benefits, industry common practice, and peer pressure. External forces such as a lack of push from suppliers and customers and a lack of strategic vision of using advanced e-business technology for competitive advantages have determinant effects on the level and scale of e-adoption in SME sector.

Chapter VII, *China and India: E-Business in the Developing World* by Peter Raven, Xiaoqing Huang, and Ben Kim, examines China and India in an attempt to understand their approaches to developing e-business. Each has taken a different path to utilizing the Internet for business. These approaches are based on a number of factors, including government initiatives and focus, infrastructure building, experience and understanding of business operations, and culture, among others. Both countries are poised for rapidly increasing e-business. However, they have huge problems of poverty and inequality between urban and rural connectivity that must be resolved to take advantage of e-business.

Chapter VIII, *Trust and Environment in Inter-Organisational E-Commerce Collaboration* by Amanda Diggles and Carol Pollard, explores inter-organisational collaboration in business-to-business e-commerce with seven informants from four Australian organisations in Tasmania. Using a qualitative case study approach, this research confirmed trust was an important prerequisite for the establishment and development of both electronic and traditional inter-organisational relationships. Collaborative relations such as communication and repeated interactions facilitated the development of trading partner trust. Other factors included trading partner size, reputation and length of pre-existing relationship. Perceived benefits of trading partner trust included general business efficiencies, business growth, faster payment, increased information sharing and confidence, improved business relations, delivery and reliability. The results enhance organisational awareness of similarities and differences between traditional and electronic inter-organisational trading relationships, and contribute to the growing body of knowledge on trust in inter-organisational relationships.

Section III: Web Services consists of five chapters. Chapter IX *Incorporating Web Services into E-Business Systems: An SME Perspective* by Ranjit Bose and Vijayan Sugumaran, investigates the existing deployment barriers from the perspectives of the three Web services (WS) stakeholders, namely the service providers, service consumers, and the WS standards organizations and presents a challenges framework that organizes and interrelates these barriers in an easily understandable manner to help study further the factors that impact the deployment and use of WS within e-business. Using the framework, this study analyzes WS incorporation challenges for small and medium-sized enterprises (SMEs) since they are a vital engine driving the world economy, and are realizing significant benefits from adoption and implementation of Internet-based business solutions. WS-based e-business system applications promise to do even more for them.

Chapter X, *Modelling in Clinical Practice with Web Services and BPEL* by Iain Morrison, Bryn Lewis, and Sony Nugrahanto, briefly describes an approach to clinical information and service modelling. This approach uses tools and techniques gaining increasing acceptance in the e-commerce domain, which shares many of the technical and interoperability problems present in e-Health. The use of BPEL supports services that are provided by both humans and computers. This allows great flexibility in service delivery and deployment, which has been demonstrated in the MCPOP asthma workflow demonstration.

Chapter XI, *Assessing the Potential Impact of Web Services on Business Processes* by Jan-Hendrik Sewing, Michael Rosemann, Marlon Dumas, and Marcello La Rosa, presents a methodology for assessing the suitability of business processes for Web service adoption, both from a strategic and from a technical perspective. It is shown that, by enriching business process models with appropriate metadata, analysts are able to identify which Web services are most relevant for the automation of business processes. The methodology can also be used to assess the impact of new Web services on existing business processes. The application of the methodology is described using a procurement scenario.

Chapter XII, *Web Service Orchestration and Choreography: Enabling Business Processes on the Web* by Florian Daniel and Barbara Pernici, introduces the reader to a relevant aspect of modern, distributed systems in the context of the service-oriented architecture (SOA) (i.e., the distributed execution of composite applications or business processes). This research clarifies the difference between orchestration and choreography, the two main techniques for the definition of service-based collaborations, discusses their most representative approaches, and binds such approaches to a concrete protocol stack. The study provides insight into some advanced service composition problems and, finally, provides our outlook over future trends in the service composition area.

Chapter XIII, *Metering and Accounting for Service-Oriented Computing* by Arun Kumar and Vikas Agarwal, and Neeran Karnik, presents an architecture for enabling usage metering in service-oriented systems. The success of Service-oriented architectures such as Web Services depends upon availability of supporting functions such as security, systems management, service level agreements, etc. Metering and accounting for service usage is one such important management component that is essential for successful deployments in commercial environments. This chapter starts by defining taxonomy of services from the perspective of usage metering, charging, and business models. The study discusses how service usage can be measured, aggregated, and communicated in a uniform way. Finally, it reports on a prototype design and implementation.

Section IV: Online Consumer Behavior consists of three chapters. Chapter XIV, *Effects of Web-Based Customer Relationship Management on Customer Satisfaction: A Structural Equation Modeling Analysis* by Wen-Jang Jih, Su-Fang Lee, Yuan-Cheng Tsai, and Shyh-Rong Fang, seeks to shed some light on how the customer perception of companies' e-CRM practices affects customer satisfaction with these practices. Web-based Internet features are becoming a standard platform for companies to implement their customer relationship management initiatives. Referred to as e-CRM in most professional literature, this practice is still in the infancy stage of its life cycle in terms of our level of understanding. A structural equation modeling analysis with the primary data collected in Taiwan reveals that online customers' perception of e-CRM practices positively impacts customers' Website satisfaction through their perception of the Website's customer orientation.

Chapter XV, *The Formation of Online Trust* by Anol Bhattacherjee, presents three processes (relational, calculative, and institutional) by which consumers form trust in online firms and describes how these processes change over time as they gain experience with online firms. These processes are tested using empirical data from a field survey of online banking users. The results indicate that relational, calculative, and institutional beliefs are indeed significant drivers of trust. However, calculative and institutional beliefs have stronger initial effects than relational beliefs for new consumers of online firms. The effect of calculative belief on trust decreases with time, while that of relational beliefs increases and that of institutional beliefs remains relatively unchanged. Research and practical implications of these findings are discussed.

Chapter XVI, *The Influence of Familiarity and Security on Decision Making Processes in E-Commerce: The Role of User Experience* by Fahim Akhter and Wendy Hui, analyzes the role of trust antecedents such as security and familiarity when they are used collectively to do online transactions. Trust, in general, is an important factor in conducting e-transaction, which revolve around uncertainty and ambiguity. The fuzzy logic approach provides a means for coping with this uncertainty and vagueness that are present in e-commerce. Therefore, in this study, the fuzzy logic approach is been deployed to develop scales to measure the effects of users' familiarity and perception of security in an online business-to-consumer (B2C) context. This research provides guidelines to vendors on how they could ascertain the trust level of their business and ways of mitigate the negative impact on the trust level.

Section V: Online Intermediaries consists of two chapters. Chapter XVII, *The Roles of Online Intermediaries in Collective Memory-Supported Electronic Negotiation* by Nongkran Lertpittayapoom and Souren Paul, highlights the use of an online intermediary as an effective location from which collective memory support can be offered. Electronic negotiation has become an alternative to face-to-face negotiation. The rise of Web sites such as electronic marketplaces or electronic brokerages also fueled the popularity of electronic negotiation. The current forms of negotiation support systems (NSS) used to support many electronic negotiations offer very little support for historical negotiation data. In order to address this issue, the idea of a collective memory support in negotiations has been proposed in recent years. This study proposes that an intermediary based collective memory support will increase confidence in negotiation, reduce overall negotiation time, and strengthen trust between negotiators.

Chapter XVIII, *Morethailand.com: Online Travel Intermediary* by Pongsak Hoontrakul and Sunil Sahadev, showcases "morethailand.com," an e-intermediary in the tourism industry. Based out of Thailand, the firm is in the process of finding a niche for itself through innovative online and offline marketing strategies with the constraint of limited resources. This case study attempts to focus on the e-business challenges in the travel and tourism sector especially in a developing country like Thailand. It specifically highlights the clash between the traditional and modern form of intermediaries in the travel and tourism sector and how it is bound to evolve in the future. A comparison between different approaches to search engine marketing offers an interesting perspective to the literature pertaining to on line e-commerce. An economic view on the case is also presented.

A large number of e-business applications have been successfully implemented in many organizations as productivity tools and strategic weapons. Coupled with the hyper-competitive global business environment, the rapid emergence of new e-business standards and technologies has accelerated the pace of organizational changes to an unprecedented level. The pervasive use of e-business applications and their inevitable effect on organizations present numerous challenges as well as opportunities for academics and practitioners. *E-Business Models, Services, and Communication (Advances in E-Business Research, Vol. 2)* is a unique collection of the latest research associated with the emerging e-business technologies and applications. As leading experts in the e-business area, the contributors did an excellent job of providing our readers with timely, critical, and thought-provoking knowledge. We expect this book to shed new insights for researchers, educators, and practitioners to better understand the important issues and future trends of e-business research and technologies. I would like to express my gratitude to the authors and reviewers for their invaluable contribution and collaboration. Finally, I sincerely thank Ms. Meg Stocking, former Assistant Executive Editor, and other members of the IGI Global for their help with this book project.

In Lee, PhD
Editor-in-Chief

Section I

E-Business Models and Organizations

Chapter I
Markets, Hierarchies, and the Evolving Nature of Interorganizational Cooperation[1]

Wonyoung Lee
Marketing Lab, Korea

Praveen Aggarwal
University of Minnesota Duluth, USA

Hyonkil Shin
Hankuk University of Foreign Studies, Korea

Taihoon Cha
Hankuk University of Foreign Studies, Korea

Seunghan Kim
Samsung SDS, Korea

ABSTRACT

The decreasing cost of IT has encouraged organizations to seek new ways of cooperating with members of the supply chain and other key strategic partners. This increased cooperation is giving rise to a new type of interorganizational system (IOS). Before the advent of the Internet, IS integration required significant investments on the part of organizations participating in an IOS. Such heavy investments, in turn, necessitated close strategic cooperation in the non-IS domain as well. Thus, IS integration went hand-in-hand with non-IS (relational) integration in the pre-Internet era. However, advances in Internet technology have commoditized IS integration to a significant extent, thereby allowing the uncoupling of IS integration and relational integration. It is now possible for organizations to have IS integration without developing strong non-IS linkages. We propose a framework to account for this recent shift and present a typology for classifying interorganizational systems based on the segregation of IS and relational integration. We also verify the typology in case studies of four large firms.

INTRODUCTION

Developments in information technology (IT) have made a significant impact on the way companies compete and cooperate with each other. As the costs of IT, especially those pertaining to hardware purchases, continue to decline, companies are discovering newer ways of cooperating with their supply chain members and other strategic partners to gain and retain competitive advantage in the marketplace. This increased use of IT also seems to be making an impact on the nature of interorganizational relationships (Clemons & Row, 1992; Giaglis, Klein, & O'Keefe, 2002). Although the role of IT in interorganizational cooperation has evolved tremendously in the last decade, the use of IT for such purposes has been around for several decades. For example, companies have long used dedicated EDI systems for efficient inventory management and materials ordering. A significant development in the use of interorganizational IT in the last decade has been the increasingly widespread usage of Internet-based IT applications for better coordination and collaboration between organizations.

Compared to a traditional EDI system, the Internet provides a lower cost communications medium. The lower costs accrue from a shared global network and standardized information exchange protocols and platforms. This lowering of cost has created new opportunities for companies to cooperate with each other. Given that Internet-based information systems (IS) require a minimal dedicated infrastructure, a unique opportunity for companies is created whereby they can integrate their IS without necessarily having any close relationships with each other (Angeles, 2000; Chan & Swatman, 2000). For example, Johnston and Mak (2000) report about a retail company in Australia that uses two types of B2B e-commerce models. In one model, the company uses IS to transact with a small number of big suppliers. In this case, the retail company integrates not only its IS with its supply chain members by investing significantly in developing the infrastructure, but also invests in building relationships with them through long-term contracts. In the other model, however, the retailer uses IS to transact with a large number of small-sized suppliers. In this case, the company transacts with these small suppliers using the low-cost Internet-based EDI. Also, there is an apparent absence of any other form of relationship development between the company and its small suppliers.

Thus, it appears that the lower cost of IT is now allowing companies to integrate their information systems without having to develop any close relationships in the non-IS domain. This is a major shift from just a decade ago when relational integration went hand-in-hand with IS integration. The two could not be separated because of the capital intensive nature of the dedicated IS cooperation, where relational integration like strategic alliances was required to integrate interorganizational systems like EDI systems (Clemons et al., 1992). However, as illustrated by the Australian retailer example above, it is now becoming increasingly possible for companies to separate the two and adopt one without adopting the other.

It is this dichotomization of interorganizational integration that forms the basis of our chapter. In this chapter, we examine the phenomenon of interorganizational cooperation and integration. We propose that the reduced cost Internet-based IS systems add a new layer to the market-hierarchy dichotomy. Prior studies that have traditionally applied transaction cost theory to this dichotomy have assumed that relational and IS integration go hand-in-hand (Clemons et al., 1992; Kambil, Nunes, & Wilson, 1999; Malone, Yates, & Benjamin, 1987). We propose that this does not always have to be the case and propose a new framework to understand this phenomenon. The rest of the chapter is organized as follows. We first present a brief overview of the distinction made by previous researchers between markets and hierarchies and how this distinction has evolved in the electronic domain. Next, we argue that the

Internet has allowed for the emergence of a variety of hierarchies, primarily because firms can now form close IS collaborations without having to integrate in non-IS domains. Following this, we present an explanation of relational integration and IS integration. Using this distinction, we develop a typology of hierarchies. Next, we discuss four case studies to examine the existence of these hierarchies. Finally, we conclude with a discussion of the hierarchies and the purchase situations in which they frequently manifest.

EXCHANGE MECHANISMS AND INTERORGANIZATIONAL SYSTEMS

The flow of materials and services between adjacent members of a supply chain can be coordinated through one of two mechanisms: markets or hierarchies (Williamson, 1985). *Markets* coordinate flow through the basic economic forces of demand and supply. For any given product or service, there are a number of suppliers who can fulfill the demand. The buyer picks and chooses from among these suppliers based on several factors including price, quantity, and delivery terms. Products and services sourced through markets are likely to benefit from economies of scale and would therefore be lower priced. *Hierarchies*, on the other hand, coordinate flow by linking various levels of the supply chain either through corporate ownership (vertical integration) or through implicit or explicit contracts. Thus, for example, instead of choosing from a number of available suppliers, a company may decide to exclusively use one supplier who has been pre-qualified for quality and service commitments. Sourcing through hierarchies involves fewer coordination problems.

To accommodate the emergence of electronic interconnections and their influence on interorganizational structures, Malone et al. (1987) discuss the evolution of electronic markets and electronic hierarchies. They extend the concepts of traditional markets and hierarchies to electronic markets and hierarchies where transactions and information exchange are facilitated by electronic means of communications. They argue that electronic communications will reduce the cost of coordination, thereby favoring market mechanisms over hierarchical structures. Given that this body of literature was developed primarily in the pre-Internet era, it is not surprising that the examples of electronic communications that are cited often showed heavy investments by one or more companies to develop the infrastructure to facilitate the information exchange. In an oft-cited example, it was American Hospital Supply Company (now Baxter) that was responsible for establishing the network for the ASAP system linking several thousand hospitals. Similarly, it was United Airlines that made investments to establish a reservation system allowing travel agents to find and book flights (Petre, 1985). Thus, even when hierarchies became electronic hierarchies (in the pre-Internet era), two key features of interorganizational integration did not change substantively: (a) the establishment of such hierarchies continued to be expensive, risky, and asset-specific, and (b) because of the expenses involved, there was a close cooperative relationship among the participants that went beyond mere IS integration. In other words, IS integration still went hand-in-hand with relational integration (see, e.g., Bakos & Brynjolfsson, 1993).

THE IMPACT OF THE INTERNET ON INTERORGANIZATIONAL RELATIONSHIPS

With the advent of the Internet, the infrastructural investments needed for IS cooperation have declined considerably. The low-cost and interactive communication capability of the Internet have made IS integration among organizations a relatively less expensive proposition. This reduced cost has increased the accessibility of IS integration, thereby allowing many more small-sized trading partners to participate in integration initiatives such as the Internet-based EDI (Chan et al., 2000).

The most interesting feature of this development is that IS integration is now possible *without* having to commit to interorganizational relational integration. Some initial evidence of this new integration type, with high IS integration and low relational integration, has already been reported in recent studies (Angeles, 2000; Chan et al., 2000; Johnston et al., 2000). As argued by Bensaou (1997), "information technology may provide a customer with the coordination and cooperation capabilities traditionally associated with vertical integration without the cost of ownership" (p. 113). Clemons, Reddi, and Row (1993b) described this emerging phenomenon in terms of coordination costs and transaction risk. They argue that markets can provide the benefits of specialization and economies of scale in the form of lower prices or better value. However, market exchanges also generally entail higher transaction costs because the buyer firm now has to not only locate the seller in a market, but also has to monitor the performance and coordinate the exchange. In order to lower these costs and risks, a firm can enter into contracts or other forms of corporate relationships. Such exclusive or explicit coordination also entails higher risks (opportunistic behavior by a party). Traditionally, firms have countered such risks through vertical integration. Clemons et al. (1993b) argue that information technology can lower the cost of coordination *without* increasing the risk of coordination. Thus, they argue, we shall see more and more outsourcing and increased coordination simultaneously (a "move-to-the-middle" hypothesis). In other words, firms will not *have to* vertically integrate to enjoy the fruits of IS cooperation. The introduction of Internet-enabled technologies coupled with the acceptance and proliferation of open standards has increased the number of options available to the members of a value chain to link up electronically, irrespective of whether they have a tight strategic relationship or not. Furthermore, the accessibility and ease-of-use of extranet connections via virtual private networks (VPNs) make IS partnerships so effortless and low-risk that they can go with varying degrees of relational commitment.

Relational Integration and IS Integration

We propose that interorganizational integration, in the context of lower-cost IT, can be segregated into two components: relational integration and IS integration. Relational integration may be understood as an alliance among two or more organizations that promotes collaboration and pooling of resources to achieve common economic goals. Generally speaking, such integration has a long-term orientation to it, and the participating firms work on a relationship built on mutual adaptation, trust, and commitment (Kwon & Suh 2004). They share strategic resources in the co-creation of value (Lavie, 2002). An example would be the European industrial marketing and purchasing (IMP) group where a large number of organizations have demonstrated stable, long-term, cooperative relationships. A dyadic example of relational integration would be an exclusive distribution arrangement between a manufacturer and a distributor where both parties make long-term commitments to work together strategically to create value. Similarly, when a manufacturing firm shares proprietary information with a vendor who would use that information to make parts and components for the firm, one can say that the two firms are relationally integrated. At times, two firms may compete in the same marketplace, but still cooperate with each other to solve some common problems. For example, Ford and GM compete aggressively for market share; they may agree to cooperate for joint R&D to develop superior fuel/battery technology. Such cooperation and integration has also been referred to as "co-opetition" (Brandenburger & Nalebuff, 1996) as participants may act competitively and cooperatively simultaneously. In the more traditional case of a manufacturer and a supplier, indicators of strong relational integration include incidence of boundary-spanning tasks and activities, exchange of personnel for collaborative decision-making, and formal, long-standing contracts designed around cooperative functions.

IS integration, on the other hand, is the creation of an interorganizational system that facilitates electronic exchanges and interactions among participating organizations. As noted by Venkatraman and Zaheer (2001), such integration involves integrating the "business processes of two or more independent organizations through the exploitation of the capabilities of computers and communication technologies" (pp. 378-79). Organizations generally use such IS systems for coordination, facilitation, and/or monitoring purposes. For such a system to work effectively and efficiently, participants need not only access to each others' information systems, but also interface integration (Truman, 2000) for interactivity and seamless flow of information. While the management of strategic integration is primarily the responsibility of general management, managing IS integration is generally the responsibility of IT and IS managers. It should be noted here that strategic integration may have IS integration as one of its components. In other words, it is possible to come across situations where a firm has IS integration goals that are subservient to the organization's overall strategic vision of integration and cooperation.

Clemons et al. (1993b) provide examples of organizations that exhibit IS integration. Philadelphia's MAC ATM network is an example of IS cooperation among competing banks to provide a seamless ATM customer experience. Philadelphia's National Bank/Core States Financial owns the MAC network. Conforming to the MAC system hardware and interface requirements, all participating banks provide the network with access to their customers' account information. Thus, even though the banks compete with each other at the corporate level, there is a certain level of cooperation and integration at the IS level to enhance value creation.

Another example provided by Clemons et al. (1993b) is that of Rosenbluth Travel Agency. Rosenbluth has created an alliance of independent but cooperating travel agents (Rosenbluth International Alliance, RIA). Rosenbluth provides its alliance members with the software necessary for IS collaboration. Using this software, the agents can access travel information on any customer originating anywhere and can provide a seamless, high-quality service to customers across forty countries. An interesting aspect of this IS integration is that the agents continue to be independent operators who are neither owned by Rosenbluth nor franchised by it.

In Table 1, we present a brief summary of concepts and illustrative references that highlight key forms of interorganizational models proposed in the literature.

A TYPOLOGY OF INTERORGANIZATIONAL SYSTEMS

Malone et al. (1987) examined the impact of IT on inter-firm interaction. They argued that with an increasing adoption of technology, we will see an emergence of electronic markets and electronic hierarchies. In order to leverage the low search cost feature of IT, firms will increasingly seek new vendors, thereby leading to the emergence of electronic markets. This proposition is generally referred to as the "move to the market" hypothesis. On the other hand, Malone et al. (1987) also encountered a competing phenomenon, which they termed "electronic hierarchies," where firms used IT to develop tightly coupled partnerships with a select few firms. Generally, such partnerships incorporated cooperation in both IS and non-IS areas. Lately, researchers have argued that network structures can be seen as falling on

Table 1. Relational and IS integration—Some illustrative examples

Types of Integration	Key Concepts	Illustrative References	Systems Studied
Relational Integration	Electronic Markets	Hess & Kemerer (1994)	Loan Origination System
		Choudhury, Hartzel, & Konsynski (1998)	Inventory Locator Service in the aircraft parts industry
	Electronic Markets and Electronic Hierarchies	Malone et al. (1987)	Airline reservation system, JIT, CAD/CAM
IS Integration	Electronic Partnerships	Hart & Saunders (1998)	EDI
	Electronic Exchange Integration	Truman (2000)	EDI
	Integrated Information Links	Srinivasan, Kekre, & Mukhopadhyay (1994)	EDI to JIT
	Internal & External Integration	Iacovou, Benbasat, & Dexter (1995)	EDI
	I/O Business Process Redesign	Clark & Stoddard (1996)	EDI
Relational and IS Integration	Move to the Middle	Clemons et al. (1992)	EDI
		Clemons & Row (1993a)	Checkout scanner systems
		Bakos et al. (1993)	N/A
		Clemons et al. (1993a)	EDI
	Mixed Mode	Holland & Lockett(1997)	Electronic Ordering System
		Lee et al.(1997)	SCM
		Kambil et al.(1999)	EDI

Figure 1. The proposed hierarchical schema for interorganizational relationships

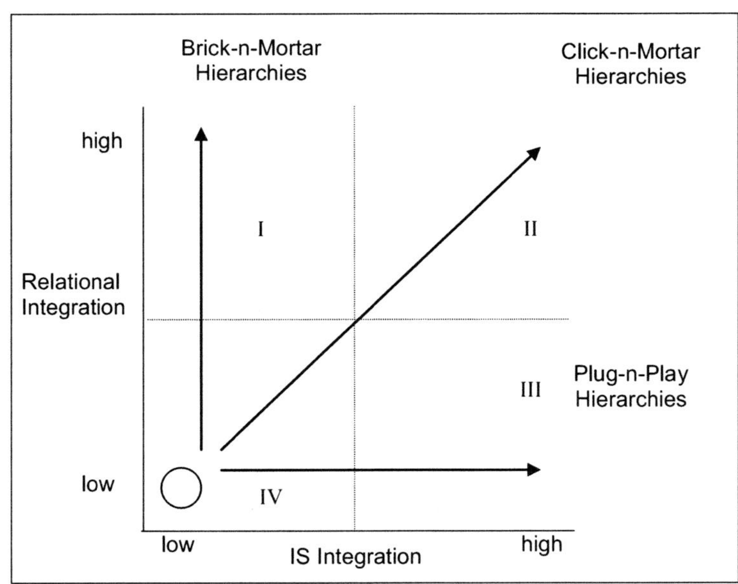

a continuum with markets and hierarchies being the two anchor points of that continuum. Holland et al. (1997) call the network structures that fall somewhere in the middle of such a continuum "mixed mode networks." Consistent with Holland et al. (1997), we would like to expand on the dichotomy of electronic markets and electronic hierarchies by proposing that hierarchies can take several different forms in the Internet-enabled world. We use the distinction between relational and IS integration to create a 2x2 matrix of IOS networks. In the base condition of low relational integration coupled with low IS integration, we have the classic electronic market scenario (quadrant IV in the figure below). In the remaining three scenarios, where either the relational integration or the IS integration is high, we get a hierarchy. Our proposed hierarchy schema is summarized in Figure 1.

Brick-n-Mortar Hierarchies

Before the development of EDI systems, most inter-firm cooperation fell in the category of brick-n-mortar hierarchies. There was relational cooperation for strategic and competitive advantage reasons, with little or no IS integration. However, even in today's world, such hierarchies are anything but extinct. Thus, a franchisor may have a strong contractual relationship with its franchisees or a manufacturer may have an exclusive distribution arrangement with an intermediary, and in either case there may be no IS integration. A significant portion of relationship marketing literature in the business-to-business context refers to such collaborations.

Click-n-Mortar Hierarchies

Click-n-mortar hierarchies are fully integrated hierarchies that exhibit a high level of relational integration coupled with a high level of IS integration. In the pre-Internet era, IS integration almost invariably required some level of relational integration as well. Researchers (such as Clemons et al., 1993a) have presented a number of reasons that can help us understand why the two were so tightly coupled in the past. First, in the absence of any universal connectivity medium such as the Internet, dedicated IOS were expensive. Second, as some of this investment was non-contractible and transaction-specific, the cost of withdrawal or switching was very high. Third, these high switching costs had the potential of shifting the bargaining power of the players involved. For example, if a supplier of a complex product made a heavy investment in an IS system to coordinate information exchange with its buyer, this created an opportunity for the buyer to engage in opportunistic behavior. Thus, it was imperative to develop relational links before incurring the expenditure on IS integration to ensure long-term viability of such an integration. Both parties had a vested interest to go beyond cooperation in the IS domain only to protect their investments in IS integration. Thus, either companies did not cooperate at all (and acted like independent parties in a market, quadrant IV of our model) or cooperated in both IS and non-IS domains (and acted like participants in hierarchies). Note, however, that the extent of integration could, and did, vary. The click-n-mortar hierarchies demonstrate the "electronic interdependence" mentioned by Bensaou and Venkatraman (1995). There is a cooperative climate among the parties and there are "rich and impersonal structural mechanisms" to promote such cooperation (p. 1483). At the same time, the two parties exchange information in a form that can be directly read by the computer of the other party, and this information exchange occurs across a wide variety of functions such as purchasing, quality control, product development, and accounting.

Plug-n-Play Hierarchies

In a traditional EDI system, one or both the parties have to make relationship-specific investments in the system. Mukhopadhyay and Kekre (2002) have even differentiated between supplier-initiated and buyer-initiated EDI systems and examined the relative strategic benefits of the two approaches. However, the Internet has brought down some of the costs of IS integration dramatically. The need for investments in non-contractible IS assets has been reduced significantly by the Internet (Johnston et al., 2000). Also, the emergence of standardized protocols and platforms has markedly reduced the switching and learning costs for organizations (Chan et al., 2000). Therefore, given the emergence of standardized protocols and the ready availability of IS exchange through the Internet, it is now possible to decouple IS integration from relational integration. Organizations can now have strong IS interdependence without having to support or supplement it with non-IS cooperation. Thus, a new type of hierarchical form, which we call plug-n-play hierarchies, has come into being. Plug-n-play hierarchies display significant IS integration without any comparable relational integration. The open architecture of the Internet (as against the proprietary architecture of the early EDI systems) allows for compatibility and easy inter-operability of IS systems across firms. The investments in IS are less asset-specific, which lessens the need for relational integration. Thus, such hierarchies are of the plug-n-play variety where there is little need to first establish an elaborate relational network to make the IS integration work.

Electronic Markets

The fourth quadrant is the base condition of our model, a non-hierarchy, where both relational integration and IS integration are low. In the absence of any integration, the scenario becomes one of an electronic market (as described by Malone et al., 1987). There are several examples in the literature where companies have simply put the low-cost search capabilities of the Internet to good use for outsourcing and purchasing without attempting to develop any kind of integration with their suppliers. For example, several companies have used reverse auction electronic markets to purchase raw materials and components. There is no long-term relational commitment in such transactions, nor is there any need for IS integration with the vendors.

EXPLORATORY EVIDENCE FOR THE PROPOSED TYPOLOGY

Although there is evidence in the extant literature to support the existence of some of the hierarchies proposed in our model, we conducted an exploratory empirical study to examine the typology structure further. Specifically, the study was designed to examine, in an exploratory sense, the following: (a) if the observed interorganizational systems can be classified into the proposed schema, (b) if a single organization can exhibit more than one type of hierarchy in its inter-firm cooperation structure, and c) if certain hierarchical arrangements are observed more often for certain types of business-to-business (B2B) purchases. Keeping with a strong tradition and history of case study method in IS literature, we chose to study four large corporations to gain insights into the proposed typology. The approach here follows the one reported by Massetti and Zmut (1996).

The four companies included in this analysis were Samsung Electronics, Hyundai-Kia Motors, SK Telecom, and LG Mart. All four are large Korean corporations that have well developed internal IS systems. The industries represented are electronics, automobile, telecommunications, and retail, respectively. Our purposive sample has many of the features commonly expected among samples for exploratory studies like ours: homogeneous representativeness, heterogeneity among cases, theoretical importance of cases, and comparability.

Interviews were held with senior managers using semi-structured interview guides. For each organization, two researchers participated in the interview in order to ensure a shared understanding that mitigates the effects of subjective interpretation of the interview data. To capture the transaction details from both purchase planning and purchase implementation perspectives, we included managers from both domains. To the extent possible, managers whose purchase responsibilities cut across several or all product categories were selected.

A set of observation criteria and coding schema was developed to help researchers record data in a consistent manner. Observations of the two researchers (for each case) were compared and evaluated for inconsistencies. Any observed inconsistency between researchers was resolved by either a third researcher or through verification from the subjects. To improve internal validity, the interview guide was designed using items and constructs from existing literature. For example, to assess relational integration, questions were asked regarding the degree of collaboration that explains how much companies cooperate with each other, the nature of contract (buying in the market, ongoing relationship, partnership, strategic alliance, backward integration), and the terms of contract (Anderson & Narus, 1990; Hibbard, Kumar, & Stern, 2001; Stock, Greis, & Kasarda, 2000). To measure IS integration, we used internal integration that is measured by the degree of connection between internal IS and inter-firm IS and external integration that is measured by the degree of connection to partner's IS (Iacovou et al., 1995; Premkumar & Ramamurthy, 1995; Truman, 2000).

Samsung Electronics

Samsung Electronics has 24 production subsidiaries, 35 sales subsidiaries, and 20 branch offices around the world, including those in North America, Europe, Southeast Asia, Central Asia, China, the CIS, and Latin America. Total sales in 2004 were U.S. $55.2 billion. Samsung Electronics' organizational structure is comprised of five business divisions: (a) digital media network division, in charge of computers and AV equipment and related products; (b) digital appliance network division, in charge of home electronics; (c) digital solution network division, in charge of semiconductor and related products; (d) telecommunication network division, in charge of the cellular phone business; and (e) business and administration support division, which is basically a staff organization.

Purchase planning for Samsung Electronics is taken care of by the Procurement Strategy Team in the Business and Administration Support Division. The actual purchasing is done in close collaboration with the procurement divisions of respective plants. All purchases at Samsung are classified in one of the three main categories: direct materials, indirect materials, and MROs (maintenance, repair, and operating supplies). The direct materials are divided into "common parts" like memory that are generic in nature (in the sense that a vendor can sell those parts to buyers other than Samsung without having to alter them in any way) and "specified parts" like video decks that are made specifically for Samsung Electronics. Specified parts are further divided into "strategic materials" and "non-strategic" materials. Strategic materials are key components that are central to a product's performance and competitive edge. For example, Qualcomm's IC chip and LCD used in Samsung's cellular phones are considered strategic materials. These parts have high strategic importance as their performance is central to the performance of the main product, and these parts also account for a significant proportion of the manufacturing cost of the cell phone. Any performance improvements or cost savings achieved in these parts can make a big difference to Samsung's bottom line. Non-strategic materials, on the other hand, are other specified materials (like the external case of a handset) that are not central to a product's core function. Indirect materials are purchases that do not get integrated into the manufactured product, but instead help in the product process. An example of indirect materials at Samsung would be infrastructural purchases such as facilities. Finally, MRO materials are mainly office supplies. To summarize, one can reclassify Samsung's purchases as procurement of strategic materials, non-strategic materials (all common parts and some specified parts), indirect materials, and MROs.

We collected data on relational integration and IS integration from three Samsung sites: the Procurement Strategy Team in the Seoul office, the Procurement Team in the Kumi Plant, and the Procurement Team in the Kiheung Complex. The data collected from these sites revealed the following. Samsung has a well developed IS network for both internal and external constituents. The internal IS system is based on SAP's R/3 system. For the interorganizational systems, Samsung Electronics depends on three different IS systems: a custom-built Web Portal, a B2Bi system called GLONETS (global logistics network system), and iMarketKorea's e-Marketplace. Samsung uses the Web portal system mainly for purchasing non-strategic materials. The Web Portal system basically allows Samsung's partners to complete a transaction online by visiting Samsung's Web site, and some level of IS compatibility is needed between Samsung and its partners. Samsung uses its B2Bi system to purchase strategic materials. GLONETS (the B2Bi system) provides Samsung with direct system-to-system connectivity with its trading partners. Thus, there is close IS integration between Samsung and vendors who supply strategic materials to the company. For MRO purchases, Samsung Electronics uses iMarketKorea's e-Marketplace, which is essentially an electronic market. Finally, given the infrequent purchase of materials classified as facilities, Samsung does not use any sophisticated information system to transact with its facilities vendors. The only IS usage in such transactions is basic email exchanges. Thus, our data indicated a higher level of IS integration for strategic and non-strategic materials compared to indirect materials and MROs.

In order to assess relational integration, we examined three aspects of such an integration: collaboration level, the nature of the contract, and

Figure 2. Interorganizational relationships at samsung electronics

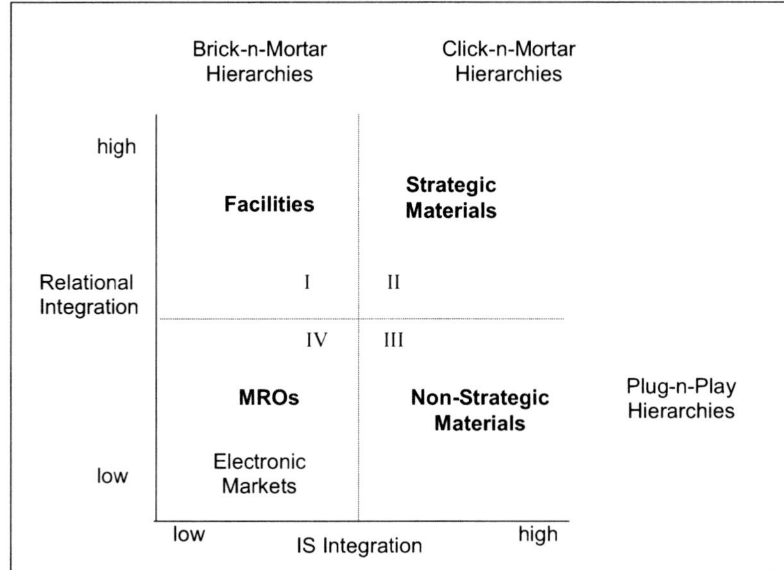

the terms of the contract. Our data indicate that Samsung had the closest relational integration with its vendors for strategic materials. As noted by one of our interviewees, "Strategic materials such as Qualcomm's IC chip are very important to the production of our cell phones. Given the lead time needed to make the chip, we use GLO-NETS to work with our partners with whom we have strong collaborative relationships." Also the company had high relational integration with its suppliers for important materials like facilities. In the case of non-strategic materials, however, the company was willing to transact with any supplier that could manufacture the materials. And in the case of MRO purchases, there was no direct relationship between Samsung and its suppliers as most MROs were procured through the e-Marketplace. To summarize, strategic materials and indirect materials displayed a higher degree of relational integration than non-strategic materials and MROs.

The results show that Samsung operates in the electronic markets mode when it is purchasing MROs (quadrant IV). Both IS and relational integration are low when MROs are bought in the e-Marketplace. Non-strategic materials display moderately high IS integration but low relational integration (quadrant III). Samsung's Web portal is a good example of a plug-n-play hierarchy as the participants need not have any significant relational integration and yet can benefit from the easy IS integration that the system offers. This is in sharp contrast to the way Samsung procures strategic materials. With vendors of strategic materials, Samsung not only has a high level of IS integration, but also has strong relational integration with the chosen vendors (quadrant II). Thus Samsung's B2Bi system is geared for those who fall within Samsung's click-n-mortar hierarchy.

Finally, Samsung is using only basic information systems like e-mail for procuring indirect materials from vendors with whom it has strong relational integration (quadrant I). This is an example of a traditional brick-n-mortar hierarchy where interorganizational bonds do not spill into the IS domain. Samsung's interorganizational hierarchies are summarized in Figure 2.

Hyundai-Kia Motors

Hyundai-Kia Motors is the leader of Korea's auto industry. Total sales in 2004 were U.S. $26.1 billion, with more than 50% of its sales originating outside Korea. At Hyundai-Kia, purchasing is handled centrally by the Procurement Headquarters of the company. The company classifies its materials purchasing into three categories: MROs, direct materials, and facilities. MROs, as the term indicates, include basic tools, office supplies, food purchases, etc. Direct materials include parts and materials that go into the manufacturing of the automobile, such as car engine, chassis, etc. Finally, facilities include capital goods such as mold press, infrastructural purchases, etc. Unlike Samsung, Hyundai-Kia does not sub-classify direct materials into categories such as strategic or non-strategic materials.

We collected information on relational and IS integration from two Hyundai-Kia sites, the Procurement Headquarters in the Seoul Office and the Procurement Team at the Ulsan Plant. Data from these two sites painted a picture of Hyundai-Kia that is quite different from that of Samsung. The level of interorganizational systems that leveraged IT was perceptibly lower at Hyundai-Kia as compared to that at Samsung Electronics.

Hyundai-Kia uses two types of IS systems for its transactions with its vendors. First, it uses an EDI system called e-SCM for procuring direct materials. The interesting part, however, is that most of the vendors' IS systems are not connected to the e-SCM system. Only a select few partners have the privilege of sharing the inventory database with Hyundai-Kia. The second IS system used by Hyundai-Kia is the e-Marketplace. This electronic market system is very similar to what

Samsung uses for its MRO purchases. As expected, Hyundai-Kia also uses the e-Marketplace primarily to make MRO purchases. For facilities purchases, the company does not use any significant IS system except email exchanges.

In terms of relational integration, Hyundai-Kia demonstrates a high degree of integration with its direct materials suppliers. In fact, when planning a new automobile, Hyundai-Kia pre-selects direct material suppliers with whom it builds extensive relationships. Throughout the pre-manufacturing phase, these vendors are consulted and kept in the loop at every step of the process. Even the production line is built to accommodate parts and materials from these exclusive suppliers. In the words of one of our interviewees, "Some of our direct material suppliers are determined up to two years before a new model is commercially produced. We maintain such relationships on a long-term basis." However, for the procurement of MROs, Hyundai-Kia does not have any extensive relationships with any specific supplier. Often, Hyundai-Kia outsources such procurement to a distribution-related sister concern like the Hyundai Department Store. Finally, Hyundai-Kia relies once again on specific suppliers with which it has strong relationships for purchasing capital goods (facilities). To summarize, our data show a high level of relational integration for direct materials and facilities purchases and a low level of relational integration for MRO purchases.

Based on the previous discussion, we can conclude that Hyundai-Kia displays three of the four types of IOS proposed in this chapter. First, MROs are transacted through the e-Marketplace, where both IS and relational integration are low. Thus, MRO purchases fall in quadrant IV (electronic markets). We did not find any evidence of plug-n-play hierarchies at Hyundai-Kia. Direct material purchases exhibit a high level of relational integration. However, when it comes to IS integration, only a few of the vendors enjoy IS integration with Hyundai-Kia. Thus, for those vendors that enjoy a high degree of relational integration and also have IS integration through e-SCM, there exists a click-n-mortar hierarchy. For the remaining direct materials suppliers and facilities suppliers, a high level of relational integration is not matched by

Figure 3. Interorganizational relationships at Hyundai-Kia Motors

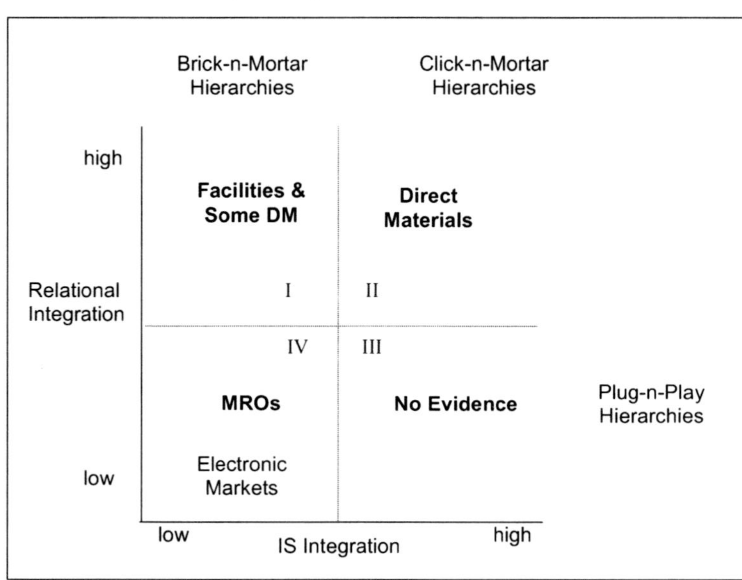

any IS integration. Therefore, they would fall into the category of brick-n-mortar hierarchies. Hyundai-Kia's interorganizational hierarchies are summarized in Figure 3.

SK Telecom

SK Telecom is the number one mobile communications company in Korea. Its total sales in 2004 were U.S. $9.6 billion. In terms of number of subscribers, the company had a 53% share of the Korean cellular market. Given that SK Telecom is primarily a service organization, it classifies its procurements into three categories: engineering materials, general materials, and MROs. Engineering materials are mostly infrastructural telecommunication equipment used for providing both wired and wireless communication access to its subscribers. These engineering materials are mostly made-to-order. SK Telecom buys large quantities of such custom-made, expensive materials. General materials are mostly promotional materials. MROs are general office supplies.

We collected data on relational and IS integration from SK Telecom's e-Management Team. The data collected revealed that despite being a telecommunication company itself, SK Telecom makes use of networked IS only for some purchases. SK Telecom has used B2B e-commerce systems since fall of 2001, but its use is limited for procurement of general materials only. For procuring MROs, SK Telecom uses electronic marketplaces such as MRO Korea. However, when it came to the procurement of custom-made engineering materials, hardly any IS system is used (except, of course, the basic email system). Thus, there is evidence of IS integration only for general materials procurement. For other purchases, IS integration is low or non-existent.

In terms of relational integration, SK Telecom transacts engineering materials with a few select suppliers because engineering materials are expensive and custom-built. Thus, there is a strong relational integration between SK Telecom and engineering materials suppliers. According to one of our interviewees, "Because engineering materials are expensive, made to order, and purchased infrequently, price and contract terms are determined through an extensive negotiation process. Using information systems for such a purchase would not be very effective." General materials are transacted with many suppliers, and SK Telecom does not have any strong relational bond with these suppliers. Finally, in the case of MROs, the company has little relationship with any specific supplier as these materials are outsourced from e-Marketplace.

Based on the discussion above, we can classify the relationships and transactions as follows: MRO purchases clearly fall in the fourth quadrant, electronic markets (both IS and relational integration are low), as MROs are transacted through e-marketplace. General materials procurement exhibits plug-n-play hierarchy, where IS integration is moderate to high but relational integration is low (quadrant III). SK Telecom is using basic information systems like email for procuring engineering materials, but has a high relational integration with the suppliers of these materials. This is an example of brick-n-mortar type hierarchy (quadrant I).

Finally, we could not identify any transactions or relationships where both relational and IS integration were strong. Thus, SK Telecom does not have any click-n-mortar hierarchical relationship with any of its suppliers. SK Telecom's interorganizational hierarchies are summarized in Figure 4.

LG Mart

LG Mart has played a leading role in transforming Korea's retail industry, and has been on the forefront of bringing a modern shopping environment to the Korean marketplace. It has four business divisions: LG25 (convenience stores), LG supermarkets, LG Mart (discount stores), and LG Department Stores. Total sales in 2004

Figure 4. Interorganizational relationships at SK Telecom

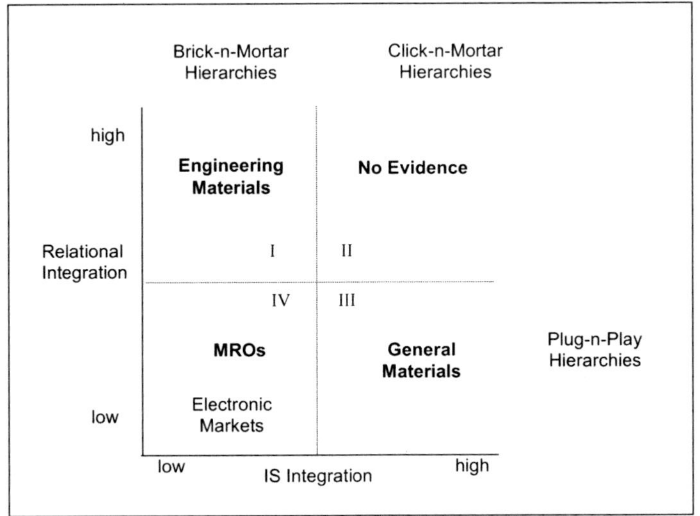

were US $2.5 billion. LG Mart itself is a part of Korea's second largest business conglomerate, LG Corp.

Given that LG Mart is primarily a retailing (distribution) company, its purchasing is different from that of manufacturers as it doesn't purchase raw materials and parts; instead it purchases goods for resale without making any major modifications or alterations. We collected our data from LG Mart's Logistics Team. Depending on the types of products being bought, LG Mart classifies its vendors into different categories: wholesale vendors, consignment vendors, VMI (Vendor Managed Inventory) vendors, and MRO vendors. One can also create another category of vendors—facilities vendors—those who supply infrastructural or capital goods to LG.

Wholesale vendors provide non-perishable merchandise. Consignment vendors provide products that need refrigeration or sub-zero temperatures. VMI vendors are a select group of strategically important vendors who are major suppliers and whose inventory systems are integrated with those of LG Mart. MRO vendors, as the name implies, sell MRO products to LG Mart. Finally, LG Mart purchases its infrastructural requirements from facilities vendors.

Based on our discussions with the logistics team at LG Mart, we can conclude that LG Mart has taken a very aggressive stance on adopting and using modern communication technology to its advantage. It developed and implemented a Web EDI system to integrate its IS with those of its suppliers. Even though it does not have any significant relationship with most of its wholesale vendors, it encourages them to integrate their IS with that of its own. It has gone even a step further with its consignment vendors and VMI vendors. In the case of consignment vendors, who typically supply LG with perishables such as dairy products, time is of essence. In order to cut down on lag time, LG Mart has transferred the responsibility and authority for logistics to its consignment vendors. Even though LG Mart takes the title of the product while it is in transit, the ultimate responsibility for inventory management rests with consignment vendors. Thus, it is no surprise that LG Mart has strong relational integration as well as IS integration with its consignment vendors. Comments our interviewee,

"The most important thing about dairy products is to keep them below a certain temperature at all times. So, LG Mart must have a tight-knit relationship with the vendor as well as allow it access to our EDI for inventory control and movement." The same kind of arrangement holds true for VMI vendors as well. LG Mart has an inventory information sharing system with two of its largest suppliers, Yuhan-Kimberly and Unilever Korea Ltd. LG Mart has a strong relational bond with these two companies and at the same time, strong IS integration with them through an SCM (Supply Chain Management) system. For its MRO purchases, LG Mart has been using LG MRO, an e-Marketplace of its parent company. Finally, the company does not have any IS integration with its capital goods suppliers and uses only basic email exchanges with them. However, there are strong relational bonds between LG Mart and its facilities suppliers.

To summarize, MRO purchases fall within quadrant IV of our model, electronic markets, and these purchases are transacted through the e-Marketplace. Wholesale vendors have high IS integration with LG Mart as they transact through Web EDI and have low relational integration. Hence, they fall within the category of plug-n-play hierarchies (quadrant III). Consignment vendors and VMI vendors display both high relational integration and high IS integration. Hence, they fall within quadrant II, click-n-mortar hierarchies.

Finally, facilities vendors have high relational integration and low IS integration. Thus they exhibit the traditional brick-n-mortar hierarchy (quadrant I). LG Mart's interorganizational hierarchies are summarized in Figure 5.

DISCUSSION

The objectives of our case studies were to examine evidence in support of our typology and to understand any relationships between the type of purchase and the IOS type. The results of our case studies are summarized in Table 2. Each column represents one company, and each entry in the table represents the purchases that fall within a given type of hierarchical relationship.

Figure 5. Interorganizational relationships at LG mart

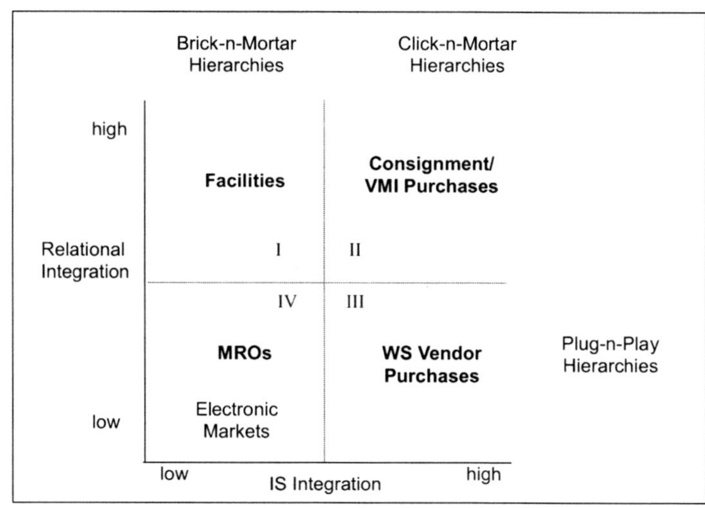

Table 2. Summary of interorganizational relationships for different purchases

Quad.	Interorganizational Relationship	Samsung	Hyundai	SK Telecom	LGMart
I	Brick-n-Mortar Hierarchies	Indirect Materials: Wafers	Facilities: Mold press	Engineering Materials: Optical repeaters	Facilities: Logistic materials such as pallets
II	Click-n-Mortar Hierarchies	Strategic Materials: Qualcomm's IC chip for cellular phones	Direct Materials: Engine, chassis	No Evidence	High Volume Direct Materials: Dairy products
III	Plug-n-Play Hierarchies	Non-strategic Materials: External case for handsets	No Evidence	General Materials: Informational brochures etc.	Non-Perishables
IV	Electronic Markets	MROs: Office furniture etc.	MROs: Basic tools, office supplies	MROs: Office supplies	MROs: Office supplies

Brick-n-Mortar Hierarchies

Brick-n-mortar hierarchies are the traditional interorganizational systems where there is a strong relational bond between the two cooperating parties with little or no IS integration. Our case studies found strong evidence in support of such hierarchies. All four organizations had brick-n-mortar hierarchical relationships with at least some of their vendors. What is interesting to note here is that even though all four organizations in our sample consider themselves to be on the cutting edge of technology, they have not felt the need (or the benefit) of integrating their IS with some of the vendors with whom they have strong relational ties.

Another interesting observation from our analysis is that the types of purchases that fall in this category are for materials and products purchased rather infrequently. These materials are mostly of an infrastructural nature. These are mostly facilities or capital goods. While it is important to purchase such materials from reliable vendors, these vendors do not seem to play any day-to-day role in the organizations' creation and delivery of value. Also, often the buyer organization has little or no expertise in these purchases. For example, Hyundai will have an immense amount of internal expertise when it comes to buying parts for its car engines. It would know precisely what to look for in these parts and how to specify the details. However, when it comes to buying an auxiliary power generator for its plant, it would have very limited knowledge of what differentiates a great power generator from an ordinary one and what specifications would be needed to meet its power needs. While a power generator could be crucial in times of need, Hyundai has little incentive to either develop any extensive in-house knowledge base on power generators or to integrate its IS systems with those of its generator vendors. Instead, it relies on non-IS relational integration and works with select vendors who are dependable and trustworthy.

Click-n-Mortar Hierarchies

We defined click-n-mortar hierarchies as those interorganizational relationships where there is evidence of strong relational and IS integration. We found evidence of click-n-mortar hierarchies in all organizations except SK Telecom. The company is primarily in the business of marketing communication services. Thus, its major purchase is of engineering materials—the infrastructure that it needs to create to offer the services. Based on our interviews with this company's representatives, we expect that SK Telecom will likely develop some form of click-n-mortar hierarchical relationships with some of its vendors whose products and services are crucial to its operations and profitability.

It is also interesting to note that the three organizations that had click-n-mortar hierarchical relationships had them with vendors that supplied materials of strategic importance. Many of these suppliers provided custom-made products or products that needed continuous R&D for enhancements and cost-savings. These materials were integral to the making and functioning of buying companies' products, and close cooperation between the buyer and the seller had the potential of creating a competitive edge for the buyer. It appeared that the relational integration helped build trust between parties, and IS integration contributed to creating efficiencies. Click-n-mortar hierarchies emerged for those product categories where the purchases were made at a moderate to high frequency and the product value was generally high.

Plug-n-Play Hierarchies

Plug-n-play hierarchies are primarily a consequence of the proliferation and standardization of the Internet. Such hierarchies became a possibility only after the cost of integrating IS systems decreased to a level that the risks associated with IS cooperation were minimal. Three of the four companies in our sample displayed Plug-n-play hierarchies. Hyundai-Kia did not have any significant plug-n-play hierarchical relationships with any of its vendors. Our discussions with its management suggested that one reason why such hierarchies do not exist at Hyundai-Kia is that all of Hyundai-Kia's production lines are custom-designed for specific models, and most vendors customize their materials and components for individual models. Thus, Hyundai-Kia works very closely with its vendors at every step of its automobile design, production, and upgrade process. This necessitates the development of relational integration in conjunction with IS integration for most production-related purchases. Note that this practice is different from that of US and Japanese auto manufacturers. Generally speaking, automobile companies in Korea have fewer suppliers than their American and Japanese counterparts (Dyer, Cho, & Chu, 1998).

There are some attributes that are common to purchases made through plug-n-play hierarchies. Materials purchased through such hierarchies are of a non-strategic nature. There is little or no customization involved, and the purchase frequency could be moderate to high. Also, speed and efficiency is essential in such purchases. Based on our interviews, we speculate that sometimes two firms may start out with plug-n-play hierarchical relationships but develop click-n-mortar hierarchies for strategic materials over time.

Electronic Markets

The main objective of this chapter was to examine interorganizational hierarchies. When relational and IS integration is absent, we call such scenarios electronic markets. Although electronic markets are not the focus of this chapter, extensive evidence exists in the literature about their existence and how they function, and our case studies further corroborate such evidence. In all four cases, we found the existence and usage of electronic markets. Without developing any long-term relational bonds or integrating IS systems, all four companies in our sample were leveraging the benefits of electronic markets to their advantage. Products most frequently procured through electronic markets were MRO supplies. Such products are generic in nature, and there are a large number of suppliers who can offer them. Thus, given the nature of these products (commodities), there are distinct advantages to procuring such products from a marketplace where vendors compete with each other for business. An electronic marketplace makes it even easier for vendors to participate in that competition. It is, therefore, not surprising that companies find procuring MROs from electronic marketplaces as an attractive option.

LIMITATIONS AND EXTENSIONS

The case study methodology employed in this study was exploratory in its scope. Thus, the evidence observed in favor of our proposed typology needs further and more rigorous corroboration. The four firms included in our sample were non-U.S. in their origin and were very large corporations. The findings need to be validated for organizations that are smaller and from other parts of the world. In an extension of this study, it will be interesting to look at the hierarchies prevalent among the suppliers of the firms examined in this study. This will help provide a comprehensive view of both sides of the dyadic relationships. Also, in this chapter we have created bipolar anchors (such as high or low IS integration), whereas in the real world, a better perspective would be to treat integration as a continuum. The reason we adopt a bipolar categorization is to bring out the contrasts among different forms of hierarchy. Thus, even when hierarchies are of a "mixed mode," we believe that it should be possible to classify them as one of the three types outlined in this chapter. An interesting extension of this study would be to examine how relational integration affects IS integration (and vice versa) among cooperating firms. It is possible that once companies start cooperating in one domain (relational or IS), they may want to extend their cooperation into the other domain, especially for purchases that can benefit from dual domain cooperation. Thus, it would be interesting to examine movement from one cell of our proposed model to the next and study the factors that motivate such migration.

CONCLUSION

Based on the arguments and evidence previously presented, we may conclude that the dichotomy of electronic markets and electronic hierarchies can be further enriched and enhanced by differentiating between relational integration and IS integration. The resulting 2x2 matrix provides a fuller array of interorganizational relationships that are emerging in the post-Internet era. Our case studies provide preliminary evidence consistent with the proposed typology. We also found evidence that a single organization can engage in different hierarchical relationships with different vendors. Thus, executives can often be expected to manage a portfolio of relationships with their trading partners. Boundary-spanning organizations involved in e-procurement, supply chain management, customer relationship management, and strategic sourcing are likely to have a diverse set of partner relationships that will differ in terms of IS and relational integration. Also, the type of hierarchical relationship appears to be a function of the kinds of materials or components being sourced from the hierarchy partner.

Standardized, commodity-type product purchases seem to fall within the quadrant of electronic markets, where the relational integration and IS integration are practically non-existent. Such purchases can even be outsourced to a specialist (such as a MRO e-marketplace) organization to benefit from economies of scale. When procuring materials of strategic importance, companies tend to prefer both strong relational integration as well as strong IS integration. Companies may need relational integration for strategic planning and IS integration for operational efficiencies. We also saw another type of hierarchy where companies engaged in IS integration without building elaborate relational commitments. We called such hierarchies plug-n-play hierarchies. Finally, for non-strategic raw materials or infrastructural facilities, reliability and trust are of paramount importance, whereas IS integration is mostly unnecessary. Thus, a traditional brick-n-mortar hierarchy seems to work best in such situations.

Kaplan and Sawhney (2000) presented a classification schema for B2B marketplaces based on what businesses buy and how they buy it. In their schema, what businesses buy is categorized into manufacturing inputs and operating inputs, while how businesses buy is segregated into systematic purchasing with long-term close relationships and spot sourcing, which is as-needed, instant purchasing. It is easy to extend their framework to the one proposed by our study. Several of the arguments and examples given by Kaplan et al. (2000) for "how businesses buy" pertain to market mechanisms used by buying firms and have a strong parallel in our relational integration dimension. Similarly, they discuss the need and importance of automating purchase processes for buying manufacturing inputs. This corresponds roughly to our IS integration dimension.

Where our model differs from their model is that we propose a typology based on type of integration, and therefore our model yields a different set of insights into the phenomenon of interorganizational systems. We treat IS integration not as a *means* of implementing an organizational integration strategy but as a strategic option itself. Thus, by segregating IS integration from relational integration, we identify additional opportunities for managers for interorganizational cooperation. Plug-n-Play hierarchy, for example, emerges only after we uncouple IS integration from relational integration. In the Internet era, we have the option of separating the two, and as shown in our case studies, managers are already segregating the two in their practice.

REFERENCES

Anderson, J. C., & Narus, J. A. (1990). A model of distributor firm and manufacturer firm working partnerships. *Journal of Marketing*, (54), 42-58, January.

Angeles, R. (2000). Revisiting the role of Internet-EDI in the current electronic commerce scene. *Logistics Information Management*, *13*(1), 45-57.

Bakos, J. Y., & Brynjolfsson, E. (1993). Information technology, incentives, and the optimal number of suppliers. *Journal of Management Information Systems*, *10*(2), 37-53.

Bensaou, M. (1997). Interorganizational cooperation: The role of information technology (an empirical comparison of US and Japanese supplier relations). *Information Systems Research* *8*(2), 107-124.

Bensaou, M., & Venkatraman, N. (1995). Configurations of interorganizational relationships: A comparison between US and Japanese automakers. *Management Science, 41*(9), 1471-92.

Brandenburger, A. M., & Nalebuff, B. J. (1996). Inside Intel. *Harvard Business Review*, *74*(6), 168-175, November-December.

Chan, C., & Swatman, P. M. C. (2000). From EDI to Internet commerce: The BHP Steel experience. *Internet Research: Electronic Networking Applications and Policy*, *10*(1), 72-82.

Choudhury, V., Hartzel, K. S., Konsynski, B. R. (1998). Uses and consequences of electronic markets: An empirical investigation in the aircraft parts industry. *MIS Quarterly*, *22*(4), 471-507

Clark, T. H., & Stoddard, D. B. (1996). Interorganizational business process redesign: Merging technological and process innovation. *Journal of Management Information Systems*, *13*(2), 9-28.

Clemons, E. K., & Row, M. C. (1993). Limits to interfirm coordination through information technology: Results of a field study in consumer packaged goods distribution. *Journal of Management Information Systems*, *10*(1), 73-95.

Clemons, E. K., & Row, M. C. (1992). Information technology and industrial cooperation: The changing economics of coordination and ownership. *Journal of Management Information Systems*, *9*(2), 9-28.

Clemons, E. K., Reddi, S. P., & Row, M. C. (1993). The impact of information technology on the organization of economic activity: The "move to the middle" hypothesis. *Journal of Management Information Systems*, *10*(2), 9-35.

Dyer, J. H., Cho, D. S., & Chu, W. (1998). Strategic supplier segmentation: The next "best practice" in supply chain management. *California Management Review*, *40*(2), 57-77.

Giaglis, G. M., Klein, S., & O'Keefe, R. M. (2002). The role of intermediaries in electronic marketplaces: Developing a contingency model. *Information Systems Journal*, (12), 231-246, July.

Hart, P., & Saunders, C. (1998). Emerging electronic partnerships: Antecedents and dimensions of EDI use from the supplier's perspective. *Journal of Management Information Systems*, *14*(4), 87-111.

Hess, C. M., & Kemerer, C. F. (1994). Computerized loan origination systems: An industry case study of the electronic markets hypothesis. *MIS Quarterly*, *18*(3), 251-275.

Hibbard, J. D., Kumar, N., & Stern, L. W. (2001). Examining the impact of destructive acts in marketing channel relationships. *Journal of Marketing Research*, (38), 45-61, February.

Holland, C. P., & Lockett, G. (1997). Mixed mode network structures: The strategic use of electronic communication by organizations. *Organization Science*, *8*(5), 475-488.

Iacovou, C. L., Benbasat, I., Dexter, & A. S. (1995). Electronic data interchange and small organizations: Adoption and impact of technology. *MIS Quarterly*, *19*(4), 465-485.

Johnston, R. B., & Mak, H. C. (2000). An emerging vision of Internet-enabled supply-chain electronic commerce. *International Journal of Electronic Commerce*, *4*(4), 43-59.

Kambil, A., Nunes, P. F., & Wilson, D. (1999). Transforming the marketspace with all-in-one markets. *International Journal of Electronic Commerce*, *3*(4), 11-28.

Kaplan, S., & Sawhney, M. (2000). E-hubs: The new B2B marketplaces. *Harvard Business Review*, 97-103, May-June.

Kwon, I. G., & Suh, T. (2004). Factors affecting the level of trust and commitment in supply chain relationships. *The Journal of Supply Chain Management*, 4-14.

Lavie, D. (2002). The competitive advantage of interconnected firms: An extension of the resource-based view. *Academy of Management Proceedings*, C1-6.

Lee, H. L., Padmanabhan, V., & Whang, S. (1997). Information distortion in a supply chain: The bullwhip effect. *Management Science*, *43*(4), 546-558.

Malone, T. W., Yates, J., & Benjamin R. I. (1987). Electronic markets and electronic hierarchies. *Communications of the ACM, 30*(6), 484-497.

Massetti, B., & Zmud, R. W. (1996). Measuring the extent of EDI usage in complex organizations: Strategies and illustrative examples. *MIS Quarterly, 20*(3), 331-345.

Mukhopadhyay, T., & Kekre, S. (2002). Strategic and operational benefits of electronic integration in B2B procurement processes. *Management Science*, *48*(10), 1301-1313.

Petre, P. (1985). How to keep customers happy captives. *Fortune*, *112*(5), 42-46, September 2.

Premkumar, G., & Ramamurthy, K. (1995). The role of interorganizational and organizational factors on the decision mode for adoption of interorganizational systems. *Decision Sciences, 26*(3), 303-336.

Srinivasan, K., Kekre, S., & Mukhopadhyay, T. (1994). Impact of electronic data interchange technology on JIT shipments. *Management Science, 40*(10), 1291-1304.

Stock, G. N., Greis, N. P., & Kasarda, J. D. (2000). Enterprise logistics and supply chain structure: The role of fit. *Journal of Operations Management*, (18), 531-547.

Truman, G. E. (2000). Integration in electronic exchange environments. *Journal of Management Information Systems, 17*(1), 209-244, Summer.

Venkatraman, N., & Zaheer, A. (1990). Electronic integration and strategic advantage: A quasi-experimental study in the insurance industry. *Information Systems Research,* 1(4), 377-93.

Williamson, O. E. (1985). *The economic institutions of capitalism*. New York: Free Press.

ENDNOTE

1 An earlier version of this chapter appeared as:
W. Lee, P. Aggarwal, H. Shin, T. Cha, and S. Kim (2006). A typology of interorganizational relationships: A marriage, a fling, or something in between. *International Journal of E-Business Research, 2*(2), 1-21.

Chapter II
Implementing E-Business Models in the Public Services: Challenges, Constraints, and Successful Elements

Francesca Andreesca
University of Greenwich, UK

ABSTRACT

Despite the significant progress made by research into e-business models, the issue of how public sector organisations can successfully make the transition from traditional approaches to e-business by taking advantage of e-technologies has received little attention. This chapter draws on qualitative, longitudinal case-study research carried out between 2001 and 2005 in Britain's national mapping agency to reveal the processes of strategic and organisational transformation engendered by e-business in an organisation evolving from the classical, bureaucratic, and centralised "public sector model" toward a new organisational form through embracing e-business as a corporate philosophy. The study also explores the key components of the new e-business model implemented by the organisation and the contextual factors that impacted on the effectiveness of e-strategy implementation in order to draw a list of best practices for the implementation of e-business in a public sector context.

INTRODUCTION

Increasing environmental pressures, global economic uncertainties, changes in public, and community expectations and pressures to increase public accountability have provided the momentum for public sector organisations in the United Kingdom to examine the effectiveness of their management structures, systems, and processes. Current economic circumstances and the growing body of opinion that public services need to be more effective have forced the British government to consider new management practices in the public services. The emphasis is on achieving efficiency, effectiveness, and economy in the activities performed by public organisations and on developing their ability to compete with private sector organisations (Boyne, 2002, 2004; Boyne & Walker, 2004). The *Modernising government* agenda has provided public sector organisations with the opportunity to operate and compete commercially, while the government retains ownership (E-Government Strategic Framework, April 2001; New Labour Modernising Government White Paper, March 1999). Commercialisation, part of these reforms, has been seen as one of the ways of reinventing public sector entities to make them more competitive in the commercial market. It was used as a way of relieving some of the government's financial pressures and described the situation whereby former government agencies were allowed to charge the public for the provision of goods and services and to adopt features of the commercial environment.

In this changing context for the public sector, public sector organisations have been urged to transform the way they do business, by taking the opportunities and meeting the challenges that e-technologies and e-ways of working presented. As a result, public sector organisations have invented new e-business models for the public services. E-business has been seen as a way of transforming these bureaucratic, centralised, and reactive organisations and their capabilities by experimenting with new ways of information and services delivery via electronic channels (Li, 2003; Mahrer & Brandtweiner, 2004). While the Internet created new commercial opportunities for public sector organisations, e-business was thus about exploiting those opportunities.

However, there has been a tendency to assume that processes of change driven by e-business in the public domain are essentially the same as those in commercial organisations in the private sector. The main problem with these assumptions is that they may ignore how both the mechanisms of change and the outcomes are different in public organisations. In particular, being a commercialising public sector organisation may add different constraints to developing an e-business strategic agenda and we may, thus, fail to do justice to what is distinctive about public sector e-business transformation in terms of the strategic priorities and demands it creates, and the kind of responses it elicits from managers.

Given the unique characteristics and the specific context within which public sector organisations operate, there is a need to develop a more tailored approach to the analysis of e-business transformation within the sector. There is an array of general influence factors specific to this particular environment that might influence the conception and implementation of the change process. However, to date, most research on e-business has focused on private sector entities with little research carried out in public sector organisations and little attention given to the contextual factors that might influence the e-business transformation processes in the public sector. It is important to analyse these factors, nevertheless, as they may enhance understanding of the challenges of applying e-business technologies and principles in the public services.

This chapter draws on qualitative, longitudinal case-study research carried out between 2001 and 2005 in a commercialised public sector organisation to reveal the processes of strategic and organisational transformation engendered by e-business during the implementation of a complex structural and cultural change programme aimed at reshaping this organisation and rethinking how it provided value to its customers. It also explores the contextual factors that challenged the implementation of the new e-business model and impacted on the effectiveness of strategic change management, by enabling or constraining the e-strategy implementation process. The discussion will examine the dilemmas and constraints identified by managers in the interpretation of the e-business strategy concept and why its implementation in practice can be challenging. While the Internet offers a technological solution, the findings of this case study suggest that the successful implementation of a wider e-business strategy depends on managing simultaneously a number of projects, which cross organisational boundaries and linking together organisational and technological factors.

The chapter is divided into five main sections. The first section discusses recent e-business literature and highlights the limitations of existing e-business models. The second section of the chapter describes the methodology used in the study. Information on the contextual developments within the case study organisation is followed by a discussion of the research findings. The case study is used as a background for discussing the challenges and constraints that this commercialising public sector organisation faces in implementing a wider e-business strategy, the key lessons learned, and the contextual factors that impacted upon the success of the e-business implementation. The final section presents some concluding comments.

E-BUSINESS MODELS IN THE PUBLIC SERVICES: LIMITATIONS OF EXISTING FRAMEWORKS

E-business models generally describe emerging business models that exploit the new capabilities of the Internet and related technologies (Afuah & Tucci, 2003; Timmers, 1998).

Research into appropriate e-business models has grown significantly over the past few years, with authors taking both theoretically- and empirically-based approaches to the development of taxonomies of business models suitable for the new economy (Barnes & Hunt, 2001; Li, 2007). However, despite the significant progress made by previous studies into e-business models, most research seem to be dealing with only some aspects of the concept, while neglecting or downplaying others (Li, 2006; Osterwalder, 2004; Osterwalder & Pigneur, 2002).

A number of business models focused upon individual business transactions that use the Net as medium of exchange, including both business to business and business to consumer (e.g., Becker & Berkemeyer, 2004; Carlton, 2001; Clay, 2001; Clegg et al., 2005; Gao, 2005; Garicano, 2001; Scott Morton, 2001). Interest has also tended to focus on new startups (Colombo, 2001; Chaston, 2001; Clarke & Flaherty, 2004) and on traditional organisations moving toward integrating electronic marketing and sales, purchasing, or customer service with their current businesses (e.g., Baida, Gordijn, Akkermans, Saele, & Morch, 2005; Barnes, Hinton, & Mieczkowska, 2005; Bhaskar, 2004; Chen & Leteney, 2000; Hansen, 2000; Kotha, Rajgopal, & Rindova, 2001; Lee & Wang, 2001), or on the technology itself (Day & Schoemaker, 2000; Smith, 2001). Much research into the use of e-models, furthermore, has tended to focus on larger firms (Dutta & Segev, 1999), new business models for digital content (Barnes et al., 2001; Boddy & Macbeth, 2000; Daniel, Wilson, & Myers, 2002; Mahadevan, 2000; Van der Wiele, Williams, Van Iwaarder, Wilson, & Dale, 2002), and the growth and development of dot-coms (Benoy, Cook, & Javalgi, 2001; Clay, 2001). Further studies revealed how the Internet has made possible types of business model previously very hard, or impossible, to implement (Mahadevean, 2000; Rayport, 1999; Timmers, 2003). The focus has been on issues related to the digital content provision (particularly online provision) and technologies or technology-based change generically, rather than specifically on the organisational transformation required for successfully making the change to e-business. This topic is critically important, nevertheless, because the majority of organisations are not start-ups and many are not solely concerned with e-commerce and electronic markets. Rather, most organisations are traditional businesses, which must grapple with finding a new architecture to meet the imperative of remaining competitive in an increasingly Internet-enhanced economy and successfully making the change. Their main concern is thus the adoption of e-business as an all embracing phenomenon and of an integrated business model to facilitate and shape the development of infrastructure and services, and to experiment with new ways of information and services delivery via electronic channels.

Osterwalder (2004, cited by Li, 2007, p. 141) defines a business model as the logic of a business system for creating value that lies behind the actual processes and argues that such a model needs to address the revenue and product aspects, the business actor and network aspects, and the marketing aspects of a business. He proposes an integrated e-business framework with four interconnected components: product innovation, customer relationship, infrastructure management, and financial aspects. Product innovation describes what business the organisation is in, while customer relationship illustrates who the organisation's target customers are. Infrastructure management describes the logistics the organisation uses, and the financial aspects describe the revenue and cost model employed by the organisation. The notion of "e-business model" is used, in this context, to describe the value an organisation offers to one or several segments of customers and the architecture of the organisation and its network of partners for creating, marketing, and delivering this relationship capital, in order to generate profitable and sustainable revenue streams. Figure 1 summarises the key components of the generic e-business model proposed by Osterwalder (2004) and the relationships amongst them, and provides a foundation for our later discussion of e-business models in the context of the case study organisation.

Within the literature drawn on public sector organisations, research has shown that government agencies are eagerly looking toward a digital future (Burn & Robbins, 2001) and they are using technology to enhance the access to and the delivery of government services for the benefit of citizens, business partners and employees (Aichholzer & Schmutzer, 2000; Heeks, 2001). To achieve these overall goals, adequate strategies have to be developed which will determine the success of failure of the ensuing e-projects (Burn et al., 2001; Gant & Gant, 2001). E-business was, in this context, directed to better meet the needs and expectations of citizens and to optimise the

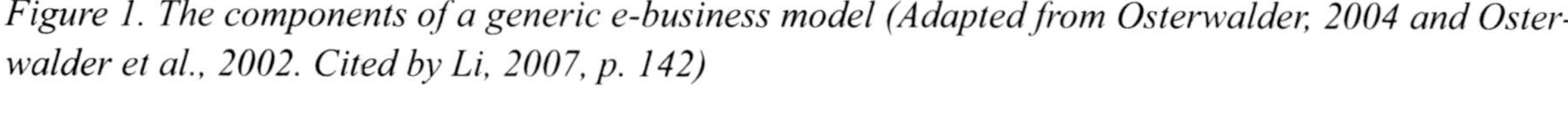
Figure 1. The components of a generic e-business model (Adapted from Osterwalder, 2004 and Osterwalder et al., 2002. Cited by Li, 2007, p. 142)

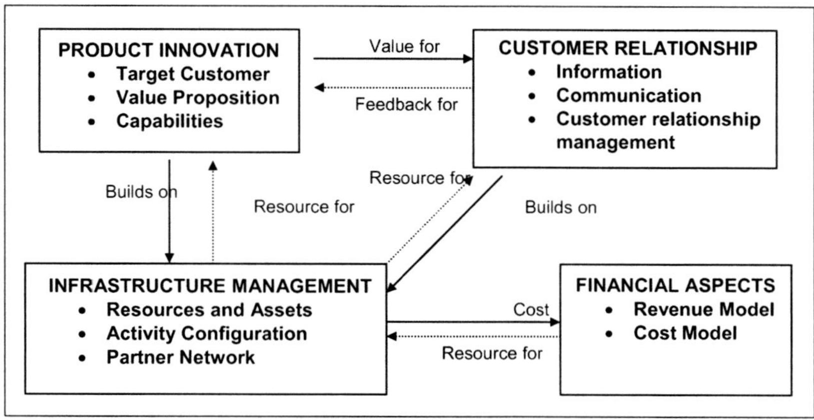

internal processes of government agencies by means of modern IT in order to reduce costs (Li, 2003).

Existing public sector literature also suggests that e-business in the public services can deliver a number of benefits (Gant et al., 2001; Graafland-Essers & Ettedgui, 2003; Heeks, 2001, 2002; Li, 2003; Osborne & Gaebler, 1997). Besides higher transparency in the public services, and therefore making processes and decisions more visible for citizens, e-business could lead to a streamlining of administrational structures, the possibility of electronic processing of public administration work leading to a reduction of internal processing time, and an enhancement of internal communication among the administration together with cost reduction. In addition, it could deliver new ways of citizen's participation in the political processes and generate more flexibility and lower response time of administrative bodies.

Much of the existing e-business literature drawn on public sector organisations has a unitarist feel, a presumption that all that "e-business" is about is the sharing of business information, maintaining business relationships, and conducting business transactions by means of Internet-based technology (Clegg et al., 2002; Poon & Swatman, 1999). However, as recent research into the use of Internet technologies in the public services has shown, e-business is not only about technology, but it also impacted every aspect of an organisation involved (Mahrer et al., 2004). Implementing e-business strategies in public sector organisations is also about these organisations' social environment and the relationships between people and technologies (Li, 2005; Mahrer et al., 2004). As elsewhere, in the United Kingdom, in the context of the increased pressures to make all the government services more cost-effective, e-business started to be seen not only as a way in which these organisations can gain value from the Internet technologies, but also as a way people within these government agencies work together, the sharing of information and effective communication, the transactions and connections across a supply chain, between suppliers and distributors and consumers, as well as the relationships between individuals and institutions (Heeks, 2002; Li, 200, Li, 2005).

Taking all these perspectives and approaches together, overall, the issue of how public sector organisations undergoing commercialisation can successfully make the transition from traditional approaches to e-business by taking advantage of e-technologies has received little attention in the existing literature. *What processes of strategic and organisational transformation are engendered by e-business implementation in public sector organisations? What challenges and constraints are they facing in implementing e-business strategies?* and *What are the key success factors?*

This chapter examines these important issues. It focuses on the processes of e-business transformation in the public services using an illustrative case study of a British public sector organisation within the geographic information industry. It aims to provide fresh insights into the change processes, which occurred in an organisation evolving from the classical, bureaucratic and centralised "public sector model" toward a new organisational form through embracing e-business as a corporate philosophy.

RESEARCH METHOD AND DESIGN

The research reported here is drawn from findings from a five-year study of organisational change carried out between 2001 and 2005. The study adopted a longitudinal perspective on change concerned with the holistic and processual character of organisational transformations over time (Pettigrew, 1985, 1990) and employed a case study methodology (Eisenhardt, 1989; Yin, 1994). The case study in this chapter was carried out at Britain's national mapping agency, a commercialising public sector organisation from the geographic information industry.

The time period for data collection was between October 2001 and September 2005. This research involved three main types of data: semi-structured interviews, documentary data, and non-participant observation.

Data were collected from the organisation at two time points during the research period to track the internal changes over time:

- Time 1 (2001/2002) corresponded to the official adoption of the new "e-business model".
- Time 2 (2003/2004) corresponded to the incorporation and consolidation of strategic changes, allowing for change to become partially "anchored" in new social structures and practices.

A total of 109 interviews were conducted with the main actors involved in the strategic initiative programmes and in the implementation of change such as deputy chief executive, corporate strategists, members of the top and middle management, other individual organisational members, and management consultants (Table 1). Most respondents had been with the organisation for a considerable period of time. This was supplemented with analysis of documentary evidence including board minutes, strategy documents, reports of the steering committee, project teams, minutes of follow-up meetings, business plans, as well as non-participant observation.

During the field study, the researcher had access to the main participants, formal and informal meetings, existing minutes, and documentation highlighting some of the historical, processual, and contextual issues relevant to the e-business strategy implementation. In addition, the interviews emphasised both individual and shared interpretations of key participants concerning actions, events, views, beliefs, aspirations, and motives. All interviews were tape-recorded.

EXAMINING E-BUSINESS STRATEGIES IN PRACTICE: THE CASE OF BRITAIN'S NATIONAL MAPPING AGENCY

Britain's national mapping agency (hereafter *NMA*) is a quasi-autonomous agency within the geographic information industry with trading fund status. It employs approximately 1850 staff, 1350 of whom are based at the head office, while the rest—cartographic surveyors and territorial sales representatives—are dispersed among a network of 80 local offices around the country.

NMA is recognised as a leading participant in the geographic information industry, within which it is forging partnerships with key private sector companies. Its principal activities are twofold: the maintenance of the National Topographic Database by recording and storing measurements of

Table 1. Number of respondents participating in interviews in Phase 1 and Phase 2

Position of Interviewee	Number in Time 1	Number in Time 2
CEO	1	1
Strategy Directors and Strategy Managers Strategic	6	6
planning responsibilities	5	2
Senior Managers	18	10
Senior Consultants	3	2
Project Managers	21	10
Line Managers	8	6
Individual Organisational Members (Sales and Finance)	6	4
Total interviews = 109	68	41

new roads, houses, and so forth and the creation of products from it such as paper map series and digital data sets used in geographic information systems.

The organisation offered an excellent opportunity to study the organisational change required in transforming a former government agency into an e-business, culturally, commercially, and technically. Confronted by powerful pressures to improve organisational performance under the government modernisation agenda, NMA implemented a complex e-business strategy, combined with a huge investment in technology new product development, which were designed to radically change the organisation's structure, management, and knowledge processes. To take advantage of the opportunities that e-technologies and e-ways of working presented, NMA charted an ambitious organisational transformation in which e-business was seen as a catalyst for change and the e-strategy as a route map.

This knowledge-intensive organisation is a particularly interesting example of how a public organisation managed to overcome the constraints of its business context to fashion its own destiny. Unlike other public sector organisations with stable, incremental environments, NMA is operating in conditions of low environmental stability with frequent, rapid changes in geographic information systems technology. Due to the emergence of new digital technology, the geographic information industry is on the verge of rapid growth, particularly in the market for location-based services. The overlay of layers of data to create new views creates good commercial opportunities for NMA, such as in the correlation of geographic, commercial catchment area and socio-demographic data for use in supermarket home delivery services.

All of these trends make the geographic information industry very different from the more traditional consumer and industrial markets in which many other public organisations operate. With an increasingly challenging environment, pressures to develop e-business under the government e-strategy in the public sector and emergence of new technologies, NMA is closer to the "relentlessly changing organisations" model of Brown and Eisenhardt (1997) in the high-velocity computer industry. There are these particular "high-tech" and "e-business" features of NMA that make this public sector organisation such an interesting case for management research in general, and for e-business change implementation in particular.

Key Facts About NMA

- Modern data collection using the geographic positioning system (GPS) and location information.
- Turnover from trading activities: £ 105.5 million in 2005/2006; most of the incomes come from computerised geographic data, which is used extensively in both the private and public sector, with around £136 billion of Britain's GDP underpinned by it.
- Core markets by 2005: Public sector and utilities (32%); land and property (5%); consumer (12%); commercial markets (mobile communications & wireless; large retailers; banking, finance and insurance; transport and distribution) (51%).
- Has operated as a trading fund since April 1999. This provides a greater degree of commercial flexibility and increased responsibility for its business planning and finances. As a trading fund, the business has to make a profit but does not receive a subsidy from the taxpayer.
- A potential change in status toward a government-owned plc. was proposed in 2002 and rejected because it did not deliver the necessary benefits to the organisation. It was decided that it was in the public interest for NMA to remain a trading fund. However, enhanced financial freedoms and flexibilities have been granted by the government

through a revised framework document in 2003.

External Context

The *e-government strategic framework* (April 2001) set out a series of guiding principles for public sector organisations centred upon building services around citizens choices, making government and its services more accessible electronically, and managing information and knowledge in more efficient ways to ensure easier online access and more effective use of all services. It set a series of e-government policies and targets for quasi-autonomous agencies, stating as main objectives that 90% of low-value procurement transactions and 100% of document management should take place electronically by 2004 and that 100% of services should be available electronically by 2005. In order to meet these aims, public sector organisations must innovate within a common framework and manage their services as a business, focusing on cost effectiveness and funding mechanisms.

In line with these targets, Britain's national mapping agency was granted trading fund powers by Parliament in 1999 to give it direct responsibility for its own finances and freedom to develop new initiatives. In effect, this meant that NMA would remain obliged to serve government by providing information across Britain while earning revenues in a commercial and increasingly competitive marketplace, reducing dependence on the taxpayer. Such a status provided the organisation with the opportunity to operate and compete commercially by earning commercial revenues for its geographical information in order to be self-funding, as well as be more accountable for the efficiency and effectiveness of its operations.

Internal Context

The organisation had a long history of unsuccessful reorganisations and frequent changes of chief executives. Since 1993, NMA has launched three different reorganisation initiatives under different governments, all of them recognised by managers and staff as "spectacularly unsuccessful."

Similar to other public sector entities undergoing public sector reform in the form of commercialisation, the efficiency and effectiveness of management processes were major challenges. NMA was a vertically integrated organisation with an excessive degree of specialisation, rigid hierarchical divisions and divided areas of activity with niches and boundaries that served no useful purpose. Underlying many of the problems of inefficiency and high costs was the monopoly situation that all costs could eventually be passed on to the market. The organisation was also a classic example of public service culture and organisational systems and processes. NMA's administrative structure based on departments and well-defined job categories had effectively prevented the organisation from operating in accordance with its own objectives and values. It was realised that, especially in the relationship between NMA's employees and its customers, too much importance was being given to resolving bureaucratic issues, to the detriment of customer service. In short, the internal structure worked against the integration of main business processes.

Drivers for Change

NMA has expanded considerably in recent years into commercial and leisure markets, both in the UK and internationally. The environment in which the organisation operated was characterised by emerging opportunities for the rapid expansion of the digital market and, in particular, location-based services offered via the Internet. That sat alongside its activities in the mature market for traditional paper-based mapping.

The severe market competition and threat of product substitution through the mass expansion of digital information and the new status of trading fund acted as drivers for revenue maximisation and for placing greater emphasis on increasing the utilisation of geographical data. A key aspect of becoming a trading fund was to move toward performance targets and a culture of measuring, and rewarding achievement linked to the business vision. This new "business model" meant that NMA had to strike the right balance between maintaining consistent and accurate geographical information for the whole of Great Britain while ensuring its operations are funded by earning income and generating profits from the licensing of data to both the public and private sectors. The organisation was also required to make an average return on the capital it employs—on average around £40 million—of at least 5.5% a year and to pay an annual dividend to the government based on each year's trading results.

In response to this challenge, a series of organisation change initiatives began.

The Change Agenda: From Bureaucracy to E-Business

With the advent of a new chief executive officer recruited from the commercial sector in September 2000, considerable impetus for change was being evidenced. A re-evaluation of the business from the customers' perspective was completed and the need for the organisation to develop innovative products and services that could be delivered electronically was identified. The review undertaken by the executive team identified that the greatest hindrance to achieving NMA's corporate goals were its structures and work practices. Another major change that had to occur was a shift from the old culture of public monopoly to the culture of a market-oriented, customer-focused, and self-financing organisation. The nature and direction of the required cultural shift was a radical change for many employees, who had spent virtually all their careers in the relative security, comfort and complacency of the old "public sector ethos" culture. The "cultural inertia" among the majority of employees, at all levels, was one of the major challenges to management in trying to achieve the transformation to the new system of efficient business operations.

Following the review, a new vision formed the foundation on which the organisation could be transformed into an e-business: *"NMA and its partners will be the content provider of choice for location based information in the new information economy."* In October 2000, a cross-functional team from across NMA was established to develop the vision into a new strategy for the organisation. The team used the mission statement as a starting point for designing the structure and process of the change programme and translating it into a new e-strategy.

Fundamentally, the e-strategy was about transforming the business commercially, technologically, and culturally by implementing a new business model combined with multi-million pound investment in technology and new product development. The main strategic priorities were as follows:

1. Commercial revenue – increase commercial revenue from existing assets.
2. Reduce costs and waste.
3. Invest in new brands, infrastructure, and capability.
4. Grow data products and help partners to develop their products.
5. Aggressive marketing for products.
6. Grow partners and enable them to add value to products.
7. Build the best data to enable "joined-up geography."

The key emphasis was on better knowledge management, focusing on the needs of businesses and individuals and helping partners to create radically new products underpinned by data maintained by NMA. At the heart of the new strategy was the idea of NMA working together with partners to become the content provider of choice for location-based information. This meant establishing commercial agreements with various partners in which NMA was providing the geographical data and the partners were developing the software required for customising this data in different ways and translating it into innovative products and services under NMA's brand.

A series of *objectives* were established:

1. Delivering excellence in all aspects of the business, employing e-business principles to exceed customer expectations.
2. Identifying, developing, and maintaining effective strategic partnerships.
3. Ensuring that the business strategy is clearly understood by staff, customers, partners, and the wider community.
4. Establishing NMA as the centre of excellence for innovation in location-based information.
5. Developing a business of progressive people with skills appropriate to an e-business.
6. Changing the internal culture.

A range of projects were identified that would exploit e-business technology and approaches to improve performance. An initial assessment of costs, benefits, and timescales were prepared. At the end of the four-week period, NMA executive and non-executive directors approved the strategy. More detailed planning and evaluation of implementation costs and benefits followed as development work began.

A major feature of the e-strategy implementation was the intention to place the organisation at the forefront of the new information economy by embracing cutting-edge technology for supplying geographical data and enhancing the versatility of NMA data. This involved the implementation of a groundbreaking new concept of mapping and the development of new products, by transforming the map-making process so that electronic data could be available to customers within twenty-four hours of being surveyed. The key aim was to replace the traditional paper map products with large-scale electronic mapping so that most of the products and services offered by the organisation could be delivered electronically; digital mapping now accounts for some 80% of the organisation's turnover.

Among the most pioneering products were a digital database and online service named MasterMap, featuring definitive digital data for the whole of Great Britain and an online integrated product called Pre-Build TM. The MasterMap database provides intelligent and accessible data with the flexibility to link information across and between organisations, while Pre-Build TM offered highly detailed digital mapping pinpointing buildings and roads tailored to the needs of utilities and telecommunication companies.

The successful implementation of the new strategy pivoted on the adoption of *e-business as a corporate philosophy*. As the chief executive remarked:

... e-business is key to our future success, opening huge new opportunities for us and our partners. It requires new ways of working and both individual and team efforts right across the business. We have the best data to underpin the Master Map of Britain. Our e-initiatives will ensure we can create and supply that data when, where and how our customers want it—and at the same times e-enable ourselves. (Chief Executive, 2001)

Collecting, maintaining, and delivering geographical data was at the forefront of NMA's activity and the implementation of the new e-business strategy acted as a driver for the transformation of its core business processes—data collection and management. The e-strategy was thus seen as the necessary framework for driving forward business change. As some senior managers argued:

... the "E" strategy allows us to reassess how we manage the collection and delivery of our data to remain at the forefront of the industry, offering

agility and flexibility to our customers. (Director –Data Collection and Management, 2001)

... The digital maps business cannot grow enough without the e-strategy. This work is critical because it will allow us to create and deliver more innovative products much faster to our customers. It will allow us to become far more efficient and cost effective across a wide range of activities. (Director – Digital Brands, 2001)

As the main supplier of geographical information in Britain, NMA needed not only to implement tangible customer benefits and to advance online services, but also to change the organisation's internal culture to a customer-led one. The prevailing view amongst over 90% of senior executives interviewed was that e-business was not only about electronic service delivery, but also that "e" should become embedded in the employees' ways of working, in terms of approach and attitude:

We must become a more agile organisation able to respond to our customers and partners needs at 'internet-speed' ... The IT technology is the engine room of this change providing the infrastructure, information systems and user support in transforming the organisation. However, if we are to succeed in achieving our strategic aims and becoming an e-business, it is essential that we develop new ways of working. We must improve our day-to-day business practices and ensure that we get the best out of people, knowledge, systems, and facilities. (Chief Technology Officer, 2001)

The process of strategy formulation resulted in a series of 21 investment projects that were grouped into five strategic initiatives reflecting their inter-connected nature (Table 2).

Table 2. Projects under the e-strategy

Strategic Initiative	**Corresponding Projects**
Putting the customer first	• *Customer Web sites* • *New Web site for the organisation* • *Customer relationship management* • *Online service* • *Digital mapping*
Strategic alliances	• *Establishment* • *Joined-up government* • *Alliance extranet*
The new mapping agency	• *New ways of working and project platinum* • *Knowledge management* • *"Help yourself" (personalised online support for all employees)* • *Raising the return (a new financial model)*
Developing the market	• *Developing the digital National Geographic database* • *E-brands* • *Location-based standards* • *E-business channels* • *Market development team* • *Pricing and licensing*
Enabling Infrastructure	• *Enhancing the IT infrastructure* • *Off-site 24*7 availability* • *Enterprise wide software suite (ESS)*

Putting the customer first initiative involved the adoption of e-business principles and technology to ensure that each customer and partner is managed at segment and individual levels. In the words of the initiative manager:

This initiative is critical because it will allow us to create and deliver more innovative products much faster to our customers and to become far more efficient and cost effective across a wide range of activities. (Initiative Manager, 2001)

Customers were offered online access to a wide range of mapping data, product demonstrations to show the versatility of NMA data and tailor-made Web gateways into the mapping agency, each fostering improved, more focused customer service. These gateways included facilities for the online ordering and delivery of existing data products at any time of the day or night or requests for special mapping surveys. Each customer Web site held information specific to that customer or partner as well as access to generic information and functionality available to wider groups.

By December 2002, the implementation of a portal Web infrastructure environment increased the efficiency of personalisation and customisation provided to customers. In parallel, the NMA Web site was redeveloped to become a gateway for location-based services and information and an enterprise-wide software was implemented to allow better customer relationship management. Users of the new Web site were able to access location-based information and services either directly provided by NMA or indirectly by partners and account holders (customers and partners) could order digital and graphic mapping online.

The strategic alliance initiative involved the establishment of a strategic alliance to help drive the location-based information industry forward in a cohesive manner and develop collaborative working between NMA and other parts of the government with the help of e-business technology. It involved joined-up geography by using NMA data and referencing framework to combine other location-based information from other government bodies, for example, land ownership, local authorities, addresses, field parcels and land use. It also marked a change in the way NMA was making available its data sets to users, by enabling partners to commercialise this data, on behalf of NMA, in a more flexible way. The initiative manager talks of the overall project as follows:

This initiative ensures that our NMA has the right strategic relationships to help grow the geographic information industry. Our organisation holds an important position in the location based information industry but must work with key players in government and the private sector to realise the vision. (Initiative Manager, 2001)

The new mapping agency initiative *focused on the people implications of the transformation of NMA into an e-business. The project manager states:*

Whilst each of the other four strategic initiatives delivers in its own way significant change to the business, this initiative is the one that touches every single person in NMA. These projects are all closely related to our people and the way we do things. The focus is on simple and more effective ways of working whilst focusing on the needs of the customer. (Initiative Manager, 2001)

A programme called "New Ways of Working" addressed issues associated with the current organisational structure, people, culture, communication, and the way employees worked. The clear target was to make these elements more streamlined, adaptive, responsive, and customer-driven. This included changing the existing working practices, the implementation of new performance management and reward systems focused on rewarding performance, changing the way information and knowledge are captured, coordinated, and made readily available within the organisation (knowledge management), and the implementation of a new software, which allowed employees to manage their personnel records online while also eliminating unnecessary paperwork, procedures, administration, and costly support functions.

The organisation needed new competencies and skills among existing managers so that they could drive forward the change programme. Current management capabilities were characterised by excellent technical abilities but poor people management skills especially in terms of managing change and risk. It was considered that in order to change the culture of the organisation, leaders and management teams had to develop themselves in readiness to embrace the new challenges and opportunities facing NMA. Therefore, a new programme entitled "project platinum" was designed to help leaders understand how they could influence the culture of the organisation, identify the competencies and skills required in leaders and set in place a programme which could develop the behaviours supporting those competencies. As part of this initiative, a set-piece event—*NMA Experience*—was organised in December 2001. The event was attended by all the employees and was designed to explain to everyone the new vision and values of the organisation as an attempt to change the strong supportive civil service culture, rich in custom and practice, develop a new culture in line with the new direction of the organisation and encourage creative and innovative behaviours. The core new values were identified as "customer focused," "quick," "working together," "able to take some risks," "interested and excited by challenge," "personally accountable," "commercially oriented" and "rewarded for results."

Developing the market initiative involved developing new partnerships and using new channels to reach new customers. In the past, NMA focused on an established core of customers in a relatively mature market with sectors such as central government, local government, and utilities. These customers increasingly expected better quality products and services in a market that was becoming more competitive. The organisation needed thus not only to develop the existing markets but also to find new markets and work with partners to develop new applications that will provide benefits to end customers. This involved adopting a proactive brand strategy, with a focus on digital location-based information and the launch of a new idea of geographic database—master map. Innovative in concept, master map was not a map in the traditional sense but a digital map framework through which customers could access the precise mapping data they needed. It offered a high level of flexibility and a complete reference system for Britain's geographical data. As the programme manager comments:

The initiative supports customers evolving needs, develops existing markets, and opens new opportunities to ensure that NMA is the content provider of choice. (Initiative Manager, 2001)

Enabling infrastructure initiative involved building a robust new infrastructure of systems to underpin the e-business. A considerable amount of infrastructure has been put in place to support the whole of the e-strategy but particularly the master map idea. The Internet, Extranet, and Intranet applications were all upgraded and, in order to enhance customer benefit and operational efficiencies, the old systems were replaced with a single, integrated, enterprise-wide software application platform. This integrated software package called *enterprise-wide software suite* (ESS) offered a single repository for all NMA's data and was implemented in association with technology partners. One of the programme managers expressed a commonly held view:

The application and technical environment that we build must provide the efficiencies that allow us to operate in an increasingly dynamic and delivery focused organisation. Information technology (IT) provides the infrastructure, information systems and user support in transforming the organisation. Without a robust IT infrastructure none of the e-business activities will be sustainable. To a lesser or greater extent, we have all been frustrated when a system let us down, whether it be our own personal Internet service provider or a corporate system. As our business becomes increasingly dependant on IT systems, we have to avoid those frustrating (and potentially damaging) failures. (Programme Manager, Enabling Infrastructure, 2002)

IMPLEMENTATION ISSUES

Organisational Restructuring

In order to successfully implement the e-business strategy, the structure of the organisation was reviewed and reorganised in November 2001. As the CEO summed up the rationale for this strategic initiative:

The need for accurate, reliable locational information underpins so many of the new services coming on stream and in Britain, no one has better locational information than us ... But to stay at the forefront of the geographical industry we must keep pace with the market. That's why we're not only investing in e-business initiatives but have already put in place a whole new organisational structure to make it a reality. (Chief Executive, 2001)

The realignment of internal group structures and board responsibilities resulted in:

1. The establishment of two brands businesses based around distinct customer groups—digital and graphic brands. The two brands' businesses were focused on introducing new and innovative ways of working with commercial and government partners to meet different customer group needs. Amongst such innovative approaches were the establishment of a joint-venture company with a commercial partner, with the aim of providing consistent and maintained points of interest data for the industry and an estimated £ 35 million content deal with a mobile phone operator that would allow mobile users to access coloured maps featuring real-time displays of various locations;
2. The creation of a business change group that was charged with championing the transformation of the way the organisation did business and in particular managing the implementation of the e-business strategy.

Ownership of the Strategy

Ownership, accountability, and leadership were essential elements of the successful implementation of the NMA e-business strategy. As change was intended to be transformational and to affect all the aspects of the organisation and the levels within it, the entire programme has been top-down driven, with the provision of a clear, sustained direction that was well resourced and coordinated. The instigators of the transformation were the leaders of the organisation and the strategy and operating board—including executive and non-executive directors—had been heavily involved in the e-business strategy and monitor its implementation. In addition, each strategic initiative had a director-level owner who was accountable to the board for delivering the benefits of that initiative. Full-time initiative managers who focused on co-ordinating activity within their initiative have been appointed.

At project level, business owners have been identified, who were champions for their projects within the implementation. Project owners were responsible for ensuring that their projects delivered the benefits anticipated in the strategy. Where IT projects were involved in the delivery, the business owners worked in close conjunction with IT programme and project managers.

Risk Management, Change Control, and Financial Monitoring at Appropriate Levels

Mechanisms have been implemented to ensure the adequate management of risks, costs, and change control during the implementation. The operating board received updates on implementation progress, including costs, on a fortnightly basis with a more detailed review undertaken six-weekly through a business health check exercise. In addition, a weekly implementation steering group (chaired by the director of business change and including the initiative owner directors) monitored strategic level risks, costs, and implementation progress. Significant changes to project contracts and business cases were approved by initiative owners and reported to the steering group. Furthermore, programme and project boards have been established within each initiative and these dealt with the day-to-day detail of implementation monitoring, cost control and minor change control.

Internal Communication

In order to engage all employees in the business transformation associated with the implementation of the e-business strategy, considerable effort has been put into a coordinated programme of internal communication, which included:

1. Face-to-face briefings with all staff including interactive and multimedia demonstrations of live and prototype systems.
2. Fortnightly update briefings at operating board—cascade briefed by managers to all staff and reported on Intranet.
3. A dynamic Intranet site—regularly updated with project aims and progress.
4. Internal branding of the implementation activity to help focus all staff on the business transformation.

... and Further Restructuring

In May 2002, a new human resources director, recruited from the commercial sector, was appointed to drive forward the people side of the change programme. At her initiative in August 2002, a team of senior managers undertook an eight-week review exercise, which involved looking forward to the future and identifying the challenges and opportunities that the organisation was likely to face in 3 to 5 years time and how the business could be driven forward.

Following this review in September 2002, the board announced a further restructuring of the organisation to help develop stronger teams and networks around the core processes (Figure 2) and to create a more flexible structure, with more flexible processes and communication patterns. This was accompanied by a review of staffing levels in different functional and sub-functional areas and 300 people were, consequently, released. A consequence of this restructuring was that a number of old divisions and functions were either eliminated or merged in order to obtain a leaner, flatter structure and increase overall efficiency of the business.

The proposed new structure involved merging the digital and graphic brands businesses into a single sales and market development group and creating a separate programmes and products group, each headed by a director. The business change group activities were absorbed within other parts of the organisation. To give greater integration to corporate communications, the corporate communications department has been integrated into the human resources and corporate services group led by the HR director. Minimal changes were introduced in the other groups. As a result of these changes, the new structure due to be implemented starting with November

2002 incorporates seven major groups (Figure 3): strategy, human resources and corporate services, finance, information systems, Web, research, and innovation, data collection and management, programmes and products, and sales and market development.

The previous structure created in November 2001, in relation to the e-strategy implementation, served its purpose of focusing the organisation of work on developing new products and markets and gave an impetus to particular projects. It allowed NMA to strengthen its digital offering and also gave the graphic side of the business the confidence and space to develop, and between them both, business groups could identify notable successes.

The new structure implemented in September 2002 offered a much higher level of functional flexibility. It gave clarity to the end-to-end processes of the business—from collecting data, through the production processes, and on the supply of data to partners and customers, while allowing the development of stronger cross-functional teams and networks around core processes. The number of hierarchical levels between top management and business groups teams has been substantially reduced and the seven groups have been organised along business processes, giving a lot of operational freedom to group managers. This freedom was balanced by a stronger planning process in the organisation with group teams working with the strategy people on the overall planning.

The different cross-functional teams created meant increased horizontal communication between groups as well as vertical between top management team and group teams, facilitated by the use of modern information technology. The new organisation of work was trying to combine the strengths of a functionally arranged organisational structure, offering a better co-ordination of the core business process with the flexibilities in terms of vertical communication offered by a process-based structure.

The transition from the old structure to the new one was a lengthy process. The old structure was effectively being moved to the new structure on a level-by-level basis. As employees in the positions made redundant under the voluntary redundancy scheme were leaving the organisation, the remaining positions were being rearranged in the new structure and staff were notified about the new positions. Transition structures were being used to prop up the old structure and keep the day-to-day operations going. The implementation of the new structure was finalised in August 2003.

In parallel with these structural changes, in order to track and predict customer, market, and

Figure 2. Core business processes in NMA

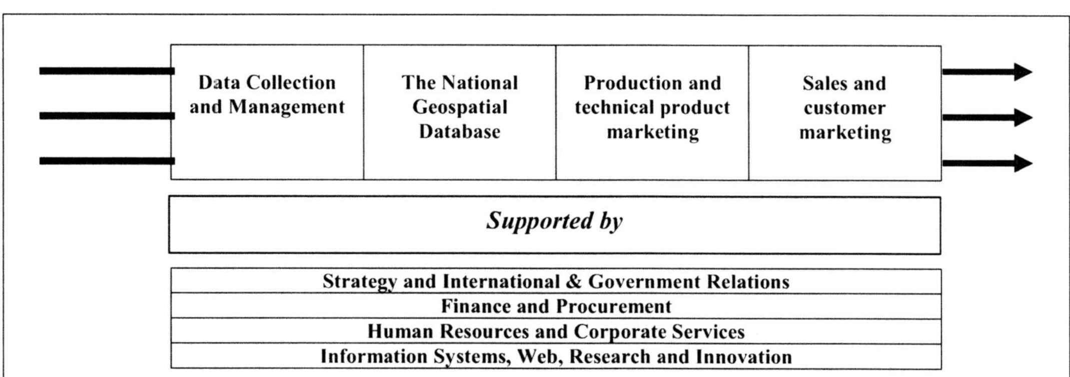

Figure 3. The new organisational structure

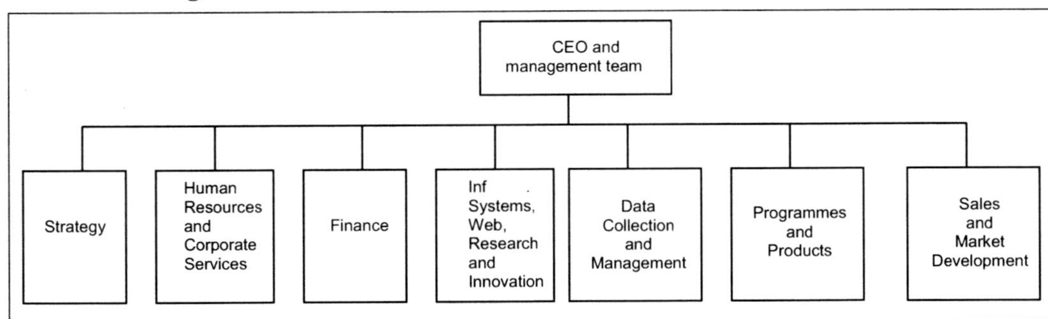

brand profitability, a corporate balanced scorecard with six performance dimensions (financial performance, quality of service, flexibility, competitiveness, resource utilisation, and innovation) has been introduced as a way of consolidating corporate performance measures and focus them upon core strategy components. The aim of introducing the balanced scorecard, in addition to other measurement tools such as customer satisfaction surveys, employee opinion, and monthly business health checks, was to provide the management board with the means to monitor the progress of the business on an ongoing basis. In addition, the strategy team could liaise better with individual business planners (business groups' directors) for coordinating business processes across teams and establish integrated performance measures.

By December 2004, all 21 projects comprising the e-strategy were fully completed and their success benchmarked against their key deliverables. An overall assessment of the change efforts driven by the e-business implementation between 2000 and 2004 suggests the e-strategy implementation was a success. The progress made toward transforming the way the organisation worked was acknowledged by customers, partners, suppliers, and e-business experts and employees noticed a marked improvement in their working environment. In addition to this feedback, the e-strategy was awarded five stars by the Government Office of the E-Envoy in 2004 and this rating indicated that the NMA's strategy was seen as a successful plan of action that has largely been met with key deliverables offering customers and staff new benefits. An operating profit of £9.4 million was forecasted by April 2005 thanks to careful management of costs, growth in revenue, and rigorous prioritisation of investments.

In July 2004, a new framework document was presented to Parliament, setting out fresh financial arrangements (the payment of an annual dividend to the government) and reconfirming the agency's trading fund status with strong links into the commercial market place. The performance of the organisation was rated as "excellent" in the context of the growing commercial partnerships of NMA with partners from the public and private sector.

A new business strategy (2005-2008) organised around four key themes—people, data, delivery, and customers—and focused on how NMA will be meeting customer needs in the next four years was created, building on some of the success aspects of the previous e-strategy: the creation of better data collection, maintenance, and management systems, as well as the development of new products and geographic solutions through partnerships with other public and private organisations. A new business plan (2005-2008) entitled " focusing upon delivery" was also launched building upon progress made in 2003-2004 and promoting the following objectives: efficiency gain in data collection by March 2006; delivery of key investment programmes by March 2007; enhancement of database quality and content, flexible data delivery by March 2007; Customer migration and improved customer experience by May 2005. An event chart of the NMA "journey" is presented in Figure 4.

INFLUENCING FACTORS

While the mechanisms used to implement e-business within the case study organisation were key to its success, it was apparent from the study that a range of enablers and constraints existed within the organisation that directly impacted upon the success of the e-business implementation in a public sector context.

Adaptive Responses to Government Policy and the Political "Ties" of the Organisations

The degree of flexibility and freedom that the organisation was allowed to have in interpreting and applying government policy acted as a facilitator for the change process.

The NMA's links with government were somewhat more at arms-length. The "radical" Labour reform has still exposed NMA to a period of turbulence and conflict, with pressures to expand the range of products and services in the context of harsh reductions in government funding provided over the last years. However, NMA board members were nominally independent directors and, indeed, technically NMA was a quasi-autonomous agency run on next steps lines

Figure 4. Event chart, e-strategy implementation, and follow-up (2000-2004)

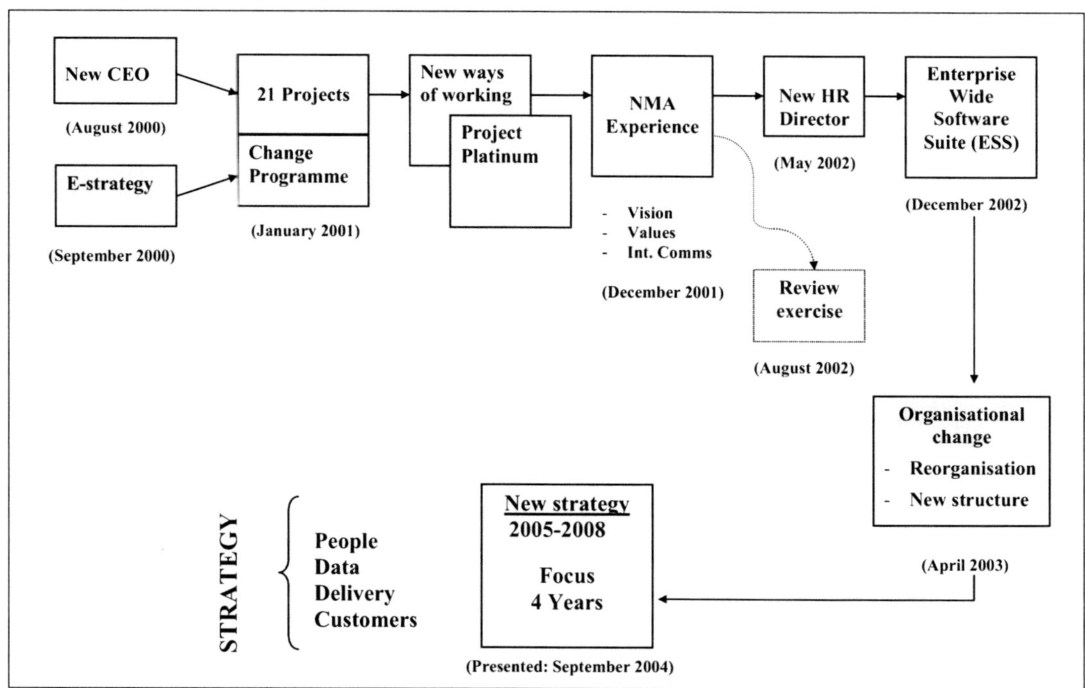

with its activities not, as a consequence, regulated by any government department or body. These weak political ties with the government allowed NMA enhanced freedoms and flexibilities in developing the business:

The government acted more as an interested observer on the side lines and wouldn't particularly have a major influence on our strategy. (Director of Business Change, 2002)

Commercialisation Framework (Degree of Commercialisation)

This dimension represents the extent to which the organisation could fully or partially commercialise their products in a commercial and increasingly competitive marketplace, reducing or eliminating dependence on the taxpayer.

As a trading fund organisation, NMA was operating under a more favourable business model, which allowed the organisation to fully commercialise its services while ensuring that its operations are funded by earning income and generating profits from the licensing of data to both the public and private sectors. NMA was, furthermore, an organisation in which commercialisation was a very viable strategy, with its geographic data an obvious commodity to market and well served by the advances in technology and satellite communications. In this case, therefore, the extent of commercialisation acted as a facilitator of strategic change:

If we had kept a low profile and stayed within the sort of things we were always doing, then maybe we would have less threat of competition and may still be competition but less threat of it. But essentially because nobody else will be able to make any money out of it, it wasn't a market that everybody else wanted to get into, and so, if it was no competition, the chances are we probably do something that our customers didn't want anyway. So, in time, we would still lose business. If it wasn't the competition, it will be that we were still looking for alternatives and people coming to us for mapping data. (Director of Business Change, 2002)

Complex Nature of Strategy

Most private sector organisations specify their overall business objective as the maximisation of profit or shareholder value. However, for "halfway" public sector organisations like NMA, the challenge was to articulate the most viable strategy that would both serve the commercialisation objectives and satisfy the multiple stakeholders (government, clients, users, staff, and the board).

In NMA, it was found that this factor acted sometimes as a barrier. The organisation had launched a comprehensive strategy aiming at transforming its traditional structure into an e-business technologically, commercially, and culturally. This was designed to be a radical change to the way the organisation worked, allowing customers to preview and buy the mapping data in much more user-friendly ways. Underpinning much of the strategy was a number of projects, highly technical, which involved good knowledge of information systems and digital mapping development. Translating such a complex strategy into clear strategic objectives at business unit level and cascading these objectives from the top down to the bottom of the organisation proved to be, at times, extremely challenging:

Given the business environment in which we operate, I think all of the change that we've been going through has been orientated toward trying to get us more externally focused, more commercially focused, but without losing our core strengths, which is we are the National mapping agency, we provide the referencing system which is unique. And is about how do we get more customer information into the business, so we guide technical developments more carefully. (Corporate Strategist, 2002)

I know that in many areas there was a major problem with senior managers communicating with middle managers. You know, get them involved and thinking about all the staff, getting them to understand what change was, and what was required, and why you need to do things in a different way, and the approach that they were adopting wasn't the right way, because we had to have this message with "marketisation" right, but we didn't have to be vertical about it. (Business Unit Manager, 2002)

Organisational Culture: The Public Sector "Ethos"

In NMA, the public sector culture was being eroded and was being replaced by a new notion: that the public services are increasingly public businesses, aimed primarily at satisfying individual client needs in the market place, in conditions of resource constraint, with the role of the state as an employer becoming subordinated to this political priority. However, there were difficulties in replacing the old public-service "silo" mentality built around consensus and adapting to the new customer-oriented, sales environment that was being demanded of them. Therefore, the old culture acted as a barrier to change:

We are still a Civil Service Agency and we can't escape from our heritage and our history, as we had a very strong corporate culture built around understanding and this notion of family, it is not necessarily a culture which is orientated toward high performance, but it is one that does allow people to learn and develop. And it's about how we actually develop some of strengths of this culture by actually bringing a bit more hard-line in terms of performance, because it's quite clear at the moment, the organisation can't quite carry financially the overhead of the current structure, the current manpower, the current skills and there is a need to do something about all three. (Corporate Strategist, 2002)

Although suddenly we said to people 'We are going to change the relationship that you have, it's not a parent-child relationship anymore, it's an adult relationship, and you got to take some responsibility.' 'You got to take some responsibility for managing your career, you got to take some responsibility for your development'... it is quite difficult for people to adjust to that change in the behaviours set. (HR Manager, 2002)

Nature of the Workforce

This factor acted as a barrier to change. The nature of work was of a predominantly intellectual nature and required a well-educated, professional workforce (surveyors and cartographers with vast knowledge in the field of geographic information systems). These categories of "knowledge workers" represented distinctive professional groups with a distinctive set of behavioural traits and values: a sense of community, loyalty to the organisations they worked for and their goals, and a sense of identification with their group activity rather than with the employing organisations. The existence of these groups often led to resistance to change, conflict of interests and pressure over the implementation or modification of certain policies and practices.

Traditionally, NMA has always employed professional staff with good technical and operational skills, but the necessary commercial skills have often been lacking. In 2002, as a result of either the voluntary redundancy scheme or the early retirement initiative, a number of long-serving members of staff with key technical and operational skills were allowed to leave on the grounds that they lacked the commercial skills required. In return, a number of new managers were recruited from the commercial sector and given authority to manage the older workforce, without the right technical and operational knowledge of the industry and operational activities. This often resulted in tensions between the surveyors in the field and the commercially-oriented managers leading them, partly generated by the lack of a clear "line of sight" between the two groups. The prevailing view among over 90% of staff interviewed was that this strategy allowed an important skill base to be lost:

NMA has brought in a lot of people from outside (from private sector) in recent times; they really do have a far better understanding of the commercial realities of markets in NMA and NMA data, and people can get better products, but they have no understanding of how this data got there to be put in the market, what are the problems. We can't be measured directly against certain indicators like in the public sector, and say 'this is how we need to do things' because the private sector doesn't actually do half of what we do, it doesn't face a lot of the challenges that we face, and having no understanding of that is bad. (Production Manager, 2003)

What was also evident from the interviews was the immense disruption in these knowledge workers' sense of personal identity. Their sense of betrayal and confusion might have been more keenly felt because of their identification with the organisation they belonged to and worked for many years:

I worked for this organisation since its beginnings, almost 30 years ago, and have been trained to be a good surveyor and this is what I know to do. I cannot use my skills in other similar organisations because there is only one National mapping agency, no one else does what we do in here! (Surveyor, Regional Office, 2003)

While the organisation was struggling to inculcate a certain corporate loyalty to the new e-vision and change programme within its operational staff, paradoxically the reduction strategy operated by the centre had the opposite effect:

Managers have this view of this organisation like a machine. The way it is going at the moment, we are going to lose the wrong people, which had the key skills and the knowledge will go with them. It takes years to train a good surveyor and we won't be able to get better people in, because not everyone knows how to collect data to make a map. This is a very distinctive kind of knowledge and we won't be able to get it back too soon, once it's lost. (Manager, 2003)

The criticism about the people coming from outside is that they have a good commercial background, but they don't understand this organisation. We need to do it better by looking at this organisation organically, as a community or an organism. Because at the end of the day, that's what we are, individuals. (Business Improvement Manager, 2003)

"Local Parochialism"

This factor, representing the extent to which the different communities within the organisation have a strong individual identity, culture, systems, ways of working, history of autonomy, and freedom to act on their own (Balogun, Gleadle, Hope Hailey, & Willmott, 2005), acted sometimes as a barrier to change and cultivated a mentality of "them" and "us" between the headquarters and regional offices staff.

Professional staff (surveyors) spread around the country in the regional offices have traditionally been loyal to their local offices rather than to wider industry groups. Each regional director responsible for data collection and management in a particular area of the country traditionally ran his own "tribe" without integration with others:

I wouldn't want them [managers from the corporate HQ] to be more involved in the planning of the changes in my area, because they don't put too much effort into really understand our field operations ... ultimately if I am responsible for the area, then I want to have the responsibility to make the decisions. (Regional Manager, 2003)

Management of the E-Business Change Programme Itself

Various factors also emerged concerned with the management of the change programme itself. Firstly, there was the problem of sustaining change over the long-term. In NMA, the complex and constant nature of change was generating difficulties in maintaining change in an environment of continually shifting goalposts. Secondly, from the point of view of the individual business groups, a challenge was achieving a balance between putting the changes in place and keeping up with the "day job":

It is too dangerous to come along with a plan that says 'this is exactly how things are going to look like in the future.' In some aspects, some of the technical aspects, for example, we were fairly sure about what we wanted to implement, then we get on and implement it. But on the cultural change, it was very much leading our way, finding out and let's get to the next stage and let's get a bit beyond that, set ourselves something in 2 years time—this is the sort of organisation we want to be, but let's do not be prescriptive of how we get there. (Director of Business Change, 2002)

Middle managers played a crucial role in change, but the incentives for them to support it were not always there. There was anecdotal evidence about middle managers being lured into contributing to the implementation of change and then released from their posts, following the voluntary redundancy programme.

At the events that I've been to, the middle managers were told: 'you are in fact the key people within the organisation that makes things happen, you know the senior managers and the directors, you know the technical staff and therefore, you create that link, therefore you are in many ways the driving force!' This was a little ironic as there hasn't been as much engaging of 'middle managers' as you would expect. (Business Unit Manager, 2003)

To make this whole process work, we need to make sure that people who are effectively running individual business units buy into the process ...it was a bad idea to initiate this procedure to release them, because if they don't get rewarded they will not deliver their today's results with the same motivation, it's like telling them 'do this, but instead of being rewarded, you will get punished. (Business Improvement Manager, 2002)

LESSONS LEARNED FROM THE CASE STUDY

Drawing on Osterwalder's (2004) analytical framework introduced earlier in this chapter as a point of departure for exploring the processes of e-business transformation in NMA, the key components of the new e-business model implemented by the organisation can be framed as shown in Table 3. The steps taken to meet the organisational challenges of implementing the e-business strategy across the organisation provide a list of best practices for this particular situation (see Table 4).

Electronic service delivery enabled NMA to become far more responsive and flexible, as well as creating the opportunity to harvest significant efficiency benefits. The digital revolution offered huge opportunities for the organisation to improve the services that it provided to its customers, enhance its interaction with partners and revolutionised the way people worked by firstly, redrawing the way in which those services are provided to capture the full benefits of technology, and secondly,

Table 3. NMA e-business model analysis based on Osterwalder's (2004) framework

Key dimensions of e-business model	Sub-categories	Explanation	What this means for NMA	Strength of dimension in NMA
Product innovation	*Target customer*	The segment of customers to whom the organisation wants to offer value.	• Traditional customers (public sector & utilities). • Emerging market segments (telecomm, retail, and insurance).	Time 1 - Weak Time 2 - Strong
	Value proposition	The overall view of an organisation's bundle of products and services that are of value to the customer.	• Data collection, data management. • Product development (translating digital data into business solutions that meet end users' needs).	Time 1 - Weak Time 2 - Strong
	Capabilities	The ability to execute a repeatable pattern of actions that is necessary in order to create value for customer.	• Data collection and data management of geographic information using global positioning system (GPS) networks.	Time 1 - Average Time 2 - Strong
Customer relationship	*Customer relationship management*	The link established between an organisation and its customers.	• Create link between different groups of customers and data collection and management.	Time 1 - Weak Time 2 - Strong
	Distribution channels	The means of getting in touch with the customers.	• Commercial partners to translate digital data into business solutions that meet end users' needs through partnership agreements.	Time 1 - Weak Time 2 - Strong
Infrastructure management	*Resources and assets*		• Topographic database of England, Scotland, and Wales. • Unique satellite navigation technology, expensive to replicate.	Time 1 - Strong, but not put to best purpose Time 2 - Strong and well capitalised on
	Activity configuration	The arrangement of activities and resources that are necessary to create value for customers.	• Organisational structure organised around core business processes (data collection and data management).	Time 1 - Weak Time 2 - Strong
	Partnerships	Voluntarily initiated cooperative agreements with others organisations in order to create value for customers.	• 193 Licensed partners from individual entrepreneurs to multinational companies who can add commercial value to NMA's datasets and bring new solutions & products to market. • Collaborative working between NMA and other parts of the government.	Time 1 - Weak Time 2 - Strong Time 1 - Average Time 2 - Strong

Table 3. continued

Financial aspects	*Cost model*	The representation in money of all the means employed in the business model.	• As a public sector organisation operating as a Trading fund, NMA had to earn commercial revenues in order to be self-financing. • NMA had to strike the right balance between maintaining consistent and accurate geographical information for the whole of Great Britain while ensuring its operations are funded by earning income and generating profits from the licensing of data to both the public and private sectors.	Time 1 - Weak Time 2 - Strong
	Revenue model	The way the organisation makes money through a variety of revenue flows.	• As a trading fund, NMA was required to make an average return on the capital it employs- on average around £40 million—of at least 5.5% a year and to pay an annual dividend to the government based on each year's trading results.	Time 1 - Weak Time 2 - Strong

Table 4. Best practices for the implementation of the e-business strategy

No.	Organisational challenges	Steps taken to meet organisational challenges	Data from NMA
1	Being "halfway" toward the private sector as a public sector executive agency moving toward a competitive commercial model.	• Design a strategy that would capitalise on the unique position of the NMA on the market, as the biggest geographical information provider in UK with market-ready cutting-edge technology and high levels of internal capability. • Establish strategic alliances to help drive the location-based information industry forward in a cohesive manner. • Develop collaborative working between NMA and other parts of the government.	"What we needed was a strategy that recognised our unique position. Something that enabled the organisation to have learning and, at the end of the experience, the learning would be resident in the organisation." (Corporate Strategist, 2001) "Who are our competitors? There is no single competitor for us. Because we are responsible for the national infrastructure of geographical information, there is no single other organisation who could and would want to replicate that, because it is hugely expensive to replicate that." (Senior manager, 2002)
2	Need to develop and communicate a clear e-business vision and the concept behind the change to the organisation as a whole and to all stakeholders, especially end-users (customers and partners).	• Communicate the why, where and how of the change to the people involved in the 21 projects and to all employees by using mobilising events such as "NMA Experience." This builds confidence in the projects, lets the team know where they stand and where they are headed, and encourage commitment to the cause through the use of various internal communication mechanisms.	"The top team and the board decided 'Right, this is our new strategy, this is where we are going, and this is our vision. We need to communicate that to everybody." (Project Platinum Manager, 2002) "The essentials are around being absolutely clear about what it is you are trying to achieve and why – and I don't just mean the reorganisation. I mean: where do you want to be as a business?" (Senior manager, 2003) "What this event (NMA Experience) did was to move the senior management up in the eyes of the workforce. It helped them understand that there was skill and ability in our senior team, and they were all committing to doing things in a different way and start leading the business more effectively." (Project Manager, 2002)
3	Create a feeling of ownership for the e-strategy at project level and a commitment at all levels of the organisation.	• Get the project leaders and initiative owners involved early in the e-strategy projects. • Communication events important in creating belief and feeling of ownership.	"We put this plan together, represented by a railway journey. It's a single-track railway, a one-way journey, because we wouldn't be going back. It didn't have a starting-point because change has been going on forever, and we couldn't say if or when we would finish." (Chief Executive, 2001)
4	Need new effective communication channels between the project teams and between the sales and marketing teams and customers.	• The project management teams were put in place to develop channels for and manage the communication between the different parties. Weekly, fortnightly, and quarterly status meetings help to keep all parties updated on each other's progress and on the progress of the e-strategy implementation as a whole,	"After about three months we had improved the relationship between the project teams and the steering group. The steering group felt more comfortable and more confident in the ability of the teams to deliver." (Director of Business Change, 2002) "Communication forms the grounding for all the organisational work I have done. The communication, consultation, and involvement strategy is what will make it happen." (Programme Manager, 2003)

Table 4. continued

5	Manage different customer segments: retain traditional loyal customers (public sector & utilities) while developing emerging markets (telecomm, retail and insurance) and commercial partnerships.	• From products to relationships: shift from a customer relationship management (CRM) focused on products or processes to a CRM philosophy focused on customer segments and the solutions they require. • Identify the most profitable customer groups. • Focus NMA's activity entirely on improving core business processes (data collection and management) and involve commercial partners in translating this digital data into business solutions that meet end users' needs through partnership agreements.	"We need partners who would come and help us find/exploit certain niches in the market place. They are very well financed (e.g., big mobile operators) and by enlarge our strategy is and will be in the future to partner with some of these companies rather than compete with them. So partnership development is an important part of our strategy, previously we worked with small partners, now we are trying to work with bigger ones, to get them develop solutions for us." (Senior manager, 2002) "We place the customer rather than the product or process at the centre of the organisation to develop a stronger link between our different groups of customers and our data collection and management side of the business." (Business Improvement Manager, 2002)
6	Establish the right model of organisational design for the organisation.	• Design and implement the right structure for an e-business starting from NMA's core business processes. • Focus on core organisational competences: data collection, data management, exploitation of new technologies and partner/customer management.	"The normal practice would be: you take the external consultants' methodology cookbook, you apply things from it and you get a sense of the right way to do things … but this organisation is different and we wanted the structure to reflect what we do, not what external consultants think that we should do!"(Board member responsible for the structural change, 2003) "We did not want again an off-the-shelf structure. Consultants came with a whole series of structural models, they came with the toolkit but didn't know how to fit it." (Strategist, 2003) "Don't expect everything to work without some adjustment and don't be afraid to review changes at an early stage to keep the reorganisation on track." (Business Group Director, 2003)
7	Top management commitment and the business case.	• CEO with experience and personally identified with the e-strategy project. • Have a multi functional leadership team (i.e., from sales, marketing, and IT). • Involve senior management from sales and marketing in the strategy implementation.	"The fundamentals are you need to have a really clear leader of the structure, somebody who has a very clear vision about what the endgame looks like." (Senior Manager, 2002) "Sales and marketing senior management buy-in was absolutely fundamental for the process to work … There must be a vision, there must be a strategy, and there must be support behind it." (Senior change manager, 2003)
8	Political resistance to change of various stakeholders and managing simultaneously their diverse expectations.	• Consistent communication allied to the use of facilitated workshops.	"Consistency of message and purpose is one of the most important success factors in making e-change happen. Crystal-clear purpose, understood by all, including 'what it means for me' should be made explicit." (Employee, 2002)

Table 4. continued

9	External "customer acceptance" barriers and problems.	• Communicate consistently with end users, at the beginning to build confidence, and throughout to communicate progress and to get feedback. • Use customer relationship management to re-build the confidence of customers who are confused about who they are actually buying products and services from.	"The changes in our business processes, for example, procurement, reporting, and customer relationship management were so massive that the smallest error could have potentially serious consequences during business processes switching, damaging customer relationships, and delivery channels for a lengthy period of time. Communicating proposed changes to our customers, users, and clients was essential. They demanded honest, consistent, and up-to-date information whether the news were good or bad." (Business Improvement Manager, 2002) "It was important to ensure all the time our customers, users, and clients that we had a back-up or disaster recovery plan should something go wrong during the transition." (Sales and Marketing Manager, 2002)
10	Aligning the objectives of the 21 projects with the overall objectives of the e-business strategy and establishing timelines in place.	• People involved in the projects have clear understanding of their roles and responsibilities. • Good project management to avoid duplications and conflicting business objectives.	"Project planning is a big machine that takes up vast amounts of time and internal resources. Managing all this complexity terrifies some people …" (Senior Manager, 2002)
11	Blending major change with major continuity.	• Integrate the e-commerce strategy with the business strategy and with the core operations from the start.	"We needed to be able to adapt to shifting circumstances in market conditions and identify potential changes in course sooner rather than later …" (Senior Marketing manager, 2003)

tailoring the services to the needs of individual citizens, customers, and businesses.

Several success factors relevant to e-business implementation emerged from this account.

Firstly, one major lesson from this experience was that a successful organisational transformation involving e-business implementation requires clear leadership from the top management team. The NMA e-strategy has been created as the strategic blueprint to develop the business and firmly position it in the new information economy. The strategy was transforming the business at all levels, culturally, technically and commercially. Fundamental to all of this activity was the requirement to create the environment in which NMA could successfully deliver its strategy for the business. This has required the Senior Management Team to clearly articulate the vision, purpose, goals and values for the organisation and to communicate them clearly business wide. It also required pulling together the leadership, communication and engagement activity, while ensuring that all existing projects, initiatives and everyday activities were aligned and integrated with this. This high-level strategic activity was also about leveraging what was already in place, and most importantly maintain consistency across cultural, behavioural, and leadership approaches.

Secondly, the case of Britain's national mapping agency shows that, in practice, the transition from government monopoly to commercial organisation while embracing e-business as a corporate philosophy can be extremely challenging to achieve. Although e-business has enabled NMA to tap new customers and new revenues and opened up a space for importation of private sector practices into NMA, the strong public interest for its activities was still present. Yet the organisation was expected to operate commercially, cover its costs, and build up reserves through its own commercial style operations. That situated the organisation in the intersection of two different spheres—the public and the private. Becoming an e-business, in this context, required collaborative working not only with commercial partners but also with different parts of the government. The "in-between" situation thus tested to the full the capability of the organisation to lead and manage change, especially in terms of finding the perfect balance between fulfilling its still strategic role as national agency and providing high-quality services to its customers in a dynamic marketplace.

One of the senior managers interviewed described this situation with the following words:

We [as an organisation] want to behave as if we were situated in the commercial business sector, but we cannot escape our origins. (Senior Manager, 2004)

Thirdly, the case findings demonstrate that successful organisational transformation involving e-business implementation relies on changing some fundamental business processes and attitudes. Close cooperation between many different sets of people—from middle managers to programmers, and from technical architects to system users within the organisation, is needed. This convergence of business process, creative and technical skills created in NMA a new dimension for teamwork, which in turn shifted the culture of the organisation from "knowledge is power" to "sharing knowledge is power." Technology can be an important enabler but not a driver of knowledge sharing.

Finally, one key challenge in NMA was how to blend major change with major continuity. In this respect, a major lesson learnt from this organisation's experience was that it is essential to integrate the e-commerce strategy with the business strategy and with the core operations from the start. This echoes the findings of Dutta et al. (1999) that successes result from close partnerships between commercial and IT managers, and that companies that make e-commerce central to their organisation do better than those that make it an afterthought.

CONCLUSION

This chapter has depicted the e-business transformation of Britain's national mapping agency over the 2001-2005 period, and analysed the nature of its reorganisation around a new e-business model. Analysis of these dynamic change processes exposed a number of dilemmas and conflicting challenges for public sector managers in relation to the interpretation of the e-business strategy concept and its implementation in practice. While the Internet offers a technological solution, the findings of this case study suggest that the successful implementation of a wider e-business strategy depends on managing simultaneously a number of projects which cross-organisational boundaries and linking together organisational and technological factors.

The case thus presents an interesting example of a commercialising public sector organisation experimenting with new e-configurations and processes. While this reflective account may be unique, it does, however, provide pointers to other large organisations undertaking a similar e-transformation, and reflects on the degree of organisational transformation required by traditional organisations in meeting this imperative and successfully making the change to e-business. In particular, the findings illustrate that an e-business strategy is not just about technology. It also embraces the business challenges that result from managing change in a fast moving environment, as well as the important issues of people, organisation, culture, communication, and how an organisation must create a process for delivering innovation.

Further empirical field studies in other public sector settings would enrich the concepts developed in this study and would produce a definitive list of best practices. The case highlights, however, the complex nature of the notion of "e-business" in a public sector context and shows that when implemented successfully, it can transform entirely these organisations and their capabilities.

REFERENCES

Aichholzer, G., & Schmutzer, R. (2000). Organisational, technological, and regulatory challenges for realising electronic government. In *Proceedings of the 8th European Conference on Information Systems*, Vienna, Austria.

Afuah, A., & Tucci, C. (2003). *Internet business models and strategies: Text and cases.* Boston: McGraw-Hill.

Balogun, J., Gleadle, P., Hope Hailey, V., & Willmott, H. (2005). Managing change across boundaries: Boundary-shaking practices. *British Journal of Management*, *16*, 261-278.

Baida, Z., Gordijn, J., Akkermans, H., Saele, H., & Morch, A. (2005). Finding e-service offerings by computer-supported customer need reasoning. *International Journal of e-business Research, 1*(2), 91-112.

Barnes, D., Hinton, M., & Mieczkowska, S. (2005). Enhancing customer service operations in e-business: The emotional dimension. *Journal of Electronic Commerce in Organizations, 3*(2), 17-32.

Barnes, S., & Hunt, B. (2001). *E-commerce and e-business: Business models for global success.* Oxford: Butterworth Heinemann.

Becker, S., & Berkemeyer, A. (2004). A case study on a security maturity assessment of a business-to-business electronic commerce organization. *Journal of Electronic Commerce in Organizations, 2*(4), 1-19.

Benoy, J., Cook, R., & Javalgi, R. (2001). Marketing on the Web: How executives feel, what businesses do. *Business Horizons, 44*(4), 32-40.

Bhaskar, R. (2004). A customer relationship management system to target customers at Cisco. *Journal of Electronic Commerce in Organizations, 2*(4), 1-19.

Boddy, D., & Macbeth, D. (2000). Prescriptions for managing change: a survey of their effects in projects to implement collaborative working between organisations. *International Journal of Project Management, 18*, 297-306.

Boyne, G. (2002). Public and private management: What's the difference. *Journal of Management Studies, 39*(1), 97-122.

Boyne, G. (2004). A 3Rs strategy for public service turnaround: Retrenchment, repositioning, and reorganisation. *Public Money and Management, April*, 97-103.

Boyne, G., & Walker, R. (2004). Strategy content and public service organizations. *Journal of Public Administration Research and Theory, 14*(2), 231-252.

Brown, S. L., & Eisenhardt, K. M. (1997). The art of continuous change: Linking complexity theory and time-paced evolution in relentlessly shifting organisation. *Administrative Science Quarterly, 42*, 1-34.

Burn, J. M., & Robbins, G. (2001). *Strategic planning for e-government: A customer value based model. Proceedings of the 7th Americas Conference on Information Systems* (pp. 1578-1583), Boston, USA.

Carlton, D. W. (2001). Free riding and sales strategies for the Internet. *The Journal of Industrial Economics, 49*(4), 521-540.

Chen, S., & Leteney, F. (2000). Get real! Managing the next stage of Internet retail. *European Management Journal, 18*(5), 519-528.

Chaston, I. (2001). The Internet and e-commerce: An opportunity to examine organisational learning in progress in small manufacturing firms. *International Small Business Journal, 19*(2), 13-30.

Clarke, I., & Flaherty, T. B. (2004). Challenges of transforming a traditional brick-and-mortar store into a bricks-and-clicks model: A small business case study. *Journal of Electronic Commerce in Organizations, 2*(4), 74-87.

Clay, K. (2001). Prices and price dispersion on the Web: Evidence from the online book industry. *The Journal of Industrial Economics, 49*(4), 441-462.

Clegg, C. W., Chu, C., Smithson, S., Henney, A., et al. (2002). *E-business prospects: Findings from an expert panel.* London: Department of Trade and Industry.

Clegg, C., Chu, C., Smithson, S., Henney, A., et al. (2005). Sociotechnical study of e-business: Grappling with an octopus. *Journal of Electronic Commerce in Organizations, 3*(1), 53-71.

Colombo, M. G. (2001). Technology-based entrepreneurs: does internet make a difference? *Small Business Economics, 16*(3), 177-190.

Daniel, E., Wilson, H., & Myers, A. (2002). Adoption of e-commerce by SMEs in the UK: Toward a stage model. *International Small Business Journal, 20*(3), 253-270.

Day, G., & Schoemaker, P. (2000). Avoiding the pitfalls of emerging technologies. *California Management Review, 42*(2), 8-33.

Dutta, S., & Segev, A. (1999). Business transformation on the Internet. *European Management Journal, 17*(5), 466-476.

Eisenhardt, K. (1989). Building theories from case study research. *Academy of Management Review, 14*(4), 532-550.

Gao, J. (2005). E-commerce issues in Australian manufacturing: A newspaper medium perspective. *Journal of Electronic Commerce in Organizations, 3*(4), 20-41.

Gant, J. P., & Gant, D. B. (2001). Web portals and their role in e-government. *Proceedings of the 7th American Conference on Information Systems* (pp. 1616-1623), Boston, USA.

Garicano, L. (2001). The effects of business-to-business e-commerce on transaction costs. *The Journal of Industrial Economics, 49*(4), 463-486.

Graafland-Essers, I., & Ettedgui, E. (2003). *Benchmarking e-government in Europe and the US*. RAND.

Hansen, M. (2000). Networked incubators: Hothouses of the new economy. *Harvard Business Review, 78*(5), 74-84.

Heeks, R. (2002). *Information systems for public sector management*. Manchester: Institute for Development Policy and Management.

Heeks, R. (2001). *Building e-government for development: A framework for national and donor action*. Manchester: Institute for Development Policy and Management.

Kotha, S., Rajgopal, S., & Rindova, V. (2001). Reputation building and performance: An empirical analysis of the top-50 pure Internet firms. *European Management Journal, 19*(6), 571-586.

Lee, H., & Wang, S. (2001). Winning the last mile of e-commerce. *Sloan Management Review, 42*(4), 54-62.

Li, F. (2007). *What is e-business? How the Internet transforms organizations*. Oxford: Blackwell Publishing.

Li, F. (2005). Social aspects of e-business. *Journal of E-Commerce in Organizations, Special issue, 3*(2), i-iv.

Li, F. (2003). Implementing e-government strategy in Scotland: Current situation and emerging issues. *Journal of E-Commerce in Organizations, 1*(2), 44-65.

Mahadevan, B. (2000). Business models for Internet-based e-commerce: An anatomy. *California Management Review, 42*(4), 55-69.

Mahrer, H., & Brandtweiner, R. (2004). Success factors for implementing e-government services: The case of the Austrian e-government service portal. *International Journal of Information Technology and Management, 3*(2/3/4), 235-245.

Labour Government. (2001). *E-government strategic framework*, April 2001.

Labour Government. (1999). *Modernising Government White Paper*, March 1999.

Osborne, D., & Gaebler, T. (1997). *Reinventing government*. London: Signum.

Osterwalder, A. (2004). *The business model ontology: A proposition in a design science approach*. PhD Thesis, Ecole Des Hautes Etudes Commerciales (EHEC), University of Lausanne, Lausanne.

Osterwalder, A., & Pigneur, T. (2002). *An e-business model ontology for modelling e-business*. Paper presented at the 15th Electronic Commerce Conference—E-Reality: Constructing the E-Economy, Bled, Slovenia, 17-19 June.

Pettigrew, A. (1990). Longitudinal field research on change. Theory and practice. *Organization Science, 1*, 267-292.

Pettigrew, A. (1985). *The awakening giant: Continuity and change in ICI*. Oxford: Basil Blackwell.

Poon, S., & Swatman, P. (1999). An exploratory study of small business Internet commerce issues. *Information and Management, 35*, 9-18.

Rayport, J. (1999). The truth about internet business models. *Strategy and Business,* Third Quarter.

Scott Morton, F. (2001). Internet car retailing. *The Journal of Industrial Economics, 49*(4), 501-520.

Smith, M. D. (2001). Consumer decision-making at an Internet shopbot: Brand still matters. *The Journal of Industrial Economics, 49*(4), 541-559.

Timmers, P. (1998). Business models for the electronic markets. *Electronic Markets, 8*(2), 3-8.

Timmers, P. (2003). *Electronic commerce* (2nd ed.). Chichester: John Wiley.

Van der Wiele, T., Williams, R., Van Iwaarder, J., Wilson, M., & Dale, B. (2002). The e-business research network: Summary of the results of the Dutch pilot survey. In *Proceedings of the British Academy of Management*, September 2002, UK.

Yin, R. (1994). *Case study research: Design and methods* (2nd ed.). London: Sage

Chapter III
Ambient E-Service: Applications and Embracing Model

Yuan-Chu Hwang
National United University, Taiwan

Soe-Tsyr Yuan
National Chengchi University, Taiwan

ABSTRACT

Most of existing mobile services were designed based on the client/server architecture. Those mobile services neither paid much attention to mobile users' interactions with their environments nor considered the collective efforts between the mobile users in a dynamic peer group. In this chapter, the notion of ambient e-service is so defined as to identify a new scope of mobile e-service, which address dynamic collective efforts between mobile users (enabled by mobile peer-to-peer technology), dynamic interactions with ambient environments (envisioned by location-based service), the moment of value (empowered by wireless technologies), and low cost service provision. The notable features of ambient e-services are the exhilarated linkage based on social context and significantly rapid growth of connections. We also present an ambient e-service framework that characterizes ambient e-services with three dimensions (value stack, environment stack, and technology stack), followed by several exemplars of ambient e-service applications. Moreover, we present the ambient e-service embracing model (ASEM) that addresses the integrated consideration of trust, reputation, and privacy required for fostering the growth of ambient e-services and steers the directions of future fruitful relevant research. The embracing model can also guide the government or service providers to implement the ambient e-service applications that satisfy customers' unique needs under various circumstances.

INTRODUCTION TO AMBIENT E-SERVICE

The notion of ambient e-service is defined to identify a new scope of mobile e-services. Until now, there are two different design paradigms in mobile commerce. Most current mobile commerce applications are grounded in the client/server architecture, where the only interactions involved are between a service provider and a mobile user.

Mobile users are standalone. Users under such service environment cannot interact with each other easily. Although the issues of human-computer interaction with mobile devices has been brought to public attention for the last several years (Paternò, 2003). In current mobile service scenarios, interactions, or cooperation between mobile users are not considered as important issues. Therefore, collective efforts from mobile user groups cannot be produced.

Fortunately, the peer-to-peer (P2P) technology with mobile devices makes it possible for mobile users to communicate with each other easily. Mobile users can exchange information wirelessly under a sensors-enabled environment. Ambient e-service is designed based on the P2P architecture that highlights the collaborative interactions of mobile users.

The notion of ambient e-services addresses dynamic collective efforts between mobile users (enabled by mobile-P2P), dynamic interactions with ambient environments (envisioned by location-based services), moment of value, and low cost service provision. The collective effort is based on the collaborative interactions of mobile users, which facilitate the low cost service provision. In a sensor-enabled environment, information presentations are embedded in everyday objects such as pens, walls, or doors. It makes the environment become an interface of the context information. Using the mobile P2P technology, users can exchange their information wirelessly and proceed with highly extensive interactions. Grounded on location-based service, location information of mobile users can be retrieved. Hence, ambient e-service can provide personal, timely, and relevant services to mobile users.

Compared to the client/server design, an ambient e-service has two major distinguished features. First, under the client/server architecture, it is not possible to effectively attain the collective efforts that are tailored to the contexts of the user. Second, with the P2P design, the number of connections grows by a significantly rapid pace especially in an open space. For a better understanding of ambient e-services, we will use an ambient

Figure. 1. Ambient e-service framework

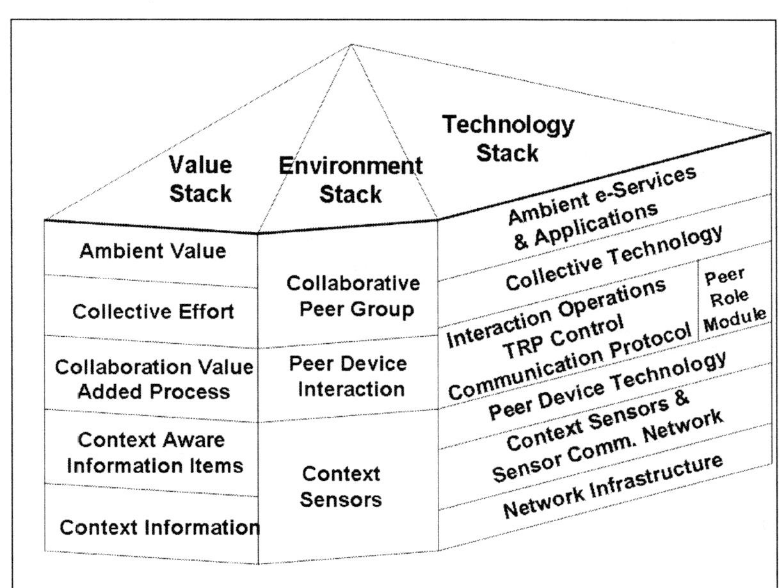

e-service framework (as shown as Figure 1) to identify some possible deliverables (values) of ambient e-services and address the technologies required to support the applications of ambient e-services.

The framework is composed of three dimensions: the value stack, the environment stack, and the technology stack. Descriptions of each stack are given next.

Value Stack

The ambient value stack comprises five layers representing the supporting value layers for ambient e-service (deliverables of higher levels requiring the provision of deliverables of lower levels). The basic layer of ambient value stack is the "context information," which is derived from the ambient sensor environments. A mobile user can interact with the environment (for example, when entering a room) and the context sensors, then retrieve context information with the device the user carries (informing the user of his or her location). Examining the user's profile, the second layer "Context aware information items" sends to the user information that matches his or her preferences. The information received from the environments may be useful to the user, but some of it may be irrelevant. Using its communication abilities, a mobile peer can collaborate with another mobile peer and exchange information stored in their mobile devices. Through these collaborative interactions, the user may discover someone whose information is valuable and thus exchange or trade with them using a micro payment or barter process. This is called the "collaboration value added process."

A peer may also interact with a peer group of multiple peers. Aiming at the same goals or interests, a peer group may combine the abilities of individual members, or explore their collective knowledge to accomplish goals that are impossible for a single peer to attain. In other words, "collective effort" represents the power of a peer group (or multiple peer groups). The ambient value would then be generated by the collective efforts of peer interactions or peer group interactions.

Environment Stack

The environment stack consists of three layers indicating the supporting environment layers for ambient e-service (environments of higher levels comprising those lower levels).The sketched stack diagram is shown in Figure 2.

"Ambient context sensors" form the bottom layer, which includes three categories of environment. Schilit, Adams, and Want (1994) argue that the important aspects of context are where the user is, who the user is with, and what resources are nearby.

The user environment includes the user context, the activity context, and the social context. The user environment represents the profile of a user such as peer identification, where the user is, who the user is, user preferences, user privacy concerns, user social situation and relations with others, and so forth. The physical environment includes the physical context and the device context. The physical environment refers to things like temperature, noise, and lighting level, along with the device context. The computing environment includes the network context and the services context. The computing environment represents the network connectivity, available processors, cost of computing, bandwidth, and available nearby services, and similar information.

The layer "peer device interaction" represents environments (featuring peer-to-peer interactions) in which mobile users may exchange their experiences and trade information with nearby peers. The "peer device interaction" layer rests on the "ambient context sensors" layer; that is, all peer information originally derives from interaction with the dynamic environments of the bottom layer.

The top layer of the environment stack represents environments featuring peer group interactions and collaboration. The peer group is capable of combine the power of every peer in the group for certain objectives, including collective purchases, forming a task-oriented workforce group, or collaborative filtering.

Technology Stack

The ambient technology stack is displayed in Figure 3. The combinative hexagon diagram represents the conceptual technology stacks, while the individual hexagon diagrams can be further elaborated into the detailed stacks. The technology stack can be categorized into four highly correlated major parts. The hexagon named "mobile communication infrastructure" represents the fundamental technologies for ambient e-service environment communications, which include the network infrastructure layer, context sensors and communication network layer, and peer device technology layer. The "ambient interaction control" hexagon represents technologies involved in enabling mobile devices to interact with other devices within the ambient e-service environment. This layer includes the peer communication protocol layer, the trust, reputation, and privacy control layer, and the ambient interaction interface and operation layer. The "interaction role module" hexagon is related to the technology for various roles involved in the ambient e-service environment. Both the ambient interaction control hexagon and the interaction role module hexagon are based on the mobile communication infrastructure hexagon. The collective wisdom hexagon is the uppermost of the three conceptual technology hexagons. It represents related collective technology that facilitates various ambient e-service applications. Advanced introduction of these ambient technology stacks is described next.

Network infrastructure is the fundamental basis of all ambient technology stacks. The wired and wireless hybrid network provides the basic communication infrastructure for context sensors and peer devices. Above the network infrastructure layer, context sensors interact with the surrounding peers via the sensor communication network. Peer devices technology lies atop the sensor communication network layer, which includes the hardware, operation systems, and software platforms of the mobile device.

The layer above the peer device technology layer has two folds: (1) For peers to interact with each other, a peer communication protocol is

Figure 2. Ambient environment stack

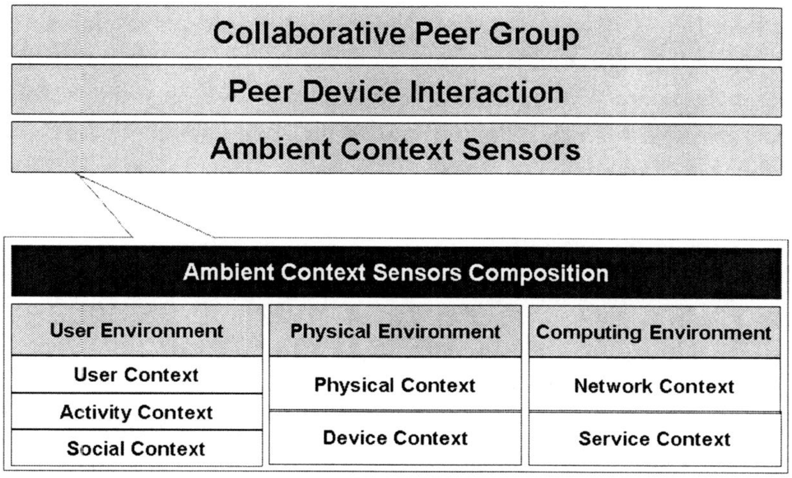

Figure 3. The ambient technology stack

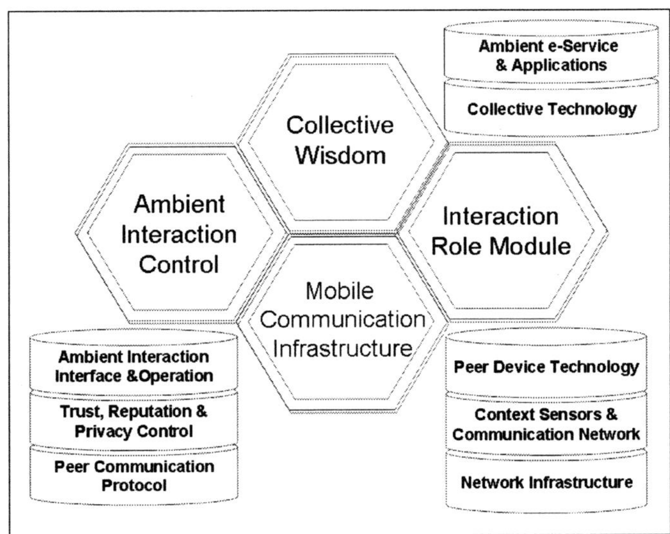

required (similar to that used in Web services). (2) In ambient environments, peers may know nearby peers for only a short period of time. How can a peer trust nearby peers? Is it possible to build a reputation system that enables peer trust? Similarly, privacy control should be addressed in an ambient e-service. With trust, reputation, and privacy control as the basis of communication, mobile users then can engage ambient interactions to handle operations between nearby mobile peers. These operations include such activities as "discovery," "request," "respond," "bargain," "transact," and "delivery."

Since a mobile user plays different roles in different interactions, the peer role module can be applied to the peer in response to the dynamic roles rendered. Mobile users who have information required by other users, play the seller role by applying the seller module. Surrounding peers (who have obtained various kinds of information) then play the broker role by applying the broker module. Mobile users who need information from others apply the buyer module and play the buyer role (they can trade or barter with other mobile users).

Beyond peer-to-peer interactions, a peer group's collective effort is the communal power for everyone. Technologies that support peer and peer group distributed collaboration constitute a key feature of ambient e-service. Collective aspects of ambient e-service will be discussed in the next section.

The remaining sections of this chapter are organized as follows: the next section exemplifies several ambient e-service application scenarios, followed by the challenges and the state of the art for embracing ambient e-services. In the ASEM section, we present an embracing model of ambient e-services in terms of its framework design. In addition, we illustrate the roadmap and impact of the embracing model in the roadmap section. Finally, a conclusion and the directions of our future work are provided in final section.

AMBIENT E-SERVICE APPLICATIONS

It is useful to begin by making a distinction between two kinds of ambient e-services, services for distributed trading, and services for distributed collaboration. The social context and the rapid growth of connections are the major incentives for using the ambient e-service design. These two characteristics are not mutually exclusive; of course, a particular scenario may apply to either or both of the ambient characteristics.

This section aims to identify several important ambient e-service application scenarios on the assumption that ambient environments for mobile commerce have been provided. Without loss of generosity, the physical context of location is referenced and considered in the ambient environments addressed in the following scenarios, naturally relating to the LBS (location-based service) research. As mentioned in the introduction section, ambient e-services aim to identify a new scope of mobile e-services that primarily address dynamic collective efforts between mobile users (enabled by mobile peer-to-peer) and dynamic interactions with ambient environments (envisioned by LBS) and low cost service provision.

LBS has been categorized into four major types: transaction services, information services, navigation and tracking services, and security services (Lim & Saiu, 2003), in this research we identify selected ambient service application scenarios that reflect the four LBS categories, as well as exhibit dynamic collective efforts based on M-P2P.

We introduce an ambient shopping mall scenario to represent ambient transaction services. The shopping mall scenario can easily be modified to represent ambient security services. An information distribution cooperation scenario is then offered as an exemplar of ambient information service provision. Finally, a peer group cooperation scenario is presented, with reference to ambient navigation and information services. The ambient location information acquisition scenario may be considered either instance of ambient information services or of ambient navigation and tracking services.

Collective efforts of mobile users are not possible in the current mobile services framework that deploys services using a client/server architecture. These applications differ from previous mobile e-services in addressing dynamic collective efforts between mobile users and dynamic interactions with ambient environments. Moreover, mobile devices in ambient e-services applications are personal to the users. The social contexts retained in personal devices (e.g., the social relationships in the vicinity) can thus generate the e-services of much higher complexity and security than the social contexts in sensor networks. E-services using a social context environment render ambient e-services capable of providing enhanced collaborative power for mobile users whenever needed.

In the following subsections, each scenario will be detailed in terms of its motivation, promised value, and interaction structure.

Ambient Shopping Mall Scenario

The ambient e-service addressed in this scenario is the case of new customers of high buyer perishability (entering the shopping mall and being in a rush to buy certain items without the knowledge of where to buy and how to buy cheaply, given relevant sales promotion). New customers carrying mobile devices can communicate with nearby peers as they enter the shopping mall. In addition to the provision of a convenient communication mechanism, secure and fair interactions are also expected in this scenario. There are various information sources within the environment, but not all of them are trustworthy. Users may collaborate with nearby peer groups to establish collective security procedures even though the period of time they will be interacting is short. Therefore, even though users may not recognize most of the participants within the shopping mall, there is still a fair transaction environment.

Figure 4 offers a view of the ambient shopping mall scenario. Compared with the traditional advertising media, electronic advertisements are low cost, easy to update, and convenient for customers to access. In a shopping mall fully equipped with wireless network infrastructure, information such as sales promotions may be broadcast to mobile devices by the Info_BC_Station. When customers passing by the Info_BC_Stations or some trusted peers, related information will be sent to customer's mobile device based on the user's preference settings. Information obtained by a given peer may thus vary based on its interactions with the various ambient environments in the mall.

In such a scenario, the major goal of the ambient shopping mall e-service is to provide a new channel for customers to obtain needed information. The assumption of this scenario is that the contents of the information retained in peers differs from peer-to-peer based on their membership status (i.e., desired e-service fields and preference settings of will-to-receive). Mobile users will receive information based on their user context and their preferences or membership data. Members with higher loyalty points will receive a higher discount e-coupon. This would encourage customers to join the membership program.

All mobile peers have a temporary peer ID number (pseudonym), preferences, context data, transaction history, and information already obtained. Peers are able to perform basic operations such as bargaining and making payments. Mobile peers can apply different role modules, the buyer module, the seller module, and the broker module for mobile peers to perform specific operations.

When a peer uses the seller module, it can respond to a buyer's product discovery operation. If a seller peer has information that the buyer requires, the seller then responds to the buyer's request and initiates a bargaining operation with the buyer peer. After the payment process, the seller delivers the desired e-service to the buyer. The operations performed by the buyer module are complementary to those performed by the seller module. But the buyer module has been designed to not only handle transactions with seller module, but also to request packaging services from the broker module.

The broker module is applied to peers who will stay in the mall for a long time and possess a more complete store of information. It is designed for peers serving as service providers and contains a "generate" package, which cre-

Figure 4. Ambient shopping mail scenario

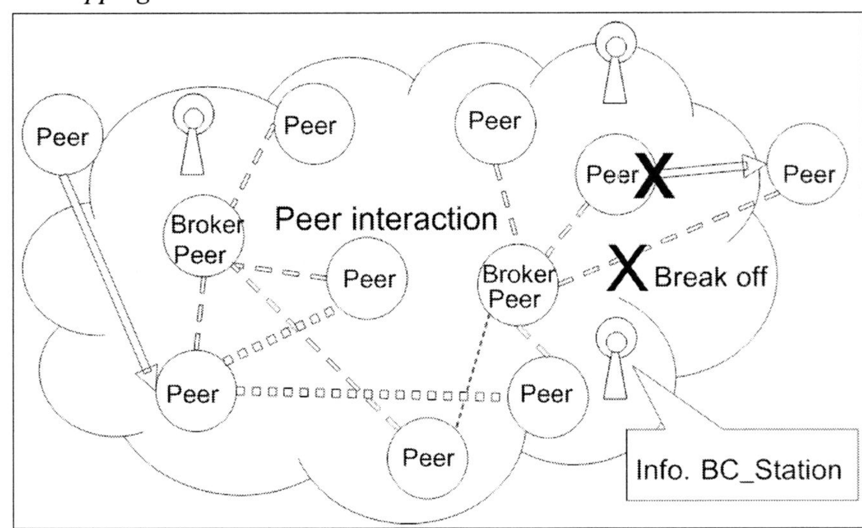

ates services that produce information tailored to the buyer's interests and preference (Similar to service bundles in Baida, Gordijn, Akkermans, Saele, & Morch, 2005). Package templates are used for the broker module to produce a service package with minimum effort. Further, the broker module has the same ability to deliver products as the seller module.

Although effective outreach is one of the shopping mall's goals, if the contents of information are the same for everyone, both client/server and P2P designs can pass the items to the public, but in different ways. However, mass broadcasts such as spam will annoy customers and make them reluctant to join the shopping program. When considering user differentiation, content differentiation will be in relation to user profiles and to ambient context sensors in the environment stack (that subsequently will involve social context and correlate to the privacy concerns of the customers). Those concerns make the P2P design more appropriate than the client/server architecture.

A UML class diagram (Figure 5) represents the relationships between the different modules as well as the peer module basic functions.

Information Distribution Cooperation Scenario

Information distribution cooperation is an ambient e-service based on a mobile advertising infrastructure. Distributor companies can broadcast shop advertisement items such as e-coupons through an ambient advertising infrastructure, which dispatches advertisement items relevant to the preferences of proximate users. Shops may be geographically distant from the broadcast stations of the distributor companies. In this scenario, e-coupons are considered valuable information items. When a mobile user passes through a shop and wants to buy certain products but is short of the relevant e-coupons, the mobile peer can probe the surrounding environment to see if any nearby peers own the desired e-coupons.

Figure 5. Class diagram of ambient shopping mall scenario

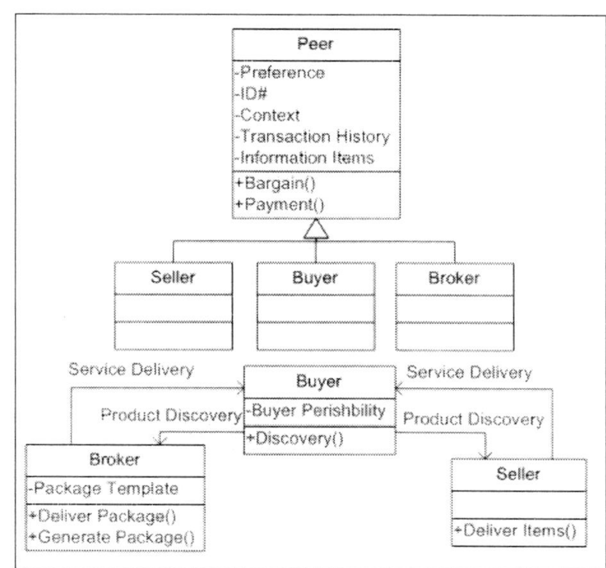

E-coupons become a valuable information item if the contents of information are different. In this business model, mobile users can obtain financial benefits by exchanging e-coupons, and thus be attracted to join the program, creating larger participant scale, which leads to more interactions, in turn bringing in even more participants, generating a cycle of positive feedback that is a win-win situation for both customers and stores. The P2P design, in conjunction with social awareness, will thus enable both rapid growth of connections and increased persuasiveness, being more powerful than the client/server design.

Figure 6 depicts a UML class diagram of the scenario, representing the relationships, attributes, and operations between all participants. When a mobile user (the barter initiator) passes through a shop and lacks desired e-coupons, the peer can search for the e-coupons in the ambient peer groups. Whenever the requested e-coupons are found and owned by another peer (the barter responder), the barter initiator requests a bartering process with the barter responder. E-coupons can be distributed not only to the mobile users falling within the broadcast range of the distributor companies, but also to the primary target peers (who desire specific e-coupons at the right time and right place).

Ambient Location Information Acquisition Scenario

Recently, mobile services have been offering location-based services for mobile users with devices using handheld positioning technologies. For instance, the mobile location service Pocket Map delivers nearby restaurant or theater information to mobile users. Those services require the location information of the mobile user as a basis for provision of various services. Some mobile services simply furnish a mobile user with the user's current position based positioning technologies.

However, it is often the case that not every mobile device is empowered with the handset positioning technology or subscribes to mobile positioning services. Consequently, such users cannot obtain desired location-based services. Instead, they can obtain location information from nearby peers who possess such information, and

Figure 6. Class diagram of the information distribution cooperation scenario

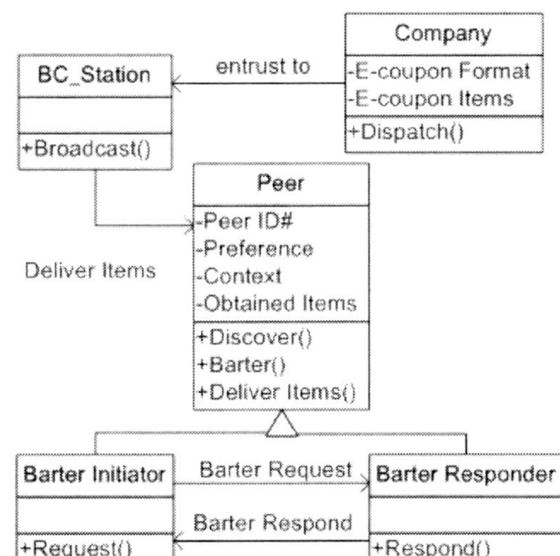

Figure 7. Ambient location information acquisition scenario

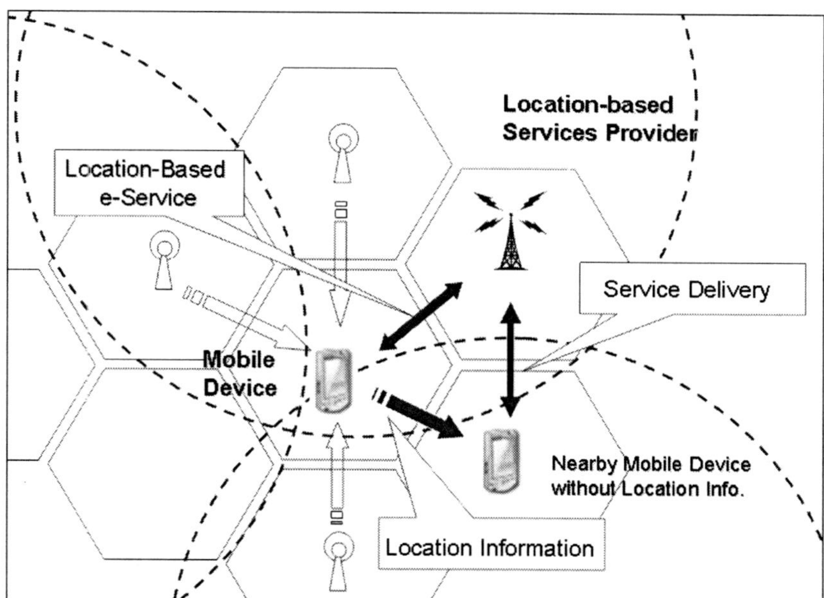

Figure 8. Class diagram of ambient location information acquisition scenario

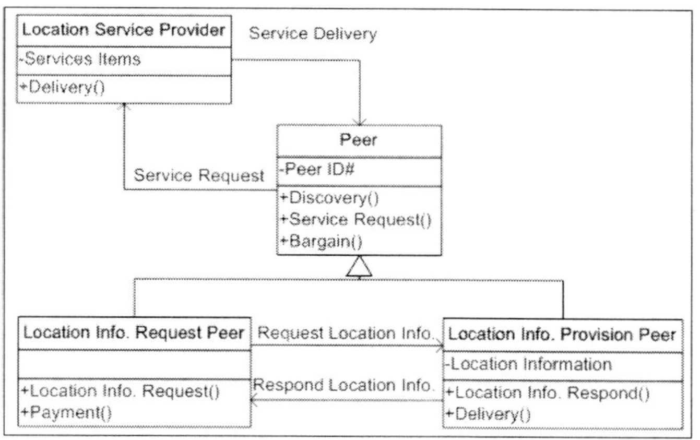

then engage their desired location-based services (as long as those location-based services do not require precise location information). Figure 7 displays this scenario.

In this scenario, location information will be useful only when the peer is within a certain distance. Each peer faces the question of what specific information should be passed to nearby peers. Should location information be given to everyone nearby or just to certain peers with specific characteristics (for example, part of the same virtual community)? Considering the possible invasion of user's sensitive data, the ambient e-service's social context with privacy concern is the better choice for this scenario. Figure 8 represents the interactions between participants.

Using location information provided by nearby peers, the mobile user then is able to use location-based services.

Cooperative Peer Group Scenario

The cooperative peer group scenario is classified into the application category of distributed collaboration (as depicted in Figure 9). In addition to one-to-one interactions, mobile users can form peer groups to work together. For example, when the workforce is dynamically deployed in the exhibition center and the environment has customers coming and going, workforces can receive and update the exhibition center task ontology from a broadcast station in the area. To support real-time collaboration of distributed group work between mobile workforces, peers may exchange their current working content information to find the best-fit candidate peers for dynamic tasks encountered based on their social context (profile, relationship, or experience) so as to maintain optimal allocation of workforce task assignments, enhancing overall performance.

Conceptual Scenario Infrastructure

The ambient e-services infrastructure is depicted in Figure 10, showing participant attributes, operations, and the relationships between them. This diagram captures the major concepts of the scenarios mentioned earlier, and highlights peer interactive efforts with others, the major concept of ambient e-services. This ability to engage in interactive collaboration enables mobile users to form peer groups able to carry out group goals.

CHALLENGES FOR EMBRACING AMBIENT E-SERVICE

Ambient e-service addresses dynamic collective efforts of mobile users and permits dynamic interactions within ambient environments in a way that is different from previous e-service applications. It enables us to explore the collective wisdom of nearby peers in an ambient e-service environment. It offers a new paradigm for mobile

Figure 9. Cooperative peer group scenario

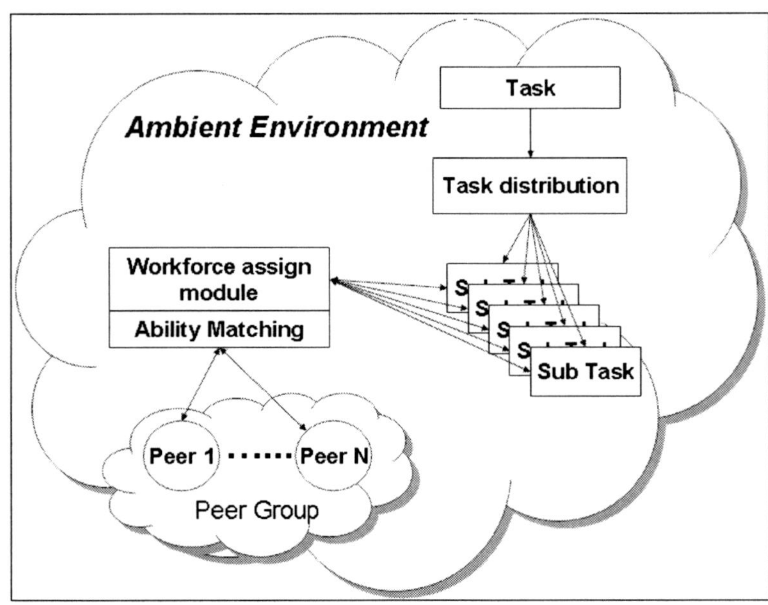

Figure 10. Class diagram of the ambient e-service infrastructure

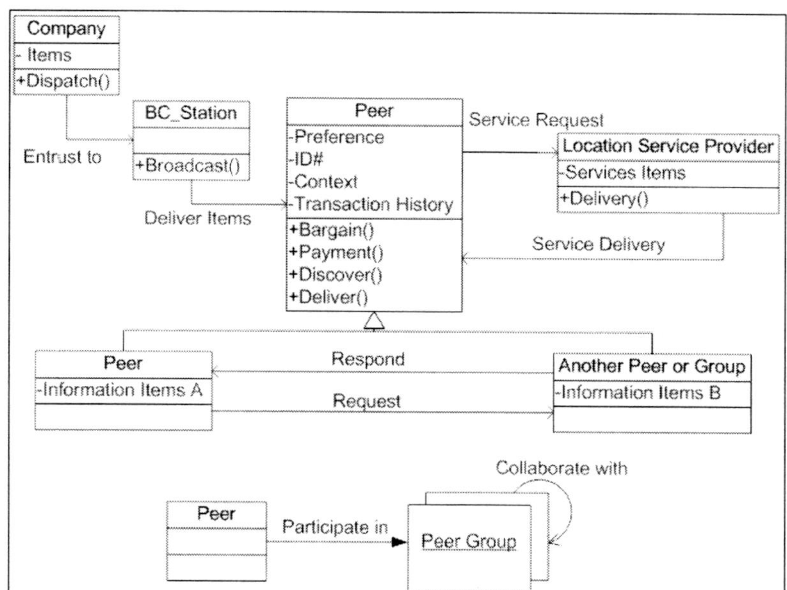

Figure 11. Issues of ambient e-services

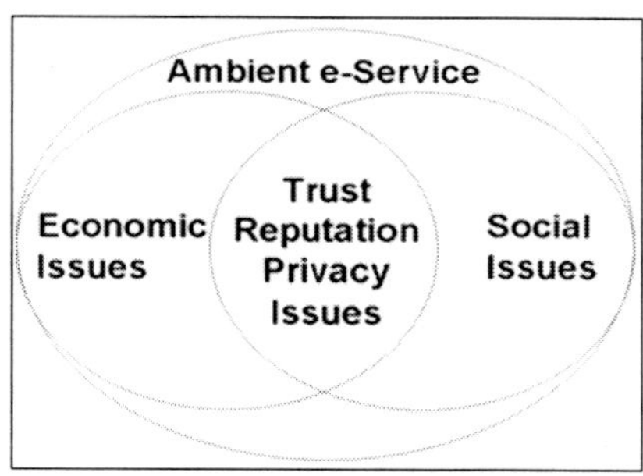

commerce and may stimulate the development of new and revolutionary business models.

Ambient e-service creates important social and economic issues. Social issues include user interaction behaviors, intellectual property rights problems, and security issues. For ambient e-service implementation, user behavior and interaction are very complex. In addition to security issues, ambient e-services also present troubling legal issues. How do holders protect their intellectual property in ambient e-services? How much access to such material should users have? These issues are vital social issues awaiting future study.

The economic issues include the pricing issues of e-services, bargaining and payment issues, and collaboration and utility issues. One of the most important issues is the service pricing issue. Ambient e-services require several kinds of supporting infrastructures such as sensor networks, wired/wireless network infrastructures, broadcast stations, and service providers. The ambient value is delivered through the combined efforts of supporting infrastructures. Accordingly, how to price ambient e-services and how to divide revenues between infrastructure and service providers will become an important issue.

However, the core issue of trust, reputation, and privacy is involved in both the social issues and the economics issues (Figure 10). Privacy and security are very important concerns of company managers today (Chou, Yen, Lin, & Cheng, 1999). In a dynamic environment of ambient e-services, who can be trusted? Is the mobile user trustworthy? What do the peers know about each other? These questions underlie the interactions and collaborations between mobile users. Accordingly, trust, reputation, and privacy issues act as the ground of ambient e-service.

Relationships Between Trust, Reputation, and Privacy

Ambient e-services rest on the interactions and collective efforts of the surrounding environments and nearby participating peers. However, in the ambient environments of ad-hoc networks, peers may not be familiar with each other. Unlike the fixed Internet environment, there are no permanent databases of historical data that can be analyzed in the ambient environments. Consequently, it is rare to see trust mechanisms with which peers interact with each other in the ad-hoc network domain. However, before cooperating with other peers, peers need to protect themselves and seek out trustworthy partners for interactions based on peer reputations.

Over the past few decades, a considerable number of studies have explored trustworthiness in different circumstances. The trust problem has recently been given added stimulus by the development of electronic commerce. Numerous attempts have been made by scholars to show that trust is the essence of e-commerce success. Trust is generally needed in every buyer-seller relationship in order to facilitate the business transaction (So & Sculli, 2002). Sufficient evidence exists to show that reputation is usually considered a core manner of how trust is manipulated and demonstrated in e-commerce scenarios. One may notice that privacy and security are foundational to user participation in e-commerce programs. Surprisingly, little attention has been given to the relations between trust, reputation, and privacy and their impact on e-commerce. Yet trust, reputation, and privacy issues are core issues for user participation in e-service business models.

On the other hand, the idea of privacy may have different meanings and significance to different mobile users. Privacy must be considered together with all other requirements including functionality, usability, performance, costs, and security (Shand, Dimmonck, & Bacon, 2003). However, the privacy concern remains a crucial barrier to mobile user participation in ambient e-services. The more participants an e-service has, the more power the ambient e-service would embody. The power comes from the number of participant users and the ability for users to obtain needed information. The collective power comes into view only when the number of the connections exceeds a certain threshold. Accordingly, transcending this threshold is a crucial problem for developing ambient e-services. Privacy-aware ambient e-services are believed to encourage users to participate in the services for attaining collective power. Figure 12 summarizes the semantic interactions of trust, reputation, and privacy that underlie the embracing of ambient e-service.

Figure 12. Semantic interactions of trust, reputation, and privacy

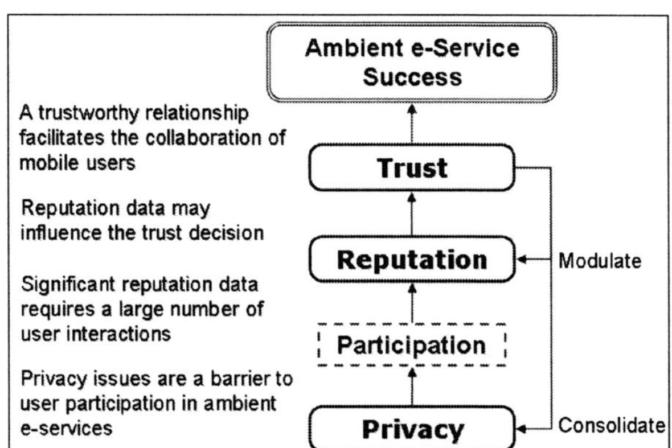

Embracing Challenges

Various features of ambient e-service applications make our lives convenient and safe. Ambient e-services facilitate people to communicate and collaborate with others. Although there might exist some technical problems for ambient e-services, those problems will be solved through the continuous new techniques and innovations.

However, user participation will become the major barrier when we boost ambient e-service applications into public. From the past experiences, no matter how good a system could be or how high the value of the system function can achieve, a system will never be popular if users can not trust the system or truly understand how it works. In other words, the problem of user acceptance toward ambient e-service applications is worthy of further discussion.

Many existing systems that might be useful to customers, users may be still reluctant to participate owing to the fear of invasions of privacy (even though the system functions provisioned are powerful and of potential benefits) (Hoy, Grubbs, & Phelps, 2003; Odlyzko, 2003). In other words, the privacy concern goes deeply into the heart of the trust problem. Users will participate in those services only when they believe their private data are well protected and feel safe to join in. With participants' trust and interactions, ambient e-service applications are then able to become popular.

Trust and reputation studies have been proposed for large open environments such as e-commerce and recommendation systems. Although trust and reputation are different in how they are developed, they are closely related. There are many researches focusing on how to translate trust from reputation data, and reputation has been the major criterion to measure the trustworthiness.

However, existing studies have been focused on reputation computation and translation from reputation to trust. What seem to be lacking are a consideration of the relationship between trust, reputation and privacy and integrating those abstract ideas into a whole framework.

In other words, it is required to devise a framework that integrates and analyzes the relationship between trust, reputation, and privacy (so as to embrace ambient e-service applications). Moreover, this framework needs to take into account the nature of ambient e-service environments (distributed interactive network environments of trust and reputation data stored in every user's handheld devices).

Moreover, for driving the values of collective actions, there are four features required for the environment of ambient e-services. As follows are these four features:

- **Convenient:** Mobile users can conveniently interact with others in the environment.
- **Safe:** Mobile users may exchange experience for safety protection cooperation but only when the environment provides a certain level of protection that satisfies their privacy requirement.
- **Fair:** In the environment, communications are free from fears and with fair interactions.
- **Collaborative:** The environment supports collaborative actions between mobile users, realizing the collective power of mobile users.

Implementation of ambient e-services thus faces two major challenges:

- **Dynamic identity management:** Dynamic identity management problem refers to the dynamic organization of ambient e-service user groups and user identities in the ambient environment. Owing to the nature of ambient e-services, every mobile device carries a temporary identity. The identity may be functional for only a short period of time for a limited communication range. Mobile users may leave or enter the e-service environment and update their user identity, refreshing the composition of the environment. Accordingly, the problem of dynamic identity management in light of the trust, reputation and privacy issues has to be carefully resolved.
- **Ambient data management:** In an ambient environment, data spreading across the devices of mobile users complicates the handling of the trust, reputation, and privacy issues. The problem of ambient data management therefore rests on the assurance of the following objectives: (1) seamless unlinkability, (2) convenient data access, (3) ambient data access, and (4) carefree heterogeneous data sources (to be addressed next).

CURRENT RESEARCH IN AMBIENT E-SERVICE IMPLEMENTATION

The existing research exhibits certain deficiencies. Ambient e-services are similar to applications on mobile ad-hoc networks, which are a collection of autonomous peers or terminals that communicate with each other over relatively bandwidth-constrained wireless links. Since the peer nodes are mobile devices, the network topology may change rapidly and unpredictably over time, and the network structures underlying ambient e-services are largely decentralized. Accordingly, all network activities, including the discovery of the topology and the delivery of messages, must be executed by the peers themselves.

To implement ambient e-services, the characteristics of the ambient e-service environments (distributed environments, peer-to-peer communication network structures, lightweight computation, limited storage, and connection-constrained wireless networks) must be taken into account. This creates a twofold problem for implementation: dynamic identity management and ambient data management. Existing relevant research (together with their deficiencies from the implementation point of view) are briefly discussed as follows.

Dynamic Identity Management for Ambient E-Service

- **Dynamic identity management:** In an ambient e-service environment, an identity is temporarily assigned to each peer. Once a peer enters an ambient e-service environment, a temporary peer ID is issued using the technology of mobile identity management (Roussos, Peterson, & Patel, 2003). In current research, in order to collect user reputation data or compute their trustworthiness, historical transaction data is opened for reference. One may trace the identity owner to find out who the user is. For the sake of privacy, the identity should be protected from others, as should sensitive data. In studies (Enzmann & Schneider, 2004, 2005), identity is issued as a one to one relationship, but the connections between identity and transaction data are restrained by using the blind signature technique.
- **Deficiencies of existing research:** In an ambient e-service environment, users may not stay in the environment for a long time and do not have permanent ID. Lacking sustained identification, trust, and reputation data for mobile peers cannot be tracked. Accordingly, trust and reputation information cannot be retained. Therefore, the ambient e-service environment should consider the refreshing of the participant composition and the checking of the updated identities. Because the ambient e-service application focuses on interactions between nearby peers, the overhead costs for checking updated identities is needed only over a finite range and thus, the communication cost is manageable. However, issues of environment identity refreshment and identity updating for ambient e-services still await the development of acceptable mechanisms in the future.

Ambient Data Management for Ambient E-Service

From the implementation standpoint, ambient data management problems include (1) seamless unlinkability management, (2) convenient data access control, (3) ambient data access control, and (4) carefree heterogeneous data sources. An in-depth discussion of these four issues is given in the following section.

- **Seamless unlinkability management:** Unlinkability means that users are unable to determine whether the same user caused certain specific operations in the services. In providing seamless unlinkability management, some studies have proposed that the transactions become public data for normal requesters but that the details of the transaction information be kept from the public (Enzmann et al., 2004, 2005). Other researchers make recommendations unlinkable and keep the reputation data unlinkable to their original identities (Golbeck, Parsia, & Hendler, 2003). Since these mechanisms were designed for fixed-Internet environments, they are not appropriate for ambient s-services owing to their nature (temporary identity, dynamic network composition, etc.). Moreover, the seamless unlinkability management problem is more complex.
- **Convenient data access control:** This refers to enabling the information requester to access needed data as easily as possible while keeping real identities from each other. Some studies address easy authentication of data access (Wilhelm, Staamann, & Buttyan, 2000) and easy data authorization (Lin, Lu, & Yu, 2004; Wilhelm et al., 2000). A pessimistic approach to trust has also been proposed to guard the agent from malicious execution environments (Wilhelm et al., 2000). Many studies work on the provision of secure data access control and authoriza-

tion/authentication procedures for secure transaction. In contrast to the complex data access control procedures proposed in existing researches, what ambient e-services require is a convenient solution.

- **Ambient data access control:** The issue of ambient data access control involves the distributed data storage problem. Most current studies related to trust, reputation, and privacy issues are focused on the fixed Internet environment (Enzmann et al., 2004, 2005; Golbeck et al., 2003; Kinateder & Rothermel, 2003; Lin et al., 2004; Sabater & Sierra, 2002). Little is known about the wireless peer-to-peer environment (Wilhelm et al., 2000). Few studies have been exploring the problems of updating trust data in wireless distributed network environments (Lin et al., 2004; Shand et al., 2003).

Due to the storage and communicational limitations of mobile devices, not all trust data can be retrieved when needed, or stored in mobile devices. There are two approaches to the problem of acquisition and retention of available trust data. The local computation design calculates the trust data only from locally obtained data (Aberer & Despotovic, 2001; Gupta, Judge, & Ammar, 2003; Shand et al., 2003; Twigg, 2003), while the global trust computation calculates from the entire trust data stored in disparate sources (Aberer et al., 2001; Castelfranchi, Falcone, & Pezzulo, 2003; Lin et al., 2004; Mui, Halberstadt, & Mohtashemi, 2003; Sabater et al., 2002). Methods to obtain trust data then involve the problem of convenient data access control.

- **Heterogeneous data source:** The trust or reputation computation based on heterogeneous data sources may be calculated either from the experience or without experience.

Over the past few decades, a considerable number of studies have been conducted on using good experience as the source of reputation computation (Golbeck et al., 2003; Mui et al., 2003; Sabater et al., 2002; Shand et al., 2003). Some studies involve recommendations based on good experience (Shand et al., 2003; Twigg, 2003). Besides good experience, bad experience is also important. Studies on trust management based on bad experience have also been performed (Aberer et al., 2001; Mui et al., 2003). Bad experiences may be used as optional information to confirm the positive experience information.

It has been recognized that trust can be generated without direct experience in three ways. The first way is grounded on prediction that is based on indirect data sources. For instance, one may get the trust or reputation data from user groups the targeted users belongs to, or have general trust ideas about those groups (Mui et al., 2003; Sabater et al., 2002) based on the trustworthy group or community certificates. The second way is to compute trustworthiness based on other persons that trusted, as with the FOAF project (Golbeck et al., 2003). Using collaborative content-based filtering is the third way to compute trust without any available direct experience.

When dealing without direct experience, the importance of prevention of malicious use of information was addressed by Castelfranchi et al. (2003). Uncertainty management and risk reasoning are also considered in Twigg (2003). Very few attempts have been made at understanding fraud and deception in the mobile environment, especially under privacy concerns.

- **The deficiencies of existing research:** Interest in heterogeneous information sources has been growing in recent years (Hertzum, Andersen, Andersen, & Hansen, 2002). Researchers have proposed trust and reputation systems, along with various methods for collecting trustworthy information from users. However, these are not suitable for the ambient e-service environment due to the difference in the environment architecture and design concepts. For instance, a distributed trust and reputation management framework for e-services was proposed to solve the trust issues in a distributed environment (Lin et al., 2004). In this framework, a distributed broker-based architecture was employed to gather information sufficient to make a confident judgment of trustworthiness. However, this solution was based on client/server architecture, compelling brokers, and users to function within the fixed Internet. It does have certain similarities to the ambient framework, depending as it does on the collective efforts of the broker peers to build up the trust and reputation management system. However, it works only on the fixed Internet and is not suitable for the ambient e-service wireless peer-to-peer environments. These challenges awaiting future research.

AMBIENT E-SERVICE EMBRACING MODEL (ASEM)

In this section, we present a framework called the ambient e-service embracing model (ASEM) that addresses the core elements (of relevance to the integrated concerns of trust, reputation, and privacy) required in dynamic identity management and ambient data management so as to assure such desired features as convenience, safety, fairness, and collaboration for mobile users when they use ambient e-services.

The ASEM framework considers the conceptual ideas of trust, privacy, and reputation as an integrated construct as shown in Figure13. The construct of Figure 13 manifests the core elements of the model together with their dependency relationships. In other words, the embracing of ambient e-services is driven by the use of carefree heterogeneous data sources that in turn relies on convenient data access control, seamless unlinkability, and ambient data access control (mutually correlated with dynamic identity management). The itemized descriptions of the core elements and their dependency relationships include:

- **Dynamic identity management:** A user identity exists only when the user is within an ambient environment, and expires when the ambient e-service is unreachable. Accordingly, dynamic identity management must enable dynamically issued identities to be different when a mobile peer leaves the environment and then re-enters the en-

Figure 13. The construct of ASEM framework

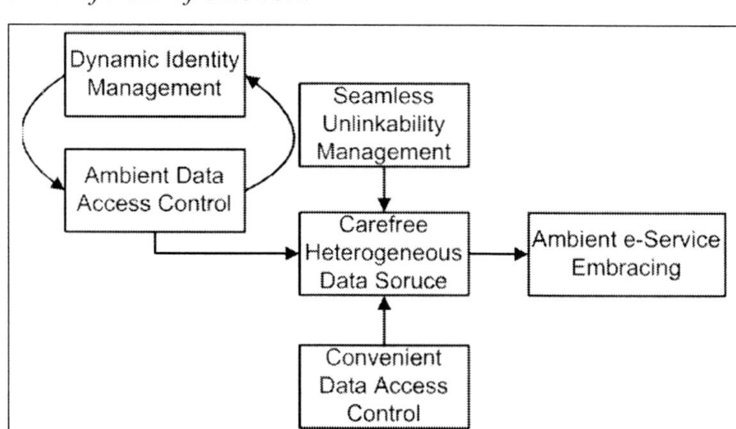

vironment (even though the mobile device used is the same).

- **Ambient data access control:** Owing to the dynamic structures of participant composition, constant updating of the environment of the distributed data storage is necessary (for subsequent accounting of the integrated concern of privacy, reputation, and trust). Ambient data access aims at facilitating the manipulation of this updating and accessing in the ambient environment.
- **Correlation of dynamic identity management and ambient data access control:** Ambient data access control relies on dynamic identity management in that the updating of the environment of the distributed data storage requires knowledge of the dynamic composition structures of participants and their dynamically issued identifiers. Conversely, dynamic identity management depends on ambient data access control because the dynamically issued identity is recorded in the device storage of the mobile user.
- **Seamless unlinkability management:** Privacy concerns allow e-service providers to retain only necessary information from mobile users. In other words, e-service providers acquire information with no traceable identities. A blind or unlinkable identity based on a given user's trust and reputation records should be furnished when a mobile user poses a query to the e-service providers. Seamless unlinkability identity aims at designing unlinkability to encourage carefree access to heterogeneous data sources when using ambient e-services.
- **Convenient data access control:** Due to the physical limitations of mobile devices of users, ambient e-services require an easy authorization and authentication process. This process has to take into account such questions as What kinds of authentication are required for different ambient e-services? How many steps or parameters may be involved in authentication execution, if the process is to be considered an "easy" authentication process? Convenient data access control aims to assure the required convenience and carefree access to the heterogeneous data sources when implementing ambient e-services.
- **Carefree heterogeneous data sources:** Since trust and reputation data is a major factor in the risk assessment of ambient e-services, the heterogeneous data sources from which trust or reputation data is obtained become significant. Heterogeneous data sources, in general, include data based on experience, information gathered without experience, and information based on the social relationships among mobile users. These heterogeneous data sources will be weighted differently in assessments of the safety and fairness of the ambient e-services. The perception of safety and fairness of the carefree heterogeneous data of the ambient e-services will significantly impact their acceptance and success.

The conceptual idea of trust, reputation, and privacy concerns for ambient e-services are consolidated into an integrated model of ASEM. Further determination of what degree of trust of different ambient e-services is necessary so as to facilitate the success of ambient e-services. Additionally, the essential requirements for trust related factor attributes and their contribution to ambient e-service implement must also be made explicit. Accordingly, a measurement matrix of ASEM should be designed in order to enable the benchmark processes of ambient e-service systems implementation.

ASEM Measurement Design

An ASEM measurement design was proposed in Hwang and Yuan (2005), which identifies possible measurements for each core element of ASEM. However, different ways of rendering the infrastructure into implementations (and the evaluation of the implementations) are beyond the focus of this chapter. In the following sections, we are trying to provide a vision about how to explore the collective effort in the ambient e-service environments. In this section, we present the framework for the core element design for ASEM as a set of required/possible measurements (Figure 14):

- **Dynamic identity management:** An ambient e-service is provided within an ambient environment, in which the peers are of a dynamic composition. Issuing an identity for a mobile peer is a complex task. A set of required/possible measurements associated with dynamic identity management may include:
    - **Identity type:** Identity type defines the role of a peer. An identity may be a real personal **identity, or a pseudonym.**
    - **Identity expiration check (Y/N):** This is an indicator of whether applications provide an identity expiration check mechanism to support dynamic interactions between mobile users.
    - **Identity list update frequency:** Due to the dynamic composition of mobile peers, the identities of the surrounding peers should be updated frequently. The identity list update frequency represents how often the identity list is updated.
    - **Identity authentication (Y/N):** For safety reasons, a peer identity should be considered in the authentication process. This is an indicator of whether a provisioned e-service application bestows an identity authentication mechanism to support the dynamic interactions of mobile users.
    - **Identity authorization (Y/N):** Not all peers within an ambient e-service have the same service privileges. This is an indicator of whether an e-service application provides an identity authorization mechanism in order to facilitate the authorization process for dynamic interactions between mobile users.

Figure 14. The measurement design of the ASEM framework

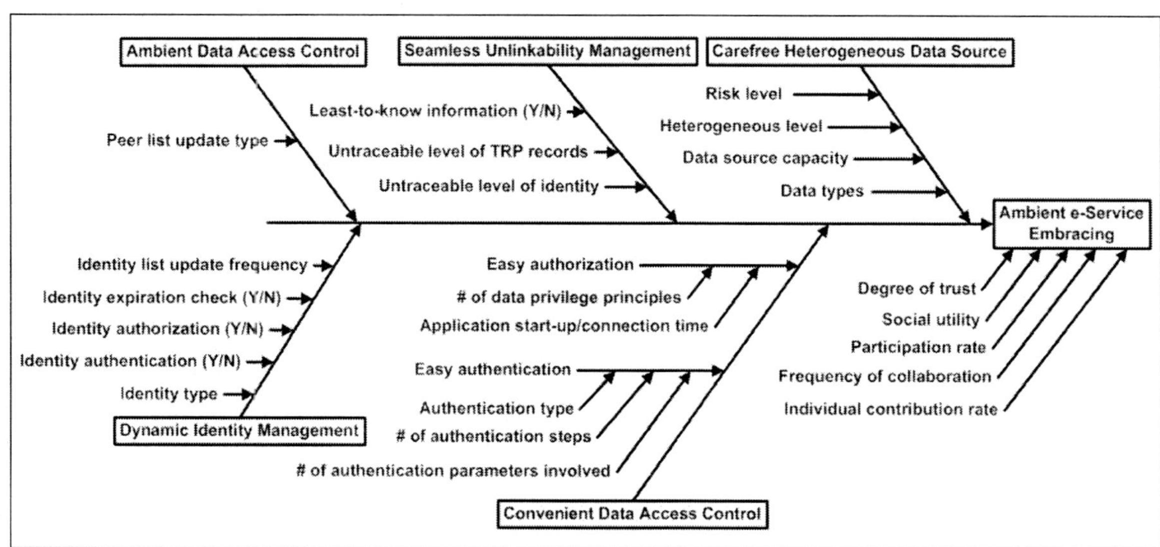

- ◦ **Ambient data access control:** An ambient e-service platform is constructed on top of a dynamic identity management environment, which provides the necessary mechanisms supporting the complex dynamic mobile identity composition. From a the viewpoint of a given mobile peer, each peer needs to manage his or her surrounding peer list and stay updated whenever necessary. Ambient data access control is designed to be capable of measuring the level of peer reachability.
- ◦ **Peer list update type:** The peer list update can be processed in different ways depending on network constraints and communication cost (e.g., real-time, periodical). Not all e-services require real time updates for nearby peers. Users may update their surrounding peer list based on the precise level of information they need.
- **Seamless unlinkability management:** When participating in an e-service, a user usually cares about what sensitive information about him or her is gathered and retained in the system. Certain problems are of deep concern to users: If sensitive data leaks out to the others, will that affect the user's safety? Is it possible for the user to hide sensitive data from others or at least to make it untraceable? Seamless unlinkability management can thus be measured by three factors:
  - ◦ **Least-to-know information (Y/N):** This is an indicator of whether an e-service application provides only necessary information when interacting with other mobile users.
  - ◦ **Untraceable level of identity:** This represents how far the personal data of the mobile users can be traced. If there is not any trace blocking mechanisms available, the level of untraceability is low. The level of untraceability is higher when users cannot learn each other's real identity, as when applications employ techniques such as pseudo identitities or electronic signatures that can conceal real identities.
  - ◦ **Untraceable level of TRP records:** This denotes how detailed records of trust, reputation and privacy (TRP) can be retrieved and traced.
- **Convenient data access control:** Convenience can be categorized into two types: easy authentication and easy authorization.
- **Easy authentication:** Indicates the comparative complexity level of the authentication processes, as measured by:
  - ◦ **The number of authentication steps:** The method of one-time sign-in authentication is considered to be more convenient (embodying only 1 authentication step) than authentication processes that require a different authentication for each process)
  - ◦ **The number of authentication parameters involved:** The fewer the number of parameters an authentication process uses, the more convenient it is considered to be.
  - ◦ **Authentication type:** Many different types of authentication techniques, including PKI, one time authentication, or some combinations of methods, may be used in an authentication process. The authentication type determines the complexity of the process, and also influences user perceptions of ease of authentication.
  - ◦ **Easy authorization:** Related to easy authentication; it represents the convenience level of mobile users when attempting to obtain authorization, and may be measured by:

- **The number of data privilege principles:** The complexity of an authorization process depends on the number of authorization principles in the process. When the authorization process uses many principles, the security level rises, but it becomes more complicated.
- **Application start-up/connection time:** The time spent by the application in start-up or connection with other peers may also be used to measure the degree of convenience. The more time spent, the less convenient it is.

- **Carefree heterogeneous data sources:** During implementation of ambient e-services, large amounts of data may be used to derive TRP and affect user perception of safety. Various heterogeneous sources of data will be considered. Different sources have different weights in calculations of trustworthiness. Carefree heterogeneous data sources may be assessed by the following four factors.
  - **Data types:** The heterogeneity of the data can be measured by the number of data types. The more genera the data sources contain, the higher the variety they embody.
  - **Data source capacity:** The greater the amount of data acquired, the more ability the system has to conduct a rich, precise analysis. Data source capacity denotes the quantity of data.
  - **Level of heterogeneity:** The level of heterogeneity represents the degree of heterogeneity of the collected data sources.
  - **Risk level:** Owing to the heterogeneity of the data sources, some of the sources may be more trustworthy than others. The degree of trustworthiness depends on user perception of the data sources. The risk level of the data sources indicates the chance of a given user being deceived when the data sources are accessed. The reputation of a source is related to its risk assessment.
- **Ambient e-service embracing:** The embracing of ambient e-services unfolds across four dimensions of use: convenience, safety, fairness, and collaborative efforts of mobile users. These four dimensions also represent the ultimate goals of the ambient e-services. The degree to which for an ambient e-service is accepted can be measured as follows:
  - **Degree of trust:** When considering the risk of fraud and deception, the degree of trust can be treated as the benchmark of safety and fairness. Trust is derived from computation involving heterogeneous data sources and various relationships of social networks.
  - **Participation rate:** Users will be willing to participate in the e-service application only when they feel it is safe and convenient. Thus, the percentage of user participation may be used as a measurement of the convenience and fairness of the e-service.
  - **Frequency of collaboration:** This is a measurement of how often a collaboration activity occurs. This measurement may be treated as an indicator of the convenience of collective activities such as collective bargaining or collective agreement made possible by an ambient e-services.
  - **Individual contribution rate:** To reduce free-rider concerns, measurements of individual contribution rates are required, as this is of relevance to the perception of the fairness of an ambient e-service.
  - **Social utility:** Social utility is a measurement of the quantified collective efforts of an ambient e-service. Different from the computation of individual utilities, social utility describes the

power of collective efforts in an ambient environment.

ROADMAP FOR AMBIENT E-SERVICES

We have proposed an ambient e-service framework, followed by an ASEM model for embracing and adopting ambient e-service applications. This model is believed to bestow ambient e-services fundamental guidelines for their future development in research, platforms, or applications. In other words, the roadmap for ambient e-services is two-fold: One is for the application service domain, which represents the remarkable diversity of ambient e-service applications grounding on ASEM. The other is for the platform design domain, which manifests possible solutions in shaping the ambient e-service platform design.

Application Service Domain

Ambient e-service application scenarios have been illustrated in the previous work by Hwang and Yuan (2007), which presumes the ambient environments for mobile commerce are provided. As mentioned in the introduction section, ambient e-services mainly address dynamic collective efforts between mobile users (enabled by M-P2P) and dynamic interactions with ambient environments (envisioned by LBS). LBS has been categorized into four major types: transaction service, information service, navigation and tracking service and safety service (Lim et al., 2003). Ambient e-service applications categories reflect LBS types as well as exhibiting dynamic collective efforts based on M-P2P.

Several major applications are demonstrated in Hwang et al. (2007). The ambient shopping mall scenario, for example, is classified as a distributed transaction service. In a shopping mall (fully equipped with wireless network infrastructures), information such as advertisements or sales promotion information can be broadcast to peers passing-by using an information broadcast station. Peers in different locations receive different information depending on the information lists in their nearby broadcast station. This means the experiences and obtained information of peers differ based on their location and user context (user preferences or interests). Customers are not required to go all over the shopping mall to receive broadcasted information, but may pay a small sum to acquire a suitable information service package based on their preferences. Alternatively, a mobile agent peer can inquire of nearby peers what they want and then, if desired, proceed to a bartering process. This will help newly entered customers in a hurry to efficiently acquire shopping mall information.

This scenario delineates not only the case of new customers with high buyer perishability (entering the shopping mall and being in a rush to buy certain items without the knowledge of where to buy and at what prices), but also presents performance of the collective efforts of mobile users (in collective bargaining, collective purchasing, or a similar collective agreement). Through a transaction e-service, information such as e-coupons can be distributed not only to mobile users falling into the broadcast range of the distributor companies, but also to the primary target peers (who truly need the e-coupons in a specific place at a specific time).

However, in such an ad-hoc structured environment, peers might not recognize each other. Should peers trust their information sources? No evidence exists that all peers are trustable. What if someone unauthorized is trying to acquire sensitive information about a given peer? The constant possibility of fraud or identity theft forces users to protect themselves from any possible form of harm. A mobile user's willingness to participate thus hinges on satisfactory resolution of the safety and privacy concerns. This in turn affects the viability of a particular e-service: if the number of participants diminishes, the e-service application will no longer be tenable. Accordingly, a convenient and safe environment supports both increased user participation and increased application viability.

Since different e-service applications require different conditions and face different restrictions, the ASEM framework outlines the guidelines for e-service implementation. For example, if the trading process employs a bartering mechanism (that does not involve real money), the required level of trust is comparatively lower than a process that uses actual currency.

The ASEM framework also diminishes the chance of fraud and deceit. Mobile users can obtain the necessary decision information of assured quality from nearby sources such as other mobile users or service providers. Different information sources may be accessed to facilitate greater user utility. Once the risk level of transactions can be reduced, the convenient interactions of ambient e-services will become more common, increasing the chance of realizing the power of the collective efforts between mobile users.

Platform Design Domain

The future design of ambient e-service platforms must consider dynamic identity management, ambient data access control, seamless unlinkability management, and convenient data access control. Dynamic identity management and ambient data access control are particularly dependent on the nature of an ambient e-service's environment, governed by factors such as wireless communication distance, handheld device storage capacity, and temporary identity. In the shopping mall scenario application, the communication ranges of the ad-hoc wireless networks centered around the mobile user vary, and it is necessary for the mobile user to update the list of nearby peers from its current location and check if any peers offer items fitting the user's needs. However, the desired update type and frequency vary between applications. In the shopping mall application, it is not necessary to engage a constant update of the list of the surrounding peers because users often move slowly. Accordingly, a periodical update type is the right choice for the update-type design for the ambient shopping mall scenario.

This short term life-time identity is a unique property in ambient environments. As mentioned in the ASEM section, dynamic identity management aims to issue different identities for a mobile peer when the peer leaves the environment and re-enters the environment again (even though the mobile device used is the same). However, existing P2P systems/solutions are still with long-lived identities. For instance, as addressed in Resnick, Zeckhauser, Friedman, and Kuwabara (2000), reputation systems generally take on three properties: (1) entities are long-lived; (2) feedback about current interactions is captured and distributed; (3) past feedback guides buyer decisions. In other words, the identities in ambient e-service environments are short-lived and localized, and thus existing methods/solutions requiring long-lived identities cannot be applied to our environments.

On the other hand, the nature of ambient environment (localized/short period life-time's identities) could result in the material change of the reputation's basics as well as other issues (trust/traceability/ privacy). How to derive a reputation system coping with the nature of ambient environments accordingly becomes new a challenge to straighten out.

The requirements for seamless unlinkability management in different ambient e-service scenarios are also different. In the ambient shopping mall scenario, if a transaction involves just information items, the volume of necessary information would be less than those transactions that involve real money. The requisite security level for privacy concerns can be handled by associating weights with respect to a user's unique needs and circumstances. A blind signature method provides higher untraceable level than the pseudo identity. Alternatively, a user may have various role identities for different transactions, and this then involves both dynamic identity management and seamless unlinkability management.

Convenient data access control facilitates ambient e-service implementation. A single sign-on authorization is more acceptable than a set of complex authorization processes. While the identity authentication can be achieved by various techniques such as strong authentication or passwords, the proper method should be based on the unique needs and preferences of the user.

Respecting the heterogeneity of data sources, since all data sources have their own risk levels, carefree heterogeneous data sources should draw upon the entire set of data sources so as to enable the computation required for decision-making. This computation should take into account the risk level, heterogeneity, and the quantity of available data. However, an economical evaluation method is indispensable due to the computational limitations of ambient handheld devices.

In the work of Hwang and Yuan (2006), a multiple layered anonymous pseudonym system was proposed which combines interaction trust and creditability investigation enabling users to collaborate with nearby peers to establish a rapid reputation under a short-lived identity environments.

Benefits of ASEM

Ambient e-service aims to exchange or integrate value-added information through proximity interactions. Thus, the contributions of this research include a focus on the value of ASEM. In the previous section, we proposed an ambient e-service framework to create the required device platforms and enable a trustworthy environment (facilitating the exchange of added values through the convergence of physical and digital means). There are five mega values of the ambient e-service platform as shown in Figure 15, discussed in the following paragraphs.

Figure 15. Values of ambient e-service embracing model

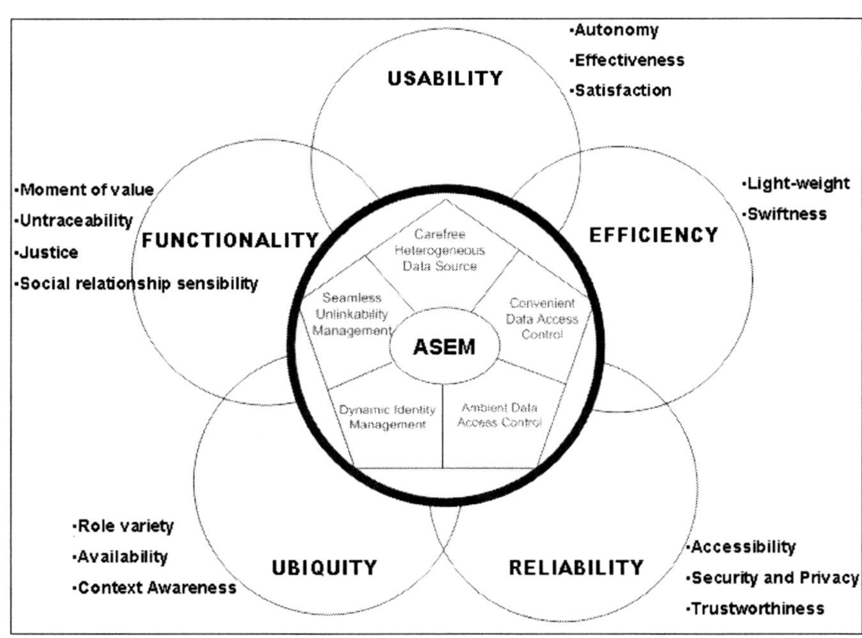

- **Ubiquity**
    - **Availability:** Wireless technology of mobile devices equipped with the platform makes it possible for users to ubiquitously acquire ambient e-services. Transactions and interactions can be carried out anywhere and at anytime without being constrained to the fixed power line or Internet plugs.
    - **Context awareness:** Context awareness may be used to design the ambient e-service platform user interface so that the device and the platform have information about the circumstances under which the mobile users operate and then can react accordingly.
    - **Role variety:** In our daily life, a user may have various roles in different communities. Through a dynamic identity management mechanism, the user can assume different roles in accord with their needs without the worry of others recognizing the private identity or roles of the user.
- **Reliability**
    - **Security and privacy:** The ambient e-service platform offers the functions of authentication and authorization so as to protect private or sensitive user data.
    - **Ambient e-service** is based on the pure P2P architecture and thus no centralized authority for security or privacy is assumed. However, there are still decentralized security protections (such as PGP) that may be deployed in the platform. Moreover, the user's transaction data and interaction logs can be retained only in the user's mobile device.
    - **Accessibility:** Access control to a user's individual information is granted by the user himself/herself. The user can either decide to keep silence or share their value-added information (what, who, where, when, how), yielding collective interactions and exchanges.
    - **Trustworthiness:** The ambient e-service platform is trustworthy because of its various security and privacy controls. The nature of P2P architecture and seamless unlinkability enables users to be free from privacy intrusions. Furthermore, the ambient e-service platform does not provide an agglomerate "trustworthiness" of each user. Instead, based on a user's social network connectivity, the user will receive a personalized set of decision data of trust, which may vary widely from person to person. This would subsequently increase the user's acceptance level of the services provisioned and enable them to feel satisfied with the platform.
- **Functionality**
    - **Moment of value:** The ambient e-service platform is empowered by the mobile technology and context awareness technology. Unlike traditional ways of broadcasting advertising information, which many consumers find annoying and intrusive, users can obtain their desired information or services in a timely and controllable way. When a user needs certain information, useful information that matches user preferences and the current context can be delivered to the user's mobile device automatically.
    - **Untraceability:** Untraceability is the most distinguishing feature of the ambient e-service platform. The platform equips users with unlinkable short-term pseudonyms for security assurance.
    - **Justice:** After each transaction, the platform issues an unlinkable evaluation token that is delivered to the

buyer as well as the seller. Since the anonymous evaluation token is not bound to any transaction data, users can evaluate the seller/buyer without the fear of retaliation.

    - **Social relationship sensibility:** The platform can enable the establishment of social connection networks that generally provide valuable and reliable exchanges of decision information. This is because opinions from a trusted source have greater impact than those of an unfamiliar source.
- **Efficiency**
    - **Light-weight:** The platform enables easy authentication and easy authorization that simplify the computation of interactions. Mechanisms for single sign-on or other lightweight digital identity assignment also contribute to the efficiency of ambient e-service interactions.
    - **Swiftness:** The platform utilizes a user's context and proximity interactions for efficient and swift service provision.
- **Usability**
    - **Autonomy:** The platform enables mobile peers to operate without the direct intervention of humans or others. Mobile peers can interact with other peers (and possibly humans) via communication channels on the ambient e-service platform. Mobile peers do not simply act in response to their environment; they are able to exhibit goal-directed behavior by taking the initiative; exercises control over their own actions.
    - **Effectiveness:** The platform ensures data suitability for user needs or decision making by providing trustworthy estimations of unfamiliar peers. Also, the platform's seamless unlinkability enables the platform users to enjoy a privacy enhanced transaction environment. That will strengthen the users to embrace ambient e-service and share their point of view voluntarily.
    - **Satisfaction:** The platform aims to improve the quality of carefree perception and assure total customer satisfaction. By adopting heterogeneous data sources combined with the social connectivity relationships as estimation resources, service quality would increase continuously. Moreover, the user interface, equipped with context awareness technology, would contribute to platform ease-of-use, while the lightweight computation and swift response time would satisfy uses.

ASEM aims to provide the design guidelines of the platforms for supporting ambient e-services within a safe and trustworthy environment, as well as aggregating the collective effort of mobile users within the environment. In this section, the benefits of ASEM from the socio-economic perspective are briefly discussed (in addition to the justification of ASEM rendered being technologically possible as addressed in previous sections).

From the economic view for privacy invasion, anecdotal evidence shows that people are willing to disclose personal information for potential monetary savings (Russell, 1989), and people do join Web sites for free gifts and catalogs. That evidence supports that individuals respond to economic incentives in deciding whether to disclose information. On the other hand, in various organizational and marketing contexts, concern of privacy invasion have been shown to depend on information control, outcomes arising from disclosures, information type and sensitivity, perceived relevancy of information use, and target of disclosures. Hoffman, Novak, and Peralta (1999) claimed that nearly 63% percent of consumers would not provide information to Web sites because of the lack of trust.

From the socio-economic view, our method is to be evaluated in terms of a cost-benefit analysis and expect the majority benefit would eliminate privacy invasion. In other words, with our method privacy, of a person's persona would be appropriately protected because all the real personal identities are hidden. Seamless unlinkability management enables users to control their owned information in accord with the information type and sensitivity; users are able to decide whether to disclosure the information or not, as well as the target of their information disclosed to.

Furthermore, users within the ambient environment may provide various data sources (i.e., experience or subjective opinions) for others to make a strategic decision. These collective efforts encourage the building of the sense of ambient trust by engaging the reliability of fraud detection in ambient e-service environments.

However, some systematical costs are required. Making decisions with heterogeneous data source provide a comparative reliability rather than depending on their own information, especially in the dynamic environment. When the number peers exceeds the limit of computation capability, the complexity of data management and computation will become a major problem especially in a peer-to-peer environment. For preliminary estimates, establishing a trustworthy ambient environment with privacy protection might have to trade with some efficiency loss. Therefore, the trade-off between the cost and benefit is a major issue for further research. At the moment, this chapter mainly focuses on the framework prospect, but we intend to provide a vision of collective wisdom within ambient e-service environment. However, the implementation or systematical evaluations are not the focus of this chapter.

In summary, with the supporting platform (delimited by ASEM), ambient e-service applications may offer a new, carefree information/service era. Again, take the shopping mall scenario for example. Mobile users can acquire desired information conveniently, either from the system or from nearby users. They can then determine their actions based on various information sources, and decide which one is most suitable for their current needs. Fraud and untruthful activities can be reduced with the collective effort of the participants.

CONCLUSION

Ambient e-services address dynamic collective efforts of mobile users dynamically engaging interactions in the ambient environments, rendering a new paradigm of mobile commerce promising revolutionary business models. This chapter presents an ambient e-services framework characterizing three supporting stacks. The ambient value stack describes the value process in ambient environments. The ambient technology stack identifies the technology process to ensure connectivity and security in ambient interactions and cooperation between peers and then realize powerful collective efforts. The environment stack then represents the ambient basics for the collaborations.

Ambient e-services applications can be divided into two types. One is for the distributed trading, another is for the distributed collaboration. However, social context and significant rapid growth of connections enabled by P2P are the two major incentives for applying ambient e-service to such revolutionary business models. We exemplify several ambient e-service applications. Those applications differ from existing mobile e-services (grounded on client/server design) in terms of the focus of the dynamic interactions between peers in dynamic ambient e-service environments.

In this chapter, we also presented another framework called ambient e-service embracing model (ASEM) that addresses the core elements (of relevance to the integrated concern of trust, reputation, and privacy) required for assuring desired features such as convenience, safety, fairness, and collaboration for mobile users when they engage ambient e-services. This framework manifests the relationship between the issues of dynamic identity management and ambient data management. The framework abstracts the trust, reputation, and privacy concerns into an integrated consideration. Since different e-service applications are of different circumstances and bear different restrictions, the framework of ASEM also outlines the guidelines for the implementation of ambient e-service applications and the platforms.

The fruitful future research includes a further in-depth evaluation of ASEM, a complete design of the ASEM core elements, and a fielded implementation of certain ambient e-services deriving economic models of ambient e-services.

REFERENCES

Aberer, K., & Despotovic, Z.(2001). Managing trust in a peer-2-peer information system. *Proceedings of the Conference on Information and Knowledge Management* (pp. 310-317). CIKM01. (Nov. 5-10, 2001). Atlanta, Georgia.

Ashrafi, N., & Kuilboer, J. P. (2005). Privacy protection via technology: Platform for privacy preferences (P3P). *International Journal of E-Business Research, 1*(2), 56-69.

Baida, Z., Gordijn, J., Akkermans, H., Saele, H., & Morch, A. Z. (2005). Finding e-service offerings by computer-supported customer need reasoning, *International Journal of E-Business Research, 1*(3), 91-112.

Chou, D.C., Yen, D.C., Lin, B., & Cheng, P.H.-L. (1999). Cyberspace security management. *Industrial Management & Data Systems, 99*(8), 353-361.

Castelfranchi, C., Falcone, R., & Pezzulo, G. (2003). Integrating trustfulness and decision using fuzzy cognitive maps. *Trust Management 2003, LNCS 2692* (pp. 195-210).

Enzmann, M., & Schneider, M. (2005). Improving customer retention in e-commerce through a secure and privacy-enhanced loyalty system (Forthcoming). *Information Systems Frontiers, 7*(4-5), 359-370, December 2005.

Enzmann, M., & Schneider, M. (2004). A privacy-friendly loyalty system for electronic marketplaces. *Proceedings of the 2004 IEEE International Conference on e-Technology, e-Commerce, and e-Service* (EEE04), Taiwan.

Golbeck, J., Parsia, B., & Hendler, J. (2003). Trust networks on the semantic Web. *Proceedings of Cooperative Intelligent Agents 2003.*

Gupta, M., Judge, P., & Ammar, M. (2003). A reputation system for peer-to-peer networks. *NOSSDAV'03* (pp. 144-152). (Jun. 1-3, 2003).

Hertzum, M., Andersen, H., Andersen, V., & Hansen, C. (2002). Trust in information sources: Seeking information from people, documents, and virtual agents. *Interacting with Computers, 14*(5), 575-599.

Hoffman, D. L., Novak, T. P., & Peralta, M. A. (1999). Building consumer trust online. *Communications of the ACM, 42*(4), 80-85.

Hoy, M.G., & Phelps, J. (2003). Consumer privacy and security protection on church Web sites: Reasons for concern. *Journal of Public Policy and Marketing, 22*(1), 58-70.

Hwang Y. C., & Yuan S. T. (2007). A roadmap for ambient e-service: Applications and embracing model. *International Journal of E-Business Research, 13*(1), 51-73.

Hwang Y. C., & Yuan S. T. (2006). *Exploring collective wisdom in ambient e-service environment: Implementation method and evaluations.* Technical report. National Cheng-Chi University, Taiwan.

Hwang, Y. C., & Yuan, S. T. (2005). Ambient e-service embracing model. *Proceedings of the 7th IEEE International Conference on E-Commerce Technology* (pp. 535-538). (CEC2005) Germany.

Kinateder, M., & Rothermel, K. (2003). Architecture and algorithms for a distributed reputation system. *Trust Management 2003, LNCS 2692* (pp. 1-16).

Lim, E., & Saiu, K. (2003). *Advances in mobile commerce technologies.* Hershey, PA: Idea Group Publishing.

Lin, K., Lu, H., & Yu, T. (2004). A distributed trust and reputation management framework for e-services. *IEEE International Conference on Services Computing*, Shanghai, China.

Mui, L., Halberstadt, A., & Mohtashemi, M. (2003). Evaluating reputation in multi-agents systems. In R. Falcone, S. Barber, L. Korba, & M. Singh (Eds.), *Trust, reputation, and security: Theories and practice* (pp. 123-137). Springer-Verlag, Berlin.

Odlyzko, A. (2003). Privacy, economics, and price discrimination on the Internet. *The 5th International Conference on Electronic Commerce* (ICEC 2003). ACM Press.

Paternò, F. (2003). Understanding interaction with mobile devices. *Interacting with Computers, 15*(4), 473-478.

Resnick, P., Zeckhauser, R., Friedman, E., & Kuwabara, K. (2000). Reputation systems: Facilitating trust in Internet interactions. *Communications of the ACM, 43*(12), 45-48.

Roussos, G., Peterson, D., & Patel, U. (2003). Mobile identity management: An enacted view. *International Journal of E-Commerce, 8*(1). 81-100.

Russell, C. (1989). Kiss and tell. *American Demographics, 11*(12), 2.

Sabater, J., & Sierra, C. (2002). Reputation and social network analysis in multi-agent systems. *The 1st International Joint Conference on Autonomous Agents & Multiagent Systems* (pp. 475-482). AAMAS'02, July 15-19, 2002, Bologna, Italy.

Schilit, B., Adams, N., & Want, R. (1994). Context-aware computing applications. *Proceedings of the 1st International Workshop on Mobile Computing Systems and Applications* (pp. 85-90).

Shand, B., Dimmonck, N., & Bacon, J. (2003). Trust for ubiquitous, transparent collaboration. *Proceedings of the 1st IEEE International Conference on Pervasive Computing and Communications* (PerCom'03).

So, W.C., & Sculli, D. (2002). The role of trust, quality, value and risk in conducting e-business. *Industrial Management and Data Systems, 102*(9), 503-512.

Twigg, A. (2003). A subjective approach to routing in P2P and ad hoc networks. *Trust Management 2003* (pp. 225-238), LNCS 2692.

Wilhelm, U. G., Staamann, S. M., & Buttyan, L. (2000). A pessimistic approach to trust in mobile agent platforms. *IEEE Internet Computing* (pp. 40-48), September-October.

Chapter IV
Superior Customer Value and Network Size in Markets Characterized by Network Effects

Fan-Chen Tseng
Kainan University, Taiwan

Ching-I Teng
Chang Guung University, Taiwan

David M. Chiang
National Taiwan University, Taiwan

ABSTRACT

Network effect indicates that the value of connecting to a network is positively associated with the current number of customers connected to that network. Network effect strengthens the strong firms, weakens the weak firms, and may lead to a winner-take-all market. Thus, managing customer perceived value is crucial in markets with network effects. This article models customer perceived value, presents ways to improve the value, and discusses the relationship between customer perceived value and network size. Implications for e-business practitioners are discussed.

INTRODUCTION

Information technologies changed business operations and customer behavior. In information economies, network effects involve a "larger gets larger" mechanism, which predicts a theoretical natural monopoly, urging e-businesses (such as net-enabled organizations and value webs) to exploit network effects.

Network effects indicate the value of connecting to a network positively correlates with the number of customers connected to the network.

Users thus prefer large networks to smaller ones, fostering the growth of larger networks. Network effects take place in physical networks such as telephone networks or virtual networks such as the networks of the members of a Web site. Typical products with network effects are image phone, e-mail, videotape, computer operating system, word processing software, TV game player, and computer keyboard. Network effects are also pervasive in the network sector such as the telecommunication and information industries. With the rise of electronic commerce, network effects are influential in online auctions, e-marketplaces, or online employment Web sites.

It is well known that network effects can tilt the market toward the largest player and result in a natural monopoly (Chou & Shy, 1990; Farrell & Saloner, 1992; Katz & Shapiro, 1986). For instance, "Microsoft's dominance is simply a manifestation of the network externality [effects], which relentlessly drives computer software to standardization" (Choi, Stahl, & Whinston, 1997, p. 4). Thus, e-businesses actively compete to be the largest to take advantage of network effects. Chen, Chen, and Wu (2005) provided a Simonian perspective that guides e-businesses to gain sustaining competitive advantages.

Inefficiencies in social welfare (the difference between the actual and the optimal social welfare) resulting from network effects were explored (Farrell et al., 1986). Although researchers shifted their research focus to competitive strategies (Tseng, Teng, & Chiang, 2005), their assumptions remain too restrictive. This article presents how to deliver superior value to customers in markets with network effects, and discusses the relationship between customer perceived value and network size.

The remainder of this article is organized as follows. Section 2 reviews the literature. Section 3 then describes the model for describing customer perceived value. Subsequently, section 4 elaborates how to deliver superior customer value, and section 5 states the relationship between customer perceived value and network size. Finally, section 6 draws conclusions.

LITERATURE REVIEW

Terms and Definitions

Katz and Shapiro (1985) utilized the term *positive consumption externality* to explain network effects as "the utility a user derives from consumption increases with the number of other users consuming the good" (Katz et al., 1985, p. 424) and then called it *positive consumption benefits* (Katz et al., 1986, p. 823). Alternative definition says that "the fact that the value of a unit of the good increases with the number of units sold" (Economides, 1996, p. 678). Choi et al. (1997, p. 4) argued that network externality is better termed *network effect* when a market price already reflects the external benefit or loss. This article agrees with Choi et al.'s suggestion and uses the term *network effect* to describe the phenomenon.

Network effects also have many variations with similar or different definitions such as *congestion externality* (Westland, 1992), *complementary network externality* (Church & Gandal, 1993), *positive demand externality* (Xie & Sirbu, 1995), *indirect network externality* (Gupta, Jain, & Sawhney, 1999), and *cross-consumer externality* (Holcombe & Sobel, 2000). Chiang and Teng (2005) provided detailed definitions and differences between those terms. Understanding those terms helps researchers to create knowledge on network effects.

Business Strategies

E-businesses operating in markets characterized by network effects can use strategies such as building alliances, taking first-mover advantages, managing customer expectations (Shapiro & Varian, 1999), and penetrative pricing (Bensaid

& Lesne, 1996; Shapiro & Varian, 1998). E-businesses can penetrate a market by setting a low price and then capture the entire market when their user network size exceeds a threshold (Bensaid et al., 1996; Shapiro et al., 1998).

Network effects also make conventional wisdoms less applicable. For instance, permitting piracy is irrational in conventional wisdoms but it can be beneficial to firms in markets with network effects. The reason is that pirates cannot pay the price for the technology usage, but they can provide utility to legal users by interacting with them by the technology (Conner and Remult, 1991). Moreover, introducing different but compatible products can also be beneficial to profits (Conner, 1995). Furthermore, Choi et al. (1997) argued that the monopolistic position of Microsoft does not lead to limited output and raising prices, contradictory to conventional wisdom that monopoly *always* limits output and raises prices.

Inefficiencies and Corrections

Previous research raised various inefficiencies regarding network effects. A leader in a market with network effects will capture the whole market, and no challenger firm can survive in those markets even when the challenger has a superior technology (Farrell et al., 1986).

A market leader capturing a whole market with network effects has incentives to introduce new products that are incompatible to their previous-version products. Such a strategy of making the previously released products obsolete is named planned obsolescence (Choi, 1994). A market leader also has incentives to first offer poorer-quality products and then offers better-quality products (Padmanabhan, Rajiv, & Srinivasan, 1997). Additionally, a market leader can also preannounce their upgrade-version product to make competing technologies less attractive to prospect users (Farrell et al., 1986).

Governmental interventions may correct, reduce, or eliminate those inefficiencies. Standard setting is intuitive for preventing anti-social-welfare research and development race. However, standard setting policy does the contrary. Such a policy urges firms to compete more than ever to be the standard chosen by the government (Kristiansen, 1998). On the other hand, the forced licensing policy, which forces the winner license his or her technology to other firms, can reduce the inefficiencies from network effects (Kristiansen, 1998). Baake and Boom (2001) proposed that firms in equilibrium always provide the converter, although firms prefer introducing high quality products that are incompatible to the product of each other. The converter effectively reduces social welfare inefficiency from network effects.

Recent studies demonstrated that network effects, adoption costs, switching costs (Zhu, Kraemer, Gurbaxani, & Xu, 2006), network topology, and density (Weitzel, Beimborn, & König, 2006) affects technology competition, explaining why not all markets with network effects are eventually occupied by a market leader. Other recent studies are summarized next.

Recent Studies

The recent research on network effects has examined numerous topics, including two-sided network effects (Parker & van Alstyne, 2005), strong ties network effects in technology competition (Suarez, 2005), product launch strategies (Lee & O'Connor, 2003; Sun, Xie, & Cao, 2004), relationship between network effects and penetration thresholds (Kornish, 2006), relationship between network effects and price of word processing software (Chakravarty, Dogan, & Tomlinson, 2006), business-to-consumer pricing strategies (Chiang & Teng, 2001; Gallaugher & Wang, 2002), business-to-business pricing strategies (Lin & Kulatilaka, 2006), innovation and strategic activities (Ehrhardt, 2004; Ende & Wijnberg, 2003), and strategies for beating the market leaders (Witt, 1997) or replacing the market leaders (Chiang & Teng, 2003; Teng & Chiang, 2006; Teng, Tseng, & Chiang, 2006; Tseng et al., 2005). Chiang et al. (2005) massively reviewed the related literature regarding network effects.

Two studies are closely related to this article. First, Chiang et al. (2003) designed a discrete-choice model describing firms and customers in markets with network effects. Chiang and Teng also proposed a *customer-targeting strategy* that the challenger can compete with the market leader. A challenger can entice some of the customers of the market leader away from the market leader's network. Once successful, this strategy may initiate a chain reaction leading to an exodus of customers away from the network of the market leader.

Second, Tseng et al. (2005) provided the *utility-threshold-raising strategy.* A challenger can increase the customer *utility thresholds* (the minimal product utility for which consumers are willing to pay the price) of the market leader, reducing customer net utilities in using the technology of the market leader. Once customer net utilities become negative, customers will not use the technology of the market leader, and the challenger may capture a market share. Moreover, Tseng et al. (2005) advanced the work of Chiang et al. (2003) by incorporating the concept of *multiple adoption*, which described the phenomenon that customers use both the market leader's and the challenger's technologies.

Simplified models were used in these studies and thus are fairly limited in practical use. For instance, the price for using the network was assumed the same for all customers, and the heterogeneity of customer utility thresholds was modeled using a simple linear function.

This article models the customer perceived value and network size in more general terms, and discusses how to deliver superior customer value. Restated, this article provides more practical insights and suggestions for firms in industries with network effects.

MODELING CUSTOMER PERCEIVED VALUE

Customer perceived value (CPV) is the difference between *total customer value* and *total customer cost* (Kotler, 2003). Total customer value comprises four parts: product value, services value, personnel value, and image value. Meanwhile, total customer cost consists of monetary cost, time cost, energy cost, and psychic cost. This article applies the CPV concept in a model of network effects.

Total Customer Value

In the proposed model, each customer of a network enjoys two values. First, network facilities provide the *stand-alone value* (V_S), regardless of whether other customers use the same network. Second, all other customers in the same network provide the *network value* (V_N) to customers. The network value ordinarily increases with the network size, which is the number of customers using the network.

Through participation in a network, every customer delivers a *unit network value* (v_n) to every other customer of the network. Consequently, the *network value* to a customer in a network with M customers is $V_N = (M-1)\ v_n$. The total customer value for a customer can be written as follows:

total customer value = stand-alone value + network value

$$= V_S + V_N$$
$$= V_S + (M-1)\ v_n.$$

Total Customer Cost

To enjoy network values, every customer must bear the equipment purchasing cost, price for network participation, training costs, and the switching cost for changing a network. These costs were summarized into *total customer cost* of network use. One may notice that a firm can set different prices for different customer segments, creating different total customer costs for customers.

The customer with the *i*th-lowest total cost was denoted as C_i. Thus in a network with M customers, customer C_1 has the lowest total cost, and customer C_M has the highest total cost. Restated, the customers are numbered *in ascending order* of total customer costs. An increasing function $f(i)$ was used to express the total customer cost for C_i, where $1 \leq i \leq M$.

Customer Perceived Value

The *customer perceived value* (CPV) for customer C_i is defined as total customer value minus the total customer cost (Kotler, 2003), or

CPV of C_i
= total customer value – total customer cost
$= (V_S + (M - 1)\ v_n) - f(i)$ (1)

Customers who stay in a network must enjoy non-negative CPV, otherwise they will suffer a loss from network participation.

Summary of Notations

The notations and descriptions used in this article are listed below:

- V_S: The stand-alone value a customer obtains by participating in a network.
- V_N: The *network value* to a customer participating in a network.
- v_n: The unit network value; that is, the value a customer brings to every other customer in the same network.
- M: The total number of customers in a network.
- C_i: The customer with the *i*th-lowest total customer cost among M customers.
- $f(i)$: Total cost for customer C_i, where $1 \leq i \leq M$

The following sections explore how to deliver superior customer perceived value and the relationship between customer perceived value and network size.

DELIVERING SUPERIOR CUSTOMER PERCEIVED VALUE

Customer perceived value can be improved by (1) increasing total customer value or (2) reducing total customer cost. This section elaborates these two approaches, respectively.

Increasing Total Customer Value

Total customer value consists of stand-alone value and network value. Firms can deliver higher stand-alone value or network value. Stand-alone value can only be increased by superior technologies or infrastructures. However, network value can be improved in several ways.

First, network value can be increased via a larger network size. Actually, the network size is a key factor of success for firms competing in markets with network effects. That is the reason why firms are pursuing the *get-big-fast* (GBF) strategy. Network size can be increased by several ways. A conventional approach is conducting intensive promotional activities and offering introductory prices (with deep discounts) to attract customers to a firm's network to build a large user network.

Acquisitions, mergers, or strategic alliances also can increase the network size and then the total customer value. Acquiring new customers and horizontal integration are effective for increasing network value. For instance, two telecommunications companies can build a strategic alliance to create a *mega-network*. Their customers can enjoy an intra-network rate when making phone calls within the mega-network. Another example in the USA is that the employment Web site CareerBuilder.com acquired HeadHunter.net to increase its network size and make itself more competitive to the market leader Monster.com.

Next, increased unit network value also increases network value. Designing more valuable services and functions that enhance customer communications can increase unit network value. For instance, cell phone companies provided text messaging services, and allowed video signals to be transmitted via cell phones. This improvement enriched communications among users. Thus, the *unit network value* v_n is increased, and the network value increases as a result.

Taobao.com demonstrated how to improve unit network value. During the first quarter of 2005, the Chinese online auction Web site Taobao.com has a trading value more than that of eBay. With far fewer members than eBay, Taobao.com delivered higher *unit network utility* to its customers. Taobao.com customized its services to suit the market conditions in China (Hu & Lin, 2005). The promising profitability of Taobao.com attracted Yahoo! to invest one billion dollars in the holding company (alibaba.com) of Taobao.com (Wang, 2005).

Reducing Total Customer Cost

Customers were numbered *in ascending order* of total customer costs, and an increasing function $f(i)$ was used. A linear function is a convenient approximation. A larger slope describes higher *heterogeneity* among customers in their total costs, and a smaller slope describes higher *homogeneity* among customers.

However, members of a network communicate and exchange information with each other. Customers will thus become more homogeneous. In this case, a sub-linear (or concave) function may be a better approximation for discussing their costs. Thus, we don't impose any specific form for the function. We use both a linear and a sub-linear function to explain the reduction of the total customer costs.

The total customer cost can be reduced by a constant amount (an offset) or by a ratio. One firm can reduce the total customer cost by a constant amount. For example, a firm may offer a fixed amount of subsidies to customers, or may lower prices uniformly by a fixed amount. Such activi-

Figure 1. Decreasing total customer cost by an offset for linear function f(i)

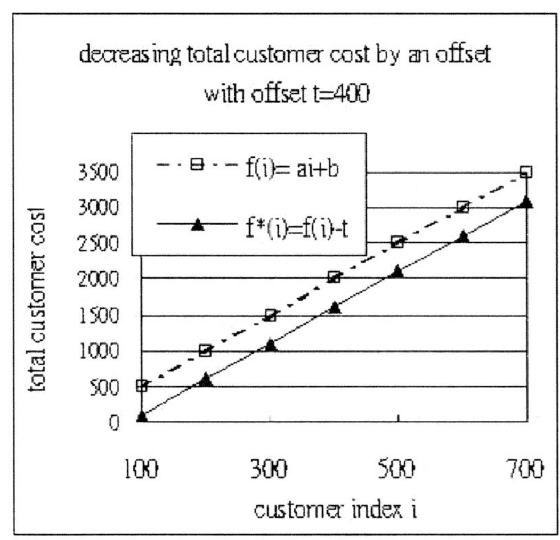

Figure 2. Decreasing total customer cost by an offset for nonlinear function f(i)

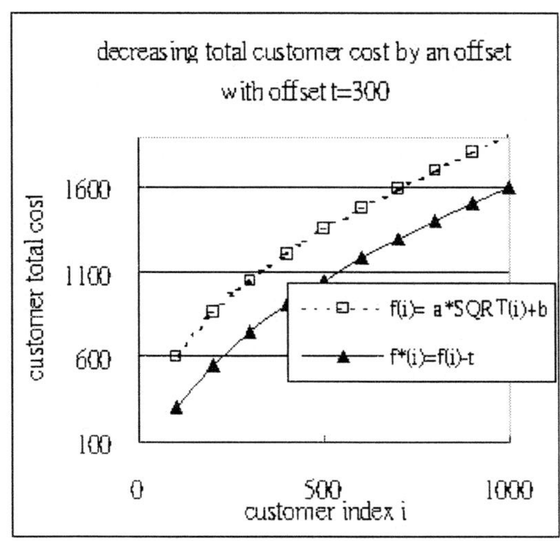

Figure 3. Decreasing total customer cost by a ratio for linear function f(i)

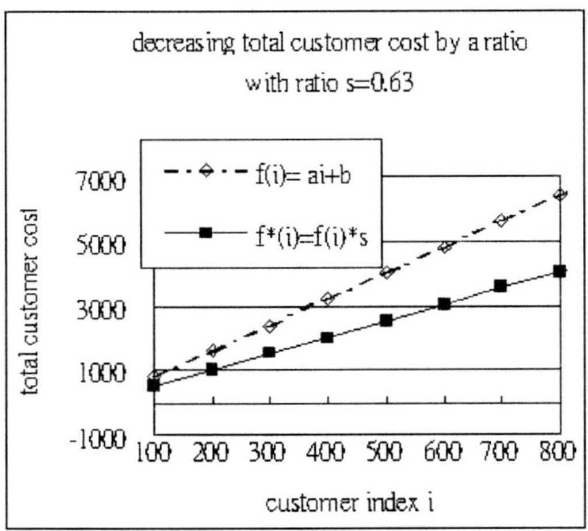

Figure 4. Decreasing total customer cost by a ratio for nonlinear function f(i)

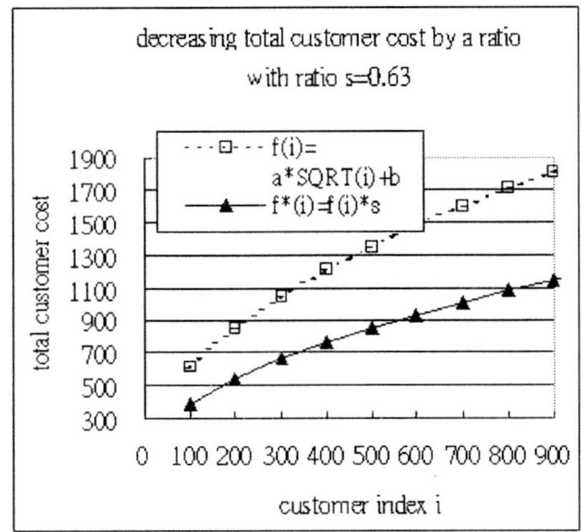

ties can be modeled as a decrease by an offset of the total customer cost. If the function $f(i)$ is a linear function, Figure 1 illustrates the effect of decreasing the total customer cost by an offset. If the function $f(i)$ is a sub-linear function (e.g. a square root function), Figure 2 demonstrates the effect of reducing the total customer cost by an offset. In both figures, dashed lines or curves denote the original function $f(i)$, and solid lines or curves represent the reduced function $f^*(i)$.

On the other hand, a firm can reduce the total customer cost proportionally (by a ratio). For instance, a firm may raise product standards to nullify the benefits offered by its competitors, or may include additional functions in their products. Raising the product standards will increase customer sensitivity to performance relative to prices. Customers who have higher costs have invested more resources in using the network and they are likely to respond more strongly to functional or technical improvements in the network. Restated, the total costs of such customers will be lowered more than those of customers with lower total costs.

Such activities can be modeled as a decrease of total customer costs by a particular ratio (i.e., multiplied with a number less than one). If the function $f(i)$ is linear, Figure 3 illustrates the effect of decreasing the total customer cost by a ratio. If the function $f(i)$ is a sub-linear function (e.g., a square root function), Figure 4 demonstrates the effect of reducing the total customer cost by an offset. In both figures, dashed lines or curves depict the original function $f(i)$, and solid lines or curves represent the reduced function $f^*(i)$.

CUSTOMER PERCEIVED VALUE AND NETWORK SIZE

The network size is determined by two opposing factors: the *network value* provided by the network, and the *customer cost* for staying in the network. Based on the model, estimating the network size means finding the maximal number of users a system provider can acquire, given the network value and customer cost functions.

Because customers are numbered in ascending order of their total customer costs, the customer perceived value (CPV) decreases with the customer index. Therefore, finding the potential size of the network is equivalent to finding the index of the marginal customer whose CPV value is zero. This article denotes this marginal customer as the *boundary customer*. Customers before the boundary customer have a willingness to stay in the network, because they enjoy positive CPV. In contrast, customers after the boundary customer will not stay in the network, because they will have negative CPV.

The index of the boundary customer, denoted as m, can be determined by setting the *customer perceived value* (CPV) of the boundary user to zero. Therefore, we are solving the following equation:

CPV of boundary customer C_m
= total customer value – total customer cost
= (stand-alone value + network value)– total customer cost
$= (V_S + V_N) - f(m)$
$= (V_S + (m-1)\, v_n) - f(m) - 0$ (2)

The previous equation can be rewritten as:

$$(V_S + (m-1)\, v_n) = f(m) \qquad (3)$$

Note the left-hand side represents the *total value* to C_m and that the right-hand side represents the *total cost* of C_m. Both are functions of m, and we can plot their curves and solve equation (3) graphically. For the boundary *customer*, the total value equals the *total cost* and the CPV is zero. Therefore, at the intersection of the curves we can find the solution for m as the potential network size, and denote this value as M.

In the previous section we suggested that customer perceived value can be increased by (1) increasing total customer value or (2) reducing total customer cost. Using the model provided in this article, we can estimate the effects or impacts of these two approaches on increasing network sizes. For ease of explanation, we assume linear functions for both network value and customer costs. The *stand-alone value* is set to 1800.

We first demonstrate the effect of increasing total customer value. The analytical results are shown in Figure 5. Originally, the unit network value is 2.5, and then increased to 3.0. We see

Figure 5. The network size can be increased by increasing customer value

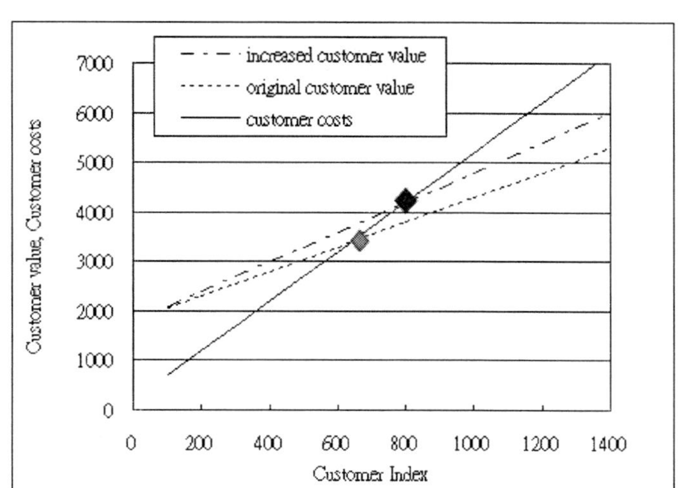

that originally there are about 600 users (total customer value and customer cost interest at about $m = 600$). When the customer value is increased, the number of users willing to pay for the network increases to nearly 800.

Next, let's demonstrate the effect of reducing total customer costs. The analytical results are shown in Figure 6. Note that the total customer costs can be reduced by an offset (a constant amount) or by a ratio.

We see that originally there are about 600 users (total customer value and customer cost interest at about $m = 600$). When the cost is reduced by an offset of 300, the number of users willing to pay for the network increases above 700. When the cost is reduced by a ratio of 0.8, the number of users willing to pay for the network increases to 1100. We see that reducing the cost by a ratio has a stronger effect of attracting more users. This can be explained as follows: While reducing the cost by an offset gives a uniform favor to all users, irrespective of their heterogeneity in costs, reducing the cost by a ratio devotes more resources to the users with higher costs and can thus increase the market share more significantly.

From this example we can see the power of this model in predicting the effectiveness of marketing strategies, and the effect of customer perceived value on network size.

CONCLUSION

Network effects are pervasive in information and network industries. The success of an eBay auction compared to Yahoo! Auction in the U.S. and in Europe demonstrates the significance of network effects. To have competitive advantages in markets with network effects, firms must deliver superior value to their customers. This article provides significant insights to firms regarding how to improve customer perceived value.

This article contains two contributions. The first is on theoretical development. This article proposes a more general model. The price no longer needs to be the same for all customers,

Figure 6. The network size can be increased by reducing customer costs

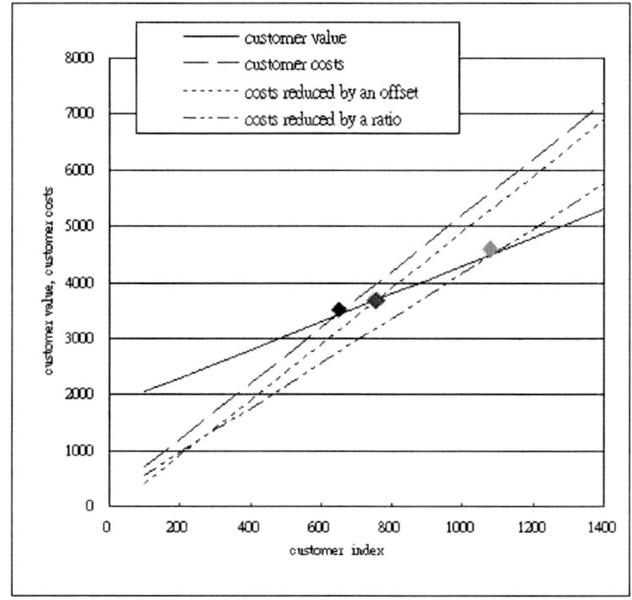

allowing analysis for firms adopting differential pricing strategies. In addition, the heterogeneity of customer costs is not required to be a simple linear function. The current model in this article has few restrictions regarding parameters, and thus it can reflect the actual situations more accurately.

The second contribution lies on practical applications for firms in markets with network effects. Firms in information industry, telecommmunication industry, and consumer electronics industry can benefit from this article. Based on this article, firms can adopt two approaches—increasing customer value and reducing customer costs—to delivering superior customer value.

A firm can increase stand-alone value, network size, or unit network value to improve customer value. For instance, Internet service providers may consider horizontal integration to enlarge their network size, creating higher value to their customers. Yahoo! Messenger and MSN adopted this strategy when they permitted their customers to communicate with each other across these two systems.

On the other hand, customer cost can be reduced either by an offset or by a ratio. A typical example took place in the cell phone service industry in Taiwan. Taiwanese government enforced the *number portability* policy (which allows customers to transfer from one telephone service provider/operator to another without changing their telephone numbers). Some firms (such as Taiwan Mobile) charge customers with a penalty fee when they switch to another operator while carrying the original phone numbers. Start-up firms (such as Asia Pacific Telecom Group), however, actively subsidize new customers for this fee. This strategy is reasonable because it reduces customer costs by an offset.

However, when a new technology is competing with existing technologies, subsidy alone may not work well. Substantial technological advances and extraordinary benefits to customers are needed to attract customers whose total costs are higher. For instance, Japan's NTT DoCoMo introduced the 3G cell phone standard, W-CDMA, of which the advantages outweighed the drawback of incompatibility with existing standards. As a result, customers were willing to embrace the 3G services. This phenomenon can be explained as reducing customer costs by a ratio.

This article models network effects using the concept of customer perceived value. Future studies can use the model presented in this article to empirically explain e-businesses successes and failures. Competitive strategies can be formulated using the two generic approaches presented in this article, namely increasing customer value or reducing customer costs. Finally, empirical studies can estimate the model parameters to apply the theories of network effects to practical situations.

ACKNOWLEDGMENT

This chapter is mainly based on the paper of Tseng, Teng, and Chiang (2007), which is sponsored by the National Science Council, Taiwan under contract: NSC-93-2416-H-182-016. Correspondence and reprint requests should be made to Ching-I Teng, chingit@mail.cgu.edu.tw.

REFERENCES

Baake, P., & Boom, A. (2001). Vertical product differentiation, network externalities, and compatibility decisions. *International Journal of Industrial Organization, 19*(1,2), 267-284.

Bensaid, B., & Lesne, J. P. (1996). Dynamic monopoly pricing with network externalities. *International Journal of Industrial Organization, 14*(6), 837-855.

Chakravarty, S., Dogan, K., & Tomlinson, N. (2006). A hedonic study of network effects in the market for word processing software. *Decision Support Systems, 41*(4), 747-763.

Chen, Y. S., Chen, G., & Wu, S. (2005). Issues and opportunities in e-business research: A Simonian perspective. *International Journal of E-business Research*, *1*(1), 37-53.

Chiang, D. M., & Teng, C. I. (2005). Consumption externalities: Review and future research opportunities. *Electronic Commerce Studies*, *3*(1), 15-38.

Chiang, D. M., & Teng, C. I. (2003). Installed base collapsing strategies with network externalities. *Journal of Management*, *20*(5), 829-857.

Chiang, D. M., & Teng, C. I. (2001). Pricing strategies with network externalities between two groups of customers. *NTU Management Review*, *12*(1), 1-36.

Choi, J. P. (1994). Network externalities, compatibility choice, and planned obsolescence. *Journal of Industrial Economics, 42*(2), 167-182.

Choi, S. Y., Stahl, D. O., & Whinston, A. B. (1997). Is Microsoft a Monopolist? *Brazilian Electronic Journal of Economics, 1*, 0 (December 10).

Chou, C. F., & Shy, O. (1990). Network effects without network externalities. *International Journal of Industrial Organization*, *8*(2), 259-270.

Church, J., & Gandal, N. (1993). Complementary network externalities and technological adoption. *International Journal of Industrial Organization*, *11*(2), 239-260.

Conner, K. R. (1995). Obtaining strategic advantage from being imitated: When can encouraging "clones" pay? *Management Science, 41*(2), 209-225.

Conner, K. R., & Rumelt, R. P. (1991). Software piracy: An analysis of protection strategies. *Management Science, 37*(2), 125-139.

Economides, N. (1996). The economics of networks. *International Journal of Industrial Organization, 14*(6), 673-699.

Ehrhardt, M. (2004). Network effects: Standardization and competitive strategy: How companies influence the emergence of dominant designs. *International Journal of Technology Management*, *27*(2,3), 272.

Ende, J., & Wijnberg, N. (2003). The organization of innovation and market dynamics: Managing increasing returns in software firms. *IEEE Transactions on Engineering Management*, *50*(3), 374.

Farrell, J., & Saloner, G. (1986). Installed base and compatibility: Innovation, product pre-announcements, and predation. *American Economic Review*, *76*, 940-955.

Farrell, J., & Saloner, G. (1992). Converters, compatibility, and control of interfaces. *Journal of Industrial Economics*, *40*(1), 9-35.

Gallaugher, J. M., & Wang, Y. M. (2002). Understanding network effects in software markets: Evidence from Web server pricing. *MIS Quarterly*, *26*(4), 303-327.

Gupta, S., Jain, D. C., & Sawhney, M. S. (1999). Modeling the evolution of markets with indirect network externalities: An application to digital television. *Marketing Science, 18*(3), 396-416.

Holcombe, R. G., & Sobel, R. S. (2000). Consumption externalities and economic welfare. *Eastern Economic Journal*, *26*(2), 157-170.

Hu, J., & Lin, H. (2005). The online auction Web site that beats eBay in China. *Business Weekly*, (921), July 18-24, 2005 (in Chinese).

Katz, M. L., & Shapiro, C. (1986). Technology adoption in the presence of network externalities. *Journal of Political Economy, 94*, 822-841.

Katz, M. L., & Shapiro, C. (1985). Network externalities, competition, and compatibility. *American Economic Review, 75*, 424-440.

Kornish, L. J. (2006). Technology choice and timing with positive network effects. *European Journal of Operational Research, 173*(1), 268-282.

Kotler, P. (2003). *Marketing Management.* Prentice Hall.

Kristiansen, E. G. (1998). R&D in the presence of network externalities: Timing and compatibility. *Rand Journal of Economics, 29*(3), 531-547.

Lee, Y., & O'Connor, G. C. (2003). New product launch strategy for network effect products. *Journal of the Academy of Marketing Science, 31*(3), 241-255.

Lin, L., & Kulatilaka, N. (2006). Network effects and technology licensing with fixed fee, royalty, and hybrid contracts. *Journal of Management Information Systems, 23*(2), 91-118.

Padmanabhan, V., Rajiv, S., & Srinivasan, K. (1997). New products, upgrades, and new releases: A rationale for sequential product introduction. *Journal of Marketing Research, 34*(4), 456-472.

Parker, G. G., & van Alstyne, M. W. (2005). Two-sided network effects: A theory of information product design. *Management Science, 51*(10), 1494-1504.

Shapiro, C., & Varian, H. R. (1999). The art of standard wars. *California Management Review, 41*(2), 8-32.

Shapiro, C., & Varian, H. R. (1998). *Information rules.* HBS Press.

Suarez, F. F. (2005). Network effects revisited: The role of strong ties in technology selection. *Academy of Management Journal, 48*(4), 710-720.

Sun, B., Xie, J., & Cao, H. H. (2004). Product strategy for innovators in markets with network effects. *Marketing Science, 23*(2), 243.

Teng, C. I., & Chiang, D. M. (2006). Triggering the chain reaction: Customer targeting strategies in markets with network effects. *Electronic Commerce Studies, 4*(1), 23-36.

Teng, C. I., Tseng, F. C., & Chiang, D. M. (2006). Customer-capturing strategies: The way to replace existing technology characterized by network effects. *Technovation, 26*(12), 1384-1389.

Tseng, F. C., Teng, C. I., & Chiang, D. M. (2007). Delivering superior customer perceived value in the context of network effects. *International Journal of E-business Research, 3*(1), 40-49.

Tseng, F. C, Teng, C. I., & Chiang, D. M. (2005). Competing on utility thresholds: The way to capture markets characterized by network effects. *Proceedings of the International Conference on Business and Information*, Hong Kong, July, 2005.

Wang, X. P. (2005). Yahoo! invests in alibaba.com. *Commercial Times*, Aug. 12, 2005 (in Chinese).

Weitzel, T., Beimborn, D., & König, W. (2006). A unified economic model of standard diffusion: The impact of standardization cost, network effects, and network topology. *MIS Quarterly, 30*(special issue), 489-514.

Westland, J. C. (1992). Congestion and network externalities in the short run pricing of information system services. *Management Science, 38*(7), 992-1009.

Witt, U. (1997). "Lock-in" vs. "critical masses"—industrial change under network externalities. *International Journal of Industrial Organization, 15*(6), 753-773.

Xie, J., & Sirbu, M. (1995). Price competition and compatibility in the presence of positive demand externalities. *Management Science, 41*(5), 909-926.

Zhu, K., Kraemer, K., Gurbaxani, V., & Xu, S. X. (2006). Migration to open-standard interorganizational systems: Network effects, switching costs, and path dependency. *MIS Quarterly, 30*(special issue), 515-539.

Section II
E-Business Strategies

Chapter V
Pure Play vs. Bricks-and-Clicks:
A Study of Their Benefits and Practices

Youlong Zhuang
Columbia College, USA

Albert L. Lederer
University of Kentucky, USA

ABSTRACT

Pure play and bricks-and-clicks represent today's two major retailing models. The current study answers four questions comparing the two models in terms of the e-commerce benefits achieved and information systems management practices used to achieve them. It applies a Web-based survey to compare 69 pure plays to 348 bricks-and-clicks retailers in terms of the market expansion, customer service, back-end efficiency, inventory management, and cost reduction benefits reaped as well as in terms of the benchmarking, process redesign, and planning practices used. It found market expansion as the top benefit for both types of retailers. Pure plays exceed bricks-and-clicks at achieving back-end efficiency, inventory management, and cost reduction benefits. Pure play retailers apply benchmarking to reap their benefits while bricks-and-clicks retailers use process redesign and planning to reap theirs. Pure play retailers are better able to utilize benchmarking to realize market expansion and customer service benefits. On the other hand, bricks-and-clicks retailers are better able to utilize process redesign to realize inventory management and cost reduction benefits. The findings suggest potential directions for future research as well as electronic retail practice.

INTRODUCTION

When Internet household usage emerged and then grew exponentially during the mid 1990s, its pioneers and pundits alike predicted that online sales were opening a new era in retailing. Pure play retailers, they asserted, would replace traditional ones in much the same manner that shopping malls had replaced downtown stores. Thousands of pure play stores appeared almost overnight while seemly infinite venture capital poured into them.

However, when pure play firms started to fail, many experts predicted that the winners of online retailing would be the bricks-and-clicks merchants who sold their goods both at traditional stores and over the Internet. Today, many pure play retailers are gone, but many others remain. At the same time, many traditional stores have become bricks-and-clicks retailers, and are earning profits through their online endeavors.

Beyond any doubt, today's retailers will continue to use the Internet to reach millions of consumers at a very low cost (Mahajan, Shrinivasan, & Wind, 2002). Likewise beyond a doubt, sales over the Internet will continue to grow (Madlberger & Kotzab, 2001; Saini & Johnson, 2005).

However, debate continues about which business model is better able to realize the benefits of virtual retailing. The two types of retailers may use different strategies to accomplish their objectives (Birkhofer, Schoegel, & Tomczak, 2000; Koo, Koh, & Nam, 2004). Many questions remain unanswered. Exactly what benefits of the Internet do pure play retailers reap? What benefits do Bricks-and-Clicks retailers reap? Are the benefits the same for both models? Or for which benefits does one type of the online retailer outdo the other type? Do the two types of retailers achieve their benefits through the same IT management practices? The purpose of the study reported here is to answer such questions as these.

Answers to them can help managers of both kinds of online retailers understand their own organization and their competitors, and accordingly adjust their business model to gain the maximum advantages of the Internet. Managers of each type of retailer can thus learn from their counterparts and better position their own firm's e-commerce strategy. Answers to the questions can help researchers understand how implementers of electronic retailing achieve its benefits in order to compete.

BRICKS-AND-CLICKS VS. PURE PLAY

Pure Play and Bricks-and-Clicks retailers are two major categories of online retail business models (Turban, King, Viehland, & Lee, 2006). Increasingly, manufacturers and wholesalers have adopted multi-channel distribution systems in which they also sell directly to the end customer. Both online and physical stores can add paper-based catalogs. However, firms vary considerably in their use of Web sites (Hsu, Kraemer, & Dunkle, 2006); the percentage of the transactions through the Web site still enables the classification of retailers into Pure Play (meaning they sell exclusively through the Website) vs. Bricks-and-Clicks (meaning they make only some of their sales through it).

Harden, Heyman, and Bruner (2000) suggested evaluating a commercial Web site from six aspects. First, e-commerce has increased the consumer awareness of products. The Web, together with television, radio, print, billboards, and other advertising media, can be a cost-effective way to build consumer awareness of a product brand. The Web can build such awareness even though the majority of Web surfers do not click on banner ads. This is a big difference from traditional media such as television, magazines, and newspapers, which do not allow click-through (Roehm & Roehm, 2005). Strong brand name recognition is an important means of capturing customers (Coltman, Devinney, Latukefu, & Midgley, 2001).

Second, e-commerce has saved the cost of direct marketing. Compared to traditional direct mail, the Web can provide much advantage when the cost of paper, postage, and other expenses are considered. Other advantages include the availability of real-time inventory data and the reduced cost of human data entry. E-commerce has also accelerated direct marketing activities (Nadherny, 1998). It takes a much shorter time to test direct marketing concepts through the Internet.

Third, e-commerce has increased the sales of products both online and off-line. The Web is a means to make e-commerce become a reality by providing online sales. Sales are the most obvious performance that management wants. With the enhanced customization capabilities available from new technologies, firms can focus their marketing effort on customer segments with the highest profit potential. After all, the 20-80 rule still holds in the virtual world (i.e., 20% of all customers may be responsible for 80% of a firm's profits).

Fourth, e-commerce has facilitated customer support. One of the Web's most important applications is customer support. Three major opportunities in this area are revenue enhancement, cost-avoidance, and other "soft benefits."

Fifth, e-commerce has enabled firms to collect more information about the market. A Web site can gather more information than traditional market research can. For example, a site can recognize patterns in users' behavior, surmise visitor demographics, and personalize content for the users on the fly.

Sixth, e-commerce has provided the means of publishing advertisements. A Web site can attract surfers and thus provide owners a chance to sell online advertising for other firms. This is the major return for content providers such as Yahoo! and Excite. Every site can be a portal. Compared to the traditional print media, a Web site is better at immediacy and unlimited space (Berman & Thelen, 2004; Kulviwat, Thaku, & Guo, 2006).

These benefits of e-commerce facilitated the creation of the benefit items used in this research. Those items permitted the creation of the categories of benefits produced by the factor analysis in this study.

The Assumed Advantages of Bricks-and-Clicks

Many experts have suggested reasons that Bricks-and-Clicks stores are better positioned to reap the benefits of Internet retailing (Muller-Lankenau, Wehmeyer, & Klein, 2006; Pitta, 2002). First, due to the brand awareness of their physical sites, Bricks-and-Clicks stores have less trouble attracting visitors (Min & Wolfinbarger, 2005; Nannery, 2000). Shoppers who buy from a physical store are more likely to buy from the online front of that store. Bricks-and-Clicks stores are more likely to attract mainstream shoppers because these same people already shop at their physical stores. Bricks-and-Clicks retailers can use the two mediums in a complementary manner. At the same time, the cost of establishing brand awareness for pure play is very high. The cost of acquiring a new customer for pure plays exceeds the analogous cost for every other sales channel (i.e., traditional, mail order, phone order, television order, and Bricks-and-Clicks).

Second, the initial investment in an online store for those Bricks-and-Clicks firms is lower. The existing physical store infrastructure, distribution systems, inventory and information systems, and both hardware and software can be used for the online store without adding excessive cost (Koller, 2001; Rayport & Jaworski, 2002). In fact, many analysts believe the Bricks-and-Clicks model is the only viable option for online retailing. Regardless, the lower initial investment leaves more resources for the Bricks-and-Clicks firm to allocate to other online store-related expenses (such as promoting its Web site address).

Third, customer service favors Bricks-and-Clicks retailers. Their virtual stores can provide in-store pickup and allow customers to return products purchased online. Large numbers of consumers do research online and actually purchase the product from a physical outlet (Mullaney, 1999).

Fourth, the Bricks-and-Clicks model is a diversified portfolio that can better withstand a difficult economy (Saunders & Cook, 2002). When the online side of the store is losing money, its physical side may still profit so that the losses reduce the taxes for its holding firm when the two sides report income taxes together. In general,

Bricks-and-Clicks companies survived during the economic downturn of 2001 while similar pure play startups failed. For example, Tesco.com, a Bricks-and-Clicks superstore with a major grocery component, performed better because of its existing supply network while Webvan, a Pure Play grocer, closed its doors with a record loss of $700 million during that same period.

In summary, experts have asserted, and intuition further suggests, that the Bricks-and-Clicks model is better positioned to reap the benefits of online retailing. However, Bricks-and-Clicks retailers have challenges of their own.

Challenges to Bricks-and-Clicks

One big challenge for many chief technology officers of Bricks-and-Clicks online stores is the integration and leveraging of the online front with the physical front (Prencipe & McCarthy, 2002) and the integration of the online store with back-office operations (Reinhardt & Levesque, 2004). Pure Play online stores do not have such problems. For example, Wal-Mart.com erred by trying to mimic its physical stores by offering a huge line of product categories online and selling items that were not economical there (Grunberg, 1999). Despite Wal-Mart's leadership in delivering truckloads of goods to its stores, Wal-Mart.com often failed to deliver to virtual shoppers on time during its first few years of operation. Even worse, inventory systems could not provide real time information for the online store.

Another major challenge for managers in Bricks-and-Clicks relative to those in Pure Play stores is the difference in competitive pace (Grunberg, 1999). Competition in the online world is faster. Information about an online store can quickly spread through e-mail and bulletin boards. Some Bricks-and-Clicks stores employ the same group of people to run the two different types of business, and those people have difficulty handling the two differently paced environments.

Still another challenge to the managers of Bricks-and-Clicks stores is the cannibalization effect on the sales of their existing physical stores (Grunberg, 1999; Nielson, Host, & Mols, 2005). Online sales may reduce off-line sales, and competition between managers of the two types of commerce within a single retailer may prevent them from cooperating with each other. Their conflicts may make reaping the benefits of the online store more difficult for Bricks-and-Clicks retailers.

Finally, Pure Play retailers do not collect sales tax unless they have a physical store in the state. In effect, they offer the same goods for lower prices than do Bricks-and-Clicks competitors, thus making it more difficult for the latter to reap the benefits of their online endeavors (Spencer, 2003).

Practices

Despite their differences, both Pure Play and Bricks-and-Clicks retailers have access to the same management practices for helping realize the benefits of a new information technology. Three such important practices are process redesign, benchmarking, and planning.

Process redesign enables organizations to respond to changes in the business environment by applying new ways of conducting their activities (Benjamin & Levinson, 1993; Keen, 1993). Many organizations disappear fairly quickly when IT makes major changes in their industry and they fail to adjust those activities (Ndede-Amadi, 2004). Other companies have been forced to learn that successful e-commerce demands more than simply a good Web site (Barnes, Hinton, & Mieczkowska et al., 2004; Lee, Jih, & Fang, 2006; Reijers & Jansen-Vullers, 2005). Interaction with customers and suppliers, they have discovered, should be seamlessly integrated with existing business processes.

Also, when IT was introduced into a firm, managers tended to focus on the isolated components of operations such as separate systems for customer orders and inventory management. Only after these systems were running for a while did managers realize the necessity for integration of these systems and thus for the redesign of their processes.

Today, e-commerce is changing the retail environment, and forcing such adjustment. Firms are reevaluating and redesigning business processes in marketing, sales, and inventory management to integrate them with e-commerce and reap its benefits (Andreescu, 2006).

Benchmarking is another popular practice for organizations developing new, competitive IT (Boar, 1994; Hammer & Champy, 1993; Whiteley, 1992). Every organization can improve by studying the practices of its competitors. Benchmarking is a popular means by which e-commerce firms learn more about themselves by comparing themselves to their competitors (Rabin, 2001).

For example, firms can compare their own Web site design to that of their competitors. Web site design may, after all, determine successful e-commerce (Tan, Lin, & Urguhart, 2006). The appearance, structure, navigation, function, and maintenance status all influence the visitor's perception of the shopping experience and the firm's image (Kim, Shaw, & Schneider, 2003), and are easily available for comparative analysis. Firms thus develop guidelines and criteria to benchmark such e-commerce features against those of their competitors.

Planning links IT strategy to business strategy, a requirement for successful information systems (Baets, 1992; Das, Zahra, & Warkentin, 1991; Henderson & Venkatraman, 1993). Planning is viewed as composed of five phases: planning the IS planning process, analyzing the current environment, conceiving strategy alternatives, selecting strategy, and planning strategy implementation (Mentzas, 1997). Both IS and business managers have consistently ranked such planning among the top IS management challenges (Luftman & McLean, 2004).

Firms must integrate IT with their strategic business planning, and they use EC planning to do so (Holland, Lockett, & Blackman, 1992). Integration in electronic retailing thus includes tying the firm's e-commerce planning to the business mission, goals, and overall planning by identifying new e-commerce projects in a strategic plan and setting their priorities (Lee & Cata, 2005). E-commerce services are not stand-alone projects, and must fit with a firm's operations for the firm to be able to reap its benefits (Apigian, Ragu-Nathan, Ragu-Nathan, & Kunnathur, 2005; Groenfeldt, 1997).

Specific Research Questions

The overarching question in this research is, how do Pure Play and Bricks-and-Clicks retailers differ in the benefits they achieve and in how they achieve them? Managers are interested in answers to this question to help guide them in how to allocate resources across process redesign, benchmarking, and EC planning in online retailing, and thus to help guide them in what benefits to expect from the allocation of those resources as a function of their pure play versus Bricks-and-Clicks retailer type.

To answer the overarching question, it is decomposed into these four questions:

1. Which benefits does each type of e-commerce realize?
2. Which type achieves greater benefits?
3. How do the types differ in using the practices to obtain the benefits?
4. Which type is better than the other type at applying the practices to realize the benefits?

METHODOLOGY

This research used an online survey to collect data from managers of their organization's e-commerce retailing. Two major retailer portals were selected because they were popular, well-respected, and represented many retailers and a wide variety of products (Willmott, 2000). The first, stores.yahoo.com, had over 5,000 retailers at the time of data collection. The second, www.mysimon.com, had over 2,000. Because many sites appeared on both, duplicates were eliminated, resulting in a sample size of 4,088 companies. E-mail addresses were collected from each site.

To improve data reliability and validity, the questionnaire was evaluated rigorously by pilot testing prior to administration. Five local retailers with e-commerce sites were selected to represent various sizes and products. These pilot subjects completed the survey and provided face-to-face comments. They discussed the benefits and features of their sites, and their oral comments were consistent with their survey answers. The survey was revised after each of the first four pilot tests to make it clearer and easier to complete. The fifth pilot study resulted in no questionnaire changes and provided the basis for the study.

A short message was first e-mailed to the participants, the managers responsible for their organizations' e-commerce sites, at the 4,088 companies on the two e-commerce retail portals. The message included a link to the survey Web site.

The survey asked participants to identify the address of their e-commerce site. It also contained 31 items of e-commerce benefits and three items for each of process redesign, benchmarking, and planning. The benefits items resulted from an extensive literature review of the advantages retailers realize from e-commerce. The practices items were initially derived from Powell and Dent-Micaleff's (1997) study of information technology in traditional retailing, and were updated based on an e-commerce literature review. Subjects responded on 1 (strongly disagree) to 5 (strongly agree) scales.

Finally, the instrument asked organizational and demographic questions including the percentage of the company's transactions coming through the e-commerce site. Those with 100% coming through it were categorized as Pure Play and those with less than 100% were Bricks-and-Clicks.

After respondents finished the survey and submitted it online, they received a request that a second subject in their organization complete a three-minute survey. The secondary survey contained the e-commerce benefits items, demographics questions, and a request for the e-commerce site address to match to the primary instrument so that validation analysis could compare primary and secondary responses to the same items

Sample

Of the 852 total responses, 379 e-mailed reasons they could not complete the survey (e.g., firm policy, site too new, they were too busy), and 473 completed it. Fifteen of the 473 were dropped as unusable. The overall response rate was 21% (852/4,088), but was 11% (458/4088) when counting only usable surveys. Of 458 finished surveys, 58 secondary subjects also provided usable data for a rate of 13% (58/458).

The average firm size in the sample was 408 employees with a median of 10. About nine employees with a median of three worked on the firm's e-commerce site. Online store profits averaged $250,000 with a median of $16,000 for the 197 firms who provided this data. Of the respondents, 20% were CEOs, 22% were owners, 16% were IT managers or Web masters, 19% were sales or marketing managers, 16% were in other managerial positions, and 5% did not provide a job title. Characteristics of the primary and secondary respondents were very similar. The Bricks-and-Clicks firms received an average of 39.25% of their transactions through their e-commerce site.

A comparison of the demographics of the two types of online retailers appears in Table 1. No statistically significant differences were found ($p<.05$).

Table 1. Demographics comparisons

	Bricks-and-Clicks			Pure Play			
Demographic	**N**	**Mean**	**Std. Dev.**	**N**	**Mean**	**Std. Dev.**	**Sig. (2-tailed)**
Age of the site (years)	348	2.06	1.34	69	1.91	1.46	.40
Total firm employees	342	486.72	5,728.35	66	16.56	36.14	.51
Employees for the site	344	6.24	17.68	67	10.86	21.40	.10
Percent of returning customers	260	43.61	66.30	54	41.45	27.70	.82
Revenue ($000)	201	2,907	20,752	36	356	649	.46
Profits ($000)	146	291	2,085	25	77	205	.61

DATA ANALYSIS

E-Commerce Benefits Validation

Because no known structure for benefits existed, an exploratory factor analysis (EFA) was applied to the 31 benefits items. The EFA used the principal component extraction method and Varimax rotation with Kaiser Normalization and Eigenvalues exceeding one (Varimax was chosen under the assumption that different retailers seek different benefits). It required that factor loadings exceed .50, and that each item load on a single factor. The initial analysis extracted five factors. After four rounds of deleting items with the smallest loading (one at a time), five factors with 27 items met the criteria. Table 2 shows the final factors with meaningful factor names, loadings, Cronbach's alpha, Eigenvalues, and variances explained.

All of the items in the final structure seem reasonably well placed. Those in back-end efficiency focus generally on accounting functions. Those in marketing emphasize the selling of products and services. Inventory management items stress procuring, storing, and repackaging merchandise. Cost reduction items focus on lower expenses in various areas of the organization. Finally, the items in customer service concern improved relations with customers.

Validation of Process Redesign, Benchmarking, and Planning Practices

Because a structure of process redesign, benchmarking, and planning did exist for the practices, a confirmatory factor analysis with EQS was applied to validate the practices as distinct constructs. EQS provides a robust statistic that compensates for potential non-normality. The model met the conventionally accepted goodness of fit standards (Bentler, 1990; Bollen, 1989). The Satorra-Bentler scaled chi square divided by degrees of freedom of 1.79 was less than 2.0; the comparative fit index of .99 and the robust comparative fit index of .99 were greater than .90; the adjusted goodness of fit index of .95 was greater than .80; the standardized root mean squared residual of .04 was less than .10; and the root mean square error of approximation of .05 was less than .08.

Convergent validity was supported via four tests (Hatcher, 1994). First, all factor loadings were statistically significant ($p<.001$). Second, item reliabilities for all three factors exceeded .80. Third, construct reliabilities for all three factors exceeded .70. Finally, an average variance-extracted (AVE) test found all three factor estimates exceeding .50. Table 3 shows the details of these tests.

Table 2. Final rotated component matrix of exploratory factor analysis (N=458)

Our e-commerce site has …	F1	F2	F3	F4	F5
Factor 1 Back-End Efficiency (Eigenvalue=4.39 , Variance Explained=16.2%, alpha=.89)					
BNFT5 … facilitated order entry processing	.73				
BNFT2 …facilitated billing	.71				
BNFT3 …facilitated electronic auditing	.71				
BNFT9 …improved control of data	.69				
BNFT12 …improved operational efficiency	.68			.42	
BNFT6 …facilitated shipment tracing	.65				
BNFT11 …improved operational effectiveness	.62			.43	
Factor 2 Market Expansion (Eigenvalue=3.98 , Variance Explained=14.8%, alpha=.86)					
BNFT18 …provided access to new markets		.80			
BNFT22 …provided opportunities for niche marketing		.74			
BNFT13 …increased customer awareness of our products/ services		.73			
BNFT14 …increased sales		.71			
BNFT21 …provided customers with better information about products/services		.60			
BNFT17 …permitted differentiating our products/services from those of competitors		.58			
BNFT19 …provided better information for management decision making		.51			
Factor 3 Inventory Management (Eigenvalue=3.35 , Variance Explained=12.5%, alpha=.88)					
BNFT30 …streamlined the inventory replenishment			.82		
BNFT31 …streamlined the procurement processes			.80		
BNFT29 …reduced the time required to repackage products/ services			.72		
BNFT27 …reduced inventory costs			.66	.44	
Factor 4 Cost Reduction (Eigenvalue=3.06, Variance Explained=11.3%, alpha=.86)					
BNFT23 …reduced administrative costs				.79	
BNFT24 …reduced customer support costs				.78	
BNFT28 …reduced marketing costs				.73	
BNFT26 …reduced information processing costs			.49	.58	
Factor 5 Customer Service (Eigenvalue=2.86 , Variance Explained=10.6%, alpha=.79)					
BNFT15 …permitted better interaction with customers					.73
BNFT20 …provided customer intimacy					.66
BNFT10 …improved customer service					.64
BNFT16 …permitted better understanding of customers		.46			.58
BNFT7 …helped maintain current customers	.46				.56

Table 3. Convergent validity of practices

		Reliabilities		
	Loadings	**Item**	**Construct**	**AVE**
Process Redesign			1.04	1.13
BUS10 We redesigned our inventory management process to fit our e-commerce.	1.07	1.15		
BUS11 We redesigned our marketing and sales process to fit our e-commerce.	1.13	1.28		
BUS12 Improving company processes is a key part of our use of e-commerce.	.98	.95		
Benchmarking			.95	.87
BUS13 We actively research the best e-commerce practices of other retailers.	.98	.96		
BUS14 We actively research the best Web practices of other Web sites.	.95	.90		
BUS15 We regularly search the Web for new features of other Web stores.	.87	.75		
E-Commerce Planning			.93	.81
BUS16 We have a long-term strategic plan for e-commerce.	.85	.72		
BUS17 We have clearly identified our e-commerce project priorities.	.94	.88		
BUS18 Our e-commerce planning is integrated with the overall business plan.	.91	.83		

Discriminant validity was supported via three tests (Hatcher, 1994). A pair-wise chi-square difference test found all three possible unidimensional models significantly different ($p<.001$) from the original model. A variance-extracted test found all three variance extracted estimates greater than the squared correlation of their two respective factors. Confidence interval tests found none of the upper and lower limits of the three pairs of estimates to contain one.

Common Method Variance

Common method variance can account, at least in part, for a relationship between similar measures (Podsakoff & Organ 1986). A multivariate analysis of variance of the 27 benefit items indicated no significant differences (Wilks' Lambda = .97, p = .94) between the 458 primary and 58 secondary subjects. In other words, the pairs of subjects did not disagree about the benefits.

Non-Response Bias

A time-trend extrapolation test (Armstrong & Overton, 1977) was used to assess non-response bias. The assumption behind the test is that non-respondents resemble late respondents more than early ones. The 458 primary responses were divided into quartiles and the earliest 25% compared to the latest 25%. A multivariate analysis of variance of the 36 items indicated no significant differences (Wilks' Lambda = .910, p = .988) across the quartiles. The results are consistent with the lack of non-response bias.

ANSWERS TO RESEARCH QUESTIONS

Question 1: Which Benefits Does Each Type of E-Commerce Realize?

Table 4 shows the ten highest means of the benefits as indicated by the Pure Play retailer managers in the survey. Eight of those benefits were from market expansion and back-end efficiency. The other two were from customer service. The table thus suggests that Pure Play retailers realize market expansion and back-end efficiency much more so than cost reduction and inventory management.

Table 5 underscores the importance of market expansion and back-end efficiency benefits by displaying the means for the benefits in each dimension as indicated by the Pure Play retail managers. The paired t-tests in the diagonal of the table indicate that the differences in the means for each adjacent dimension are not due to chance ($p<.05$); in other words, for example, the mean

Table 4. Top ten benefits of the e-commerce site to Pure Play stores

Benefits	Categories	Rating
BN22 Provide opportunities for niche marketing	Market Expansion	4.42
BN5 Facilitate order entry processing	Back-End Efficiency	4.42
BN18 Provide access to new markets	Market Expansion	4.36
BN13 Increase customer awareness of our products/ services	Market Expansion	4.30
BN14 Increase sales	Market Expansion	4.29
BN21 Provide customers with better information about products/services	Market Expansion	4.23
BN10 Improve customer service	Customer Service	4.19
BN11 Improve operational effectiveness	Back-End Efficiency	4.17
BN12 Improve operational efficiency	Back-End Efficiency	4.13
BN15 Permit better interaction with customers	Customer Service	4.09

Table 5. Pure Play means and paired t-tests

	Means	Market Expansion	Back-End Efficiency	Customer Service	Cost Reduction	Inventory Management
Paired t test						
Market Expansion	4.17		.050	.001	.001	.001
Back-End Efficiency	4.03			.038	.001	.001
Customer Service	3.87				.017	.001
Cost Reduction	3.61					.031
Inventory Management	3.37					

of back-end efficiency (4.03) was greater than the mean of customer service (3.87) with p<.038. Each off-diagonal cell with a number in it further shows the level of statistical significance of the difference in the means of the dimensions of its row and column.

The top seven benefits realized by Bricks-and-Clicks retailers were from market expansion and customer service (see Table 6), and eight of the top ten also came from those dimensions. Two benefits from the top ten came from back-end efficiency. Table 7 underscores the importance of market expansion and customer service benefits with the means of each dimension. The paired t-tests in the diagonal in the table indicate that the differences in the means for each adjacent dimension are not due to chance (p<.001).

QUESTION 2: WHICH ELECTRONIC RETAILING TYPE ACHIEVES GREATER BENEFITS?

Table 8 shows the 22 benefits for which Pure Play had higher a mean than Bricks-and-Clicks. The difference between the means for the two types appears under the "Difference" column. Asterisks indicate the level of statistical significance of each difference. Fourteen of those differences are statistically significant with p<

Table 6. Top ten benefits of e-commerce site to Bricks-and-Clicks stores

Benefits	Categories	Rating
BN14 Increase sales	Market Expansion	4.42
BN13 Increase customer awareness of our products/ services	Market Expansion	4.41
BN18 Provide access to new markets	Market Expansion	4.32
BN22 Provide opportunities for niche marketing	Market Expansion	4.24
BN21 Provide customers with better information about products/services	Market Expansion	4.24
BN15 Permit better interaction with customers	Customer Service	4.06
BN10 Improve customer service	Customer Service	4.00
BN5 Facilitate order entry processing	Back-End Efficiency	3.98
BN11 Improve operational effectiveness	Back-End Efficiency	3.86
BN17 Permit differentiating our products/services from those of competitors	Market Expansion	3.86

Table 7. Bricks-and-Clicks means and paired t-tests

	Means	Market Expansion	Customer Service	Back-End Efficiency	Cost Reduction	Inventory Management
Pared t test						
Market Expansion	4.16		.001	.001	.001	.001
Customer Service	3.77			.001	.001	.001
Back-End Efficiency	3.61				.001	.001
Cost Reduction	3.24					.001
Inventory Management	2.85					

.05 to p<.001. Thirteen of those fourteen are in back-end efficiency, inventory management, and cost reduction. These findings thus suggest that Pure Plays achieve greater benefits in those three dimensions.

On the other hand, Bricks-and-Clicks had higher means of only five of the 27 (see Table 9). All of the five belong to market expansion and customer services, but none of the differences are statistically significant.

Table 8. Top differences: Advantages of Pure Play over Bricks-and-Clicks

Benefits	Categories	Difference
BN2 Facilitate billing	Back-End Efficiency	.65***
BN3 Facilitate electronic auditing	Back-End Efficiency	.61***
BN30 Streamline the inventory replenishment	Inventory Management	.59***
BN27 Reduce inventory costs	Inventory Management	.58***
BN31 Streamline the procurement processes	Inventory Management	.51***
BN24 Reduce customer support costs	Cost Reduction	.50**
BN5 Facilitate order entry processing	Back-End Efficiency	.44**
BN23 Reduce administrative costs	Cost Reduction	.42*
BN26 Reduce information processing costs	Cost Reduction	.42**
BN29 Reduce the time required to repackage products/ services	Inventory Management	.41*
BN12 Our e-commerce site has improved operational efficiency	Back-End Efficiency	.32*
BN7 Our e-commerce site has helped maintain current customers	Customer Service	.31*
BN9 Our e-commerce site has improved control of data	Back-End Efficiency	.31*
BN11 Our e-commerce site has improved operational effectiveness	Back-End Efficiency	.31*
BN6 Our e-commerce site has facilitated shipment tracing	Back-End Efficiency	.25
BN19 Our e-commerce site has provided better information for management decision making	Market Expansion	.22
BN10 Our e-commerce site has improved customer service	Customer Service	.19
BN22 Our e-commerce site has provided opportunities for niche marketing	Market Expansion	.18
BN28 Our e-commerce site has reduced marketing costs	Cost Reduction	.14
BN16 Our e-commerce site has permitted better understanding of customers	Customer Service	.05
BN18 Our e-commerce site has provided access to new markets	Market Expansion	.04
BN15 Our e-commerce site has permitted better interaction with customers	Customer Service	.03

**p<0.05, **p<0.01, ***p<0.001*

Table 9. Top differences: Advantages of Bricks-and-Clicks over Pure Play

Benefits	Categories	Difference
BN17 Permit differentiating our products/services from those of competitors	Market Expansion	.16
BN14 Increase sales	Market Expansion	.13
BN13 Increase customer awareness of our products/ services	Market Expansion	.11
BN20 Provide customer intimacy	Customer Service	.03
BN21 Provide customers with better information about products/services	Market Expansion	.01

Table 10. Categories and differences

Categories	Pure Play	Bricks-and-Clicks	Difference
Inventory Management	3.37	2.85	.52***
Back-End Efficiency	4.03	3.61	.42***
Cost Reduction	3.61	3.24	.37**
Customer Service	3.87	3.77	.10
Market Expansion	4.17	4.16	.01

***p<.01, ***p<.001*

Table 10 reinforces the finding that Pure Play retailers achieve greater benefits in the three more productivity-oriented categories. The greater means for the three were different at a statistically significant level with p<.01 to p<.001. The table also shows that Pure Play retailers achieved marginally higher benefits for the other two categories.

Question 3: How do theTypes Differ in Using the Practices to Obtain the Benefits?

According to a MANOVA for Pure Play retailers with three practices as independent variables and the five benefits as dependent variables, only benchmarking significantly predicts benefits (Table 11). It does so for back-end efficiency, market expansion, and customer service.

According to an analogous MANOVA for Bricks-and-Clicks retailers in the same table, only process redesign and EC planning significantly predict benefits. Process redesign predicts all five benefits, and EC planning does so for back-end efficiency, market expansion, and customer service. The column "Sig." under "Bricks-and-Clicks" shows the significance levels for those dimensions.

In other words, Pure Play retailers use benchmarking to obtain back-end efficiency, market expansion, and customer service benefits whereas Bricks-and-Clicks retailers use process redesign to obtain all five benefits, and they use EC planning to obtain back-end efficiency, market expansion,

Table 11. MANOVAs for Pure Play and Bricks-and-Clicks

		Pure Play				Bricks-and-Clicks			
Source	Dependent Variable	B	Mean Sq.	F	Sig.	B	Mean Sq.	F	Sig.
Process Redesign Pillai's Trace= B&C: .234*** PP: .119	Back-End Efficiency	.135	.63	1.43	.236	.321	32.52	54.10	.000***
	Market Expansion	.185	1.18	3.16	.080	.107	3.64	10.302	.001***
	Inventory Management	.103	.36	.40	.530	.461	67.08	88.15	.000***
	Cost Reduction	-.060	.12	.12	.733	.378	45.13	51.21	.000***
	Customer Service	.264	2.40	5.50	.022	.139	6.13	11.21	.001***
Benchmarking Pillai's Trace= B&C: .022 PP: .276***	Back-End Efficiency	.357	4.17	9.48	.003**	.079	1.26	2.10	.148
	Market Expansion	.493	7.96	21.35	.000***	.092	1.72	4.87	.028
	Inventory Management	.133	.58	.64	.427	-.005	.01	.01	.930
	Cost Reduction	.135	.60	.57	.454	.008	.01	.01	.909
	Customer Service	.352	4.07	9.31	.003**	.029	.17	.31	.577
EC Planning Pillai's Trace= B&C: .065*** PP: .072	Back-End Efficiency	.216	1.40	3.17	.080	.160	4.49	7.48	.007**
	Market Expansion	-.100	.00	.01	.930	.209	7.69	21.79	.000***
	Inventory Management	.074	.16	.18	.674	.067	.78	1.03	.311
	Cost Reduction	.291	2.52	2.40	.127	.115	2.32	2.64	.105
	Customer Service	.072	.15	.35	.557	.182	5.85	10.70	.001***

$*p<.05$, $**p<.01$, $***p<.001$

and customer service (i.e., the very same three that the Pure Plays achieve via benchmarking).

Question 4: Which Type is Better than the Other type at Applying the Practices to Realize the Benefits?

According to a MANOVA with retailer type as an interaction term, Pure Play retailers are better able than Bricks-and-Clicks retailers to use benchmarking to realize market expansion and customer service benefits (as indicated in the second and fifth lines within the "Group x Benchmarking" row in Table 12). On the other hand, Bricks-and-Clicks retailers are better able than Pure Play retailers to use process redesign to realize inventory management and cost reduction benefits (as indicated in the third and fourth lines within the Group x Process Redesign row in Table 12). Neither type was better able than the other to use EC planning to realize the benefits (as indicated by the lack of significance in the Group x Ecommerce Planning row in Table 12).

DISCUSSION

Question 1: Which Benefits does each Type of E-Commerce Realize?

Both Pure Play and Bricks-and-Clicks reap their top ten benefits within market expansion, customer service, and back-end efficiency. Market expansion dominates both types of retailers, thus indicating that both types receive the greatest benefits from increasing sales by entering new markets.

Pure Play retailers reap the most benefit from "Provide opportunities for niche marketing"

Table 12. Tests of between-subjects effects

Source	Dependent Variable	B	Mean Square	F	Sig.
Group: Pure Play (1) vs. Bricks and Clicks (0) Pillai's Trace=.047***	Back-End Efficiency	-0.554	0.59	1.03	.311
	Market Expansion	-1.334	3.43	9.63	.002**
	Inventory Management	1.113	2.39	3.05	.082
	Cost Reduction	0.628	0.76	0.84	.360
	Customer Service	-1.530	4.52	8.54	.004**
Process Redesign Pillai's Trace=.204***	Back-End Efficiency	0.321	32.52	56.51	.000***
	Market Expansion	0.107	3.64	10.21	.002**
	Inventory Management	0.461	67.08	85.49	.000***
	Cost Reduction	0.378	45.13	49.68	.000***
	Customer Service	0.139	6.13	11.58	.001***
Benchmarking Pillai's Trace=.018	Back-End Efficiency	0.079	1.26	2.19	.139
	Market Expansion	0.092	1.72	4.83	.029
	Inventory Management	-0.005	0.01	0.01	.931
	Cost Reduction	0.008	0.01	0.01	.910
	Customer Service	0.029	0.17	0.32	.571
Ecommerce Planning Pillai's Trace=.055***	Back-End Efficiency	0.160	4.49	7.81	.005**
	Market Expansion	0.209	7.69	21.60	.000***
	Inventory Management	0.067	0.78	1.00	.319
	Cost Reduction	0.115	2.32	2.56	.110
	Customer Service	0.182	5.85	11.05	.001***
Group x Process Redesign Pillai's Trace=.029***	Back-End Efficiency	-0.186	1.07	1.86	.174
	Market Expansion	0.078	0.19	0.53	.469
	Inventory Management	-0.358	3.98	5.07	.025*
	Cost Reduction	-0.438	5.95	6.55	.011*
	Customer Service	0.125	0.49	0.92	.339
Group x Benchmarking Pillai's Trace=.034***	Back-End Efficiency	0.278	2.17	3.78	.053
	Market Expansion	0.400	4.52	12.70	.000***
	Inventory Management	0.139	0.54	0.69	.406
	Cost Reduction	0.127	0.46	0.50	.478
	Customer Service	0.323	2.95	5.57	.019*
Group x Ecommerce Planning Pillai's Trace=.016	Back-End Efficiency	0.057	0.08	0.14	.706
	Market Expansion	-0.219	1.22	3.42	.065
	Inventory Management	0.007	0.00	0.00	.967
	Cost Reduction	0.176	0.79	0.87	.352
	Customer Service	-0.111	0.31	0.59	.444

$^*p<.05$, $^{**}p<.01$, $^{***}p<.001$

(BN22 within market expansion) and "Facilitate order entry processing" (BN5 within back-end efficiency). The former perhaps illustrates their careful choice of product line, and the latter their dependency on the single online channel for sales.

After market expansion, Pure Play retailers' second highest benefit category was back-end efficiency. Such a finding may reflect the potential advantages of dealing with customers without face-to-face contact and of having all customer sales data in digital form.

Bricks-and-Clicks retailers reap the most benefit from "Increase sales" (BN14 within market expansion). Such an outcome perhaps quite directly reflects their major motivation of going online.

After market expansion, Bricks-and-Clicks retailers' second highest benefit category was customer service. Such a finding reflects the use of electronic retailing as the means for expanding their market.

Question 2: Which Electronic Retailing Type Achieves Greater Benefits?

Pure Play retailers reap substantially greater benefits in inventory management, back-end efficiency, and cost reduction, the three categories perhaps more directly dependent on technology. "Streamline the inventory replenishment," "Streamline the procurement processes," and "Reduce inventory costs" (BN30, BN31 and BN27 of inventory management); "Facilitate billing," "Facilitate electronic auditing," and "Facilitate order entry processing" (BN2, BN3, and BN5 of back-end efficiency); and "Reduce customer support costs" and "Reduce information processing costs" (BN24 and BN26 of cost reduction) had the greatest differences and do appear more directly related to technology than do many in market expansion and customer service. The finding of superiority in the three technology-related categories may be consistent with the Pure Play retailers' reliance on that technology as their single channel for sales and as their single source of sales information for accounting and control.

Although Bricks-and-Clicks appear to reap greater benefits in market expansion and customer service, areas with which they would already be familiar, no differences were statistically significant. In effect, one might attribute the apparent differences to chance, and conclude that in no instances were those retailers clearly superior to Pure Plays.

Question 3: How do the Types Differ in Using the Practices to Obtain the Benefits?

Pure Play and Bricks-and-Clicks retailers use different practices to reap e-commerce benefits. The former depends on benchmarking while the latter relies on process redesign and planning. This is an interesting finding because it demonstrates distinct differences between the two types of retailer. Pure Play retailers depend heavily on the rapidly changing technology of e-commerce, and competitors' advances are readily apparent. Benchmarking can thus play an important role in helping Pure Plays keep up with those changes.

Unlike Pure Plays, Bricks-and-Clicks retailers already have extensive traditional sales-related activities. As a result, redesigning their current business processes and planning future undertakings can, and apparently do play an important role in the achievement of their e-commerce benefits.

Also, the benefits they reap with these e-commerce practices differ. For Pure Plays, benchmarking significantly predicts back-end efficiency, market expansion, and customer service. For Bricks-and-Clicks, planning predicts the same three while process redesign significantly predicts all five benefits. Apparently, process redesign, the effective tool of Bricks-and-Clicks, is a more powerful practice than benchmarking and planning. At the same time, inventory management and cost reduction benefits, predicted only by process redesign for Bricks-and-Clicks, are more elusive.

Question 4: Which Type is Better than the Other Type at Applying the Practices to Realize the Benefits?

Pure Plays are better able to use benchmarking to realize market expansion and customer service benefits, while Bricks-and-Clicks are better able to use process redesign to realize inventory management and cost reduction benefits. This again demonstrates distinct differences between the two types of retailer.

Pure Plays, we speculate, excel at benchmarking to compare themselves to their technology-dependent competitors. They realize the effects of this comparison in their selling activities in terms expanding their markets and serving their customers.

On the other hand, Bricks-and-Clicks excel at redesigning processes that are conceivably tied to their physical stores. They realize the effects of this redesign by controlling inventories and costs, key issues in those physical stores.

Perhaps surprising, neither type of retailer excels at planning to realize the benefits of e-commerce. Such planning is certainly essential, but neither Pure Plays nor Bricks-and-Clicks are able to use it to better achieve any particular benefits of e-commerce.

IMPLICATIONS FOR RESEARCHERS

Although this chapter is not grounded in any particular theory, the finding that Pure Play retailers realized more benefits than did Bricks-and-Clicks retailers is consistent with the transaction cost economics (TCE) theory of Williamson (1975, 1985). TCE explains where a company's boundaries (i.e., the choices of in-house vs. outsourced functions) should be established based on the costs of various production and coordination mechanisms. Pure Play firms may be able to realize more benefits because a single online channel might be more cost effective and efficient than multiple channels would be. The finding is thus consistent with the online store outsourcing of many large retailers. ToysRus, target, and office depot thus outsource their online stores to amazon.com to more narrowly define those boundaries and achieve better cost effectiveness and efficiency

The current research found market expansion as the benefits most realized by both Pure Play and Bricks-and-Clicks retailers while Pure Play's second most realized was back-end efficiency and Bricks-and-Clicks second was customer service. We speculate that the absence of customer contact enables Pure Plays to realize better back-end efficiency and that Bricks-and-Clicks are more motivated to provide better customer service. However, future researchers might investigate that speculation and any other reasons for the differences.

The current research found that Pure Play retailers realized more benefits than Bricks-and-Clicks retailers. We speculate that the Pure Play's greater reliance on technology is the reason, but future researchers might further investigation this issue too. Future researchers may also want to find out whether such differences in those benefits can be sustained.

The current research found that Pure Plays use benchmarking to achieve their benefits while Bricks-and-Clicks use process redesign and planning to realize theirs. One would expect both types of retailers to use all three practices to do so. Hence, future researchers might investigate why Pure Plays do not use process redesign and planning as well as why Bricks-and-Clicks do not use benchmarking effectively. They might also investigate the effects of other practices.

The current research found Pure Plays better able to use benchmarking to realize market expansion and customer service benefits, and Bricks-and-Clicks better able to use process redesign to realize inventory management and cost reduction benefits. We speculate as to reasons for these differences, but leave their confirmation to future researchers.

In the current research, the total firm employees, profits, and revenues were much larger for Bricks-and-Clicks than for Pure Play firms whereas the number of employees who work on the Web site was greater for Pure Play firms than for Bricks-and-Clicks. Future researchers might investigate the impact of such differences on firm behavior.

This study had two main limitations. First, although a control for common method variance was used, a single subject was the source of both independent and dependent variables. Second, the variables relied largely on the perceptions of the subjects rather than on independently collected tangible data.

In summary, this research found fundamental differences between the two types of retailers. Finding such differences inspires researchers to look for others, not only in the benefits achieved and the IS management practices used to achieve them, but also in other management and retailing issues.

IMPLICATIONS

The current study found that Pure Play retailers generally realize more benefits than do Bricks-and-Clicks. This suggests that managers of Bricks-and-Clicks may want to manage their online stores more as a Pure Play than as a subdivision of their physical store.

The current study found that Pure Plays reap more benefits in the particular areas of back-end efficiency, inventory management, and cost reduction than they do in customer service or market expansion. This may imply they should emphasize product lines that require less customer service.

The current study found that Pure Plays are better at using benchmarking to reap benefits. This implies that managers of Pure Plays might consider applying this advantage more extensively than they currently do in order to reap more benefits and better compete.

The current study found Bricks-and-Clicks better at using process redesign to reap benefits. Managers of these retailers may want to consider applying this advantage more extensively than they currently do.

CONCLUSION

This study found that both Pure Play and Bricks-and-Clicks firms realize their top benefits from market expansion, but Pure Play firms reap them secondly from Back-End Efficiency and Bricks-and-Clicks do so secondly from customer service. Moreover, Pure Play retailers outperform Bricks-and-Clicks in the achievement of benefits in inventory management, back-end efficiency, and cost reduction.

Pure Play firms depend on benchmarking and Bricks-and-Clicks firms rely on process redesign and planning to achieve the benefits of e-commerce. Pure Plays are better able than Bricks-and-Clicks to use benchmarking to realize market expansion and customer service benefits, while Bricks-and-Clicks are better able than Pure Plays to use process redesign alone to realize inventory management and cost reduction benefits. Neither was better able to use EC planning to achieve any benefits.

The study thus contributes by showing clear distinctions between the two types of online retailers. Not only do they differ in terms of having or not having a physical presence, but they also differ in terms of how they achieve the benefits of e-commerce. The study suggests that Pure Plays can gain the greatest benefits from benchmarking while Bricks-and-Clicks can do so via process redesign. It thus provides an empirical look at the similarities and differences between the two types of retailer, and suggests future research areas and management practices.

REFERENCES

Andreescu, F. (2006). Organisational challenges of implementing e-business in the public services: The case of Britain's National Mapping Agency. *International Journal of E-Business Research, 2*(4), 39-60.

Apigian, C. H., Ragu-Nathan, B. S., Ragu-Nathan, T. S., & Kunnathur, A. (2005). Internet technology: The strategic imperative. *Journal of Electronic Commerce Research, 6*(2), 123-145.

Armstrong, J. S., & Overton, T. S. (1977). Estimating non-response bias in mail surveys. *Journal of Marketing Research*, (14), 396-402.

Baets, W. (1992). Aligning information systems with business strategy. *Journal of Strategic Information Systems, 1*(4), 205-213.

Barnes, D., Hinton, M., & Mieczkowska, S. (2004). Managing the transition from bricks-and-mortar to clicks-and-mortar: A business process perspective. *Knowledge and Process Management, 11*(3), 199-209.

Benjamin, R., & Levinson, E. (1993). A framework for managing IT-enabled change. *Sloan Management Review, 34*(4), 23-33.

Bentler, P. M. (1990), Comparative fit indexes in structural models. *Psychological Bulletin*, (107), 238-246.

Berman, B., & Thelen, S. (2004). A guide to developing and managing a well-integrated multichannel retail strategy. *International Journal of Retail and Distribution Management, 32*(2/3), 147-156.

Birkhofer, B., Schoegel, M., & Tomczak, T. (2000). Transaction- and trust-based strategies in e-commerce—A conceptual approach. *Electronic Markets, 10*(3). Retrieved August 26, 2004, from http://www.electronicmarkets.org/modules/pub/view.php/electronicmarkets-221

Boar, B. (1994). Information technology and business alignment: a strategic assessment. In B. Voss, & D. Willey (Eds.), *Handbook of Business Strategy* (pp. 173-188). New York: Faulkner & Gray.

Bollen, K. A. (1989). *Structural equations with latent variables*. New York: Wiley.

Coltman, T., Devinney, T. M., Latukefu, A., & Midgley, D. F. (2001), E-business: Revolution, evolution, or hype? *California Management Review, 44*(1), 57-78.

Das, S. R., Zahra, S. A., & Warkentin, M. E. (1991). Integrating the content and process of strategic MIS planning with competitive strategy. *Decision Sciences, 22*(1), 953-984.

Groenfeldt, T. (1997). Who's in the driver's seat? *Journal of Business Strategy, 18*(1), 36-41.

Grunberg, D. B. (1999). Internet: Friend or foe? *Franchising World, 31*(5), 39.

Hammer, M., & Champy, J. (1993). *Reengineering the corporation: A manifesto for business revolution*. New York: Harper Business.

Harden, L., Heyman, B., & Bruner, R. (2000). *Net results.2: Best practices for Web marketing.* Indianapolis, IN: New Riders.

Hatcher, L. (1994). *Step-by-step approach to using the SAS system for factor analysis and structural equation modeling.* Cary, NC: SAS Institute Inc.

Henderson, J., & Venkatraman, N. (1993). Strategic alignment: Leveraging information technology for transforming organizations. *IBM Systems Journal, 32*(1), 4-16.

Holland, C., Lockett, G., & Blackman, I. (1992). Planning for electronic data interchange. *Strategic Management Journal, 13*(7), 539-550.

Hsu, P., Kraemer, K. L., & Dunkle, D. (2006). Determinants of e-business use in U.S. firms. *International Journal of Electronic Commerce, 10*(4), 9-45, summer.

Keen, P. G. W. (1993). Information technology and the management difference: A fusion map. *IBM Systems Journal, 32*(1), 17-39.

Kim, S., Shaw, T., & Schneider, H. (2003). Web site design benchmarking within industry groups. *Internet Research, 13*(1), 17-26.

Koller, M. (2001). Grocer builds net traffic—Albertson's expands in Seattle, pushes online/storefront strategy. *InternetWeek*, (872), 13-14.

Koo, C. M., Koh, C. E., & Nam, K. (2004). An examination of Porter's competitive strategies in electronic virtual markets: A comparison of two online business models. *International Journal of Electronic Commerce, 9*(1), 163-179.

Kulviwat, S., Thaku, R., & Guo, C. (2006). An exploratory study of consumer adoption of online shopping: Mediating effect of online purchase intention. *International Journal of E-Business Research, 2*(2), 68-82.

Lee, C. S., & Shu, W. (2005). Four models of Internet-enabled distribution structures. *Information Systems Management, 22*(3), 14-22.

Lee, S., Jih, W., & Fang, S. (2006). Investigating the impact of customer relationship management practices of e-commerce on online customer's Web site satisfaction: A model-building approach. *International Journal of E-Business Research, 2*(4), 61-77.

Lee, S. M., & Cata, T. (2005). Critical success factors of Web-based e-service. *International Journal of E-Business Research, 1*(3), 21-40.

Luftman, J., & McLean, E. R. (2004). Key issues for IT executive. *MIS Quarterly Executive, 3*(3), June, 89-104.

Madlberger, M., & Kotzab, H. (2001). Adapting the Internet as distribution channel for stationary retailers: The Austrian case. *Electronic Markets, 11*(1). Retrieved August 26, 2004, from http://www.electronicmarkets.org/modules/pub/view.php/electronicmarkets-118

Mahajan, V., Shrinivasan, R., & Wind, J. (2002). The dot.com retail failures of 2000: Were there any winners? *Journal of the Academy of Marketing Science, 30*(4), 474-486.

Mentzas, G. (1997). Implementing an IS strategy—A team approach. *Long Range Planning, 10*(1), 84-95.

Min, S., & Wolfinbarger, M. (2005). Market share, profit margin, and marketing efficiency of early movers, bricks and clicks, and specialists in e-commerce. *Journal of Business Research*, (58), 1030-1039.

Mullaney, T. J. (1999). Needed: The human touch: Online retailers are beginning to discover the importance of customer-service reps who can talk and thank. *BusinessWeek*, (3659), EB 52.

Muller-Lankenau, C., Wehmeyer, K., & Klein, S. (2006). Multi-channel strategies: Capturing and exploring diversity in the European retail grocery industry. *International Journal of Electronic Commerce, 10*(2), 85-122, winter.

Nadherny, C. C. (1998). Technology and direct marketing leadership. *Direct Marketing, 61*(7), 42-45, November.

Nannery, M. (2000). HMV's Cooler Britannia. *Chain Store Age, 76*(8), 84-85.

Ndede-Amadi, A. A. (2004). What strategic alignment, process redesign, enterprise resource planning, and e-commerce have in common: Enterprise-wide computing. *Business Process Management Journal, 10*(2), 184-199.

Nicholls, A., & Watson, A. (2005). Implementing e-value strategies in UK retailing. *International*

Journal of Retail and Distribution Management, 33(6/7), 426-443.

Nielson, J. F., Host, V., & Mols, N. P. (2005). Adoption of Internet-based marketing channels by small-and-medium-sized manufacturers. *International Journal of E-Business Research, 1*(2), 1-23.

Pitta, D. A. (2002). Internet currency. *The Journal of Consumer Marketing, 19*(1), 86-87.

Podsakoff, P. M., & Organ, D. M. (1986). Self-reports in organizational research: Problems and prospects. *Journal of Management, 12*(4), 531-543.

Powell, T. C., & Dent-Micallef, A. (1997). Information technology as competitive advantage: The role of human, business, and technology resources. *Strategic Management Journal, 18*(5), 375-405.

Prencipe, L. W., & McCarthy, J. (2002). Battle of the shopping carts. *InfoWorld, 24*(40), 46-47.

Rabin, S. (2001). Providing a high-performance commerce site. *Information Systems Management, 18*(4), 40-51.

Rayport, J. F., & Jaworski, B. J. (2002). *Introduction to e-commerce.* Boston: McGraw-Hill/Irwin.

Reijers, H., & Jansen-Vullers, M. J. (2005). Better processes = better e-commerce. *Quality Progress, 38*(3), 57-63.

Reinhardt, G., & Levesque, M. (2004). A new entrant's decision on virtual versus bricks-and-mortar retailing. *Journal of Electronic Commerce Research 5*(3), 136-152.

Roehm, H. A., & Roehm, M. L. (2005). The hybrid split ad technique and onsite rewards. *Journal of Consumer Behaviour, 4*(3), 173-184.

Saini, A., & Johnson, J. L. (2005). Organizational capabilities in e-commerce: An empirical investigation of e-brokerage service providers. *Journal of the Academy of Marketing Science, 33*(3), 360-375.

Saunders, A., & Cook, S. (2002). E25 after the deluge. *Management Today*, 40-45.

Spencer, J. (2003). "I ordered that?' Web retailers make it easier to return goods. *The Wall Street Journal*, (Eastern Edition), D. 1.

Tan, F. B., Lin, H. J., & Urguhart, C. (2006). An exploratory study of the design preferences of U.S. and Chinese virtual communities. *International Journal of E-Business Research, 2*(3), 46-70.

Turban, E., King, D., Viehland, D., & Lee, J. (2006). *Electronic commerce—A managerial perspective*. Upper Saddle River, NJ: Prentice Hall.

Whiteley, R. (1992). *The customer driven company.* Reading, MA: Addison-Wesley.

Williamson, O. E. (1975). *Markets and hierarchies: Analysis and antitrust implications.* New York: Free Press.

Williamson, O. E. (1985). *The economic institutions of capitalism: Firms, markets, relational contracting.* New York: Free Press.

Willmott, D. (2000). The top 100 Web sites and the technologies that make them work. *PC Magazine, 19*(2), 144-159.

Chapter VI
Engaging SMEs in E-Business: Insights from an Empirical Study

Mark Xu
University of Portsmouth, UK

Ravni Rohatgi
University of Portsmouth, UK

Yanqing Duan
University of Bedfordshire Business School, UK

ABSTRACT

The rapid rise of e-business has brought profound impact on, as well as significant challenges to, businesses of all sizes. The lack of anticipated engagement in e-business by small- and medium-sized enterprises (SMEs) is still a concern to the UK government. Findings from the literature appear to have revealed a contradictory picture of SMEs' engagement in e-business. There is limited systematic research into how companies, especially small companies, are adopting the Internet technologies. This chapter reviews current research on SMEs' e-business adoption by following various adoption models. The chapter examines the driving forces and inhibitors that affect the adoption of e-business technology in SMEs. Through interviews with 40 owner/managers in the electronic components industry, the chapter reveals that most of the small firms in this industry are at the lower level of the "e-adoption ladder"—predominantly using the Internet for searching information and e-mail. SMEs in this industry have not yet widely engaged in online transactions. The current level of adoption is driven by both internal and external factors, including operational benefits, industry common practice, and peer pressure. External forces such as a lack of push from suppliers and customers and a lack of strategic vision of using advanced e-business technology for competitive advantages have determinant effects on the level and scale of e-adoption in SME sector.

INTRODUCTION

Small- and medium-sized enterprises (SMEs) play an important role in local, national, or even global economy. In the UK, there are 3.7 million firms employing over 12 million people, which generates 55% of UK employment and contributes approximately 51% to the UK Gross Domestic Product with an annual turnover of over 1 trillion pounds sterling (Dixon, Thompson, & McAllister, 2002). SMEs are not miniature versions of large firms, they are unique in their own right (Barnett & Mackness, 1983). Certain characteristics make up the SME organizational environment in which it operates; this includes a small management team, strong owner influence, multi-functional management, limited ability to obtain finance, and a lack of control over the business environment. SMEs provide an environment in which structures and processes are and must remain simple, flexible, and adaptable (Carmichael, Turgoose, Older, & Todd, 2000). In small firms, firm and managerial factors are merged due to the high locus of control exerted by the key decision makers (Boone, Brabander, & Hellemans, 2000). Kula and Tatoglu (2003) argue that SMEs have fewer resources than large firms, which lead to weaknesses in planning, training, finance, and organization of internal information.

Studying e-business adoption in the SMEs sector is of particular importance. The Internet is described as the SME's gateway to global business and markets (Liikanen, 2001), and e-business technologies are expected to allow SMEs to gain capabilities that were once the preserve of their larger competitors. These new technologies offer the potential for creating entirely new ways of working, giving rise to a new breed of SMEs whose management and employees use a more flexible and more effective way of working. E-business is expected to become a key driver in the way companies across the globe conduct business. However, whether these new technologies are put to efficient use by SMEs and what driving forces that push SMEs up the adoption ladder remains a question that attracts considerable attention of researchers and policy makers (Fillis, Johannson, & Wagner, 2004; Parish, Kibblewhite, Woodley, & Richardson, 2002; Ramsey, Ibbotson, Bell, & Gary, 2003).

The unique characteristics of SMEs affect their Internet technologies adoption. Research suggests that there is a correlation between the size of a business and the level of IT adoption (McDonagh & Prothero, 2000). The typical micro enterprise exhibits much lower rates of e-business activities than larger firms when excluding smaller high-technology firms (Smyth & Ibbotson 2001). Large organizations are inclined to adopt the click and mortar model by integrating offline and online business or spin-off online operations. In contrast, small- and medium-sized firms lack a general pattern on adoption of Internet technologies (Chavez, Leiter, & Kiely, 2000). The extent of adopting Internet technologies may vary widely among small- and medium-sized enterprises (Kula et al., 2003). This creates great demands and challenges to construct a clear picture of the level of e-business adoption in the SME sector.

Research into the level of adoption of e-business technologies in the SMEs sector reported very contradictory results, which exacerbates the current situation of confusion. For example, Smyth et al. (2001) reported from a multiple industry survey that an extremely low adoption rate was found in Ireland and Northern Ireland. Daniel, Wilson, and Myers (2002a) found 50% of e-business adoption in UK SMEs. The statistics of the European Observatory for SMEs show that most SMEs are not using the Internet and the World Wide Web (WWW) for commercial transactions despite the allure of e-business benefits (Ramsey et al., 2003). A multi-industry survey conducted in the North and South of Ireland by Ramsey et al. (2003) revealed that only 33% of the firms had a Web site, 10% of the firms used Web sites to generate online orders, and none of the Web sites could facilitate online payments. However, in a study of the adoption of e-commerce in the UK electronics industry (Parish et al., 2002), a relative high level of adoption of Internet technologies has been reported (i.e., 85% the firm (larger than 100 employees) buy online, and 43% of the firms sell online). The disparity of those empirical findings reflects a lack of consensus and the complexities in gaining a holistic view of e-business adoption in the SME sector.

In view of this, this chapter aims to examine the current level of adopting e-business technologies by SMEs in a specific industry. It is believed that an industry specific study can produce accurate results showing the level of e-business adoption that are appropriate to that industry, based on which practical solutions can be postulated to improve the effective usage of e-business technologies.

DEFINITIONS OF E-BUSINESS AND SME

The terms "e-business," "e-commerce," and "Internet commerce" are often used interchangeably. Fillis et al. (2004) define e-business as companies that utilize e-technology in their business operations, but exclude sending and receiving text-based e-mail messages. Stone (2003) states that e-business is not just the World-Wide-Web (www), it involves technology (e.g., intranets, portals, content management, middleware, mobile) to enhance profitability. The UK Department of Trade and Industry (DTI) specifies e-business as the integration of all the activities within the internal processes of a business through ICT (information communication technology). The activities include full integration of information and communication technologies (ICTs) into a firm's operations and potentially include redesigning its business processes around ICT or completely reinventing its business model. In this chapter, e-business refers to the incorporation of Internet technologies into entire enterprise's operations and management.

The term SMEs is commonly referred to as small- and medium-sized enterprises but these firms can differ significantly in terms of employee numbers. The European Union's definition of SMEs suggests that a small business includes 10-99 employees, and that a medium sized business includes 100-250 employees. A microenterprise includes less than 10 employees (Ramsey et al. 2003). A study of Internet adoption in Turkey by Kula et al. (2003) defines SME as one that employs less than 100 persons. In this study SMEs refers to VAT (value added tax) registered companies in the UK with employee numbers between 10 to 250. This is a working definition defined and used by the UK Department of Trade and Industry (DTI).

MODELS OF E-ADOPTION/GROWTH

Molla, Heeks, and Balcells (2006) stress that e-commerce adoption is not necessarily an one-time activity. Instead, small firms can gradually develop more complex, more integrated e-commerce capabilities (Chen, Haney, Pandzik, Spigarelli, & Jesseman, 2003; Daniel & Grimshaw, 2002b). With increasing attention to e-business application, a number of e-business growth/adoption models have been developed. Gary (2003) suggests that ICT adoption is driven by two theories. One is social network theory where adoption is encouraged by the everyday influences that shape opinions, attitudes, and behavior coming from individual expectations, peer pressure, and the business milieu in which firms operate. The second is technology determinist—a rational process where the benefits of simple ICT applications attract small firm owners. The owners move to another stage of business development and become aware of the benefits of more advanced ICT applications. Some examples of adoption models, growth models are cited as follows:

- DTI e-business adoption ladder (DTI 2001).
- British library staircase of Internet engagement model (Allcock, Webber, & Yeates, 1999).
- The stage of growth for e-business maturity (SOGe) model (McKay, Prananto, & Marshall, 2000; Prananto, McKay, & Marshall, 2003).
- SMEs stages of adoption and use of e-commerce OUBS model (Gary, 2003).
- A stage model of SMEs e-commerce development (Lawson, Alcock, Cooper, & Burgess, 2003; Rao, Metts, & Monge, 2003).
- The IBM model of stages and states of e-business (Stone, 2003).
- An e-commerce adoption process model incorporating adoption stages, phases, and influential factors (Molla et al., 2006).

The e-adoption ladder addresses the technology complexity of e-business technology, whereas the British library staircase model addresses non-technological factors affecting e-adoption, thus both of the models are reviewed next.

The "E-Adoption Ladder"

Martin and Matlay (2001) suggest that there are different levels of e-business in SMEs known as "e-adoption." In a DTI benchmarking study report, e-adoption is defined as incremental tiers or steps and can be represented in the form of an "e-adoption ladder" with each stage increasing in level of sophistication as depicted in Figure 1.

The first two stages involve acquiring basic ICT skills and technology to operate e-mail for messaging and simple brochure Web sites for online marketing. The e-commerce stage involves online interaction between a business and its customers, or a business and its suppliers, for the placement of an order and online payment processing. The e-business stage allows integration of the supply chain. The final stage enables open information sharing between customers, suppliers and partners based on which existing business processes are radically transformed or new business models are formed. The adoption ladder emphasizes e-business technology adoption along with organizational change. The final three stages require advanced technology and

Figure 1. Extent of organizational change and sophistication

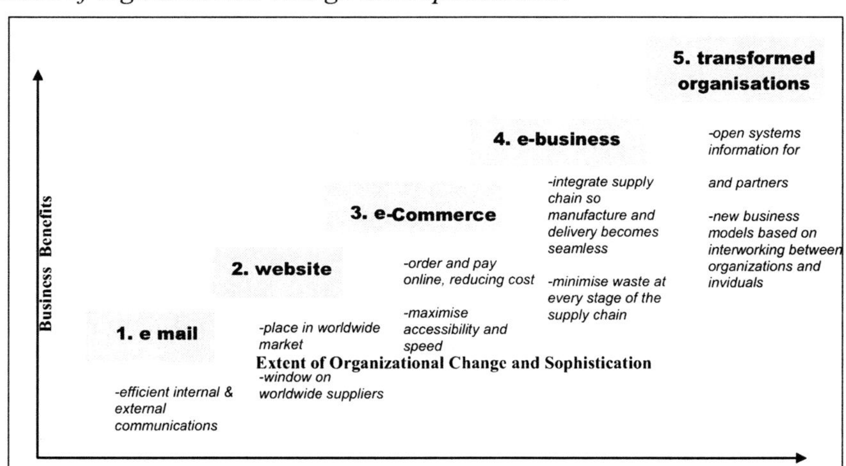

a wide range of specialist business skills and expertise in areas such as management, strategy, and marketing.

Criticism of the adoption ladder points to the linear progression and technology sophistication aspects. Gary (2003) commented that the adoption ladder is a simple technology stage model, which provides a useful sense of technological progression, but it is too linear to fully describe processes that are often non-linear and very complex. Ramsey et al. (2003) argued in line with Gary (2003) that the e-adoption ladder assumes a linear progression from being less mature to increased sophistication over time. Ideally the organization will move through the stages of using e-commerce purely for informational purpose, then transactional, and ultimately progress to having a strategic e-focus. They speculate that the majority of SMEs may have very low-level requirements and/or follow a non-linear/discontinuous path. In reality, the diffusion and assimilation of Internet commerce by SMEs is likely to follow a "zig-zag" path based on a "trial and error" approach (Poon, 2002; Poon & Swatman, 1999).

The Staircase of Internet Engagement

Based on information needs rather than technology push and considering SME sector characteristics, Allcock et al. (1999) introduced a 4-stages staircase model adopted by British Library. The model includes four stages of Internet engagement along with technology sophistication. The first stage is "threshold" featured by using computers, but not the Internet. This is followed by the second stage "beginner," which uses connected computers, but not a Web site. The third stage is "intermediate," on this stage, e-mail and static Web sites are used (e.g., link to suppliers), but the usage is not aligned with any strategy. The last stage is "advanced," which uses interactive Web sites and Web-based networks to support business strategy. At this stage, companies demonstrate high ICT skills. The staircase model also considers the non-technology forces (e.g., external pressure, increased ICT skills, business driver) that influence the level of Internet engagement; this differentiates the model from the adoption ladder. The driving forces may push SMEs up the stairs, whilst the influential factors (e.g., lack of resource and skills, system changeover, etc.) may send the firm down the stairs. Gary (2003) positively commented that the British library staircase model takes the perspective of the SMEs owner-managers, linking technology evolution to their capability to learn, to manage new ICT knowledge, and to introduce business changes.

FACTORS IMPACTING E-BUSINESS ADOPTION IN SMES

Numerous attempts have been made to study the factors impacting the e-business adoption and growth. Stokes (2000) uncovered factors such as inertia and lack of interest, resource-based issues that hamper the development of new competencies. Smyth et al. (2001) identified barriers such as lack of skills and investment in staff training and poor knowledge of the Internet start-up process. Fillis et al. (2004) developed a model of factors impacting on adoption in small firms. The model comprises of three tiers of influential factors including macro-factors (e.g., globalization, competition, government policy, etc.), industry/sectoral factors and firm/managerial factors at micro level. Fillis et al. (2004) emphasize that macro-level factors are the drivers behind technological change and specific industry and sectoral factors will influence the SME in its demand for e-business. At the firm level, resource-based issues, competencies, managers' attitudes and benefits are highlighted as the main factors drive adoption or non-adoption. Some key influential factors effecting SMEs are discussed next.

Resource-Based Issues

Limited resources (e.g., financial, time, management, personnel) are often highlighted as major factors impacting on the decision to adopt. SMEs cannot afford to experiment with these technologies and make expensive mistakes (EBPG, 2002). Consequently, this leads many SME managers to adopt a "wait and see" attitude in order to minimize risks. Lawrence (2002) argues that resource limitations such as time and capital coupled with preferences for traditional mechanisms to do business, inhibited the firms from gaining benefits from introducing e-commerce technology. In contrast to this notion, Mehrtens, Cragg, and Mills (2001) found that financial resource does not affect the decision on whether to adopt Internet technologies. SMEs have been seen as spending little on technology, therefore they do not use the optimum solutions for much of their business, which ultimately causes slow growth of the business. As a result, they are unable to invest in new technology that could actually help put them on the fast track.

Competency/Skills Gap

Fillis et al. (2004) suggest that some of the barriers are grounded in a competency/skills gap framework (i.e., in adequate development of appropriate skills, investment in staff training, and poor knowledge of the Internet start-up process). A recent report (IBM.com) on Canadian SMEs found that Canadian small business owners are lagging far behind their American counterparts. One of the reasons is Canadian businesses in general tend to be more reluctant to embrace for sophisticated applications. Gary (2003) argues that whether the adoption is driven by business demand or technology push, the owner manager needs to be personally ready before moving to the next stage and that the process involves learning and new knowledge.

Duan (2004) argues that e-commerce offers companies tremendous opportunities to improve their business performance in new and innovative ways, but its potential benefit would only be realized by capable managers and skilled employees who can deal with these emerging technologies and implement them wisely. A number of studies (Drew, 2003; Jones, Hecker, & Holland, 2003; Lawson et al., 2003; Matlay & Addis 2003; Quayle 2003) have been conducted to address competency and skill issue and identified that lack of skills and knowledge is one of the barriers for the uptake and use of Internet and e-commerce. Abundant evidence from literature on skills and knowledge deficiency in SMEs suggests that competency and skills gap are and will continue to be a significant impediment to the uptake of new technology, and will increasingly disadvantage the competitiveness of SMEs.

Managerial Orientation and Attitudes

A conservative, risk-averse orientation of an owner/manager may mean that a dominant negative attitude is displayed toward its adoption. There may be a sense that business is dictated mainly by the end customer, supplier, or distributor who does not want to embrace technology, instead preferring conventional, traditional methods (Fillis et al., 2004). This supports Cyert and March's (1992) notion that managers of SMEs prefer the comfort of what they perceive as familiar rather than indulging into any new venture. They are reluctant to "think outside the box" to seek new business solutions. Risk aversion generally tends to be more common than the acceptance of risk and change. Managers of SMEs are more likely to be resistant to change. Maurer (1996) claimed that only one third of technological changes in SME organizations succeed. He identified three main levels of resistance to change: informational—where there is not enough information or understanding of what is required; gut reaction—emotional, psychological, and even physiological individual reactions; and cultural.

The attitude of the owner managers toward IT adoption is identified as an influential factor (Chong, 2001; Drew, 2003; Levy & Powell, 2002). It is found that some managers do not believe Internet technologies can provide significant improvement in service compared with traditional methods (Mehrtens et al., 2001). Successful companies that embrace IT and Internet technologies are often the ones that the owner takes on the role as innovation champion of the IT adoption. In addition, such champions will have a reasonable level of knowledge and understanding regarding the specific technology.

Benefits Awareness

Levy, Powell, and Yetton (2002) suggest that SMEs tend to be driven by short-term efficiency and operational benefits to the detriment of strategic, long-term business benefits. It is imperative that growing awareness and understanding of the benefits and uses of e-commerce among SMEs can positively influence their desire and interest in adopting e-commerce (Ramsey et al. 2003). Lack of understanding of the benefits SMEs can achieve (Goode, 2002) and of unrealistic expectations of benefits and the difficulties of evaluating them (Poon, 2000) contribute to the low level of e-commerce adoption in SMEs (Stockdale & Standing, 2004). Kula et al. (2003) suggest that SME managers tend to be unfamiliar with the technology and its benefits. They perceive it to be both costly and a source of security concerns. Most SMEs innovate only when they clearly perceive business opportunities involved with their firms, or because they are under pressure from suppliers and clients. On the other hand, Schlenker and Crocker (2003) point out that the technology suppliers have largely failed to demonstrate the business value of Internet technologies to the SME, which may exacerbate the situation.

Contextual Factors

Contextual factors such as the influence from sectors, customers, suppliers, completions, location, etc. have been considered as one of the major factors for small business e-business adoption (Fillis et al. 2004; Molla et al. 2006,). For example, in Daniel et al.'s (2002b) study, they reveal that the use of e-commerce for responding to competitors, providing enhanced customer services and improving relations with suppliers was driving the uptake by smaller businesses to a greater extent than by their larger counterparts. Drew's survey with SMEs in the East of England also finds that the most important forces were industry changes and trends, opportunities to growth and the need to keep up with competitions.

KEY FINDINGS FROM AN UK EMPIRICAL STUDY

Research Method

Rather than to construct a holistic picture of the whole SME sector cross multiple industry, an empirical study was carried out with the electronic components manufacturer and supplier industry. There are three reasons to choose this industry for sampling:

- Firstly, according to Ramsey et al. (2003), this industry has been under researched relative to other industry sectors such as retail chain, services or travel industry. For example, the highest Internet presence is in the hospitability/leisure sector and the lowest is in agriculture and transport sectors.
- Secondly, the aforementioned studies are primarily multiple industry-based and country-specific surveys, which lead to disparity in findings. The aggregated findings on the level of e-business adoption of multiple industries are inconclusive due to industry

sectoral differences. This is evident from Fillis, et al. (2004) who argue that specific industry and sector factors will influence the demand for e-business technologies in SMEs, and Internet usage will not be consistent across SMEs in every business sector. They explain that e-business is not appropriate for all firms across all industry sectors. Specific sectoral circumstances may mean that more traditional methods of securing business will still dominate. Thus an accurate national or international picture of e-business adoption in SMEs is difficult to construct due to macro, industrial, firm and owner manager differences.

- Lastly, according to executives from Business Link (a UK government-enabled support agency that provides business solutions to SMEs), specialist manufacturers are more likely to be pro-e-business, and would adopt future technologies if they have not already done so. The electronic components industry fits well into this category.

The extensive literature review (i.e., the e-adoption ladder, the British Library Staircase model, and the factors influencing e-adoption) inform the research design of this study. Most of the measurements used in the interview are drawn from this literature. The approach for data collection conforms to both qualitative and quantitative techniques. With the help of the Southampton and Fareham Chamber of Commerce and Industry, which maintains close contacts with regional SMEs, 40 companies in the South of England have been contacted and chosen to participate in the study. The selection process assumed that there is no pre-knowledge as to the usage of Internet technologies within those firms, thus the sample is framed in random nature.

The primary method is structured interview with managing directors, which was conducted during April and May 2004. A questionnaire was used during the one to one interviews. In the case where managing directors were not available for an interview, a substitute such as sales director, IT director, or finance director was interviewed. Interviewing owner managers or directors for this topic is based on the consideration that investment in Internet technology is a major strategic decision of owner managers for small and medium firms. Ramsey et al. (2003) used a similar approach in their study. We echo their view that due to the dynamic nature, e-business decision-making is based largely on the intuitive competencies of the entrepreneurial owner/managers. Most of the interviews lasted approximately half an hour. A number of standard questions were asked at each interview, this is to ensure that minimum consensus can be tabulated in data analysis. The interviewees were invited to discuss the topics and their concerns relevant to the study without prompting them with directions or constraints. Each interview was recorded with the consent of the interviewee. Copies of the interview transcriptions were given to each interviewee shortly after the interview. Where appropriate, they could add any extra information as appropriate. Due to the qualitative nature of data and the small size of sample, statistical tests are not used to analyze the data.

Company Profile and Use of the Technology

To understand the context of the responses, the sample companies were broken down by the number of employees and the position of the interviewees. As indicated in Table 1, 70% of the interviewees are managing directors, and the vast majority of the sample are small companies with employee less than 50.

Position in the Ladder—The Level of Adoption of E-Business Technology

The adoption of e-business technology in those SMEs is examined in light of the e-adoption lad-

Table 1. The profile of the sample

Number of Employees	Managing Director	Directors (Other)*	Total (%)
10-49	20	5	62.5%
50-99	5	3	20.0%
100-149	3	0	7.5%
150-199	0	2	5.0%
200-249	0	2	5.0%
Total (%)	70%	30%	100%

**Other directors include sales director, finance director, IT director, production director, and marketing director*

Figure 2. Usage of e-business technology

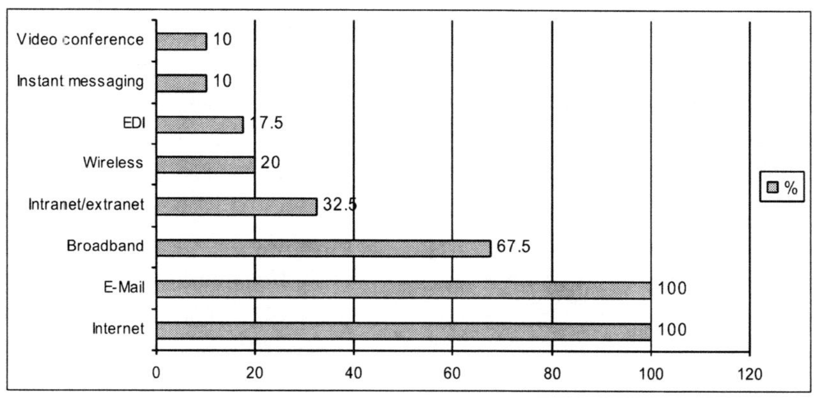

der. Figure 2 shows the extent of usage of these technologies in this industry.

The data shows that all the companies interviewed have access to the Internet. E-mail has been widely used by small and medium firms. Sixty-eight percent of the firms are using broadband, which enables fast access to the Internet and e-mail and 20% uses wireless access. One third of the companies used Intranets for internal communication and an Extranet to link to suppliers. However, using instant messaging, video conferencing, and other tools for business are low in these firms.

A further inquiry on the level of complexity of the firms' Web site and the primary purposes of the Web site reveals that 88% of Web sites are static (i.e., displaying information about the company and products). Fifteen percent of the Web sites have only one Web page showing contact details. Only five companies (12%) enabled customers to buy products online, and those five companies are medium-sized companies with employees over 100. The primary purposes of using the Web site are discussed with the managers, which are summarized in Figure 4.

The data shows that the top four (over 70%) usages of Web sites are related to Internet marketing and information communication, which suggests that the Web sites are predominantly used as a marketing and communication tool. It

Figure 3. Purposes and functionality of the Web site

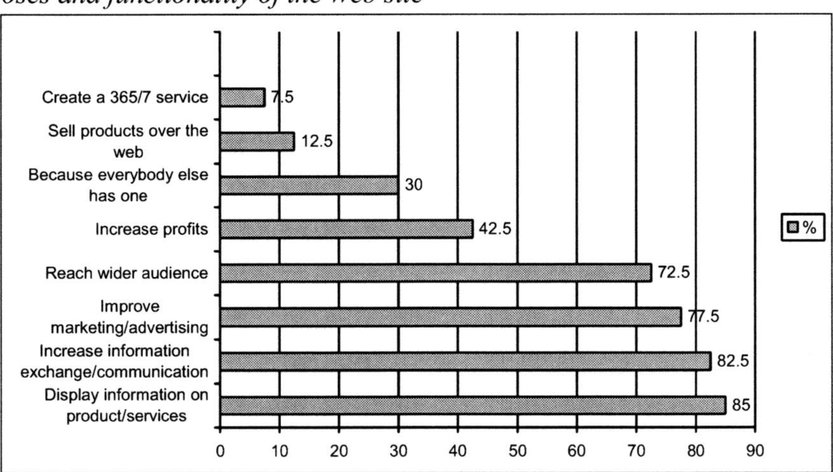

is worth highlighting that only 12.5% of the Web sites offer an online buying or selling e-commerce function. This is in contrast to some of the findings mentioned earlier where higher level of e-business applications was reported (Daniel et al., 2002; Parish et al., 2002; Stone, 2003). It also differs from Ramsey et al.'s (2003) finding that there was no indication (0%) of high-level functionality—the ability to buy and pay for service/product online.

The high-level usage of Web site and e-mails confirms many findings reported in other similar studies. For example, Kula et al. (2003) report the ranking of Internet application usage from the highest to lowest level are e-mail, browsing company homepages, market, and product searches. They suggest that Internet applications are principally concerned with external communications and gathering information for market and product research. Ramsey et al. (2003) reported that owner managers perceive e-mail as an important function for their business. Managers interviewed in this study acknowledged that the reasons of high-level usage of Internet and e-mails are the great benefit as comparing to other means (i.e., using the Internet and e-mail can increase the response rate of receiving and sending information, which in turn reduces the cost of postage).

Other benefits include sharing information, improving marketing and communication, and access to a wide range of information. It needs to note that only four managers regard an additional benefit being increased profits through interactive Web sites, which enable customers to purchase components and parts over the Internet. Only five medium-sized companies actually sell products on the Web. This is in line with Lymer, Nayak, Johnson, and Spaul's (1998) findings that the main Internet tools identified as available for small business were a Web site, e-mail, and access to online information and networking.

Although one third of the firms acknowledged using intranet and/or extranet, the main benefit is enabling information communication and sharing, not online buying or selling. Referring to the e-adoption ladder, firms in this particular industry widely adopt the most common Internet technologies (e-mail and Internet) that constitute the first and the second levels of the ladder. This firmly positions the SMEs in this industry on the lower two ladders. The adoption of broadband (68%) and wireless technology (20%) shows the firms attempt to maximize accessibility and speed. Even though these technologies are used, there is little sign to show that the firms are moving up to the full e-commerce stage. This adds to criticism over the e-adoption model that technology complexity may not necessarily lead to a higher degree of e-commerce or e-business adoption. In terms of the British Library Staircase, there are influential factors that can hold firms up on the adoption ladder. The next section will examine these factors.

The Driving Forces of E-Business Adoption

Business Benefits

Business driver has been regarded as a main driving force for technology adoption as shown in the Staircase model. Levy et al. (2002) suggest that SMEs tend to be driven by short-term efficiency and operational benefits to the detriment of strategic, long-term business benefits. Evidence shown in Figure 4 confirms this assertion.

The data shows that the vast majority of the owner managers believe their firms gained immediate operational benefits from using Internet technologies, for example, cost reduction, sharing information, improved marketing, and communication. A few managers comment that the cost of postage and postal mail were significantly reduced due to the introduction of using e-mail. Another key benefit is faster responses to customers needs. Carmichael et al. (2000) suggest that the key driver for SMEs to innovate is competition and customer feedback. SMEs realized that they need to remain competitive in order to survive, thus responding to customer feedback is an important weapon of competition. One manager owes the benefits to increased profit due to their interactive Web site enabling customer to purchase components and parts over the Internet. These operational benefits and response to competition needs clearly constitute the main driving forces that push firms up the adoption ladder.

Industry Common Practice or Peer Pressure

Kula et al. (2003) suggest that most SMEs innovate only when they clearly perceive business opportunities for their firms, or because they are under pressure from suppliers and clients. It is interesting to note that one third of the companies interviewed (30% in Figure 3) don't have a clear idea about the reasons for having a Web site.

Figure 4. Benefit of adopting e-business technologies

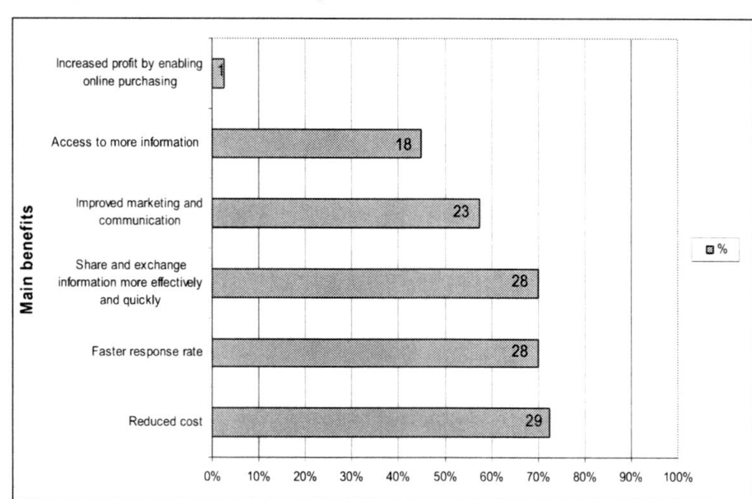

Some managers said that it is common to have a company Web site in the industry, as everyone else has one. The reason "everyone else has one" shows the effect of benchmarking or peer pressure from the industry. The finding appears to suggest that peer pressure or industry standard is a main driving force to pushing firms up the ladder of adoption of e-business technologies. However, this could become an inhibitor to adopting new technologies if there is no industry leader or champion to innovate and to demonstrate the strategic advantages of using advanced e-business technologies.

Awareness of E-Business Function

It is evident from this study that over 90% of the managers have some understanding of the e-business function and its potential, although the degree of understanding varies significantly. Table 2 presents the awareness level against e-adoption ladder. The four categories are based on the responses generated from the interviews.

The synthesized data shows that 25% of the managers can relate e-business to buying and selling over the Internet. A few managers are quoted as saying that:

- *"E-business is buying and selling over the Internet, also including instant messaging, chatting to customers."*
- *"E-business is electronic business activities, for example internal and external communications, being able to e-mail customers—current and potential, to buy and sell products."*
- *"Conducting business through the Internet using Web Technology, using the Internet to extend business overseas."*

Those remarks reflect managers' understanding/awareness of the "e-commerce" function—the third level of the e-business adoption ladder. Three managers can even relate e-business to supply chain for procurement, or to integrate with ERP (enterprise resource planning) system. For example:

- *"Using the Internet for information gathering. The ability to procure electronically. Using ERP systems, portals to place orders, appearing on industry wide Web sites, and placing orders via electronic means."*
- *"Using the Internet to process orders and communicate between companies. To make more contacts internationally and to ease the communication between suppliers and customers via digital technology such as Broadband."*
- *"Doing everything electronically—the next evolution from the 3rd party stage. Getting suppliers online and clients online and doing*

Table 2. Managers' awareness of e-business function

E-business function awareness against adoption ladder	Responses	%
On e-business ladder Doing business over the Internet involving procurement, supply chain	3	7.5
On e-commerce ladder Doing business over the Internet including taking orders and selling	10	25.0
On Internet ladder Using Web site for marketing, information gathering, or something to do with the Internet	20	50.0
Under the ladder Do not know e-business function	7	17.5

> *every bit of business online. The Web site has 4 stages: static, interactive, transactional, involves the whole supply chain.*"

This shows sufficient awareness of the higher level of e-business sophistication (i.e., the e-business ladder of the adoption model. However, none of the managers indicate that there will be a radical transformation of the way of doing business in the industry.

It is interesting to note that the combination of the first two categories adds up to 32.5%, which shows that over one third of the managers are aware of the e-commerce/e-business functionality, but actual online selling is conducted within only 5 companies (12.5%). There must be factors that hold firms up from adopting technology to the level as managers perceived.

Table 2 also shows that half of the owner managers do not relate e-business to online buying, selling and transforming business process, but regard e-business as the same as online marketing, information searching, a part of customer process, or simply something to do with the Internet. For example:

> "*E-business complements other business channels but cannot replace it. Ten years ago, banks, shops etc. closed many of their physical premises, just to find they were not generating as much business because people were not familiar with using the Internet and were not comfortable. There is no point adopting something new where no one is going to use it. E-business is about making business processes a part of the customer process. It is a way of interacting more technically with the customer.*"

> "*E-business is a marketing and advertising tool with the ability to promote products and services (e.g., using the WWW to have company information listed on search engines so people can see what you do on a global scale).*"

There are 17.5% owner managers who do not know e-business functionality and its potential opportunity. One manager even perceived e-business as,

> "Doing business in Europe" (!).

Overall, the findings are in contrast to some of the claims that a lack of understanding of the benefits (Goode, 2002) and the difficulties of evaluating them contribute to the low level of e-commerce adoption in SMEs (Stockdale et al., 2004). Our study reveals that the majority of managers' understanding of e-business tends to be consistent with the current level of e-business adoption in their firms.

The Barriers to E-Business Adoption

The barriers that hold companies back from adopting e-business technology are discussed with the directors through a structured question. The question adopted several measurements appeared in literature, and used 5 likart scale in order to identify the most influential inhibitors that hold-up firms in climbing up the adoption ladder. The results are summarized in Figure 5.

Lack of Resources and Training

Lack of resources has been seen as a main obstacle to adopting e-business technologies. This refers to limited personnel, training, and expertise. Managers explained that being small companies, the employees have to train themselves on how to use the functions of the technologies that the company has adopted (i.e., how to use the Internet, how to access information, and how to use search engines to obtain higher numbers of hits. As the usage of complex e-business technology is minimal in these firms, formal training is not required by the users, nor is such training provided by the firm.

Figure 5. Barriers to implementing e-business technology

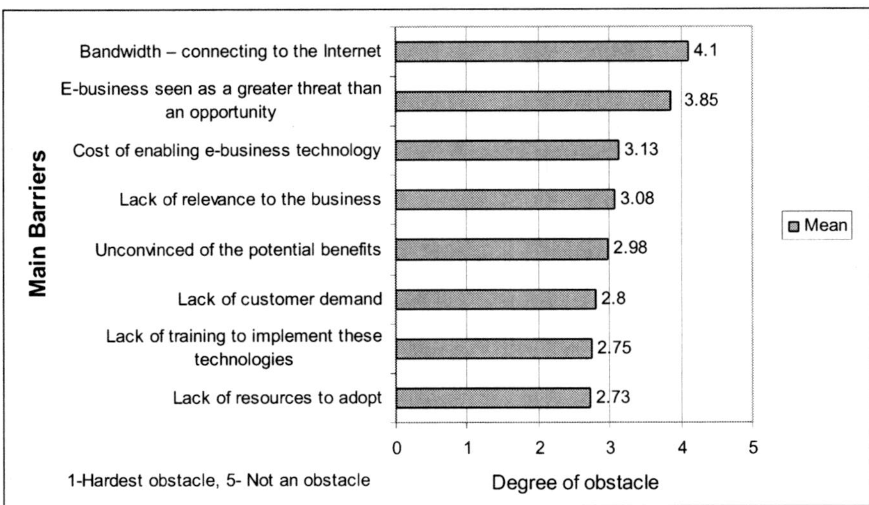

SMEs have been seen as spending little on technology, therefore they do not use the optimum solutions for much of their business. As a result, they are unable to invest in new technology that could actually help put them on the fast track. However, this study shows that the cost of enabling e-business technology appears not to be a barrier to these firms as shown by the mean score (3.13). This support the arguments that financial resources do not affect the decision on whether or not to adopt Internet technologies (Mehrtens et al., 2001), and that cost is not a main concern when making e-business decisions (Ramsey et al., 2003).

The Industry Nature and Tradition

Some managers commented that e-business technologies are not relevant to the industry and there is no demand from customers for using these technologies. Managers explained that the nature of the industry requires regular face-to-face or telephone contact when describing electronic components. Another reason is that people are used to using traditional methods such as phone or fax. They feel more comfortable continuing to use these technologies, as opposed to investing in new technologies, which may require considerable training. This suggests that the nature of the industry, the common practice, and the traditional way of doing business impose a significant impact on the adoption of new technologies. Ramsey et al.'s (2003) addresses the unique nature of an industry in relation to utilization of Internet technology. They assert that each day the owner manager is more preoccupied with "fire-fighting" to realize and fulfill customer orders, where there is a heavy reliance on face-to-face contact. The service is highly tangible and is not really suited to the e-business environment. The high level of intangibility of the service/product mix can be viewed as one of the major impediments to future utilization of Internet commerce by this particular business.

Lack Of Push From Supply Chain (Customer Demand)

Fillis et al. (2004) speculate that there may be a sense that business is dictated mainly by the end customer, supplier, or distributor who does not want to embrace e-business technology, instead preferring conventional, traditional methods. The data in Figure 5 shows that the SME managers in this industry feel there is a lack of demand from customers to use online selling and buying. This implies that the downstream supply chain (could also be from the upstream chain) demand has a notable impact on the level and scale of adopting advanced e-business technologies.

Lack of Vision and Industrial Champion

Some managers don't perceive (or are not convinced by) the potential strategic benefits of being the first to utilize new technologies. Some managers do not perceive the relevance of using new technologies to their business, although they understand the online buying and selling functions offered by the technologies. A lack of vision and risk taking may be speculated as the reason leading to the current situation. We echo Gary's (2003) argument that whether the adoption is driven by business demand or technology push, the owner managers need to be personally ready before moving on to the next stage and that the process involves learning and new knowledge.

In summary, a lack of resources and a lack of vision of the potential benefits are influential factors that are internal to the SMEs, whereas the industry common practice and a lack of push from supply chain constitute external factors. These factors hamper SMEs in proactively adopting e-business technologies (i.e., holding up the firms on the adoption ladder/staircase). Other internal factors such as Internet access, bandwidth, and cost appear not to be critical obstacles in adopting e-business technologies in those firms.

A Forward View of E-Adoption Pattern

Regarding the importance and the future of adopting e-business technology, 65% of the managers interviewed think e-business technology (predominantly Internet and e-mail) is important to their companies. Figure 6 shows managers' perceptions of the future of adopting e-business technology within their firms.

The dominant view is to adopt e-business technology in conjunction with conventional methods of doing business (i.e., the "clicks and mortar" pat-

Figure 6. The future outlook of e-business

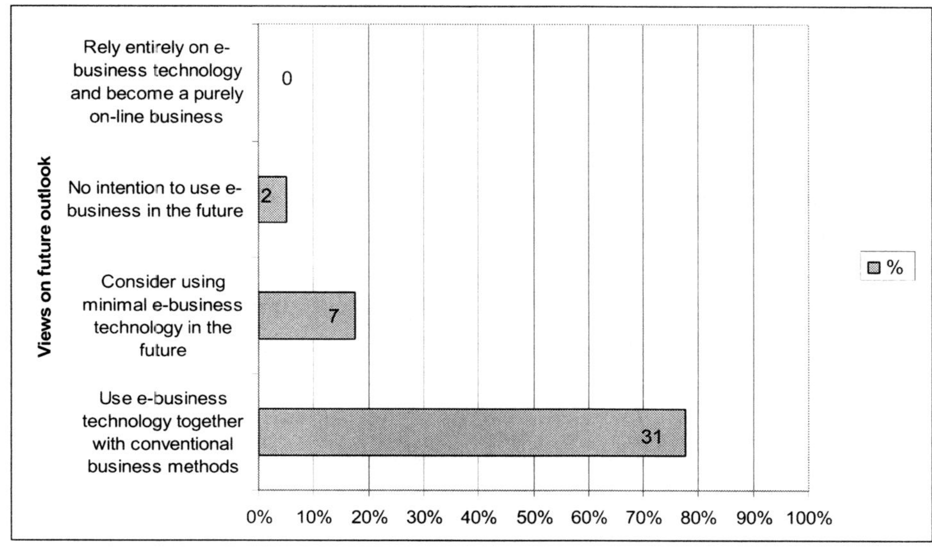

tern. None of the firms interviewed are considering transforming into a purely online business. This has been emphasized by the managers that the industry requires regular face-to-face or telephone contact with customers and employees prefer to adhere to the traditional way of doing business. It is noted that 17.5% consider using e-business technology to a minimum level and 5% of firms never intend to use e-business technologies. It appears that industry common practice has a strong influence on these SMEs. This situation may not change significantly in a short period of time, as 67.5% of the managers interviewed are satisfied with the e-business technology adopted, and less than a quarter (22.5%) of the managers expressed dissatisfaction, unless significant pressure and push from external stakeholders, particularly from suppliers and customers emerge.

CONCLUSION AND IMPLICATIONS

This chapter reviews the current research concerning the e-business adoption in SMEs regarding the adoption models and the associated influential factors. Focusing on a specific industry sector, this study found that SMEs in the electronic components industry are at the lower ladder of adopting e-business technology. The technologies used are predominantly e-mail and Internet, and are used primarily as an additional marketing tool to display company's products and services information, rather than as an e-commerce platform to enable online transactions and organizational transformation. The problems underpinning the low adoption of sophisticated e-business technology lie not in Internet access, cost, and managerial understanding, but in the external forces including industry/sector practice, lack of push from supply chain, as well as internal factors such as lack of resources, expertise and strategic vision to lead. Even though half of the owner managers are aware of e-business functions, awareness of e-business strategic benefits can be further improved. As far as this industry is concerned, a push from external forces could quickly change the picture of the level and the scale of e-business adoption. The findings also suggest that e-business adoption may not follow a linear path and the adoption pattern may be specific to each industry/sector.

Although some of the findings tend to be common to all SMEs (e.g., lack of resources) some findings are unique in the context of this study. These distinct findings have implications in providing guidance on practical application of e-business technologies in SMEs and in developing e-adoption models. The findings recommend that industry common practice, peer pressure, and customer push need to be recognized as major external forces that influence the level of adoption of e-business technology in SMEs. Even though this study is not aimed to scientifically test whether external forces outweigh internal forces, its results indicate that external forces tend to be a strong influential factor in affecting the level and scale of e-technology adoption in this particular industry. The findings approve that most SMEs are followers in their sector in terms of adopting technology. It can be envisaged that an industry champion/ or leader who demonstrates strategic benefits of adopting advanced technologies, together with a strong demand from suppliers or customers could influence many SMEs moving up to the higher level of the adoption ladder, although there are internal resource constraints. This implies that the pattern of adopting e-business technologies may not be linear as depicted in Figure 1 (i.e., SMEs may not necessarily move from Internet level to e-commerce level and then to e-business level). It is possible that many SMEs in the electronic components industry may engage in business process change based on an intranet-based supply chain infrastructure while conducting online buying and selling. This is a non-linear path of adopting e-business technology. Based on such speculation, the e-adoption model may need to be modified to include a non-linear path with consideration of the driving forces from a firm's internal and external environment. Figure 7 depicts such a model.

Insights gained from the investigation also suggest that owner managers need to develop a strategic vision, and the industry needs a champion to lead. As far as the SMEs in the electronics components industry is concerned, there needs to be an external push as well as an internal business driver to make small firms proactively engage in adopting advanced e-business technologies. This could be achieved by inspiring owner managers with immediate benefits and strategic (competitive) advantages of using e-business technologies. The key to success is to provide a cost/time saving as well as flexible learning opportunity for the owner managers who are busy in managing daily business and seeking new business opportunities. The IT industry that provides e-business solutions needs to articulate explicitly the potential and added value of technologies to owner managers. The products and services need to be tailor-made to suit the unique needs of SMEs, and vendors' support and training should be prioritized to SMEs clients, due to the significant lack of expertise, specialist knowledge, and resources in the SME sector. The e-business environment and infrastructure need to be continuously improved to facilitate e-business application in SMEs. This includes easy Internet/broadband access, government incentives for SMEs, secure order processing and payment systems, distribution infrastructure supporting online transactions, online taxation and legislation. These are generally uncontrollable factors to SME managers but they could pose direct impact on the level of adoption as external forces.

It needs to be noted that findings reported in this chapter should be interpreted with caution due to the limitations of the unique industry selected and the small sample size. However, the findings help raise the question as to whether there exists a general pattern or model of e-business adoption that can fit all SME sectors. It also opens a door for future study to examine if external forces have more influence than internal forces in the SME sector. Aggregated findings on the level of e-business adoption from multiple industry-based studies neglected sector difference, and the results are not consistent to generate a common adoption pattern/model. Therefore, further study of a similar nature in specific industry needs to

Figure 7. An E-Adoption Ladder with influential factors

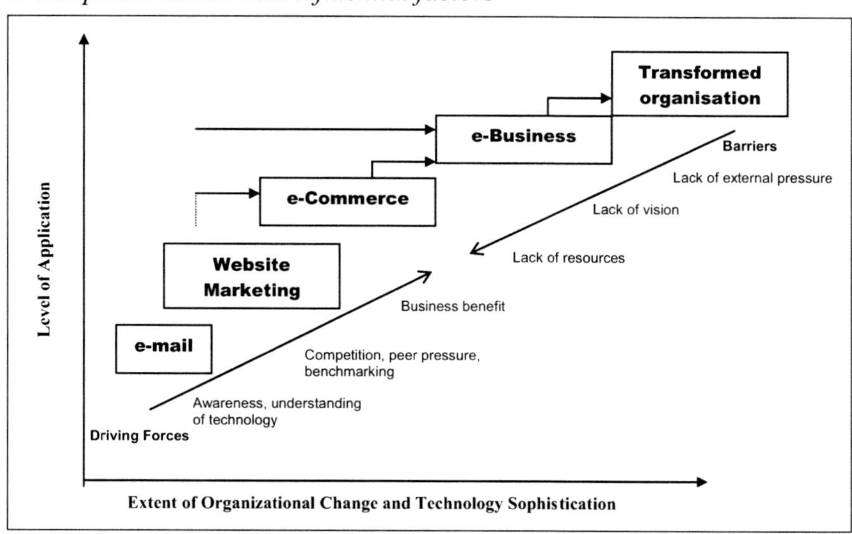

be conducted, so that the unique needs and problems related to that industries/sectors in adopting e-business technology can be appropriately addressed, and the findings generated from different industry/sector can be compared in the context of developing an e-business adoption model.

REFERENCE

Allcock, S. P. A., Webber, S., & Yeates, R. (1999). Business information and the Internet: Use of the Internet as an information resource for SME. *British Library Research and Information Report,* (136).

Barnett, R. R., & Mackness, J. R. (1983). An action research study of small firm management. *Journal of Applied Systems, 10*, 63-83.

Boone, C., De Brabander, B., & Hellemans, J. (2000). Research note: CEO locus of control and small firm performance. *Organization Studies, 21*(3). 641-646.

Carmichael, C., Turgoose, C., Older Gary, M., & Todd, C. (2000). Innovation and SMEs. *Journal of Industry and Higher Education*, 244-248.

Chavez, R., Leiter, M., & Kiely, T. (2000). Should you spin off your Internet business? *Business Strategy Review, 11*(2), 19-31.

Chen, L., Haney, S., Pandzik, A., Spigarelli, J., & Jesseman, C. (2003). Small business Internet commerce: A case study. *Information Resources Management Journal, 16*(3), 17-42.

Chong, S. (2001). *Electronic commerce adoption by small-medium sized enterprises in Australia and Singapore.* Working Paper, School of Information Systems, Curtin University of Technology, Perth, Western Australia.

Cyert, R. M., & March, J. G. (1992). *A behavioural theory of the firm* (2nd ed.). Oxford: Blackwell.

Daniel, E., & Grimshaw, D. J. (2002b). An exploratory comparison of electronic commerce adoption in large and small enterprises. *Journal of Information Technology, 17*(3), 133-147.

Daniel, E., Wilson, H., & Myers, A. (2002a). Adoption of e-commerce by SMEs in the UK. *International Small Business Journal, 20*(3), 253-270.

Dixon, T., Thompson, B., & McAllister, P. (2002). *The value of ICT for SMEs in the UK: A critical review of literature.* Report for the Small Business Service Research Programme.

Drew, S. (2003). Strategic use of e-commerce by SMEs in the East of England. *European Management Journal, 21*(1), 79-88.

DTI. (2001) *Business in the information age—International Benchmarking Study 2000.* (UK Department of Trade and Industry). Retrieved from www.ukonlineforbusiness.gov.uk

Duan, Y. (2004). E-commerce training for SMEs. In M. Khosrow-Pour (Ed.), *Encyclopedia of information science and technology* (pp. 962-965). Hershey, PA: Idea Group Reference.

EBPG. (2002). eEurope go digital: Benchmarking national and regional e-business policies for SMEs. Final report of the EBusiness Policy Group, 28 June 2002.

Fillis, I., Johannson, U., & Wagner, B. (2004). Factors impacting on adoption and development in the smaller firm. *International Journal of Enterpreneurial Behaviour & Research, 10*(3), 178-191.

Gary, C. (2003). *A stage model of ICT adoption in small firms.* Workshop in Rimini—Firms and Consumers Facing E-Commerce: Strategies to Increase Its Adoption and Usage. Open University Business School, UK

Goode, S. (2002). Management attitudes toward the World Wide Web in Australian small business. *Information Systems Management*, 45-48.

Jones, C., Hecker, R., & Holland, P. (2003). Small firm Internet adoption: Opportunities forgone, a journey not begun. *Journal of Small Business and Enterprise Development, 10*(3), 287-297.

Kula, V., & Tatoglu, E. (2003). An exploratory study of Internet adoption by SMEs in an emerging market economy. *European Business Review, 15*(5), 324-333.

Lawrence, K. (2002). Factors inhibiting the collaborative adoption of electronic-commerce among Australia SMEs. In S. Burgess (Ed.), Managing information technology in small business: Challenges & solutions (pp. 178-192). Hershey, PA: Idea Group Publishing.

Lawson, R., Alcock, C., Cooper, J., & Burgess, L. (2003). Factors affecting adoption of electronic commerce technologies by SMEs: An Australian study. *Journal of Small Business and Enterprise Development, 10*(3), 265-276.

Levy, M., & Powell, P. (2002). SME transformation: Modelling progressions. In S. Wrycza (Ed.), *Information systems and the future of the digital economy, Proceedings of the 10th European Conference on Information Systems*, Gdansk, Poland, June 2002.

Levy, M., Powell, P., & Yetton, P. (2002). The dynamics of SME information systems. *Small Business Economics, 19*(4), 341-354.

Liikanen, E. (2001). *eEurope and the role of SMEs.* Paper presented at the European Commission Go Digital Meeting, 6 April.

Lymer, A., Nayak, A., Johnson, R., & Spaul, B. (1998). *UK business and the information superhighway: The impact of the Internet on SMEs.* ACCA Occasional Research Paper, No. 23: The Association of Chartered Certified Accountants.

Martin L. M., & Matlay, H. (2001). Innovative use of the Internet in established small firms: The impact of knowledge management and organisational learning in accessing new opportunities. *Qualitative Market Research: An International Journal, 6*(1), 18-26

Matlay, H., & Addis, M. (2003). Adoption of ICTs and e-commerce in small business: An HEI-based consultancy perspective. *Journal of Small Business and Enterprise Development, 10*(3), 321-335.

Maurer, R. (1996). *Beyond walls of resistance.* Bard Press.

McDonagh, P., & Prothero, A. (2000). Euroclicking and the Irish SME: Prepared for e-commerce and the single currency. *Irish Marketing Review, 13*(1), 21-33

McKay, J., Prananto, A., & Marshall, P. (2000). *E-business maturity: The SOGe model.* Paper presented at the proceedings of the 11th Australasian Conference on Information Systems (ACIS), 6-8 Dec, Queensland University of Technology, Brisbane, Australia.

Mehrtens, J., Cragg, P. B., & Mills, A. M. (2001). A model of Internet adoption by SMEs. *Information & Management, 39*(3), 165-176.

Molla, A., Heeks, R., & Balcells, I. (2006). Adding clicks to bricks: A case study of e-commerce adoption by a Catalan small retailer. *European Journal of Information Systems, 15*(4), 424-438.

Parish, A., Kibblewhite, G., Woodley, M., & Richardson, J. (2002). *The UK electronics industry e-commerce initiative—A study of the adoption of e-commerce.* Retrieved from www.intellectuk.org/publications/reports

Poon, S. (2000). Business environment and Internet commerce benefits—A small business perspective. *European Journal of Information Systems, 9*, 72-81.

Poon, S., & Swatman, P. M. C. (1999). An exploratory study of small business Internet commerce, *Information & Management, 35*(1), 9-18.

Prananto, A., McKay, J. A., & Marshall, P. (2003). A study of the progression of e-business maturity in Australian SMEs: Some evidence of the applicability of the stages of growth for e-business model. *Proceedings of the 7th Pacific Asia Conference on Information Systems (PACIS)*, July 10-13.

Quayle, M. (2003). E-business in a turbulent world: Usage in European small and medium size enterprises. *International Journal of Electronic Business, 1*(1), 41-52.

Ramsey, E., Ibbotson, P., Bell, J., & Gary, B. (2003). E-opportunities of service sector SMEs: An Irish cross-boarder study. *Journal of Small Business and Enterprise Development, 10*(3), 250-264.

Rao, S. S., Metts, G., & Monge, C. A. M. (2003). Electronic development in small- and medium-sized enterprises: A stage model and its implications. *Business Process Management Journal, 9*(1), 11-32.

Schlenker, L. & Crocker, N. (2003). Building an e-business scenario for small business: the IBM SME Gateway project. *Qualitative Market Research: An International Journal, 6*(1), 7-17.

Smyth, M., & Ibbotson, P. G. (2001). *Internet connectivity in Ireland.* Retrieved from www.bankofireland.co.uk

Stockdale, R., & Standing, C. (2004). Benefits and barriers of electronic marketplace participation: An SME perspective. *The Journal of Enterprise Information Management, 17*(4), 301-311.

Stokes, D. (2000). Marketing and the small firm. In Carter, S. & Jones, D. *Enterprise and small business: Principlies, practice and policy.* Pearson Education, Harlow (pp. 354-383).

Stone, M. (2003). SME e-business and supplier-customer relations. Journal *of Small Business and Enterprise Development, 10*(3), 345-353.

Chapter VII
China and India:
E-Business in the Developing World

Peter Raven
Seattle University, USA

Xiaoqing Huang
Guangxi Institute of Supervising and Testing on Product Quality, China

Ben Kim
Seattle University, USA

ABSTRACT

The Internet has changed the way many companies do business, but has also tended to increase the disparity between firms in developed countries and those in developing countries. As the digital divide seems to grow, the question becomes how will developing countries catch up? We examine two large developing countries, China and India, in an attempt to understand their approaches to developing e-business. While both countries had access to the technology at about the same time, each has taken a different path to utilizing it. These approaches are based on a number of factors including government initiatives and focus, infrastructure building, experience and understanding of business operations, and culture, among others. China appears to be ahead of India in the mechanics and infrastructure, but India is ahead in e-readiness. Both countries are poised for rapidly increasing e-business, however, they have huge problems of poverty and inequality between urban and rural connectivity that must be resolved to take advantage of e-business.

INTRODUCTION

The personal computer and the Internet have changed the nature of business worldwide—in both developed and developing countries. People geographically isolated are now able to communicate in real time. But, how has this ability to communicate affected global businesses, especially among developing nations? This is not a trivial question, as the notion of the "digital divide" appears to be expanding, rather than contracting, as businesses in developed countries are increasingly connected, while those in developing countries lag relatively further behind. The promise of the Internet and efficiencies of e-business are not equally distributed.

In this study, we examine the adoption and use of Internet strategies in furthering e-business in two large developing nations—China and India. We will see that each country has chosen a different path to utilizing the Internet in business. This may be instructive for other developing countries as they increasingly adopt the Internet and utilize its efficiencies for business and development.

Industrialized countries adopted the Internet for business purposes at different rates. The U.S., where the Internet first developed, appears to be furthest along in business usage and near the top at a consumer level, although many other countries have significantly increased their use of the Internet (see Table 1). The Internet penetration of China and India is shown in Table 2.

Most U.S. firms have an Internet presence, but not all use the Internet in the same way or to the same extent. Increasingly, U.S. firms feel the need to have a Web presence to reach their customers and to serve them efficiently. Sometimes the result is a full-service, e-business exchange site, but for other firms the result is merely an informational site.

For marketers in developing countries, though, the question may be to what extent can the Internet be used to increase business efficiency as well as in marketing products both locally and globally? Firms from industrialized countries have successfully done this, but there is little information about developing countries using the Internet to do so. This study examines the commercial use of the Internet in China and India in an attempt to understand their approaches to e-business. We examine several key areas we think may explain the adoption of e-business in these developing countries: regulatory issues, infrastructure, policy, and culture.

Table 1. Growth of Internet—World Wide

World Regions	Population (2006 Est.)	Population % of World	Internet Users 2006	% Population (Penetration)	% Growth 2000-2006
Northern America	331,473,276	5.1	232,057,067	70.0	114.7
Oceania	33,956,977	0.5	18,430,359	54.3	141.9
Europe	807,289,020	12.4	312,722,892	38.7	197.6
Latin America & Caribbean	553,908,632	8.5	88,430,359	16.0	391.3
Asia	3,667,774,066	56.4	387,593,457	10.6	239.1
Middle East	190,084,161	2.9	19,382,400	10.2	490.1
Africa	915,210,928	14.1	32,765,700	3.6	625.7
Total World	**6,499,697,060**	**100%**	**1,091,730,861**	**16.8**	**202.4**

Note 1: % Pop. is the Penetration Rate, expressed as population percentage. Note 2: Internet Growth Percent is between December, 2000 and June, 2005 (Stats, 2007)

Table 2. Comparisons of China and India. Sources: iWatch (2005); Strauss, El-Ansary, & Frost (2006); Stats (2007)

Economic or social factor	Unit of measurement	China	India
Electrical Generation Capacity	Megawatts	258,000	89,000
Electricity Generated	Billions of kilowatts	1,166	417
Telephone lines connected	Millions	240	43
Mobile/cellular phones	Millions	400	75
Internet connections	Millions	45	9
GDP	USD – billions	1121	460
Population	Millions	1260	1060
Population Increase per year	Millions	10	19
Birth Rate	Numbers per 1000	8.8	27
Per Capita Income	USD/year/person	1060	480
Internet Users (2006)	Millions	132	40
Internet Penetration (2006)	Percent	10.1	3.6

BACKGROUND AND LITERATURE REVIEW

Both China and India have large, growing populations and are frequently compared to each other because of this fact. However, they also have very different cultures and political traditions that affect the dynamics of a direct comparison. While Internet usage is growing rapidly in both India and China, each country suffers from poverty, illiteracy, and poor information and communication technology (ICT) infrastructure. As these countries approach Internet business strategies differently, can we learn from their experiences? Are the strategies and metrics used in describing China and India of use for other developing countries—or even to developed countries? We anticipate that an understanding of the ways in which the Internet is used in China and India, especially in business-to-business (B2B) transactions, will help firms in both developing and developed countries utilize better Internet strategies to compete globally. Although our focus is on B2B e-business, we will also discuss business-to-consumer (B2C) e-business where it is appropriate. While there are differences between the two in target customers, there are also many similarities and the lines between them are often blurred. Previous work has shown that B2B is primarily driven by global forces in more of a "push" mode, while B2C is more internally driven; "pulled" by consumer markets (Gibbs, Kraemer, & Dedrick, 2003).

Why compare China and India in this study? Both countries are developing rapidly in certain sectors and represent the largest of the emerging markets. China is the largest communist country with a population of 1.3 billion and India is the largest democracy with a population of 1.08 billion (CIA, 2006). Besides their respective sizes, each country has similar problems of disparate ethnicities, languages, and skewed distributions of wealth. Both China and India are developing economies, encountering many of the same problems of transition from traditional to developing to global economy. Both are now members of the global trading community, the World Trade Organization (WTO). They have approached their entry into the WTO, though, in different ways. India, probably because of its British-colonization heritage, has approached the world markets in a more market-driven fashion. China having no such market tradition, is still feeling its way into the world marketplace and seems to perceive a greater need to control the process. These approaches result in different paths to development and to e-business (Kshetri, 2005; Levinson, 2004).

Economic Development

The level of development of a country impacts its ability to trade with other countries, improve its standard of living, and prosper (Economist, 2006; Harrison, 1996). It should be no surprise that countries develop at different rates and in different ways. Each country has a different set of inherent resources—from natural resources to human resources—which have influenced their history, culture, and personality. Until recently, these phenomena, including wars, have had the greatest impacts on rates of development and development typically proceeded at a relatively slow and predICTable pace. The industrialized countries of Europe and North America, for example, took about 200 years to become developed. Today, however, technology, especially the Internet, is seen as helping developing countries "leapfrog" the traditional stages of development (Levinson, 2004). In fact, developing countries are often too impatient to wait for the slow pace of traditional development processes, as they fall further and further behind developed countries.

There are many barriers to Internet and e-business adoption in developing countries. For example, incentives for the integration of the Internet in businesses may be low due to poverty and perceived low demand for goods and services. The infrastructure may be inadequate to sustain growing adoption of Internet business strategies and government policies may not support technology development. There may also be deep cultural problems acting as barriers, such as illiteracy and language issues, credit problems, and a limited tradition of entrepreneurship and innovation (Levinson, 2004).

Development is a complex process. Many developing countries do not have a tradition of a market economy and wrestle with the notion of privatization of public enterprises (Yoder, Borkholder, & Friesen, 1991). While developing countries open to international capital flows are likely to receive advanced technology through foreign investments, policy measures are more likely to be successful if directed towards stimulating the accumulation of location-specific assets, including ICT, rather than investment incentives to foreign investors (Nordas, 2002). Technology transfer is also affected by cultural and political differences (Al-Ghailani & Moor, 1995). Other indicators of a "chicken/egg" dilemma suggest that economic development precedes Internet development, thus contributing to the "digital divide" (Norris, 2000).

Outward-oriented countries are those that look elsewhere for growth. They seem to grow at a more rapid pace than more inward-oriented countries (CIA, 2006; Santos-Paulino, 2005; Young, Huang, & McDermott, 1996). Dollar (1992) cites the recent rapid growth of Asian developing economies compared to those of Africa and Latin America as support for an outward-orientation. An outward-orientation implies that trade liberalization, devaluation of the real exchange rate, and stabilized real exchange rates improve growth in developing countries.

With that, what is the role of technology, and specifically the Internet, in development planning? Akel (2001) suggests a four step process she calls the "Internet advantage," consisting of creating a technology intensive environment, offering services to create a unique community, encouraging a climate of entrepreneurship, and providing appropriate assistance. These steps seem to apply to development within the U.S., but can they also apply to developing countries? We explore the applicability of this process in subsequent sections.

Because of its relative newness and the rapid rate of development of the industry, the theoretical literature on e-business in developing countries is relatively sparse. However, the literature provides a basis for modeling the diffusion of e-business, including some of the barriers facing early adopters (Travica, 2002). Limitations and/or barriers to e-business in developing countries include limited Internet accessibility, lack of competition in international telephone traffic (which increases the cost of a network), lack of intra-regional infrastructure, and disproportionate penetration of the telephone in urban areas. E-business depends on several layers: an infrastructure layer—transportation (roads, air, railroads, etc.); a telecommunications layer (pervasive, modern, secure, and affordable channels); a software industry to support e-business; the opportunity for e-payments; and a cultural layer including a tradition of remote shopping such as catalogs and mail-order, and standardized goods and services assuring consumers of consistent quality, leading to trust.

Development of Technology

Technology predICTably enhances existing inequalities between economies. Scientists rely on information to be current, but much is available electronically today, so even if it is free, scientists in developing countries may not have access to it. Ninety-five percent of all computers are in developed nations. Ten nations, accounting for just 20% of world population, have three-quarters of the world's telephone lines (Arunachalam, 1999; Buinessline, 2004). The unequal availability of information in developing economies may also inhibit business knowledge and decision-making. Developing countries with better access to current information of their own and other markets, such as economic trends, consumer preferences, demand, currency exchange rates, and other business information, should be able to be more successful in business.

A number of factors affect the rates of adoption of technologies including industrial organization, reliance on IT (information technology), local resources, management styles, political influence, regulatory requirements, etc. (Lanjouw & Mody, 1996). For example, stringent environmental requirements have encouraged adoption of pollution control and recycling technologies in Germany and Japan. Policies and economic incentives can retard or accelerate the rates of technology adoption by businesses (Chien & Salem, 2001; Colaco, 2003). In addition, cultural issues such as entrepreneurship and leveraging first mover advantage influence adoption of e-business (Gregorio, Kassicieh, & de Gouvea Neto, 2005).

Managers have control over organizational factors, but little control over broader environmental factors such as increased competition, liberal government policies, and market stability—all of which have a positive impact on IT adoption (Dasgupta, Agarwal, Ionnidis, & Gopalakrishnan, 1999). There is also a strong correlation across countries between GDP/capita and Internet connectivity. While information technology is believed to be a new source for global economic growth (Friedman, 2005), there is also concern that the Internet may be a factor in widening the income differentials between countries. The regulatory environment's influence on competition also has an impact on Internet connectivity (Kiiski & Pohjola, 2002). These issues suggest the extremely complex phenomena of technology adoption and development in developing countries. Without efficient access to the Internet, e-business is likely to be retarded.

With the possible exception of China, India has been affected more by changes in IT than any other developing country, yet it remains very poor. India has lagged far behind many other Asian countries in the adoption of the Internet. In a population of one billion people, there are fewer than two million Internet subscribers, a figure that contrasts with India's closest comparator in size, China, which has more than three times as many telephone lines and four times as many Internet users. However, Internet users in India are estimated to be four times that of subscribers (Miller, 2001).

Former UN Secretary General Kofi Anan has warned of the dangers of excluding the world's poor from the Internet suggesting that being cut off from telecommunications services is a hardship almost as acute as other deprivations such as jobs, shelter, food, health care, and drinkable water. The fact there are absolute inequalities between rich and poor nations in the virtual world is hardly surprising given the substantial disparities in every other dimension of life from health care and nutrition to education and longevity. The more interesting question concerns relative inequality of opportunities. Relative opportunities may lie in equalizing technological resources, such as through distribution of computer hardware, skills training, and network connections (Norris, 2000). Thus, many developing countries see a way out of their never-ending cycle of poverty through technology, especially the Internet.

CHINA'S APPROACH TO E-BUSINESS

In this section, we examine the ways in which China has approached e-business. Chinese universities joined the Internet six years after those in India, but policy makers and politicians soon realized its potential (Press, Foster, Wolcott, & McHenry, 2002). China's leaders saw the impact of the Internet on Western and other Asian economies and understood its importance for China in the future (Hachigian, 2001). Chinese businesses are encouraged to embrace new technologies to be competitive in world markets and to be connected to the information needed through regulation and other initiatives.

China has taken to the Internet rapidly and has become the second largest Internet market in the world with around 8.5% of its population of 1.3 billion now connected. This translates to about 120 million users by the end of 2005 (Communications, 2006). More than half of China's Web users access it through broadband, attracting firms such as Amazon.com, eBay, and Google.

Regulatory Environment

The Chinese government has made a concerted effort to develop the infrastructure necessary to fully utilize the Internet. However, because of the vastness of this country, most infrastructure development has occurred in urban areas. Rural areas are largely untouched by the promise of the Internet and e-business (Chen, 2003). This disparity does not seem to be a big issue to central planners, as their focus is more on consumers than on business (CII, 2000). By the end of June 2006, Internet penetration in urban areas was six times of that in rural areas. PredICTions indicate that this disparity will continue to increase in the near future (CNNIC, 2006).

Government regulations play a much more important role in China than in the U.S. (Xu, Zhu, & Gibbs, 2004). Other facilitators of e-business in China include technology competence, enterprise integration, and competition intensity. In China, firms lag in using e-business related technologies, especially inter-organizational technologies.

Infrastructure

China's development of the Internet was in three phases—(1) First Phase (1987-1993)—when a few scientific research institutions were allowed access, (2) Second Phase (1994 to 2002)—implementation of full services (Lu, Du, Zhang, Feicheng, & Le, 2002). The Third Phase (2002 to the present) is characterized by stepping into the diversity of Internet applications (Qiaoqiao, 2004). By 1999, most government departments were connected and had their own sites. The Chinese government had hoped to have one million enterprises connected by 1999 and double that in the following few years. Five main Internet applications were approved: (1) electronic government; (2) electronic business, including the Golden Bridge, Golden Card, and Golden Gate projects; (3) distance education; (4) distance medical treatment; and (5) digital library. However, problems of slow speeds, high usage costs, poor information quality, ineffective management, incomplete policies, and unbalanced information flow remain.

China has improved its infrastructure and readiness for e-business considerably, but there is much room for further improvement. In order to take full advantage of the Internet in managing the supply chain, fast and accurate information is needed, along with the ability to adjust inventory, production, and transportation systems and react quickly to market changes (Daly & Cui, 2003).

Between 1999 and 2002, China added 106 million landlines, 163 million cell phone subscribers, and 36 million new cable television subscribers—considerably more than other country (WEF, 2004). Currently, China is adding four million mobile subscribers a month and has the world's largest broadband Internet market with almost 25 million users, growing at more than a million per month (Economist, 2005). Clearly, China is building an infrastructure to sustain future growth.

Policy

For reasons of national pride and prestige in the world community, China seems to focus on increasing the number of people using the Internet. This strategy has long-term implications for development. In what might be called a pull strategy, by emphasizing the consumer use of the Internet, China may be hoping that demand will eventually be filled by local businesses meeting the needs of local Internet consumers. Indeed, PC penetration has had rapid growth—from only 1600 in 1994, 80,000 in 1996, to 22.5 million in 2000. However, still only a small portion of the total population (<4%) has a PC (Sina, 2006), but the number is now up to 130 million online (Eschenbacher, 2006). In the new development stage, China continually focuses on improving its infrastructure to increase Internet penetration and to improve e-business (Yaoping, 2005).

Culture

Culture plays a significant role in adoption of technology and use of the Internet (Bagchi, Hart, & Peterson, 2004; Levinson, 2004). For example, the technology adoption model (TAM) helps explain IT adoption by suggesting that perceived ease of use and perceived usefulness of technology influence attitudes toward technology. Attitude toward technology in turn influences intentions and then behaviors, including adoption. The TAM has demonstrated its usefulness in several cultures, but notably not in Japan. An explanation for the differences in technology adoption is in cultural values (Bagchi et al., 2004). Japanese tend to rank lower than many other cultures on individualism and higher on collectivism and power distance, the opposite of cultural values necessary for positive attitudes toward technology adoption. Culture, of course, does not act alone in technology adoption, as suggested by the technology transfer literature, which also indicates a role for income per capita, human capital, openness, type of government, and others (Bagchi et al., 2004).

The technology adoption model (extended version) has been tested in several industries in China, where it was supported (Di Benedetto, Calantone, & Zhang, 2003). In addition, the authors suggest that cultural factors such as cosmopolitanism and mobility may lead to diffusion patterns across countries.

Other Chinese cultural characteristics that influence technology adoption include a preference not to be in debt, a desire to touch and feel articles before buying them, a fear of a disappointing shopping experience, security issues with providing credit or debit card numbers to strangers, and the perils of an ineffective distribution system where purchased items may be lost or delayed in transit. Chesse (2001) also depICTs the reliability and efficiency of distribution systems in China to be an issue in e-business acceptance. In addition, transparency is not universal among Chinese firms and many companies are reluctant to share operational and financial details, which could reduce the effectiveness of B2B e-business.

Interpersonal relationships in doing business are important to the Chinese. Chinese tend to prefer face to face business negotiations and rely on long-term trust and family relationships in doing business (University, 2004). These cultural business characteristics may be difficult to facilitate through the Internet and may make Chinese business leaders more reluctant to accept e-business.

There is also a language barrier for Chinese Internet users (University, 2004). Although Chinese language Web sites are increasing, most business sites are still in English, or other Western languages. To compensate, Chinese students are learning English and other Western languages in schools. In comparison to India, this may be facilitated by the considerably higher literacy rates in China—90.9% compared to 59.5% in India (CIA, 2006).

The literature suggests that technology could be at odds with traditional cultures—that "Western" technologies may negatively influence "non-Western" cultures (Shoib & Nandhakumar, 2003). While this may have some merit, the reverse could also be true—that "non-Western" cultures may use "Western" technology in different ways that are innovative and mesh better with their non-Western cultures. For example, collaborative Internet programs have been used by Navajo tribal elders in traditional consensus decision-making (Keating et al., 2001).

China's one-child policy may have influenced technology adoption in unanticipated ways. A focus on education and getting into the right schools has left little time to cultivate friendships, except through instant messaging and online games (Eschenbacher, 2006). More than 130 million online PCs and 300 million mobile phones attest to the extent of this growing digital culture, which has liberated Chinese youth.

The Internet has facilitated innovativeness and entrepreneurship in the developed countries which adopted it early on. While China is not well known for producing entrepreneurs, adoption of the Internet in China is helping to develop a number of entrepreneurs who do not rely on official connections or government sinecures. These new Net entrepreneurs are becoming role models for a future generation of Chinese business owners (McCarthy, 2000). However, competition among Chinese B2B enterprises is still in its early stages, limited by a lack of trust in partners and a reluctance to share information (University, 2004).

Taken together, these factors of e-business adoption suggest that China is progressing rapidly toward integrated e-business, but still has a long way to go to reach the level of many developed countries.

E-Business

It is difficult to determine the exact nature and extent of e-business in China, as data varies widely by source, if it is even available. It does appear that B2B online transactions far surpass B2C, with one estimate suggesting 75% are B2B (E-commerce, 2005a). Estimates suggest that about 18% of surfers in China buy online. Internet use has been especially rapid in online financial services. At the same time, broadband usage is growing at a rate of about 75%, putting it on track to exceed the U.S. rate by a large margin (Morris, 2006).

China's potential for e-business is huge. With more than 130 million currently online and that number expected to pass that of the U.S. in a few years, e-business can only grow (Panlogic, 2006). In addition, the user profile lends itself to online buying—90% of users are under 40 and 2/3 of users are expected to buy online. However, e-business will be held back by low credit card usage and intellectual property issues. Most Web sites in China still do not support transactions.

China's infrastructure, especially transportation, is inadequate to support sustainable e-business, especially in rural areas (Country Profile, 2006). However, a great deal of money is being pored into transportation to upgrade the systems. The railway system carries more than a third of all cargo and passengers and is expanding with new track linking key areas. Port facilities have also improved to where the 200 seaports handled 25 billion metric tons in 2005. The telecommunications infrastructure is a bright spot. China now has more cable television subscribers and mobile phone customers than does the U.S.

The value of e-business in China is difficult to discern as estimates vary greatly. One Chinese language report (CCID, 2005) indicates that the B2B market grew from 107.5 billion Yuan ($12.97 billion) in 2001 to 178.4 billion Yuan ($21.528 billion) in 2002 and to 346.4 billion Yuan ($41.803 billion) in 2003. The B2C market grew from 790 million Yuan ($95.33 million) in 2003 to 1.6 billion Yuan ($193.08 million) in 2004. Another estimate for general e-commerce revenue suggests it is expected to reach USD 16 billion in 2006 (E-commerce, 2005a). In any case, the various state and local governments continue to influence e-business, with Beijing, for example, wanting 80% of department stores in the capital to offer online shopping in 2005.

Western firms continue to have difficulties in doing e-business in China, however. EBay recently shut down its China site and has, instead, replaced it with a joint venture run by a Chinese company (Hopkins, 2006). EBay apparently found that its highly successful business model did not work quite as well in China, where Chinese firms are able to satisfy consumer tastes and preferences better.

There are also Web design issues that make direct transfer of business models difficult in China (Koziol, 2006). China's Web sites tend to be much richer than the clean lines used in Western e-mail and Web site designs. Chinese Web sites and e-mail tend to incorporate many messages and graphics, whereas Western users tend to prefer simpler and clearer messages. Chinese sites may look cluttered and busy to the Western eye.

Several high profile cases have dealt with China's censorship of the Web. MacMillan (2006), for example, recently describes a protest by Reporters Without Borders to curb censorship. Although by no means the only country restrICTing the Internet, China is as a pioneer in Internet censorship, devoting more resources than any other country to restrICT online freedoms.

INDIA'S APPROACH TO E-BUSINESS

The Indian economy has been growing between 6.0 and 6.5% annually (James, 2002).

In a country well known for its role in outsourcing of IT and offshore call centers for industrialized countries, it is perhaps surprising that India has not progressed further in Internet penetration and e-business. Despite a large number of high-tech employees, only about 0.4% of the population was connected to the Internet in 2000 (Kiggen, 2001). However, current information suggests a combination of low broadband costs and inexpensive computers has increased Internet connectivity in India to about 38.5 million in 2005—and that is expected to increase to 100 million in 2007 (eMarketer, 2006). It is also interesting to note that the proportion of women Internet users will increase to about 40% of the user population.

Like China, India is a large and heterogeneous country with many dialects and cultures. It is still expensive to get online and the quality of the infrastructure needs improving, but India is moving rapidly towards greater Internet penetration.

One advantage India may have over China is widespread fluency in English, arguably the business language of the Internet. This is especially true in urban areas, where Internet connectivity is likely to be highest. Several other issues that influence Internet use in India follow.

Regulatory Environment

The Indian government has strongly encouraged the development of the Internet and information technology through various incentives, including exempting the industry from burdensome regulations and controls (Miller, 2001). The government has followed up its encouragement by allocating 2-3% of its budget for IT and encouraging innovative uses of the Internet, such as using solar power and locating cyber-cafes near railway stations (Rao, 2002a). Unfortunately, while Internet backbone costs have dropped, last mile costs are still high in India. In addition to more traditional uses, India anticipates that the Internet will empower poor, rural villagers to improve their lives (Quibria, Tschang, & Reyes-Macasaquit, 2002).

Infrastructure

The IDC expects India's ISP (Internet service provider) sector to grow by 27% in coming years and to reach 8.2 million subscribers by 2005 (Corp., 2003). As personal computer (PC) prices fall, increasing PC penetration will lead to greater Internet penetration. The IT sector, in fact, seems to be propelling the Indian economy forward. The Indian Government, through the Ministry of Information and Communication Technology is developing infrastructure to support IT (Colaco, 2003), but there is considerable variation between states (Press et al., 2002). However, between 1999 and 2002, India added only 15 million land-lines, while China added 106 million (WEF, 2004). In the race between India and China in infrastructure development, India is coming in at a distant second. India is adding mobile subscribers at one quarter the rate of China (one million/month) and has only 3 million broadband accounts to China's 25 million (Economist, 2005).

Indeed, the outsourcing of IT from western countries has stretched the infrastructure in many cities to its breaking point; resulting in power outages, increasing costs, and a shortage of qualified graduates, in what some refer to as the Bangalore Effect (Aspden, 2006).

Policy

Like China, India has a large rural population, much of which is not connected to the Internet. However, India has developed several initiatives to help connect rural villages (Rao, 2002c). The Indian model uses unique combinations of low-cost indigenous technology with low-cost delivery that utilizes the ability of the informal sector to respond and adapt to local needs (James, 2003). Examples of "pro-poor innovations" include small-scale rural telephone exchanges and very low cost computers that are accessible to poor, often illiterate users. The results suggest that sustainable Internet models for developing economies may look quite different from those in industrial countries.

As early as 1998, Prime Minister Vajpayee proclaimed that "IT is India's tomorrow," implying that the Internet is a key to this vision as an enabler of technology-based change (Wolcott & Goodman, 2003). Although the Indian government is still overly bureaucratic, its attitude toward regulation is beginning to change. Foreign investment in India has increased dramatically and the government has raised the levels of permitted foreign direct investment (FDI) in the oil and private banking industries (Walsh, 2004).

India provides an example of how fundamental, focused changes in policy and legislation can set free forces that accelerate Internet diffusion. While private sector initiatives expanded the Internet infrastructure and Internet services markets, government initiatives promoted the expansion of the Internet into parts of the country not well served by private ISPs (Wolcott et al., 2003).

Prakash (2005) considers the importance of ICT (Information and Communications Technology) in "leapfrogging" India into the knowledge era. Not everyone agrees, however, with the Indian Government's focus on ICT. Rather than acting to leapfrog India into the forefront of the global knowledge community; Mir & Mir (2005) suggest its role should be more of "catalysis." As such, ICT works better when integrated into existing institutional programs of growth and welfare. Catalysts have more of an accelerating or facilitating role, rather than a transforming one, and work upon activities already taking place.

Culture

As with China, the societal culture, as well as the organizational culture, influences the adoption rate of IT in India (Dasgupta et al., 1999). Poverty levels are high in India, but some of the best run software firms also exist there (Cheung, 2001a). Only a fraction of the population can be considered a target for Internet use, but that part is well-educated, media-savvy, and an early adopter of new technology. Indian users tend to be young, male, and members of the middle class and above. Indian users prefer e-mail and Web surfing, rather than online shopping. Their reluctance to use credit cards also reduces the rate of growth of B2C activities (Cheung, 2001b).

India has a relatively high capacity for entrepreneurship, especially necessity-based, rather than opportunity-based entrepreneurship (Rao, 2002b). Young, moderately educated and well-off men are more likely to be entrepreneurs, as social rigidities still reduce the chances for women. However, changes are occurring. Poverty stricken rural areas are being targeted in India for IT development (Rao, 2002c). Some of these initiatives encourage women entrepreneurs to develop Web based businesses. For example, an Indian Institute of Technology project put women in charge of running 80% of the fast-growing number of Internet cafes and kiosks in Madras (News, 2004).

Most IT commercial initiatives are focused on products for global markets, but there are also "pro-poor" initiatives that have been generated by Indian IT institutions in an attempt to narrow the digital divide (James, 2003). Some of these have included small-scale rural telephone exchanges and ultra-low cost computers to provide the rural poor with access to the Internet. For example, less than 1% of the Indian population has access to a computer and more than 40% are illiterate, but a government initiative has developed the SIMPUTER, an inexpensive, portable, battery-operated, hand held computer. The SIMPUTER has text to speech capabilities and voice mail, but no keyboard. It can break written words into sounds in English, Tamil, Hindi, and Kannada (Meall, 2002). One interesting application has been in the Bay of Bengal, where fishing villages now have access to U.S. Navy weather forecasts, helping to keep fishermen safe, as well as showing locations of fish and current market prices.

Other direct impacts of ICT on development in India include providing market and other information, acting as electronic marketplaces in poor communities, farm cooperative information, farm management tasks, and other applications in education, healthcare, and governance (Quibria et al., 2002).

Traditional farmers in remote Indian villages are now conducting e-business through ITC, one of India's largest agribusiness companies, which has created the e-choupal concept (Sawhney, 2002). Using ITC computers charged by solar panels and backed by batteries, e-choupals are like an integration of Internet kiosk, village gathering place, and e-business hub. Since their launch in June 2000, e-choupal services have reached 600,000 farmers in 6000 villages. Farmers gain by lower transaction costs and better prices and ITC benefits from better quality produce, higher prices in the international marketplace, and savings on procurement.

E-Business

Such data as exists indicates that e-business is limited in India, although it appears ready for rapid growth in the near future. Online consumer purchases were about USD 130 million in 2004/5 and are expected to increase to USD 550 million by 2006/7 (E-commerce, 2005b). Low PC and Internet penetration, security issues, among others, are holding back e-business in India. E-mail is used by 98% of Internet users in India, while banking is used by 32%, online bill payment by 18%, and stock trading by 15% (eMarketer, 2006). Both urban and rural banking customers are now increasingly demanding the convenience that online banking offers (Kannabiran & Narayan, 2005). This data suggests a slow, but steady increase in e-business.

DISCUSSION

While Internet usage is growing rapidly in both India and China, both countries suffer from poverty, illiteracy, and poor ICT infrastructure. Technology transfer is affected by cultural and political differences. Thus, we should see a difference in rate of technology adoption and direction of economic growth between China and India.

A number of observers see technology as enabling developing countries to "leapfrog" the development process (Miller, 2001). While technology can be an enabler, the development process is much more complex than technology alone can rectify (Quibria et al., 2002). Government policies and regulations must not restrICT businesses excessively. Infrastructure development and educational levels need to increase to allow e-business to occur. Economic growth will rely on complex interactions between private firms, the public and private sectors, and within and between governments. Foreign Direct Investments (FDI) and exports are seen as key to continued growth of the China economy (Yao, 2006). However, IT is also expected to have an important role in the continued development of China (Lemon, 2005).

China appears to have several advantages over India in the race to economic development through ITC (Thiagarajan, 2002).

- The general infrastructure is superior to that of India, both in fixed-line subscribers and Internet penetration. China has invested about ten times as much in telecommunications as India and is spending about three times more than India on telecommunications, as a percentage of GDP.
- China attracts more foreign direct investment (FDI)—many times that of India. Much of this investment is going into the China IT industry, creating significant opportunities for employment.
- China policies allow for rapid clearances and approvals for technology businesses, especially those located in five economic zones and technology parks.
- China has a stronger domestic sector than does India, allowing it to absorb production that may not be exported.

In addition, the centrally-planned policies of China have focused on developing infrastructure nation-wide and especially in rural markets, and are quite dispersed. On the other hand, India's market–oriented policies are not focused on the broad access to broadband, but rather on serving relatively few outsourcing companies serving the global community (Economist, 2005).

Yet, a number of obstacles stand in the way of adopting e-business. Wang (2002) lists ten obstacles he thinks are most important. Among them are three critical issues for China that differ from obstacles in India: computer and English illiteracy among elderly business decision-makers; insufficient technical and legal protection; and incomplete understanding of the real sense of e-business.

Computer and English literacy are lower in China than in India. Colonization by the British in India required English as the *lingua franca* used for business and government communications. There has been no such systematic use of English in China. Computer literacy is probably also higher in India because of the huge software outsourcing business. Technical and legal protection in China is lacking. The legal system in India tries to protect intellectual property rights. Finally, an understanding of e-business has come late to China (Wang, 2002). E-business is not merely the use of e-mail and Web sites—it includes all the business processes that can be made more efficient through the Internet. India has substantial experience with software outsourcing to aid in their use of supply chain management, including the ordering, producing, marketing, paying, and delivering processes.

E-payment has been an obstacle to e-business in China, although Alibaba and its subsidiary auction site, Taobao, plan to use Taobao's online payment tool, AliPay, for Alibaba's B2B e-business site (Agency, 2005).

Also, China still has control issues, which it attempts to address by prohibition of certain activities. China is thought to have the most sophisticated Internet filtering regime in the world and uses it in various ways to prevent citizen access to political, religious, and other sensitive information (Bambauer et al., 2005). A recent example is the registering of bloggers and enlisting ISPs to help prohibit content that refers to democracy or political change (Chan, 2005). Even more recently, a controversy about Google, Yahoo!, and Microsoft's presence in China brings to light the issues of censorship, free markets, and Internet control (Elgin, 2006).

On the other hand, India has some advantages over China (Thiagarajan, 2002).

- India has a greater fluency in English, the language of the Web. This, and the training of a large number of skilled technology workers, has enabled India to capitalize on its offshore outsourcing initiatives. China will have a difficult time in catching up on outsourcing.
- The Indian government has also favored the software industry and encouraged it through tax incentives.
- India probably has the highest number of SEI-CMM (Software Engineering Institute—Capability Maturity Model) Level 5 engineers in the world. The combination of this certification of quality and good management systems and processes has allowed Indian software suppliers to perform projects with great efficiency.

The rapid growth of Indian software and outsourced IT services has been a catalyst for continuing technology-based change and integration into the global economy (Sarkar & El Sawy, 2003). It has not hurt, either, that this growth is primarily outward focused on providing the large economies of North America and Western Europe with software and back office services. China, on the other hand, has focused more on internal e-business and the production of electronic products (Xu et al., 2004).

The Indian experience of integration of the Internet into business is an example of how fundamental, focused changes in governmental policy and regulations can accelerate Internet diffusion. While private sector initiatives expanded the infrastructure for the Internet, governmental initiatives promoted Internet expansion to parts of the country poorly served by ISPs (Wolcott et al., 2003). Like China, India still has problems of poverty and unequal distribution of wealth, as well as infrastructure problems to overcome.

China has promoted a strategy of competition among government-owned organizations, while India has set policy through publicly visible task forces. India's approach is relatively more transparent and market driven than China's (Press et al., 2002). It is unclear at this stage which approach will yield faster economic growth in e-business, although China seems to have the advantage currently.

By many measures, China is ahead of India in the ITC race and is likely to remain so at least in the near future (see Table 3). However, we see India as progressing rapidly in adoption of ITC especially in business applications. In fact, the Economist Intelligence Unit (EIU, 2006), in its 2006 e-readiness rankings, lists India at 53 out of 60 countries measured and China at 57 (Table 3). The e-readiness rankings are based on a number of items comprising six weighted categories: connectivity and technology infrastructure—25%; business environment—20%; consumer and business adoption—20%; legal and policy environment—15%; social and cultural environment—15%; and supporting e-services—5%.

Both countries dropped in ranking somewhat from the previous year. China's consumer and business adoption, legal and policy, social and cultural environments, and supporting e-services indices are lower than India's. China's lower level of entrepreneurial initiatives is also reflected in the rankings. China does do slightly better in connectivity and technology infrastructure and business environment. The drop from the previous year, and growth in the top ranked countries, should be of concern to both countries, though. The e-business rankings are interesting because they suggest that to succeed in e-business, a number of business and cultural factors must be in place, not just technological factors. Also, the rankings suggest that although e-business is growing rapidly in both countries, it is not yet large enough to transform large parts of their economies. However, both countries continue to attract foreign direct investment in technology.

The e-readiness rankings and other sources suggest that adoption of Internet and e-business technologies does not automatically result in increased e-business. Like other businesses, e-business requires good management, finance, marketing, and other business processes (Oyclaran-Oyeyinka & Lal, 2004). In order for any business, but especially e-business to succeed in international markets, understanding these markets and their consumers, whether other businesses or final consumers, is critical. Export promotion councils set up by industry and government can help entrepreneurial e-businesses in both India and China market to appropriate markets. Governments and industry should not neglect this critical element.

Table 3. E-Business Readiness Rankings and Scores—2004 - 2006. Source: EIU (2006)

	2006		2005		2004	
	Rank	Score (of 10)	Rank	Score (of 10)	Rank	Score (of 10)
Denmark	1	9.00	1	8.74	1	8.28
India	53	4.25	49	4.17	46	4.45
China	57	4.02	54	3.85	52	3.96

CONCLUSION AND RECOMMENDATION

A number of studies have confirmed that China is generally ahead of India in Internet infrastructure development and e-business (Press, Foster, & Goodman, 1999; Press et al., 2002), but others see it differently. Kshetri (2005), for example, argues that because India has a higher e-readiness rank (Table 3), it is actually better prepared for e-business than is China. The e-readiness rankings consider a number of factors and India has better "legal support for virtual transactions and digital signatures, well-developed private sector and entrepreneurship, the regulatory environment including taxation, and openness to trade and investment" (p. 11), among others. Improving IP protection and more consistent application of the rule of law will help China achieve greater development through the Internet and e-business. It is interesting that both China and India dropped in e-readiness rankings, although both indices were higher in 2006. This has been true of most Asian-Pacific countries, except for Japan and South Korea, which remain unchanged. *Business India Intelligence* (2006) suggests this is due to the comparatively larger growth in other countries. Europe and North America, for example, are catching up to Northeast Asia's broadband density. One area of real concern for developed nations is the number of technically trained people entering the workforce. India and China are graduating 125,000 computer science graduates every year, more than twice that of the EU (Hewitt, 2005).

While the adoption of technology to enable e-business in China is occurring rapidly, conducting e-business transactions is lagging, due to barriers

Table 4. Summary of E-business Differences between China and India (data from various sources indicated in text + or _ indicates the degree of difference).

Factor	China	India	Advantage
Regulatory Environment	+ focus on consumers	+ focus on business, but primarily offshoring	China
Infrastructure	+++ broadband high penetration +++ mobile	+ broadband - mobile	China
Policy	++ central policy is very focused on growth throughout China	+ less planning for growth – mostly focused on key offshoring centers	China
Culture	+ literacy >90% - English & computer (low literacy levels) - entrepreneurship - Poverty	- literacy < 60% + English and computer (higher literacy levels) ++ entrepreneurship - Poverty	India
Internet Users (2004)	95.8 million (2005 est. 100 million)	18.481 million	China
Internet Penetration (2004)	7.48%	3.77%	China
E-readiness	54	49	India
Current e-business * (2004/5)	$41.99 billion (Chinese source)	$150 million	China
Expected e-business * (2006/7)	$16 billion (non-Chinese source)	$550 million	China

** As indicated in the text, estimates vary depending on source. These are reported values for both B2B and B2C. B2B is the largest portion in both China and India.*

in business, legal, and cultural perspectives that fail to adapt to the potential of the technology (Tan & Ouyang, 2004). The major differences between e-business in China and India are summarized in Table 4. While India will probably not overtake China in the ITC race anytime soon, we do see India attempting to uplift its poor rural areas through technology and also penetrate large foreign markets. Of course, there is a long way to go and as urban areas in both countries advance, the distances between urban and rural, as far as technology and development go, continue to widen. This disparity between urban and rural connectivity may have long range internal implications for both countries.

What should other countries, developing and developed, learn from the technology experiences of China and India? Can their experiences be a guide for development and utilization of the Internet and e-business? The answer is yes, with the caveat that what has worked for both countries will likely need localization and modification to work well in individual countries. With that caveat, we offer the following observations and suggestions:

- The Internet is a compelling communications system that, properly used, can inform and educate people in ways that have not been possible before. While urban areas benefit initially, rural areas can also benefit if the proper infrastructure is built.
- The Internet can change business models through e-business. E-business has the potential of unleashing innovative and entrepreneurial ways of thinking and doing business that will aid in economic development.
- Landline-based Internet models are rapidly being overtaken by mobile Internet connections in developing countries. Mobile technology has the potential of allowing even more users access to the potential of the Internet and e-business.
- Developing countries can take advantage of the experiences of both developed countries and other developing countries as models for their own growth.
- Governmental policy is an influential driver of Internet usage and e-business. Countries with a focused policy of infrastructure development (e.g., China) will likely outpace those with confused and unfocused policies (e.g., India).
- Intellectual property protection and the rule of law must be enforced for sustained development, but has apparently not been critical in development during the initial stages (e.g., China).

REFERENCES

Agency, X. N. (2005). Competition on China's e-commerce market intensifies. *Business CustomWire*.

Akel, M. (2001). The Internet advantage: A process for integrating electronic commerce into economic development strategy. *Economic Development Review, 17*(3), 13-19.

Al-Ghailani, H. H., & Moor, W. C. (1995). Technology transfer to developing countries. *International Journal of Technology Management, 10*(7, 8), 687-703.

Arunachalam, S. (1999). Information technology: What does it mean for scientists and scholars in the developing world? *American Society for Information Science, 25*(4), 21-24.

Aspden, R. (2006). The Bangalore Effect. *New Statesman, 135*(4777), 26-27.

Bagchi, K., Hart, P., & Peterson, M. (2004). National culture and information technology product adoption. *Journal of Global Information Technology Management, 7*(4).

Bambauer, D., Diebert, R. J., Palfrey, J. G., Jr., Rohoziniski, R., Villeneuve, N., & Zittrain, J. (2005). Internet filtering in China 2004-2005: A country study. *Berkman Center for Internet & Society at Harvard Law School, Research Publication No. 2005-10.*

Buinessline. (2004). Tele-density, Net connectivity low: Policy thrust on spectrum, broadband must. *Businessline Chennai*, 1.

CCID. (2005). Report on the Status of EC in the World—April 2004. *Chinese Center for Information Industry.*

Chan, K. (2005). China tightens censorship of foreign broadcasters. *The Christian Post.*

Chen, X. (2003). *Comparison of Internet development between China and Korea.* Retrieved from http://news.cinhuanet.com/newsmedia/2003-02/09/content_720249.htm

Chesse, J. P. (2001). Distribution: It's more than moving the goods.

Cheung, E. (2001a, January 4). *Profiling Indian Internet users: Part 1.* eMarketer. Retrieved from www.mail-archive.com/gkd@phoenix.edc.org/msg00368.html

Cheung, E. (2001b). *Profiling Indian Internet users: Part 2.* Retrieved August 21, 2004, from www.mail-archive.com/gkd@phoenix.edc.org/msg00368.html

Chien, A., & Salem, E. (2001, Nov 5). *Building an e-business strategy for Mainland China.* Retrieved May 29, 2004, from http:// www.cio.com/research/ec/edit/110501_China.html

CIA. (2006). *World Fact Book.* Retrieved from https://www.cia.gov/cia/publications/factbook/geos/ch.html

CII. (2000). CHINA E-Commerce Index Report. Retrieved May 29, 2004, from http://tech.sina.com.cn/Internet/China/2000-08-08/33014.shtml

CNNIC. (2006, July). *185th Statistical Survey Report on the Internet Development in China.* China Internet Network Information Center Retrieved January 21, 2007, from http://www.cnnic.net.cn/en/index/0O/02/index.htm

Colaco, S. (2003). *Internet potential in India.* Retrieved August 21, 2004, from http://www.stylusinc.com/Internet_potential_India.htm

Communications, M. (2006). China's Web users increase 18% in 2005. *Telcomworldwide*, 1.

Corp., I. D. (2003). India's Internet subscriber base to grow 27%. *World IT Report*, N.

Country Profile, C. (2006). Transport, communications, and the Internet. *Economist Intelligence Unit*, 26-29.

Daly, S. P., & Cui, L. X. (2003). E-logistics in China: Basic problems, manageable concerns, and intractable solutions. *Industrial Marketing Management, 32*, 235-242.

Dasgupta, S., Agarwal, D., Ionnidis, A., & Gopalakrishnan, S. (1999). Determinants of information technology adoption: An extension of existing models to firms in a developing country. *Journal of Global Information Management, 7*(3), 30-40.

Di Benedetto, C. A., Calantone, R. J., & Zhang, C. (2003). International technology transfer. *International Marketing Review, 20*(4), 446-462.

Dollar, D. (1992). Outward-oriented developing economies really do grow more rapidly: Evidence from 95 LDCs, 1976-1985. *Economic Development and Cultural Change, 40*(3), 523-544.

E-commerce. (2005a). Country commerce: China. In *Country Commerce 2005* (pp. 123-134).

E-commerce. (2005b). Country commerce: India. In *Country Commerce 2005* (pp. 93-99): Economist Intelligence Unit Limited.

Economist. (2005). India vs. China. *Business China*, 4-5.

Economist. (2006). Exporting success. *Economist, 378*(8463), 69.

EIU. (2006). The 2006 e-readiness rankings. *The Economist Intelligence Unit*, 1-27. Retrieved December 30, 2006, from http://a330.g.akamai.net/7/330/2540/20060424215053/graphics.eiu.com/files/ad_pdfs/2006Ereadiness_Ranking_WP.pdf

Elgin, B. (2006, February 15). The Web and China: Not so simple. *Business Week Online*.

eMarketer. (2006). Indian Internet users to reach 100 million. *eMarketer.com*.

Eschenbacher, D. (2006). Insider's view China. *Campaign*, (32), 15.

Friedman, T. L. (2005). The world is flat: A brief history of the twenty-first century. In. New York: Farrar, Strauss and Giroux.

Gibbs, J., Kraemer, K. L., & Dedrick, J. (2003). Environment and policy factors shaping global e-commerce diffusion: A cross-country comparison. *Information Society, 19*(1), 5-20.

Gregorio, D. D., Kassicieh, S. K., & de Gouvea Neto, R. (2005). Drivers of k-business activity in developed and emerging markets. *IEEE Transactions on Engineering Management, 52*(2), 155-166.

Hachigian, N. (2001). China's cyber strategy. *Foreign Affairs*, 118-133.

Harrison, A. (1996). Openness and growth: A time-series, cross-country analysis for developing countries. *Journal of Development Economics, 48*(2), 419-447.

Hewitt, P. (2005). Taking the lead in global digital excellence. *Computer Weekly, 16*.

Hopkins, J. (2006, December 20). EBay shuts down China site, teams with Beijing partner. *USA Today*, p. 03b.

Intelligence, B. I. (2006). Up and down the ladder. *Business India Intelligence, 13*(9), 3-4.

iWatch. (2005). Wake up call for India.

James, D. (2002). Dark clouds should part for international market. *Marketing News, 36*(1), 9, 13.

James, J. (2003). Sustainable Internet access for the rural poor? Elements of an emerging Indian model. *Futures, 35*, 461-472.

Kannabiran, G., & Narayan, P. C. (2005). Deploying Internet banking and e-commerce—Case study of a private-sector bank in India. *Information Technology for Development, 11*(4), 363-379.

Keating, G., Ramussen, S., Raven, M., Tso, E., Cocq, J., & Dotson, P. (2001). *Use of Web-based consensus building and conflICT clarification process for the Navajo Nation governmental efficiency evaluation*. Unpublished manuscript.

Kiggen, E. (2001, January 8). *Study: High-tech scores low in India*. Retrieved February 2, 2002, from www.newsfactor.com/

Kiiski, S., & Pohjola, M. (2002). Cross-country diffusion of the Internet. *Information Economics and Policy, 14*(2), 297-310.

Koziol, M. (2006). Advice for e-mail marketing to China. *B to B, 91*(15), 19.

Kshetri, N. (2005). What determines Internet Diffusion Loci in developing countries: Evidence from China and India. *Pacific Telecommunications Review, 23*(3), 25-34.

Lanjouw, J. O., & Mody, A. (1996). Innovation and the international diffusion of environmentally responsive technology. *Research Policy, 25*(4), 549-571.

Lemon, S. (2005). Chinese official calls for expanding IT use. *Computerworld, 39*(47), 12.

Levinson, N. S. (2004). Developing nations. In H. Bidgoli (Ed.), *The Internet Encyclopedia* (Vol. 1, pp. 434-443). Hoboken, NJ: John Wiley & Sons.

Lu, W., Du, J., Zhang, J., Feicheng, M., & Le, T. (2002). Internet development in China. *Journal of Information Science, 28*(3), 207-223.

MacMillan, D. (2006). Nations that censor the net. *Business Week Online*, p. 8.

McCarthy, T. (2000). China's Internet gold rush. *Time, 155*(8), 50-51.

Meall, L. (2002). Eastern promise. *Accountancy*, 60-61.

Miller, R. R. (2001). Leapfrogging? India's information technology industry and the Internet. Retrieved May 10, 2002, from http://www.ifc.org/economics/pubs/dp42/dp42.pdf

Mir, R., & Mir, A. (2005). Catalysis, not leapfrog: An institutionalist argument for a limited role of ICTs in India's Development. *Asian Business & Management, 4*(4), 411-429.

Morris, I. (2006). China's broadband boom. *Telecommunications—International Edition, 40*(11), 16-18.

News, B. (2004, July 7). *Women lead rural India's Internet rush.* BBC News Retrieved August 21, 2004, from http://newsvote.bbc.co.uk/mpapps/pagetools/print/news.bbc.co.uk/2/hi/south_asia/3871529.stm

Nordas, H. K. (2002). Patterns of foreign direct investment in poor countries. *Journal of International Trade & Economic Development, 11*(3), 247-266.

Norris, P. (2000, Aug 1-6). *The global divide: Information poverty and Internet access worldwide.* Paper presented at the International Political Science World Congress, Quebec City.

Oyclaran-Oyeyinka, B., & Lal, K. (2004). Determinants of e-business adoption: Evidence from firms in India, Nigeria, Uganda. *INTECH Discussion Paper Series* (2004-14).

Panlogic. (2006). *Connecting with China.* Panlogic.

Prakash, G. (2005). Leapfrogging into the knowledge era: Use of ICT for development. *IIMB Management Review, 17*(3), 47-56.

Press, L., Foster, W., & Goodman, S. (1999). *The Internet in India and China.* Retrieved from http://www.isoc.org/inet99/proceedings/3a/3a_3.htm

Press, L., Foster, W., Wolcott, P., & McHenry, W. (2002). The Internet in India and China. *First Monday, 7*(10).

Qiaoqiao, Z. (2004). *Xinhuanet.com.* Retrieved January 18, 2007, from http://news.xinhuanet.com/it/2004-08/04/content_1708666.htm

Quibria, M. G., Tschang, T., & Reyes-Macasaquit, M. L. (2002). New information and communication technologies and poverty: Some evidence from developing Asia. *Journal of the Asia Pacific Economy, 7*(3), 285-310.

Rao, M. (2002a, Jan 25). *E-government services to create billion-dollar market in India.* Kotak Street Retrieved April 11, 2002, from http://kotakstreet.com/webapp/kotak/MarketMonitor/KotakByLanesID.jsp?id=63

Rao, M. (2002b, Apr 18). *New report highlights entrepreneurial drive in India, calls for better infrastructural and educational support.* Retrieved April 22, 2002, from www.Indiainfoline.com/nevi/inwi/

Rao, M. (2002c, Feb 25). *Rural community networks: Growing social capital via interactive technologies.* Retrieved May 2, 2002, from www.Indiainfonline.com

Santos-Paulino, A. (2005). Trade liberalisation and economic performance: Theory and evidence for developing countries. *World Economy, 28*(6), 783-821.

Sarkar, M. E., & El Sawy, O. A. (2003). The four tigers of global e-business infrastructure: Strategies and implications for emerging economies. *Communications of the Association for Information Systems, 12*, 1-22.

Sawhney, M. (2002). Fields of online dreams; e-commerce can flourish anywhere if you build the right business model. *CIO*, 128-130.

Shoib, G., & Nandhakumar, J. (2003). Cross-cultural IS adoption in multinational corporations. *Information Technology for Development, 10*(4), 249-261.

Sina. (2006). *Tech Sina.* Retrieved January 22, 2007, from http://tech.sina.com.cn/it/2006-09-29/07251165444.shtml

Stats, I. W. (2007). *Internet usage in Asia.* Retrieved January 9, 2007, from http://www.Internetworldstats.com/stats3.htm

Strauss, J., El-Ansary, A., & Frost, R. (2006). *E-marketing* (4th ed.). Upper Saddle River, NJ: Pearson/Prentice Hall.

Tan, Z. A., & Ouyang, W. (2004). Diffusion and impacts of the Internet and e-commerce in China. *Electronic Markets, 14*(1), 25-35.

Thiagarajan, K. (2002, March 31). China: The hidden dragon. *Businessline,* 1.

Travica, B. (2002). Diffusion of electronic commerce in developing countries: The case of Costa Rica. *Journal of Global Information Technology Management, 5*(1), 4-24.

University, B. (2004). B2B e-commerce: Is Chinese enterprise getting ready? Retrieved May 29, 2004, from http://www.Chinabyte.com/20010904/1416727.shtml

Walsh, J. K. (2004). India. *Global Markets Update.*

Wang, G. A. (2002). On obstacles to e-business development in Mainland China. *Quarterly Journal of Electronic Commerce, 3*(4), 417-427.

WEF. (2004). WEF Report: Developing Countries lead in ICT Access. *Economic Bureau of the World Economic Forum.*

Wolcott, P., & Goodman, S. (2003). Global diffusion of the Internet : India: Is the elephant learning to dance? *Communications of the Association for Information Systems, 11*, 560-646.

Xu, S., Zhu, K., & Gibbs, J. (2004). Global technology, local adoption: A cross-country investigation of Internet adoption by companies in the United States and China. *Electronic Markets, 14*(1), 13-25.

Yao, S. (2006). On economic growth, FDI and exports in China. *Applied Economics, 38*(3), 339-351.

Yaoping, J. (2005, Sept. 6). *ChinaIRN.com.* Retrieved January 21, 2007, from http://www.Chinairn.com/doc/4080/40189.html/

Yoder, R. A., Borkholder, P. L., & Friesen, B. D. (1991). Privatization and development: The empirical evidence. *The Journal of Developing Areas, 25*, 425-434.

Young, S., Huang, C. H., & McDermott, M. (1996). Internationalization and competitive catch-up processes: Case study evidence on Chinese multinational enterprises. *Management International Review, 36*(4), 295-314.

Chapter VIII
The Role of Trust in Business-to-Business E-Commerce Collaboration in a Unique Environment in Australia

Carol Pollard
Appalachian State University, USA

Amanda Diggles
Tasmanian State Government, Department of Health & Human Services, Australia

ABSTRACT

This research explores interorganisational collaboration in business-to-business e-commerce, and the factors that influence its development in a unique Australian environment. Using a qualitative case study approach, seven informants from four Tasmanian organisations were interviewed. The data confirmed trust was an important prerequisite for the establishment and development of both electronic and traditional interorganisational relationships. Collaborative relations such as communication and repeated interactions facilitated the development of trading-partner trust. Interestingly, trading-partner size did not influence trading partner trust, although "volume of business conducted" between trading partners was an influencing factor. Other factors included trading-partner reputation and length of preexisting relationship. Perceived benefits of trading partner trust included general business efficiencies, business growth, faster payment, increased information sharing and confidence, improved business relations, delivery, and reliability. The results enhance organisational awareness of similarities and differences between traditional and electronic business-to-business trading relationships, and contribute to the growing body of knowledge on interorganisational trust and business-to-business e-commerce. The influence of the unique Tasmanian environment was acknowledged and discussed as a mediating variable in considering the findings.

INTRODUCTION

Trust does not reside in integrated circuits or fibre optic cables. Although it involves an exchange of information, trust is not reducible to information. A "virtual" firm can have abundant information coming through network wires about its suppliers and contractors. But, if they are all crooks or frauds, dealing with them will remain a costly process involving complex contracts and time-consuming enforcement. (Fukuyama, 1995, p. 25)

Business-to-business electronic commerce covers a broad range of applications that enable an enterprise or business to form electronic relationships with their distributors, resellers, suppliers, and other partners (Turban, Lee, King, & Chung, 2000). A number of studies have reported on the benefits of information exchange between the various constituents of the supply chain (Cachon & Fisher, 2000; Garvirneni, Kapuscinski, & Tayur, 1999; Li, 2002). These benefits include improved ordering and inventory allocation. Lack of trading-partner trust has been identified as a significant factor contributing to the slow adoption rate of business-to-business e-commerce in the developing research that reports on interorganisational trust between firms conducting business online (Aschonmeit & Lenz, 2002; Hsiao, 2001; Keen, 2002; Scott, 2000). In a recent study of supply-chain information sharing, Lee and Whang (2000) identified confidentiality as one of the major hurdles that prevent firms in the supply chain from sharing information, and stress the importance of establishing trust to encourage information sharing within the supply chain. Some researchers propose that the issue of trust is the biggest obstacle to information sharing in business (Lewicki & Bunker, 1996; Li 2002), and there has been some speculation that geographic location may have an influence on the development of trust in online collaborations (Pavlou, Tan, & Gefen, 2003; Ratnasingham & Kumar, 2000).

This study goes beyond existing literature that focuses primarily on the role of trust in business-to-consumer transactions (Pennington, Wilcox, & Grover, 2004) to explore the nature of trust, its development and influences within direct, intermediated, and direct/intermediated business-to-business (B2B) e-commerce collaborative relationships in a unique Australian environment. The objective of the research is to provide some guidance for those currently involved in, or considering future adoption and participation in business-to-business electronic commerce, and to provide empirical evidence to the current body of literature. We begin by presenting definitions of interorganisational relationships and trust, and follow with a discussion of previous trust and e-commerce literature. Next, research design, data collection, and analysis processes are described. Finally, findings are presented, along with conclusions and suggestions for practice and future research.

DEFINING CONCEPTS

Interorganisational Relationships

It is widely held that to survive and thrive in competitive environments, organisations must seek cooperative relationships with other organisations (Kumar, Stern, & Anderson, 1993). These cooperative relationships are regarded as interorganisational relationships (IORs) or interfirm partnerships (Kumar et al., 1993). Recently, technology has begun to support the development and maintenance of IORs through the introduction of interorganisational systems (IOS).

Collaboration through IOS can cover a variety of activities, such as supply-chain management, outsourcing, strategic planning logistics, and demand forecasting (Kwok, Lee, & Turban, 2001). Factors such as technology, leadership, and culture have been shown to influence the process of interorganisational relationships (Westley & Vredenburg, 1997). The definition of IOS provided by Cash and Konsynski (1985) and Johnston and Vitale (1988) as cited in Karahannas and Jones (1999, p. 346) is accepted for this study:

Automated information systems shared by more than one company and allowing information flow across organisational boundaries.

Trust

The emerging body of research on trust in e-commerce has been based on the findings and principles derived from the existing traditional research on trust (Papadopoulou, Kanellis, & Martakos, 2001). For the purposes of evaluating the contribution of the current study, it is important to note that a large amount of this research has been from a theoretical or conceptual standpoint, and empirical evidence has been limited.

The concept of trust has received interest from many disciplines including psychology, sociology, history, economics, management, marketing, law, economics, information systems, and computer science (Keen, 2002; Lewicki & Bunker, 1996; McKnight & Chervany, 2000; Mishra, 1996; Sheppard & Tuchinsky, 1996), with each discipline viewing trust from its own unique perspective (Lewicki & Bunker, 1996; McKnight & Chervany, 2000).

It has been suggested that trust can occur at an *interpersonal* or *intraorganisational* level (Cummings & Bromily, 1996; Lewicki & Bunker, 1996; McKnight & Chervany, 2000), between organisations (*interorganisational*) (Allen, Colligan, Finnie, & Kern, 2000; Aschmoneit & Lenz, 2001; Doney & Cannon, 1997; Karahannas & Jones, 1999; Smeltzer, 1997) and in relation to *characteristics of the technology* (Pennington et al., 2004)

McKnight, Cummings, and Chervany (1998) developed a useful typology of the concept of trust and define three types of trust: interpersonal trust, system trust, and dispositional trust. *Interpersonal trust* is defined as a party's willingness to depend on the other party with a feeling of security. *System trust* is the belief that proper impersonal structures are in place to protect or support a successful interaction. *Dispositional trust* is a person's tendency to trust across a broad spectrum of situations and persons. These three types of trust will be explored empirically in the context of B2B interorganisational collaboration in this study.

RESEARCH QUESTIONS

A review of previous literature led to the development of four research questions that provided the structure for the literature review presented next:

1. What role does trust play in B2B e-commerce collaborations?
2. What factors facilitate trust in B2B e-commerce collaborations?
3. What factors inhibit trust in B2B e-commerce collaborations?
4. Does environment matter in B2B e-commerce collaborations?

BACKGROUND LITERATURE

Upon examination of the trust literature, it appears that while there is extensive research into both interpersonal and organisational levels of trust, there is limited research on interorganisational trust, and an even greater paucity of research on trust with respect to interorganisational collaborations in a business-to-business e-commerce environment. Given the burgeoning number of interorganisational relationships now operating across time and space, trust in B2B e-commerce collaborative relationships would appear to be an important topic to address. It is this gap in the trust literature that is being addressed empirically in this study with a view to assisting organisations currently involved, or considering involvement, in interorganisational e-commerce to gain greater benefits from these collaborative relationships, and to raise awareness of the importance of nurturing and maintaining a high level of trust in the e-commerce relationship.

Research Question 1: What role does trust play in B2B e-commerce collaborations?

Research into online trust has reported mixed results. On one hand, trust has emerged as an extremely important aspect of business-to-business e-commerce (Allen et al., 2000; Aschmoneit & Lenz, 2001; Ba, Whinston, & Zang, 1999; Hart & Saunders, 1997; Hsiao, 2001; Keen, 2002). Indeed, some (Kim, 2001; Scott, 2000) assert that trust is one of the most important issues in e-commerce. Some researchers attribute the importance of trust to the impersonal nature of the online setting, the geographic distance, and the increased uncertainty of the online setting. For example, Pavlou et al. (2003) explain that the absence of physical proximity, handshakes, and body signals; lack of face-to-face interaction; and capacity for interruption and feedback make trading-partner trust even more important in an online environment.

According to Hart and Saunders (1997), electronic access to information introduces a new source of vulnerability into an interorganisational relationship, and to manage these uncertainties, organisations need to build trustful relationships with their electronic partners.

The lack of interorganisational trust has been identified as a barrier to business-to-business e-commerce adoption (Aschmoneit & Lenz, 2001; Hsiao, 2001; Keen, 2002), and Pavlou et al. (2003) suggest that engendering information technology (IT) to encourage online interorganisational relationships should be considered as a strategic initiative. In support of these claims, a market research study in March 2001 by Jupiter Media Metrix Inc. found that almost half of all managers studied blamed a lack of trust for the slow adoption rate of business-to-business e-commerce (Costello, 2001).

On the other hand, in a study of 20 organisations that used interorganisational systems as part of strategic alliances (Karahannas & Jones, 1999), it was reported that trading-partner trust was not always considered relevant to interorganisational systems development and use. Similarly, the influences of supplier selection have been studied (Doney & Cannon, 1997), and results suggested that buying organisations were not influenced by trust, but instead were more interested in their supplier's delivery performance and relative price/cost. The results indicated that trust operated as a qualifier, not a winner, increasing the likelihood that buyers anticipate doing business with the supplier. While the majority of the limited evidence collected to date suggests that trust is fundamental in building and retaining online relationships (Gefen, 2002; Pavlou et al., 2003), it is contended that empirical evidence, particularly with respect to the role that trust plays in B2B e-commerce vis-à-vis more traditional interorganisational relationships, is lacking, and it is the purpose of this research to begin to address this lack of in-depth empirical evidence.

Research Question 2: What factors facilitate trust in B2B e-commerce collaborations?

Research Question 3: What factors inhibit trust in B2B e-commerce collaborations?

A number of influencing factors have been reported in the trust literature. These include *reputation*, *size*, *communication*, and *confidentiality of information shared.* In support of the first two factors, Doney and Cannon (1997) and Song and Zahedi (2002) indicate that reputation and size have been most frequently suggested as factors that contribute significantly to trust in buyer-seller relations. Others agree, for example Jarvenpaa and Tractinsky (1999) propose that a company's *reputation* is a valued asset which provides assurances of another party's ability, integrity, and goodwill and are directly related to levels of buyer-seller trust. Similarly, Shapiro, Sheppard, and Cheraskin (1992) explain that the threat of loss of reputation and resulting loss of business from the spread of word about untrustworthy behaviour is often quite an effective deterrent to untrustworthy behaviours. While, Smeltzer (1997) found that having a good history and past performance is a trust-enhancing factor, others suggest the threat of loss of reputation and resulting loss of business is an effective deterrent to trust and third-party gossip, which have been identified as a powerful means of social control (Jarvenpaa & Tractinsky, 1999; Shapiro et al., 1992), and Burt and Knez (1996) suggest it is a possible influence on increased cooperation and trust.

With respect to firm *size,* Jarvenpaa and Tractinsky (1999), propose that being a larger organisation implies significant resources invested in the business, and that there is much to lose by acting in an untrustworthy manner.

Another interesting factor is *time.* Zand (1972) suggests that it takes time to develop trust, a view supported by several other trust theorists (Lewicki & Bunker, 1996; Sheppard & Tuchinsky, 1996). However, by speculating that trust develops over time, it is implicitly assumed that trust begins at a low level and gradually increases. When contrasted with subsequent findings, these theories present an interesting paradox. For example, Kramer (1994) surveyed participants who were previously unknown to each other and found high-trust levels. McKnight et al. (1998) suggest two factors that account for high initial levels of trust. These are *participant disposition to trust* (the tendency to be willing to depend on others) and *system trust* (the belief that impersonal structures are in place to protect or support the likelihood of success).

In a similar vein, the *communication process* is another significant facilitator of trust (Shapiro et al., 1992). An important dimension of communication that has been identified in the literature is frequency of interaction. This acts as a mediator of distrustful behaviour that can potentially jeopardise future benefits (Sydow, 1998). It has been suggested that repeated interactions allow parties to better interpret prior outcomes and provide a basis for assessing predictability that should be encouraged (Doney & Cannon, 1997; Shapiro et al., 1992).

On the other hand, Hardy, Phillips, and Lawrence (1996, p. 69), propose that interorganisational "trust grows out of a communication process in which shared meanings develop to provide a foundation for non-opportunistic behaviour." Another dimension of communication is the *length of the relationship.* The longer the relationship, the larger the investment made by trading partners over time, and the easier it is to predict future behaviour, thus increasing trust in a partner (Doney & Cannon, 1997).

The *nature of the information* communicated can also influence trust levels. Doney and Cannon (1997), contend that buyers tend to have greater trust in suppliers who share confidential information in that it provides a signal of good faith to the buying organisation; that they are willing to make themselves vulnerable. Hart and Saunders (1997) suggest that willingness to share this information demonstrates openness and reinforces trust.

Joint projects and goals are also important vehicles for increasing the level of perceived trust between trading partners (Shapiro et al., 1992).

The combination of these influencing factors has resulted in a number of benefits to the organisations involved in interorganisational relationships. Perceived benefits of trust have been classified into three distinct categories: *economic, personal,* and *symbolic* (Shapiro et al., 1992), in that *perceived economic benefits* include cost savings from lower administrative costs, timeliness from speed and automation, and simplicity from structured business processes. *Perceived personal benefits* include competitive advantage, reduced lead times, increased productivity and customer satisfaction. *Symbolic perceived benefits* of trust include building/enhancing reputation, increased commitment and business stability, competitive edge, and a strategic outlook. In addition, Hart and Saunders (1997) suggest that trust increases the probability of a trading partner wanting to expand the amount of information sharing and exploring mutually beneficial arrangements.

Research Question 4: Does environment matter in B2B e-commerce collaborations?

According to Barret (1999), different cultures have different expectations of technology, and can potentially impede levels of technology implementation and use. Begin and Boisvert (2002) offer support to Barret's position, in their assertion that:

A culture oriented toward traditional approaches hinders the deployment of electronic commerce... where sales contracts are habitually concluded with a handshake and when customers value direct contact or are not familiar with the use of the Internet. (p. 18)

More recently, it has been suggested that geographic distance between participants increases the importance of trust in e-commerce relationships (Pavlou et al., 2003; Ratnasingham & Kumar, 2000). These findings imply that technology alone is insufficient for successful e-commerce participation, and that building and maintaining positive and trusting trading-partner relationships across different cultures and environments is critical and as such, is worthy of further exploration.

It is estimated that in 2004, some 945 million people will be connected to the Internet (Computer Industry Almanac, 2002), providing significant opportunities for firms in sparsely populated geographically remote countries to expand their markets and gain operational efficiencies. Australia, with a population of approximately 20 million (ABS, 2002), is one such country.

Within Australia, it would seem that businesses in the unique environment of the Island of Tasmania, which have a limited local market, are particularly well placed to reap the benefits of these new online business opportunities. According to Begin and Boisvert (2002), however, the Tasmanian culture may be expected to impede the uptake of e-commerce. Tasmania has a population of approximately 400,000 people, located primarily in two closely situated main population centres. Although Tasmania is only 130 miles across the Bass Strait from mainland Australia, it is widely accepted that when you arrive on the island of Tasmania, you step back 20 years into a close-knit community where contracts are still decided by a handshake and business reputations rise and fall on personal endorsements. In essence, it is the type of culture that is likely to resist the deployment of electronic commerce and online interorganisational systems (Begin & Boisvert, 2002). The presence of these more pronounced local differences between traditional vs. online interorganisational relationships make Tasmania an interesting environment in which to begin to explore the role of trust in online business-to-business collaborative relationships, and to add to the current body of literature.

METHOD

The purpose of this research is to gain insight and understanding into the role of trading-partner trust within an interorganisational business-to-business e-commerce environment through considering the perceptions and experiences of individuals within this environment. As such, interorganisational business-to-business e-commerce is viewed as a social construct, and a subjective approach was considered to be the most suitable for this research (Creswell, 1994; Neumann, 2000). Case-study research is the most common qualitative method used within information systems (Orlikowski & Baroudi, 1991). Case-study research investigates a contemporary phenomenon within real-life context when the boundaries between the phenomenon and context are unclear (Myers, 1997). Therefore, it can be seen that case-study research is particularly suited to information systems research due to the ambiguity between the boundaries and context of information systems, technology, and organisations. This is particularly true for the current research, which involves people, organisations, trading partners, technology, and electronic commerce information systems, and the relationships between these. Table 1 provides a comparison of the main characteristics of case studies suggested by Benbasat, Goldstein and Mead (1987) with the characteristics of the current research to demonstrate the appropriateness of the case-study technique in the current research.

To probe the research questions and to facilitate replication (Benbasat et al., 1987; Miles & Huberman, 1989) an interview protocol was developed to guide semistructured face-to-face interviews.

Table 1. Comparison of Key Characteristics of Case Studies with the Current Research (Adapted from Benbasat, Goldsein, & Mead, 1987)

Key Characteristics of Case Studies	Current Research Study Characteristics
The phenomena under investigation is being studied in its natural environment	The participants were interviewed within their own working environment, or in an environment which they felt most comfortable
Data is collected by several means	Interview data and observation of the participants were collected during the interview
One or few people, groups or organisations are investigated	Four organisations were included within this study and seven participants within these organisations were interviewed
The intricacy of the entity under study is deeply investigated	The concept of inter-organisational trust within e-commerce was the major focus of this research and was investigated in detail
This method suits exploratory research	Inter-organisational e-commerce is a relatively new phenomenon as is the concept of trust within this environment
There are no experimental controls or manipulations within case study research	No experimental controls or manipulations were used
The researcher does not state any independent and dependent variables within the research	No independent or dependent variables were stated
The outcomes produced from the research depends upon the ability of the researcher to synthesise observations	Interviews and observations were summarised and synthesised
The site and data collection methods chosen may alter as the researcher forms new hypothesis and theories	Not addressed
Case study method is helpful when the research is interested in asking 'why' and 'how' type questions. These types of questions are adept in assisting the researcher in understanding the community of interacting individuals as apposed to frequency or rate of reoccurrence	This research asks 'why' and 'how' questions. However, in addition to these, 'what' questions are also asked. Neuman (2000) suggests these 'what' questions are also important in case study research.
The focus of the research is centred upon current events	Web-based B2B e-commerce is an emerging concept.

Questions emerged from a thorough review of the research literature provided in the previous section. In the interviews, initial socioeconomic data were collected to provide a profile of participants and the organisations they represent, followed by a number of trust-related questions that emerged from careful reading of previous relevant findings reported in the literature.

A purposeful sample of four organisations was chosen on the basis of size, nature of electronic trading relations with their trading partners (direct vs. intermediary), and industry sector (public vs. private; manufacturing vs. service).

Within these four organisations, individual face-to-face interviews were conducted with a total of seven upper-level managers. Originally, two interviews were planned in each organisation. However, in approaching the organisations, it was discovered that Organisation B had only one person who had the knowledge to answer the questions posed in the interview protocol. A decision was made to proceed with two interviews in organisations A, C, and D, and one in Organisation B. Each 1-hour interview was tape recorded, with the consent of the informant, and transcribed in accordance with the 24-hour rule advocated by Yin (1994). In keeping with the need to test the interview process (Miles & Huberman, 1994), the interview protocol was pilot tested for flow, timing, content, and comprehensibility by a business manager who had similar attributes to the informant's and two academic staff members of a large Australian university. Based on feedback from the pilot test, minor refinements in terminology and flow of questions were made to the interview protocol before formal data collection began. The interview protocol is available on request from the authors.

Interview transcripts were analysed using a combination of a top-down/bottom-up approach based on three stages of coding: open, axial, and selective (Strauss, 1987). The initial open-code categories were used to develop relationships through axial coding that led to the emergence of the final selective codes. This approach is similar in nature to the approach adopted by Karahannas and Jones (1999) who explored theoretical and originally unanticipated trust themes simultaneously.

Three types of validity suggested by Neuman (2000) were addressed within this research to ensure research accuracy: member validity, natural history validity, and ecological validity.

To address *member validity*, all seven informants were provided with a copy of their interview transcript and subsequently with a copy of the research findings. Each was asked to ensure both the transcript and the findings accurately reflected their beliefs and perceptions. All informants indicated agreement with the interview transcript and the subsequent research findings.

To address *natural history validity* and thus facilitate replication of the study by future researchers, a comprehensive case-study database was developed to allow others to follow the path from initial research questions through the coding process to the final conclusions, as suggested by Benbasat et al. (1987), Yin (1994), and Babbie (2002). This was achieved through the input of the interview data into Microsoft Excel spreadsheets to show the evolution of the open, axial, and selective codes, and to link the analysis back to the raw data. In this way, the relationships established in the early stages of data analysis and their subsequent refinements throughout the various phases of coding were fully documented to provide a chain of evidence. Summary sheets for each interview documented observational data to allow the researchers to further reflect on the content of the interview transcripts.

Finally, to address *ecological validity*, which assesses whether the participants' natural setting is disturbed by the researcher's presence or procedures, the participants were encouraged to continue to accept phone calls, deliveries, and queries from people within their workplace during the interviews. In addition, the information gathered from the participants related to their *past* experiences and/or perceptions of their electronic trading partners, both of which were formed prior to the occurrence of the interview.

SAMPLE

The selection of participants for the interview procedure was purposeful since in this research, the focus was "less to generalise to a larger population than it is to gain a deeper understanding of types" (Neuman, 2000, p.198). The participants in this study were from the Tasmanian business community, and were contacted through industry representatives and network contacts. Each participant was selected based on the type of business they represented, and their involvement with electronic trading partners. This electronic commerce participation was through "supplier management, inventory management, distribution management, payment management, or channel management" (Kalakota & Whinston, 1999, p.18).

The sample selection meets the guidelines for in-depth case studies suggested by Eisenhardt (1989). She recommends using 4 to 10 cases in a number of diverse industry sectors.

Table 2. Profile of participants and organisations

Organisation	**A – Government**		**B – Wholesale**	**C – Information Services**		**D – Manufacturing**	
Type of E-Commerce System	Intermediated		Direct & Intermediated	Direct		Direct	
Position	Supply Chain Manager	Acting Supply Chain Manager	Managing Director	Director of Information Systems	Marketing Manager	Group Logistics Manager	Sales Manager
Yrs. with Organisation	17	12	12	14	7	18	12
Yrs. In current Position	3	12	12	3	5	1.5	1
No. of Employees	350		8	42		500	
Yrs in Operation	70		147	122		132	
No. of traditional trading partners	1800		250	3000		3000	
No. of electronic trading partners	2		2	695		15-20	
Location of electronic trading partners	Local & Interstate		Local, interstate & international	Local & interstate		Local, interstate & international	
E -Trade Contact	Suppliers		Suppliers & Buyers	Buyers		Distributors	
Pre-existing relationship?	Yes		Yes	Yes		Yes	
Length of Relationship (years)	4-7		7-147	Up to 122		Up to 40	
Years system Utilised	2		D: 6 months I: 2 yrs	2		3	

Table 1 shows that these four organisations were from the government, wholesale, manufacturing, and information services sectors.

To preserve anonymity, organisations who participated in this research are referred to as organisation A, B, C, and D, and the individual informants are referred to by their job title. A profile of each of the participant organisations is provided in Table 2. The e-commerce relationships explored include one intermediated, one intermediated/direct, and two direct e-commerce systems. Organisation A utilises a Web-based intermediary system to import its suppliers' catalogues from the intermediary's e-commerce application. Orders are collated and entered into organisation A's purchasing system and sent through the intermediary system, where the order is placed. The supplier also updates the status of the order on the intermediary application, allowing organisation A to view the status of the order. Organisations C and D have direct e-commerce systems and choose not to use an intermediary, with the systems consisting of secure online and interactive ordering and account facilities that are developed and maintained internally. Organisation B utilises two separate e-commerce systems, one provided by its supplier and one by its buyer, one of which is intermediated and one direct.

All informants are in upper-managerial positions and were chosen because of their close proximity to their trading partner(s) and the e-commerce system. Each organisation is described in more detail in the following sections.

Organisation A: Government

Organisation A utilises an e-commerce system provided by an intermediary. The intermediary designed, developed, implemented, and maintains the e-commerce system. The e-commerce system allows the organisation to obtain quotes, search catalogues, compare prices, place orders, and also provides electronic notification during the ordering and delivery process. Organisation A communicates this way with two of its major suppliers: one local and one mainland-based supplier.

The intermediary system is used to import supplier catalogues from the intermediary's e-commerce application and repurpose the data for a variety of uses. Orders are collated and entered into the organisation's purchasing system and sent to the intermediary system, where the order is placed. The supplier also updates the status of the order on the intermediary's application, allowing the government organisation to view the status of the order. This intermediary system is linked in with the organisation's internal management system.

Prior to the current intermediated e-commerce system, various other unsuccessful attempts to develop an e-commerce system were undertaken by other intermediaries.

Organisation B: Wholesale

Organisation B has, in place, two major business-to-business e-commerce systems: a direct Web-based system with a major supplier and an intermediated Web-based system with a major buyer. Remaining orders are processed using e-mail and more traditional methods. Information generated from both systems is imported into the organisation's accounting software, MYOB. Both electronic systems are perceived very differently, whereby one is considered a success and the other is not.

The direct system is a Web-based interface provided by a mainland-based supplier. This system allows the buyer to select from a variety of goods with multiple prices (e.g., duty free) and place such orders, instantly providing the purchaser with related business records, and allowing the ability to track such orders. The system allows the ability to pay for such goods online, and for goods to be ordered and picked up within the hour.

The intermediary e-commerce system used by Organisation B is the same system utilised by Organisation A, however, Organisation B is a supplier, not a buyer.

Organisation C: Information Services

Organisation C offers business customers' access to a Web site to facilitate access to their services and information, and an electronic means of exchanging and accessing secure information (their core business function). Business customers must register with Organisation C to gain access to its electronic commerce system. A subscriber to the company's Web site has instant secure access to available information and services. Information is presented and accessed via a Web browser. Customers can also lodge business information. E-mail is also used for sending reports requested by the business customer. A fee is charged per transaction regardless of the mechanism utilised (e.g., online or by telephone).

Organisation D: Manufacturing

Organisation D supplies its products in local, interstate, and international markets. The organisation utilises e-commerce with their distributors, while traditional methods are still used with their suppliers.

Organisation D uses business-to-business e-commerce in the following ways:

- A Web site containing a catalogue of its products and contact details for its registered distributors in Australia and throughout the world.
- A secure online interactive ordering and account facility for its partners.
- A secure document management system.

Purchase orders can be created 24 hours a day, and entered instantly and directly into the manufacturing system. Invoices are automatically generated when orders have been fulfilled and shipped.

The organisation's registered distributors have a 24-hour a day, secure, self-service, interactive interface to the organisations database for placing and tracking the progress of orders and managing their account details. Trading partners have access to their own secure areas containing all their ordering and invoice information.

FINDINGS

A number of themes related to the role of trust emerged from an analysis of the data. These include the *importance* and *locus* of trust, and a number of *influencing* factors and *benefits* emerged. Each theme is discussed separately below. Then the influencing factors and the benefits associated with interorganisational trust are reported.

Analysis of the qualitative data strongly suggests that trust was considered to be an essential element of online interorganisational relationships. Indeed, the Sales Manager (Organisation D) perceived trust to be so important that he felt that his organisation "couldn't trade (electronically)... without that (high) level of trust".

Providing further support for this, the Supply Chain Manager in Organisation A perceived trust as being a prerequisite for trading electronically, and also that this trust was implied by the invitation to trade electronically:

I don't think that we would ever have entered into any agreement... with anyone that we had had poor dealings with or had been found to be unreliable, in either: the delivery of orders or their timeliness, responses to us, pricing, or anything like that, because the whole thing would have collapsed.

I think that the high degree of trust was implicit in getting it up and running to start with. Like with most systems ... they are only as good as the people at the other end, you'd definitely need a degree of trust and select your people quite carefully. (Group Logistics Manager, Organisation D)

Interestingly, trust was not perceived as being more important in the online environment, but rather as a prerequisite to conducting business relations with trading partners both online and off-line.

It (trust) is a prerequisite to dealing with any customer. It is important to recognise that you are trying to make a differential between a B2B is different to a traditional or vice versa and that's not the case. It is just a different method of trading. The same conditions apply. We wouldn't put an assessment on someone that wanted to come to us and B2B trade, any differently than if we wanted them to sell to them retail. We wouldn't even make a distinction between the two. (Group Logistics Manager, Organisation D)

It (trust) is important whether you are dealing with them (trading partner) manually or electronically. (Acting Supply Manager, Organisation A)

Some informants indicated that trust in their trading partners had existed before development of the e-commerce system, and that their trust had remained constant. The following statements demonstrate this:

The trust issue is well and truly decided before e-commerce....the majority of that is already established on a traditional basis, and the trust is the same. (Group Logistics Manager, Organisation D)

I don't believe that there was any major trust issues there, it was more, the trust was already there for the clients that are using us on the e-trading basis. (Marketing Manager, Organisation C)

It (trust) was evident before we ever looked at trading electronically with them, I suppose they were also deciding factors that these were the groups that wed deal with, where they already demonstrated reliability, because of our relationship with them. (Acting Supply Chain Manager, Organisation A)

In addition, the informants stressed that the *method* of trading had changed — not the *relationship.*

It (trust) hasn't been lost at any stage. I can't say it has been gained either, I think because we had such good relationships anyway, it's just remained as a good relationship, so we haven't lost or gained, we had just had such a firm relationship before...I haven't gained any more trust since electronic trading. (Acting Supply Chain Manager, Organisation A)

The method of dealing with them has changed, not the integrity and ethos that goes around it. (Supply Chain Manager, Organisation A)

I think...there is no more trust than if you were dealing with them normally, it's like that level of trust should be the same. (Managing Director, Organisation B)

Also, when the Managing Director was asked whether trust in his electronic trading partners was any different to his traditional trading partners he replied, "no...because they are still traditional trading partners really, the order might come over some fancy system..." From this it can be seen that the Managing Director did not think that the e-commerce system should have affected his trust in his trading partners.

Locus of Trust

Despite informants being questioned specifically about trust in their electronic trading partners, trust emerged in a number of loci:

- *Individual* (i.e., person)
- *Electronic trading partner* (i.e., organisation)
- *E-commerce system/technology*
- *Information* or *orders* within the e-commerce system

A common theme that emerged across all organisations was that informants appeared to place their trust in the *orders (information)* and *people* within their trading partner's organisations, rather than the system itself.

Trust of the client and the person and the people they are and the type of the orders that they give us is still one hundred percent, but the system...I have some doubts about. But as a client themselves, the trust is perfect. And that trust is not built up because of something that spits out of my computer...so there is a huge amount of trust. But it doesn't flow through to the ordering system and the electronic commerce system; it is a waste of my time basically. (Managing Director, Organisation B)

Like with most systems...they are only as good as the people at the other end, you'd definitely need a degree of trust and select your people quite carefully. (Group Logistics Manager, Organisation D)

Ultimately I think trust, where it could be lost would not be as a result of what's happening with the information system, I think it would ultimately have to come back to what's actually done in a human terms. (Marketing Manager, Organisation C)

The individual people, yep, they are open and honest and if there is a problem they come out with it, there seems to be nothing hidden. Yeah I have trust in them... (Acting Supply Chain Manager, Organisation A)

The Acting Supply Chain Manager introduced the concept of trust in information, indicating that their electronic trading parner would *have to trust us and the information that we give them, because that is what they are acting on,* indicating their trading partner would need to trust both the trading partner and the information they provided.

The varying loci of trust are reflected in the factors that positively and negatively influence the development of trust. These factors are described next.

Facilitators of Trust

Facilitators of trust reflect a differentiation between factors that develop "system" trust in the *technology,* and its inherent mechanisms that are in place to facilitate a successful transaction (e-commerce system, information) and those that develop "interpersonal" trust in *relationships* between individuals and/or organisations. Trust in the human dimension of the relationship appears to be more influential than trust in the mechanisms that are in place to ensure success of the e-commerce system. Perceptions of the importance of some factors, as noted next, are mixed.

Interpersonal Trust

Length of relationship: Regardless of the type of interorganisational relationship entered into (direct, intermediated, mixed) there was general agreement that time facilitated the development of trust in their online interorganisational relationships.

The length of our relationship, the length of their existing contracts and a good relationship that we'd had with them that would have to be the big one and the volume of our business with them. I think our history...as I say the length of time we dealt with them, the length of time we are still to deal with them... (Acting Supply Chain Manager, Organisation A)

Trust develops over time just from your interaction with them, their performance, their willingness to work with you, if there is a problem, so trust develops over time and a lot of that's just based on good communication between the two of you and that's what's happened in this case. (Acting Supply Chain Manager, Organisation A)

(trust) is something that obviously takes a little time to build up, initially. (Managing Director, Organisation B)

Ultimately, I think that trust is gained over time. (Marketing Manager, Organisation C)

Communication mode: Informants emphasised the importance of *traditional communication* in developing and maintaining trust. To demonstrate, the Director of Information Systems commented:

traditional communication is the only way to achieve that (trust). While in support of this the Managing Director expressed that trust is not built up because of something that spits out of my computer, but because I speak to them every week.

Others concurred:

traditional communication methods build a trust relationship, in addition to the Web site .... traditional communication is the only way to achieve that (trust) ..... (we) still hold the manual forms of communication as being important for building relationships. (Director of Information Systems, Organisation C)

(it allows the ability to) understand any problems that they are having at their end or what they'd like to see done and we can tell them any problems we can see. (Acting Supply Chain Manager, Organisation A)

Reputation: When asked whether a trading partner's reputation influenced their decision to trust, informants' responses were mixed. All participants from the Organisations A, B, and D indicated that reputation and background influenced their decision to trust their trading partners.

You have to have some trust before you enter into a relationship, into a contractual relationship with them, so a lot of that trust is based on the market knowledge, your own negotiations with them, that sort of thing. (their trading partner) had a good reputation . . . reputation came into it (their decision to trust). (Acting Supply Chain Manager, Organisation A)

We are trying very hard to get on with a good company with a good reputation, so we can say that we are dealing with those people B2B. (Group Logistics Manager, Organisation D)

In contrast, participants from Organisation C did not consider their trading partner background and reputation as influencing factors.

(Reputation) didn't have any bearing...any of our clients can use it. (Director of Information Systems, Organisation C)

Disposition to trust: Not surprisingly, given the environment in which the data were collected, many of the participants indicated they were predisposed to trusting behaviours, regardless of the communication medium:

Human nature is such that there is a basic desire or a basic behaviour that people do trust people. (Marketing Manager, Organisation C)

I have a very high degree of trust in everybody, I always trust that people are doing the right thing...I don't look for dishonesty or unreliability.

If we are talking about trust in terms of reliability, to do what they say, you have to have it because if you don't think that you can rely on them to do something, there is no point in setting up the arrangement to start with. (Supply Chain Manager, Organisation A)

Risk propensity: In contrast, another participant perceived their electronic trading partners to be more inclined to trust, compared to traditional trading partners, due to the fact that they were willing to take the risk to trade electronically. This can be seen from the following statement:

I think that the level of trust is actually higher with the electronic trading partners. Because I think predominantly they are more inclined to trust-the fact that they are using an electronic commerce medium to send the information. (Marketing Manager, Organisation C)

Volume of Transactions: While *size* of a trading-partner organisation was reported to be irrelevant in the formation of informants' decision to trust, that is:

It doesn't really matter what size they are or anything; I mean we want everyone we deal with to come on (to the system). So size wasn't a determining factor of who we'd get on. (Acting Supply Chain Manager, Organisation A)

we've got some of our biggest companies using it, and we've got some of our smallest ones. (Sales Manager, Organisation D)

(one of our trading partners is) a very small company with just a couple of employees, whereas <Other Trading-Partner Name> is a national organisation with thousands of employees. (Supply Chain Manager, Organisation A)

It is interesting to note that informants commented favourably on the influence of their trading-partner *volume of transactions* on their decision to trust.

If someone came and said hey we want to be part of <Intermediary Name> and we are going to give you orders worth $500 bucks a year, we would say forget it ... We could have a sole trader who accesses us electronically that still provides a benefit to us and vice versa and particularly with the large volume users there are enormous scales of economy to be had... (Marketing Manager, Organisation C)

System Trust

A different view was provided by the Director of Information Systems (Organisation C). He expressed the belief that the online interorganisational system itself, and its inherent support mechanisms, is an important facilitator of trust. This facilitation occurs by allowing electronic trading partners to be part of the business process, as opposed to those who only communicate with staff by telephone or fax:

Traditional clients wouldn't see the level of detail that we provide to our electronic trading partners...For people that are actually using the Web site they are actually looking and monitoring files a whole lot more than our traditional paper-based clients or fax-based clients. The only time that our traditional clients hear from us is when we need to know something...they don't actually see the mechanics of the processing in action. Whereas the people that actually use us through the Web site actually see more of what actually happens within our organisation...I think it would actually build a little bit of trust in those people and it actually helps to engender the relationship between us and them as well.

The Acting Supply Chain Manager (Organisation A) agreed. She expressed the view that the perception of her electronic trading partner had improved since they had agreed to take on the risk associated with participating in an online interorganisational system:

The only real difference is we are both exploring something new and we both put in resources into it and we both put in time and effort into it, which is probably something in addition to any of our other trading partners, is that we are just going down this whole new avenue and we are both doing it. That creates a bit more of a bond between us...We are both sharing risk...it's not just shovelling off onto one or the other, it is a sharing of risk, we are not transferring it.

They (trading partner) are prepared to work with us and look at a better way of doing things, this has sort of raised them a little in my estimation in that sense.

Inhibitors of Trust

Only three factors emerged as inhibitors of trust. One related to "interpersonal" trust, reliability of the trading partner, while the other two related to "system" trust, the reliability of the system and the mechanism of anonymity offered by the online environment. Each of these is discussed next.

Reliability of trading partner: The Managing Director explained that if his trading partners perceived his organisation as being unreliable, they would discontinue trading with him and go elsewhere, indicating, "They are going to get it somewhere else that they know that they can get it." From this it can be seen that a consequence of the trading partner's unreliability may be a termination of the trading relationship. Others agreed:

If they've mucked you up on supply, if they've made costs for you, or those sorts of issues. That's more the reason that you are not going to deal with them ... You'd effectively cease trading with customers whether it's through lack of trust in non-payment, or lack of trust in accessing data or using your information in inappropriate way. (Group Logistic Manager, Organisation D)

Interestingly, the Marketing Manager indicated that a breach of trust in an individual would not necessarily reflect on the organisation as a whole, giving an example of how this had occurred:

That was an isolated situation where an individual within a client organisation took an opportunity that was before them to access information on a person without that person's authority and used the information...for their own personal...thing...I don't believe that is something that needs rebuilding; I just think that's something that needs a good boot up the tail. I wouldn't say trust has been lost irreparably...that was seen for what it was, which was an inappropriate action from someone who had their own personal axe to grind...I think that was very isolated incident, I don't think it was a case of wide scale breach of trust, that organisation still has legitimate reasons to do (business with us).

Reliability of system: The Managing Director from Organisation B indicated that his organisation would often question the reliability of the system, and does not trust the system enough to recommend it to his other trading partners:

We are always questioning what is happening. And whether it's right and whether the information going onto the site is direct, whether the pricing is correct, like constantly questioning that.

We talk about that (the system), bitch about that (the system) every day of the week. Like that would be part of our topic of discussion every week, without a doubt. Like we were down there yesterday and we had a meeting for two hours and we spent an hour talking about this bloody electronic ordering.

I am very hesitant to recommend it to anyone, from the experience that I have had with it. Very hesitant. If we had to go through the performance we go through with the <Trading-Partner Name> with every client, it would be a pain an absolute pain and so I wouldn't want to be part of that. And I could then see it costing us money and it could diminish our reputation with our customer by recommending something that we know will cost them money.

Anonymous Online Environment: Interestingly, a participant indicated that e-commerce might enable a trading partner to take advantage of their trading partners, in relation to pricing and unseen goods. The Managing Director at Organisation B explained that people could hide behind the guise of e-commerce being unscrupulous by supplying goods at dishonest prices without electronic trading partners being aware, due to the lack of ability to check prices, to negotiate, and to provide feedback.

Furthermore, the Marketing Manager indicated that untrustworthy behaviour could be facilitated by the e-commerce medium due to its anonymity, rather than over the telephone or personal interactions, as explained here:

Similarly if somebody was to ring up and lodge a spurious account ... it is a lot less likely that they would do that over the phone or in person while talking to somebody, than potentially doing it over the Internet...the more remote something is the greater the potential it is that somebody won't perhaps be honest.

Does Environment Matter?

The data documented in the previous sections suggests that the business environment influences the development and maintenance of trust. The feelings of a number of informants are expressed in the following quote in which one informant refers to the importance of trading-partner trust in small-sized markets such as the local Tasmanian market.

In order to operate in a closed or a small market like Tasmania...companies must have a certain degree, no a high degree of honesty or they simply go out of business. Without everyday normal honesty in their dealings then they are going to fall down and they are not going to continue. So I believe that to be in business honesty is essential and I take that as a given. (Supply Chain Manager, Organisation A)

Furthermore, the Director of Information Systems at Organisation C indicated that he tended to trust his trading partners because of a "Tasmanian attitude I suppose if you like to call it that way." This could be interpreted that Tasmanians are trusting in general and that a person's culture and/or environment influences their trusting beliefs.

DISCUSSION

The current findings provide further support for the importance of interorganisational trust within an electronic environment as suggested by existing literature (Aschmoneit & Lenz, 2001; Ba, Whinston & Zang, 1999; Hart & Saunders, 1997; Hsiao, 2001; Keen, 2002). In doing so, they contrast with those reported by Doney and Cannon (1997) and Karahannas and Jones (1999), who suggest that trading-partner trust was not always considered relevant to interorganisational systems development and use, and trust was seen as a qualifier, not a winner.

However, in contrast to a previous study by Pavlou et al. (2001) that suggests trust is even more important in an online environment because of the impersonal nature of the online setting, the present study found that trust was *equally* as important in an online environment as in an off-line environment, regardless of the method of interacting. This is an extremely important and interesting finding of this research. A possible explanation for these differences in findings may be that most organisations in this study were located in the same geographic region, and so could still depend upon traditional communication methods. Most of these organisations communicated with their trading partners on a regular basis, both face-to-face over the phone and electronically, whereby the speculated increased need for trust in an online environment may not have applied.

The findings also revealed that trading-partner trust existed before the e-commerce systems were established, and that trust remained relatively constant despite the development of the e-commerce system. These findings conflict with Smeltzer (1997), whose informants perceived that the sharing of technical advances (e.g., the e-commerce system) facilitated trust, and Shapiro et al. (1992), who indicate that taking on joint projects and goals increases trust.

An explanation for this constancy of trading-partner trust may be due to the fact that the organisations studied already had mature relationships at the time of the development of the e-commerce system. This could be an indication that some of the organisations may have reached the final stage of trust development (identification-based trust) as previously suggested by Lewicki and Bunker (1996), who suggest that not all relationships evolve through to the last level of trust development, whereby these organisations may have reached the "peak" in their trusting relationships.

Different placement of trust emerged from the data, these being the *individual* (i.e., person), *electronic trading partner* (i.e., organisation), *e-commerce system/technology*, and the *information* or *orders* within the e-commerce system. These different trust loci emerged despite informants specifically being asked about *trading-partner trust*. Here it could be seen that the informants perceived that trust was important in a number of areas, not just their trading partners. These findings support those reported by Huang and Janz (2002).

It should be noted that in the current study, "interpersonal" trust facilitators outweighed facilitators of "system" trust. Collaborative relations such as *communication* and *repeated interactions* were perceived to be facilitators of the development of trading-partner trust, in support of previous studies that reported communication is a means of facilitating trading-partner trust (Hardy, Phillips, & Lawrence, 1996; Shapiro et al., 1992; Sydow, 1998) and those of Doney and Cannon (1997) who propose that repeated interactions facilitate trust.

Contrary to those who propose trading-partner size is an influence of trading-partner trust (Doney & Cannon, 1997; Jarvenpaa & Tractinsky, 1999; McKnight et al., 1998; Smeltzer, 1997), the findings in the current study revealed *trading-partner size* was not perceived as an influence. However, the new notion of *"volume" of business* between trading partners was suggested as an influence of trading-partner trust. Support was also provided for Smeltzer (1997) that having a *good history and past performance* was perceived as a trust-enhancing factor.

Support was also found for those who suggest that there are various economic, personal, and symbolic benefits of trading-partner trust (Shapiro et al., 1992). For example *increased information sharing, increased confidence, good relations, business growth, and efficiencies such as faster payment, improved delivery, and reliability* were all benefits mentioned. These findings support those of Hart and Saunders (1997) who indicate that trust increases the probability of a trading partner's willingness to expand the amount of information sharing.

Throughout the interviews, the participant's *individual disposition to trust* emerged, where certain participants indicated that they were naturally trusting, had faith in humanity, and did not tend to look for dishonest or untrustworthy behaviour. These findings support those of McKnight et al. (1998), Kramer (1994) and Pennington et al. (2004), whereby dispositional trust positively influenced the level of trust invested in others. One participant specifically mentioned that his/her disposition to trust, or "attitude" to trust might have been related to the Tasmanian culture. This suggests that willingness to trust could in part be explained by the influence of their environment. It would be interesting to investigate this further by conducting a quantitative cross-cultural analysis between organisations in different environments to explore this phenomenon.

IMPLICATIONS AND LIMITATIONS

This research has *practical* implications for ways in which electronic trading partners might increase interorganisational trust. Since trading-partner trust is essential to developing and maintaining successful trading-partner relationships, it is suggested that trading partners should try to facilitate such trust by fostering a level of trust prior to moving to an e-commerce environment, and for those relationships that are exclusively electronic in nature by encouraging collaborative activities such as repeated interactions supplemented with traditional forms of communication to the extent possible.

It is suggested that *future researchers* investigate further the issues explored in this study within organisations which:

- Only trade electronically.
- Have no preexisting trading-partner relationships.
- Are geographically distant and face-to-face interaction is minimal.
- Are contemplating adopting business-to-business e-commerce.
- Are located in various types of environments (urban, rural, third-world, etc.).

In addition, it is suggested that longitudinal studies of development of interorganisational trust would also add to our understanding of this interesting phenomenon.

In considering the findings presented here, it is important to consider the limitations imposed by the sample selection and extent of data collection. First, it is important to consider the implications in light of the somewhat unique Australian community in which the data were reported. To raise an awareness of the need to report on (and consider the effects of) the environment when reporting research findings, data were intentionally collected in the unique Tasmanian. To enable more valid comparisons of research findings, other researchers are alerted to the need to consider that the current findings might be quite different if conducted in a large city such as London, Sydney, or New York, or in a third-world country such as Bangladesh, India, or Mali.

Second, it should be noted that most of the online interorganisational relationships reported continued to include face-to-face communication after the introduction of the e-commerce system. Using the terminology associated with virtual teams, these interorganisational relationships are by nature "amalgamated," using traditional methods in combination with electronic trading methods and cannot be strictly construed as "virtual."

The authors also wish to clearly acknowledge they are not attempting to generalise the results of this study to all other organisations conducting business-to-business e-commerce. It would be unrealistic to expect that the perceptions and experiences of the seven informants within four organisations could necessarily be generalised to other individuals and organisations using business-to-business e-commerce. However, given the invaluable insights provided by researchers such as Mintzberg (1971), in his study of five chief executive officers, the contribution of an exploratory study such as the current one in providing valuable insights into the perceptions of a small number of organisations in a somewhat unique environment using a rigorous and carefully planned research method and design, should not be dismissed lightly. The data collected and reported here are designed to be exploratory in nature: to provide a point of departure for the further study of online interorganisational relationships in different environments, and the factors associated with developing and maintaining trust in business-to-business e-commerce collaborations.

ACKNOWLEDGMENT

The authors wish to gratefully acknowledge the invaluable, discerning comments of three anonymous reviewers and the associate editor on previous versions of the paper.

REFERENCES

ABS. (2002). *Yearbook Australia, 2002.* Retrieved November 10, 2004, from http://www.abs.gov.au/ausstats/abs%40.nsf/94713ad445ff1425ca25682000192af2/1647209ef7e25faaca2568a900154b63?OpenD

Allen, D. K., Colligan, D., Finnie, A., & Kern, T. (2000). Trust, power and interorganisational information systems: The case of the electronic trading community TransLease. *Journal of Information Systems, 10*, 21-40.

Aschmoneit, P., & Lenz, M. (2001). The role of trust in business-to-business electronic commerce. In *Proceedings of the Seventh Americas Conference on Information Systems*, Boston (pp. 1-9).

Ba, S., Whinston, A., & Zang, H. (1999, December 13-15). Building trust in the electronic market using an economic incentive mechanism. In P. De, & J. I. DeGross (Eds.), *Proceedings of the International Conference on Information Systems 1999*, Charlotte, NC (pp. 218-212).

Babbie, E. R. (2002). *The basics of social research.* Belmont, CA: Wadsworth/Thomson Learning.

Barret, M. I. (1999). Challenges of EDI adoption for electronic trading in the London insurance market. *European Journal of Information Systems, 8*(1), 1-15.

Begin, L., & Boisvert, H. (2002). E-commerce: Evaluating the external business environment. *CMA Management, 76*(2), 16-21.

Benbasat, I., Goldstein, D., & Mead, M. (1987, September). The case research strategy in studies of information systems. *MIS Quarterly*, 369-384.

Burt, R. S., & Knez, M. (1996). Trust and third-party gossip. In R. M. Kramer, & T. R. Tyler (Eds.), Trust in organisations: *Frontiers of theory and research* (pp. 68-89). Thousand Oaks, CA: Sage Publications.

Cachon, G., & Fisher, M. (2000). Supply chain inventory management and the value of shared information. *Management Science, 46*(8), 936-953.

Cash, J. I., & Konsynski, B. R. (1985). IS redraws competitive boundaries. *Harvard Business Review, 64*(2), 134-142.

Computer Industry Almanac, Inc. (2002). Internet users will top one billion in 2005. Retrieved November 10, 2004, from http://www.c-i-a.com/pr032102.htm

Costello, S. (2001). *Study: Companies slow to adopt B2B*. Retrieved September 28, 2002, from http://www.computerworld.com/management-topics/ebusiness/story/0,10801,58375,00.html

Creswell, J. W. (1994). *Research design: Qualitative and quantitative approaches.* Thousand Oaks, CA: Sage Publications.

Cummings, J., & Bromily, P. (1996). The organisational trust inventory (OTI): Development and validation. In R. M. Kramer, & T. R. Tyler (Eds.), *Trust in organisations: Frontiers of theory and research* (pp. 302-330). Thousand Oaks, CA: Sage Publications.

Doney, P., & Cannon, J. (1997). An examination of the nature of trust in buyer-seller relationships. *Journal of Marketing, 61*, 35-51.

Eisenhardt, K. (1989). Building theories from case study research. *Academy of Management Review, 14*(4), 532-550.

Fukuyama, F. (1995). *The virtual handshake: E-commerce and the challenge of trust.* Merrill Lynch. Retrieved from http://www.ml.com/

Gavirneni, S., Kapuscinski, R., & Tayur, S. (1999). Value of information in capacitated supply chains. *Management Science, 45*, 16-24.

Gefen, D. (2002). Reflections on the dimensons of trust and trustworthiness among online consumers. *DATA BASE for Advances in Information Systems, 33*(3), 38-46.

Hardy, C., Phillips, N., & Lawrence, T (1996). Forms and facades of trust. In R. M. Kramer, & T. R. Tyler (Eds.), *Trust in organisations: Frontiers of theory and research* (pp. 65-85). Thousand Oaks, CA: Sage Publications.

Hart, P., & Saunders, C. (1997). Power and trust: Critical factors in the adoption and use of electronic data interchange. *Organisation Science, 8*(1), 23-42.

Hsiao, R. (2001, December 16-19). Technology fears: Barriers to the adoption of business-to-business electronic commerce. In V. Storey, S. Sakar, & J. I. DeGross (Eds.), *Proceedings of the International Conference on Information Systems 2001*, New Orleans, LA (pp. 181-192).

Huang, Z., & Janz, B. D. (2002, August 9-11). Internet EDI adoption: Trust in technology and application knowledge. In *Proceedings of the Eighth Americas Conference on Information Systems*, Dallas, TX (pp. 2222-2227).

Jarvenpaa, S. L., & Tractinsky, N. (1999). Consumer trust in an Internet store. *Journal of Computer-Mediated Communication, 5*(2), 1-33.

Johnston, H., & Vitale, M. (1988). Creating competitive advantage with interorganisational systems. *MIS Quarterly, 6*, 153-65.

Kalakota, R., & Whinston, A. B. (1999). *Electronic commerce: A managers guide.* Reading, MA: Addison-Wesley.

Karahannas, M., & Jones, M. (1999, December 13-15). Interorganisational systems and trust in strategic alliances. In P. De, & J. I. DeGross (Eds.), *Proceedings of the International Conference on Information Systems 1999*, Charlotte, NC (pp. 346-357).

Keen, P. (2002). *Electronic commerce and the concept of trust*. Retrieved February 22, 2003, from http://www.peterkeen.com/ecr1.htm

Kim, E. (2001, August 3-5). A model of sustainable trust in B2C e-markets. In *Proceedings of the Americas Conference on Information Systems*, Boston (pp. 804-809).

Kramer, R. (1994). The sinister attribution error: Paranoid cognition and collective distrust in organisations. *Motivations and Emotions, 18*, 199-230.

Kumar, N., Stern, L. W., & Anderson, J. C. (1993). Conducting interorganisational research using key informants. *Academy of Management Journal, 36*(6), 1633.

Kwok, R., Lee, M., & Turban, E. (2001). On interorganisational EC collaboration—The impact of inter-cultural communication apprehension. In *Proceedings of the 34th Hawaiian Information Conference on Systems Sciences* (Vol. 1, pp. 1011-1019). IEEE Publishing.

Lee, H. L., & Whang, S. (2000). Information sharing in a supply chain. *International Journal of Technology Management, 20*, 373-387.

Lewicki, R. J., & Bunker, B. B. (1996). Developing and maintaining trust in work relationships. In R. M. Kramer, & T. R. Tyler (Eds.), *Trust in organisations: Frontiers of theory and research* (pp. 114-139). Thousand Oaks, CA: Sage Publications.

Li, L. (2002). Information sharing in a supply chain with horizontal competition. *Management Science, 48*(9), 1196-1212.

McKnight, D. H., Cummings, L. L., & Chervany, N. L. (1998). Initial trust formation in new organisational relationships. *The Academy of Management Review, 23*(3), 473-490.

McKnight, D. H., & Chervany, N. L. (2000). What is trust? A conceptual analysis and an interdisciplinary model. In *Proceedings of the Americas Conference on Information Systems 2000*, Long Beach, CA (pp. 877-883).

Miles, M. B., & Huberman, A. M. (1989). *Qualitative data analysis: A sourcebook of new methods.* Thousand Oaks, CA: Sage Publications.

Miles, M. B., & Huberman, A. M. (1994). *Qualitative data analysis—An expanded source book* (2nd ed.). Thousand Oaks, CA: Sage Publications.

Mintzberg, H. (1971). Managerial work: Analysis from observation. *Management Science, 18*(3), B97-B112.

Mishra, A. K. (1996). Organisational responses to crisis—The centrality of trust. In R. M. Kramer, & T. R. Tyler (Eds.), *Trust in organisations: Frontiers of theory and research* (pp. 261-287). Thousand Oaks, CA: Sage Publications.

Myers, M. D. (1997). *Qualitative research in information systems.* Retrieved April 3, 2002, from http://www.qual.auckland.ac.nz/

Neuman, W. L. (2000). *Social research methods: Qualitative and quantitative approaches* (4th ed.). Sydney: Allyn and Bacon.

Orlikowski, W. J., & Baroudi, J. J. (1991). Studying information technology in organisations: Research approaches and assumptions. *Information Systems Research, 2*(1), 1-28.

Papadopoulou, P., Kanellis, P., & Martakos, D. (2001). Investigating trust in e-commerce: A literature review and a model for its formation in customer relationships. In *Proceedings of the Seventh Americas Conference on Information Systems*, Boston (pp. 791-798).

Pavlou, P., Tan, Y., & Gefen, D. (2003). The transitional role of institutional trust in online interorganisational relationships. In *Proceedings of the 36th Hawaii International Conference on Systems Sciences—Track 7, 2003* (p. 215a). IEEE Publishing.

Pennington, R., Wilcox, H. D., & Grover, V. (2004). The role of system trust in business-to-consumer transactions. *Journal of Management Information Systems, 20*(3), 197-226.

Ratnasingham, P., & Kumar, K. (2000). Trading partner trust in e-commerce participation. In *Proceedings of the 21st International Conference in Information Systems*, Brisbane (pp. 544-552).

Scott, J. (2000). Facilitating interorganisational learning with information technology. *Journal of Management Information Systems, 17*(2), 81-113.

Shapiro, D. L., Sheppard, B. H., & Cheraskin, L. (1992, October). Business on a handshake. *The Negotiation Journal*, 365-378.

Sheppard, B. H., & Tuchinsky, M. (1996). Micro-OB and the network organisation. In R. M. Kramer, & T. R. Tyler (Eds.), *Trust in organisations: Frontiers of theory and research* (pp. 140-165). Sage Publications.

Smeltzer, L. R. (1997, Winter). The meaning and origin of trust in buyer-supplier relationships. *International Journal of Purchasing and Materials Management*, 40-48.

Song, J., & Zahedi, F. (2002, August 9-11). A theoretical framework for the use of Web infomediaries. In *Proceedings of the Americas Conference on Information Systems*, Dallas, TX (pp. 2250-2256).

Strauss, A. (1987). *Qualitative analysis for social scientists*. New York: Cambridge University Press.

Sydow, J. (1998). Understanding the institution of inter-organisational trust. In C. Lane, & R. Bachmann (Eds.), *Trust within and between organisations* (pp. 31-63). New York: Oxford University Press.

Turban, E., Lee, J., King, D., & Chung, H. M. (2000). *Electronic commerce: A managerial perspective*. New Jersey: Prentice Hall.

Westley, F., & Vredenburg, H. (1997). Organizational collaboration and the preservation of global biodiversity. *Organization Science, 8*(4), 381-403.

Yin, R. (1994). *Case study research* (2nd ed.). Thousand Oaks, CA: Sage Publications.

Zand, D. E. (1972). Trust and managerial problem solving. *Administrative Science Quarterly, 17*, 229-239.

ENDNOTE

* Each author contributed equally to the development of this paper.

This work was previously published in the International Journal of E-Business Research, Vol. 2, Issue 3, edited by I. Lee, pp. 71-80, copyright 2006 by Idea Group Publishing (an imprint of IGI Global).

Section III
Web Services

Chapter IX
Incorporating Web Services into E-Business Systems:
An SME Perspective

Ranjit Bose
University of New Mexico, USA

Vijayan Sugumaran
Oakland University, USA

ABSTRACT

There are a multitude of benefits and challenges that can be derived from the convergence of two major current technologies: (a) Web services (WS)—technology that allows application development and integration using the service-oriented computing paradigm; and (b) e-business systems—using the Internet as the basis for interacting with customers, suppliers, and other business partners. This combination called WS-based e-business systems promises to provide a dynamic e-business environment. We investigate the existing deployment barriers for such an environment from the perspectives of the three WS stakeholders, namely the service providers, service consumers, and the WS standards organizations, and present a challenges framework that organizes and interrelate these barriers in an easily understandable manner to help study further the factors that impact the deployment and use of WS within e-business. Using this framework, we analyze WS incorporation challenges for small- and medium-sized enterprises (SMEs) since they are a vital engine driving the world economy, and are realizing significant benefits from adoption and implementation of Internet-based business solutions. WS-based e-business system applications promise to do even more for them.

INTRODUCTION

Electronic business or e-business—the process of doing business electronically—is more than electronic commerce. While e-commerce describes the world of business-to-consumer commercial transactions, the term e-business usually refers to a broader scope of electronically enabled and integrated front-end and back-end business operations, within business-to-business (B2B), business-to-consumer (B2C), and business-to-government (B2G) models. E-business is a large, fast growing industry, and organizations of all sizes are looking for fast, effective ways to implement e-business. E-business applications have significantly matured in functionality and reliability over the years. Currently B2B e-business systems have gained in popularity with many organizations of different sizes (Gonsalves, 2002).

The service-oriented computing paradigm (Bichier & Lin, 2006), which also is gaining in popularity as a viable and cost-effective application software development option for organizations, is designed to utilize services as the basic constructs to support the development of rapid, low-cost and easy composition of distributed applications. Web services (WS), based on service-oriented computing, enables different software components to be integrated within an application without having to develop these components from scratch and without the hassle of custom coding (Chen, 2005; Stal, 2002).

The idea behind the WS technology is that the service provider defines a service description of the service and publishes it to a client (or service discovery agency) through which a service description is published and made discoverable. The service client (requestor or consumer) discovers a service and retrieves the service description directly from the service (through meta-data exchange) or from a registry or repository; it uses the service description to bind with the service provider and to invoke the service or to interact with the service. Service provider and service client roles are logical constructs and a service may exhibit characteristics of both.

There are a multitude of benefits and challenges that can be derived from the convergence of the two major current technologies: (a) WS—technology that allows application development and integration using the service-oriented computing paradigm; and (b) e-business systems—using the Internet as the basis for interacting with customers, suppliers, and other business partners. This combination called *WS-based e-business systems* promises to provide a dynamic e-business environment.

WS-based e-business systems make it possible to provide the ability to deliver a standards-based, interoperable infrastructure for e-business. Interoperability in an e-business environment allows information to be presented in a consistent manner between business systems, regardless of technology, application, or platform. It thus provides organizations with the ability to transfer and use information across multiple technologies and systems by creating commonality in the way that business systems share information and processes across organizational boundaries. Additionally, WS-based e-business systems make it possible to enable dynamic e-business by providing a standard mechanism for supporting complete automation through all aspects of the end-to-end business process that include finding suitable business partners, getting information about their products and service offerings, negotiating and establishing business terms and conditions, service level agreements (SLAs), payment options etc., to use those services, and invoking those services; all automatically.

WS technology application is resulting in significant changes in the way applications and supporting infrastructures are integrated (Schmidt, 2003). These changes have led to the design and development of service-oriented architecture (SOA) of application systems (Fowler, 2003). SOA is a way of logically designing an application system to either provide services to service-consumer applications or to other services distributed in a network, via published and discoverable interfaces. WS are becoming the basic building blocks out of which new applications are being created, and service composition is becoming the main focus of the application development process (Peltz, 2003). Service composition combines two or more WS following a certain composition pattern to achieve a business process goal. Thus, service composition provides a mechanism for seamless integration of cross-enterprise and intra-enterprise applications (Chung, Lin, & Mathieu, 2003).

The SOA is built on a foundation of standards, which define the roles and activities of the architectural elements to help support the interoperability of incompatible systems across the Web. The SOA is distributed, permitting elements of an application to be deployed on multiple systems and executed across connected networks (Geng, Gopal, Ramesh, & Whinston, 2003; Kleijen, & Raju, 2003). Because the transport mechanism is built on HTTP (hypertext transfer protocol), it is possible for application elements to interact within and across enterprises. The elements of an application are designed to support specific tasks within a broader workflow or business process. Each of these service elements of an application is responsible for defining its inputs and outputs using the standards for WS, so that other elements are able to determine how this element operates, how to make use of its functionality, and what result to expect from its execution (Papazoglou, 2003).

An element or component of an application is implemented as a Web service, which is a self-contained and self-described modular element of the application that uses a set of open standards to facilitate program-to-program interaction by specifying a programmatic means to describe, publish, discover, and bind application interfaces. The set of standards include a standard specification for public registries known as universal description discovery and integration (UDDI), a description language for Web based services namely WS description language (WSDL), a distributed object communication protocol called simple object access protocol (SOAP) and a dynamic, self-defining information specification protocol with semantic support known as extended markup language (XML). These technologies together make the notion of WS possible. WS provide significant opportunities for technical and business innovation (Arsanjani, Hailpern, Martin, & Tarr, 2003; Maruyama, 2002).

Since WS technologies provide a language-neutral, environment-neutral programming model that accelerates application development and integration inside and outside the enterprise, they encourage an approach to application development that is evolutionary, building on investments previously made within an IT organization, and developing new capabilities incrementally (Khalaf, 2002; Rust & Kannan, 2003). Consequently, within the last few years companies of all sizes have begun to explore the use of WS technologies within their e-business context (Hagel, 2002). The incorporation of WS into e-business provides several business benefits that include lowering costs, improving application sharing, increasing flexibility, streamlining business processes, and opportunity to create innovative business models among others. However, there are several obstacles that need to be overcome before widespread incorporation of WS into e-business is realized (Tilley et al., 2004). As with any emerging technology, WS till date have single-mindedly focused on the technical aspects of partner discovery and application interfacing while neglecting most business aspects such as security, access control, business partner selection, service level agreement management, monitoring, and payment for those services.

WS-based e-business systems are currently in the early phase of deployment, primarily within large organizations that have well-established IT infrastructures and technically savvy staff (Chen, Chen, & Shao, 2003). The deployments are currently focused in two areas: (1) enterprise application integration, for integrating disparate components, mainly legacy applications, of an enterprise wide system; and (2) business partner integration and secure exchange of data with dedicated partners without using a proprietary approach (Manes, 2003).

In spite all these advantages of using WS, several barriers still exist with their further development and use (Tilley et al., 2004). A thorough and systematic investigation of these deployment barriers is needed to help overcome them and improve the rate of WS deployment across organizations. WS-based computing poses significant challenges as developers determine how to leverage emerging technologies to automate individual applications based on cross-organizational, heterogeneous software components. While WS standards permit application-to-application interoperability, the coordination of a set of WS working toward a common end is currently an open issue (Orchard, 2002). Furthermore, service providers need to better learn how to develop WS interfaces that perform well, identify performance problems when they occur, and to fix them.

For effective implementation of WS-based e-business applications, the barriers for their deployment from the perspectives of the three stakeholders of WS, namely the service providers, service consumers, and the WS standards organizations need to be identified and studied. The service providers offer WS. These are organizations that procure the service implementations, supply their service descriptions, and provide related technical and business support. The service consumers are the end users of the services as well as application assemblers who assemble several WS to build an application for the organization. A service agreement, which is a contract between a service provider and a service consumer, is used regarding the attributes of a Web service and its usage. The standards organizations are bodies that are involved in developing open standards for both the providers and consumers to use.

In this study, we investigate the deployment barriers that exist from the perspectives of each of the previous stakeholders and present a challenges framework that organizes and interrelates these barriers in an easily understandable manner to help study further the factors that impact the deployment and use of WS within e-business. We analyze using the framework WS incorporation challenges for small and medium-sized enterprises (SMEs) since they are a vital engine driving the world economy, and are realizing significant benefits from adoption and implementation of Internet-based business solutions. WS-based e-business system applications promise to do even more for them.

SMES AND E-BUSINESS

There is no universal definition of SMEs; each country has its own. However, in general, SMEs are defined as non-subsidiary, independent firms, which employ fewer than a stated number of employees. This number varies across nations. The United States defines SMEs as firms with the size of the employees fewer than 500, the European Union sets the limit to 250 employees, while some other countries at 200 employees. Small firms are generally those with fewer than 50 employees, while micro-enterprises have at most ten, or in some cases five, employees. Financial assets are also used to define SMEs. The United States, in its definition, also assumes that the SMEs are independently owned and operated, and they are not dominant in their field of operation within the overall marketplace.

Characteristics of SMEs

There have been many studies in the literature that have attempted to define several unique characteristics of SMEs compared with large enterprises. Central to all of these studies is the realization that many of the processes and techniques that have been successfully applied in large enterprises do not necessarily provide similar outcomes when applied to SMEs. In other words, SMEs are not "small large enterprises" but are a separate and distinct group of organizations compared to large enterprises. Therefore, it is appropriate to know some of their characteristics reported in the literature.

Some of these characteristics include lack of technical expertise as well as adequate human resources in SMEs to develop complex technological solutions and to undertake technical enhancements (Barry & Milner, 2002). Most SMEs avoid sophisticated software and applications and often suffer from inadequate organizational planning (Tetteh & Burn, 2001). They tend to have a small management team and are strongly influenced by the owner's background and personal traits. Auger and Gallaugher (1997) identified a variety of business characteristics that affect the adoption and use of IT in SMEs. These business characteristics include business size, business age, business sector, market focus, and level of IT expertise among others.

IT Adoption in SMEs

SMEs in the United States, Canada, Australia, and leading European economies are realizing significant financial benefits from adoption and implementation of Internet-based business solutions (Beckinsale, Levy, & Powell, 2006). These Internet-based solutions fall under two broad categories: the first category is customer-focused such as customer development and e-marketing, whereas the second category is internally-focused such as accounting and supply chain management solutions. A recent study reported that 25 million SMEs in the United States generate 53% employment and 51% turnover and 18 million in the European Union generate 66% employment and 55% turnover.

In spite of these impressive statistics, the state of adoption and implementation of Internet-based business solutions in SMEs worldwide can be divided into four evolutionary categories ranging from limited use of information technology through to full integration of business automated processes as seen in the digitized firm (Knol & Stroken, 2001; Mehrtens, Cragg, & Mills, 2001). These categories are (1) no adoption—there is no information and communication technologies usage or limited usage, (2) basic adoption—e-mail and static Web pages are implemented within the business, (3) intermediate adoption—e-business platforms are being used including B2C online payment systems, and (4) advanced adoption—e-business platforms are used including B2B processes/exchange.

Factors Influencing the Adoption and Non-Adoption of E-Business in SMEs

The advent of e-business in the 1990s offered considerable opportunities to SMEs to expand customer base, enter new product markets and rationalize their businesses (EMPG, 2002). Many smaller firms have started using e-business to customize products and services, manage supply processes and inventories, and reduce the time between order and delivery. The significant benefits achieved by those SMEs that adopted e-business include cost reduction, sales increase, and the ability to reach a global market.

The literature reports several factors that influence the decision to adopt and use e-business in SMEs (Fariselli, Oughton, Picory, & Sugden, 1999; Mirchandani, & Motwani, 2001). They include the size of the business in terms of the number of employees, the age of the business, the business sector (i.e., service, manufacturing, or retail), the market focus (i.e., local, regional, national, or international), level of IT expertise available amongst staff, and the annual turnover of the business.

A firm's past experience with information technologies in terms of exposure and organizational learning ultimately affects its future choices in adopting advanced information and communication technologies. At the business sector or industry level, the factors include the availability of external know-how (for example, technology suppliers), the degree of innovativeness of the industry, the requirements imposed by major customers and external markets, and overall levels of competition and technological sophistication in the industry. The greater the computer literacy and computing skill of the owner, the more likely the firm will adopt e-business through awareness of its benefits, especially for the strategic management of the business.

The literature also reports several factors that influence the decision to not adopt and not use e-business in SMEs (Scupola, 2002). They include lack of awareness and knowledge of e-business, limited understanding of the complexity of electronic operations, inadequate skills and high initial investment required to develop a viable e-business strategy, infrastructure access and costs, lack of suitable software standards, lack of easily accessible, independent, and inexpensive advice and assistance in e-business development to SMEs, and concerns with security and privacy.

State of E-Business Adoption in SMEs

More and more SMEs are adopting e-business by implementing Web sites with portals while focusing on the quality of these Web sites and the choice of functionalities that they offer to users (Jeffcoate, Chappell, & Feindt, 2002). The SMEs are defining the scope of their e-business operations by identifying (1) the functionalities and services they will provide, (2) the clienteles they will target, and (3) the geographic scope of their operations. The technological solutions that the SMEs have adopted for e-business fall within a range of options to complement their traditional operations (Cote, Sabourn, & Vezina, 2004).

These technological solution options are as follows. E-shop—information or information requests, sale and distribution of the business's products and services; E-procurement is a site on which vendors sell to big buyers; E-auction is an electronic auction site; E-mall—several vendors operate on the same site; 3rd party marketplace—provides transactional support for vendors; Virtual communities are designed to foster communication between the members of a given community.

Current e-business adopters intend to continue adopting new forms of e-business applications. Governments and other national bodies in several countries are promoting and assisting SMEs through various incentives to embrace and use e-business (Salleh, Rohde, & Green, 2006). Modern Web-based technologies also are becoming an important way for SMEs to acquire information systems capabilities to support their business transformation. Web service technology is identified as a key driver for SMEs to gain operational and strategic advantages within their e-business systems (Joshi, Singh, & Phippen, 2004). Web service enabled collaborations will enable SMEs to work with large enterprises quickly, cheaply, and seamlessly by integrating themselves into a larger company's supply chain and manufactured systems, thus reducing the coordination costs of business relationships for both parties. WS technology creates the potential to enable a network of SMEs to collaborate and provide customers with an end-to-end, wide ranging service that gives the impression of a single and large scale enterprise. However, barriers to WS adoption within SMEs must not be underestimated since in the SME arena information technology is all too often perceived as simply a route to operational efficiencies and cost savings as opposed to gaining competitive advantage (Wu, 2004).

WEB SERVICES DEPLOYMENT BARRIERS

Web services-based applications are being developed to increasingly support sophisticated e-business processes (Lin, Ho, & Zhang, 2004). The application development trend can be categorized into three categories:

1. **Category 1—Enterprise application integration:** The first step is to integrate internal

applications. WS allow enterprises to expose legacy applications to business applications in heterogeneous environments without having to rewrite significant amounts of code.

2. **Category 2—Interoperability with key business partners:** The next developmental step for most enterprises is to integrate one or two key partners outside the enterprise. Enterprises use WS because they allow for interoperability between applications across the public Internet. Currently, due to the lack of broadly adopted specifications, enterprises must agree upon the technologies they will use to develop these interoperating WS applications.
3. **Category 3—Interoperability across multiple enterprises:** The subsequent developmental step for most enterprises is to extend their computing out to more business partners and customers. Currently, due to the lack of broadly adopted specifications, enterprises are forced to implement a series of agreed upon ad hoc solutions to ensure secure and reliable cross-enterprise interoperability.

Stakeholders of Web Services

A survey of the literature shows that the variables at play in WS adoption and use can be grouped into two levels: (a) organization, and (b) industry. Much of the research on WS has focused on the industry level and examination of WS-based software development has been ignored at the organizational level (Casati, Shan, Dayal, & Shan, 2003). In order for WS to take off, simultaneous progress has to be made at all levels. Issues at one level are invariably linked to issues at play at the other level. Thus, variables at play at the industry level such as emergence of standards for WS, methodologies for service identification, composition, and advertising have an impact on organizational level adoption and use of WS. Organizational level variables in turn, such as, WS reuse strategy, technological infrastructure, training and education, management support, metrics and incentives, etc., can influence WS adoption and use at both project and individual levels.

One important factor in the implementation of WS reuse programs is the relationship between suppliers and consumers. Thus, it is essential to examine the issues related to WS from the perspectives of all the stakeholders. Figure 1 schematically depicts these stakeholders and their inter-relationships. The three major stakeholders are (1) WS providers, (2) WS consumers, and (3) standards organizations. The WS providers primarily consist of WS vendors and WS integrators and publishers. The WS vendors are the companies that provide the actual WS themselves. The WS integrators and publishers are third party services that get requirements from consumers for applications and identify appropriate services and integrate them to create the applications needed by the consumer (Daniel, White, & Ward, 2004). In other words, consumers outsource the service identification and integration aspects to these vendors who deliver the complete application. WS consumers are organizations that utilize one or more WS in their e-business applications. These organizations may have two types of consumers. Application assemblers are usually IT department employees who are charged with developing organizational wide applications using WS. They are aware of all the available WS in a particular domain and particularly, the ones that their organization has subscribed to in developing prior applications. End users are individual users who are trying to develop simple applications using just one or two WS. Standards organizations oversee the specification and development of appropriate standards that govern all aspects of WS creation, identification, integration, and execution.

The relationships between suppliers, consumers, and standards organizations have to be understood at all levels. For example, at the industry level, suppliers will be organizations that design

Figure 1. Major stakeholders in WS application development

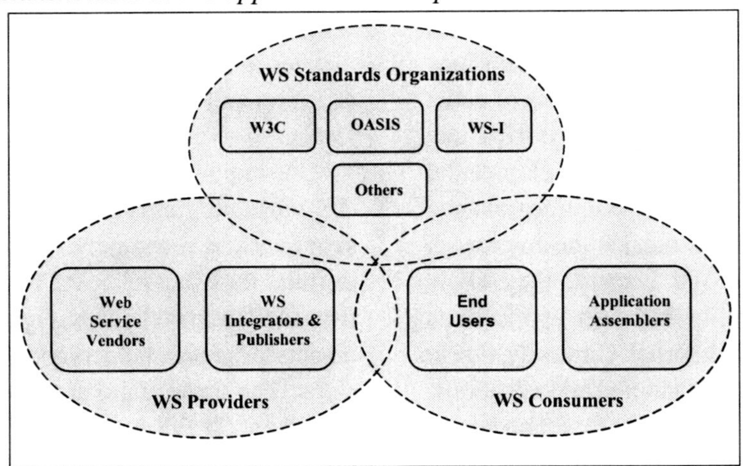

and develop WS and make them available for sale through their Website or via publishers and integrators to consumer organizations. Similarly at the organizational level, suppliers and consumers may be project teams and individuals. It is important to keep in mind, that a given organization, a project team, or an individual can be a Web service supplier, a Web service consumer, or both.

The following sub-section identifies the typical challenges that exist for each of the three stakeholders, and presents a framework that organizes these challenges in a coherent manner.

Stakeholder Challenges

Much of the current excitement about WS is based on two factors. First, WS are designed to improve interoperability across information systems at lower cost by extensively using open Internet and Web standards. Second, the decision by WS vendors to initially cooperate on setting key standards and compete later has greatly reduced investment uncertainty and increased incentives for others to provide complementary applications, thus potentially reinforcing adoption of standards. The technical objective of WS is to provide an integration mechanism facilitating the loose coupling of systems and hence the dynamic replacement of a service with another one of the same characteristics. Currently the most important issues regarding the wide adoption of WS are: (1) in the areas of still outstanding or insufficient standardization, (2) low acceptance of service consumers, and (3) critical mass of available useful services (Kreger, 2003).

Most of the problems related to WS-based software development deals with its adoption and use in organizations (Lee & Runge, 2001). The IS discipline has a long history of having developed theories and frameworks to address such problems. These theories and frameworks should be drawn upon to provide frameworks to study non-technical issues related to WS adoption. Such frameworks will provide a systematic basis on which different propositions regarding organizational, and industry level use of WS can be tested. Sound experimental design procedures and research methodologies also need to be drawn upon to study them. Based on the above discussion, we believe that a good framework for studying the challenges of WS adoption and use will need to look at both the technical issues and non-technical issues associated with WS deployment. Both of these types of issues have to be investigated for each of the major stakeholders, namely, Web service providers, Web service consumers, and standards organizations. The following three subsections briefly discuss the aforementioned issues related to each of the major stakeholders respectively and the last subsection puts together these issues into an overall challenges framework for further study.

Providers

A number of processes such as identifying new WS requirements, design, implementation, and testing of these services, eliciting customer feedback, etc., are involved in WS creation by WS vendors. Their WS development processes are impacted by many factors such as WS development strategy, architecture standards, design requirements, etc. Vendors make these services available to consumers by publishing them in one or more WS directories (Geng et al., 2003). Consumers use these services by identifying and subscribing to them from the directory. Based on their experience with the services, they may provide feedback to suppliers so that they can refine their services. Consumers' use of WS may involve many processes, such as, methodology standardization, project management, resource allocation, etc. and is impacted by many factors, such as, reuse strategy, organizational culture, technological infrastructure, etc.

There are a number of ways in which Web services can be published such as UDDI, simple URI-based registry publishing, exchanging schemas, etc. A service provider has to carefully consider how and where to publish its services. Depending upon the application domain, type of service, and the target audience, some approaches may be better compared to others. For example, ebXML is being adopted and pushed by some government institutions and is being evaluated by some industries (medial, traveling), while UDDI is pushed by some large software vendors. Hence, a Web services provider needs to understand the market space they are trying to target and publish their services accordingly so that consumers can easily find them.

A key "hidden" inhibitor is the lack of complementary WS including support for service-provider-specific processes such as metering, accounting, and billing. Overcoming the lack of third party WS and service-provider support is difficult because it requires foresight about how to decompose an automation problem and how to deliver it. Yet, doing so is critical because modularity and sharing are typically subject to positive demand-side network externalities. Service delivery overhead is another major obstacle to creating external services.

Research on semantic Web is on the rise and semantic Web services are accompanied by mechanisms for "smart" invocation of Web services. Thus, this new breed of Web services will greatly impact the whole WS paradigm. Semantic Web services (SWS) support automatic discovery, composition, and execution across heterogeneous users and domains. To this end, several frameworks have been developed, namely, Internet reasoning service (IRS-II) (Motta, Domingue, Cabral, & Gaspari, 2003), OWL-S (OWL-S Coalition, 2004), and Web service modeling framework (WSFM) (Fensel & Bussler, 2002). IRS uses a knowledge-based approach for SWS and allows applications to semantically describe and execute Web services. OWL-S provides an ontology for describing Web services capabilities. WSFM focuses on e-commerce requirements for Web services including trust and security.

A service provider needs to consider many aspects of quality of service (QoS). One of them is its QoS policy. Some WS adopt a best-effort policy, which offers no guarantee that requests for services will be accepted (they could just be dropped in case of overload), and no guarantees on response time, throughput, or availability are provided. While this type of policy may be acceptable in some cases, it is totally unacceptable in others, especially when a Web service becomes an important part of an application composed of various WS. In these cases, Web service providers may want longer-term relationships with users of their services. These relationships generate service level agreements (SLAs), legally binding contracts that establish bounds on various QoS metrics.

Providers must monitor the load they receive from consumers (users) and check whether the service they provide to them meets the agreed-upon SLAs. Consumers, therefore, must also check on the quality of the service they obtain. QoS monitoring may be outsourced to QoS monitoring services such as the ones that monitor Web sites (such as www.keynote.com). However, the consumers also have many other challenges to address.

Consumers

One of the main issues in WS based application development is the difficulty in identifying relevant WS and integrating them to generate a cohesive application (McIlraith, Son, & Zeng, 2001). UDDI requires consumers to manually search for WS, typically by completing a Web form to search a repository. This is fine if only one Web service is needed and once it is found it will never change. Unfortunately, this is usually not the case. In order for a Web-based application to adjust to changing WS, intelligent interfaces are needed that makes use of the semantics of the application domain.

Application assemblers and individual end users of WS can create integrated solutions by combining distributed WS over the Internet. However, there are several issues that such integrators face. For example, some of the integration solution requirements that WS would have to address are:

1. **Efficiency:** To scale on an industrial basis, WS execution must be very efficient.
2. **Expressiveness:** B2B interactions in supply chain scenarios are complex, requiring an expressive set of supported integration concepts.
3. **Security:** Interactions within, as well as across, enterprises must be secured to prevent security attacks of all types, and non-repudiation must be provided for reliable record keeping.
4. **Reliability:** Remote and distributed communication must be reliable, and messages must be sent exactly once to ensure dependable interactions.
5. **Manageability:** Inter-enterprise communication changes frequently, requiring easily manageable technology. These requirements pose a high demand on a technology that addresses their implementation.

Security is a major concern for organizations attempting to deploy WS-based applications. One of the key aspects of Web services management is to ensure that services can be delivered and accessed securely according to the organization's security policies. Some of the security concerns are addressed through the WS-security (WSS) specification, which has been developed through OASIS. WSS defines SOAP extensions to implement client authentication, message integrity and message confidentiality. It is built on current XML security technologies, including XML digital signature, XML encryption, and X.509 certificates. It is designed to provide authentication and authorization for secure message exchange between Web services.

Service requesters find required services by searching the service broker's registry. Requesters then bind their applications to the service provider to use particular service. The lack of ready-to-use WS from either internal sources or third parties compels system architects and engineers to write most of the functionality from scratch. Because WS disregard the traditional separation between local and global applications, developers must carefully consider and anticipate design requirements related to trust, semantics, and coordination

(Curbera, Khalaf, Mukhi, Tai, & Weerawarana, 2003). By piggybacking on existing infrastructure, a company reduces the size and specificity of its investments while providing customers a customized service that can be seamlessly integrated with their personal software.

Successful deployment of WS, particularly in the context of mission critical applications, requires adequate methods for performance management and monitoring. The Web services used should be reliable, extensible, scalable, and provide high performance. There should be mechanisms in place to check the service quality, end-point integrity, and runtime performance. WS monitoring and performance management tools are still evolving and organizations need to adopt a comprehensive and proactive strategy as opposed to piece meal approach. Typical tests that are carried out in monitoring Web services are stress test, integrity test, reliability test, and corrective measures monitoring. Some of the key factors for improving WS performance are: monitoring the whole transaction in real-time as a single unit, service level agreements and corrective actions, use of patterns, and clearly defining exception conditions.

From the consumers' point of view, several inhibitors of WS adoption exist. They include: (1) a lack of service provider processes such as metering, accounting, and billing; (2) a lack of semantic consistency in business processes such as ordering, billing, or shipping; and (3) a lack of workflow management mechanisms to orchestrate a group of specialized WS in support of a single business process. The QoS measure is also observed by WS users. Typically, these users are not human beings but programs that send requests for services to WS providers. QoS issues in WS have to be evaluated from the perspectives of the providers of WS and from the perspective of the users of these services. To support Web service management, factors that must be addressed include: WS monitoring, alert and notifications, alarm and traps handling, WS instrumentation at the application level, and WS interoperability with network management protocols. The standards organizations, therefore, are challenged to guide the development of several different standards in order to ease the WS adoption process.

Standards Organizations

There are several standards bodies that exist related to WS such as the World Wide Web Consortium (W3C), the organization for the advancement of structured information standards (OASIS), and WS interoperability organization (WS-I).

World Wide Web Consortium (W3C), which developed XML and SOAP is a major contributor to WS standards. Its "Web services activity" group builds a set of technologies that allow application-to-application interactions on the Web: an XML-based protocol for communication, a description language for describing interfaces to services, etc. In other words, the goal of the WS activity group is to develop innovative technologies in order to lead Web services to their full potential.

OASIS is a not-for-profit, international consortium that drives the development, convergence, and adoption of e-business standards. Members of OASIS set the technical agenda, using a lightweight, open process expressly designed to promote industry consensus and unite disparate efforts. OASIS produces worldwide standards for security, WS, conformance, business transactions, supply chain, public sector, and interoperability within and between marketplaces.

WS-I is an open, industry organization chartered to promote WS interoperability across platforms, operating systems, and programming languages. The organization works across the industry and standards organizations to respond to customer needs by providing guidance, best practices, and resources for developing WS solutions. WS-I's goal of promoting standards-based interoperability between Web services will have wide-ranging repercussions for the Web services, enterprise application integration (EAI), and middleware industries.

The three organizations previously mentioned, along with other standard setting bodies such as the IETF, OAGI, OMG, and UDDI are working on addressing some of the shortcomings of integrating WS into e-business applications, as discussed next. One of the fundamental shortcomings of WS is that business process dynamics and nonfunctional properties of service-enabled processes are poorly addressed by existing service description languages and WS flow languages. These languages seem to target service signatures and signature interactions only. Another basic shortcoming of WS is that current standards do not put forth a methodology to assist designers in building WS on top of legacy assets.

The Web services stack provides a conceptual framework for establishing the relationships and dependencies between various standards. It consists of several layers with well defined functionalities that facilitate the development of WS-based applications. The WS-stack consists of the following layers: transport, messaging, description, discovery, quality of service, and orchestration/integration. Each of these layers has one or more protocols (standards) associated with it. For example, the transport layer supports HTTP, BEEP, IIOP, JMS, SMTP etc., while the messaging layer utilizes XML, SOAP, and REST protocols. The quality of service layer deals with WS-reliability and WS-security. The orchestration layer focuses on choreography and employs standards such as BPEL4WS, WSCI, and BPSS. This layer also deals with transaction and coordination. While considerable efforts have lead to the acceptance of several standards at the lower layers of the WS-stack, the WS choreography and orchestration standards are still evolving. These standards have a tremendous impact as the organization and customer business processes get more intertwined. Vendors that provide a complete and coherent WS-stack would attract early adopters and gain competitive advantage.

To support the SOA, WS must provide standards-based definition of an interoperability communication protocol, mechanisms for service description, discovery, and composition as well as a basic set of quality of service protocols. The unique strengths and limitations of WS suggest unique design guidelines, including large granularity of messages, asynchronous messaging, bi-directionality of services, endpoint discovery, service agents, request pipeline, context, and content-based routing.

Web Services Incorporation Challenges Framework

Based on the discussions in the previous three subsections, we present a framework that classifies the challenges that are being faced in integrating WS into application development, particularly e-business applications, which have a very short development cycle. The challenges are organized under two broad categories, namely, technical and managerial. We present these challenges from the three stakeholders' perspective.

The major challenges faced by the stakeholders are provided in Table 1. The WS Suppliers consists of two groups: the vendors that actually provide services and third parties that support Web Service integration and publication services. Suppliers of WS face several challenges. The technical challenges that they face relate to:

1. Service description and profile.
2. Web service accessibility, and documentation.
3. Architecture standards and infrastructure,
4. Design requirements.
5. WS evolution.

The managerial challenges that they face are:

1. Pricing and quality of service commitments
2. Identifying new services
3. Customer feedback and support
4. Partnerships with third party providers
5. Demand management and liability

The WS consumers are essentially application developers in the IT department within an organization who are responsible for integrating WS into applications or individual end users that merely use these applications and articulate specific requirement to application developers. One of the major challenges these groups face in using WS is finding the appropriate WS to integrate that meet the application requirements. Simple applications with a single Web service may be easy to accomplish; however, large-scale applications that incorporate a variety of heterogeneous WS are very difficult to develop because of a number of interoperability issues. Some of the technical challenges that are still faced by this group of stakeholders are:

1. Search and identification of relevant WS
2. Customization and integration
3. Metrics and security
4. Dynamic and trusted environment
5. Necessary tools and infrastructure

In addition to these technical challenges, organizations also face the following managerial challenges in order to institutionalize WS based application development:

1. WS utilization strategy
2. Promoting WS training and education
3. Resource allocation and support
4. Incentives and rewards
5. Partnership management and security

The standards organizations play a vital role in moving the WS technology forward. While there exists some basic standards such as SOAP, WSDL, and UDDI that are used as building blocks for transport, describing, publishing, and invoking WS at the physical level, there is lot more work to

Table 1. WS challenges for the stakeholders

Stakeholder	Technical Challenges	Managerial Challenges
Web Services Supplier	• Service description and profile. • WS accessibility and documentation. • Architecture standards & infrastructure. • Design requirements. • Web services evolution.	• Pricing and quality of service commitments. • Identifying new services. • Customer support and feedback. • Partnerships with third party providers. • Demand management and liability.
Web Services Consumer	• Search and identification of relevant WS. • Customization and integration. • Metrics and security. • Dynamic and trusted environment. • Tools and infrastructure.	• WS utilization strategy. • Promoting WS training and education. • Resource allocation and support. • Incentives and rewards. • Partnership management and security.
Web services Standards Organization	• Service description, publishing, and invocation. • WS technology stack components. • Modeling Web services. • Architectures for WS applications. • Specifications for all aspects of WS.	• Future directions for WS research and practice. • WS implementation guidelines. • Vendor cooperation for common standards. • Open standards and interoperability. • Consistency between standards.

be done in standardizing various aspects of WS such as coordination, transaction, semantics, quality of service, security, etc. Since members of the standards organizations come from both IT users (mainly enterprise customers) and IT vendors communities, managing conflicts of interests, and getting vendors with competing interests and products to agree on "open" standards is a non trivial task. Some of the technical challenges that the standards organizations face are:

1. Open standards for service description, publishing and invocation
2. Identifying appropriate WS technology stack components
3. Modeling WS
4. Overarching architectures for WS applications
5. Specifications for all aspects of WS

From a managerial perspective, the leadership of these standards organizations face the following challenges:

1. Future directions for WS research and practice
2. WS implementation guidelines
3. Vendor cooperation for common standards
4. Open standards and interoperability
5. Consistency between the various standards

WEB SERVICES INCORPORATION CHALLENGES FOR SMEs

As mentioned in the previous section, there are several technical and managerial challenges that SMEs face in order to fully integrate Web services into their e-business applications. Regardless of whether an SME plays the role of a consumer or a supplier or both, it may not be able to contribute much in terms of solving technical problems in the Web services area due to lack of man power and expertise. Thus, solutions to technical challenges have to come from the large corporations in the industry and standards organizations. SMEs can adapt the solution architectures and configurations developed as industry standards in order to implement Web services based e-business applications. However, SMEs would still face a number of managerial challenges in order to successfully integrate Web services into their e-business applications. In the following paragraphs, we elaborate on these challenges first from the perspective of SMEs that are Web services consumers and then from the point of view of SMEs that are suppliers of Web services.

SMEs as Web Services Consumer

Technical Challenges

Search and Identification of Relevant WS
The main challenge of service discovery for SMEs is the use of automated means for accurate discovery of services in a manner that demands minimal user involvement. Improving service discovery would require explicating the semantics of both the service provider and the service requester. Improving service discovery would involve adding semantic annotations and including descriptions of QoS characteristics (for example in DAML/OWL or other semantic markup languages) to service definitions in WSDL and then registering these descriptions in registries. The use of standard ontologies that support shared vocabularies and domain models for use in the service description would also facilitate service discovery by making the semantics implied by structures in service descriptions explicit (Acuna & Carlos, 2006). To achieve automated discovery of services, the needs of service requesters have to be explicitly stated. Such needs have to be expressed as goals, which would correspond to the description of what services are sought, in some formal request language.

While WS enable SMEs as providers to offer their services on-line, they currently do not specify business essentials to the consumers such as how these services can be configured, integrated, monitored, metered, and protected. Current lack of standardization around WS specification for each business process in each industry leads service providers to publish similar WS with different parameters and signatures. The implication of this is that when a WS customer (also referred to as service requestor) receives a WSDL specification for a WS from a public registry, developers need to specifically implement each WS call to support each service provider's method.

In the current specification of UDDI registry, once published, the business information and the business service descriptions are available for anyone to view and invoke. There is no notion of security and access control on the information posted in the public registries supported by UDDI. It is seldom the case that the services to be offered by an enterprise can all be made public and can be accessed by anyone. While the individual service provider's WS applications can implement their own security within their domain and prevent unwanted parties from making use of their services, the security exposures and overheads in scanning and parsing all incoming requests (including Spam) discourage many businesses from publishing any mission critical services on the public registry, which hinders the search process for many genuine potential consumers to identify relevant WS that match their needs.

Customization and Integration

The terms "orchestration" and "choreography" are used to describe business interaction protocols comprising collaborating services (Agarwal et al., 2005). Orchestration describes how services must interact with each other at the message level, including the business logic and execution order of the interactions from the perspective and under control of a single endpoint. Choreography on the other hand is typically associated with the public (globally visible) message exchanges, rules of interaction and agreements that occur between multiple business process endpoints, rather than a specific business process that is executed by a single party.

Choreography is more collaborative in nature than orchestration. Choreography offers a means by which the rules of participation for collaboration can be clearly defined and agreed to, jointly. Choreography tracks the sequence of messages that may involve multiple parties and multiple sources, including customers, suppliers, and partners, where each party involved in the process describes the part they play in the interaction and no party "owns" the conversation. Orchestration is targeted by a family of XML-based process standard definition languages, most representative of which is the business process execution language for WS (WS-BPEL).

Therefore, for SME WS to interact properly with each other as part of composite applications that perform more complex functions by orchestrating numerous services and pieces of information, the consumer and provider entities must agree both on the service description (WSDL definition) and semantics that will govern the interaction between them (Talib, Yang, & Ilyas, 2005). The development of a complete semantic solution would therefore require that semantics are addressed not only at the terminology level but also at the level that WS are used and applied in the context of business scenarios, i.e. at the business process-level. This would imply that there must be an agreement between a service consumer and provider as to the implied processing of messages exchanged between interacting services that are part of a business process.

Metrics and Security

Quality of service (QoS) metrics encompasses important functional and non-functional service quality attributes, such as performance metrics, security attributes, reliability, scalability, and availability. Traditionally, QoS has been measured by the degree to which applications, systems, networks, and all other elements of the IT infrastructure support availability of services at a required level of performance under all access and load conditions. While traditional QoS metrics apply, the characteristics of WS environments bring both greater availability of applications and increased complexity in terms of accessing and managing services and thus impose specific and intense demands on organizations, which QoS must address. Delivering QoS on the Internet is therefore a critical and significant challenge because of its dynamic and unpredictable nature. To be successful, both the consumer and the provider must understand and respect each other's QoS policies, performance levels, security requirements, etc.

Validation of the security aspects in SOA-based applications will require a full system approach to test end-to-end security solutions from both network level and application level security angles (Gutierrez, Fernandez-Medina, & Piattini, 2005). As far as security is concerned, broadband connections remain "always on," exposing SMEs to the same hackers, and fraudulent behaviors that have plagued the government and large enterprises lately. SMEs, unlike larger enterprises, have not developed the means of effectively thwarting such attacks. They also face a maze of "new" security issues surrounding virus protection, integrity of data in transit and in storage, and control of what flows into and out of the company. Additionally, security infrastructure solutions that protect against these exposures require administration and overhead. SMEs therefore need security solutions to protect against these risks and minimize administrative overhead.

SMEs require different solutions than those incorporated by larger corporations. At one level, SMEs need the same security basics that larger organizations require, such as firewall and virtual private network (VPN) capabilities. Beyond that, a large portion of SME consumers look for the flexibility to integrate virus scanning and content control (such as URL filtering) into their environments. Since SMEs often rely on third parties for IT functions, rather then staffing their own IT departments, they need solutions that install easily, run without much administrative overhead, and fit seamlessly into their current network infrastructure. Their solution of choice, and the answer to a majority of their requirements, is the security appliance, which is a network-enabled device explicitly designed to provide a single dedicated service, such as a firewall, or a predefined suite of services.

Dynamic and Trusted Environment

Providing an effective dynamic e-business environment is technical challenge for organizations of all sizes, not only for the SMEs. The capabilities of a dynamic e-business environment are:

1. Open application interfaces to enable interaction between trading partners, service providers, and other entities that enable e-commerce.
2. Communication paths supported primarily by the Internet and extending to other public or private systems.
3. Open standards representing business transaction processes that facilitate automated business to business interaction and minimize or eliminate manual intervention.
4. Facilities that support dynamic connection while permitting easy reconfiguration of connections and adaptation when market conditions change.
5. Systems that foster automated functions and services such as identification, negotiation, and agreement among trading partners and services providers (Gurguis & Zeid, 2005).

WS enable many of these key prerequisites for dynamic e-business. Based on open standards, they define a means by which business services can be published, discovered, and invoked. They support directories of businesses and services where entries are added modified or deleted dynamically, thereby deliver the most current search and identification results to business applications. They define a standard way to describe and invoke a WS interface so that the business application can easily connect to it. They support an unrestricted message package supporting all forms of business processes and embody an unlimited range of businesses and services.

A trusted environment for e-business to facilitate the Web-enabled services provided by the consumers and the suppliers should be conceptualized, developed and established. The development of this trusted environment should be undertaken by all interested parties who would participate directly for building consensus. Establishing the trusted environment is crucial for conducting e-business interactions, especially between partners who do not know each other in advance, e.g. on Internet trading platforms. Transparency is essential. The technical building blocks should include the definition of common interfaces, service types and services, representation and presentation issues related to trust. The service building blocks should include naming and identification, discovery, mediation, usage, metering, monitoring and service management, coordination, payment, etc., which constitute the real trust issues. These issues are closely related to QoS metrics.

Tools and Infrastructure

One of the major limitations of the state-of-the-art technologies that prevent effective automated composition of WS-based application is the lack of tools for supporting the evolution and adaptation of business processes. It is hard to define compositions of distributed business processes that work properly under all circumstances (Hull & Su, 2005). Misunderstanding in the agreement between different organizations/entities, as well as errors in the specification and implementation of the interaction protocols, can easily occur, especially for complex processes and interaction protocols. Typical problems are business processes that wait forever, or for too long, to receive an answer from another process or that expect a different answer; or, business processes that fail to invoke another process as required and do not allow the distributed business to correctly proceed. Moreover, even in the case where business interactions are initially correctly defined and implemented, they frequently stop working when some processes involved in the interactions are autonomously redefined by an external organization; this kind of evolution is very common in distributed and highly dynamic environments.

SMEs would have to overcome these technical challenges of providing infrastructure support for application integration (Malloy, Kraft, Hallstrom, & Voas, 2006). That is, the run-time environment should be able to possess the ability to support service-based application integration by enabling better-structured integration solutions that deliver applications compromised of interchangeable parts, evolutionary application portfolios that protect investment and can respond rapidly to new requirements and business processes, and facilitate 'best of breed' portfolio strategies, which automatically combine legacy applications, acquired packages, external application subscriptions, and newly built components.

Managerial Challenges

Web Services Utilization Strategy

Until the WS standards and technologies mature and become universally accepted by the stakeholders, all organizations including SMEs should create a roadmap that will guide them to adopt WS in a manner that avoids risks to deliver the expected business benefits. The strategy should be to implement WS incrementally, first within the organization and then expanding outward as standards and technologies mature. By deploying WS first within their own organizational boundaries, SMEs can gain operational efficiencies and a unified understanding of how best of breed WS could be potentially utilized in their complex business processes. Once they are comfortable and knowledgeable with the use of WS internally, the deployment domain could expand to include their trading partners.

To quickly gain operational efficiency, SMEs should focus on integrating internal legacy systems by exploring different WS interface mechanisms to extract data and make them available to existing and new e-business applications. Therefore, instead of making the data and transaction only available to the specific application that the legacy code was developed for, they can be made available to any application across the enterprise and can be reused as often as necessary.

Two levels of integration are possible: data integration and process integration. With the use of standard WS interfaces, it is relatively easy to create applications that bring together data from multiple, possibly remote, locations. Similarly, existing functionalities can be integrated as well as new functionality can be incorporated using standard SOAP interfaces to make them available across the organization. Additionally, these integrations help create a Web-enabled environment for the execution of the business functions.

Promoting Web Services Training and Education

Since most SMEs lack adequate human resources and technical expertise available internally to develop complex technological solutions, promoting enterprise clusters can enhance SME performance and competitiveness. The SMEs working in clusters—formed through partnerships and networks at the business sector or industry level—can attain the advantages of large firms while retaining the benefits of specialization and flexibility. Grouped in local systems of production, these SMEs can often be more flexible and responsive to customer needs than large integrated firms. They can pool resources and share the costs of training, research and marketing. Clustering will facilitate exchange of personnel and diffusion of technology and creates new possibilities for efficiency gains. More importantly, these local networks of support systems can help SMEs meet the challenges of globalization by increasing their ability to reach a global market.

SMEs' deployment of WS-based e-business systems depends on their perception of the opportunities afforded by such systems and the relevance of these opportunities to their business. SMEs can be made more aware of the benefits and opportunities of such systems by providing more hands-on, customized delivery of information, assistance, and demonstration tailored to specific business sector needs or specific business functions. Thus SMEs should promote WS through awareness campaigns within and between the enterprise clusters. Knowledge of best practice, what works elsewhere, is also important in formulating the awareness campaigns.

Resource Allocation and Support

As SMEs gain expertise and knowledge on WS use in their e-business environment, they need to develop methods for monitoring and managing WS for better utilization of their resources. With any new technology, customers are first concerned about how the technology can benefit them. As the technology matures and first versions of products utilizing the technology are released, the emphasis invariably shifts to performance. Not only do customers expect the new technology to improve ease of development and interoperability but they also want it to perform at an optimum level. Through their experiences with WS technologies, SMEs need to constantly improve the methods for configuring, building, and calling WS to obtain optimal performance.

The benefits of integration and flexibility that WS bring to an enterprise are wonderful, but if an enterprise cannot determine an effective way to manage their services, the benefits are unattainable in any sort of meaningful way. Thus, it becomes paramount for SMEs to adopt a comprehensive services management solution to ensure rock solid services execution and in turn, guarantee smooth business operations for customers and partners. Such a service management solution should include components such as access mechanism, which includes authentication and authorization effectiveness; WS provisioning, which includes effective subscription, service level agreement (SLA) with the supplier, license (contract) management, monitoring, metering and billing; secure communications; and workflow management.

Incentives and Rewards

The WS technologies potentially facilitate a new trend toward products and services that can be designed and delivered to customers, who can pick and choose only the desired ones. To the consumers or customers, WS technologies can provide greater flexibility and promote integration. Because theoretically, customers can buy different pieces from multiple product and service providers, put these pieces together the way they want, and do not worry about the communication and interfacing problem. That is, customers can choose "best of breed" products and/or services and put them together in a way desired to build their system architecture in achieving their business and technical objectives. At the same time, due to the use of WS technologies, the cost of switching product or service providers will be reduced to minimal.

The incentives and rewards structures in SMEs should be designed around the tangible and intangible benefits that will be derived from the deployment of WS in their e-business context. The tangible benefits could include such things as reduced administrative costs, reduced production costs, reduced lead time, increased sales, and creation of additional revenue streams. The intangible benefits could include such things as quality of information, improved internal control of the business, and improved relations with business partners.

SMEs as Web Services Supplier

Technical Challenges

Service Description and Profile

One of the technical challenges faced by Web service suppliers is describing and advertising their Web services correctly and efficiently. They also face the problem of how to publicize their services so that service seekers can easily find these services and evaluate their suitability. After all, if the service seekers can't find or get appropriate information about a particular Web service, then the likelihood of some one using that service is grim and hence the service provider stands to lose lot of market share (Zhang, 2005). Web service profiles are created for quick and easy identification of appropriate services. In articulating their Web service profiles, providers should go through the same exercise of modeling the requirements and functionalities that the Web service can satisfy, and then transforming this model into appropriate specification. Thus, a well-established approach can be very valuable to *providers* in appropriately describing and publishing relevant information about their Web services to facilitate easy discovery by service seekers.

The main purpose of the service profile is to advertise or communicate to the rest of the world as to what the service does. The service profile provides current information about the service to the user; so constant update is not needed. Thus, the service profile should reflect the static information about the service. A common challenge faced by service providers is how to model and structure the service profiles using standard modeling techniques. Since a class diagram in UML represents static information about the system, it is suitable for representing the service profile. Also, the structure of a service profile is similar to the structure of a class and hence standard templates should be developed to represent service profiles. Thus, when a specific service is defined, the elements of the service are described as instantiations of the template.

Web Services Accessibility and Documentation

One of the major problems faced by Web application developers is the difficulty in accessing relevant Web services that meet the set of requirements for the application under consideration (Zhou, Chia, & Lee, 2005). This is partly because developers don't have a systematic way to translate the system models generated at the end of the requirements analysis phase into a format that could be used to easily search and compare against the service descriptions published by Web service providers (Sirin, Parsia, & Hendler, 2005). Thus, the challenge is whether developers can identify the requirements and important elements of the application and transpose it into a canonical representation and match it against the service profile documentation of available Web services. The developer can then determine to what extent a particular service meets the requirements and select the most appropriate ones. This process can be done manually or even partially automated through intelligent agents (Jabisetti & Lee, 2005). The service suppliers should provide an environment in which the user can focus on the requirements modeling and documentation. The resulting models can be provided to a set of agents that can do the mapping and automatically search their respective domains to find appropriate Web services and make recommendations. The developer can evaluate this initial agent feedback, select a few services to investigate further, and eventually select the most suitable Web services to use in the application. With time, more and more Web services are becoming available and the agents can maintain an up-to-date documentation of these services in their respective domains.

Architecture Standards and Infrastructure

A Web service architecture provides a model and context for understanding the constituent services and the relationships between them. This model describes the characteristics that are common to all Web services and the ones that are needed by many. Enterprises often use Web services to distribute data and conduct business transactions. Such business transactions may require a service to access other services to perform global transactions and there are no universally accepted standards for such global transactions. Standards are necessary for coordination among services and such standards are in the process of being developed.

Architecture standards and adequate infrastructure are essential for developing applications using service oriented architecture. Several component based architectures exist and coarse-grained components and services have become more common in application development and system integration. Mature enterprise architectures built from multiple components and services that support the business processes can be joined into blocks of increasingly larger, coarser grained components. The key challenge is to determine how best to combine the functionality of large enterprise level components, fine-grained business objects, and the legacy systems.

Design Requirements

As Web services implementation is on the rise, SMEs are looking for an evolutionary approach for the design of "open" and "modular" Web services technology to support agile businesses. While an organization can focus initially on opportunities that can deliver immediate gains to efficiency, more advanced capabilities of this technology can provide new opportunities for a business. However, there is hardly any guidance available today for the efficient design of Web services and the necessary tool set. Organizations, particularly the SMEs that want to become Web services suppliers, need to determine what services to design and build, how to build them at the right level of granularity, and how to build them loosely coupled (Fontana, 2004). Web services providers face the challenge of developing a framework with multiple perspectives that will characterize the process complexity from a Web service design and deployment point of view. Service providers need to develop guidelines to make decisions on the content and granularity of services that will make up the Service Oriented Architecture of a firm adopting one or more of their services.

Design of Web services from the provider's perspective involves a number of issues. First, providers need to determine which services will be in demand and how to design them for maximum utility. Second, these services might replace a small portion of an existing system or interface with major subsystems within existing systems. Thus, the granularity and viability of Web services is an important issue. Stated differently, how large or small the services should be, their interface design, and how they can be clustered. Third, the Web service should provide necessary and sufficient metadata. Fourth, how will the Web service handle exceptions and recover from failures. Fifth, the service providers have to pay special attention to issues related to authentication, authorization, single sign-on, confidentiality, and non-repudiation.

Web Services Evolution

A key challenge in integrating Web services into applications is that Web services are still evolving. They provide interoperability across platforms, operating systems, and programming languages through a collection of technologies and specifications. However, many of these technologies are still being introduced. Additional standards are being defined to enable Web services to realize their full potential. When organizations design their applications using service oriented architecture, one problem that arises is version control as Web services evolve over a period of time. A key question is, when should the organization switch to new services and how to ensure that this transition will be smooth. Thus, the version management of Web services involves challenges such as how to alert users that its functionality and interface has changed and how to deal with the applications that may rely on the previous version of a Web service.

Managerial Challenges

Pricing and Quality of Service

As WS evolve in the industry, there will be an increasing need for WS providers to create business models that will measure the value of their service. These business models should efficiently measure WS invoked by service requestors, particularly those services of high value. SMEs face several managerial challenges in creating WS pricing models, which depend on a number of factors such as reliability and security, transactions and scalability, accessibility, integrity, performance, accounting, etc. SMEs need to gain experience in pricing and negotiating WS contracts and maintaining them over a period of time. This issue becomes even harder if different customers require different billing rates.

Current specifications don't have an agreed upon mechanism for handling WS metering and accounting; hence, SMEs providing WS tools have to build their own solutions. This can lead to problems when moving from one vendor's tools to another. Companies providing WS for their business partners typically do not post their services on public registries and can therefore control access and billing. SMEs typically face challenges in providing adequate monitoring and billing facilities because of their lack of resources and expertise.

SMEs that provide WS with a high degree of value have to develop service level agreements (SLA's) or their equivalent, which implies that the parties involved have to agree to the contract. The contract lays the foundation for metering the services to be used and also includes environmental prerequisites for the use of the Web service. The contract should provide details concerning the type of contract, start dates and expiration dates of the contract, time model to be used, limits to the amount of service to be provided, and security signatures or certificates for encryption and authentication. SMEs have to clearly spell out the details of the contract, which is important for billing purposes and prevents inaccurate charges to the service requestor.

Identifying New Services

SMEs need to identify how WS can truly serve the business needs of its users. They must be seen not only as a technology but also as an *enabler* for delivering new forms of business value. End users might not realize that WS are responsible for delivering value-added services but enterprise strategic planners and IT executives are aware of them as a fundamental way of conducting business. Hence, SMEs have to identify potential new WS that serve as the strategic enabler for delivering business services to the right person, at the right time, on the right device.

SMEs that once positioned themselves as WS companies might feel pressured to differentiate their products further as WS become standard. Emerging technologies often have life spans that match market changes. Specialized markets exist for a technology, but over time, the market expands and the technology becomes widely adopted and commoditized. Hence, SMEs need to be aware of the changes in the WS market place and make changes accordingly in terms of identifying new services. Also, the SME sector may not have access to highly qualified software developers with WS skills and be subjected to design solutions from amateur and inexperienced designers. This may lead to WS that are highly static, not scalable, and exceedingly difficult to enhance.

Customer Support and Feedback

Typically, a language gap exists between SMEs promoting technical features of their products and organizations looking for business value. SMEs must better articulate the business benefits of their technologies to bridge this gap. For instance, if SMEs can back up their products claims using real case studies and metrics that drive home their points and provide industry-relevant details.

Problems are encountered when WS use a different platform than the client application. This leaves the developers building a client application unable to understand and appreciate the strengths and limitations of services their applications call. Typically, WS are developed and maintained by groups other than those building the application. Application developers working with WS lack insight into the application details, and even the platform upon which the service is built. Providing customer support would facilitate technical appreciation of how the Web service does its chores. This may assist with issues surrounding how to make calls to that service or help developers resolve problems that are inherent within the service itself. Hence, SMEs should allocate enough resources to help developers analyze and diagnose problems they encounter with the Web service.

Web service developers have a good understanding of what the Web service should do and how to implement those requirements. However, they lack the real-world experience of designing an application directly in support of end users. Developers of client applications can assist WS providers by providing real-world feedback on their performance and reliability. This enables application developers to better understand Web service strengths and limitations, while providing service developers with invaluable information on service use. This type of information is essential to SMEs when architecting and building new services. Service consumers can field test the work of service providers, which may provide the only true test of the Web service.

Demand Management

A great benefit of WS is that it can be reused. This may have unintended consequences. For example, many different consumers can reuse these services that the provider did not anticipate.

Since Web service providers are loosely coupled from their consumers, a service can experience an unexpected demand as consumers increase their usage. The risk that an SME service provider faces as its services find new users is an increased risk of downtime or lower performance for critical users. The application servers used by the SMEs can address some of the risks of downtime that results from unexpected WS traffic, but not all of the risks. Thus, an SME has to create an active WS management solution that provides dynamic routing, load balancing, and prioritized messages.

CONCLUDING REMARKS

This chapter has discussed the integration of Web services into e-business applications from the perspective of SMEs. E-business adoption and use in organizations including SMEs have resulted in significant financial benefits to them worldwide. In recent years, WS have generated considerable excitement in the global computing industry because of its promise of full-fledged application software that needn't be installed on ones local computer, but that allow systems running in different environments to interoperate via XML and other Web standards. The integration of WS in e-business, consequently offers an enterprise considerable opportunities for integration within the enterprise, either with legacy applications or new business processes that span organizational silos.

However, WS computing offers significant technical and managerial challenges to its stakeholders—suppliers, consumers, and standards organizations—as they determine how to help leverage the emerging technologies to create service components and automate individual applications. WS technologies are maturing and industry analysts predict that the market for WS components is either about to take off or has already arrived. This study investigated the challenges that exist for each of the stakeholders and presented a framework that organized and inter-related these challenges in an easily understandable manner to help study the factors that impact the deployment of WS. SMEs were studied and then analyzed using the framework to provide insights into the technical and managerial challenges they need to overcome to deploy WS based e-business systems. It was suggested that SMEs should start deployment of these technologies now, but they should start within the firewall, inside the enterprise, and work outwards as they gain experience and knowledge along the way.

The challenges framework presented in this paper is by no means exhaustive; however, it does provide a useful insight into the factors that impact the deployment of WS. The next stage of our research is to investigate some of these factors in more detail. We expect this article to shed some light for researchers and practitioners to better understand the important issues and future trends of Web services based e-business systems.

REFERENCES

Acuna, C. J., & Carlos, R. J. (2006). Modeling semantic Web services: A case study. *Proceedings of the 6th International Conference on Web Engineering* (pp. 32-39), Palo Alto, California.

Agarwal, V., Dasgupta, K., Karnik, N., Kumar, A., Kundu, A., Mittal, S., & Srivastava, B. (2005). A service creation environment based on end to end composition of Web services. *Proceedings of the 14th International Conference on World Wide Web* (pp. 128-137), Chiba, Japan.

Arsanjani, A., Hailpern, B., Martin, J., & Tarr, P. (2003). Web services: Promises and compromises. *ACM Queue, 1*(1), 48-58.

Auger, P., & Gallaugher, J. M. (1997). Factors affecting adoption of an Internet-based sales presence for small businesses. *The Information Society, 13*(1), 55-74.

Barry, H., & Milner, B. (2002). SME's and electronic commerce: A departure from the traditional prioritization of training? *Journal of European Industrial Training, 25*(7), 316-326.

Beckinsale, M., Levy, M. & Powell, P. (2006). Exploring Internet adoption drivers in SMEs. *Electronic Markets, 16*(4), 361-370.

Bichier, M., & Lin, K. J. (2006). Service-oriented computing. *IEEE Computer, 39*(3), 99-101.

Casati, F., Shan, E., Dayal, U., & Shan, M. (2003). Business-oriented management of Web services. *Communications of the ACM, 46*(10), 55-61.

Chen, M. (2005). An analysis of the driving forces for Web services adoption. *Information Systems and eBusiness Management, 3*(3), 265-279.

Chen, M., Chen, A., & Shao, B. (2003). The implications and impacts of Web services to electronic commerce research and practices. *Journal of Electronic Commerce Research, 4*(4), 128-139.

Chung, J., Lin, K., & Mathieu, R. G. (2003). Web services computing: Advancing software interoperability. *IEEE Computer, 36*(10), 35-37.

Cote, L., Sabourin, V., & Vezina, M. (2004). *Electronic business models—A study on the adoption of electronic business by small and medium-sized Canadian enterprises.* Retrieved from http://www.cefrio.qc.ca

Curbera, F., Khalaf, R., Mukhi, N., Tai, S., & Weerawarana, S. (2003). The next step in Web services. *Communications of the ACM, 46*(10), 29-34.

Daniel, E. M., White, A., & Ward, J. M. (2004). Exploring the role of third parties in inter-organizational Web service adoption. *Journal of Enterprise Information Management, 17*(5), 351-360.

EMPG. (2002). *eEurope go digital: Benchmarking national and regional e-business policies for SMEs.* Final Report of the E-business Policy Group, 28 June.

Fariselli, P., Oughton, C., Picory, C., & Sugden, R. (1999). Electronic commerce and the future for SMEs in a global market place: Networking and public policies. *Small Business Economics, 12*(3), 261-275.

Fensel, D., & Bussler, C. (2002). The Web service modeling framework WSMF. *Electronic Commerce: Research and Applications, 1*(2002), 113-137.

Fontana, J. (2004). Service-oriented hype to meet hard realities. *Network World, 21*, 68-69.

Fowler, M. (2003). *Patterns of enterprise application architecture.* Boston: Addison-Wesley.

Geng, X., Gopal, R. D., Ramesh, R., & Whinston, A. B. (2003). Scaling Web services with capacity provision networks. *IEEE Computer, 36*(11), 64-72.

Gonsalves, A. (2002). GE unit adds Web services. *Information Week.* 30 April.

Gurguis, S. A., & Zeid, A. (2005). Towards autonomic Web services: Achieving self-healing using Web services. *Proceedings of the Workshop on Design and Evolution of Autonomic Application Software* (pp. 1-5), St. Louis, Missouri.

Gutierrez, C., Fernandez-Medina, E., & Piattini, M. (2005). Web services enterprise security architecture: A case study. *Proceedings of the 2005 Workshop on Secure Web services* (pp. 10-19).

Hagel III, J. (2002). *Out of box: Strategies for achieving profits today and growth through Web services.* Boston: Harvard Business School Press.

Hull, R., & Su, J. (2005). Tools for composite Web services: A short overview. *ACM SIGMOD Record, 43*(2), 86-95.

Jabisetti, N., & Lee, Y. (2005). OWL-S-based autonomic services for grid computing. *Proceedings of the IEEE International Conference on Web services* (pp. 825-826), July 11-15, 2005.

Jeffcoate, J., Chappell, C., & Feindt, S. (2002). Best practice in SME adoption of e-commerce. *Benchmarking: An International Journal, 9*(2), 122-132.

Joshi, P., Singh, H., & Phippen, A. D. (2004). Web services: Measuring practitioner attitude. *14*(5), 366-371.

Khalaf, R. (2002). Enterprise services. *Communications of the ACM, 45*(10), 77-82.

Kleijen, S., & Raju, S. (2003). An open Web services architecture. *ACM Queue, 1*(1), 38-47.

Knol, W. H. C., & Stroken, J. M. H. (2001). The diffusion and adoption of information technology in small and medium sized enterprises through IT scenarios. *Technology Analysis & Strategic Management, 13*(2), 227-246.

Kreger, H. (2003). Fulfilling the Web services promise. *Communications of the ACM, 46*(6), 29-34.

Lee, J., & Runge, J. (2001). Adoption of information technology in small business: Testing drivers of adoption for entrepreneurs. *Journal of Computer Information Systems, 42*(1), 44-57.

Lin, K. J., Ho, J., & Zhang, L. J. (2004). First wave of Web services adoption in research. *International Journal of Web services Research, 1*(4), 1-4.

Malloy, B. A., Kraft, N. A., Hallstrom, J. O., & Voas, J. M. (2006). Improving the predictable assembly of service-oriented architectures. *IEEE Software, 23*(2), 12-15.

Manes, A. T. (2003). *Web services: A manager's guide.* Boston: Addison Wesley.

Maruyama, H. (2002). New trends in e-business: From B2B to Web services. *New Generation Computing, 20*, 125-139.

McIlraith, S., Son, T. C., & Zeng, H. (2001). Semantic Web services. *IEEE Intelligent Systems.* Special issue on semantic Web, *16*(2), 46-53.

Mehrtens, J., Cragg, P. B., & Mills, A. M. (2001). A model of Internet adoption by SMEs. *Information and Management, 39*, 165-176.

Mirchandani, D. A., & Motwani, J. (2001). Understanding small business electronic commerce adoption: An empirical analysis. *Journal of Computer Information Systems, 41*(3), 70-73.

Motta, E., Domingue, J., Cabral, L., Gaspari, M. (2003). IRS-II: A framework and infrastructure for semantic Web services. In D. Fensel, K. Sycara, & J. Mylopoulos (Eds.), *The semantic Web—ISWC 2003. Lecture Notes in Computer Science* (Vol. 2870, pp. 306-318). Heidelberg: Springer-Verlag.

Orchard, D. (2002). *Web services pitfalls.* Retrieved from http://www.xml.com/pub/a/2002/02/06/Webservices.html

OWL-S Coalition. (2004). *OWL-S 1.0 Release.* Retrieved from http://www.daml.org/services/owl-s/1.1/

Papazoglou, M. P. (2003). Web services and business transactions. *World Wide Web: Internet and Web Information Systems, 6*, 49-91.

Peltz, C. (2003). Web services orchestration and choreography. *IEEE Computer, 36*(10), 46-53.

Rust, T. R., & Kannan, P. K. (2003). E-service: A new paradigm for business in the electronic environment. *Communications of the ACM, 46*(6), 36-42.

Salleh, N. A. M., Rohde, F., & Green, P. (2006). The effect of enacted capabilities on adoption of a government electronic procurement system by Malaysian SMEs. *Electronic Markets, 16*(4), 292-311.

Scupola, A. (2002). Adoption issues of business-to-business Internet commerce in European SMEs. *Proceedings of the 35th Hawaii International Conference on System Sciences* (Vol. 7), Hawaii, USA.

Schmidt, R. (2003). Web services-based architectures to support dynamic inter-organizational business processes. In M. Jeckle, & L. J. Zhang (Eds.), *International Conference on Web services, ICWS-Europe 2003, LNCS 2853* (pp. 123-136), Berlin.

Sirin, E., Parsia, B., & Hendler, J. (2004). Filtering and selecting semantic Web services with interactive composition techniques. *IEEE Intelligent Systems*, *19*(4), 42-49.

Stal, M. (2002). Web services: Beyond component-based computing. *Communications of the ACM, 45*(10), 71-76.

Talib, M. A., Yang, Z., & Ilyas, Q. M. (2005). A framework towards Web services composition modeling and execution. *Proceedings of the IEEE EEE05 International Workshop on Business Services Networks* (pp. 4-10), Hong Kong.

Tetteh, E., & Burn, J. (2001). Global strategies for SME-business: Applying the SMALL framework. *Logistics Information Management, 14*(1-2), 171-180.

Tilley, S., Gerdes, J., Hamilton, T., Huang, S., Miller, H., Smith, D., & Wong, K. (2004). On business value and technical challenges of adopting Web services. *Journal of Software Maintenance and Evolution: Research and Practice, 16*, 31-50.

Wu, C. (2004). A readiness model for adopting Web services. *Journal of Enterprise Information Management, 17*(5), 361-371.

Zhang, D. (2005). Web services composition for process management in e-business. *The Journal of Computer Information Systems*, *45*(2), 83-91.

Zhou, C., Chia, L. T., & Lee, B. S. (2005). Semantics in service discovery and QoS measurement. *IT Professional*, *7*(2), 29-34.

Chapter X
Modelling in Clinical Practice with Web Services and BPEL

Iain Morrison
The University of Melborne, Australia

Bryn Lewis
The University of Melborne, Australia

Sony Nugrahanto
The University of Melborne, Australia

ABSTRACT

The aim of increasing the quality of health care has led to the development of a number of "guideline" systems whereby clinicians receive assistance in decision making in a given care context—for example in areas such as prescribing or therapeutics. These guidelines range in complexity and functionality from simple textual references through to executable modules which can subsume some of the clinical decision making process. In the latter case, ensuring consistent and interoperable engagement between the guideline engine, clinical information system and patient record can become problematic. Critical areas include vocabulary and terminology (in differing use contexts) and the interfaces and interaction between different sub-systems where traditional approaches have been focussed on tightly coupling of sub-systems and in the generation of special purpose "glue" languages and logic. In this paper, we briefly describe an approach to clinical, information and service modelling. This approach uses tools and techniques gaining increasing acceptance in the e-commerce domain, which shares many of the technical and interoperability problems present in e-health.

INTRODUCTION

Integrating decision-making and computing practices in the clinical environment is a key objective of health informatics. A key factor in the adoption of new computing practices in clinical contexts is the careful survey of clinical practices and decision-making, in order to design and develop applications that can be used within accepted practices rather than orthogonal to them.

The Modelling the Clinical Processes of Prescribing (MCPOP) project (Liaw, Morrison, Lewis, Deveny, 2004) uses the FRAMS (Falls Risks Assessment and Management System) methodology, based on expert and professional reference groups and rigorous modelling, to translate clinical practice into computing structures.

In the MCPOP project we faced the requirement to (1) have a model for the underlying patient record systems (2) anticipate a clinical information system for use by a GP (3) refine/extend vocabularies and term-sets for use in the project domain (4) elucidate and define "best practice" in prescribing for asthma through researching an appropriate clinical process/workflow model, and (5) define interfaces to services such as guideline systems, decision support systems or terminology/taxonomy services.

In this paper we will focus mainly on the last two requirement areas. Their more generic features are shared by many similar projects in the domain.

As a precursor from requirements (1-3), we note that we used the general practice data model (GPDM) (General Practice Computing Group, 2000) as our underlying information model for the Clinical Information System. The GPDM is a patient-centric data model developed in Australia following wide stakeholder representation. At the level of clinical data (transactions/events) it has much in common with openEHR/CEN13606 but lacks the management and organising structures of that emerging standard.

We translated the GPDM Entities and Data Elements into accessible electronic forms including UML and XMI to produce a base structure. These were then imported into two tools for further modelling, instantiation and development. We used Eclipse for Java-based development (with the eclipse modelling framework) and Protégé, a Knowledge Engineering Tool developed at Stanford Medical Institute and in use in a number of existing Health Informatics Projects, as a decision support aid. By using Protégé, we obtain the capacity to also capture instance (patient) data and a means of researching decision support artefacts through its built-in query language and constraint modelling plug-ins, without committing to prior application software development. Protege also has a Java API and through its XML-based persistence mechanism (ontology and instance data) and also Java-XML Binding (JAXB), we are able to export

Figure 1. Modelling outputs

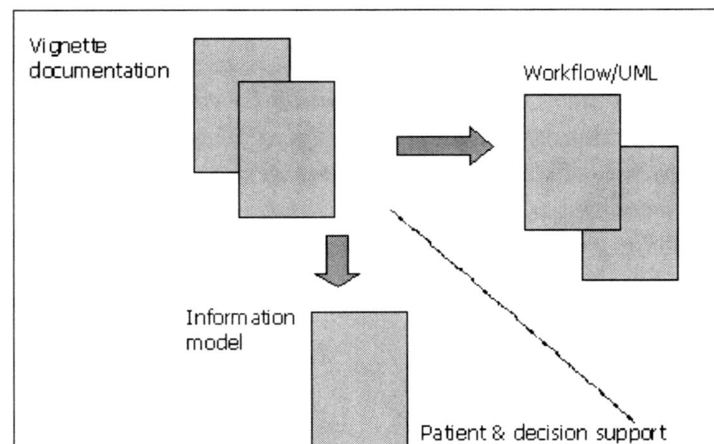

the information models and instance data as XML data or as Java classes and objects.

In Figure 1, we show a schematic of the FRAMS outputs — the methodology produces (1) a set of information constructs necessary in the clinical use context (to be sourced from the GPDM in the case of patient data or from external sources such as medication descriptions) and (2) a best-practice workflow representation of clinical decision making including, where necessary, decision points and variables and information flows. We note that the workflow may include referrals to other health providers (such as diagnostic scanning).

PROCESS MODELLING

Workflow Modelling and SOA

We have investigated modelling the clinical processes of prescribing for asthma. The modelling required is multilevel as it (1) describes the clinical processes/pathways, (2) describes the linkages to the clinical information systems (CIS) and actors/agents in the use context (GP in practice) and it (3) describes the information flows.

The model describes systems, sub-systems and their interactions. An implementation that

Figure 2. Actor representation

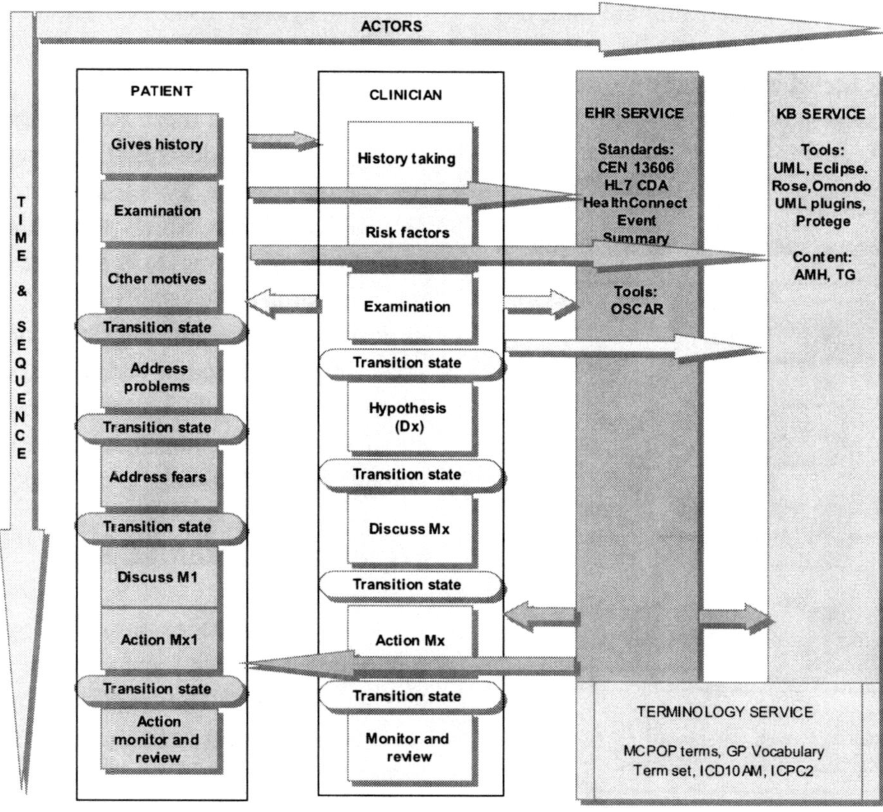

satisfies the specifications of the model can best be realised using a Service Oriented Architecture (SOA).

In Figure 2, we provide an "actor" representation where the roles being enacted are evident as are the associated information flows. Overlaying this, and set out in Figure 3, we provide a high level graphical representation of one of our clinical model flows that emerged from the FRAMS methodology. The latter flow can, of course, be iteratively expanded to expose information flows and activities at lower levels of granularity. In enactment, the clinical model workflow informs and manages the activities of the actors and their information flows and is in turn informed by them.

What we are seeking are representations of clinical processes and models that are both descriptive and executable and that facilitate linkage to other (sub-) systems which carry out activities and support services.

Figure 3. High level clinical model workflow

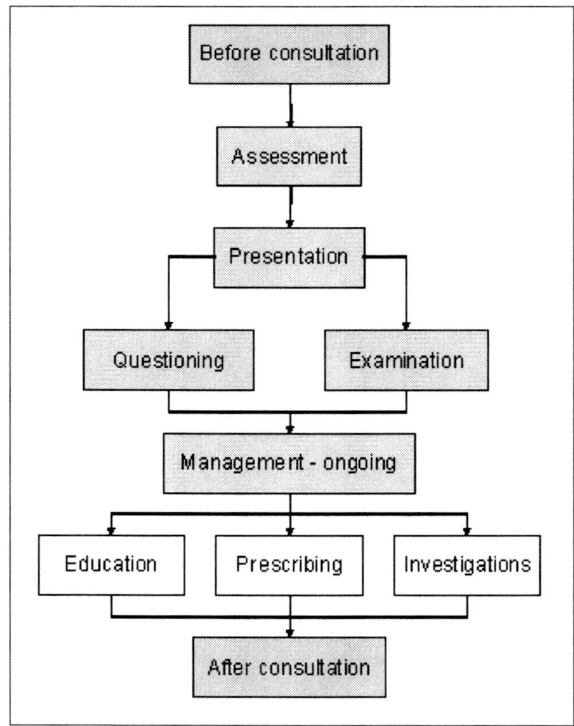

The distributed and multiple sub-systems nature of "on-demand" e-commerce systems means that they have the following characteristics and design goals:

- The sharing of information and data models in some application domain between disparate and independently operating systems, which requires reaching agreement on the syntax, semantics and vocabulary for structured dialogue in computer mediated interactions,
- Achieving automated interoperability in functional areas (order, invoicing, finance,..) critical to the supply chain (business processes), and
- Integration of functional interoperability into synchronised transactions that serve a business aim.

The first two of these have given rise to the emergence of "self-describing" message exchange between disparate systems, based on XML and XML Schema which allow hierarchies of namespaces (meaning) to be imported and shared understanding to be established.

Rapid advances are being made on the second and third point through widespread adoption of SOAP (Simple Object Access Protocol) and, with extension to incorporate multiple communication and engagement models, Web services.

Workflow in Health Care

Some of the solutions provided by SOA and e-commerce answer some of the challenges of health informatics. The use of workflow diagrams to depict high-level decision logic is not new to health informatics. Several current guideline systems use workflow diagrams, of one form or another, to express their business logic and flow of activities (Peleg et al., 2001, 2003; Tu, 2003).

Figure 4. Assignment of service roles

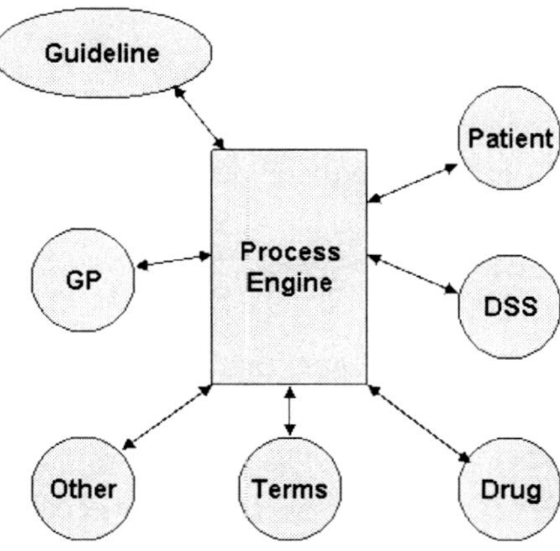

Although the high-level workflow descriptions are accessible to experts and clinical practitioners for validation, there is a lack of standardisation and consistency across guideline systems in terms of:

- Their description and construction
- Vocabulary
- Linkage to underlying "implementations" which embody the CIS and EHR.
- To external services.

The drivers and developments in e-commerce technology that are prima facie applicable to those in a health care context include:

- The emergence of service-based, loose coupled, architectures.
- Common, standards-based, languages for interfaces and information flows.
- Process description languages and (executable) process models.
- Applications/systems design based on standards conforming (meta-) information and service descriptions.
- The capacity to discover and transact with services at run-time.
- The movement to model-driven approaches where these lead to executable workflow linked to, and built upon, the previously-described service models and implementations.

As a central thought given the last point one can ask what value is modelling, and indeed UML-based modelling, in health care contexts. The answer to this partly lies in the underlying specification language that the modelling (UML) representation compiles to, and the constructs in the UML representation set. These areas are quite fluid at the moment but initial indications are positive (Anzbock, 2005; Bastos, 2002; Dadam, 1997; Knape, 2003; Ouvry, 2002).

In the next section, we provide an introduction to (and our rationale for adopting) an emerging process modelling and execution language that provides a basis for exploration of the above in the context of this project. We will then develop a prototype implementation using this language that binds together our information and clinical models in practice.

Business Process Execution Language

In looking at particular workflow definition and execution languages, we decided to implement our project on BPEL (initially the IBM-variant BPWS4J and then the Collaxa BPEL Engine [now Oracle Process Manager]).

Characteristics of this architecture and associated implementations, include a service orientation model that emphasises standards compliance and XML encoding. As well as a formal basis to the language, services are loose coupled and can support synchronous and asynchronous activation. It should be noted also that critical review of BPEL as a workflow description language has been positive (Wohed, 2003) and BPEL well supports the separation of domain and workflow information artefacts and derivation of executable workflow descriptions from use-cases (vignettes in our case) (Anzbock, 2005).

In our model (Figure 4), for example, "service" roles can be assigned to a health care provider, a patient (and patient health record), the DSS/Workflow engine and associated services, such as terminology or medicines information.

In proposing BPEL as a language for expressing/representing the workflow, it should be noted that it makes transparent the information flows which are defined by application syntax and semantics—that is, BPEL is information flow agnostic as long as the information can be represented in XML syntax and XML Schema.

The important contributions of each of the above are that they allow us to: (1) develop a model or description of a workflow in suitable modelling notation (such as UML), (2) express the model in a formal language (BPEL) that also links in information flow, and (3) execute the statements of the language. We note that our approach can facilitate:

- Artefact re-use.
- Computer-mediated decision support.
- Rapid expert review, and rapid update and distribution.

We should also note that there are signs that the benefits of the architectural approach are being recognised in the practice of health care whereby complex clinical processes are being decomposed into sequences of service activations driven by decision variables through formal workflow and process languages as referenced earlier. There appears acceptance of the utility of an UML-based modelling approach at the process level. Although earlier techniques (Knape, 1997) then exported a translation of the model description (from UML to XMI) for hand coding of activities to machine interpretable form; the sequence of drill down from graphical process description to executable form is revealed.

In Figure 5, we show the relationship of this "hand-coded" methodology to that proposed in this project using BPEL. In methods which model then code (the top section of the diagram), the UML Activity Diagram for the process is exported in

Figure 5. Hand coded vs. Automatic BPEL generation

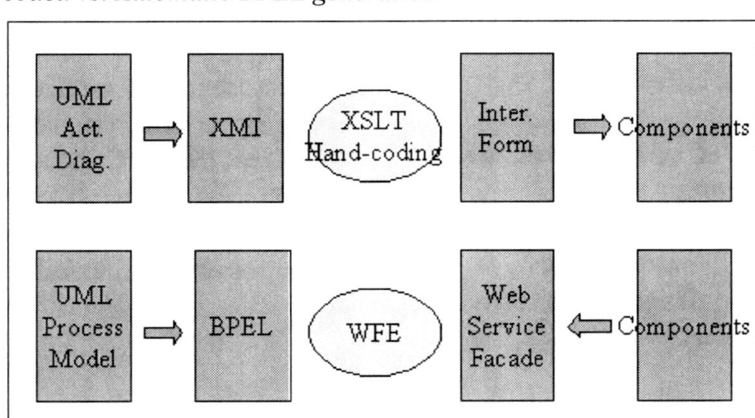

Figure 6. Asthma workflows

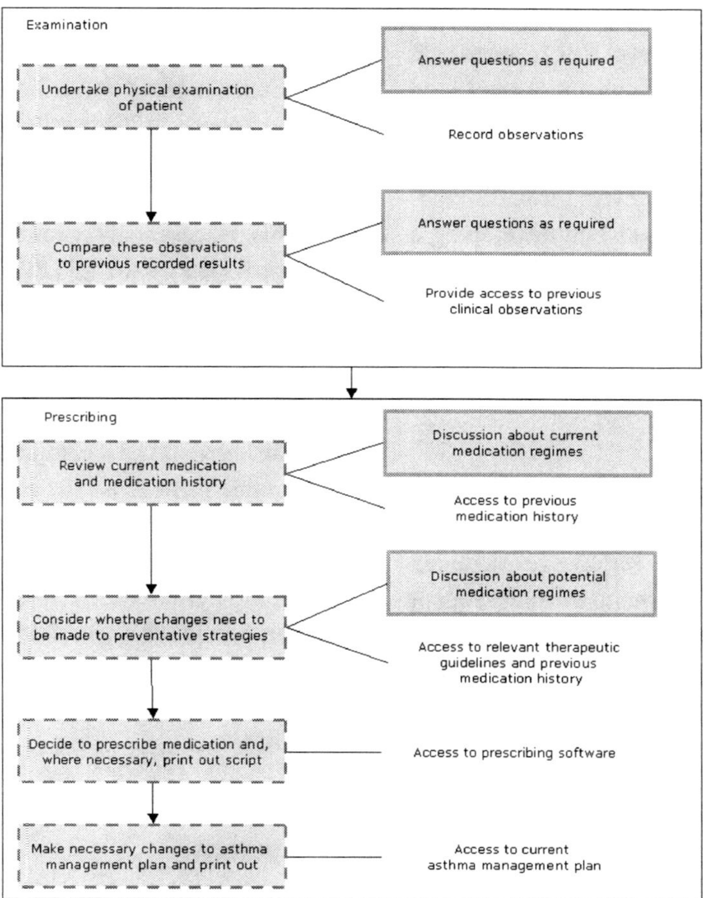

XMI and XSLT tools are used to transform the XML representation of the flow diagrams into an intermediate form. The hand-coded computation languages are added. In the BPEL approach, the process UML representation is machine translated directly to BPEL that is interpreted and run by a Work-Flow-Engine to invoke Web service implementations acting as the front end of a traditional computer modules.

The last step in our methodology as applied to this project is to link UML model artefacts for clinical use (possibly restricted in our use case) to process descriptions to be computer generated automatically in the BPEL language. This UML-to-BPEL auto-generation has already been achieved in an e-commerce context through stereotypes developed using the UML standard. We are developing UML behavioural models in terms of activity and sequence diagrams using a UML-Profile specifically designed for process modelling to extend this to the clinical domain as part of an ongoing research effort in our group. This will provide an end-to-end translation from visual clinical flow representation to execution in terms of accessible services.

Initial attempts to model a workflow in UML and to then generate BPEL have been made (e.g., Iyengar, 2004). The results of these efforts so far indicate that it is not yet possible to use UML to model a workflow at a complex domain level in health care such that BPEL is generated. It is possible to represent a workflow in BPEL at a low level, that is, in which low level BPEL constructs are explicitly represented. Such a representation is so close to being BPEL that little if anything is gained by the UML representation. The work at IBM (http://www.ibm.com/developerworks/webservices/library/ws-uml2bpel/) on developing a UML mapping to BPEL is encouraging however as is the initial work on generating UML profiles for domain level mapping (Gardner, 2003).

APPLICATION: WORKFLOW FOR ASTHMA

The Asthma prototype flow we have developed in "proof-of-approach" implements two subsequent flows of Asthma generic workflow: "examination" and "prescribing" shown in Figure 3. In Figure 6, dotted boxes describe GP activities while bold boxes represent the patient and unbordered boxes the computer.

Based on the high level process description, we have developed an executable workflow as shown in Figure 6. In "Examination", GP initiates the workflow and sends an examination request to practice nurse. After examination, the nurse sends back the result to GP. Once the activities in "Examination" have been completed, the patient moves to "Prescribing" where GP may prescribe a new medication or consult a medication guideline.

This process incorporates use of the instance data provided by the GPDM (with data loaded), clinical activities by the GP (practice nurse or external provider), and associated flows of information between their sources/sinks and the workflow engine.

The above is not a complete representation in executable form of all the clinical process flows contained in our guideline but sufficient to test the methodology for turning such descriptions into computer-coordinated service exchanges and human-computer interactions.

The following steps are involved in developing workflow descriptions and executable workflow.

1. Select a vignette and associated clinical process.

Figure 7. Web service distribution[1]

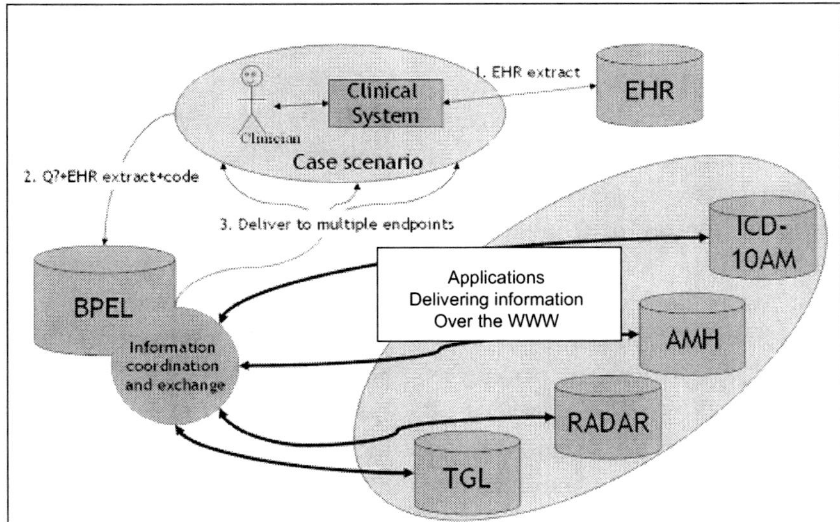

2. Map the process to BPEL following the high-level workflow model (Note that currently this translation [as discussed in the previous section] to BPEL needs to be done by hand.).
3. Identify the information requirements of the EHR or patient to support the clinical workflow and link to the "patient data" service that accesses vignette data in the instance of the GPDM.
4. Link to "provider or test data" service (that is then written to GPDM).
5. Prompt the GP for input data—suggest "best-practice" action, such as selected medication.
6. Allow GP to input and record setting to GPDM—event data, medication record, and prescription.
7. Allow the scheduling of, and access to, external information and service providers.

The prototype demonstrates information flows between multiple actors, some of whose activities may be computer mediated through Web services (in computer-to-computer interaction) and some of which may lead to the requirement for manual inputs (in our case we use the task manager interface to the BPEL Engine to map information flow requirements into a browser-based human-computer interaction).

DEVELOPMENT OF WEB SERVICES

Figure 7 provides an idea of what we are trying to project. To explore issues in interoperability, the services were developed and deployed as Web services implemented in both Microsoft (.NET over ISS) and Sun (Java over Tomcat) as Web-based applications to test if the workflows could be supported by services deployed on either platform without any change to the BPEL descriptions of the workflow elements. The information and data exchanged was specified in a platform independent way and mapped both to and from this common, standards compliant external form. In Health Informatics, XML and XML Schema are emerging as the preferred information and data model encoding mechanisms to ensure exchange of self-describing messages.

XML not only provides the means of describing data in a portable format, but can also be used to describe remote procedure invocations (XML-RPC) and to encode the distribution, communication, information and data models associated with remoted services (using the WSDL dialect).

Logical Level Interoperability

At a *logical* level, there are two types of application semantics able to be supported as the application is decomposed into a collection of services and activations:

1. Document-exchange where the endpoint of the remote service needs to interpret the meaning in the document.
2. RPC (Remote Procedure Call) invocation where the endpoint reads and decodes the document and interprets it as providing a remote procedure signature, parameters and type system.

The semantics are thus either *RPC* or *Document*. The decision of which to use depends on whether responsibility of semantic interpretation is to rest with the application or the container.

Implementation Level Interoperability

At an *implementation* level interoperability is concerned with how messages are formatted, encoded and carried "on-the-wire" (rather than their semantic meaning). In Web services, this is done with "binding" and "services" descriptions. In Web services the usual choices involve SOAP over SMTP or HTTP. The SMTP method is used more for asynchronous messaging/activation and HTTP for synchronous.

The design or application semantics of an RPC- and Document-based Web Service is a separate issue to the *formatting* and *representation*. The SOAP message (i.e., the XML-encoded message body) can be *formatted* as RPC-style (style=rpc in WSDL) or document-style (style=document). In "style=rpc", the XML message body is constructed by the endpoint to encode a representation of a method call and there are rules for the formatting to ensure that this conforms with the SOAP formatting rule-set (SOAPEncodingStyle).

Toolkits usually make choices from the above as to what they support. As a default, Microsoft .NET uses document-literal, while SUN JAX-RPC specification and toolset uses RPC. With the toolkits, you can write or develop from the WSDL directly or auto-generate from the service specification (signature) having nominated the formatting/encoding required. Until recently, most J2EE Web Service tools defaulted to RPC/encoded and .NET to Document/literal.

There are pros/cons in each approach/choice, the most important for our purposes being validation, use of standards compliant (externally set) schemas and exposure of language features. "Document-Literal" formatting/encoding is "safer" as it is widely implemented and also offers schema validation.

Practical Implementation Issues

Using tools to derive Web service semantics in WSDL from implementation code (as in the case of our Protege-Java API) is straightforward but ignores the design of the messaging schemas, which is central to WS Interoperability. In a single homogenous environment, generating WSDL Web service descriptions of service implementation is not difficult as all type and platform dependencies are hidden. In heterogeneous environments there are (at least) two independent mappings that may not be in synchronisation at several levels. In our general service architecture, we also have to deal with the Workflow Engine and service implementation dependencies.

The popular RPC/encoded style is well understood and attractive but there is difficulty in synchronising the implementations of the SOAP encoding implementation data model. On the other hand, in a document/literal approach, tools can find it hard to interpret XML schemas representing certain application types and architectural "nuances" so discipline is required in application design.

So at a *logical* level, there may be a predisposition to use RPC semantics whereas at an *implementation* level, to assist interoperability, a Document/Literal representation is preferred. If we view WSDL as carrying an IDL description of the service, we can remind ourselves of the canonical service production process—(1) the service is defined in its IDL (methods, parameters, types); (2) the stub (client) and skeleton (service helper) is compiled; and (3) the client and service implementations attached. That is, the production proceeds from a logical definition down to the implementation (not the other way round).

Writing canonical WSDL and using XML Schema (XSD) as a first step therefore promotes interoperability. For a complex service you could use a tool to generate a WSDL template then hand-edit. Collaxa (our BPEL Engine) promotes this approach (messages, schemas, documents, etc.) which in effect gives a message-driven or data driven development approach. In general, schemas, message parts and data bindings should use XSD and WS-Interoperability recommendations.

"Wrapped" Encoding

The "Wrapped" convention produces document/literal WSDL style/use Web services and yet supports an RPC-style programming interface (i.e., it performs automatic marshalling of input and output parameters) under schema control. The "Wrapped" convention simulates RPC while providing the benefits of schema validation and, hence, does place constraints on the schema used and the use of reference linkages within the WSDL itself.

As an approach to combining Web services into our SOA for process modelling in clinical practice, we have adopted a canonical WSDL focus (schemas and message orientation) using document/literal style (for implementation interoperability) and wrapped services (for simulation of the standard RPC interface). This approach (document/literal) is recommended and supported by our BPEL Workflow Engine and also supported by .NET and Java toolsets and containers.

External Service Description

The way in which external services are interfaced to the workflow supports their extension and further development. We have used tools which allow us to automatically construct computational objects (components/classes) from the data structures they represent. We constructed some information artefacts (e.g., pharmaceutical descriptions), pending their standardisation, in order to enact these as external services within our asthma example workflow. The techniques we have used are schema driven and we can easily deploy changed structures as these are developed or agreed upon.

In a similar vein, we aim to "attach" open XML-based medical terminology services (such as UMLSKS) to our prototypes in a further demonstration of the utility of our architectural approach.

In cases where the workflow requires more complex decision support than that available directly within BPEL, we have implemented a simple DSS Web service-based on an initial Java Rule Engine API (Java, 1994). This enables rule-based reasoning based on relationships between domain-level objects which are transmitted between services in XML representation. We expect this to be a fruitful area for further research in health informatics as standards-languages for rule representation evolve.

Transaction-Based Processes

We should also note at this point that our prototype is built using BPEL and services represented as Web services. Web services are autonomous and network-located. They can activate other services independent of the requesting service through which they were activated. This allows sequences such as the referral of a drug recommendation for checking for a particular patient to be queried by the DSS against the EHR, on its own behalf. BPEL provides information flows and activation trails for audit on a per sequence basis. That is, the services are self-logging and facilitate audit of decision making and clinical sequence.

CONCLUSION

The MCPOP Process Modelling uses the role-based approaches and models emerging in the e-Commerce domain to model the clinical process, workflow, and decision support. A significant emphasis in this project has been the development of a scalable and flexible services oriented architecture (SOA) to develop the role-based MCPOP reference implementation.

The workflow, as determined by the clinical modelling process and extracted from the clinical vignettes, is mapped into the information model and implemented automatically as BPEL scripts, which invoke underlying services. The BPEL script, as run by Collaxa, orchestrates the workflow according to the (clinical) process model, presenting and collecting information appropriately according to the various scenarios of clinical practice. Earlier derivation of BPEL workflow descriptions from use-cases in diagnosis (Anzbock, 2005) provide more detailed discussion of mapping of workflow artefacts and noted that it would be useful to execute flows within a BPEL Workflow Server given initial indications were that the BPEL language would be an effective tool in medical workflow. In this paper we have carried this out for asthma and support their optimism.

The MCPOP methodology and architecture is "agnostic" regarding vocabularies of the messaging and terminology formats used by services — except to the extent that the current implementations require XML encoded representations, which most systems support. The use of BPEL also supports services that are provided by both humans and computers. This allows great flexibility in service delivery and deployment, which has been demonstrated in the MCPOP asthma workflow demonstration.

In further developing this approach, our current research involves the automation of the mapping of domain-level process descriptions and artefacts to BPEL (through development of suitable UML profiles and meta-models), assisting semantic interoperability at the information model level, and exploration of different process pathways such as in e-prescribing.

REFERENCES

Anzböck, R. & Dustdar, S. (2005, September 5-7). Semi-automatic generation of Web services and BPEL processes—A model-driven approach (extended version). *Lecture Notes in Computer Science* (Vol. 3649, pp. 64-79).

Bastos, R. M. & Ruiz, D. D. A. (2002). Extending UML activity for workflow modelling in production systems. In *Proceedings of the 35th Hawaii International Conference on Systems Sciences* (pp. 3786-3795).

Dadam, P., Reichert, M., & Kuhn, K. (1997, November). Clinical workflows—The killer application for process-oriented information systems? Ulmr Informatik Berichte. Nr 97-16. Fakultat fur Informatik. Universitat Ulm.

General Practice Computing Group. (2000). *The general practice data model.* Retrieved from http://www.gpcg.org/publications/docs/GPCG_standards_activity.PDF

Gardner, T. (2003, May). Mapping from UML to BPEL4WS. In *OMG MDA Implementers' Workshop*, Orlando, FL).

Iyengar, S. (2004, March 18-19). Business process integration: Using UML and BPEL4WS. In *SI-SE 2004 10th Anniversary Symposium*, University of Zurich.

The Java Rule Engine API. (n.d.). JSR000094. Retrieved November 1, 2005, from http://www.jcp.org/aboutJava/communityprocess/final/jsr094/

Knape, T., Hederman, L., Wade, V.P., Gargan, M., Harris, C., & Rahman, Y. (2003). A UML approach to process modelling of clinical practice guidelines for enactment. In R. Baud (Ed.), *The new navigators.* IOS Press.

Liaw, S-T., Morrison, I., Lewis, B., & Deveny, E. (2004). Modelling the clinical processes of prescribing (MCPOP)—Information, clinical workflow, and processes. In K. Walduck & B. Cesnik (Eds.), *HIC 2004: Twelfth National Health Informatics Conference* (pp. 194-199). Brunswick East, Vic.: Health Informatics Society of Australia.

Ouvry, A. S. (2002). Workflow analysis and modeling in medical it projects. *Medicamundi, 46*(2), 47.

Peleg, M., Boxwala, A.A., Tu, S., Greenes, R.A., Shortliffe, E.H., & Patel, V.L. (2001). Handling expressiveness and comprehensibility requirements in GLIF3. In V. Patel et al. (Eds.), *Medinfo 2001.* Amsterdam. IOS Press.

Peleg, M., Tu, S., Bury, J., Ciccarese, P., Fox, J., Greenes, R.A., et al. (2003). *Comparing models of decision and action for guideline-based decision support: A case study approach.* Stanford University Report, No: SMI-2002-0922.

Tu, S. W., Campbell, J. et al. (2003). The structure of guideline recommendations: A synthesis. *American Medical Informatics Association Symposium* (pp. 679-83).

Wohed, P., van der Aalst, W. M. P. Dumas, M., & ter Hofstede, A. H. M. (2003, October). Analysis of Web services composition languages: The case of BPEL4WS. In *Proceedings of the 22nd International Conference on Conceptual Modeling (ER'2003)*, Chicago (pp. 200-215).

ENDNOTE

1 EHR: Electronic Health Record. ICD: International Classification of Diseases. AMH: Australian Medicines Handbook. RADAR: Rationale Assessment of Drugs and Research. TGL: Therapeutic Guidelines Ltd.

Chapter XI
Assessing the Potential Impact of Web Services on Business Processes

Jan-Hendrik Sewing
Siemens Management Consulting, Germany

Michael Rosemann
Queensland University of Technology, Australia

Marlon Dumas
Queensland University of Technology, Australia and University of Tartu, Estonia

Marcello La Rosa
Queensland University of Technology, Australia

ABSTRACT

Though Web services offer unique opportunities for the design of new business processes, the assessment of the potential impact of Web services on existing business information systems is often reduced to technical aspects. This chapter proposes a four-phase methodology, which facilitates the evaluation of the potential use of Web services on business information systems both from a technical and from a strategic viewpoint. It is based on business process models, which are used to frame the adoption and deployment of Web services and to assess their impact on existing business processes. The application of this methodology is described using a procurement scenario.

INTRODUCTION

Web services (WS) is an emerging set of technologies that aims at facilitating the flexible and standardised implementation of interoperable software systems. Considerably hyped in recent years, Web services are expected to ease many current IT problems such as the large-scale integration of heterogeneous software applications or the cost-effective establishment of e-business interactions. From a more technical viewpoint, investment in Web services is seen as a prerequisite to adopt a service-oriented architecture, an IT systems architecture paradigm that uses the concept of service as a basis for managing inter-connected software applications.

Although the intensity of development efforts and standardisation activities is very high, systematic approaches to assess the actual impact of Web services on existing business information systems are still missing. Thus, many organisations are struggling to assess the real impact of Web services and the accompanying opportunities and threats. Without appropriate business alignment, Web services might be perceived as a technical solution without a clear value proposition, in the sense that their potential benefits might not justify associated software reengineering efforts. This constitutes a potential risk factor in light of current IT spending practice and could eventually hamper a wider adoption.

Addressing the alignment of Web services to business priorities is therefore a critical step toward the success of this emerging technology—it will determine whether Web services can fit into (and more importantly improve) existing business practices and thus increase the competitiveness of the organisations that adopt them.

Business process modelling encapsulates all forms of graphical visualisation and structured documentation of business processes and related elements such as events, data, material flows, and external interactions. Business process modelling may be conducted for a wide variety of purposes including among others process documentation, process improvement, compliance, software implementation, or quality certification (Becker, Rosemann, & Von Uthmann, 2000; Curtis, Keller, & Over, 1992). It is an established approach for analysing and improving existing business processes. Business process models, extended with relevant information, have the potential to serve as a decision support instrument for assessing the potential of Web services. They are able to show the process context and ways of how Web services can enable business process innovation.

This chapter proposes a methodology for identifying and assessing opportunities for introducing Web services into existing business information systems by means of business process modelling. After briefly outlining and justifying the research approach, a framework is presented for selecting the most appropriate processes for potential incorporation of Web services. Following this, information domains and types are identified that need to be contained in a business process model to support systematic Web services assessments and to facilitate Web services deployment. This information is then mapped into a specific representation in the context of the ARIS toolset (Scheer, 1998a), a widely used solution for business process modelling. This mapping as well as the conceptual possibilities of the methodology are then illustrated through an example from the area of e-procurement. Finally, related work, conclusions, and directions for future work are discussed.

RESEARCH APPROACH

The proposed assessment methodology is grounded in related literature and complemented by focus group discussions with early and prospective Web services adopters. The purpose of the focus groups was to explore the current practice of Web service implementations, and industry's perception and approaches on how to address the challenge of business alignment. Specifically, two focus groups were organised—one for discussing the uptake and adoption of Web services technologies and a second one for discussing the use of business process models for assessing Web services adoption opportunities.

The participants of the focus groups were selected on the basis of their experience with Web services or their affiliation to organisations that were considering the deployment of Web services. The choice of participants was also guided by the objective of covering different organisations and industry sectors, and striking a balance between participants with a technical and a management background. Overall, the focus groups included 15 participants from eight organisations and covering four different groups (IT users, vendors, consulting firms, and research).

The reason for choosing focus groups as the empirical basis for this study lies in their effectiveness for gathering the general opinion of a target audience by providing an environment that allows probing for clarification and justification of opinion (Morgan, 1988; Saulnier, 2000)). Focus groups are especially suitable for generating hypotheses when little is known in a specific research area (New Mexico State University—College of Agriculture and Home Economics 1999). Sofaer, Kreling, Kenney, Swift, and Dewart (2001) suggest that if the previous work in a field is limited (which is the case here) then the research needs to be, at least initially, exploratory in approach.

IDENTIFYING SUITABLE PROCESSES FOR WEB SERVICE DEPLOYMENT

Two main assessment scenarios can be differentiated: (1) an organisation has a specific need and wants to evaluate the applicability of Web services within a selected business process, or (2) an organisation wishes to identify those business processes, which would benefit most from the deployment of Web services. In both cases, it is assumed that the organisation has conducted business process modelling and business process redesign activities beforehand, in order to start from an informed perspective.

Decision Methodology: Overview

In the following, a general decision methodology for the deployment of Web services is proposed for scenario (2). It is shown what information would be required at which phase and to what extent business process models can be utilised.

The methodology is intended to serve as a guideline for systematically assessing the potential of business processes regarding the deployment of Web services and selecting the most appropriate processes and Web services. It helps answer "outside-in" questions (Bibby & Brea, 2003) such as "to what business processes could Web services be best applied," and "what economic impact could that have?"

The methodology consists of a framework that follows a top-down structure with four decision phases. It includes several checklists to make it a practical instrument. A process' Web services potential (i.e., the technical and economic feasibility and suitability of Web services integration within a selected business process is the main outcome of this methodology). The assessment is based on a scoring model in which criteria and their weighting can be adapted and modified, making the tool highly flexible.

The assumed starting input are business process models, which could be the result of a comprehensive process modelling or business process improvement project. In the first phase, this existing set of business processes is evaluated against a shortlist of criteria, which allows to immediately disqualify some business processes for the deployment of Web services. These criteria could be that the processes are definitely unable to be Web services enabled or are already working very well so that running the risks associated with the change process would be unreasonable.

Within the second phase, the remaining subset of processes is evaluated with respect to its "Web service—process suitability." Processes can be classified into four categories based on organisation-independent characteristics (i.e., (a) strong Web service suitability, (b) Web service "learning chance," (c) future Web service potential, and (d) limited Web service potential.

The processes which fall into the categories (a), (b), and (c) are subject to further investigation within a third phase. Here, organisation-dependent criteria come into play, further reducing the set of potentially suitable business processes. This includes among others an assessment of the strategic importance of Web services for the organisation.

During the fourth and final phase, the organisation finally prioritises the remaining potential Web services projects largely based on methods and measures known from conventional evaluation of alternative IT investments such as return on investment and net present value (Remenyi, Money, Sherwood-Smith, & Irani, 2000).

The following sections describe the different phases and the required input in more detail.

First Phase: Process Rejection Based on Disqualifying Criteria

At this phase, business processes that match at least one of a list of disqualifying criteria are rejected. These organisation-independent criteria should be easy to assess without requiring a detailed investigation of the process models. Care must be taken to ensure that the criteria are chosen in such a way that they do not reject potential processes over-hastily. On the other hand they should be selective enough to reject as many unsuitable processes as possible and reduce the effort of detailed evaluations in the following phase. Thus, there is a trade-off between the amount of accidental disqualification of business processes and the workload at the following decision point.

Given that Web services are driven toward automated program-to-program interactions, and given the cost of reengineering existing processes and software to introduce Web services, a conservative set of criteria could be:

- The process involves only physical performance that cannot be digitised.
- Human intelligence or sophisticated interpretation is required.
- Isolated process which is working well, stable, efficient, and cannot be leveraged (i.e., does not represent "hidden value").

Second Phase: Assessing General Web Services Suitability

At this phase the remaining subset of business processes from the first phase is evaluated using a "Web service-process suitability" scoring table. The criteria are still independent from the specifics of an individual organisation. The goal of the scoring table is to assess the suitability of the business process for the application of Web services based on two dimensions.

- The first dimension measures whether the business needs match with potential business drivers for Web services.
- The second dimension evaluates whether the technical requirements could currently be met by available Web services technology.

Each dimension is represented by a number of criteria, which can be weighted and contain weighted sub-criteria. For both dimensions, possible criteria are summarised in Table 1. The criteria and framework are based on criteria proposed by Burdett (2003), Hagel and Brown (2002), Hagel, Brown, and Layton-Rodin (2002), Linthicum (2002), Patricia Seybold Group (2002), Robins, Sleeper, and McTiernan (2003), The Stencil Group (2002), Wilkov (2002), Wright (2002), and findings from our two focus groups.

Scores are then calculated independently for both dimensions. Every criterion which has been answered with a "yes" gets a score of one, every

Table 1. Process evaluation for Web services

Second Phase—Qualifying Analysis Criteria	
Business Need	**Business Process Characteristics**
Reduction of asset investment:	Unique expensive resources are currently used to support the process and could be replaced.
Reuse and easier maintenance:	Redundant functionality in several application systems exists and shall be reduced/existing functionality shall be leveraged.
Support for heterogeneous endpoints:	Business process requires support for multiple, heterogeneous interfaces.
Automation of manual interventions and intensive data entry (human intervention for exceptions only):	Multiple manual, error-prone interventions dealing with digitized data are currently required for the business process.
Automation of transaction chains:	Multi-step process, involving different business parties, shall be automated.
Introduction of self-service mechanism (enabling direct access to core system rather than cached or replicated data):	A batch process shall be replaced by a self-service, real-time mechanism.
Higher transparency/visibility:	Frequent access to dynamically produced data has to be supported.
Ad-hoc business:	Ad-hoc business with previously unknown parties shall be supported.
Higher flexibility and business agility, dynamic process support:	"On demand" reconfiguration of business process required.
Low impact of failure:	Financial risk of system failure is low for the business process.
Technical Need	**Business Process Characteristic**
Processing speed:	No extremely short responses are required.
Processing time guarantees:	No precisely predictable response time is required.
Distribution of transaction volume:	Low transaction burst probability.
Response to failure:	No failure compensation, roll-back, "state capture" are required.
Security Requirements:	No non-repudiation, "chains of trust" and tamper-proofness are required.
Semantic heterogeneity:	Shared meaning can be defined.
Process repetition:	High repetition frequency.
Process stability:	Process and involved application systems are likely to change over time.
Transaction mode:	Real-time mode is required.
Support for heterogeneity:	Multiple, diverse hardware and software systems are involved.
Implementation effort:	Significant custom development would be required for conventional approach.

"no" results in a score of zero. The scores are then weighted and added as shown in Table 2. It is not in the scope of this work to determine how the scores should or could be derived, but we can note that traditional multi-criteria decision-making methodologies (Keeney & Raiffa 1993) could be employed for this purpose.

The resulting score for each dimension of the business process under evaluation can then be visualised as a dot in a two dimensional matrix,

Table 2. Simple scoring table for each of the two dimensions

Characteristic	[No = 0, Yes = 1]	Weight; Σ(rows) = 1 (each ranging [0..1])	Score per Characteristic
xyz	{0;1}	[0..1]	= ({0;1} x [Weight])
...	...	...	...
		Σ(rows) = 1	Σ(rows)

which represents its potential for Web services deployment. A possible matrix is given in Figure 1.

Third Phase: Organisational Characteristics

The third phase evaluated the general process suitability for Web services. After this phase, at least the processes marked with "limited applicability" can be eliminated. The following evaluation is not based on general process characteristics anymore but on *organisational-dependent* criteria. Here, it has to be established whether the qualified processes from phase 2 are suitable for Web services with regard to the specific characteristics of the organisation. For example, in spite of high costs and risks, an organisation could decide to experiment with a "future Web service" application etc. Potential questions leading to assessment criteria were identified with the help of the focus group sessions:

Figure 1. Web services suitability matrix

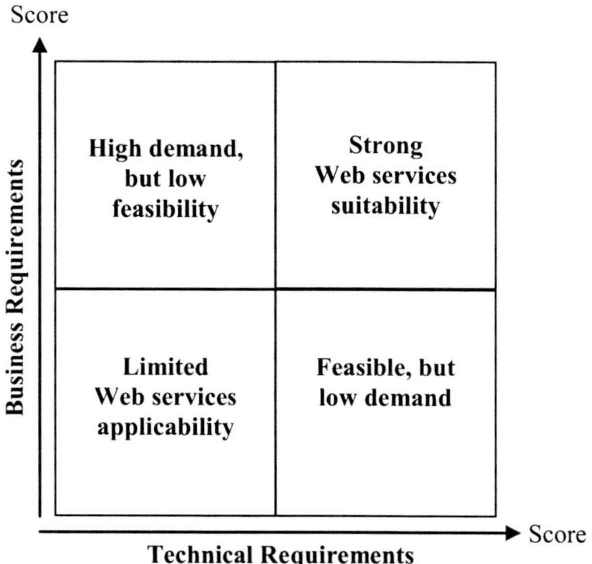

- Who are the involved business partners for the business process under consideration?
- What is the level of trust and the level of knowledge about their internal processes and systems? Do the partners already use standardised data formats or are they in the process of adopting Web services?
- Would the required technical resources be available?
- Would the required skill set be available?
- Are there example implementation and/or best practice available?
- What are potential risks? Consider risk affinity.

Some of these questions relate to internal organisational factors while others deal with external market characteristics. Clearly, the organisational assessment of Web services should consider criteria along both of these categories. The set of criteria presented in Table 3 derive from the previous questions as well as relevant literature (Chen, 2003; Christiansen, 2002; The Stencil Group 2002)).

Scores can then be calculated and combined in the same way as for the process analysis in phase 2. The resulting degree of current importance of Web services for an organisation could be again visualized as a dot in a two-dimensional matrix similar to the process evaluation phase. This is shown in Figure 2 and Table 4.

Table 3. Organisational assessment criteria

Organisational Assessment Criteria	
Internal Factors	
Funding & backing:	Business units specify and fund most major IT projects.
Role of IT for organisation:	Use of IT is a competitive advantage.
Role of innovation for organisation:	Innovation is a competitive advantage, organisation is risk taking.
Current application architectures:	IT maintenance and integration costs are high.
Importance of optimisation:	Increasing productivity is a strategic need.
Current IT resources:	Current development & deployment platforms support service-oriented architectures.
Current available IT skills:	Adequately skilled personnel is available.
External Factors	
Industry characteristics regarding specified data formats:	Industry uses standardised data formats (esp. XML).
Industry characteristics regarding data regulations:	Use or sharing of data is regulated by law.
Industry e-commerce capabilities:	Industry has experience using B2Bi.
Support from current IT vendors:	IT vendors have strategic support for Web services.
Current business partners IT capabilities:	Partners have heterogeneous B2B capabilities.
Market structure:	Oligopoly, more than one dominating player are present.
Current business relationship characteristics:	Several trust-based relationship with deep mutual understanding of internal structures exist.

Figure 2. Matrix for WS strategic importance with respect to organisational criteria

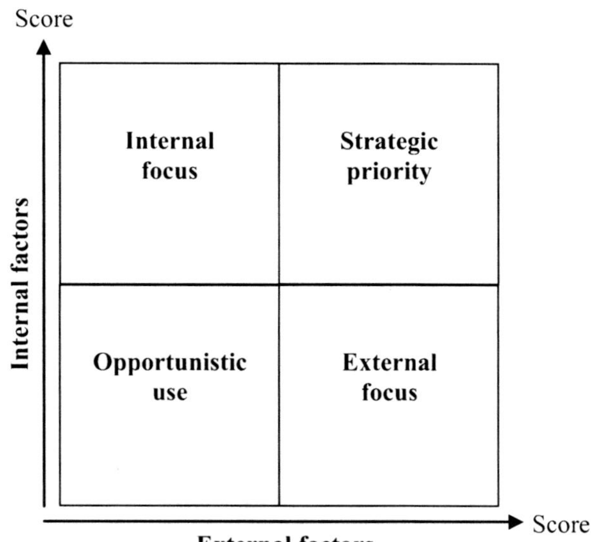

Table 4. Explanation of the cells in the matrix of Figure 2

Field in Matrix	Description	Likely Approach	Potential Risks
NE = Strategic priority	Web services should represent a significant element of the overall IT strategy. Strategic business processes will be affected. All major IT efforts should be considered in the context of fulfilling the Service Oriented Architecture vision.	Going for vision of service-oriented enterprise.	Over architecting.
NW = Internal focus	The organisation is positioned to make use of Web services. However, many of the partners and customers may not be. Therefore, it makes most sense to look at how Web services-based integration can optimise internal processes and help better utilise existing assets.	Focusing on fixing while ensuring performing applications.	Ignoring interesting market opportunities.
SE = External focus	Web services represent an important way to connect to customers and business partners because of market dynamics. Web services-based offerings could represent a potential competitive advantage for first movers.	Using innovation for competitive advantage.	Opening holes regarding security and scalability.
SW = Opportunistic use	Web services may be an appropriate solution for specific projects. However, they do not represent a critical element of the overall IT strategy. Nevertheless, developers should be encouraged to experiment with the Web service standards and related software tools.	Small steps for incremental benefits.	Missing the strategic vision.

Fourth Phase—Assigning Web Services Implementation Priority

The remaining business processes that were generally suitable regarding their process characteristics (2nd phase) and met the organisations' specific situation (3rd phase) are prioritised in a last step. The goal here is to define for which processes should Web services be deployed in the first instance. This can be determined by considering organisation-dependent factors. A list of proposed factors is presented in Table 5. Different weights could be assigned to the factors depending on the importance the organisation attaches to them. The set of criteria is based on Christiansen (2002), Estrem (2003), Hammer and Champy (1993), Hagel and Brown (2002), Patricia Seybold Group (2002), Samtani and Sadhwani (2002), and the focus groups.

Based on these outlined logical steps an organisation should be able to systematically integrate Web service technology as a facilitator of its business processes. The questions proposed for an assessment and their sequence guarantee that the most suitable and feasible activities and business processes for Web services support are identified. The framework can moreover be tailored to the individual characteristics of an organisation, as the criteria and their weighting are adaptable. Figure 3 summarises the outlined phases.

IDENTIFYING WEB SERVICE REQUIREMENTS FROM PROCESS MODELS

Information for the Assessment of Web Service Potential

Business process modelling can support the decision making process described previously in all phases. Apart from presenting an overview of an organisation's processes, assigned actors and resources and their interrelationships, which is of great value in order to gain a fundamental understanding of how the enterprise works (e.g., compare with Schmelzer & Bloomberg, 2002), a wide spectrum of information can be captured in the process model and help answer the questions above. A list of identified critical information for the evaluation of Web services and their deployment is presented in Table 6 and Table 7. This list

Table 5. Priority criteria

4th Phase—Priority Criteria
• Choose main "pain areas" where business partners or customers would like to be able to do things they cannot do at the moment.
• Consider importance of involved business partner/customer for organisation.
• Choose projects where a new business need has to be satisfied and aggregated applications from remote systems can be leveraged.
• Choose projects for identified stable (proven) core business functionalities. However, the pilot area should not endanger established, mission-critical processes.
• Choose highly repeatable scenarios.
• Evaluate project's feasibility.
• Analyse of value proposition with (risk-adapted) return on investment analysis, economic value added (EVA) etc. for Compare estimated costs.
• Compare estimated project duration.
• Compare potential benefits.
• Compare potential risks.
• Financial decision for evaluating investment alternatives, likely to be based on strategic cost management methods like total cost of ownership.

Figure 3. Identifying and evaluating Web service opportunities

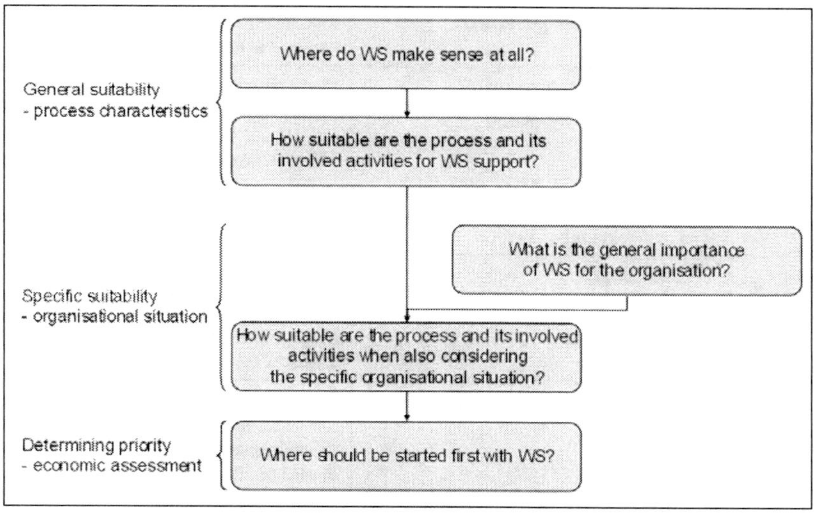

Table 6. Information for Web services evaluation: Processes and transactions characteristics

Related Phase	Information Domain and Type	Detailed Description
	Process characteristics	
2	**Process stability**	Adaptability requirements (process' ability/likelihood to change).
2	**Process repetition frequency**	Frequency process is carried out with.
2, 4	**Process's level of mission-criticality**	Degree to which the organisation relies on the process under consideration.
2, 4	**Process's estimated monetary value if quantifiable**	Quantification of the value of the business process if possible.
	Transactions characteristics	
2	**Business transaction type** E.g. Request/confirm, Request/response, Notification, Distribution	Transaction type information supports an estimation of the degree of complexity of a potential service.
2	**Composition requirements**	Required interrelations with other services, supports an estimation of the degree of complexity of a potential service.
2	**Interaction mode** Synchronous, asynchronous or "as-agreed-by-parties"	"As-agreed-by-parties" indicates that the flow of control would be specified in trading partner agreements.
2	**Message exchange requirements**	
	Reliable delivery	Delivery of message until acknowledged.
	Ordered delivery	Messages are to be delivered and processes in the order they are sent.
	Atomic delivery	"All or nothing" delivery of messages to multiple partners.
	Message expiry	Definition of validity of involved message.
2	**Processing speed requirements**	Time constraints that have to be met.
2	**Processing speed guarantees**	Accepted level of speed/time deviation.

Table 6.continued

2	**Throughput requirements**	Rate (and peak rate) at which potential service is required to be able to process requests.
2	**Scalability requirements**	Based on estimation of service's future use .
2	**Security requirements**	
	Authentication	Identification and validation of message sender.
	Authorisation	Assignment of rights to message sender.
	Confidentiality	Transport security/encryption requirements.
	Data integrity	To ensure that data has not been altered between communication entities.
	Non-repudiation	To ensure that transaction route is traceable and no aspect of the transaction can be denied.
2	**Failure response requirements**	Compensation requirements for sub-transactions, roll-back, sub-transactions might also produce valuable results that should not be completely lost in case of failure (state capture).

Table 7. Information for Web services evaluation: Systems, data, and partners characteristics

Related Phase	Information Domain and Type	Detailed Description
	Involved systems' characteristics	
1, 2	**Description of modules and functionality**	Description of functionality to track redundancies, encourage re-use etc.
2	**Capacity utilisation level**	Description of system's current degree of utilisation and relationships to processes.
2	**Costs (initial & maintenance)**	Description of current costs for, supporting potential reduction of asset investments etc.
2	**Existing interfaces**	Description of interfaces to assess degree of required support for heterogeneity.
2	**Used communication protocols**	Description of communication protocols.
2	**Systems ability to change**	System's adaptability support and requirements.
	Involved data's characteristics	
3	**Data format & standards compliance**	Description of data structure.
2	**Dynamics, frequency of change**	Description of current level of dynamics of involved data.
2	**Importance of timeliness**	Requirements for timeliness of involved data.
2	**Required level of data security**	Description of required degree of end-to-end security for data.
	Involved business partners' characteristics	
2, 3	**Total number of involved parties**	Higher number usually means higher complexity that has to be supported.
4	**Assumed frequency of cooperation**	Information could be used for assigning priority to potential supporting IT project.
4	**Importance of business partner to organisation**	Information could be used for assigning priority to potential supporting IT project.

Table 7. continued

3	**Autonomy, degree of individuality**	Partner's IT compliance to existing "global" standards and agreements.
3	**Existing level of business trust**	A high level of business trust is especially considered to be important for near-term external Web service projects.
3	**Existing process insight, manageability, shared meaning**	External visibility, understanding, and manageability of partners' applications.
3	**Existing technological base**	Description of partners' current IT systems.
3	**Existing IT skill base**	Description of partners' current IT skills.

was developed based on the information which has been identified as important for the different evaluation phases as well as with the help of additional literature (e.g., ebXML Business Process Team, 2002; Papazoglou, 2003). Furthermore, a classification into separate domains has been carried out.

Information for Facilitating Web Services Deployment

Apart from supporting the *identification and evaluation* of opportunities for Web services deployment to improve business processes, business process models are also a valuable tool for facilitating Web services deployment. Business process models could capture (a) patterns, (b) Web services taxonomies, and (c) Web services semantics.

Patterns may be identified in Web services practices and added as additional, classifying information to a model. Once patterns are identified and captured they provide opportunities for simplifying structures and processes. Besides, these identified patterns promote the re-use of knowledge and functionality, which reduces the development effort. Encouraging and reinforcing consistency and standardisation (e.g., compare with Glushko & McGrath, 2002) can also lead to reduced maintenance. IBM, for example, offers a set of e-business patterns to facilitate the process of developing Web-based applications. As a general rule, they expect that the emerging Web services affect the implementation of all their presented patterns (i.e., business, integration, and application patterns whenever there is a boundary between businesses, applications, or logical components of a solution across which information must be exchanged (Adams, Gisolfi, Snell, & Varadan 2002).

Because Web services are presumed to be re-used, a prerequisite for efficient service development is also the creation of a comprehensive reusability strategy. One of the bases for this strategy should be a taxonomy of services (Scholler, 2003). *Web service taxonomies* help categorise Web services, e.g. based on their role or function they provide within an overall enterprise. Scholler (2003), for instance, proposes a 2 x 2 matrix taxonomy consisting of the dimensions provider scope (e.g., the provider may be a particular organisational unit, and its associated applications or the provider may also be enterprise wide in scope) and consumer scope (e.g., consumers may be local to a particular organisation, or the consumers may be global and outside the boundaries of the enterprise). These dimensions result in at least four classes of services with accompanying different strategies that should be followed (Scholler, 2003). Other examples for possible Web services taxonomies include the business purposes that trigger Web services implementations. Web services taxonomy information could be attached to the Web services implementations that are captured in business process models.

Apart from capturing patterns and Web service taxonomies, *Web service semantics* (i.e., service capabilities, additional functional and

Table 8. Identified critical information for Web service deployment

Information Domain and Type	Detailed Description
Business purpose for Web service	
Capturing the business purpose of Web services implementations provides a basis for identifying knowledge and know-how for future implementation projects.	
Interaction pattern	
Web services transactions could potentially also automate more complex interaction patterns to great advantage in the future. Capturing the interaction patterns supported by existing Web services implementations would offer the chance to identify reusable knowledge if the same interaction pattern was to be supported in a new project.	
Simple Transaction (1:1)	Any Web services where the objective is for the provider to execute an operation on behalf of the consumer. (e.g., order taking, billing, buying, reporting, finding, reserving).
Agent (1:1:n)	A Web services that acts as an agent providing intelligence in the selection of other services. (e.g., search engine, travel agent that maintains up-to-date arrangements, automatic trading agent).
Dealer/Intermediary (n:1:n)	A third party that locates, aggregates, potentially inserts value-adding services.
Auction (1:n)	An auction service allows an individual or enterprise to offer various forms of auction service on a private or public basis. (e.g., personal auction service, bid processes).
Virtual hub (n:n)	Core business services are exposed and executed directly by other parties in a collaborative process. (e.g., supply chain process).
Relationship type	
Buyer to major supplier, buyer to small supplier, buyer/supplier via e-marketplace, buyer/supplier via a third party ("exchange hub"), ad-hoc, previously unknown	Identified patterns would encourage re-use of functionalities, thus facilitate deployment etc.
Service semantics	
Service ontology & capabilities	Description of what the service is about and how it can be discovered (e.g., synonyms for name etc.).
Functional service properties (e.g., identification, location, etc.)	Potentially supporting re-use of services and communication with business partners.
Non-functional service properties (e.g., availability, costs, ownership, quality, etc.)	Potentially supporting provider evaluation etc.

non-functional properties) can also be recorded in business process models to facilitate Web services deployment. Documentation of Web services capabilities and additional functional properties will support the re-use of services and facilitate communication with internal and external parties involved in the Web services implementations. Furthermore, capturing non-functional service properties will be necessary for Web services (provider) evaluation.

Table 8 lists information that is important for Web services deployment and can be captured in a business process model. The information domains and types presented are based on ebXML Business Process Team (2002), National Health Supply Chain Taskforce Interoperability Working Group (2002), and Scholler (2003).

INTEGRATION IN ARIS AND EXAMPLE

This section discusses how the proposed methodology for Web services assessment and deployment can be supported by a mainstream business process modelling solution, namely ARIS. The implementation of the methodology is then illustrated through an e-procurement scenario.

Introduction to ARIS

ARIS is a mature business modelling tool, which is regularly ranked in market studies as the most advanced solution for process modelling and analysis. Its sophisticated capabilities and its wide distribution is practice motivated us to select ARIS for the purpose of this research. ARIS (architecture of integrated information systems) is a process-oriented business process documentation, analysis, and improvement framework (supported by a toolset) that attempts to span the gap between business theory and information/communication technology (Scheer, 1998a). In ARIS, business processes are represented in diagrammatic form as chains of events and functions (EPCs). Apart from processes, ARIS can be used to model systems, resources, data, software, information flow, organisation, knowledge, skills, business objectives, risks, and costs (Davis, 2001). The result is a highly intricate model, which is divided into views in order to reduce its complexity. With such division, the contents of the individual views can be described by special methods. The description may either be performed from a purely functional point of view, or the applications may be considered from the point of view of the data. A third perspective is the organisational one, where organisational units and responsibilities are presented. In order to maintain the relational structure between functions, data, and organisation, the control view shows, for instance, what data is processed by which functions (Scheer, Abolhassan, Jost, & Kirchmer, 2002, p. 17). A fifth view, the output view, represents resulting products and services. Output is the result of processes and describing output is seen as one of the key processes in describing business processes (Scheer, 1998b, p. 93).

The ARIS toolset supports a range of modelling techniques. Several model types were evaluated regarding their suitability for supporting the integration of the identified critical information for Web service assessment and deployment. Among them are the extended event-driven process chain (eEPC), column eEPC, process chain diagram (PCD), and the recently introduced e-business scenario diagram. In our example, the latter was used for the top-level modelling. The extended event-driven process chain is the chosen model type for modelling greater levels of detail. Both techniques, e-business scenario diagram and the event-driven process chain, are also used within the enterprise system SAP. Thus, we believe that our examples can easily be understood by the wide community involved in SAP-related modelling activities.

ARIS Model Types Employed

EPCs are activity-oriented diagrams, which are depicted in the process view. The structure of an EPC is that of a directed graph with active nodes ("functions") and passive nodes ("events"). A process is described via an EPC as a chain of business functions, where each function describes an activity and is preceded by and succeeded by events. The latter represent the prior and subsequent situation regarding the function (Soderstrom et al., 2002). In ARIS, events are graphically represented by a hexagon shape; functions are displayed as soft rectangles. In addition to that, rule operators, represented by circles, illustrate AND, OR, and XOR decisions and are used to model the internal structure of a process (e.g., branching, re-branching, parallel sub-processes etc.). Dotted arrows connect the elements depicting the control flow.

eEPCs are event-driven process chains which are "extended" by the inclusion of elements that are specified in greater detail in other views. That way eEPCs can represent how the available resources implement a process and how the process interacts with its environment. Based on such a model the following types of questions could be answered: (a) who does it? (organisational unit), (b) what do they do? (function, information carrier), (c) how do they do it? (knowledge, application system), (d) why do they do it? (objective), and (e) when do they do it? (event) (Davis, 2001, p. 162-163).

Table 9 shows common object types that were also used for the implementation of the exemplary business process model presented later. Their description has been adapted from the ARIS Methods Manual (IDS Scheer AG, 2002).

To facilitate the modelling of e-business processes, the ARIS framework incorporates a dedicated type of diagram, namely "e-business scenario diagram." Using this type of diagram it is possible to view a value-added chain holistically (i.e., from the end customer through all the companies involved in the process). By adopting

Table 9. Common objects within the ARIS toolset

Symbol	Object Type Name	Description
	Event	Events trigger functions and are the results of functions.
	Function	A function is a technical task or activity performed on an object.
	Process Interface	A process interface indicates from which process the related event has been created, or which process the event triggers.
	Rules X-OR AND OR	The rules describe how the events and functions are related. The X-OR means that one and only one input/output is possible, the AND that all the inputs or outputs must be true, and the OR when any combination may be possible.
Resource objects		
	Organisational Unit Type	An organisational unit type represents a typification of individual organisational units, i.e. performers of the tasks required to attain the business objectives.
	Information Carrier	An information carrier is a means to store information.
	Cluster	A cluster represents the logical view on a collection of entity types and relationship types of a data model.
	Application System Type	The Application System Type is representative of a related group of IT systems.
	Objective	An objective is the definition of future company goals
	Knowledge Category	A knowledge category is used to classify knowledge by topic

the column representation style, the e-business scenario diagram provides an abstraction of the interfaces between different process partners.

Apart from involved business participants that are placed in the "header row" and the central elements, business processes, different information carrier objects (e.g., Internet) are also available to present the underlying media by which business documents are passed across boundaries (Davis, 2001, p. 345). Business component objects, which represent the application system type used in normal eEPCs, can also be included. Furthermore, security protocol objects can be attached to the business documents to specify security requirements. As with eEPCs, the organisational, data and systems description can be specified in greater detail within additional assignable models. The symbols (representing different objects) offered by the e-business scenario diagram type are shown in Figure 4.

Description of Relevant Modelling Constructs in ARIS

The following sections present the modelling constructs and techniques that could be used—in addition to the standard elements "function," "state," "operator," and "connection"—to capture the information relevant to Web services assessment and deployment (hereafter referred to as "Web service modelling") in an ARIS business process model.

Hierarchical Decomposition

It is a natural design technique to start by creating a high-level concept and then to drill down into successive levels of detail (Davis, 2001, p. 242). Process decomposition is achieved by assigning hierarchies of eEPCs to functions (Davis, 2001, p.

Figure 4. Modelling symbols for e-business scenario diagrams

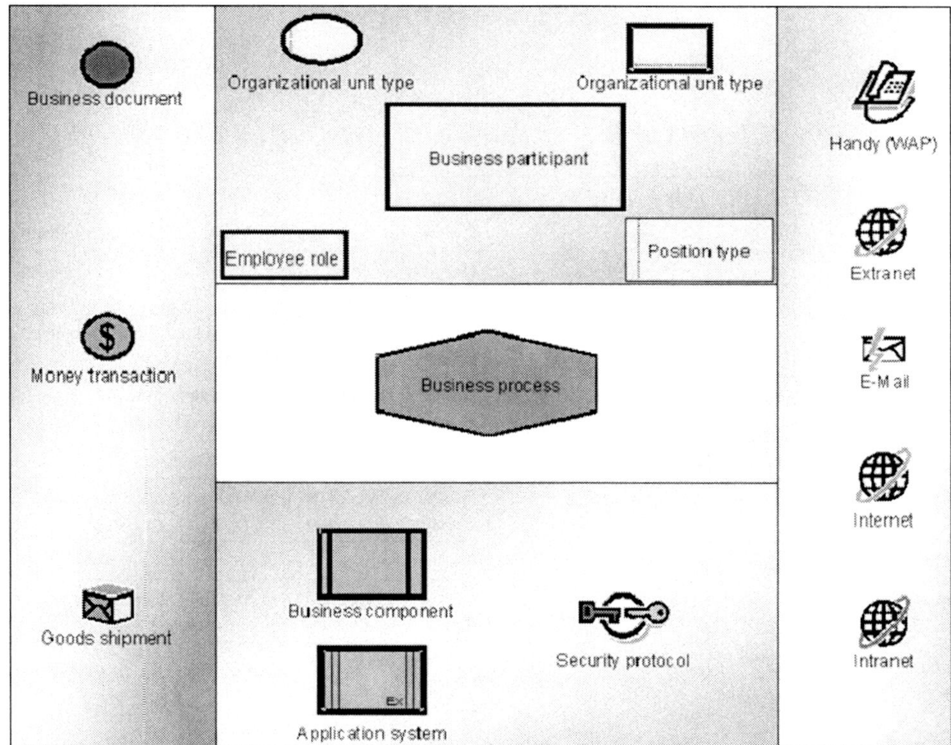

243). Apart from that, most model assignments in ARIS are made to models that provide additional details about the particular object. The most relevant for this work are presented in Table 10.

Attributes

Attributes are populated with values either through the process of drawing the models or by inserting them manually. Apart from storing modelling related information that is necessary for the administration of the databases, models, and its objects, additional information about the real world items that the model represents can be added. Special attributes further allow for linking business documents and Web sites or other applications to objects, models, and databases. Thus, although ARIS' attributes are not intended for storing vast amounts of detailed information about the items themselves, a business process model can act as a central repository (Davis, 2001, p. 25, 97). For convenience, the attributes can also be displayed directly on the model graphic (Davis, 2001, p. 91).

Organisational Objects

Organisational objects represent information on business participants that are involved in the process tasks. Many practitioners model every organisational object, be it a single person, department or a whole organisation, as an organisational unit object which is feasible and keeps the models simple (Davis, 2001, p. 145, 147). However, a hierarchical approach is more appropriate if complex projects shall be modelled and shared to ensure a common, standard-based approach. Therefore, the detailed relationships between organisational objects can be modelled within the organisational chart model. In both model types, eEPCs and e-business scenario diagram, it is possible to assign organisational chart models to organisational objects (Davis, 2001, p. 145).

Application System Objects

Application system objects represent the IT assets in ARIS that are used to support the business. Many objects exist to define detailed hierarchies

Table 10. Hierarchical models in ARIS that can be assigned to objects, adapted from Davis (2001)

Object	Assigned Model	Hierarchical Representation
Function	eEPC	Decomposition of the function into a more detailed sub process.
Application System Type	Application System Type Diagram	Decomposition of the systems into sub-systems, modules, and IT functions.
Organisational Unit Type	Organisation Chart	Description of the organisational set-up of the involved businesses.
Information Carrier	None	However, the technical terms model or the eERM model can be assigned to show structure of carried data.
Cluster	eERM Model	Formal description of the data structure.
Technical Term	Technical Terms Model	Decomposition of the technical term into its information structure.
Knowledge Category	Knowledge Structure Diagram	Description of the structure of business knowledge.
Business Objective	Objective Diagram	Composition/decomposition of the business objectives and description of related critical factors.

of systems, sub systems, software modules, and even specific IT functions. Although in practice only the application system type element is used within the majority of eEPCs, an application system's internal relationships can be displayed in the assignable application system model type (Davis, 2001, p. 148).

If processes are entirely carried out by application systems the corresponding function symbol can be replaced by a designated object called system function (Davis, 2001, p. 150).

Data Objects

Involved data in IT systems and communication can be modelled formally (i.e., using recognised modelling standards such as ER-diagrams, or less formally using "business language). Whereas the technical term object is used for modelling data informally from a business perspective, the cluster, entity type and attribute objects represent formal data modelling in ARIS (Davis, 2001, p. 150). Their internal relationship can be shown via the eERM model type. The technical terms model can be used to model how technical terms map to clusters, entities and attributes of the formal data model (Davis, 2001, p. 151).

Information Carrier Objects

Information carriers can be thought of defining how the data is stored and delivered or "carried" to and from the functions (Davis, 2001, p. 155). Symbols are available for EDI, Intranet, Internet, e-mail, fax, etc. Explicit relationships between the involved data and its carrier can also be modelled (resulting in so called "secondary relationships)" (Davis, 2001, p. 157). However, this relationship cannot be modelled (visually) in the e-business scenario diagram type.

Objective Objects

A hierarchy of business objectives and related critical success factors can be modelled within the objectives diagram model. The specific objectives could then be added to an eEPC and assigned on a function/EPC level to show which process steps support their realisation (Davis, 2001, p. 161).

Knowledge Objects

Knowledge is considered everything that is known to be of relevance to a process (Davis, 2001, p. 158). In process modelling one would not want to try to model all of the knowledge related to the process but only where it was key to a process step (Davis, 2001, p. 158). The ARIS object chosen for knowledge here is the knowledge category object. For more detailed levels (e.g., to represent the structure of knowledge or interrelationships, specific designated model types exist as with the other resources as well). The knowledge structure diagrams are useful models for representing and structuring aspects of business knowledge, thus also facilitating communication and re-use of the latter. For Web services modelling they can be redefined in order to depict available case studies, benefits realised through Web services application etc.

Matching Web Service Information with ARIS Constructs

In the following, it is outlined how necessary information supporting Web services evaluation and deployment could be captured as elements of a collaborative business process model created with the ARIS Toolset. Here, a matching between the identified critical information supporting Web services assessment and deployment (Table 6, Table 7, and Table 8) on the one hand and the outlined appropriate ARIS constructs for representation in a collaborative business process model on the other hand is performed. The outcome is shown in Table 11, Table 12, and Table 13.

E-Procurement Scenario

Figure 5 depicts the high-level business processes of the e-procurement scenario modelled with the ARIS toolset. These processes are presented in an e-business scenario diagram. The header row contains the involved business parties; the following row holds the related business processes and resources. This model is of the "swim lane" type. The column presentation therefore visualises the interface between the two business partners. Electronic communication takes place in form of business document exchanges. Most of the business processes carry an "assignment" symbol in their bottom right corner which depicts the fact

Table 11. Capturing WS-relevant process and transaction characteristics in process models

Phase	Information domain and type	How to capture in a process model?
	Process characteristics	
2	**Process stability**	To be specified on function/EPC level as discrete attribute (predefined list).
2	**Process repetition frequency**	To be specified on event level as attribute.
2, 4	**Process' level of mission-criticality**	To be specified on function/EPC level as discrete attribute (predefined list) or through colour coding (i.e., representing value of attribute by displaying corresponding function objects in different, designated colours).
2, 4	**Process's estimated monetary value if quantifiable**	To be possibly specified on function/EPC level as attribute or through colour coding.
	Involved electronic transaction characteristics	
2	**Business transaction type**	Information implicitly available through process structure.
2	**Composition requirements**	Relationships of constituting parts of transaction are implicitly available through process structure.
2	**Transaction mode**	To be modelled as a discrete attribute (predefined list).
2	**Message delivery requirements**	Information may be attached as to information carrier or function.
2	**Failure response requirements**	Information may be attached to information carrier or function.
2	**Required processing speed**	To be specified on functional level as attribute.
2	**Processing speed guarantees**	To be specified on functional level as attribute.
2	**Throughput requirements**	To be specified on functional level as attribute.
2	**Scalability requirements**	To be specified on functional level as attribute.
2	**Security requirements**	Can be modelled in e-business scenario diagram as designated symbol with own attributes. However, no mapping of the symbol to other diagrams (e.g., eEPCs) is possible. Could alternatively be modelled as attributes of other practical object that was assignable to information carriers or as direct attributes of information carrier or function.

Table 12. Capturing WS-relevant system, data, and partners characteristics in process models

Phase	Information domain and type	How to capture in a process model?
	Involved systems' characteristics	
1, 2	**Description of internal structure and functionality**	To be described as attribute of application system type module or IT function.
2	**Capacity utilisation level**	To be specified as attribute of application system or module.
2	**Costs (initial & maintenance)**	Same as above.
2	**Existing interfaces**	Supported input and output formats to be specified as data objects and/or as attributes of application system.
2	**Used communication protocols**	Depicted through information carrier.
2	**Systems ability/likelihood to change**	To be specified as discrete attribute (predefined list) of application system or module.
	Involved data's characteristics	
3	**Data format, standards compliance**	To be described as attribute of cluster object and specified in eERM model if complex.
2	**Dynamics, frequency of change**	To be specified as attribute of cluster object.
2	**Importance of timeliness**	To be specified as discrete attribute (predefined list) of cluster object.
2	**Required level of data security**	To be described as attribute of cluster object.
	Involved business partners' characteristics	
2, 3	**Total number of involved parties**	Derived from relationships with organisational units.
4	**Frequency of cooperation**	Discrete attribute (predefined list) of organisational unit.
4	**Importance of business partner**	As above.
3	**Autonomy, degree of individuality**	As above.
3	**Existing level of business trust**	As above.
3	**Existing process insight and manageability, shared meaning**	As above (possibly multiple attributes).
3.	**Existing technological base**	Implicitly contained in model through application systems if process & resource insight is granted.
3.	**Existing IT skill base**	Same as **frequency of cooperation.**
	Types of characteristics of the involved business parties could also be modelled as redefined knowledge category objects and be assigned to the organisational objects representing the business participants via the knowledge map model type.	
	Examples, first implementations and maturity, risks, and pitfalls	
3, 4	Can be referenced as attribute on function/EPC level. Colour coding could be used to assign the implementation's level of maturity on the function/EPC level (designated colours for discrete levels of maturity). Could alternatively be modelled as redefined knowledge category objects that could be assigned on function/EPC level and colour coded according to the maturity. The advantage of using knowledge category objects is that they could carry further details (e.g. experienced issues, benefits) in assigned knowledge structure diagrams.	

Table 13. Capturing information for Web service deployment in a business process model

Information domain and type—Web service deployment	How to capture in a process model?
Business purpose for Web service	
Business drivers could be captured in several plausible ways, as: 1. Discrete attribute (predefined list + free text if value not yet in list) on function/EPC level. 2. Redefined specific knowledge category objects. The advantage would be that these objects could then be directly assigned to functions as well as be included in knowledge structure diagrams detailing known Web service implementations. Objective objects can only be assigned to functions. 3. A discrete attribute (predefined list + free text if value not yet in list) of the knowledge category objects which refer to first implementations and are assigned to functions. 4. Objective objects in a hierarchical objective diagram + assigned on function/EPC level after first Web services projects.	
Interaction patterns	
Interaction type classifications could be captured in several plausible ways, as: 1. A discrete attribute (predefined list + free text if value not yet in list) on function/EPC level. 2. Redefined specific knowledge category objects (that could be part of a knowledge structure diagram attached to a knowledge category object for first implementations) 3. Comments, after first own or reported projects. 4. A discrete attribute (predefined list + free text if value not yet in list) of the knowledge category objects which refer to first implementations and are assigned to functions. This is recommended, because it constitutes a simple, discrete type of information.	
Relationship type	
See previous **Interaction patterns**	
Service semantics	
Functional service properties	To be described on function/EPC level as attributes or as attributes of the knowledge category objects representing Web services examples.
Non-functional service properties	To be described on function/EPC level as attributes or as attributes of the knowledge category objects representing Web services examples.
Service ontology & capabilities	To be described on function/EPC level as attributes or as attributes of the knowledge category objects representing Web services examples.
Misc.	
Information can be included that is critical or has proven to be important in the past	To be captured in model as attributes, comments, or knowledge objects.

that an associated eEPC is available that further details the business process.

The user can quickly browse through the models with the help of these visual links. The modelling symbols have been introduced in Figure 4.

The scenario starts with the product catalogue provision by the seller. The catalogue can be provided as a Web service, which would be a service to the buyer. An advantage would be the support for heterogeneous systems (i.e., the catalogue Web services could be integrated on a Web site), as a small desktop application at the buyers site etc. Upon identification of a specific product need, a purchase requisition is triggered on the buyer's side, who assigns a source of supply, which may lead to an update of contract information. Thereafter a purchase order (PO) is created and the material planning system is updated. Upon reception of the purchase order

Figure 5. High-level processes for e-procurement in e-business diagram

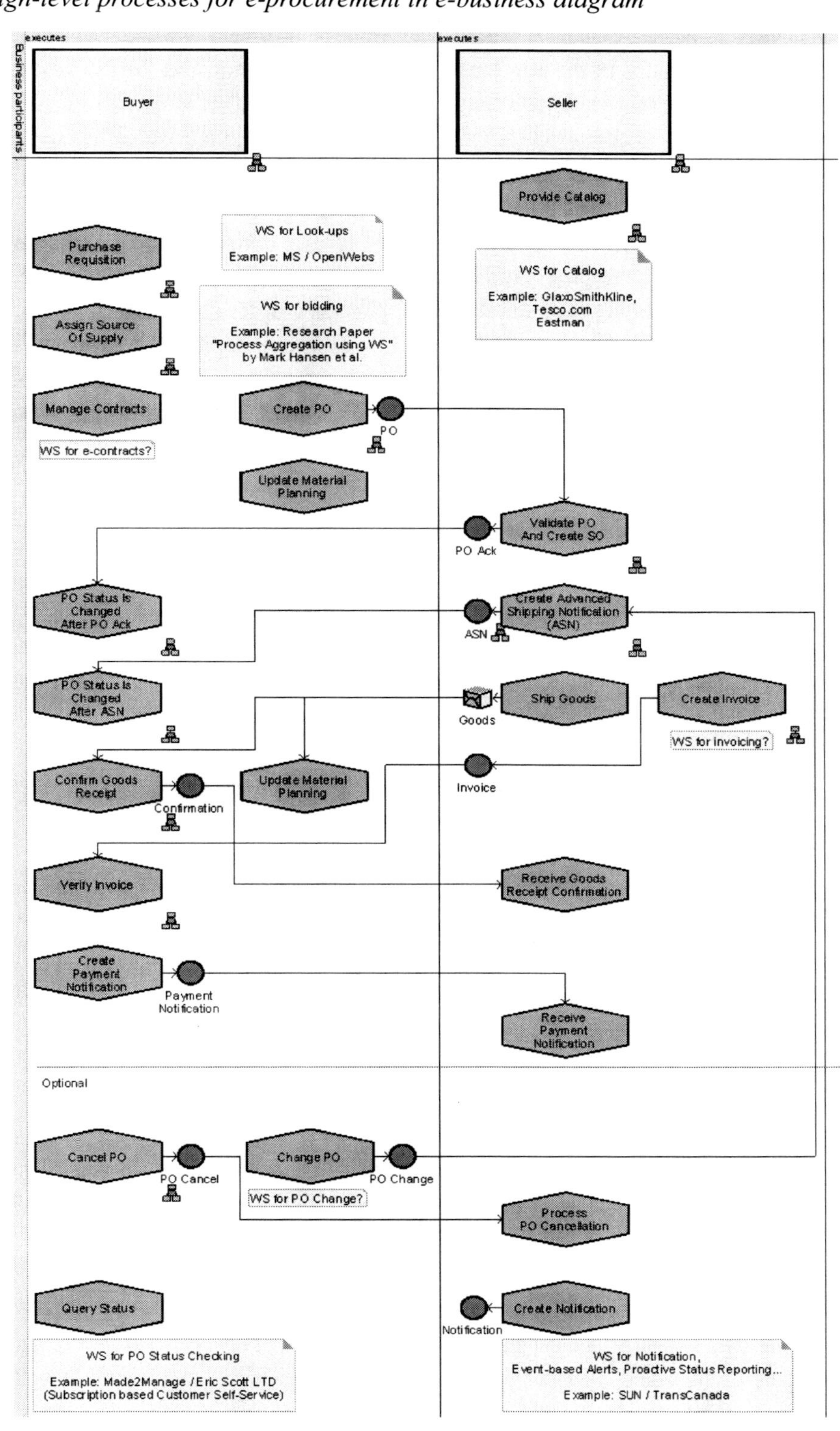

the seller validates it and creates a sales order (SO). A PO acknowledgement (PO Ack) is sent to the buyer who changes the status of the purchase order. The seller provides the required goods and sends an advanced shipping notification (ASN) to the buyer, which leads to another update of the PO at the buyer's side. Finally, the goods are shipped and an invoice is created and transmitted to the buyer. Although no examples could be found, the invoicing process might prove suitable for Web services integration. The buyer confirms the reception of the goods, updates his material planning and verifies the invoice upon arrival. A payment notification is sent to the seller when the invoice has been verified. In addition, message exchange is required for PO amendment, status querying and further notifications. Existing Web services solutions are attached to the model in the form of comments. Comments are also attached to processes where Web services applications should be clearly considered (e.g., automation of (parts of) contracts, support for the invoice process, and purchase order changes).

Figure 6 depicts the process "Create ASN" in greater detail. The representation chosen is an eEPC model. The column type gives a correspond-

Figure 6. Seller's process "Create ASN" in greater detail via an eEPC

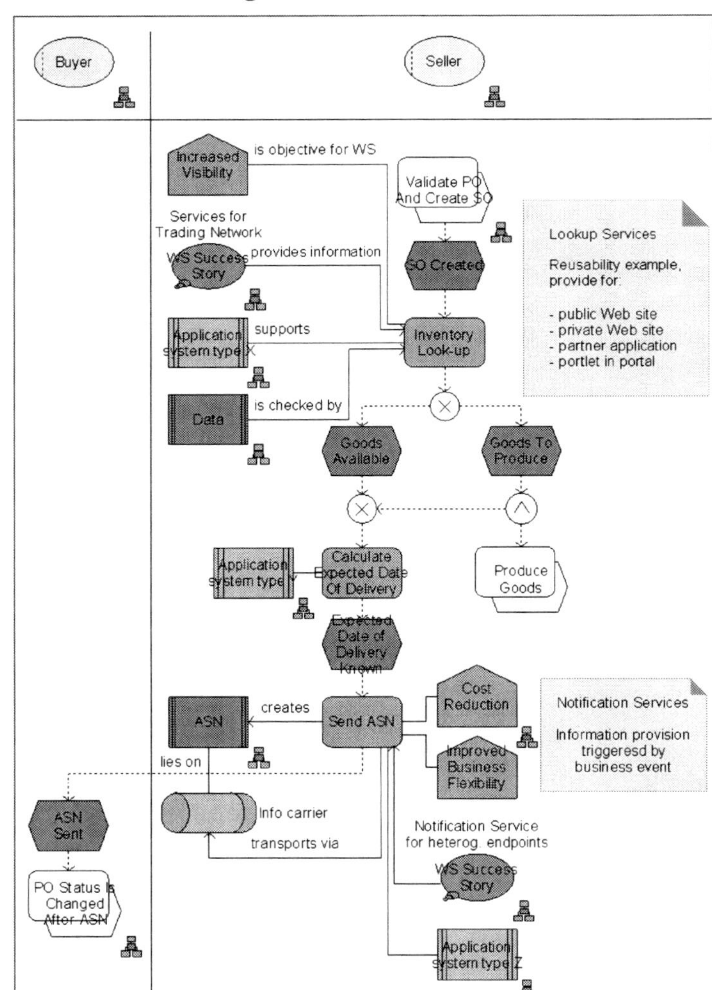

ing "swim lane" view on the involved business parties. In ARIS the model shows up after a double click on the assignment symbol of the "Create ASN" process in the e-business diagram. The model shows the required activities and resulting states to carry out the business process. It also includes involved application systems, data and information carriers and their interrelationships. Applications systems and data can be further detailed in related diagrams such as the eEPC in Figure 6. The activities (Function objects) supported through Web services carry a Knowledge object that represents the corresponding type of Web services example, differentiated according to their maturity (i.e., research prototype, vendor proposal, success story). The different degree of maturity is depicted through colour coding of the knowledge objects (i.e., predefined colours for low maturity, moderate maturity, high maturity: red-yellow-green). The Web services examples can be detailed in knowledge structure diagrams, which can include information about benefits, issues, and hyperlinks to relevant documents.

RELATED WORK

The methodology proposed in this chapter is closely related and complementary to other methodologies proposed in the area of service analysis and design (SAD). SAD refers to the stages in the lifecycle of a service-oriented architecture where the purpose, scope, and interfaces of individual services are identified, and a priori relationships between services are documented. It is also in these stages that the relationships between service models and other enterprise modelling artifacts such as organisational charts, document flow charts, and business process models are specified. Various methodologies for SAD have been proposed. In this section, we discuss three SAD methodologies and relate them to the methodology proposed in this chapter.

Jones (2005) proposes a top-down approach for the definition of a *business services architecture*. The methodology revolves around four questions (what, who, why, and how), which are considered at different levels of granularity. The methodology relies on a recursive identification of the business services of an organisation (the so-called *what*), through the analysis of the consumers of functionality provided by the services (*who*), the interactions involved (*why*), and the details of the implementation (*how*). A systematic consideration of these questions leads to the identification of services, actors and interactions, which can be represented in "interaction diagrams," out of which interaction scenarios can be subsequently discerned. A service, according to this methodology, is a discrete domain of control containing a collection of tasks to achieve related goals, and can be identified with a business function. Thus, the methodology primarily emphasises the identification of coarse-grained business services. These coarse-grained services are then be decomposed into finer-grained services, down to the level of "technical Web services" which are identified at the lowest level of the decomposition, and are seen as an implementation of the business services.

Erl (2005) proposes a methodology for identifying technical Web services and their interaction points (called "operations"). This three-step methodology starts with the definition of the business requirements relevant to a service-oriented solution. The author works out two possible approaches for this first step, depending on the source from which business requirements are drawn: (1) the *process-based approach*, which takes business processes as the starting point for the requirement analysis; and (2) the *entity-based approach*, which takes business documents and transactions as starting points. Having discerned the business requirements, the second step in Erl's methodology is to identify existing application logic, which already automates any of these requirements. This step helps to scope the potential systems affected by the introduction of a service-oriented architecture, and it is particularly useful for large-scaled solutions. The last step aims at identifying suitable *service operations* that can fulfil the business requirements (e.g., a service operation that provides an implementation for a process step or that supports a business transaction) and that encapsulate or replace the legacy application logic. These service operations are then grouped into *services* according to their logical context.

The IBM service-oriented analysis and design methodology (Zimmermann et al., 2004) is essentially an adaptation of traditional object oriented analysis and design (OOAD) methods to the realm of Web services. The purpose is to identify a suitable set of technical Web services to be deployed, from the analysis of a given business scenario. The starting point is the definition of a class diagram of the software objects involved, which aids the construction of a *services model*. Here services are identified by their operations on the basis of related behaviour. Next, business processes are defined as state transition models, in order to capture the behaviour involving each software object that has been previously identified. Finally, the interaction behaviour of business processes and services is sketched in a sequence diagram leading to a so-called *service choreography*.

A classification of service analysis approaches is depicted in Figure 7. Each quadrant in this figure identifies a distinct combination of an *abstraction level* and an *analysis driver*. The abstraction level can be *business* or *technical*, and depends on the purpose of the methodology and its deliverables. Meanwhile, the main analysis drivers can be *business processes* or *business entities*, depending on which of these is taken as a starting point.

According to this classification, our methodology is process-driven, as we start from the analysis of candidate business process models. Besides, the scope of applicability of the methodology can be placed in-between the business and technical

Figure 7. Classification of the SAD approaches

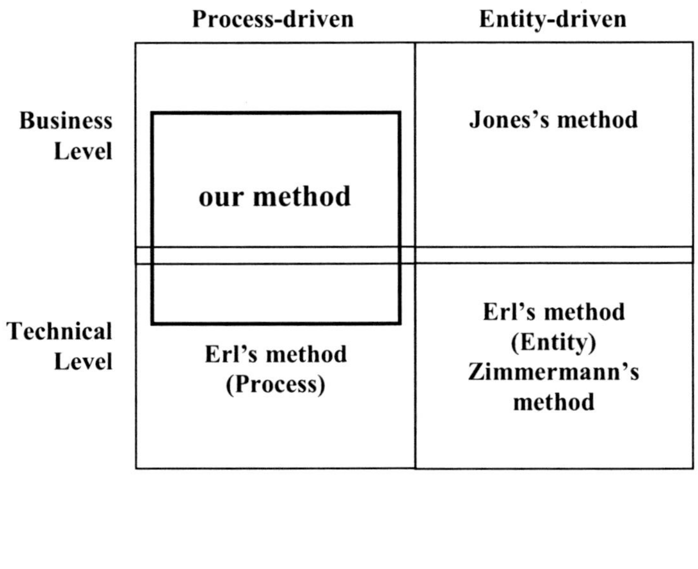

	Process-driven	Entity-driven
Business Level	our method	Jones's method
Technical Level	Erl's method (Process)	Erl's method (Entity) Zimmermann's method

levels, as we do not drill down into the details of Web services implementation, although we identify technical requirements for Web services based on process models.

Jones's methodology (Jones, 2005) falls in the business level and entity-driven quadrant: it aims at defining a business services architecture and it starts with the identification of business services corresponding to organisational functions. The methodologies of Erl (2005) and Zimmermann (2004) are at the technical level, as they aim at defining technical interfaces of Web services. They take business process models as analysis driver (in the case of Erl's process-based approach) or entity models (in the case of Erl's entity-based approach and Zimmermann's object-oriented approach).

Technical and process-driven approaches, as the one proposed by Erl, are suitable for organisations with detailed business process models or as part of an SOA transition plan. They focus on meeting immediate requirements (i.e., the SOA automation of an existing business process) and require little service analysis effort. These approaches can also enable reuse and prepare business processes for integration with partner processes. However, in order to provide immediate benefits, they usually focus only on a business process model at a time. As a result, these approaches can limit the long-term reusability potential of the resulting Web services, as an initial study of multiple process models is often required to identify commonalities. Therefore, they should be complemented with other methodologies.

On the other hand, entity-driven approaches like Jones's, Erl's entity-based approach and Zimmermann's methodology, identify highly reusable services due to their inherent generic nature, and can significantly increase the agility through which service-oriented processes can be redesigned. However, they require more up-front analysis and thus they usually increase the cost and time for service production. Besides, if applied in an overly abstract manner, they may yield conceptual service models of little practical use in practice.

Process-driven approaches naturally lead to situations where processes are the dominant feature. If applied in a simplistic manner, they may lead to extreme scenarios where each task is equated to a service, there is little reuse of services across processes, and hence fine grained services proliferate and are too hard to manage (Jones, 2005). Meanwhile, entity-driven approaches are more suitable for SOA deployment in "green field" scenarios. However in the real world such situations are quite rare due to the legacy applications that need to be taken into account (Zimmermann, 2004). In addition, entity-driven approaches may lead to the design of services that are not aligned with business operations.

As a perspective for future work, we plan to design a hybrid methodology aiming at reconciling top-down entity-driven approaches with bottom-up business-driven approaches, so as to combine the benefits of both.

CONCLUSION

This chapter addressed one of the currently perceived issues surrounding Web services, namely the lack of a sound methodology to demonstrate the actual business impact of Web services adoption in specific settings. The main contributions are: (a) a process-oriented framework for systematic assessment of Web service adoption opportunities including checklists and scoring tables; (b) a structured set of identified critical information for Web services evaluation and deployment through business process models; and (c) a mapping of this information types into ARIS constructs, thus enabling the representation of this information in a business process model.

The study has drawn on an extensive review of the literature as well as reported case studies and best practices. From these resources, a list of assessment criteria for potential application areas of Web services could be derived. These criteria were then tested through an e-procurement scenario and refined through feedback obtained from focus groups.

Further research leading to the refinement, extension, and testing of the proposed assessment methodology is needed. In particular, the methodology could be extended by depicting trade-offs between benefits and risks of Web services deployment. Also, additional requirements for the methodology should be identified through further case studies, and the implementation of the proposed methodology in other tools than ARIS should be considered. Finally, it would be highly desirable to validate the proposed methodology through more case studies in order to identify and understand the risks and pitfalls of its application.

Another relevant direction for future work is the exploration of requirements that collaborative e-business interactions impose on business process modelling and Web services as well as their implications. Issues that still need to be addressed and overcome include dealing with business trust, semantic heterogeneity, and exceptions, all of which were identified as crucial during the focus groups.

ACKNOWLEDGMENT

An earlier version of this book chapter was published with the title *Process-oriented Assessment of Web services* in the International Journal of e-Business Research (vol. 2(1), 19-44, January 2006, Idea Group Publishing. The authors are grateful to the participants of the focus groups who remain anonymous due to a confidentiality agreement. The work of the third author has been partly funded by a Queensland Government "Smart State Fellowship" co-sponsored by SAP Research.

REFERENCES

Adams, H., Gisolfi, D., Snell, J., & Varadan, R. (2002). *Best practices for Web services: Back to the basics, Part 2*: IBM Developer Works.

Becker, J., Rosemann, M., & Von Uthmann, C. (2000). Guidelines of business process modeling. In W. van derAalst, J. Sedel, & A. Oberweis (Eds.), *Business process management: Models techniques and empirical studies* (pp. 30-49). Berlin: Springer-Verlag.

Bibby, A., & Brea, C. (2003). Business process reengineering through Web services: A user-experience perspective. *Web services Journal.*

Bielski, L. (2003). Web services goes live: One deployment at a time. *American Bankers Association. ABA Banking Journal, 95*(7), 49-58.

Burdett, D. (2003). *The business Web services scorecard: Using Web services for business—The present and the future.* Commerce One Operations Inc.

Chen, M. (2003). Factors affecting the adoption and diffusion of XML and Web services standards for e-business systems. *International Journal of Human—Computer Studies [H.W. Wilson - AST], 58*(3), 259.

Christiansen, S. (2002, December 8-13 2002). *The business case for XML Web services.* Paper presented at the XML Conference 2002, Baltimore.

Curtis, B., Keller, M. I., & Over, J. (1992). Process modeling. *Communications of ACM, 35*(9), September.

Davis, R. (2001). *Business process modelling with ARIS: A practical guide.* London: Springer.

Erl, T. (2005). *Service-oriented architecture (SOA): Concepts, technology, and design.* Prentice Hall PTR.

ebXML Business Process Team. (2002, April 2002). *Business process and business document modeling worksheets and guidelines*. Retrieved January 6, 2003, from http://www.collaborative-domain.com/standards/documents/bpWS-1.05-2%20DRAFT%20(May%2016).doc

Estrem, W. A. (2003). An evaluation framework for deploying Web services in the next generation manufacturing enterprise. *Robotics and Computer-Integrated Manufacturing, In Press, Corrected Proof.*

Glushko, R. J., & McGrath, T. (2002). *Document engineering for e-business*. Paper presented at the Document Engineering 2002, McLean, Virginia, USA.

Hagel III, J., & Brown, J. S. (2002). *Orchestrating business processes—Harnessing the value of Web services technology*. Retrieved January 6, 2003, from http://www.johnhagel.com/paper_orchestratingWebservices.pdf

Hagel III, J., Brown, J. S., & Layton-Rodin, D. (2002). *The secret to creating value from Web services today: Start simply*. Retrieved January 6, 2003, from http://www.johnhagel.com/paper_startsimply.pdf

Hammer, M., & Champy, J. (1993). *Reengieneering the corporation. A manifesto for reengineering*. New York: Harper Business.

IBM. (2003). *IBM patterns for e-business*. Retrieved January 9, 2003, from http://www-106.ibm.com/developerworks/patterns/

IDS Scheer AG. (2002). ARIS methods (for Version 6).

Jones, S. (2005). *Enterprise SOA adoption strategies*. InfoQ Mini-Book Series, 2006. Retrieved January 21, 2007, from http://www.infoq.com/minibooks/enterprise-soa

Jost, W., & Wagner, K. (2002). The ARIS toolset. In A. W. Scheer, F. Abolhassan, W. Jost, & M. Kirchmer (Eds.), *Business process excellence: ARIS in practice* (pp. 16-31). Berlin Heidelberg New York: Springer.

Keeney, R., & Raiffa, H. (1993). *Decisions with multiple objectives: Preferences and value trade-offs*. Cambridge University Press.

Linthicum, D. S. (2002, Jan 17). *An application integration value-add? expoQ's David Linthicum on Web services in EAI*. Retrieved August 18, 2003, from http://searchWebservices.techtarget.com/originalContent/0,289142,sid26_gci788646,00.html

Morgan, D. L. (1988). *Focus groups as qualitative research* (Vol. 16). Newbury Park, CA: SAGE Publications.

National Health Supply Chain Taskforce Interoperability Working Group. (2002). *Electronically connecting trading partners: A proposed interoperability standard*. National Health Supply Chain Taskforce Interoperability Working Group.

New Mexico State University—College of Agriculture and Home Economics (1999-2003). *Evaluation handbook*. Retrieved January 6, 2003, from http://www.cahe.nmsu.edu/grants/evaluation/eval_section2.html#focus

Papazoglou, M. (2003). *Web services and business transactions*.

Patricia Seybold Group. (2002). *An executive's guide to Web services*. Patricia Seybold Group.

Remenyi, D., Money, A., Sherwood-Smith, M., & Irani, Z. (2000). *Effective measurement and management of IT costs and benefits* (2nd ed.). Butterworth-Heinemann.

Robins, B., Sleeper, B., & McTiernan, C. (2003). *Web services rules: Real-world lessons from early adopters*. The Stencil Group.

Samtani, G., & Sadhwani, D. (2002). ROI and Web services. In *Web service Business Strategies and Architectures*: Expert Press.

Saulnier, C. F. (2000). Groups as data collection method and data analysis technique: Multiple perspectives on urban social work education. *Small Group Research, 31*(5), 607-627.

Scheer, A. W. (1998a). *ARIS—Business process frameworks*. Berlin: Springer.

Scheer, A. W. (1998b). *ARIS—Business process modelling*. Berlin: Springer.

Scheer, A. W., Abolhassan, F., Jost, W., & Kirchmer, M. (2002). *Business process excellence: ARIS in practice*. Berlin; Heidelberg; New York: Springer.

Schmelzer, R., & Bloomberg, J. (2002, June 18). *Want to service-enable your enterprise? Model first!* Retrieved January 6, 2003, from http://searchWebservices.techtarget.com/tip/1,289483,sid26_gci833705,00.html

Scholler, D. (2003, 07/04/2003). *Web services Architecture: Part 1 - Service Development Excellence*. Retrieved 01/06/2003, from http://www.gebac.com/article.php?story=20030407225246949

Singh, M. P., & Huhns, M. N. (2005). *Service-oriented computing: Semantics, processes, agents*. John Wiley & Sons.

Soderstrom, E., et al. (2002). Towards a framework for comparing process modeling languages. In A. Banks Pidduck et al. (Eds.), *Proceedings of CAiSE 2002* (pp. 600-611). Heidelberg; Berlin: Springer.

Sofaer, S., Kreling, B., Kenney, E., Swift, E. K., & Dewart, T. (2001). Family members and friends who help beneficiaries make health decisions. *Health Care Financing Review; Washington, 23*(1), 16.

The Stencil Group. (2002). *The laws of evolution: A pragmatic analysis of the emerging Web services market*. The Stencil Group.

Wilkov, R. (2002). *How to get real value fro Web services... Today*. Retrieved January 6, 2003, from http://www.ebizq.net/topics/dev_tools/features/1567.html

Wright, D. (2002). *Beyond the hype: How to make Web services work for your organization, Part 2—How to begin to use Web services in your business*. Retrieved January 6, 2003, from http://www.lightshipinc.com/lightship/download/download.aspx?Title=BeyondHypePart2

Zimmermann, O., et al. (2004). *Elements of service-oriented analysis and design: An interdisciplinary modeling approach for SOA projects*, IBM. Retrieved January 21, 2007, from http://www-128.ibm.com/developerworks/Webservices/library/ws-soad1/

Chapter XII
Web Service Orchestration and Choreography: Enabling Business Processes on the Web

Florian Daniel
Politecnico di Milano, Italy

Barbara Pernici
Politecnico di Milano, Italy

ABSTRACT

The Web service domain is a fast growing and fast changing environment. From a business perspective, the trend over the last few years in the Web services area firmly points toward seamless business logic integration and inter-enterprise collaboration. However, in order to accomplish such goals, both technological and conceptual advances are required. Some already have proven their viability, others still have to be made. Among them, Web service orchestration and choreography are of crucial importance, but still lack a widely agreed on development framework comprising both technological and conceptual aspects. In this chapter, we try to provide a critical snapshot of current standards for Web service development and particularly we focus on Web service orchestration and choreography. We discuss problems and solutions from a conceptual point of view, exemplify the illustrated ideas by means of real-world technologies and standards, and highlight the mutual dependencies that exist among orchestration and choreography of Web services.[1]

INTRODUCTION

When analyzing the current literature on Web services and the main problems the authors focus on, it is possible to identify one main trend toward the adoption of novel and emerging Web service technologies as basis for the next generation of (Web) applications and composite Web services. In this context, especially the need for flexible solutions for composing Web services into composite applications or services is manifest. Composite applications or services leverage the functionalities provided by their individual component services by combining them in a value adding manner.

Web services are driven by the paradigm of the so-called *service-oriented architecture* (SOA), which describes the relationships that exist among service *providers*, service *consumers,* and service *brokers* and thereby provides an abstract execution environment for Web services. The research area of *service-oriented computing* (SOC) endorses the SOA paradigm and aims at producing technologies and solutions that address the efficient development, flexible composition, and execution of (composite) Web services. From their first appearance, SOA and SOC have emerged as key factors for the success of the world of Web services.

Just as the advent of *object-oriented programming* (OOP) was based on the notion of *objects* as means to modularize programming functionality, SOC could be defined as a paradigm that looks at *services* as basic functional modules that can be composed or newly defined. OOP per se did not suddenly provide revolutionary new programming capabilities with respect to conventional procedural techniques, it rather proved to be an efficient means for abstraction and isolation and thus fostered reuse, robustness, and scalability. These factors encouraged the emergence of higher-level concepts like object brokers, Java Beans, object containers, which finally enhanced interoperability.

Analogously, current specification proposals for Web services can be interpreted as a transition toward a robust SOC framework. Several Web service standardization bodies are currently addressing issues that can be interpreted as definition of a proper new programming framework. For example, even if we are already speaking about service composition and seamless inter-enterprise integration, there is still discussion over standardization of other system aspects (e.g., reliable messaging or transaction support) that have already been solved or are under study in other research areas. Past experiences taught us, however, that as long as there are no robust and commonly agreed on standards, real interoperation, and composition problems cannot be addressed adequately.

In this chapter, we will introduce the reader to the orchestration and choreography of Web services, which are becoming the cornerstones for the execution of business processes on the Web, and we will discuss the state of current research and open issues. More precisely, we will first try to clarify the main terminology in use, and then we will give an explanation for the actual need for coordination protocols and composition technologies. We will exemplify such a discussion by means of a possible protocol stack for Web service composition, and we also discuss some advanced issues. Finally, we will provide an outlook over expected future trends and draw our conclusions.

USING THE RIGHT TERMINOLOGY

Specifications and technologies for Web service composition in many cases still have to reach stable definitions and usage scenarios. Accordingly, also authors writing about service composition are far from using a commonly agreed on terminology. Peltz (2003a) defines *orchestration* as executable business process that interacts with both internal and external Web services, and *choreography* "...tracks the message sequences among multiple parties and sources—typically the public message exchanges that occur between Web services—rather than a specific business process that a single party executes..." (Peltz, 2003b).

Alonso, Casati, Kuno, and Machiraju (2004) prefer the terms coordination (protocol) and composition rather than choreography and orchestration. Literally, they clarify "...we will use the term *conversation* to refer to the sequences of operations (i.e., message exchanges) that could occur between a client and a service as part of the invocation of a Web service. We will use the term *coordination protocol* to refer to the specification of the set of correct and accepted conversations..." And "...we refer to a service implemented by combining the functionality provided by other Web services as a *composite service*, and the process of developing a composite Web service as *service composition*..."

The W3C's Web services choreography working group defines *choreography* as the definition of the sequences and conditions under which multiple cooperating independent agents exchange messages in order to perform a task to achieve a goal state. Web services choreography concerns the interactions of services with their users. Any user of a Web service, automated or otherwise, is a client of that service. These users may, in turn, be other Web services, applications, or human beings. An *orchestration* defines the sequence and conditions in which one Web service invokes other Web services in order to realize some useful function (i.e., an orchestration is the pattern of interactions that a Web service agent must follow in order to achieve its goal) (W3C, n.d.).

This terminological comparison shows that different authors prefer different names and thereby emphasize different aspects even within the same Web service domain. Figure 1 attempts to characterize and aggregate the currently used terminology through contextualizing the most commonly used terms. For this purpose, we distinguish two main dimensions: the perspective of the observer and the kind of observer along with its observation time. According to a common approach, the perspective is divided into *public* and *private*, with respect to the observer's view, whereas Figure 1 also represents the dimension *actor*, which allows the distinction between composition designers and execution engines. An *execution engine* executes a composite service (runtime orchestration: the engine is already provided with the set of component services, the *orchestra*) that has previously been defined by a composite service designer (design time composition: the orchestra is *composed* by selecting the right services). A *service designer* thus composes a new service driven by a final goal and by taking into account the restrictions imposed by the coordination protocols of the component services and by specifying the composition rules for the selected services and the coordination rules which constrain possible interactions with the services. At runtime, externally visible coordination effects can be interpreted as choreography with respect to the orchestra of compound services.

Figure 1. A contextualized view on currently used terminology; the two main nomenclatures concerning respectively public and private perspective on Web services can further be specialized by designer and execution time (Daniel & Pernici, 2006).

		Perspective	
		public	**private**
Actor	**Composition Designer (design time)**	Coordination	Composition
	Execution Engine (runtime)	Choreography	Orchestration

The taxonomy described in Figure 1 should provide the reader with a coarse contextualization of the most used terms and serves merely orientation purposes; it should not be considered a widely acknowledged categorization.

THE NEED FOR COORDINATION PROTOCOLS

According to the previous characterization, coordination and choreography describe the external message exchanges that occur between a Web service and its client or among several collaborating Web services. The main concerns that have to be addressed within the coordination layer are: Can messages be sent and received in any order? Which rules govern message sequences? Is there a relationship among incoming and outgoing messages? Is it possible to undo (parts of) already executed sequences? In the following, we will try to provide answers and details to some of these questions by discussing the conceptual backgrounds and core ideas of the most representative coordination approaches.

Conversation Between Service and Client

WSDL, the *Web service description language* (W3C, 2001), in its function of interface description language already provides a limited set of constructs that aim at specifying how to correctly interact with a particular Web service. Several extensions have been investigated that tried to extend the basic WSDL description with concepts for better describing conversation-related aspects. Figure 2, for example, graphically depicts the

Figure 2. Ordered message exchange between a Web service and its client

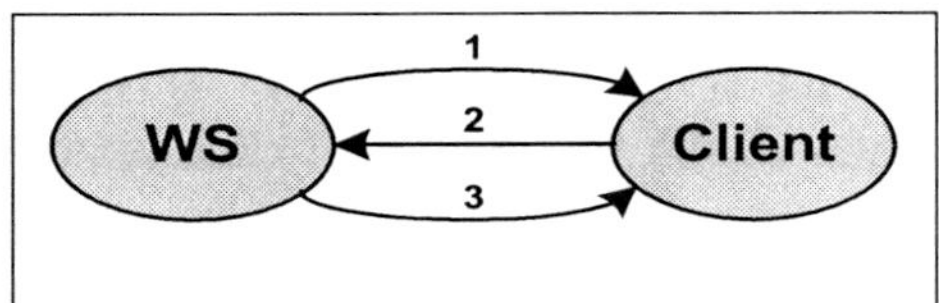

Figure 3. Interaction involving multiple Web services; messages depend semantically and chronologically from one another.

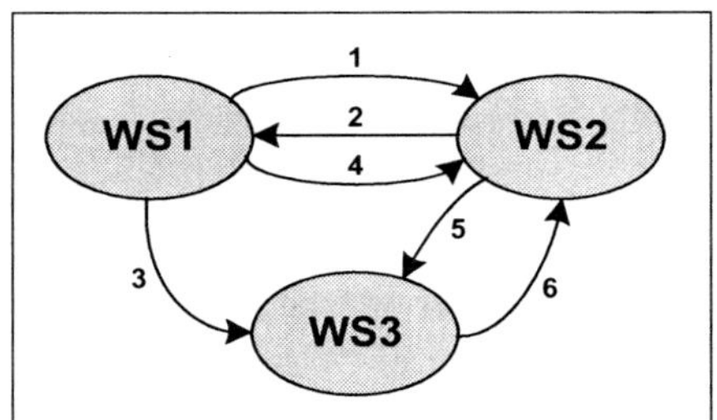

problem of ordering messages exchanged between a Web service and its client.

WSDL extensions such as WSCL (*Web services conversation language;* Hewlett-Packard Company, 2002) only had limited success, most likely due to the fact that its underlying client-server conversation model does not really fit into the service-oriented architecture of Web services. Graphically, the functionality of WSCL could best be described by a state machine model, whose expressive power allows the description of conditions and ordered messages, but does not distinguish between involved actors.

Multi-Service Conversations

Figure 3 depicts a slightly more complex conversation scenario that, for example, cannot be adequately described by means of a client-server protocol. The main novelty with respect to Figure 2 here is, that now support for an arbitrary number of interacting services is required. Each of them plays a different role within the overall conversation, and only the strict adherence to such roles leads to the fulfillment of the common (business) goal. Roles are usually labeled with names like *supplier*, *purchaser*, or *broker*.

As a first representative choreography protocols, WSCI (*Web services choreography interface*; Arkin et al., 2002) goes one step further in its support for long lasting, choreographed, and stateful message exchanges with respect to WSCL. In particular, it supports order, rules, and boundaries of messages, correlation, transactions and compensation as well as exception handling. Through its concept of *interface*, it goes beyond simple client-server interface descriptions and supports interaction contexts with different external services, despite lacking an overall global view of the conversations a service is involved in. A WSCI interface in fact only describes one partner's participation in a message exchange and, therefore, a WSCI choreography must include a set of WSCI interfaces, one for each partner constituting an interaction. The sample scenario in Figure 3 would thus require three different WSCI interface descriptions.

WS-CDL (*Web services choreography definition language*; Kavantzas et al., 2005; Ross-Talbot & Fletcher, 2006), the latest choreography protocol proposal, finally provides a global view over multiparty coordination through the explicit modeling of all the involved roles. Its purpose can be considered as twofold: on the one hand, it provides syntactical primitives for describing involved roles and the messages exchanged during interaction; on the other hand, it can be interpreted as well as binding interaction agreement between business partners that are intended to start a cooperation and require a language for formalizing their cooperation.

Advanced Protocols and Specifications

As opposed to the previous coordination protocols, which all can be considered domain-independent, there also exists a set of proprietary, domain-specific vertical protocols such as RosettaNet (RosettaNet, 2006), or xCBL (XML Common Business Library; xCBL.org, 2006), which provide conversation description mechanisms for specific domains. RosettaNet, for example, aims at facilitating dynamic and flexible trading relationships between business partners in the context of IT supply chains. xCBL, in the context of order management, combines an XML version of EDI (*electronic data interchange*) with predefined business protocols.

Along a somewhat orthogonal dimension of the composition problem, there further exists specifications such as *WS-coordination* or *WS-transactions* that can be considered as meta-specifications that provide a framework for the definition of proper coordination protocols with particular characteristics. For example, WS-coordination proposes some solutions for the problem of message correlation within conversations involving several different partners. For this purpose, it defines a reference data-structure called *coordination context*, to be added to the exchanged SOAP headers, that serves the purpose of passing a unique identifier between interacting Web services.

Vinoski (2004)—in a quite critical way and without the claim for completeness—discusses an impressive list of WS-* specifications, each concerned with the support for particular functionalities: WS-Addressing, WS-Agreement, WS-Attachments, WS-BusinessActivity, WS-Coordination, WS-Discovery, WS-Enumeration, WS-Eventing, WS-Federation, WS-Inspection, WS-Manageability, WS-MetadataExchange, WS-Notification, WS-PolicyFramework, WS-Provisioning, WS-ReliableMessaging, WS-Resource, WS-Security, WS-Topics, WS-Transactions, and WS-Transfer.

The careful reader might have derived from the names of the single specifications how all WS-* efforts together are laying the foundation for a distributed computing platform on top of standard Web technologies. Comparable to the number of APIs available to .Net or Java/J2EE developers, the amount of WS-* specifications is continuously growing, in order to provide suitable APIs and wire protocols for satisfying emerging novel interoperability requirements. The first steps towards a commonly agreed on, proper programming environment for the envisioned SOP infrastructure are thus being made.

Coordination Middleware

Before going on and discussing the composition of Web services, it is worth noting that the coordination protocol specifications described so far are all so-called *description languages*. They are not executable languages to actively coordinate conversations among different Web services. The necessary runtime logic that adheres to the described protocol must be implemented either by the services themselves or by higher-level process management languages.

Alonso et al. (2004), in order to actively support service coordination, suggest an additional middleware layer on top of the coordination layer, containing so-called *conversation controllers* with message routing and protocol compliance verification capabilities. Such conversation controllers could, for example, address the message dispatching problem arising when it comes to one Web service being engaged in several concurrent conversations. For this purpose, the *coordination context* as pushed forward by WS-coordination could be exploited for message correlation purposes.

FROM COORDINATION TO COMPOSITION

We have noted that coordination protocols are characterized by an intrinsic passive behavior with respect to the execution of a coordinated interaction. However, despite such a passive behavior, coordination protocols have proven to have enough expressive power in the context of service *coordination*, which indeed does not require any executable logic. Yet, when it comes to *orchestration*, things change and active support for the execution of explicitly provided process or flow definitions is required. Process execution implies the need for dedicated execution environments, so-called execution or process engines, able to interpret process definitions and to control the flow of data and service invocations.

There are several different interpretations of what orchestration actually should be. Some authors refer to it as proper programming languages, others tend to prefer a more general and evolutionary interpretation: "...these systems are often labeled the second generation *workflow management systems* (WfMSs) because they provide much richer integration capabilities than traditional WfMSs..." (BPMI.org, n.d.). This second interpretation is probably too simplistic and puts too much emphasis on the business perspective of the problem.

Nevertheless, current orchestration approaches definitely inherit their core modeling concepts from research in the field of WfMSs. To orchestrate Web services, their composition rules have to be specified at design time. Various structured process models have been proposed using traditional workflow constructs at their basis. A classification of typical workflow constructs that originate from a structured programming language approach to workflow definition and also can be found in today's service composition languages has been proposed by Van der Aalst, ter Hofstede, Kiepuszewski, and Barros (2003).

In the following subsections, we will provide insights into the most prominent composition approaches and issues in the context of Web services.

Model-Based Composition

Model-based service composition approaches concentrate on the explicit definition of the possible process flow that governs a composite Web service or application. Such process definitions are fed into a process or execution engine that manages the overall execution of the compound activities and thus actively orchestrates the composite service. Commercial composition tools usually provide intuitive high-level visual modeling tools that aid designers in the predominantly explicit definition of processes, such as Microsoft's BizTalk *orchestration designer* (Microsoft Corporation, n.d.) or Oracle's *BPEL process editor* (Kennedy, 2005). Internally, these models are then translated into low-level process models for execution purposes.

Several approaches for internal process models and structures have been proposed in literature. In the following, we provide a brief overview, without going too deep into detail.

State Charts and Petri Nets

State charts and Petri nets (or extensions of them) are classical and well-known formalisms within computer science. They have already proven their viability in the context of workflow modeling, and are mentioned here merely for the sake of completeness; further details can be found in (Alonso et al., 2004). Within the Web service domain, IBM's WSFL, for example, internally uses Petri net models for expressing the process logic. Benatallah, Sheng, and Dumas (2003) ground their declarative service composition approach *Self-Serv* on state charts.

Pi-Calculus

Less intuitive and without graphical representation are process specifications based on Pi-Calculus (Alonso et al., 2004). Pi-Calculus is a process algebra and an attempt at developing a formal theory for process models. As happens with Petri nets, the main advantage is represented by the fact that a precise and well-studied formalism can provide the basis for the verification of process properties and correctness analyses. Microsoft's XLANG specification, for example, is inspired by Pi-Calculus theory.

Rule-Based Orchestration

Another textual technique for specifying orchestration schemas is provided by rule-based orchestration languages, which provide constructs for the specification of processes by means of sets of rules (Alonso et al., 2004). Usually, such rules are based on the so-called *event-condition-action* (ECA) paradigm known from active database management systems. This technique is less structured with respect to the previous models and is mainly suited to model orchestrations that have only few constraints among activities.

Two Representatives of Structured Process Models: BPEL(4WS) vs. BPML

BPEL (*business process execution language*; Weerawarana & Curbera, 2002) is an XML-based Web service composition language that has its roots in both Microsoft's XLANG and IBM's WSFL. In BPEL, a composite service is named a *process*; processes export and import functionality by using Web service interfaces exclusively. Two main kinds of processes are distinguished: *abstract processes* describe business protocols, specifying the mutually exchanged messages and their invocation order by each of the parties involved, *executable processes* bind the specified behavior to concrete services. According to this twofold applicability, BPEL presents both coordination as well as composition characteristics. Services participating in a process are called *partners*, and message exchanges or intermediate result transformations are called *activities*. BPEL distinguishes between basic and structured activities. *Basic activities* represent synchronous and asynchronous calls (<invoke>, <invoke>...<receive>), *structured activities* manage the overall process flow (<flow> to denote parallelism, <switch> for alternatives, etc.).

BPEL is primarily designed as a composition language, but developers can use the same formalism for both service composition and conversation definition. As for the definition of conversations, it however lacks some necessary and, from a discovery and binding perspective, particularly useful properties that would be required for defining conversations (e.g., for service activation). As for the composition of services, the structure of BPEL is flat (i.e., sub-processes cannot be defined).

BPML (*business process management language*; BPMI.org, 2002) provides similar modeling capabilities as BPEL, but also supports some additional constructs making it more flexible in general, such as sub-processes, etc. In particular, the BPML specification provides an abstract model and an XML syntax for expressing executable business processes. Nevertheless, BPML itself does not define any application semantics, it rather defines an abstract model and grammar for expressing generic processes. This allows BPML to be used for a variety of purposes that include, but are not limited to, the definition of enterprise business processes, the definition of complex Web services and the definition of multi-party collaborations. BPML is conceived as block-structured programming language, i.e., recursive block structures play a significant role in scoping issues that are relevant for declarations, definitions and process execution.

Both BPEL and BPML provide support for long-running business transactions and robust exception handling facilities. BPML does not provide constructs for the definition of message coordination protocols as BPEL does, but developers easily can use WSCI for this purpose, which shares the same underlying process execution model. This apparent shortcoming of BPML, on the other hand, allows for a more flexible use of BPML and WSCI when it comes to defining conversations, due to the good separation of concerns. Yet, there is still less industry support for BPML in comparison to BPEL, which is reflected by the higher availability of commercial tools for process definition and execution based on the BPEL specification.

Semantics-Based Composition

Model-based service compositions are explicit process modeling approaches in that the desired process flow needs to be explicitly provided (i.e., modeled) by composite application/service designers. The semantic Web and Web service ontologies offer alternative ways for the composition and execution of compound services, which do not rely on explicit definitions of the flow or process logic. Such approaches typically aim at providing suitable frameworks for the semantic description and the automatic discovery and selection of Web services and the automatic derivation and execution of composite services defined in an implicit manner by means of goals and pre- and post-conditions over service inputs and outputs.

The recent W3C effort for the definition of *semantic annotations for WSDL* (SAWSDL) (Farrel & Lausen, 2006) aims at standardizing the first three of the previous concerns (i.e., semantic description, automatic discovery, and selection. SAWSDL does not prescribe any formalism for the specification of the semantics of a Web service, it rather concentrates on how to flexibly annotate a WSDL description with pointers to external semantic descriptions to disambiguate Web service descriptors during automatic discovery and composition. To enable semantic annotation of WSDL components, SAWSDL defines three new extensibility attributes to WSDL 2.0 elements, while remaining completely agnostic to the language used for the external semantic representation.

Concerning the semantics-based, automatic composition of Web services, Arpinar, Aleman-Meza, Zhang, and Maduko (2004) for example propose an ontology-driven Web services composition platform where the requirements of the desired composite services are specified by the user in form of provided inputs and expected outputs. The described approach allows the automatic generation and execution of a composite service that produces the expected outputs by combining existing individual services based on their semantic descriptions. A human-assisted and an automatic composition mechanism are outlined.

Two Emerging Standards: OWL-S vs. WSMO

OWL-S (*ontology Web language for Web services*; Martin, 2003) allows providers of Web services to describe properties, capabilities, and behaviors of their services by means of ontologies and provides proper language primitives for their semantic description. Final goal of OWL-S is to provide a machine-interpretable description of Web services, in addition to the human-understandable descriptions already provided by WSDL, and thus to support automatic discovery, execution and composition. The core of OWL-S, the ontology-driven description approach, builds on the *ontology Web language* (OWL), which provides the necessary constructs for explicitly representing knowledge, the meaning of terms and the relationships that exist among those terms within a specific domain. OWL and OWL-S are evolutions of DAML+OIL, a semantic markup language for Web resources.

OWL-S ontologies are structured into three main parts: A *service profile* serves the purpose of advertising and discovering services published by service providers and contains a semantically enriched and machine-interpretable service description. A *process model* describes how a service operates (by means of proper control constructs and conversation descriptions) and comprises inputs, outputs, preconditions, results, and effects of the service. According to their complexity, *atomic*, *simple*, and *composite* processes are distinguished, being the latter the most complex process. The third part, the service *grounding*, provides the necessary details to access a specific service (i.e., protocols and message formats). Whereas *profile* and *model* provide rather abstract representations, the *grounding* refers to the concrete specification. The semantics- and ontology-based approach adopted by OWL-S is particularly suited for advanced service and conversation description.

WSMO (*Web service modeling ontology*; Roman, Lausen, & Keller, 2004) as well aims at describing relevant aspects of Web services in a semantically rich fashion. Within the *Web service modeling framework* (WSMF), WSMO provides an open, semantics-based formalism for goal-driven service composition through extensive use of ontologies, semantic service descriptions and pre- and post-conditions for service descriptions. Besides ontologies, goals and service descriptions, so-called mediators allow the bypassing of interoperability problems among different services. Efficient interoperability is one of the main issues that WSMO tries to solve, differentiating it from OWL-S.

Just as for OWL-S, also in WSMO *ontologies* are adopted to provide the formal semantics that allows the automatic processing of information and the human- and computer-understandable goal definition. A *goal* specification expresses the final objective that a client may have when interacting with a service and consists primarily of constrains over post-conditions after service execution. *Mediators* provide the necessary support for integrating heterogeneous elements when combining several component services, i.e., they define mappings and transformations between connected elements. Four types of mediators exist, according to the elements they link: goal-goal mediators, ontology-ontology mediators, service-goal mediators, and service-service mediators. Finally, *Web services* are described by means of their non-functional properties, the mediators they use, their capabilities, interfaces, and groundings.

In Roman and Scicluna (2006) the authors describe how choreography requirements of Web services can be specified in WSMO, so to express an individual service's communication behavior exposed to its clients. The description of the behavior is based on the abstract state machine model and defined in terms of one or more WSMO ontologies and a set of transition rules, leading to the notion of evolving ontology for the representation of the state of the choreography.

For the execution of WSMO-based Web services, DERI has developed the so-called *Web services modeling execution environment* (WSMX) (Haller, Cimpian, Mocan, Oren, & Bussler, 2005), a comprehensive execution environment for semantic Web services and DERI's reference implementation of WSMO. WSMX is designed to allow the dynamic discovery, invocation, and composition of Web services. It offers a complete support for interacting with semantic Web services and also supports the interaction with non-WSMO services. WSMX is made available as Web service that requires in input a formal description of the requester's goal and the data the requester wants to use for the invocation. Starting from these data and the single services' choreography requirements, WSMX takes care of all other computations, such as dynamic discovery, selection, and composition of the Web services that fulfill the requester's requirements.

Quality of Service-Based Approaches

Orthogonally to semantics-based approaches, which provide open and domain-independent means for service description, there are approaches that particularly focus their attention on *quality of service* (QoS) parameters for service selection and composition. Once the functional compatibility between candidate services is ascertained, service selection in QoS-based approaches is driven by quality properties like response time, accuracy (of results), completeness (of covered data), price, availability, reputation, or similar. Representations of QoS parameters in literature range from simple parameter-value pairs to complex QoS ontologies.

In Meteor-S, process composition is annotated with information for selecting services according to quality of service characteristics (Sivashanmugam, Miller, Sheth, & Verma, 2003). Optimization of service selection has been considered and evaluation functions discussed. The approach is mainly oriented to design, giving the possibility of transforming the process representation into BPML or BPEL process specifications.

In MAIS, services are selected at runtime according to constraints on functionalities and quality of service expressed at design time and the current context for process execution (De Antonellis et al., 2006; Maurino, Modafferi, Mussi, & Pernici, 2004). Service substitution can be performed to guarantee QoS constraints at runtime in a variable execution environment.

With QoSOnt (Dobson, Lock, & Sommerville, 2005) the authors aim to provide a common QoS conceptualization to be used by all actors involved in a QoS-based service selection (i.e., clients, providers, and third party intermediary systems). The QoS ontology QoSOnt is formalized in OWL and describes non-functional aspects of Web services, which may be used by clients to judge the services' quality. QoSOnt allows the specification of QoS attributes (e.g., reliability or performance), the metrics that are used to measure the values of attributes and possible conversions between different measuring units. The ontology is modular and extensible.

Other Composition Approaches

Several further (academic) research works go one step further in service composition and also investigate the potential of additional aspects of the composition problem, such as personalization or context. We only cite two representatives of such work; the discussion of other valuable work would be out of scope for this chapter.

Maamar, Mostefaoui, and Yahyaoui (2005), for instance, extend their state-chart-based service composition model with an agent-based and context-oriented approach to composite service execution. The term *context* reflects the point of view of services rather than the one of users. At runtime, agents are engaged in conversations with their peers on behalf of the user to agree on the actual Web services to participate in the process, according to the runtime context conditions and the global composition model.

Baïna, Benali, and Godart (2003) finally provide a valuable approach to Web service composition within the initially mentioned workflow domain and with special focus on enterprise workflow interconnection. The process interconnection model presented by the authors builds on Web service-based workflow integration and allows the coexistence of heterogeneous workflow systems in a so-called "workflow of workflows." The main contribution of the work consists in the introduction of a certain level of dynamism, proper of the Web services area, into workflow definitions; more precisely, the authors postpone the selection of nested sub-processes from build-time to runtime, by introducing proper discovery, negotiation, and wrapping mechanisms for so-called process services.

In all the mentioned approaches, traditional composition patterns are enriched with additional features that allow flexible process specifications and executions. The principal trends are toward providing a precise definition of context and of local and global constraints and dynamic service selection and invocation. No new composition constructs are defined; however, new composition mechanisms and optimisation of composed services are discussed in the literature.

In choreography specifications, typically there is less attention to such quality related aspects, except for temporal constraints on the conversations. However, in this chapter we do not discuss in depth these issues since they are only marginally relevant in the comparison of coordination and composition approaches.

A POSSIBLE PROTOCOL STACK

The previous sections have shown that research on service coordination and composition has led to a variety of different approaches and protocol or language specifications. Figure 4 describes a possible protocol stack as it could be adopted for the development of composite applications or services, starting from a set of individual component services. The protocol stack is horizontally split according to two dimensions (i.e., the perspective of the observer and the conceptual approach underlying the described specification). The perspective is divided into public and private, where the *public* perspective refers to choreography, and the *private* perspective refers to orchestration. The conceptual approaches are divided into coordination-based, execution-based, semantics-based, and quality-based approaches.

Interaction among services is based on traditional transport protocols such as HTTP, SMTP, or IIOP. The widely acknowledged basic message protocol is SOAP (nevertheless, other protocols could be used), and Web service description is primarily achieved by means of WSDL. But as can be seen in Figure 4 by moving along the vertical axis, when it comes to more advanced features, such as coordination and composition, the number of possible solutions grows, and the agreement becomes less.

In the following, we position the previously discussed approaches and technologies in the overall protocol stack and complete the resulting stack with some further specification, so as to provide an overview as complete as possible of the technologies that are at the basis of each approach. The proposed stack is not intended as exact picture of each single approach (some approaches indeed do not cover all aspects addressed in Figure 4), but rather represents reasonable configurations, as they could be adopted in a working system.

Coordination-Based Approaches

- **ebXML (electronic business using extensible markup language):** (UN/CEFACT, OASIS; Eisenberg & Nickull, 2001). ebXML is a (vertical) suite of specifications of how electronic commerce exchanges should be specified, documented, and conducted, and can be subdivided into three different protocols:
- **CPP (collaboration protocol profile):** A CPP is similar to a UDDI registry entry and includes interface and message descriptions

Figure 4. Web service composition-oriented protocol stack of vendor-specific and standardized protocols and languages. Within the composition layer, we propose BPML on top of WSCI as they share a common process model. However, other executable BPM languages could be adopted as well.

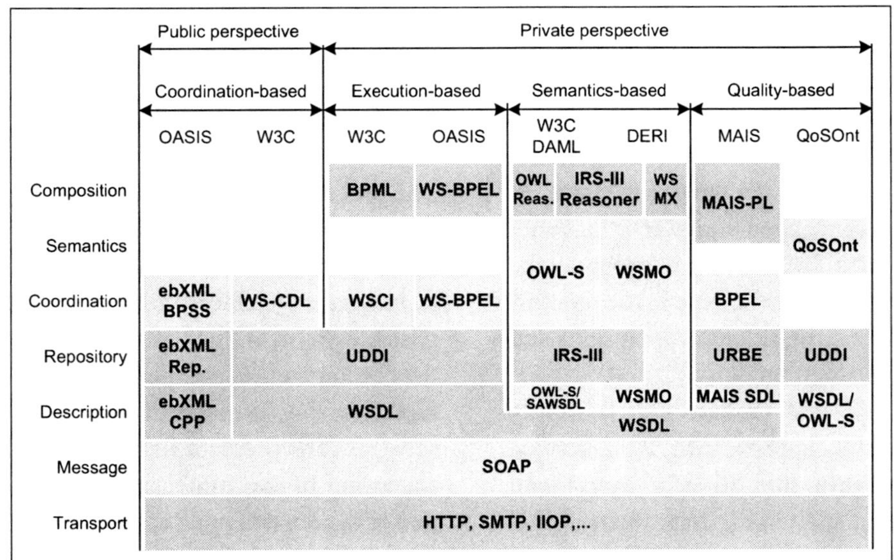

as well as business data and data exchange capabilities of a particular trading partner.

- **BPSS (business process specification schema):** The BPSS protocol can define both the choreography and communications between services. The definition of a proper business process execution language is explicitly outside the scope of ebXML.
- **Repository/Registry:** The ebXML Registry is similar to UDDI in that it allows the discovery and binding of businesses, the definition of agreements between trading-partners, the exchange of XML messages in support of business operations. The goal is to allow all these activities to be performed automatically, without human intervention, over the Internet.
- **CPA (collaboration protocol agreement, not shown in Figure 4):** A CPA contains the business agreement among cooperating partners. It is derived from the intersection of the CPPs of the cooperating trading partners.
- **WS-CDL (Web services choreography definition language):** (W3C Working Draft; Kavantzas et al., 2005; Ross-Talbot et al., 2006). WS-CDL is an XML-based language that describes peer-to-peer collaborations of parties by defining, from a global viewpoint, their common and complementary observable behavior, where ordered message exchanges aim at accomplishing a common business goal. It is neither an executable business process description language nor an implementation language.

Execution-Based Approaches

- **WSCI (Web services choreography interface):** (Initially Sun, SAP, BEA, and Intalio; now W3C Note; Arkin et al., 2002). It is an XML-based interface description language that describes the flow of messages exchanged by a Web service participating in choreographed interactions with other services. WSCI is a coordination protocol, in that it does not address the definition and the implementation of the internal processes that actually drive the message exchange.
- BPML (business process management language): (Business Process Management Initiative (BPMI.org, 2002). BPML is a language for the modeling of business processes and was designed to support processes that a business process management system could execute. BPML and WSCI share the same underlying process execution model; therefore developers can use WSCI to describe public interactions among business processes and reserve, for example, BPML for developing private implementations. However, other coordination protocols than WSCI can be adopted as well.
- **BPEL:** (also BPEL4WS, business process execution language for Web services or WS-BPEL; initially Microsoft, IBM, Siebel Systems, BEA, and SAP; now OASIS; Web services business process execution language; Weerawarana et al., 2002). It provides an XML-based grammar to describe the control logic required to coordinate Web services participating in a process flow. BPEL can act both as coordination protocol and proper composition language. BPEL orchestration engines can execute this grammar, coordinate activities and compensate activities when errors occur.

Semantics-Based Approaches

- **OWL-S (ontology Web language for Web services):** DAML.org; Martin, 2003). OWL-S is an ontology-based description language that supplies Web service providers with a set of markup language constructs for describing the properties and capabilities of their Web services at a semantic level and in an unambiguous, computer-interpretable form. It allows the definition of semantic descriptions as well as coordination rules. Previous releases of the language were built upon DAML+OIL and known as DAML-S. Theoretically, OWL-S is not limited to one specific grounding, but its current version provides a predefined grounding for WSDL that maps OWL-S elements to a WSDL interface (Polleres & Lara, 2005); alternatively, service descriptions could also leverage SAWSDL. On top of OWL-S, proper reasoners allow automatic service composition and execution.

- **WSMO (Web service modeling ontology):** (DERI; Roman et al., 2004). Based on the conceptual basis provided by the WSMF (Web service modeling framework) (Fensel & Bussler, 2002), WSMO serves the purpose of describing various aspects of semantic Web services, ranging from coordination constraints over semantics to composition issues, and aims at solving existing integration problems. The vision of WSMO is that of an automated, goal-driven service composition that builds on pre- and post-conditions associated to component services. In its current version, WSMO is grounded on WSDL, but DERI is planning to allow multiple groundings for their service descriptions.
- **IRS (Internet reasoning service):** (Confalonieri, Domingue, & Motta, 2004). IRS is KMi's semantic Web services framework for semantically describing and executing Web services. The IRS supports the provision of semantic reasoning services within the context of the semantic Web. The primary goal is to support the discovery and retrieval of knowledge components (i.e., services) from libraries over the Internet and to semi-automatically compose them according to specified goals. It is based on problem solving methods, using task descriptions in terms of input roles, output roles, pre-conditions, assumptions, and goals and ontologies. With the current version of IRS3, it is possible to execute WSMO services, but the binding of services occurs still at design time (Haller et al., 2005).
- **WSMX (Web service modeling execution environment):** (Haller et al., 2005). WSMX is the reference implementation of the WSMO execution environment developed by DERI International and allows the run-time discovery, selection, and composition of WSMO-based Web services. Discovery and selection are performed over a WSMO service repository, which is part of the WSMX implementation. WSMX internally adopts the WSML (Web service modelling language) for execution purposes.

Quality of Service-Based Approaches

- **MAIS (multichannel adaptive information systems):** (Bianchini, De Antonellis, Pernici, & Plebani, 2006; Cappiello, Missier, Pernici, Plebani, & Batini, 2004; Maurino et al., 2004). The Italian MAIS research project proposes a quality-based approach to service description, selection, and composition. Web services, described with a MAIS-SDL (service description language) based on WSDL and annotated with quality properties defined in WSOL (Tosic, Pagurek, Patel, Esfandiari, & Ma, 2003), are dynamically composed in context variable process executions. Web services are selected from URBE, a UDDI-compatible registry with a service ontology and service quality information (Bianchini et al., 2006). Flexible process descriptions are specified in MAIS-PL (MAIS process language) and formulated associating to BPEL local and global quality constraints on the basis of information available in the current context of execution.

- **QoSOnt:** (Dobson et al., 2005) provides means for semantically rich, QoS-based descriptions of Web services in OWL. The proposed approach adopts a standard UDDI registry for the discovery of service descriptions, which may be provided in either WSDL or OWL-S. QoSOnt is best used in combination with OWL-S; if service descriptions are provided in WSDL, OWL-S concepts cannot be referenced anymore, which slightly restricts the expressiveness of QoSOnt.

Based on Figure 4, one could say that composite service designers are confronted with a huge amount of partly mutually exclusive, partly dependent specifications in their composition task. Fortunately, they are not supposed to know and master all the above specifications together with their peculiarities. In fact, once they have chosen the composition or coordination approach that best matches their individual requirements, they only need to focus on those technologies and specifications that are necessary. Undoubtedly, the choice of the right approach is of crucial importance.

Besides due to real, functional needs, the high number of candidate standards is mainly due to two reasons: firstly, vendor-related political and strategic aspects (each one wants his own specification to become a common standard); secondly, the relatively young age of the overall Web service technologies themselves. Unavoidably, this results in a proliferation of proprietary (or not) specifications and a lack of stability when it comes to choose reference specifications.

Figure 5. Emergence and evolution of today's principal standards and languages concerning WS composition. The figure tries to reflect the official release or publication dates of the specifications (to the best of the authors' knowledge), first appearance of or discussions about them could differ from the proposed dates.

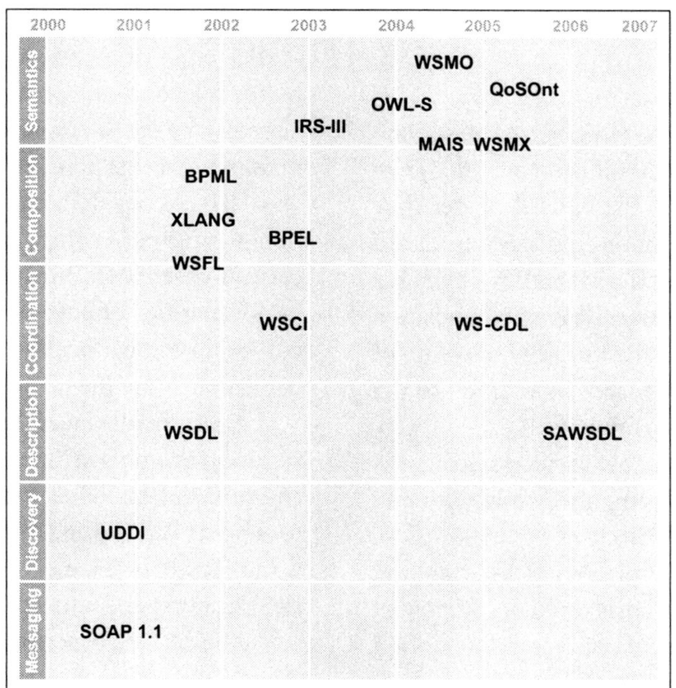

Figure 5 graphically depicts the temporal emergence of the previously listed standards and/or specifications. Along the diagram's diagonal, a trend toward high-level and semantically rich specifications can be derived (i.e., a trend toward enabling designers to comfortably specify or to automatically derive executable service compositions).

ADVANCED COMPOSITION PROBLEMS

The previous sections introduced some Web service coordination and composition solutions and characterized them by positioning them with respect to their driving conceptual approaches. Independently from the approach a developers chooses for his composite service or application, there are however a few typical, crosscutting composition problems that need to be addressed and which we did not yet cover. In this section we discuss a few of the most prominent ones of such problems (i.e., service selection, message correlation, transactions, and exception handling).

Service Selection

In one of the previous sections, we described two research efforts by Maamar et al. (2005) and Baïna et al. (2003). As the careful reader may have noticed, one of the main novelties introduced by these two research efforts (but also by some of the quality- or semantics-driven composition approaches) consists in the *dynamic selection* of the services to be composed, in addition to the dynamic service composition itself.

The purpose of dynamic service selection is mostly that of guaranteeing the availability and robustness of a composite service or application, being the Web a highly variable and fast changing environment. The question is whether component services are to be selected at process *definition time* or at *runtime*, during process execution; some authors distinguish between service selection at *design time* and *deployment time*. Service selection is probably the point where Web service orchestration approaches could learn from, but also add flexibility to traditional WfMSs, which typically include a (centralized) resource manager that, at runtime, decides to which resource instance, respecting a precise role definition, a specific task should be assigned (WfMC, n.d.).

Currently, *static* (i.e., hard-coded within the process definition) selection approaches prevail over dynamic ones (Alonso et al., 2004). The URIs for locating the necessary services are typically defined at design time, and each process instance refers to the same set of services. Instead of hard-coding the URIs within the process definition, they may be assigned to process variables and thus determined for example as result of a runtime operation call; this kind of service selection is known as *dynamic by reference*. A further degree of flexibility is provided by so-called *dynamic by lookup* binding mechanisms that support, for each activity, the definition of a query to be executed on some service directory and thus also require a certain level of middleware support.

Selection decisions are not only influenced by the selection time, but—and even to a higher degree—by the selection algorithm itself. As the ontology-driven approach shows, semantics- and goal-driven considerations could drive the selection algorithm (Arpinar et al., 2004), as well as context-based or QoS-driven ones. Also, syntactical similarities or abstract services as representatives for a specific class of equivalent services could constitute the decision domain.

UDDI provides basic functionalities to retrieve services according to their classification, providers and/or tModels. Recent proposals have emerged to support WSMO and OWL-S service selection using IRS (Confalonieri et al., 2004), using the IRS discovery and retrieval mechanisms, mapping semantic service descriptions provided by those two approaches to the knowledge representation language OCML (Hakimpour, Domingue, Motta, Cabral, & Lei, 2004).

In the URBE registry developed for MAIS, services are selected from the registry according to their functional characteristics, organized according to a service model), their quality characteristics, the invocation context, and application or user requirements (Bianchini et al., 2006). Similarity functions are provided to assess the functional suitability of a service, according to given functional and non-functional requirements, in conjunction with a lightweight ontology model. MAIS flexible process descriptions allow dynamic, context-aware selection, and binding at runtime.

Message Correlation

The next step after service selection is message correlation. For instance, there may be several concurrent instances of an individual service running in a specific execution environment (e.g., a service container) and engaged in different conversations with other services. Message correlation deals with the unique identification of such instances and the conversations they are involved in with external Web services in order to guarantee the overall, correct execution of the separate processes that are running.

As already seen earlier, WS-coordination proposes identifiers (the *coordination context*) carried by SOAP headers for uniquely associating messages to conversations. When using WSCI, designers can identify certain data items within exchanged messages that act as unique identifiers of the conversation. A possible process specification on top of these protocols must explicitly provide the necessary logic that implements the described mechanisms.

On the other hand, BPEL already proposes a solution at process level, namely so-called *correlation sets* that—similar to WSCI—allow the definition of sets of data items as unique identifiers. By assigning the same correlation set to multiple messages, the composition designer can specify that messages—whenever the respective data items have the same values—belong to the same process instance or conversation.

Transactions and Exception Handling

Composite Web services and applications aim to support collaborations between business partners; such collaborations typically require robust transaction support. The classical ACID properties of relational databases have proven being too strict in a service-oriented environment involving several autonomous business partners. Thus, in the context of Web services, some of the ACID properties need to be slightly relaxed. Furthermore, proper compensation mechanisms need be taken into consideration, as already done for WfMSs (Grefen, Pernici, & Sanchez, 1999).

In August 2002, IBM, Microsoft, and BEA proposed WS-Transaction, a standard protocol for long-running business transactions that builds on the framework provided by WS-coordination. Transactions are one way to handle exceptions, but due to their compensation mechanism not in every exceptional situation transactions provide the right functionality. Several exception handling approaches are known, the most important ones are *try-catch-throw* mechanisms as provided (e.g., by Java and currently implemented in BPEL), or *flow-based* mechanisms that consist in explicitly modeling the error checking logic within the proper process description. Also, *rule-based* approaches exist, which are particularly suited for handling temporal exceptions.

HOW ORCHESTRATION DEPENDS ON CHOREOGRAPHY

Choreography and orchestration represent two different conceptual interpretations of the collaboration problem, but the two ideas are far from being independent the one from the other. In this section, we therefore briefly highlight to what extent orchestration depends on choreography by concentrating on three main dimensions (i.e., structural, functional, and resource dependencies).

Structural Dependencies

Structural dependencies drive the overall structure and organization of a process definition and thus concern activities, conditions and routing decisions in the process specification.

Alonso et al. (2004) well explain the dependencies between coordination protocols and composition schemas by stepwise refining the portion of a process definition relative to only one of the services participating in a coordinated conversation. Starting from an overall activity diagram of the process, the authors first extract the role-specific view of the process (the one of the chosen service) and then refine it in order to reach a granularity level where the single activities of the remaining diagram reflect the single service invocations required for achieving the role-specific functionality. This so-called process skeleton on the one hand describes the role-specific view of the process; on the other hand, it provides a proper protocol description of that participant's public interactions. In this way, the authors show how the definition of the executable process intrinsically must match the constraints imposed by the underlying coordination protocol.

Functional Dependencies

Functionalities or capabilities like transaction support, security, reliability, correlation, etc., may lead to functional dependencies among orchestration languages and coordination protocols, like those provided by the wealth of WS-* specifications. Dependencies arise, whenever the functionalities they provide are used at the process specification level, and the composition language "delegates" the relative competencies to the underlying coordination protocols.

As already exemplified earlier, coordination can for example be achieved either explicitly at process level or implicitly at coordination level. For example, once the choice of adopting the WS-coordination framework has been made, the process definition does not anymore require explicit coordination constructs. The same considerations also hold in case of transaction support, reliable messaging, or the like.

Resource Dependencies

Most of the process definition languages have inherited their modeling approaches from the field of workflow management. At process or composition design time, however, service composition presents some methodological differences that are rooted in the dependencies that exist between coordination and composition.

WfMSs allow for a straightforward top-down structure of the process model, describing, for example, an administrative workflow. Resources executing a specific work item are provided with the exact amount of data that is required for the correct execution of that task. To execute one task, there is no need to know about possible other tasks before or after that specific task within the same process flow. Possible task constellations are subject only to the constraints imposed by the final goal of the underlying business process. Involved resources do not have a task-surviving behavior with constraints affecting the overall process definition. Rearranging tasks (i.e., putting some in parallel), when specifying process definitions, is common practice to improve process efficiency.

When defining the logic that constitutes a composite Web service, a strict top-down approach does not guarantee anymore that the resulting process definition is always executable. In fact, a Web service may by subject to individual conversation rules in order to be executed correctly. For example, before accepting a user's credit card number for payment, a service typically must be provided with the appropriate list of goods the user wants to buy. This externally visible behavior of Web services distinguishes the resource *Web service* from those we have in WfMSs. Single tasks cannot anymore be rearranged arbitrarily without loosing functionality.

Composite service designers must know about the coordination requirements of the services they use in order to take them into account when defining composite services. Thus, starting from an initial process idea (top-down), designers select the services providing the right functionality, and then refine their initial idea (by rearranging initially presumed invocations or adding new ones) in order to conform with the coordination requirements imposed by the selected services (bottom-up). Therefore, the resulting process definition combines a coarse-grained top-down approach with a fine-grained bottom-up approach.

FUTURE TRENDS

In light of the developments and the evolutions achieved so far in the Web services area, one is inclined to ask what will happen next to orchestration and choreography of Web services and, thus, to processes on the Web. In the following, we provide our personal ideas about some of the most interesting questions.

Coordination or Composition?

In the previous sections, we argued that coordination protocols are public documents focusing on external interactions, and composition schemas are private documents that describe the internal implementation of composite Web services. In our view, both perspectives will be needed also in the future, and more research work should focus on formally relating the two approaches, also in order to be able to prove formal properties, which are published against formal properties of private process descriptions.

The difference between coordination and composition in fact cannot just boil down to mere technical considerations; legal aspects also play an important role: While orchestrated interactions have one central entity in charge of guaranteeing the correctness of the interaction, choreographed interactions do not. In the former case, there is one partner who has a higher responsibility concerning the success of the cooperation, while in the latter case each partner has the same responsibility.

Trends in Private Process Descriptions

As hinted at in the introduction when comparing SOC with OOP where really valuable and novel concepts primarily emerged as result of the object-oriented paradigm and less because of the availability of object-oriented languages, also in the context of Web services the real potential resides in what will be build on top of the languages and specifications developed in the context of SOC, rather than in the languages or specifications themselves. Just as today's enterprise application servers run so-called *object containers* as execution environment for business logic and offering various services to its components, similar concepts are being investigated also for Web services and probably will substantially enhance current composition capabilities.

Benatallah et al. (2003), in their *Self-Serv* research project, are concentrating on a middleware infrastructure for the composition of Web services that allows multi-attribute dynamic service selections within composite service and peer-to-peer orchestrations. Furthermore, they build on the concept of *service container*, aggregating several substitutable services.

A similar approach is followed by the MAIS project (MAIS, n.d.) that—among others—aims at the definition of a platform for dynamic service selection and provision on the basis of context and QoS information. Compatible services are grouped into so-called *abstract services* and allow dynamically selecting and when necessary substituting (concrete) services at runtime according to the current context and the result of a negotiation over QoS parameters.

In general the trend is towards providing a middleware (environments supporting WS-*) to support dynamic process execution and more integration with programming environments, both in the Semantic Web service line, which is strictly related to logic programming, and in the composition line, such as for instance in BPEL extensions allowing Java code to be included in the process specification.

Trends in Public Process Description

In this area, the trend is to define constraints on messages being exchanged among several partners, without enforcing coordination through execution engines. Some support can be provided to verify, at runtime, whether a given coordination specification has been violated (such as, for instance, in Maamar et al., 2005).

Open or Closed Worlds?

Slightly different approaches are emerging from the recent trend toward Semantic Web services and still have to be profoundly investigated. Most of the efforts in this context, like OWL-S and WSMO, are covered by research and academic communities and still have to prove their commercial viability. Nevertheless, especially for dynamic service selection the potential seems to be promising.

However, in this research area much effort is devoted to the capability of handling multiple ontologies, such as in OWL-S, or in providing mediators between them, such as in WSMO. The ability of combining logics and providing general reasoning mechanisms is limited, so the trend could be a greater focus on closed world or communities of service providers and users such as defined in Marchetti, Pernici, and Plebani (2004).

From Web Services to Grid Services

Recently, also researchers from the field of grid computing have started to investigate the potential of orchestration and composition technologies, stemming from the world of Web services, for the distributed execution and management of complex processes on the grid. Grid computing is an emerging computing model that leverages a multitude of networked computers to model a virtual computer architecture that is able to distribute process executions across a parallel infrastructure. Especially in the context of large-scale scientific computations, such as genetic analyses, geological investigations or weather predictions, grid computing already provides promising results.

In Emmerich, Butchart, Chen, Wassermann, and Price (2006), the authors concentrate for example on grid services, that is, Web services that are deployed and executed in service-oriented grid computing infrastructures. By means of a real world scientific workflow problem, the authors show how BPEL can successfully be adopted to orchestrate complex, scientific workflows in grid systems, despite the typically huge number of activities that compose a scientific process (e.g., several thousands of work items!). Also in Fox and Gannon (2006), workflows of tens of thousands of participating entities or activities are described, and especially the role of robust exception handling mechanisms (as for example the one provided by BPEL) is highlighted. Scalability and robustness of orchestration and composition solutions are key ingredients for the success of Web services in grid computing.

CONCLUDING REMARKS

The time being seems of crucial importance for the success of Web services. Decisions have to be made about future standards, which will heavily influence the potential for success. In his critical article on the practice of standardization, *WS-nonexistent standards* (Vinoski, 2004), Vinoski not only complains about the numerous proposed standards, but also about the way they are proposed. As a charter member of the World Wide Web Consortium's Web services architecture working group, he asks for more consensus in the standardization processes. Today, he says, traditional standardization procedures are often bypassed by powerful vendors, which develop their own specifications and only afterwards submit them to an official standards body with the hope for fast acceptance and minimal changes. In this short-circuited standardization effort he identifies both a disadvantage for users and a threat for the overall success of the technologies to be standardized.

Therefore, let us hope in shared and agreed on standards as basis for the next generation applications and services, because "...a standard that is not generally agreed on is a standard on paper only" (Vinoski, 2004).

ACKNOWLEDGMENT

This work has been partially supported by the European FET-STREP project WS-Diamond and the Italian PRIN 2005 project Quadrantis.

REFERENCES

Aissi, S., Malu, P., & Srinivasan, K. (2002). E-business process modeling: The next big step. *IEEE Computer*, *35*(5), 55-62.

Alonso, G., Casati, F., Kuno, H., & Machiraju, V. (2004). *Web services—Concepts, architectures, and applications*. Berlin Heidelberg: Springer-Verlag.

Arkin, A., Askary, S., Fordin, S., Jekeli, W., Kawaguchi, K., Orchard, D., Pogliani, S., Riemer, K., Struble, S., Takacsi-Nagy, P., Trickovic, I., & Zimek, S. (2002). *Web service choreography interface (WSCI) 1.0. W3C Note*, August 2002. Retrieved January, 2005, from http://www.w3.org/TR/wsci

Arpinar, B., Aleman-Meza, B., Zhang, R., & Maduko, A. (2004). Ontology-driven Web services composition platform. *Proceedings of the IEEE International Conference on E-Commerce Technology*, IEEE.

Baïna, K., Benali, K., & Godart, C. (2003). Dynamic interconnection of heterogeneous workflow processes through services. The *11th International Conference on Cooperative Information Systems* (CoopIS'03), In *Confederated International Conferences (DOA/CoopIS/ODBASE'03), (LNCS) 2888*, Catania, Sicily, Italy, November 3-7, 2003. Springer-Verlag.

Benatallah, B., Casati, F., & Toumani, F. (2004). Web service conversation modeling: A cornerstone for e-business automation. *IEEE Internet Computing*, *8*(1), 46-54.

Benatallah, B., Sheng, Q. Z., & Dumas, M. (2003). The self-serv environment for Web services composition. *IEEE Internet Computing*, *7*(1), 40-48.

Bianchini, D., De Antonellis, V., Pernici, B., & Plebani, P. (2006). Ontology-based methodology for e-service discovery. *Information Systems*, *31*(4-5), 361-380.

Bieber, G., & Carpenter, J. (2001). *Introduction to service-oriented programming* (Rev 2.1). Retrieved January 2005, from http://www.openwings.org/download/specs/ServiceOrientedIntroduction.pdf

BPMI.org. (2002). *BPML/BPEL4WS—A convergence path toward a standard BPM stack*. BPMI.org Position Paper. Retrieved January 2005, from http://www.bpmi.org/

BPMI.org, Business Process Management Initiative. (n.d.). Retrieved January, 2005, from http://www.bpmi.org/

Cappiello, C., Missier, P., Pernici, B., Plebani, P., & Batini, C. (2004). QoS in multichannel IS: The MAIS approach. *Proceedings of the International Workshop on Web Quality (WQ'04) in conjunction with the ICWE 2004*, Munich, Germany.

Cardoso, J., Bostrom, R. P., & Sheth, A. (2004). Workflow management systems and ERP systems: Difference, commonalities, and applications. *Information Technology and Management, 5*, 319-338, Kluwer Academic Publishers.

Chappell, D. (2004). *Understanding BPM servers*. Chappell & Associates. Retrieved December 2004, from http://www.microsoft.com/biztalk/techinfo/default.asp

Confalonieri, R., Domingue, J., & Motta, E. (2004). Orchestration of semantic Web services in IRS-III. In *Proceedings of the 1st AKT Workshop on Semantic Web Services (AKT-SWS04)* KMi, The Open University, Milton Keynes, UK, December 8, 2004.

Daniel, F., & Pernici, B. (2006). Insights into Web service orchestration and choreography. *International Journal of E-Business Research, 2*(1), 58-77. Hereshey, PA: Idea Group Publishing.

De Antonellis, V., Melchiori, M., De Santis, L., Mecella, M., Mussi, E., Pernici, B., & Plebani, P. (2006). A layered architecture for flexible e-service invocation. *Software Practice & Experience, 36*(2), 191-223.

Dobson, G., Lock, R., & Sommerville, I. (2005). QoSOnt: An ontology for QoS in service centric systems. *Proceedings of the eScience All Hands Meeting*, Nottingham, September 2005.

Dustdar, S., & Schreiner, W. (2004). *A survey on Web services composition*. Distributed Systems Group, Technical University of Vienna.

Eisenberg, B., & Nickull, D. (2001). *ebXML technical architecture specification v1.04*. Retrieved January 2005, from http://www.ebxml.org/specs/index.htm

Emmerich, W., Butchart, B., Chen, L., Wassermann, B., & Price, S. L. (2006). Grid service orchestration using the business process execution language (BPEL). *Journal of Grid Computing, 3*(3-4), 283-304.

Farrell, J., & Lausen, H. (2006). *Semantic annotations for WSDL*. W3C Working Draft, September 2006. Retrieved January 2007, from http://www.w3.org/TR/sawsdl/

Fensel, D., & Bussler, C. (2002). The Web service modeling framework WSMF. *Electronic Commerce: Research and Applications, 1*(2002), 113-137.

Fox, G., & Gannon, D. (2006). Workflow in grid systems. *Concurrency and Computation: Practice & Experience, 18*(10), 1009-1019, August 2006.

Grefen, P., Pernici, B., & Sanchez, G. (1999); Database support for workflow management—The WIDE Project. Kluwer.

Hakimpour, F., Domingue, J., Motta, E., Cabral, L., & Lei, Y. (2004). Integration of OWL-S into IRS-III. *Proceedings of the 1st AKT Workshop on Semantic Web Services (AKT-SWS04)*; KMi, The Open University, Milton Keynes, UK.

Haller, A., Cimpian, E., Mocan, A., Oren, E., & Bussler, C. (2005). WSMX—A semantic service-oriented architecture. *Proceedings of the International Conference on Web Service* (ICWS 2005). Orlando, Florida, 2005.

Hewlett-Packard Company. (2002). *Web services conversation language (WSCL) 1.0. W3C Note,*

March 2002. Retrieved December, 2004, from http://www.w3.org/TR/wscl10/

Jung, J., Hur, W., Kang, S., & Kim, H. (2004). Business process choreography for B2B collaboration. *IEEE Internet Computing, 8*(1), 37-45, Jan-Feb 2004.

Kavantzas, N., Burdett, D., Ritzinger, G., Fletcher, T., Lafon, Y., & Barret, C. (2005). *Web services choreography description language version 1.0.* W3C Candidate Recommendation, 9 November 2005. Retrieved January 2007, from http://www.w3.org/TR/ws-cdl-10/

Kennedy, M. (2005). *Oracle BPEL process manager quick start guide, 10g (10.1.2)*; Beta Draft, April, 2005. Retrieved May 2005, from http://download-uk.oracle.com/otndocs/products/bpel/quickstart.pdf

Khalaf, R., & Nagy, W. A. (2003). *Business process with BPEL4WS: Understanding BPEL4WS, Part 7, Adding correlation and fault handling to a process.* Research report, IBM developerWorks, April 2003. Retrieved January 2005, from http://www-106.ibm.com/developerworks/webservices/ library/ws-bpelcol7/

Langdon, C. S. (2003). The state of Web services. *IEEE Computer, 36*(7), 93-94.

Leavitt, N. (2004). Are Web services finally ready to deliver? *IEEE Computer, 37*(11), 14-18, Nov. 2004.

Maamar, Z., Mostefaoui, S. K., & Yahyaoui, H. (2005). Toward an agent-based and context-oriented approach for Web services composition. *IEEE Transactions on Knowledge and Data Engineering, 17*(5), 686-697.

MAIS. (n.d.). *MAIS project home page.* Retrieved January 2005, from http://www.mais-project.it

Marchetti, C., Pernici, B., & Plebani, P. (2004). A quality model for multichannel adaptive information. *WWW (Alternate Track Papers & Posters) 2004*, New York City, pp.48-54.

Martin, D. (2003). *The OWL services coalition. OWL-S: Semantic markup for Web services.* White Paper. Retrieved December 2004, from http://www.daml.org/services/owl-s/1.0/owl-s.html

Maurino, A., Modafferi, S., Mussi, E., & Pernici, B. (2004). A framework for provisioning of complex e-services. *IEEE International Conference on Services Computing (SCC 2004)*, Shanghai.

Microsoft Corporation. (n.d.). *Microsoft BizTalk Server.* Retrieved January 2005, from http://www.microsoft.com/biztalk/

Milanovic, N., & Malek, M. (2004). Current solutions for Web service composition. *IEEE Internet Computing, 8*(6), 51-59.

Paulson, L. D. (2002). Choreographing Web services. *IEEE Computer, 35*(11), 25-25.

Peltz, C. (2003). Web services orchestration—A review of emerging technologies, tools, and standards. Hewlett-Packard Company.

Peltz, C. (2003). Web services orchestration and choreography. *IEEE Computer, 36*(10), 46-52.

Polleres, A., & Lara, R. (2005). *D4.1v0.1 A conceptual comparison between WSMO and OWL-S.* WSMO Working Draft, January 2005. Retrieved January 2005, from http://www.wsmo.org/2004/d4/d4.1/v0.1/20050106/

Roman, D., Lausen, H., & Keller, U. (2004). *D2v1.0. Web service modeling ontology (WSMO).* WSMO Working Draft; September 2004. Retrieved January 2005, from http://www.wsmo.org/2004/d2/v1.0/20040920/

Roman, D., & Scicluna, J. (2006). *Ontology-based choreography of WSMO services.* WSMO Final Draft, May 2006. Retrieved January 2007, from http://www.wsmo.org/TR/d14/v0.3/

RosettaNet. (2006). Retrieved December 2006, from http://www.rosettanet.org

Ross-Talbot, S., & Fletcher, T. (2006). *Web services choreography description language: Primer*. W3C Working Draft, June 2006. Retrieved January 2007, from http://www.w3.org/TR/ws-cdl-10-primer/

Sivashanmugam, K., Miller, J., Sheth, A., & Verma, K. (2004). Framework for semantic Web process composition. *Special Issue of the International Journal of Electronic Commerce (IJEC)*, Eds: Christoph Bussler, Dieter Fensel, Norman Sadeh, Feb 2004.

Smith, M. K., Welty, C., & McGuinness, D. L. (2004). *OWL Web ontology language guide*. W3C Recommendation, February 2004. Retrieved January 2005, from http://www.w3.org/TR/2004/REC-owl-guide-20040210/

Tosic, V., Pagurek, B, Patel, K., Esfandiari, B, & Ma, W. (2003). Management applications of the Web service offerings language (WSOL). *CAiSE 2003*, 468-484.

Van der Aalst, W. M. P., ter Hofstede, A. H. M., Kiepuszewski, B., & Barros, A. P. (2003). Workflow patterns. *Distributed and Parallel Databases*, *14*(3), 5-51, July 2003.

Vinoski, S. (2004). WS-nonexistent standards. *IEEE Internet Computing*, *8*(6), 94-96.

Weerawarana, S., & Curbera, F. (2002). *Business process with BPEL4WS: Understanding BPEL-4WS, Part 1, Concepts in business processes*. Research report, IBM developerWorks, Aug. 2002. Retrieved January 2005, from http://www-106.ibm.com/developerworks/webservices/library/ws-bpelcol1/

WfMC - Workflow Management Coalition (n.d.). Retrieved January, 2007, from http://www.wfmc.org

W3C - World Wide Web Consortium (n.d.). Retrieved January, 2007, from http://www.w3.org

W3C. (2001). *Web services description language (WSDL) 1.1. W3C Note*, March 2001, http://www.w3.org/TR/wsdl

xCBL.org. (2006). *XML common business library*. Retrieved December, 2006, from http://www.xcbl.org

ENDNOTE

[1] The present work is a revision, extension and update of the survey work published by the authors in January 2006 in Daniel and Pernici (2006).

Chapter XIII
Metering and Accounting for Service-Oriented Computing

Arun Kumar
IBM India Research Laboratory, India

Vikas Agarwal
IBM India Research Laboratory, India

Neeran Karnik
Veritas Software India Ltd., India

ABSTRACT

Distributed systems of today have evolved from tightly coupled architectures such as CORBA and DCOM to loosely coupled service-oriented architectures such as Web services. The success of such architectures depends upon availability of supporting functions such as security, systems management, service level agreements, and development environments with associated tooling. An important management component of such an infrastructure is the metering and accounting for service usage, which is essential for successful deployments in commercial environments. This chapter explores the problem space and presents an architecture that addresses this need. We start by defining taxonomy of services from the perspective of usage metering, charging, and business models. We discuss how service usage can be measured, aggregated, and communicated in a uniform way. Finally, we report on a prototype design and implementation.

INTRODUCTION

Services that can be programmatically accessed over the network have become the dominant component technology for distributed applications. They use standardized interfaces, through which their clients can remotely access their functionality or resources. Research around software services has resulted into a service oriented computing (SOC) paradigm that proposes to utilize self-describing, platform-agnostic computational elements as fundamental components for developing distributed systems (Papazoglou & Georgakopoulos, 2003).

Web services (see http://www.w3.org/TR/ws-arch/) and *grid services* (Foster, Kesselman, Nick, & Tuecke, 2002) communities have defined the core of service-oriented computing. Web services is a particular realization of service-oriented architecture (SOA) with three key elements (Vogels, 2003) that include a well defined interface using WSDL (see http://www.w3.org/TR/wsdl20-primer/), a standardized messaging protocol such as SOAP (see http://www.w3.org/TR/soap12-part0/), and a service address that a requester can use to access the service. A grid service is a Web service that conforms to a set of conventions for such purposes as service lifetime management, inspection and notification of service state changes, and also handling of faults. Grid services address the need for management of distributed and long lived state that is required in distributed applications. To unify server based state management concepts in grid services with Web services concepts, the open grid services infrastructure specification (Tuecke et al., 2003) recently underwent refactoring and evolution. The resulting specification—WS-resource framework (WSRF, 2006) establishes a distinction between the concept of a "service" and the stateful entities acted upon by the service.

As more and more services are being deployed for commercial purposes, metering and accounting of *service usage* becomes an essential component of the services infrastructure. Even in non-commercial settings or for flat-rate services, metering and accounting are needed for enforcing policies such as usage quotas, and for purposes such as provisioning or analyzing usage patterns. In commercial environments, service providers need to charge their users based upon some measure of their usage. Lack of support for such complementary and service provider-specific components has been a key inhibitor to the success of Web services (Langdon, 2003). Compared to metering of usage of resources such as CPU, disk space, bandwidth etc., the metering, accounting, and pricing considerations can be quite different in the services world for various reasons. First, the *software* function of a service often is as important as the resources that it encapsulates, and may even dominate the pricing. Secondly, complex services may be created by *composing* simpler ones—this composition must be reflected in their accounting and pricing. Also, unlike traditional scenario where a user's job directly consumes physical resources, we can now have remote users sending requests to services, indirectly consuming the service provider's resources. This limits the user's ability to observe server-side resource usage, making such metrics less acceptable for charging purposes. It is apparent that enabling service provider support for management components such as metering and accounting is non-trivial.

This chapter presents an architecture that deals with various aspects of metering and accounting in a service-oriented architecture. We anchor our discussion by defining some background concepts and terminology in the "Basic Concepts and Terminology" section. The "Metering and Accounting for Services" section presents in detail the proposed metering and accounting architecture. The "System Design and Implementation" section describes our prototype implementation and the "Discussion" section informally evaluates the proposed architecture. We discuss some prior art in this area in "Related Work" section and finally, we conclude the chapter and present our thoughts on future work.

BASIC CONCEPTS AND TERMINOLOGY

Monitoring, Metering, and Accounting

This sub-section describes the typical modules of a runtime accounting infrastructure and briefly discusses their function. Next is a discussion on the metrics that are required to capture service usage. Finally, it presents our understanding of accounting terms such as pricing, charging, etc.

Typical Accounting Infrastructure

Figure 1 depicts the modules required in the runtime infrastructure, and shows the information that must flow to enable accounting of service usage. The service provider's resources are usually instrumented to collect data for usage metering, as well as other purposes like quality of service management and load balancing. The *monitoring* module collects the raw data and provides usage-related metrics to the *metering* module. Metering is responsible for computing *service* usage metrics, using the monitored *resource* usage data if appropriate. An *accounting* module aggregates the service usage by specific users (or accounts), while the *billing* module applies service provider-defined pricing schemes to the aggregated usage data, and generates bills for the users.

Usage Metrics

The *metering* module, which expresses the usage of a service, must choose the appropriate metrics ("units") for this purpose. A usage metric should be intuitive to the customer and help him or her in estimating the usage charges before submitting a request. Previous efforts such as (Buyya,

Figure 1. Information flow for usage accounting

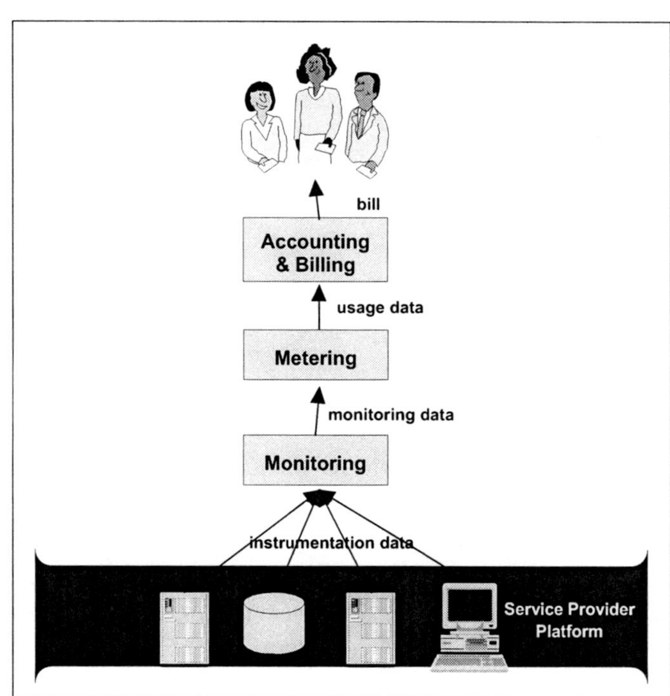

Abramson, and Giddy (2001) and Kenyon and Cheliotis (2002) that dealt with accounting of services in the context of grid computing proposed to use a *grid-unit* as a universal service access cost metric. However, since services may vary dramatically in their functionality, it is often counter-intuitive to have a common unit applicable across all services. The grid-unit previously referred to is actually a monetary unit—a currency for the grid—since it has the notion of price embedded in its definition. It does not really measure service *usage*, since the usage values reported for the same request in this case can differ if the price fluctuates. Service-specific usage metrics are more intuitive to the user and more easily auditable as well. Another motivation to exclude pricing from the usage unit is that metering information should only report usage and not charges. This would allow the information to be used for purposes other than charging customers, such as capacity planning, statistical studies, reporting to funding agencies, etc. Furthermore, it would allow service pricing to be independent of service usage, if so desired.

We suggest that a set of metrics instead of a single metric may be used as a (compound) usage unit. This chapter, therefore, assumes that a service is free to choose its set of usage metrics that may constitute its usage-unit. To enable the customers to estimate the cost before submitting a request the services specify their charging rates in terms of metrics included in their usage-unit.

Pricing, Charging, and Business Models

Service providers may have different types of *business relationships* with their customers (Gisolfi, 2001). For instance, some customers may be *subscribers* having a long-running association, while others may be one-off users on a *pay-per-use* model. This determines how the customer's usage is aggregated over time. The business model that defines the relationship between the customer and the service thus affects the Accounting module.

The set of usage metrics used to charge for a service, under a particular business model, is obtained by intersection of two sets. The first set consists of the metrics that are made available by the service. For instance, an e-mail delivery service may report *number of bytes processed* but not the *time taken* to process the e-mail delivery. The second set of metrics consists of those that the service provider wishes to use for charging. Some service providers may use resource consumption measures (e.g., for a compute service), CPU cycles consumed by the user's job may be the preferred charging metric. Other service providers may charge a pre-defined cost per request, or a cost that varies predictably with certain parameters of the request (such as *number of bytes processed* in the e-mail delivery example). The choice of charging metrics primarily depends upon the revenue that can be generated under the business model, and upon the ease or difficulty of measuring those metrics. The intersection of these two sets of metrics forms the *charging policy* of the service. It thus directly affects the design of the metering module.

Different markets can employ different pricing mechanisms. Some services may be commoditized, while others may offer more value-addition and be priced accordingly. The prices may vary from one *billing cycle* to the next or even within a billing cycle. The *pricing policy* of the service and the billing cycle thus determines how billing is done. In this chapter we do not delve into pricing and billing issues, because these are primarily dictated by market economics and do not significantly influence the metering and accounting infrastructure. We do however consider the impact of the charging policy and business models on our proposed architecture.

Service-Oriented Architectures

Service oriented architectures such as Web services (see http://www.w3.org/TR/ws-arch/) and the open grid services architecture (OGSA)

(Foster et al., 2002) (now WSRF) define the *service* abstraction along with associated concepts and components needed to build applications on top of it. This sub-section classifies various kinds of services that can be created, from the point of view of metering and accounting. It starts off by describing the scenario of a simple service that may encapsulate a resource, followed by a classification of such simple services. Finally, the most general scenario of composite services is described with the classification applied to them.

Atomic Services

The simplest type of service is one which encapsulates a resource and offers its functionality through a well defined service interface. Both hardware resources (e.g., compute servers) and software applications (e.g., scientific subroutines) can be encapsulated in this manner. Such services that do not depend upon other services in order to provide their functionality are called *Atomic services*. Figure 2 depicts an atomic service, which encapsulates a storage resource (a disk or filesystem).

Apart from their core function, services require management functionality such as security, monitoring, fault management, capacity planning, accounting, etc. Each service could implement such functions on its own, but typically service providers rely on standardized platforms built specifically for this purpose. Examples of such platforms that exist today include the Globus toolkit (see http://www.globus.org) from the Globus Alliance, IBM WebSphere Application Server (see http://www.ibm.com/software/Webservers/appserv/was/) and others.

Atomic services can be classified into the following types:

- **Resource-centric services:** These can be thought of as *wrappers* around traditional resources. A compute service, file storage service, or a remote interface to a scientific instrument fall into this category. These services offer their clients the use of a re-

Figure 2. An atomic service

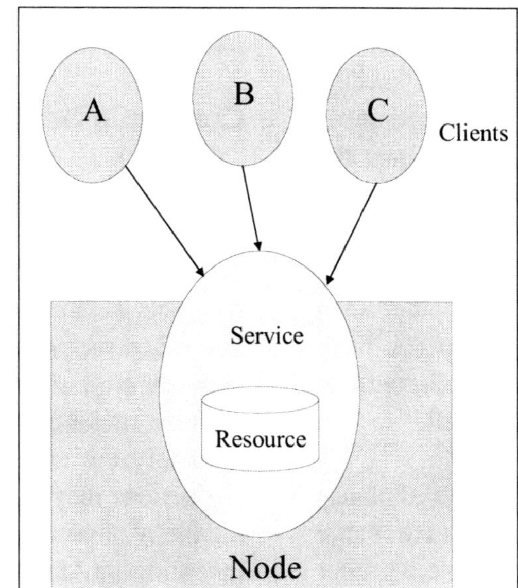

source—either by *allocating* a fraction of the resource *capacity*, or by allowing the client to *consume* a certain *amount* of the resource. When capacity is allocated, the service reports chargeable metrics that measure *resource usage over time* (e.g., the file storage service may report megabyte-hours of storage). When resources are consumed, the chargeable metrics represent the amount of resource used (e.g., a printer service may report the sheets of paper printed and the amount of ink consumed); a compute service may report CPU cycles consumed. Apart from basic resource-wrapper services, certain software services such as those offering scientific subroutines may also belong in this category. Thus, an equation solver or optimization engine would report, and thus could be charged for, on the basis of the resources required to solve the problem instance submitted by the user.

- **Transactional services:** These are software services with a transactional (or request-response) character. The user requests a certain *function* from the service, and the usage is measured for that function and *not for its resource consumption*. Consider the e-mail delivery service example again. Its client sends it a message, addressing information, etc. and requests message delivery. Typically, it would report usage in terms of the number of messages (or bytes) delivered—not the CPU, disk, or network bandwidth consumed by the service in delivering the messages. The service usage is thus expressed using *application-level* parameters rather than *server-side* resource usage metrics. Such usage metrics are more intuitive for the user and more easily auditable as well.

It is possible that a service *inherently* belongs to one category, but its provider chooses to charge for it according to another. For example, a printer service is inherently resource-centric (since it consumes resources in providing its service and the consumption cannot be determined easily from the print request). But the service provider may choose to charge on the basis of the size of the document printed, since this makes the cost more easily predictable by the client. This makes for a transactional service model. In some markets, services may be commoditized and therefore charges are fixed (they may vary from provider to provider on the basis of quality of service but not usage). For instance, local telephone service is commoditized in many places. Providers merely charge a fixed monthly fee and offer unlimited usage of the service. From the perspective of the metering and accounting infrastructure, the provider's choice of model dominates over the inherent model.

These distinctions result in fundamental differences in the way such services need to be metered and accounted for. In general, the *service usage* metrics chosen by the service provider may consist of *resource usage* metrics, *application-level parameters*, or some combination of both. Resource-centric services need active metering of underlying resource usage, because their usage cannot be predicted from the request parameters. In contrast, transactional services only need passive logging of requests and their parameters for later accounting.

Composite Services

Complex services are often created by *composing* simpler ones. Figure 3 shows an example, a financial portal service that is composed using other services for stock trading, technical analysis, etc. When such a composite service receives an end-user request, its business logic may require multiple requests to other autonomous services to satisfy the end-user request. Each underlying service may in turn be composite. Thus, a hierarchy of service invocations results from the incoming top-level request. Each service treats its immediate caller as its client, and charges it for its usage. To do this, it needs to take into account the charges it incurs from the underlying services that it invokes. Thus, apart from pair-wise charging, the accounting infrastructure must also cascade the charges up the invocation graph, all the way to the end-user's request. Composition, therefore, places significant requirements on the metering and accounting infrastructure.

The bottom-most nodes in composition hierarchies tend to be resource-centric services, whereas services at higher levels are often transactional in nature. Pair-wise composition of <caller, callee> services results in the following categories of composite services:

- **Transactional service over resource-centric service (Type T-over-R):** Transactional services are often hosted on infrastructure that is offered as a resource-centric service. An example is a yellow pages directory deployed using a storage service. The type-R service would treat the hosted service as its customer, meter its resource consumption and charge accordingly. On the other hand, the type-T service would charge its customers based upon its request parameters, irrespective of its usage of the underlying service. The metering information of the type-R service would contain resource consumption metrics, whereas that of the transactional service would contain service usage metrics.
- **Resource-centric service over resource-centric service (Type R-over-R):** This class represents resource centric services that utilize other resource-centric services. For instance, a scientific algorithm may be offered as a service running on top of a compute service. In this model, the software being offered is treated like a resource and metered internally. This approach is required when the software's resource usage varies

Figure 3. A composite service

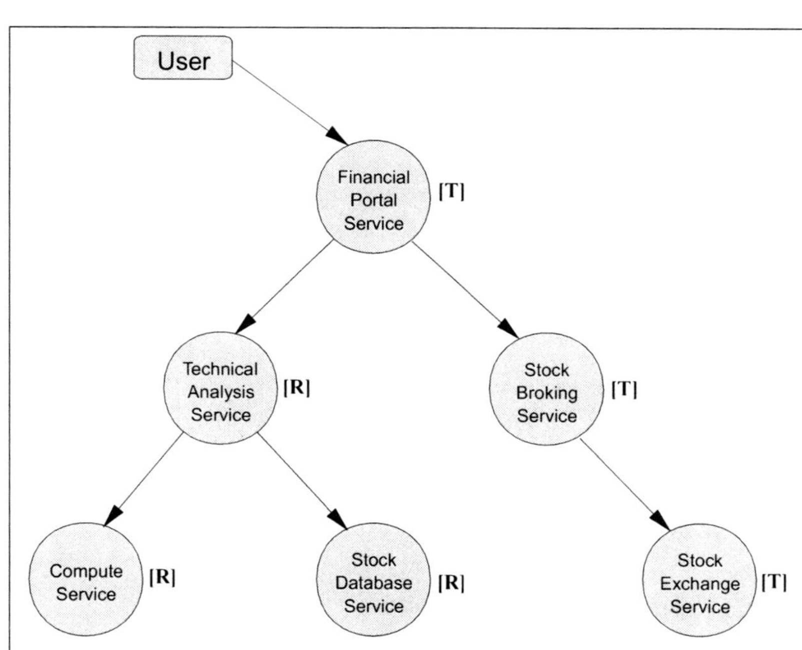

widely with its input parameters, and cannot be easily predicted. The underlying type-R service would charge the top-level service based on the actual hardware resources consumed. The top-level service would in turn charge its users using software usage metrics as well as the metrics exported by the lower-level service. Therefore, active metering is required for both services.

- **Transactional service over transactional service (Type T-over-T):** This class represents transactional services invoking other transactional services. The metering information for each of these services would contain the respective application-level usage metrics. For example, a message delivery service may use either an e-mail service or an instant messaging service for delivery, based on user presence and preferences. Each of these services is transactional.
- **Resource-centric service over transactional service (Type R-over-T):** Sometimes, a resource centric service requires the use of a transactional service. Whereas it reports its usage in terms of resource consumption, it may be charged by its underlying service on a per-transaction basis. For example, the scientific algorithm mentioned above may also need to process sensor data. The algorithm itself is resource-centric because it may not be able to predict how many times it would read the sensor or how many CPU cycles it would need to finish its task. A sensor service on the other hand can provide the latest sensor readings on request using a transactional model.

Since the caller of a composite service only interacts with the top-level service, the charging model of the top-level service determines the charging model of the pair-wise composition. Thus when the pair is itself used as a component in another composition, the resultant charging model may be unambiguously determined. Further, within a given service one operation may be Type R whereas another may be type T. Composi-

Figure 4. Metering and accounting for service-oriented computing

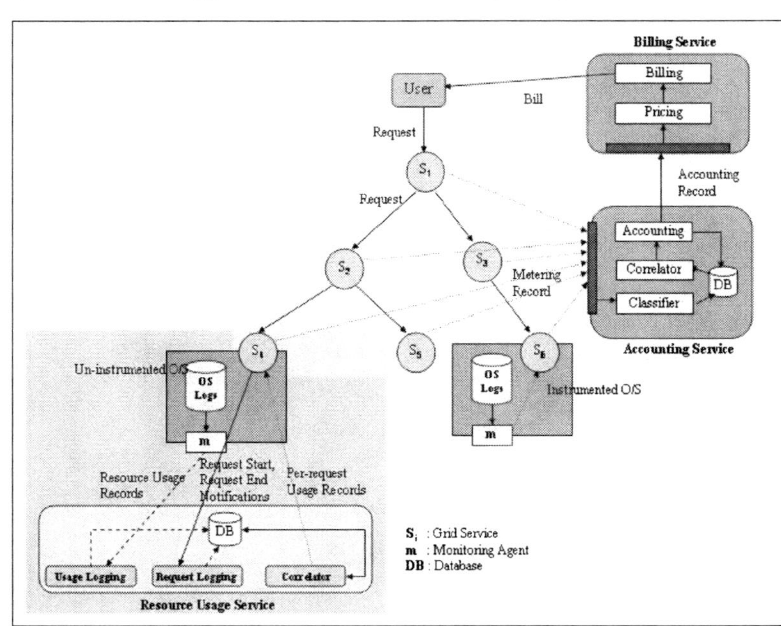

tion could then be considered at the granularity of each operation of a service.

METERING AND ACCOUNTING FOR SERVICES

Figure 4 shows the metering and accounting architecture for service-oriented systems. It shows a composite service 1 and a hierarchy of its component services 2 through 6. Besides these, there is a *resource usage service* (RUS), an *accounting service* and a *billing service*, each of which could be built into the services middleware platform or they could be available as independent services. Each service 1 through 6 registers with the accounting service and specifies the following:

- The business model(s) it supports.
- Its usage metrics and how to aggregate/compose them (Kumar & Agarwal, 2006).
- The type of each operation—R or T.

This information is needed for handling different charging scenarios. It is also used while correlating requests for that service, as explained later. A request issued by *user* to service S_1 results in invocations to services S_2 and S_3. These further result in requests to S_4, S_5 and so on. Each of these services incorporates metering functionality that computes per-request metering metrics for the service. This per-request usage is then reported to the accounting service in a *partial metering record.* The metering record is partial because it reports usage pertaining to that service alone; the usage of underlying services remains to be accounted for. Depending upon the complexity of the computation involved and the information required, construction of this record may be done in one of the following ways:

- By the service alone without any external help.
- By the service but with some inputs from its environment such as local monitor data in the operating system, data from the services middleware platform such as the IBM WebSphere Application Server, Globus Toolkit, etc.
- By the middleware on which the service is running. This enables the service implementation to be independent of the metering functionality.
- By another entity such as the resource usage service.

Generally, transactional services do not require active metering—they compute their partial metering records locally. In Figure 4, service 1, 2, 3 and 5 fall into this category. Services 4 and 6 on the other hand are resource-centric services that require resource usage data in order to compute metering metrics. However, it is not always possible to obtain the desired information for computing the metrics. In Figure 4, 6 resides in an operating system that is instrumented to provide monitor data at the desired level of granularity. In contrast, 4 has to rely on an external service such as RUS to compute or approximate the desired metrics from the available monitor data. On receipt of an incoming request, 4 sends a request_start notification to the RUS. When request execution at the local node completes, it sends a request_end notification to RUS and receives a *per-request usage record* from it. Using the metrics reported in this record it constructs its partial metering record. 6 may not need to use RUS – the monitoring agent for 6 obtains resource usage information from operating system logs and/or middleware platform logs to construct its partial metering record.

The partial metering record sent to the accounting service is self-sufficient for usage accounting for a leaf node (such as 4, 5 and 6), but is incomplete for other nodes in the composition hierarchy. The accounting service must create the *complete metering record* of a request to a non-leaf service, by correlating its partial metering record with the *corresponding* complete metering records of underlying services. These complete metering records are then aggregated over the customer-service interaction to generate accounting records. The billing service acts upon these accounting records to generate bills for the customers.

In Figure 4, two shaded rectangles split the architecture into two logical pieces. The bottom-left part illustrates the metering infrastructure required for atomic services whereas the top-right one covers metering of composite services. We first discuss the issues and provide a mechanism for metering atomic services. Next, we present an algorithm for metering composite services. These two pieces integrate with each other seamlessly and enable a management infrastructure that is capable of metering and accounting for any ecosystem of services.

Metering for Atomic Services

An atomic service can be metered in two ways, viz. *request-based (transactional) metering* or *resource-usage metering.* Request-based metering is straightforward, as it involves following simple steps:

- **At start of request execution:** Log the start time, input parameters (if required), and other details of the request.
- **At end of request execution:** Log the end time, and any other metric.

From these two logs, the metering record can be constructed. Some services may use request parameters and in addition may log other metrics, at request end time. For instance, "bytes written" or "messages sent" could be logged and used as metering metrics too. The rest of this subsection covers the details of resource-usage metering for atomic services.

Resource Usage Metering

In a typical scenario, a client application makes a request to a service. In fulfilling that request, the service consumes resources in its local environment. These resources may be heterogeneous, and distributed across the service provider's infrastructure. The client needs to be charged on the basis of this resource usage. We thus need to actively monitor the consumption of various resources, and assign it in appropriate proportions to the client requests that were serviced using those resources. This resource usage information for a service invocation needs to be derived from operating system logs. Traditional OS accounting mechanisms keep track of resource usage on a per-process basis. We can operate a monitoring agent (shown as "m" in Figure 4) on each node, which is tasked with reading such OS logs and reporting the relevant metrics to the resource usage service (RUS).

A service can be implemented in two ways—it can either start a new process for each client/request, or as a long running process serving multiple requests. In the first case, a new process is created for each client/request. This process can be destroyed once the client is finished using it. In such a scenario, the OS accounting module would typically log a resource usage record for the entire client session (spanning multiple invocations from a single client) with a process. The cumulative resource usage by the client is obtained from this entry. This may be sufficient for many scenarios. However, per-request usage information is needed sometimes. For example, when multiple clients use a service using a single 'corporate-id', the usage may still need to be attributed to those individual clients. To obtain per-request usage, the usage reported in the OS log would have to be split among different requests by correlating it with the request start and end times.

In the second scenario, the process representing the service executes indefinitely, serving requests from various clients as and when they arrive. In between, the process may be idle. The client must only be charged for the process' resource usage in the time interval when its request is active. If the OS is instrumented to provide resource usage information on per-request basis then it can be directly used, but the current OSes only provide usage information on per-process basis. Therefore, the resource usage information from OS logs must be apportioned amongst different requests, especially since those requests may have come from different clients.

To enable this, usage information based on two timelines (see Figure 5) needs to be correlated, so that the resource usage can be charged to the appropriate requests—and thereby, clients. The *request logging timeline* records points in time when a request starts or stops executing. Such points can be captured by configuring the service/middleware to send request_start and request_end notifications to the RUS. This timeline is continuous, since requests can arrive and depart at any time. The *usage logging timeline* is typically discrete because the OS measures and logs resource usage (and monitoring agent reports it) periodically. Requests are free to start and stop executing between successive readings taken by the operating system. Therefore, we may not be able to accurately assign resource consumption to specific requests. For example, in Figure 5(a) the usage logging windows for requests A and B overlap although the requests themselves do not. Therefore some heuristic needs to be used to allocate the overlapping usage to the two requests. For example, the usage could be evenly split between A and B. More appropriately, it may be split in weighted fashion, based on the durations of A and B in that window.

Further complication arises when multiple clients may access a service at the same time. There are two possibilities:

- The service queues up the requests and serves them one at a time.
- The service is multi-threaded, and serves the requests concurrently.

In the first case, the service/middleware can send a request_start notification to the RUS

Figure 5. Request logging timeline

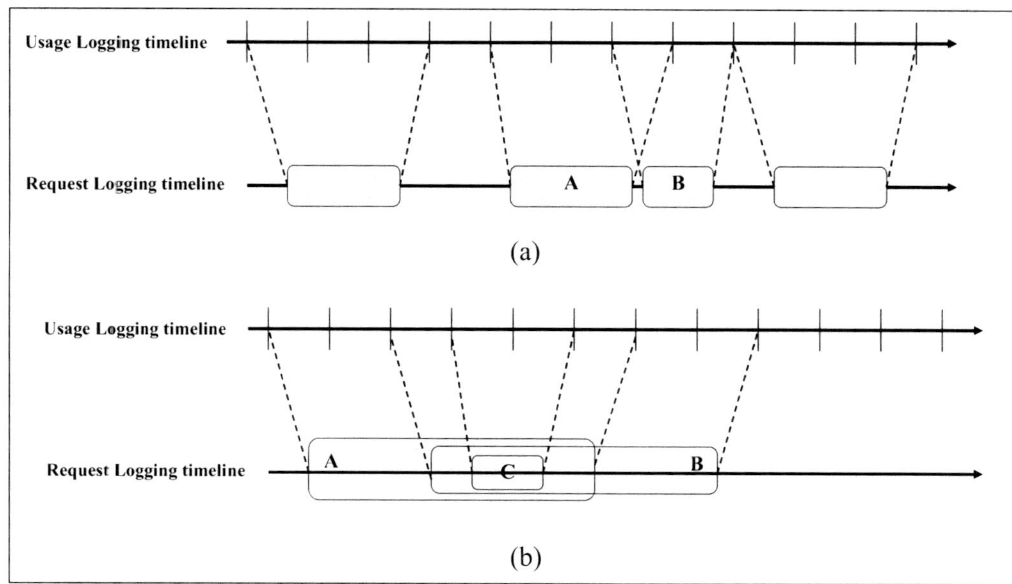

when it dequeues a request for processing, and a request_end notification when it has computed and sent back the response. This ensures that the requests do not overlap on the request logging timeline. This corresponds to the scenario shown in Figure 5(a) with requests A and B which has already been dealt with.

In the second case however, multiple threads within the same process may service requests from different clients. Thus their windows will overlap on both timelines (refer to Figure 5(b)). If the operating system is instrumented and therefore capable of providing thread-level accounting information, the monitoring agent merely reports per-thread information and the problem reduces to the earlier case. However if, as is more likely, only process-level accounting is available, the RUS must deal with the overlapping windows—it must amortize the reported resource usage over the active requests during a time window. Again, this could either be done uniformly, or weighted based on the length of each request's time window. The resource usage correlation mechanism given below uses the latter approach and correlates/aggregates the usage reported on the two timelines to compute the per-request usage records.

Resource Usage Correlation

The RUS receives usage information from two sources—the monitoring agents and the services/middleware themselves. The monitoring agent on each machine sends per-process *resource usage records* to the *usage logging* module of RUS (refer Figure 4). Figure 6 shows the format of this record. It contains the machine id (e.g., DNS name or IP address of the server), the process id, a sequence number (maintained per process and used for time window computation), a timestamp, which is the time at which usage has been measured, and one or more usage metrics and their values. The usage metrics depend on what the underlying operating system makes available via the OS Log. These typically include CPU time, memory usage, I/O operations performed, etc.[1]

Figure 6. Resource usage record structure

machine-id	process-id	seq-no	timestamp	metric-1		metric-n

Figure 7. Request_Start message

request-id	service-id	timestamp

Figure 8. Request_End message

request-id	timestamp	machine-id	process-id		machine-id	process-id

Figure 9. Per-request resource usage record structure

request-id	service-id	start-time	end-time	metric-1		metric-n

Similarly, services/middleware sends the request_start and request_end notifications asynchronously to the *request logging* module of RUS. Figure 7 shows the format of the request_start message. It contains a request id that is guaranteed to be globally unique[2]. Service id allows the RUS to identify the service that served the request. Timestamp captures the start-time of the request. Similarly, Figure 8 shows the format of a request_end message. The request id is same as the one reported in the corresponding request_start message and is used by the RUS to correlate the two entries. This is followed by a timestamp that reports the end-time of the request. For asynchronous requests, the service releases the connection from the client immediately after

Figure 10. Resource usage amortization algorithm

```
function correlate_amortize(ResUsageRecord)
begin
   MachineId = getMachine(ResUsageRecord)
   ProcessId = getProcess(ResUsageRecord)
   SeqNo = getSeqNo(ResUsageRecord)
   WindowStartTime = getRecordTimestamp(MachineId, ProcessId, SeqNo - 1)
   WindowEndTime = getRecordTimestamp(MachineId, ProcessId, SeqNo)
   TimeInterval = WindowEndTime - WindowStartTime
   TotDuration = 0
   List = getActiveRequests(MachineId, ProcessId) // list of requests that were active
                                                   // in the Time Interval, i.e. whose
                                                   // request end msg has either not
                                                   // arrived or arrived in this window
   for each request ReqId in List do
      ReqEndTime = getEndTime(ReqId)               // time at which this request ended
      if ReqEndTime = 'null'                       // if request has not ended
         ReqEndTime = WindowEndTime                // then set request end time
                                                   // to end time of time window
      endif

      ReqStartTime = getStartTime(ReqId)           // time at which this request started
      if ReqStartTime < WindowStartTime            // if request started before start
                                                   // of time window
         ReqStartTime = WindowStartTime            // then set request start time
                                                   // to start of time window
      endif

      ReqExecDuration = ReqEndTime - ReqStartTime // duration for which this request was
                                                   // executing in the time window
      TotDuration = TotDuration + ReqExecDuration // Add to cumulative duration of
   endfor                                          // all active requests

   MetricsList = getUsageMetrics(ResUsageRecord)
   NewMetricsList = 'null'
   for each request ReqId in List do
      ReqWeight = ReqExecDuration / TotDuration      // compute weight of this request
      for each Metric in MetricsList do
         UsageOfReq = getValue(Metric) * ReqWeight  // compute weighted usage for this req
         insert(NewMetricsList, Metric, UsageOfReq) // insert metric usage into new list
      endfor
      AmortRecord = createAmortizedResUsageRecord(ReqId, NewMetricsList)
   endfor

   for each request ReqId in List do
      if ReqEndTime < WindowEndTime                // if request has ended in this  window
         remove(ReqId, List)                       // then remove it from List
      endif
   endfor
end
```

initiating the job. The end_time in such a case denotes the time at which the local processing for that request completes and not when the client connection gets released. Next in the record are <machine id, process id> tuples. These are required if a service dynamically spawns processes to service a request, and will be discussed later in this section. All these usage records and notifications are stored in the RUS' local database for later processing.

Periodically, the *correlator* module of RUS processes the accumulated resource usage records of a machine to correlate and amortize the reported usage over various requests active, on that machine, in a time window. This processing is done only after all the request_start and request_end notifications have arrived for the time window to which the resource usage record corresponds. This is to ensure that irrespective of network and other delays, all the notifications of that time window have arrived before the correlation/amortization process starts. For this purpose, correlation for a resource usage record is done after a delay (from its reception) that can be of the order of minutes or even hours. This does not affect service performance since usage accounting is typically done off-line, and does not lie in the service request-response path. The correlator then aggregates all the amortized usage records, for each finished request, computed over successive time windows. This results in the creation of a per-request usage record, which is sent to the corresponding service. To receive these records, each service that uses RUS needs to implement a metering interface using which the RUS supplies those records. However, if the metering functionality is implemented by the middleware then the RUS forwards it to the middleware rather than the service. The format of a per-request usage record is shown in Figure 9.

The algorithm for resource usage amortization is presented in Figure 10. It is invoked for each unprocessed resource usage record that is ready for correlation (i.e., sufficient delay has elapsed since this resource usage record was received and all the start/end notifications for the requests active in that time window would have arrived by now). It first calculates the time interval of the window to which the resource usage record corresponds, by computing the difference of the timestamps of two consecutive resource usage records for a process. Then for each active request it calculates the duration for which that request was active in that window. For this purpose, the correlator creates and maintains a list of *active requests* by using the timestamp information obtained from the request_start and request_end notifications. Active requests are those which were

Figure 11. Resource usage aggregation algorithm

```
function record_aggregation(ReqEndRecord)
begin
   ReqId = getRequestId(ReqEndRecord)
   PerReqUsageRecord = null
   List = getAmortizedRecords(ReqId)
   for each record AmortRecord in List do
      MetricsList = getUsageMetrics(AmortRecord)
      for each metric MetricId in MetricsList do
         newMetricValue = aggregate(AmortRecord(MetricId), PerReqUsageRecord(MetricId))
         PerReqUsageRecord(MetricId) = newMetricValue
      endfor
   endfor
end
```

still executing after the last time window, besides any new requests. The list contains active request information for each service process running on different machines in the infrastructure. Next, the algorithm calculates the weight of each request and proportionately assigns the usage metrics to each request. Finally, it updates the active request list by removing those requests that have ended. The algorithm for aggregation of amortized records into per-request usage records is shown in Figure 11.

We now expand to a more general scenario. As before, clients use the services by making requests to them. However, a service may have a distributed implementation within the service provider's infrastructure – in servicing client requests it may consume resources on multiple nodes.

When a service is deployed onto a middleware platform, it may spawn a set of processes onto various servers in the service provider's infrastructure. These distributed processes constitute the implementation of the service. In Figure 12 for example, S_1 creates processes on servers A and B. As before, the monitoring agent (m) on each server periodically sends resource usage records to the RUS. Resource usage is reported for each process of interest, that is, each process belonging to a service. Since services may dynamically spawn processes, and new services may be deployed onto a server at any time, the monitoring agent must be configurable. It must be supplied with the ids of processes to be monitored, or the names of installed programs whose instances need to be monitored, for example. Also, the correlator in RUS cannot be pre-configured to know which processes belong to which service. Each request gets served by a different set of processes identified by <machine id, process id> tuples. Therefore, the service makes this information available to the RUS correlator as part of request_end notification and this information is used to obtain the list of active requests for a resource usage record dur-

Figure 12. Resource usage metering for a single but distributed service

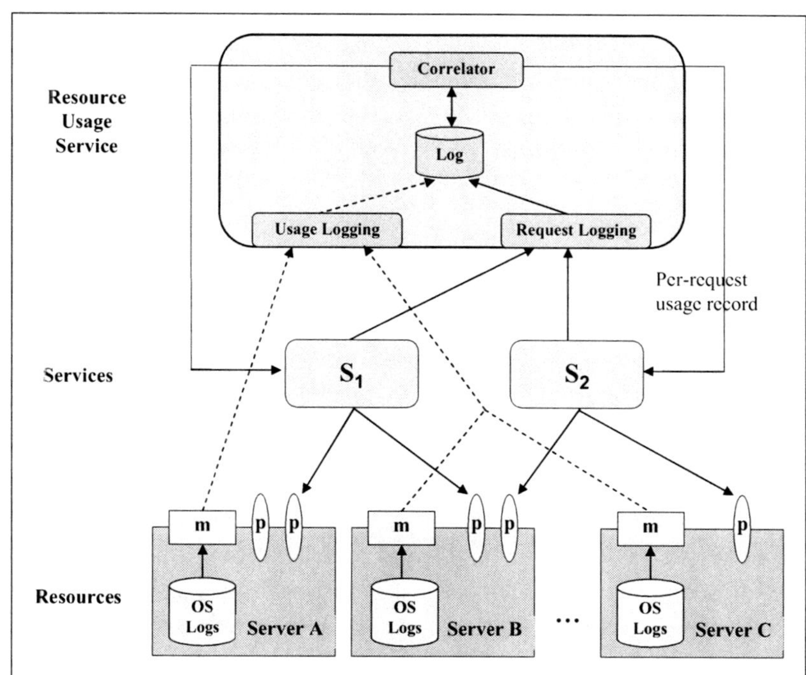

ing resource usage correlation and amortization. On the other hand, if a service consists of a set of pre-created processes on various machines, each of those must be modeled as a service, and metered as composite services.

As explained in the non-distributed scenario, the RUS correlator reconciles the resource usage records with request_start and request_end messages, to compute a per-request usage record, which it stores in the local database and also sends to the corresponding service. However, an extra step is required, in the distributed service scenario, while computing the per-request usage record. Since each request potentially executes on multiple machines, corresponding amortized usage records from all those machines need to be aggregated. This is taken care of automatically since the amortized usage records are all labeled with request id (refer Figure 10) instead of machine id and/or process id. Therefore, the aggregation algorithm as shown in Figure 11 works well.

The resource usage service could also follow a *pull* model instead of the *push* model (previously followed) to make the per-request usage records available to its clients. Under the push model, it sends the generated records to the clients registered for them. To support the pull model it must provide a query API, using which clients may retrieve desired per-request usage records. In Figure 4, it pushes the generated records to the service for which the record has been computed.

For installations consisting of atomic services alone, some of the accounting functionality in the *accounting service* may be shifted either to the resource usage service or to the service itself. The per-request usage records (generated either by service itself as for S_5 or by resource usage service, as in the case of S_4) could then be simply aggregated to generate accounting records. These accounting records can then directly be fed into *billing service* to generate the bills. However, if the system consists of composite services that may be geographically dispersed then metering of service usage has to be handled differently. This is covered in the next subsection.

Metering for Composite Services

The top-right portion of Figure 4 depicts the metering infrastructure required for composite services (Agarwal, Karnik, & Kumar, 2003). It also incorporates the accounting and billing modules of the infrastructure. Each service in the composition hierarchy reports to the accounting service per-request partial metering records that are computed as per the techniques described in the previous subsection. The *classifier* module in the accounting service indexes each such incoming metering record on per service, per user basis and stores it in the database. The *correlator* module reads these metering records from the database and correlates them to create complete metering records. It passes these complete records to the *accounting* module, which aggregates them to generate *accounting records*.

The heart of the composite service metering and accounting mechanism consists of usage reporting by services, and the correlation and aggregation of this information by the accounting service. A usage reporting protocol defines the sequence of messages to be exchanged and the corresponding message format and contents, while the correlation mechanism specifies the steps to create consolidated metering records for composite services from the reported usage information.

Since each service is autonomous, every request to a service must therefore be independently accounted for. In addition, it potentially contributes to the usage of a higher-level request in the composition hierarchy. We thus require that each request be uniquely identifiable—at any time, no two requests in the system can have the same identifier (this was also an assumption for resource usage metering). The service autonomy assumption also implies that different services in a composition hierarchy may subscribe to different accounting services. The usage reporting and correlation should support such distributed accounting as well.

Further, we do not assume that the composition hierarchy is known to the accounting service beforehand. Callers are free to make runtime choices regarding which services to invoke. The composition hierarchy must therefore be *discovered* by the accounting service at runtime. The correlation mechanism and usage reporting protocol have been designed to take care of this requirement.

Usage Reporting Protocol

Each incoming request to a service contains a globally unique request identifier generated by the caller. If the caller is a user application, it may not generate such ids—the called service must then locally generate an id for the incoming request. A service generates a metering record once it has finished its processing of the request. This implies that service usage metrics for local usage can be computed and all invocations to underlying services have also been initiated by that time. These invocations may be asynchronous—we do not require that the underlying processing be complete, before generating the metering record. Moreover, metering records arrive at the accounting service in unpredictable order. Hence, the correlation mechanism needs to ensure that all required records have arrived before aggregating the usage.

Figure 13 shows the format of the metering record sent by a service to the accounting service. It contains a request-id identifying the incoming request, identifiers for the called service and the caller (client), the name of the operation invoked, a list of request-ids of invocations to underlying services, and the usage metrics and their values. The operation name is required to look up the charging model, business model, and pricing information for this request.

Service Usage Correlation

The classifier stores incoming metering records in the database on a per user, per service basis. The correlator retrieves and processes these records either periodically or when triggered by billing queries. All records are initially assumed to be *partial*. As shown in the algorithm (refer to Figure 14) the record being processed is marked as *complete* if it is for a transactional operation, because the correlator does not need to aggregate the usage of underlying services. The record is also marked as *complete* if the list of ids of initiated requests is empty (it is the metering record of a leaf-node). If the record is still marked as *partial*, the algorithm checks whether *complete* metering records for all the underlying invocations have been computed. This is where the list of "child" request ids from the metering record (refer Figure 13) is needed. It helps the correlator to determine when it has constructed the resulting service invocation graph, and can therefore aggregate the usage reported by all underlying services.

For metering record aggregation if the values belong to the same metric or related metrics with same units, the aggregation is straightforward. However, if they are incompatible (such as CPU cycles of two different hardware platforms) then there are two options available. The aggregate service could hide this incompatibility by export-

Figure 13. Metering record format

request–id	service–id	user–id	operation	list of req ids	metric–1	...	metric–n

Figure 14. Service usage correlation algorithm

```
function correlate(Record)
begin
   if operationType(Record) = 'T'               // a record for transactional
      mark (Record, 'complete')                 // operation is always complete
      return                                    // no need to aggregate further
   endif

   List = getInvocationList(Record)             // requests to underlying services
   if (List is empty)                           // if record is for a leaf node
      mark (Record, 'complete')                 // then it is complete
      return                                    // trivial case
   endif

   if (complete(List))                          // check if all records in the list
                                                // are complete
       for each request ReqId in List
          MetRec = getMeteringRec(ReqId)        // get complete record from DB
          aggregate(Record, MetRec)             // compute the aggregate usage
       endfor
       mark (Record, 'complete')
   else
       skip this record                         // will be processed later
   endif
end
```

ing only a single metric to its clients and using an internal conversion function to translate values of one metric to another. However, if the conversion function is not carefully chosen then this method might implicitly encode pricing information. The other option for the aggregate service is to explicitly export all the different metrics of its underlying services and report their usage separately. This technique, however, is brittle since a change in the interface of an underlying service requires a change in all the aggregate services that directly or indirectly depend upon it. Moreover, this exposes the details of the underlying components to the end user, which may be undesirable. For instance, reporting a metric such as "RS6000MachineCpuCycles" while using an airline reservation service would be completely out of place. To support the former method of hiding the details of underlying metrics, the conversion function could be expressed in a flexible, declarative language such as the metric service policy (MS-Policy) (Kumar et al., 2006) that could be used by the accounting service for aggregation.

As mentioned earlier, services in a composition hierarchy may subscribe to different accounting services. Hence, we may need to correlate metering records in a distributed fashion, across accounting services. To support this, the correlator checks whether the caller's accounting service is different from itself. If so, it sends the complete metering record to the caller's accounting service for further correlation along the composition hierarchy. To enable this, the correlator of the *callee's* accounting service must know the accounting service to which the *caller* subscribes. The identity of the caller's accounting service can be communicated during an initial handshake between caller and callee services, prior to any requests. This may not add any overhead, since such a handshake may be required in any case, for purposes such as setting up service-level agreements. Alternatively, the caller can send the address of its accounting service along with each request. The callee can then include this address in the metering record sent to its own accounting service. To reduce the overhead, the address field may be omitted, indicating that a previously communicated address is still valid.

Usage Accounting

Users and services have *accounts* registered with the accounting service. Multiple users in an organization may share an account. Similarly, all services offered by a single provider may share an account. The accounting module maps user and service identifiers to their respective accounts.

A service provider offering a service identifies one or more business models under which it is willing to accept customer requests. At the time of registration, each customer selects the business model, from the offered ones, under which she prefers to use the service. It is the job of the accounting service to maintain these business relationships between the customer and service provider accounts. We consider three common business models (Agarwal, Karnik, & Kumar, 2002; Eibach & Kuebler, 2001; Gisolfi, 2001):

- **Subscription:** A customer subscribes to a service by pre-paying or guaranteeing to post-pay a fixed amount. In return, he or she gets the right to use the service up to a certain limit—based on the service price and the amount paid. The contract may also have limited validity in terms of time. In addition, the customer is allowed to exceed her specified limits but she pays for the extra usage.
- **Lease:** A customer pays a flat fee for leasing a service for a certain period of time. Limits may be imposed on the instantaneous usage by the customer. In other words, a fraction of the service capacity is allocated to the customer, and he or she may use the service freely within that capacity limit.
- **Pay-per-use:** In this model, no long-term contract needs to exist. The customer uses the service and is billed for it according to the usage incurred.

The business model agreed upon by the user and the service dictates whether and how the metering records are accounted for. This amounts to determining whether a metering record contributes to the charges made to a user's account or not. For instance in the lease model, the metering record is not used for accounting, because the user pays a flat fee for leasing the service for a given duration. The fee is independent of the customer's cumulative usage. It may, however, require monitoring of *instantaneous* usage, to enforce the capacity limit. The metering record, in this model, is only used for maintaining an audit trail. In the subscription model too, the metering record does not contribute to the charges made to user's account as long as the user stays within the specified limits for *cumulative* usage. However, usage must be metered, on a per-request basis, and aggregated in order to monitor cumulative usage and to levy extra charges if the usage exceeds these limits. But in the pay-per-use model, the metering record definitely contributes to the actual charging. Our architecture does not constrain other kinds of business models, since usage information is always available at the granularity of a request.

After determining how the metering records contribute, the accounting module aggregates those metering records into *accounting records* for each <customer, provider> pair. These accounting records are either pulled by or pushed to the *billing service* at pre-specified intervals of time—a billing cycle. Its *pricing module* contains the pricing formula (charging rates, etc.) to be used. These may vary from customer to customer depending upon their contract with the service, discounts, etc. The pricing module computes the amount to be charged by applying the appropriate pricing formula to the accounting records. This information is passed to the billing module, which prepares the bill and sends it to the user using the preferred delivery mechanism such as postal mail, e-mail, etc.

SYSTEM DESIGN AND IMPLEMENTATION

In this section, we describe our system design followed by an implementation of a prototype metering and accounting system for the composite service example introduced earlier.

Design

We carefully designed our system so as to make it generically applicable to different application domains, rather than just the example scenario. To accomplish that purpose, we developed a data model for representing usage metering and accounting information. Here we briefly present the model and more details can be obtained from Agarwal, Karnik, and Kumar (2004).

The data model was created using DMTF's common information model (CIM, 2005) that uses object-oriented modeling for managing systems, software, users, networks etc. Management applications can query and utilize information modeled through CIM to achieve various goals such as runtime application management (Keller, Kreger, & Schopmeyer, 2001). We leveraged the CIM metrics (Metrics, 2003) schema, proposed extensions to it, and proposed a new CIM schema to address information modeling issues that arise while representing metering and accounting information.

Figure 15 shows an information model that captures the conceptual view of an accounting system as described in this chapter. *BaseMetricValue* represents metrics that are generated for some managed element; *BaseMetricDefinition* allows the "types" of these metrics to be defined. Metric values are associated with their corresponding managed element through the *MetricForME* association (see the CIM metrics model (MetricsSchema, 2003)). A software operation (such as a service invocation, or job execution)

Figure 15. Metering and accounting information model

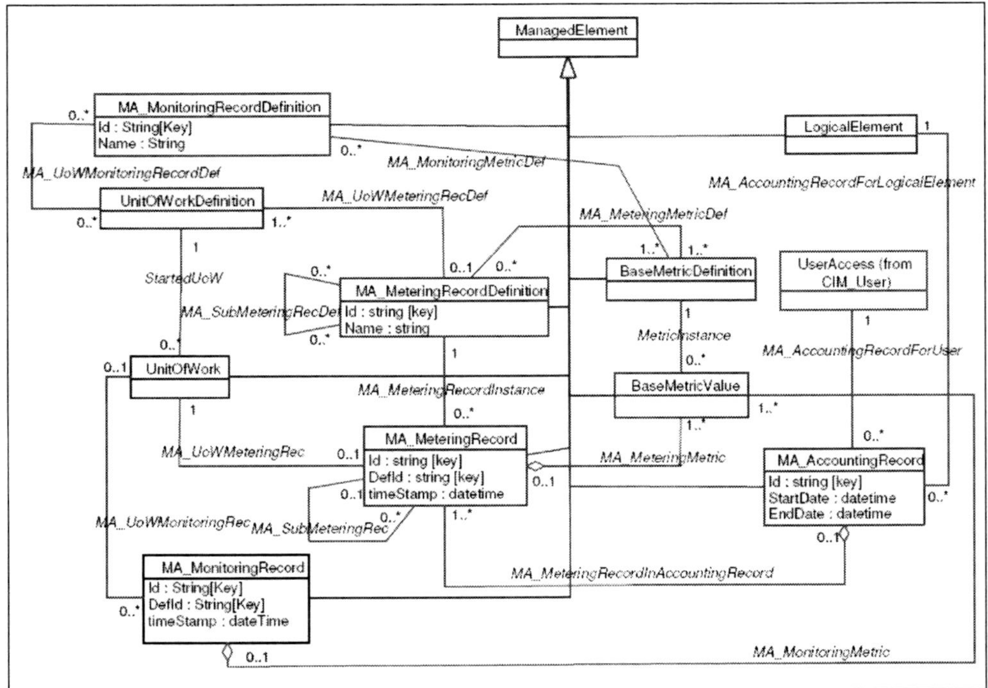

or an access to hardware that needs to be metered is represented as a *UnitOfWork* (Metrics, 2003). The *UnitOfWorkDefinition* class gives information about the *type* of unit of work.

Monitoring information is captured in a *MA_MonitoringRecord* that contains the state of the software operation or hardware access, represented by a unit of work, at an instant of time. The *MA_MonitoringMetric* aggregation allows us to identify the individual metrics that comprise the record. Each monitoring record conforms to a "schema" represented in the model as a *MA_MonitoringRecordDefinition*. Definitions of its component metrics are available via the *MA_MonitoringMetricDef* association. Each type of unit of work (i.e., each *UnitofWorkDefinition*) has an associated monitoring record definition. Similarly, each unit of work is associated with its monitoring record via the *MA_UoWMonitoringRec* association.

Metering information is also represented using similar structures. A *MA_MeteringRecord* represents the information needed to measure the usage of a unit of work. The metering record is an aggregation (*MA_MeteringMetric*) of metering-specific metrics. These metrics are derived from metrics contained in the monitoring records of the *UnitOfWork* under consideration. A unit of work may have several monitoring records representing its state at different instants of time, but it must have only one metering record (associated via *MA_UofWMeteringRec*). Moreover, a monitoring record may contain metrics that are used for purposes such as capacity planning and fault monitoring, apart from those used in metering. A *MA_MeteringRecordDefinition* describes the contents of a metering record, in conjunction with the definitions of its component metrics.

The CIM metrics model includes composite *UnitOfWorks*. The metering record of a composite unit of work would be computed from those of its components. The components' metering records are associated with that of the composite unit of work via the *MA_SubMeteringRec* association. This enables the correlation of instances of metering records. The corresponding definition classes are also similarly associated. If *UnitOfWork* hierarchies are predefined, *MA_SubMeteringRecDef* could be used to express the anticipated relationship between the corresponding *MA_MeteringRecordDefinitions*. In this way, the model allows precise specification of what constitutes the metering record of a composite unit of work.

Unlike metering, which is tied to a unit of work, accounting involves two participants—a producer and a consumer. In our schema, a *LogicalElement* represents the producer, and a consumer is the user who used that *LogicalElement*. A user is represented by *UsersAccess* from the CIM User schema. The use of a *LogicalElement* is modeled by a unit of work. An *MA_AccountingRecord* represents the accounting information that needs to be captured. It is an aggregation of metering records corresponding to one or more *UnitOfWorks*, which were executed on behalf of a user.

The association *MA_AccountingRecordForLogicalElement* in the figure relates multiple instances of *MA_AccountingRecord* to an instance of *LogicalElement*. This association specifies to which instance of *LogicalElement* those accounting records belong. Similarly, all the accounting records are associated with their corresponding users via the *MA_AccountingRecordForUser* association.

The Composite Service Example

Figure 3 depicts a financial portal service, which maintains and manages stock portfolios of its customers. It uses a *technical analysis service* to analyze stock performance and recommend stocks to buy/sell. It also uses a *stock brokering service* to trade stocks in the market. A value-added service that the financial portal offers to its customers is consultancy. The financial portal service periodically (or on explicit request) examines a customer's stock holdings and evaluates their current and expected performance through technical analysis. On the basis of this evaluation and the customer's preferences it may sell under-performing stocks, or it may notify the customer of the evaluation with its recommendations. In addition, when the customer wishes to invest in the market, the financial portal service may suggest the top few stocks based upon the customer's portfolio and preferences. The technical analysis service uses a *compute service* to run its algorithms. It also uses a *stock database* that provides historical information about various stocks. The stock brokering service trades stocks in the *stock exchange*.

Consider a typical scenario in which a user wishes to invest a certain amount in stocks—he or she invokes the invest(amount) operation on the financial portal service. This service in turn invokes recommendStocks (userProfile) on the technical analysis service, to determine the stocks to buy, given this user's profile (risk appetite, sectoral preferences, etc.). The technical analysis service executes its algorithm using the compute service's submitJob() operation. The algorithm uses the Stock Database service to obtain historical data for various stocks, using the getStockHistory(stockId) method. After getting the list of recommended stocks and the respective amount to invest from the technical analysis service, the financial portal invokes the stock broking service's executeTrade(trade) method to purchase stocks on behalf of the user. The broking service in turn uses the stock exchange service's placeOrder(order) operation to actually buy the stocks.

Figure 3 also labels each service with a category (R or T), and the various types of pair-wise compositions (described in the "Basic Concepts and Terminology" section) are thus apparent in the example. The financial portal charges its customers on the basis of application-level metrics such as the actual amount invested. The stock broking service too is of type T, since it charges a fixed brokerage per trade. The stock exchange service charges each stock broking service a monthly or annual fee for subscription to the exchange. The compute service and the stock database are resource-centric, since they act as wrappers for resources (CPU and database respectively). Their charging is based on the resource consumption. The technical analysis service's algorithm could execute for varying periods depending upon the user portfolio and historical data of the stocks under consideration—its usage of underlying services cannot be predicted from the input parameters. Therefore, its charging metrics consist of an algorithm "license fee" as well as the metrics reported by the underlying services.

Implementation

To demonstrate our architecture we implemented an Accounting service and a mock-up of the above example. For the purposes of this prototype, the implementation of resource-oriented services was simplified so that each request results in a new process. Therefore, the resource usage information was directly available from operating system logs. The prototype uses grid services (Foster et al., 2002) running on the Open grid services Infrastructure (Tuecke et al., 2003). The services are written in Java, and SOAP-over-HTTP was used for making RPC-style invocations. Each service publishes a WSDL document describing its portTypes (interfaces) and binding information. The accounting service has a *registration* portType with a registerService() operation. This is used by services to sign up with the accounting service. It also has an *accounting* portType, whose reportUsage() operation is used by other services to send their metering records. The getUsage() operation is used by the billing service to query the usage of a given <customer, provider> pair over a specified duration. The request id[3] for each request, being context information, was inserted into SOAP message headers using Axis[4] handlers.

In our prototype the service usage metrics described in the above example are computed, and metering records are sent to the accounting service. The accounting service supports all the types of service composition described earlier. It maintains accounts corresponding to each <user, service> pair in the composition hierarchy. It also generates accounting records for these accounts at each billing cycle, by aggregating the corresponding metering records.

Figure 16 shows the *partial* metering records generated by various services for a request to financial portal service. Notice that there are no usage metrics in metering records for the stock exchange service (indicated by "X" in the figures), because it is a subscription-based service that charges a monthly or annual fee for its usage. The corresponding *complete* metering records are shown in Figure 17. The complete metering records for the stock exchange, stock broking and financial portal services are essentially the same as their partial metering records, since these are type T services, and do not need to aggregate the usage of lower-level services. Also, the complete metering records for the compute and stock database services are the same as their partial metering records, since they are leaf nodes in the composition hierarchy. The complete metering record for the technical analysis service contains its own usage as well as the usage of requests to other services, as it is a type R service. In this example, it made one request (request-id 3) to Compute service and two requests (request-ids 4, 5) to the stock database service. Hence, its complete metering record contains the metrics for these requests as well.

Figure 16. Partial metering records generated by a request to FinancialPortal service

requestId	serviceId	userId	operation	listOfRequestIds	metric-1		metric-2	
					name	value	name	value
1	FinancePortal	user1	invest	2, 6	amount	1000.0		
2	TechAnalysis	FinancePortal	recommend Stocks	3, 4, 5	license	2.5		
3	Compute	TechAnalysis	submitJob		CPU	12.45	avgMem	24.38
4	StockDatabase	TechAnalysis	getStockHistory		numRec	2		
5	StockDatabase	TechAnalysis	getStockHistory		numRec	3		
6	StockBroking	FinancePortal	executeTrade	7, 8	brokerage	5.0		
7	StockExchange	StockBroking	placeOrder		X			
8	StockExchange	StockBroking	placeOrder		X			

Figure 17. Complete metering records

requestId	serviceId	userId	operation	metric-1		metric-2		metric-3		metric-4	
				name	value	name	value	name	value	name	value
1	FinancePortal	user1	invest	amount	1000.0						
2	TechAnalysis	FinancePortal	recommend Stocks	license	2.5	CPU	12.45	avgMem	24.38	numRec	5
3	Compute	TechAnalysis	submitJob	CPU	12.45	avgMem	24.38				
4	StockDatabase	TechAnalysis	getStockHistory	numRec	2						
5	StockDatabase	TechAnalysis	getStockHistory	numRec	3						
6	StockBroking	FinancePortal	executeTrade	brokerage	5.0						
7	StockExchange	StockBroking	placeOrder	X							
8	StockExchange	StockBroking	placeOrder	X							

DISCUSSION

We now present an informal evaluation of our architecture, with respect to various design issues and parameters.

- **Static vs. dynamic composition:** A major advantage of the proposed architecture is that it does not require static composition of services (i.e., the service composition hierarchy need not be known a priori). This would be essential for adaptive service composition systems (Chafle, Dasgupta, Kumar, Mittal, & Srivastava, 2006) where the composition may adapt in response to environmental changes such as service failures. For each request, a service invocation graph is implicitly constructed by the accounting service at runtime. This feature enables metering for composite services that dynamically select the underlying service instances to be used. As a result, fault tolerance and availability of the composite service are not constrained by the metering system.
- **Scalability:** Our architecture chooses a centralized approach for correlation of metering data. We support distributed correlation to the extent that different services of a composition hierarchy can subscribe to different accounting services. This significantly improves the scalability of the system. An overloaded accounting service acting as a bottleneck could be split up into multiple accounting services that serve different client services. To make the architecture even more scalable, an alternative is to distribute the correlation functionality into individual services themselves (Agarwal et al., 2002). Each service would then compute its local usage and report it to its caller service. The topmost service of the hierarchy would finally aggregate the usage to charge the end customer. For auditing, usage records could also be sent to the accounting service as well. Though much more scalable, this approach increases the management tasks that a service needs to perform, over and above its business logic. Also, it would increase metering related message exchanges since a message now is sent to both the caller service and the accounting service. Some of these issues can be taken care of by pushing the metering functionality into the underlying middleware.
- **Push vs. pull paradigm:** The architecture proposed in the chapter uses the push paradigm for reporting metering records to the accounting service. An alternative is to use a pull-based mechanism. In both the cases, either the existing services need to be modified or the hosting infrastructure (i.e. middleware) has to provide the functionality required for participating in the architecture. To enable the push-based system the hosting infrastructure could provide metering modules that can retrieve accounting information from logs generated by the service or through an accounting interface provided by the service (Agarwal et al., 2002). To enable pull-based system, the hosting infrastructure could provide agents that interact with the existing service through its non-standard interface and implement the interface required by the architecture.
- **Coherence across Web services and grid standards:** The proposed metering and accounting architecture is equally applicable to both Web services as well as grid services and does not introduce new disparity among the two standards. It can be supported in middleware platform implementations of both the standards.
- **Tooling, development, and deployment of services:** The usage reporting protocol requires services to generate request ids, create partial metering records, and communicate with an accounting service. Similarly, a service using RUS needs to generate

start_request and end_request notifications. However, much of this functionality is independent of the service's business logic. It could thus be either generated automatically using tools, or provided by a service hosting platform. The architecture, therefore, does not burden the service developers.

- **Messaging overhead:** Metering messages add some overhead to the number of messages exchanged in the system. However, services can minimize their effect by accumulating them and sending them to the accounting service, after some delay, as a bunch. This is possible since metering and accounting is an offline task and a delay does not affect system performance.
- **Service autonomy:** The architecture does not compromise the autonomy of individual services. Each service is free to select its own accounting service and resource usage service. It may even choose to implement its own accounting functionality. However, conformance to the proposed architecture is necessary to enable accounting of composite services. This requires that usage reporting protocol, RUS interface, service metering interface and accounting service interfaces be standardized so that distributed metering and accounting can be supported across services and hosting platforms.
- **Pairwise accounting:** The benefits of the notion of pair-wise accounting, in the proposed architecture, appear to be counter-intuitive. It seems inefficient to have different request ids for each service invocation rather than a single correlation id using which each service could charge the end user directly. However, pair-wise accounting and charging helps in keeping each service-to-service interaction independent of the other. This allows each service to enforce the business model(s) of its choice irrespective of which part of the composition hierarchy it contributes to. Similarly, different charging mechanisms, different types of services (i.e., type R, type T) are enabled by this notion (having a single correlation id actually assumes the resource centric model where the charges cannot be predicted in advance). It also enables distributed accounting and makes it possible to partition the end-user charges into shares of each individual services. Service level agreement violation, if any, can also be pin-pointed to the exact service that violated them.

RELATED WORK

Metering and accounting systems have existed in various forms in the pre-services world. Operating systems like Unix (and its variants) perform rudimentary accounting of resource usage (Burk & Horvath, 1997). For example, per-user disk usage is tracked and quotas can be enforced. IBM's mainframe operating systems (SMF, 2002) provide detailed logs of resource usage on a per-process basis, and utilities to generate accounting information using these logs. Naturally, these accounting mechanisms do not apply in the services domain, where per-request metering is needed.

Prior work on accounting for services has focused mainly on shared hardware resources (such as CPU time and disk space) and the economies of trading and bartering such resources (Anglano et al., 2002; Buyya et al., 2001; Kenyon et al., 2002). Barmouta and Buyya (2003) describe a grid bank used as a payment system for the grid. All these efforts are focused on pricing of resources and charging the users for using resources rather than metering and accounting of usage which has other goals also such as capacity planning, SLA monitoring, fraud and intrusion detection, etc. apart from charging. Also, their focus is on resource-centric accounting, and composite services have not been addressed. Moreover, these systems use *grid-units* as the reporting metric—a *monetary* unit with price embedded in its definition, and not a *usage* unit, which is required for metering. The resource usage WG (RUS, 2003) of global grid forum is trying to build a resource usage service that will be used for storage and retrieval of usage records. But, it does not support correlation and aggregation of those records. Also, it does not deal with composite services. The format of the usage record has been defined by usage record WG (UR, 2003), but here also they are mainly dealing with resource usage of a computational job and not services in general.

More recently, the distributed grid accounting system (DGAS) defines a layered architecture similar to ours where usage metering is done by lightweight sensors installed on the computing elements followed by usage accounting and account balancing (see http://www.to.infn.it/grid/accounting/main.html). The usage of grid resources by grid users is registered in appropriate servers, called home location registers (HLRs) that manage both user and resource accounts. The job cost is determined (by the HLR service) from resource prices and usage records. Account balancing is done by exchanging virtual credits between the user HLR and the resource HLR. However, job execution is not distributed, i.e. each job is executed on a single computing element whereas our architecture supports job execution to be distributed on a cluster of servers. Also, they assume presence of gridUserId, JobId and ResourceId in each entry of the collected data which requires specific instrumentation of applications. Composite services are also not dealt with.

Several research efforts in the past have contributed to different aspects of usage metering and accounting. Redmond and Wade (1998) discussed accounting for Internet and Web environments. Redmond and Wade (2002) discussed economic feasibility of accounting based on service value—independent of resource usage. The authentication, authorization, and accounting (AAA) working group of IETF is working on defining a standard for accounting as applied to network access. It has documented the requirements for accounting attributes and record format in an RFC (Brownlee & Blount, 2000). IPDR.org has been instrumental in defining standards to specify the record formats of data records (accounting records) which can cater to the requirements of non-voice based services such as short message service (SMS), Web browsing, etc. in the telecom domain (IPDR, 2002).

Peer-to-peer systems such as JXTA (Gong, 2001) provide support for peer metering, which is the capability to account for a peer's activities. In particular, a peer is allowed to query for simple metrics such as uptime and amount of data handled. There is no notion of composition, and the issues of correlation and aggregation of metering information do not arise.

There have been very few efforts at accounting for Web services. Eibach et al. (2001) have defined a simple metering and accounting model for individual Web services, based upon a single metric—response time. They do not support metering using resource consumption metrics or request parameters. Composite services are also not dealt with. Utility management infrastructure (UMI) metering (Albaugh & Madduri, 2004) describes a metering architecture for Web services. However, only atomic services are supported and composite services are not dealt with. An interesting aspect of the architecture is the flexible notion of *unit of work*. It could be request based, session based or time based. Supporting such a notion of unit of work would be non-trivial in the context of composite services due to many issues. Different sensors in the service provider's infrastructure monitor resource usage for different users and report them in metering records. The details of sensors/monitoring agents that deal with mapping of resource usage to users are not discussed. Composition/aggregation of metrics from different resources is supported for resources that exist inside a service provider's infrastructure. In contrast, our architecture supports composition/aggregation of usage metrics across services.

The correlation problem has been dealt with in the context of event correlation, request-response correlation and transactions. For example, the application response measurement API (ARM, 2004) supports the correlation of performance metrics reported by nested transactions. Sahai, Ouyang, and Machiraju (2001) extend ARM to enable end-to-end management of e-service transactions. In our scenario, the autonomous nature of the participating nodes posed additional challenges. Our protocol is also more efficient, since we only require one message to the correlator per request. In contrast, the protocol by Sahai et al. (2001) needs at least two messages, demarcating the start and end of each transaction.

CONCLUSION AND FUTURE WORK

In this chapter, we have explored the problem of metering and accounting of usage, in the context of service-oriented architectures such as Web services and grid services. We analyzed the different types of services and their compositions, and presented a comprehensive metering and accounting architecture for composite services. We analyzed and took into account the impact of some common pricing, charging and business models on the metering and accounting infrastructure. The infrastructure includes services like accounting and resource usage service that can be part of a middleware platform. The system can perform metering at the granularity of a client request, and amortize resource usage among overlapping requests. A CIM information model for representing metering and accounting information was also presented.

Further investigation can be done into tooling and platform support, so that much of the metering infrastructure can be automatically provided. Extensions to WSDL may allow services to specify their charging and pricing policies. The hosting platform can use this information to provide the appropriate service monitoring, and for automated generation of partial metering records.

Given such platform support, we can contemplate an alternate architecture that simplifies the Accounting service by distributing the correlation functionality into the services themselves. Each service can be made responsible for *partial* correlation of the metering records of its immediate child nodes in the composition hierarchy, and for cascading the correlated information to its immediate caller.

NOTE

Portions reprinted, with permisssion, from ("Metering and Accounting for Composite e-Services", in Proceedings of the IEEE International Conference on Electronic Commerce (CEC 2003), Newport Beach, California, 2003, and, "An Information Model for Metering and Accounting" in Proceedings of the IEEE/IFIP Network Operations and Management Symposium (NOMS 2004), Seoul, Korea, 2004, by the same authors). © 2007 IEEE.

REFERENCES

Agarwal, V., Karnik, N., & Kumar, A. (2002, April). *Architectural issues for metering and accounting of grid services.* IBM Research Report No. RI02010. Retrieved from http://domino.watson.ibm.com/library/cyberdig.nsf/Home

Agarwal, V., Karnik, N., & Kumar, A. (2003). Metering and accounting for composite e-services. *Proceedings of the 2003 IEEE International Conference on Electronic Commerce (CEC 2003)* (pp. 35-39), Newport Beach, California.

Agarwal, V., Karnik, N., & Kumar, A. (2004). An information model for metering and accounting. *Proceedings of the IEEE/IFIP Network Operations and Management Symposium (NOMS 2004)* (pp. 541-554), Seoul, Korea.

Albaugh, V., & Madduri, H. (2004). The utility metering service of the universal management infrastructure. *IBM Systems Journal*, *43*(1), 179-189.

Anglano, C., Barale, S., Gaido, L., Guarise, A., Lusso, S., & Werbrouck, A. (2002, March). *An accounting system for the DataGrid Project*. Retrieved January 2007, from http://www.to.infn.it/grid/accounting/techrep/DataGrid-01-TED-0115-3_0.pdf

ARM. (2004). *Application response measurement (ARM)*. Open Group Technical Standard. Retrieved January 2007, from http://www.opengroup.org/management/arm

Barmouta, A., & Buyya, R. (2003). GridBank: A grid accounting services architecture (GASA) for distributed systems sharing and integration. *Proceedings of the 17th Annual International Parallel & Distributed Processing Symposium (IPDPS 2003) Workshop on Internet Computing and E-Commerce* (pp. 245-252), Nice, France.

Brownlee, N., & Blount, A. (2000, September). *Accounting attributes and record formats*. IETF working group on authentication, authorization, and accounting. Retrieved July 2003, from http://www.ietf.org/rfc/rfc2924.txt

Burk, R., & Horvath, D. B. (1997). *Unix unleashed: System administrator's edition*. Sams.

Buyya, R., Abramson, D., & Giddy, J. (2001). A case for economy grid architecture for service oriented grid computing. *Proceedings of the 10th IEEE International Heterogeneous Computing Workshop (HCW 2001)* (pp. 776-790).

Chafle, G., Dasgupta, K., Kumar, A., Mittal, S., & Srivastava, B. (2006). Adaptation in Web service composition and execution. *Proceedings of the IEEE International Conference on Web services (ICWS 2006)*, Chicago (pp. 549-557).

CIM. (2005). *Common information model*. Distributed management task force. Retrieved May 10, 2005, from http://www.dmtf.org/standards/cim

Eibach, W., & Kuebler, D. (2001, July). *Metering and accounting for Web services*. IBM DeveloperWorks. Retrieved July 2000, from http://www-106.ibm.com/developerworks/Webservices/library/ws-maws/? dwzone=Webservices

Foster, I., Kesselman, C., Nick, J. M., & Tuecke, S. (2002). Grid services for distributed system integration. *IEEE Computer*, *35*(6), 37-46.

Foster, I., Kesselman, C., & Tuecke, S. (2001). The anatomy of the grid: Enabling scalable virtual organizations. *International Journal of High Performance Computing Applications*, *15*(3), 200-222.

Gisolfi, D. (2001, April). *Web services Architect Part 2: Models for dynamic e-business*. Retrieved July 2002, from http://www-106.ibm.com/developerworks/Webservices/library/ws-arc2.html

Gong, L. (2001). JXTA: A network programming environment. *IEEE Internet Computing*, *5*(3), 88-95.

IPDR. (2002, October). *Network data management—Usage (NDM-U) For IP-based services version 3.1.1.* Retrieved January 2003, from http://www.ipdr.org/download-docs/index.html

Keller, A., Kreger, H., & Schopmeyer, K. (2001). Towards a CIM schema for runtime application management. *Proceedings of the 12th IFIP/IEEE International Workshop on Distributed Systems: Operations & Management (DSOM)*, Nancy, France. Retrieved January 2007, from http://www.loria.fr/~festor/DSOM2001//proceedings/S7-2.pdf

Kenyon, C., & Cheliotis, G. (2002). Architecture requirements for commercializing grid resources. *Proceedings of the 11th IEEE International Symposium on High Performance Distributed Computing HPDC-11 (HPDC'02)*, Edinburgh, Scotland (pp. 215-224).

Kumar, A., & Agarwal, V. (2006). A customizable engine for metrics collection, aggregation, and composition. *Proceedings of the 10th IEEE/IFIP Network Operations and Management Symposium (NOMS 2006)*, Vancouver, Canada (pp. 162-173).

Langdon, C. S. (2003). The state of Web services. *IEEE Computer*, *6*(7), 93-94.

Metrics. (2003, June). *Common information model (CIM) metrics model, Version 2.7.* Distributed management task force. Retrieved July 2003, from http://www.dmtf.org/standards/documents/CIM/DSP0141.pdf

MetricsSchema. (2003, March). *CIM metrics schema, Version 2.7.* Distributed management task force, Retrieved January 2007, from http://www.dmtf.org/standards/documents/CIM/CIM_Schema27/CIM_Metrics27-Final.pdf

Papazoglou, M. P., & Georgakopoulos, D. (2003). Service-oriented computing. *Communications of the ACM*, *46*(10), 25-28.

Redmond, C., & Wade, V. (1998). Towards flexible metering and charging for information services. *Proceedings of the ICCC/IFIP Conference on Electronic Publishing*, Budapest, Hungary. Retrieved January 2007, from http://citeseer.ist.psu.edu/630476.html

Redmond, C., & Wade, V. (2002). Service level accounting in telecommunications. *Proceedings of the 8th IFIP/IEEE Network Operations and Management Symposium (NOMS)* (pp. 283-296), Florence, Italy.

RUS. (2003). *Resource usage service working group, global grid forum.* Retrieved November 2004, from http://forge.gridforum.org/projects/rus-wg/

Sahai, A., Ouyang, J., & Machiraju, V. (2001). End-to-end transaction management for Web based services. *Proceedings of the 3rd International Workshop on Advanced issues of E-Commerce and Web based Information Systems (WECWIS)* (pp. 128-135).

SMF. (2002, March). *z/OS MVS system management facilities (SMF).* Retrieved July 2002, from http://publibz.boulder.ibm.com/epubs/pdf/iea2g230.pdf

Tuecke, S., Czajkowski, K., Foster, I., Frey, J., Graham, S., Kesselman, C., Maguire, T., Sandholm, T., Vanderbilt, P., & Snelling, D. (2003). *Open grid services infrastructure (OGSI) Version 1.0.* Global grid forum draft recommendation. Retrieved January 2007, from http://www.globus.org/alliance/publications/papers/Final_OGSI_Specification_V1.0.pdf

UR. (2003). *Usage record working group, global grid forum.* Retrieved November 2004, from http://forge.gridforum.org/projects/ur-wg/

Vogels, W. (2003). Web services are not distributed objects: Common misconceptions about the fundamentals of Web service technology. *IEEE Internet Computing*, *7*(6), 59-66.

WSRF. (2006). *Web services resource framework (WSRF)—Primer v1.2.* OASIS Web services resource framework (WSRF) TC. Retrieved January 2007, from http://docs.oasis-open.org/wsrf/wsrf-primer-1.2-primer-cd-02.pdf

ENDNOTES

1. We do not specify a set of metrics here, as it is being addressed by GGF's Usage Record working group.
2. UUIDs Universally Unique ID can be used for this purpose. See http://www.opengroup.

org/dce/info/draft-leach-uuids-guids-01.txt

3 For generating globally unique ids we used the Java UUID Generator available from http://www.doomdark.org/doomdark/proj/jug/

4 Axis is a SOAP implementation available at http://xml.apache.org/axis/

Section IV
Online Consumer Behavior

Chapter XIV
Effects of Web-Based Customer Relationship Management on Customer Satisfaction:
A Structural Equation Modeling Analysis

Wen-Jang Jih
Middle Tennessee State University, USA

Su-Fang Lee
Overseas Chinese Institute of Technology, Taiwan

Yuan-Cheng Tsai
Overseas Chinese Institute of Technology, Taiwan

Shyh-Rong Fang
National Chung Hsing University, Taiwan

ABSTRACT

This study addresses the effect of e-customer relationship management (e-CRM) practices on online customers' satisfaction with their experience in interacting with the company Web sites. Recognizing the importance of maintaining a healthy relationship with customers, companies are actively seeking ways to enhance the customer value of their offerings through relationship marketing. Since effective managing of customer relationship essentially involves managing customer information flow, Internet technologies have become an important element of a firm's e-CRM program. The company Web site is functioning as the focal point of contact for interacting with existing and prospective customers. An important concern is how the company's CRM activities via Web site affects customers' overall perception of the Web site. Using the concepts of Internet-mediated market orientation in marketing and user satisfaction in information systems, this study analyzes causal as well as correlation relationships between e-CRM practices and online customer Web site satisfaction. Based on the primary data collected in Taiwan, the study found that e-CRM practices positively impact online customers' Web site satisfaction through their perception of the Web site's customer orientation.

BACKGROUND

As the Internet technology evolves into a convenient platform for communications, organizations in all sectors are acting aggressively to develop and implement truly value-creating innovations in pursuit of sustainable competitive advantage. An important technological foundation in this endeavor is a viable corporate information infrastructure that supports a wide-range of creative business strategies. In general, the open and flexible communication protocols that collectively define today's Internet technology are now playing a critical role in processing highly distributed transactions, supporting knowledge-intensive decision making, and facilitating ambitious organizational collaboration (Turban, King, Lee, & Viehland, 2004). The ubiquitous connectivity and user-friendly interfaces have also offered a rich set of technological capabilities, allowing for development of value-creating systems to attract customers' attention (Fahey, Srivastava, Sharon, & Smith, 2001).

In the e-marketing discipline, Internet technology is viewed as "a market space where a firm interacts, makes transactions, and builds relationships with suppliers, distributors, competitors, as well as consumers" (Min et al., 2002, p. 3). In addition to the functional capabilities, the appeal of Internet technology also comes from the rapid growth of consumer acceptance it has enjoyed since the network was made available for commercial usage. An industry research from Jupiter Research (http://www.find.org.tw/), for example, indicates that annual online retail sales in the United States will reach 65 billion dollars during the year of 2004 and 117 billion dollars for the year of 2008 with the composite annual growth rate of 17%. According to this research, although the growth rate of first-time online shoppers in the United States will slow down as the Internet population saturates, the average purchasing amount is expected to increase steadily as a growing number of customers gain and feel satisfied with their experience with Internet shopping. This growth trend is confirmed by the census data collected by the U.S. Census Bureau (2006); the combined retail e-commerce sales of the first three quarters had reached $79 billion dollars. A similar trend is observed in Taiwan—the compound growth rate from 2006 to 2010 is estimated to be 25.3%, with 3.1% of annual percentage of total retail sales for 2006 (Luo, 2006). The strategic role of Internet technology becomes even more obvious as one observes how companies in various sectors are integrating sophisticated knowledge management capabilities (e.g., online communities and blogging) into their new product development process and other customer-facing functions (Gebert, Geib, Kolbe, & Brenner, 2003).

An important e-marketing area that has received much attention from marketing researchers is relationship marketing. The aim of relationship marketing is to build long-term, mutually satisfying relations with customers, suppliers, and distributors with the objective to earn and retain their long-term preference and businesses (Kotler, 2000, p. 13). Today's highly competitive business environment requires the adoption of both offensive marketing strategy (recruiting new customers) and defensive marketing strategy (retaining existing customers) (Stefanou, Sarmaniotis, & Stafyla, 2003). To implement these customer-centric strategies, companies' must have access to information about customers and provide customers with valuable knowledge to help them use the products they purchased from the company. In addition, instead of treating all customers equally, it is essential for companies to understand customers' requirements and customize the product and service offerings accordingly. Maintaining constant two-way communications with customers, therefore, is an important prerequisite for successful management of meaningful customer relationship.

A variety of information systems have been used to help with interactions with the customers. Often referred to as e-CRM systems, these systems are usually integrated under Internet protocols to provide user-friendly interfaces with customers, usually via a company Web site. From customers' point of view, a company's Web site represents the company itself. Customer satisfaction with or complaining about the ways the company Web site treats customers can lead to brand loyalty, repurchase intention, and repeat sales (Stefanou et al., 2003). An important concern, therefore, is how online customer's Web site satisfaction is affected by the company's e-CRM practices as demonstrated by its Web site design and management.

In light of the central role played by the Web site in a company's e-CRM practices, this study was conducted to examine the correlation and causal relationships between the CRM aspect of Web site design and management and online customers' satisfaction with their experience of Web site visits. For the purpose of measurement, the study adopts a framework proposed by Min et al. (2002), labeled as "Internet-mediated market orientation (IMO)" to measure the construct of CRM practices.

The remainder of the chapter is structured as follows. The section of literature review briefly describes the concepts of customer relationship management, Internet-mediated market orientation, and online user/customer satisfaction. This is followed by the section on research method, which includes the description of a theoretical model linking e-commerce companies' Web-enabled customer relationship management practices with the user/customer satisfaction. The section also describes the data collection method and instrument validation. The results of data analysis are then reported in the next section. The conclusion summarizes the study, elaborates on the implication of the findings, and suggests directions for future e-commerce research.

LITERATURE REVIEW

Customer Relationship Management

The theoretical foundation of customer relationship management (CRM) is relationship marketing. Shani and Chalasani (1992) defined relationship marketing as an integrated effort to identify, maintain, and build up a network with individual customers and to continuously strengthen the network for the mutual benefit of both sides through interactive, individualized, and value-added contacts over a long period of time. In a comprehensive literature review research on CRM, Ngai (2005) pointed out the absence of a universally accepted definition of this term. Researchers have provided various definitions from different points of view. For example, Swift (2002, p. 12) focused on customer communications and defined CRM as an "enterprise approach to understanding and influencing customer behavior through meaningful communications in order to improve customer acquisition, customer retention, customer loyalty, and customer profitability." Kincaid (2003, p. 41) emphasized the importance of resource integration and considered CRM as "the strategic use of information, processes, technology, and people to manage the customer's relationship with your company (marketing, sales, services, and support) across the whole customer life cycle." Parvatiyar and Sheth (2001, p. 5) stressed the concept of value creation and viewed CRM as "a comprehensive strategy and process of acquiring, retaining, and partnering with selective customers to create superior value for the company and the customer."

From information management's perspective, CRM is actually an amalgamation of relationship marketing and information technology. Whereas relationship marketing provides strategic foundation for the CRM concept, information technologies are used to automate and integrate marketing, sales, and service activities (Turban et al., 2004). A successful execution of the relationship marketing strategy often requires using sophisticated information systems to move information and knowledge smoothly across multiple complex customer-related processes. These CRM systems create customer value and contribute to company revenue by offering three categories of knowledge: knowledge for customers, knowledge about customers, and knowledge from customers (Gebert et al., 2003). At the core of CRM, capabilities often are the technological features that promote interactivity and customization (or even personalization) (Lee-Kelley, Gilbert, & Mannicom, 2003). These requirements can be naturally fulfilled with "technology-enabled relationship management (Schneider, 2002, p. 159)."

An important goal of CRM is to maximize customer retention. Since the best means to accomplish customer retention is to keep customers satisfied, it is reasonable to use customer satisfaction as an important criterion for measuring the success or failure of a firm's CRM practices (Stefanou et al., 2003). Furthermore, when the company Web site is used as the main interaction vehicle with customers, such as commonly practiced by many e-commerce companies, it is also reasonable to assume that customer satisfaction with Web site visits is a significant determinant of customer retention (Winer, 2001).

A comprehensive set of CRM programs usually consists of customer service, frequency/loyalty programs, customization, rewards programs, and community building (Winer, 2001). From the customer point of view, however, what matters the most is often their perception of the overall interaction experience with the firm. Customers shop for and are attracted to the vendors that maximize customer value. Much of the value-creating activities are related to information and knowledge flows (Winer, 2001). The company Web site, when properly designed and managed, can serve as a flexible and convenient mechanism for satisfying customers' requirements. The information and knowledge-intensive nature of CRM has been actively discussed in both marketing and information system literature (e.g., Gebert, et al., 2003; Stefanou et al., 2003; Min et al., 2002; Romano & Fjermestad, 2003). Most discussions about CRM, however, are either conceptual or anecdotal in nature. More empirical studies are needed to verify the concepts and frameworks for the purpose of theory advancement.

Since the concept of CRM is strongly supported by the concept of market orientation, and the practicing of CRM via Web sites can be related to the concept of Internet-mediated market orientation, the following two sections discuss market orientation and Internet-mediated market orientation.

Market Orientation

A well-researched construct, the concept of market orientation is defined by some researchers as a component of organizational culture, consisting of a set of shared values and beliefs that put the customer first in business planning (Deshpade, 1999; Narver & Slater, 1990; Slater & Narver, 1994). The effect of market orientation on a firm's learning capability and innovative activity has been investigated by research in marketing. For example, Jaworski and Kohli (1993) identify market orientation as a significant determinant of overall business performance. Market orientation is also viewed as a fundamental concept underpinning a company's business strategy and innovative operations (Day, 1994; Han, Kim, & Srivastava, 1998; Harmsen & Hensen, 2004; Hurley & Hult, 1998; Farrel, 2000; Matsuno & Mentzer, 2000; Ruekert, 1992; Wu, 2004). Guided by the market orientation concept, companies recognize the value of the activities relating to collection, dissemination, and application of market information as they seek to improve their operational performance and competitive advantage (Kohli & Jaworski, 1990; Morgan & Hunt, 1994; Narver et al., 1990).

Market orientation is a composite concept. Researchers identify its components in an attempt to better relate this concept with other marketing concepts. Narver et al. (1990) suggest that market orientation consists of five components: customer orientation, competitor orientation, functional coordination, long-term perspective, and profit orientation. Kohli et al. (1990) also contend that market orientation is the manifestation of a firm's marketing concept and comprises five components: customer orientation, competitor orientation, intelligence gathering, inter-departmental information exchange, and responses to market intelligence.

In order to bring the market orientation concept to the operational level, Jaworski et al. (1993) define market orientation as a set of specific activities a firm carries out to put the marketing concept into practice, and that the concept may be measured by three sets of organization-wide activities: (1) intelligence generation, (2) intelligence dissemination, and (3) response design. These activities involve the collection and distribution of market information pertaining to current and future customer needs, and the use of the information in managerial action. This information usage perspective of the market orientation concept offers a convenient avenue for evaluating a company's marketing activities and thereby examining its impact on the other organizational concerns, such as business performance or learning capability.

Internet-Mediated Market Orientation

The main stream of marketing research has examined the role of market orientation in the traditional business operational environment. Despite the success of various Internet-centric business models demonstrated by innovative companies, there are few, if any, attempts to examine the significance of the market orientation concept in the context of e-commerce. Min et al. (2002) theory of Internet-mediated market orientation represents the first attempt to explicitly take account of Internet technology and examines the role of market orientation in an e-commerce firm's online marketing activities. Internet-mediated market orientation essentially is market orientation in the Internet context.

At the implementation level, a firm's market orientation is witnessed by how it obtains market intelligence from its trading partners and other sources (Evans & King, 1999; Nordstrom & Pinkerton, 1999). As a convenient vehicle for interactive communications, Internet technologies have enabled the inclusion of a variety of forms of electronic communications such as videoconferencing, voicemail, Webcasting, usenet, e-mail, bulletin board, etc. in a company's marketing activities. These new capabilities have essentially "transformed traditional ways of market information generation, dissemination, and organizational responsiveness to it into a networked computing environment in which a firm interacts and collaborates with end customers as well as suppliers, distributors, competitors (Min et al., 2002, p. 3)." As a result, numerous innovative business models have emerged, including the ones compiled by Turban et al. (2004)—online direct marketing, electronic tendering systems, name your price, affiliate marketing, viral marketing, group purchasing, online auctions, etc.

Min et al. (2002) proposed the Internet-mediated market orientation theory by extending the concept of market orientation to incorporate Internet services. They defined Internet-mediated market orientation as "the Internet-mediated, information rich, seamless, agile, and boundary spanning process of generating, dissemination, and responding to market information on the Internet (p. 3)." Drawing from the major research literature on market orientation, they developed a conceptual framework to highlight the significant benefits of an Internet-mediated market orientation process: improved customer service, reduced marketing cost, and overall business performance. Hoping to advance the theory to a better maturity level, they call for more systematic inquiries to be conducted in both inductive and deductive manners to challenge or strengthen their framework: "Future research is called for to ... empirically test the theory with proper measures for solid deduction (Min et al., 2002, p. 8)."

We contend that, since the three dimensions of the Internet-mediated market orientation (market information generation, market information distribution, and organizational response to market information) are essentially about interacting with customers through information exchange and the subsequent application of the market information, they ought to be investigated within the broader framework of CRM.

Online User/Customer Satisfaction

Customer satisfaction is a perceptual measure of the effectiveness of an organization's customer relationship management. A satisfied customer tends to return for future business and thereby contributes to the retention rate of the existing customers. In addition, a satisfied customer is likely to offer positive word-of-mouth service about the experience of interacting with the vendor. A number of previous researches have consistently demonstrated that customer satisfaction is an important means for firms to gain an overall competitiveness in today's information and knowledge economy (Berry, 1995), contributes to a firm's profitability, and is increasingly becoming a critical organizational objective in pursuit of a sustainable competitive advantage (Reicheld & Sasser, 1990).

The World Wide Web represents a virtual market space for customers to search for and purchase products and services. Shankar, Smith, and Rangaswamy (2003) investigated the unique characteristics of online shopping and the differences between online and offline shopping environments. They found no significant difference with regard to customer satisfaction. Szymanski & Hise (2000) conducted focused group studies with selected online shoppers to identify the significant components of the customer satisfaction framework for the online shopping environment. Most of the components they identified are related to the customer relationship management concept, including Web site convenience, provision of product information, Webpage design, and security concerns.

In the field of information system, user satisfaction has been on the research agenda for more than 20 years (Khalifa & Liu, 2004). Early studies examined satisfaction of primary users who dealt with the information products generated by the systems (Davis & Olson, 1985). The target of the study was a specific type of information systems or information technology applications. For example, DeSanctis and Gallup (1987) measured manager (decision maker) satisfaction with a group decision support system. User satisfaction is generally defined as the "multidimensional attitude towards various aspects of MIS such as output quality, man-machine interface, EDP staff and services, and various user constructs such as feelings of participation and understanding (Raymond, 1987, p. 37)." With the subsequent proliferation of personal computing and end user computing, the main focus of user satisfaction research was the individuals who directly interacted with the information system. Several factors have been examined to account for the direct interaction between end-users and specific technology applications (e.g., content, accuracy, format, ease of use, and timeliness) (Bollen, 1989).

The recent emergence of e-commerce has further blurred the distinction between end-users and online customers due to the use of Web-based user interfaces for both internal and external communications. Not only have customer-facing applications of information technology been constructed to operate under the integrating framework of Internet protocols, back-office applications are also being hyperlinked to Web browser interfaces to provide stakeholders with single user interface. The technological integration is leading to the integration of the information systems and marketing theories. The traditional information system models for user satisfaction research that mainly focused on system/information characteristics are no longer sufficient to explain user/customer satisfaction in the new online environment (Palmer & Griffith, 1998). The traditional focus of marketing on product/service features also must be expanded to incorporate system and content characteristics. Therefore, a growing number of information system studies have adopted the marketing approach to measure online user/customer satisfaction. Many of the recent researches used the disconfirmation model, a primary theory in marketing literature for explaining customer satisfaction, to examine various aspects of user satisfaction (e.g., Khalifa et al., 2004; Mckinney, Yoon, & Zahedi, 2002; Susarla, Barua, & Whinston, 2003).

The literature previously reviewed led to the conceptual framework for the study, formed by three research constructs (CRM practices, customers' perception of e-commerce firm's customer orientation, and customer Web site satisfaction) and their relationships. Three research hypotheses were formulated to represent these presumed relationships. The conceptual framework, research hypotheses, data collection and analysis methods, as well as validation of measurement instrument are described in the next section.

RESEARCH DESIGN

Research Constructs and Hypotheses

Customers satisfied with their Web site visit experience are more likely to repeat their visits and also more likely to purchase products. The immediate goal of e-CRM implementation is, therefore, to increase Web site visitors' satisfaction with their visiting experience. E-commerce companies would like to assume that everything they do with their Web site is aligned with customers' characteristics and requirements. Literature reviewed in the previous section also has suggested that customer satisfaction might be affected by their perception of the firm's customer orientation

Figure 1. Research framework

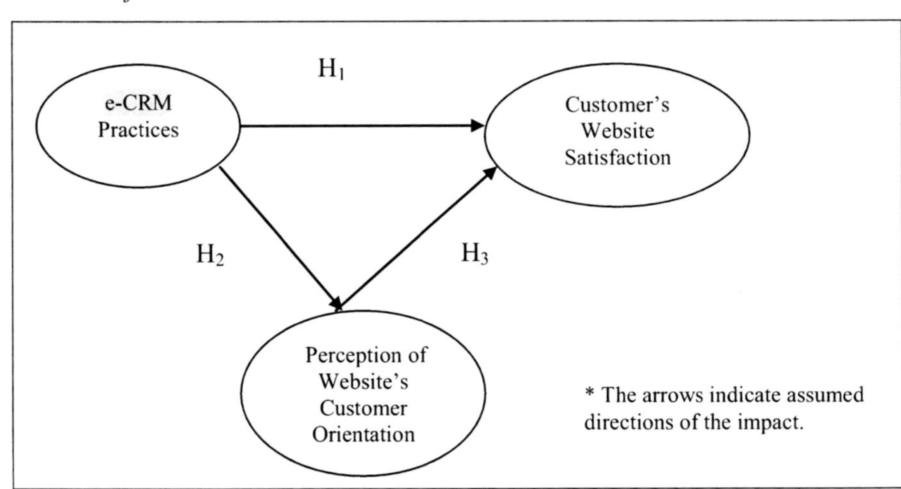

(Lee-Kelley et al., 2003). The objective of this study was to clarify these speculations. Figure 1 is a graphical depiction of the relationships between the three research constructs. Following the research framework is a list of our three research hypotheses.

- **H1:** Online customers' Web site satisfaction with their Web site visit experience is positively affected by the e-CRM practices of the e-commerce firm.
- **H2:** Customers' perception of customer orientation of an e-commerce firm is positively affected by its e-CRM practices.
- **H3:** Online customers' satisfaction with their Web site visit experience is positively affected by customers' perception of customer orientation of the e-commerce firm.

The construct e-CRM practice perception consisted of three dimensions: market information generation, market information dissemination, and organizational responses to market information. All three dimensions were evaluated from the user/customer perspective. Generation of market information represented availability of market information and was gauged in terms of the richness of the information content on the Web site. Dissemination of market information was judged by how rapidly the Web site updated and shared its market information. The organizational response was measured by the Web site's rapidity in responding to customer inquiry or request for information. Each of these three dimensions was addressed by three question items in the questionnaire.

Perception of online customer (or e-customer) orientation was operationally defined as the extent to which an e-commerce company sought to satisfy its e-customers' needs and to enhance e-customer value, and was measured by three question items: (1) "The Web site understands and satisfies customers' needs," (2) "The Web site seeks to enhance customer value," and (3) "The Web site frequently evaluates its customer satisfaction situation." Customer satisfaction with the Web site visit experience was defined as the subjective evaluation of the overall value perception resulting from the interaction experience. Three question items were devised to represent this variable: (1) "I enjoy the experience visiting the Web site," (2) "I am satisfied with the services I received from the Web site," and (3) "I trust the correctness of the content." All variables are subjectively measured using the Likert Scale, with 5 representing "Strongly Agree" and 1 for "Strongly Disagree".

Data Collection and Data Analysis

The primary data were collected from college faculty, staff, and students in Taiwan in the summer of 2004. The respondents were instructed to use one of their favorite Web sites as they responded to the questionnaires. Most respondents referred to popular local portal Web sites or major global e-commerce Web sites such as www.amazon.com and www.e-bay.com. As noted in Jih (2002, 2003) and Jih and Lee (2004), e-commerce has been a major thrust in Taiwan's economic, educational, and public sectors during the past several years. Most people in the college population have had some e-commerce experiences. The development of the survey instrument involved three steps:

- **Step 1:** An initial version of the survey questionnaire was designed to identify the question items synthesized from the literature. This version was presented to three practitioners and two academicians in the e-marketing and e-commerce fields. The questionnaire was revised to incorporate their feedbacks.
- **Step 2:** One hundred copies of the revision were distributed to the students in e-commerce and e-marketing classes. This pilot testing resulted in further modification and improvement of the questionnaire.

- **Step 3:** The new version of the questionnaire was then tested online with the college students with e-commerce experience, who were instructed to evaluate a Web site of their own choice. More modifications to the questionnaire were made to accommodate feedback from the online respondents. The final version of the questionnaire was administered to another group of college students and university employees, who were invited via e-mail to participate, during the period of April and May of 2004. A total of 160 effective questionnaires were obtained and used for analysis after removal of the incomplete ones.

Two statistical analysis software packages, SPSS 10.0 and AMOS 3.6, were used to analyze the collected data. The Cronbach's α value was calculated as the reliability indicator for each research variable. The validity of the variable measurements was quantitatively tested using exploratory factor analysis, correlation analysis, and confirmatory factor analysis, in addition to the qualitative assessment of the experts in the field. The validation of the theoretical model was then performed using structural equation modeling analysis. For the model-testing study, Hair, Anderson, Tatam, and Black (1998) suggested an appropriate size from 100 to 200. Structural equation modeling analysis using a large sample (sample size > 200) might result in poor fitness of the model. The sample size 160 used by this study satisfied this requirement. Among the respondents, 43% were males, 57% were females, 30% were ages 19 or below, 37.5% were ages 20-29, 20% were ages 30-39, and 12.6% were ages 40 or above.

Reliability and Validity of Variable Measurements

An exploratory factor analysis was performed to identify the dimensions of the latent variable that represented the research construct e-CRM practices. The resulting dimensions were then evaluated by a confirmatory factor analysis. As shown in Table 1, the result of principal component analysis identified three factors (dimensions) from the nine question items. The accumulated variance was 72.99%, an indication of high construct validity. The reliability measures of the three factors were 0.835, 0.766, and 0.810, respectively. These reliability measures were greater than the commonly accepted minimum of 0.7, demonstrating a good reliability of our measurement of e-CRM practices. All factor loadings associated with each of the three factors were greater than 0.7, an evidence that the e-CRM practices measurement in this study possessed both convergent validity and discriminant validity. The convergent validity and discriminant validity of the e-CRM practices measurement were further confirmed by the fitness indices produced by the confirmatory factor analysis: specifically, the goodness-of-fit index (GFI) and the adjusted goodness-of-fit index (AGFI). The GFI represents the amount of variances and covariances in the sample covariance matrix, which can be used as an estimate of the population matrix. In essence, the GFI is analogous in interpretation to the R2 in the multiple regression analysis. The AGFI is GFI that has been adjusted for degrees of freedom, and is essentially analogous to the adjusted R2 in multiple regression. The cutoff value for GFI is usually considered to be 0.9, and for AGFI, it is 0.8 (Sharma, 1996). In this study the GFI value was 0.943, and the AGFI value was 0.893. Additionally, all t-value estimates were significantly greater than zero, with the exception of the reference indicators, which were fixed at 1 for each of the latent variables. These characteristics of the measurements allowed for using the mean values of the three question items as the measures of the observable variables for e-CRM practices.

The factor analysis procedure was applied to confirm the constructs for our theoretical model: e-CRM practices, perception of online

Table 1. Reliability, convergent validity, and discriminatory validity measures of e-CRM practice perception dimensions

Construct Dimensions	Measurement Items	Exploratory Factor Analysis	Confirmatory Factor Analysis		Cronbach's α
		Factor Loading	Standardized Structure Coefficient	T value	
Generation of market information	The Web site provides detailed product/service information.	0.874	0.838	Fixed*	0.835
	The Web site always has the information I need.	0.834	0.739	9.367	
	The Web site provides plenty of useful information.	0.802	0.806	10.029	
Distribution of market information	The Web site frequently mails me information, saving me time and effort.	0.826	0.675	7.539	0.766
	The Web site frequently mails me information on new product, new technology, and something educational.	0.783	0.705	7.800	
	The promotion information from this Web site works for me.	0.767	0.786	Fixed*	
Organizational responses to market information	The Web site responses to competition in the market.	0.836	0.741	9.758	0.810
	The Web site responses to customer complaints and suggestions.	0.792	0.666	8.655	
	The Web site is sensitive to changes of customers' requirements for products and services.	0.700	0.881	Fixed*	

**: Factor loading set to the value of 1.0*

customer orientation, and customers' Web site satisfaction. Each analysis produced exactly one factor, with 1 used as the threshold value of the eigenvalues (Table 2). This result confirmed the single dimensionality of the factors. The high factor loadings and extracted variances of all variables and model constructs indicated a good convergent validity of the variable and construct measurements. Table 2 also showed that, with the exception of e-CRM, which was close to 0.7, all other constructs had a Cronbach's α greater than 0.7. Our evaluation of discriminant validity of the measurements was based on Fornell and Larcker's work (1981), suggesting that the discriminant validity between two constructs was good when their extracted variances exceeded the squared correlation coefficient between the two constructs. Table 3 shows the constructs in our theoretical model pass this test: the extracted variances (values on the diagonal) are all greater than the squared correlation coefficients (the rest of the values in the table).

MODEL VALIDATION

James et al. (1982) recommended that testing a causal model required a two-step approach: A

Table 2. Reliability and validity tests of model constructs

Research Constructs	Measurement Items	Factor Loadings	Cronbach's α	% of Extracted Variance
e-CRM Practices	Organizational response to market information (crm1)	0.864	0.699	62.62
	Distribution of market information (crm2)	0.771		
	Generation of market information (crm3)	0.733		
Perception of Online Customer Orientation	Web site understands and satisfies customer needs (occ1)	0.890	0.828	74.46
	Web site seeks to enhance customer value (occ2)	0.862		
	Web site frequently evaluates customer satisfaction situation (occ3)	0.837		
Customers' Web site Satisfaction	I enjoy visiting this Web site (cws1)	0.902	0.870	79.41
	Web site offers satisfying services (cws2)	0.899		
	I believe that I've made the right choice using this Web site (cws3)	0.872		

Table 3. Discriminant validity test of model constructs

Constructs	CRM Practices	Online Customer Orientation	Customers' Web Site Satisfaction
e-CRM Practices	0.626		
Perception of Online Customer Orientation	0.366	0.745	
Customers' Web site Satisfaction	0.319	0.454	0.794

Note: Values on the diagonal are extracted variances. The rest are correlation coefficients.

confirmatory factor analysis is first conducted to obtain evidence for determining whether the indicators (or observed variables) appropriately measured the latent variables.

Once an appropriate measure model was identified, items could be combined to form scales of the latent variables. The second step then utilizes these scales to test the hypothesized structural models. The theoretical model of this study consisted of three constructs (latent variables), each of which in turn was represented by three observable variables. The latent variables, the relationships to be tested between these three latent variables (expressed as oval symbols), and their corresponding observable variables (expressed as rectangular symbols) are graphically depicted in Figure 2. The factor loadings of the observed variables are indicated on the arrowed lines.

In order to determine the relationships between the three latent variables, the statistical analysis software AMOS 3.6 was used to test the research hypotheses. In addition to the chi-square test statistics, six fitness indices were used to evaluate the adequacy of the theoretical model. The $\chi 2$ test evaluated the discrepancy between the theoretical model and the collected data. The smaller the $\chi 2$ value, the better the model fit. According to Carmines and McIver (1981), the $\chi 2$ to degrees of freedom ratios ($\chi 2$ /d.f.) around 3:1 or less were indicative of an acceptable model fit. The $\chi 2$ /d.f. in this study is 1.6272, an indication of an acceptable fitness of our theoretical model with the data. The results of testing the three alternative models are summarized in Table 4. Model 1 consisted of all three relationships represented by the three research hypotheses, and therefore was the first one being tested. The results showed that both the absolute and incremental fitness indices indicated good fitness of the theoretical model. The absolute indices were GFI (0.945), AGFI (0.898), and RMSEA (root mean square error of approximation = 0.063). Ideally, both GFI and AGFI should be greater than 0.9. The GFI value was greater than 0.9, and the AGFI value was close to 0.9 in this

Figure 2. Result of model validation

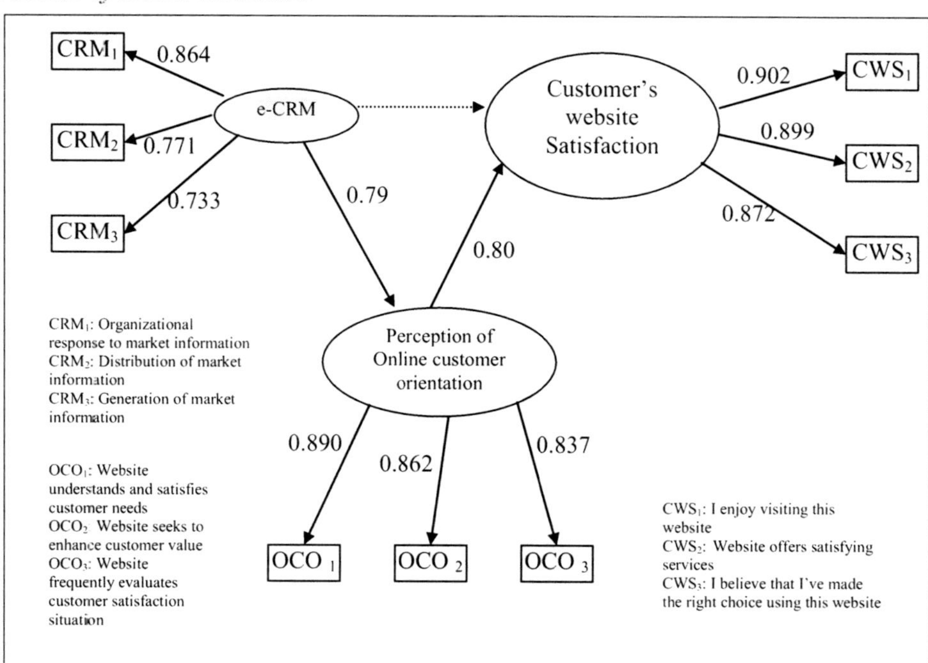

Table 4. Validation of three alternative models

path	hypothesis	expected sign	model 1		model 2		model 3 (rival)	
			Standardized Regression weights	t value	Standardized Regression weights	t value	Standardized Regression weights	t value
e-CRM→ Customer's Web site satisfaction	H1	+	0.17	1.20	Not Applicable	Not Applicable	0.281	3.31*
CRM→ Perception of online customer orientation	H2	+	0.78	6.24*	0.79	6.23*	Not Applicable	Not Applicable
Perception of online customer orientation → Customer's Web site satisfaction	H3	+	0.65	4.35*	0.80	9.29*	0.691	7.62*
χ2 / d.f.	Acceptable if < 3:1		1.6409		1.6272		4.6999	
Fit index	Critical value		Goodness-of-fit		Goodness-of-fit		Goodness-of-fit	
GFI	>0.9		0.945	good	0.945	good	0.878	poor
AGFI	>0.9		0.898	acceptable	0.901	good	0.780	poor
NFI NNFI	>0.9 >0.9		0.946 0.967	good good	0.946 0.968	good good	0.840 0.810	poor poor
CFI	>0.95		0.978	good	0.978	good	0.868	poor
RMSEA	<0.08		0.063	good	0.063	good	0.153	poor

**: Level of significance = 0.05*

case. The very small value of RMSEA (< 0.08) also confirmed adequate model fit. The incremental indices used in the study included NFI (normed fit index = 0.946) and CFI (comparative fitness index = 0.978 > 0.95). Both values were high enough to present consistent evidences in support of adequate fitness of the theoretical model (Bollen, 1989; Hair et al., 1998).

Table 4 also shows that, of the three research hypotheses in the first alternative model:

- **H1:** (Online customers' Web site satisfaction with their Web site visit experience is positively affected by the e-CRM practices of the e-commerce firm) was rejected due to the low structural coefficient 0.17 (t-value is 1.20) and was dropped from the subsequent analysis. Both H2 and H3 passed the statistical significance test and therefore were accepted:
- **H2:** The perception of online customer orientation of an e-commerce firm is positively affected by its e-CRM practices ("e-CRM —> perception of online customer orientation," structural coefficient = 0.78, t-value = 6.24).
- **H3:** Online customers' satisfaction with their Web site visit experience is positively affected by the perception of customer orientation of the e-commerce firm ("perception of online customer orientation —> online customer Web site satisfaction," structural coefficient = 0.65, t-value = 4.35).

With H1 removed from the theoretical model, the second alternative model consisted of only two paths: e-CRM -> online customer orientation (H2) and online customer orientation -> online customer satisfaction (H3). Both hypotheses passed the significance test. In addition, all fitness indices passed the fitness evaluation criteria. The AGFI value (0.901) with this model was better than this value (0.898) with the first alternative model. In short, the second alternative model had a better model fit than the first one.

Despite the acceptance of both Model 1 and Model 2, a theoretical possibility still existed that e-CRM and perception of online customer orientation individually might directly impact online customer satisfaction. Morgan et al. (1994) pointed out the possibility of an antecedent directly impacting a consequence in some structural models and the significance of formulating and testing such a rival model. The rival model tested in this study, as the third alternative model, was formed by H1 (e-CRM -> online customer Web site satisfaction) and H3 (perception of online customer orientation -> online customer Web site satisfaction). However, although the structural coefficients of both hypotheses passed the significance test, the ratio of $\chi 2$ to degrees of freedom (4.70) was higher than 3. In addition, none of the fitness indices passed the evaluation criteria. The rival model was rejected based on these results. The second alternative appeared to be the best theory (i.e., e-CRM practices did not directly impact online customers' satisfaction). Instead, online customers' Web site satisfaction was affected by the e-CRM practices indirectly through an intervening variable, perception of online customer orientation.

SUMMARY AND CONCLUSION

As with many other technological breakthroughs in the recent history, misconceptions and hypes surrounding Internet technologies have caused much confusion on the part of investors and business decision makers. Following the rise and fall of public expectations for the Internet's revolutionary impact on traditional business models at the turn of the century, researchers have reminded that the Internet would not render traditional economic and business principles obsolete (e.g., Litan & Rivlin, 2001; Porter, 2001). Rather, the convenient communication capabilities and user-friendly interfaces provided by the Internet technology only represent a collection of technological capabilities that enables the implementation of innovative applications for businesses in all sectors to strengthen their competitive advantage in the knowledge economy. Identifying the synergy between traditional business wisdom and new information technologies is a core organizational competence that can only be learned through aggressive and creative experimentation.

Emerging as a strategic initiative involving the integration of a variety of information technologies with relationship marketing, e-CRM has received much attention from both e-commerce practitioners and academicians. Using various technological tools such as Web site design, database, data mining, software agent, Web logs, and group work software in their marketing activities, companies are seeking to enhance existing customers' loyalty while attracting new customers' attention at the same time. In light of the central role played by the Web site in the e-CRM practices, this study was conducted as an attempt to shed some light on the role of e-commerce Web sites in the e-CRM practices and the customers' satisfaction with their Web site visit experience. We constructed a tentative theoretical model based on the literature in marketing and information systems. The model links three research constructs: e-CRM practices, perception of the Web site's customer orientation and customer satisfaction with Web site visits. We then used structural equation modeling analysis to validate the model. The result of model validation generated evidence for rejection and acceptance of the research hypotheses. The first hypothesis, "Online customers' Web site satisfaction is positively affected by the e-CRM practices of the e-commerce firms," was rejected. The other two hypotheses were both accepted: "The perception of online customer orientation of an e-commerce firm is positively affected by the e-CRM practices of the firm," and "online customers' satisfaction with their Web site visit experience is positively affected by the perception of customer orientation of the e-commerce firm." Interpreted collectively, these results indicated that the customers' Web site satisfaction was not affected directly by e-CRM practices, and the effect was made indirectly through the perception of online customer orientation. In other words, the perception of a Web site's online customer orientation played a pivotal role in the impact of e-CRM practices on the customer Web site satisfaction.

An important implication for e-commerce managers may be drawn from the research results. The study confirmed that the traditional wisdom about customer satisfaction is applicable as well to the e-commerce as to the traditional business environment. E-commerce companies must actively engage themselves in interacting with customers to ensure that what they do with their Web sites is all aligned with what the customers want and need. Furthermore, the challenges of time compression in transaction processing and the lack of physical contact in the e-commerce environment require even more careful design and monitoring of customer-facing business processes than in the pre-Internet era. The focus on customer requirements must be emphasized constantly to ensure that the information flows both ways via the Web site in the optimal fashion. After all, the Internet-enabled cyberspace now provides an information-symmetric scenario for both consumers and suppliers. Customers can freely switch between vendors. Customer relationship management is not just a smart business slogan. It must be thoroughly blended into the organizational culture and drives every major business decision made by the organization.

This study contributes to e-commerce research by demonstrating the use of a model-building method to test hypotheses regarding the impact of a major business initiative on customer satisfaction. E-CRM has received much attention in the management literature. Most discussions are conceptual or anecdotal in nature. Systematic inquiries involving empirical data are needed to verify the relationships between the concepts and, thereby, further this inter-disciplinary field to better maturity.

The linkage between e-CRM and Internet-mediated market orientation is also a new adventure in e-commerce research. Min et al. (2002) proposed the concept of Internet-mediated market orientation to extend the traditional market orientation to the Internet-enabled business environment. They discussed the concept and called for more follow-up research being conducted to validate their framework. This study built on their framework and used it to measure the information aspect of e-CRM practices.

Readers are cautioned in generalizing the findings reported herein for several reasons. First, the use of college faculty, staff, and students as respondents limits the generalization power of the research results. Second, the subjective nature of the responses may further pose another limitation on the external validity of the study. Third, since the data was collected in Taiwan, the research must be replicated in other cultures in order to expand the scope of applicability. Despite these limitations, since the study is confirmatory in nature, the significance of the study should not be severely reduced.

Promising directions for further research are suggested in the following directions. For a relatively new field such as e-CRM to become well established, more deductive and inductive inquiries are needed to advance the theory to a more mature level. The specific context of inquiry in this study is general Web site visit experience. Other contexts, such as online purchasing or online auction, may be used to obtain evidence from different angles of observation. Findings from research conducted in a variety of contexts will increase the theory's generalization power. Another area of research is using the controlled experiment approach to investigate issues surrounding e-CRM concepts. The controlled experiment research methodology complements survey research by keeping irrelevant factors under control in a lab setting. Examples of significant issues for controlled examination are the effect of different personalization designs, frequency of Web site update, and extent of Web site update on customers' perception of market orientation and their Web site satisfaction. The third area for future research concerns gathering data in different cultural settings to allow for cross-cultural comparison. The emerging trend of Web 2.0 services also is a challenging but promising research direction. Web 2.0 services are characterized by maximum user participation and leveraging of collective intelligence resulting from user participation in content contribution and dissemination (O'Reilly, 2003). The principle and spirit of Web 2.0 is closely aligned with that of e-CRM. Both the practitioners and researchers would find it promising to aggressively act to identify innovative approaches to incorporating Web 2.0 features in the e-CRM strategies. Finally, with the global nature of e-commerce, an in-depth understanding of cultural impact on Internet-enabled CRM practices is an essential capability to operate in today's highly globalized business environment.

REFERENCES

Berry, L. L. (1995). Relationship marketing of services: Growing interest, emerging perspectives. *Journal of the Academy of Marketing Science, 23*, 236-245.

Bollen, K. A. (1989). *Structural equations with latent variables*. New York: Wiley.

Bowen, D. E., & Schneider, A. (1988). Services marketing and management: Implications for organizational behavior. *Research in Organizational Behavior, 10*, 43-80.

Carmines, E. G., & McIver, J. P. (1981). Analyzing models with observed variables. In G. W. Bohrnstedt & E. F. Borgatta (Eds.), *Social measurement: Current issues*. Beverly Hills: Sage.

Davis, G. B., & Olson, M. H. (1985). *Management information systems: Conceptual foundations, structure, and development*. New York: McGraw-Hill.

Day, G. S. (1994). The capabilities of market-driven organization. *Journal of Marketing, 58*, 37-52, October.

DeSanctis, G., & Gallupe, R. B. (1987). A foundation for the study of group decision support systems. *Management Science, 33*(5), 589-609.

Deshpade, R. (1999). *Developing a market orientation*. Sage Publications, Inc.

Doll, W. J., Xia, W., & Torkzadeh, G. (1994). A confirmatory factor of the end-user computing satisfaction instrument. *MIS Quarterly 18*(4), 453-461.

Evans, J. R., & King, V. E. (1999). Business-to-business marketing and the World Wide Web. *Industrial Marketing Management, 28*(4), 343-358.

Fahey, A., Srivastava, R., Sharon, J. S., & Smith, D. E. (2001). Linking e-business and operating processes: The role of knowledge management. *IBM Systems Journal, 40*(4), 889-907.

Farrel, M. A. (2000). Developing a market-oriented learning organization. *Australian Journal of Management, 25*(2), 201-222.

Fornell, C., & Larcker, D. F. (1981). Evaluating structural equations of market orientation with unobservable variables and measurement error. *Journal of Marketing Research, 18*, 39-50, February.

Gebert, H., Geib, M., Kolbe, L., & Brenner, W. (2003). Knowledge-enabled customer relationship management: integrating customer relationship management and knowledge management concepts. *Journal of Knowledge Management, 7*(5), 107-123.

Hair, J. F., Anderson, R. E., Tatam, R. L., & Black, W. C. (1998). *Multivariate data analysis* (5th ed.). NJ: Prentice-Hall.

Han, J. K., Kim, N., & Srivastava, R. K. (1998). Market orientation and organizational performance: Is innovation a missing link? *Journal of Marketing, 62*, 30-45.

Harmsen, H., & Hensen, B. (2004). Identifying the determinants of value creation in the market: A competence-based approach. *Journal of Business Research, 57*(5), 533-541.

Hurley, R., & Hult, T. M. (1998). Innovation, market orientation, and organizational learning: An integration and empirical examination. *Journal of Marketing, 62*(3), 42-54.

James, L. R., Mulaik, S. A., & Brett, J. M. (1982). *Causal analysis: Assumptions, models, and data*. Beverly Hills: Sage.

Jaworski, B. J., & Kohli, A. K. (1993). Market orientation, antecedent, and consequences. *Journal of Marketing, 57*, 53-70, July.

Jih, W. J. (2003). Simulating real world experience using accumulative system development projects. *Journal of Information Systems Education, 14*(2), 181-192.

Jih, W. J. (2002). Effects of electronic commerce implementations in Taiwan. *Journal of Computer Information Systems, XXXXII*(3), 68-76.

Jih, W. J., & Lee, S. F. (2004). Exploring relationships between motivating factors and life styles of cellular phone users. *Journal of Computer Information Systems, XLIV*(2), 65-73.

Khalifa, M., & Liu, V. (2004). The state of research on information system satisfaction. *Journal of Information Technology Theory and Application, 5*(4), 37-49.

Kincaid, J. W. (2003). *Customer relationship management: Getting it right!* Upper Saddle River, NJ: Prentice-Hall PTR.

Kotler, P. (2000). *Marketing management* (10th ed.). NJ: Prentice Hall.

Kohli, A. K., & Jaworski, B. J. (1990). Market orientation: The construct, research propositions, and managerial implications. *Journal of Marketing, 54*(2), 1-18.

Lee-Kelley, L., Gilbert, D., & Mannicom, R. (2003). How e-CRM can enhance customer loyalty. *Marketing Intelligence & Planning, 21*(4/5), 239-248.

Lings, I. N. (2004). Internal market orientation construct and consequences. *Journal of Business Research, 57*, 405-413.

Litan, R. E., & Rivlin, A. M. (2001). Projecting the economic impact of the internet. *The American Economic Review, 91*(2), 313-317.

Luo, J. C. (2006). *The 2006 report on current conditions and future trends of e-commerce businesses in Taiwan.* Institute of Information Industry Research Report Series. Retrieved from http://gcis.nat.gov.tw/ec/knowledge/topics/detail.asp?DocID=1028&picName=basic

Min, S., Song, S., & Keebler, J. S. (2002). An Internet-mediated market orientation (IMO): Building a theory. *Journal of Marketing Theory and Practice, 10*(2), 1-11.

Matsuno, K., Mentzer, J. T. (2000). The effects of strategy type on the market orientation-performance relationship. *Journal of Marketing, 64*(4), 1-16.

Mckinney, V., Yoon, K., & Zahedi, F. W. (2002). The measurement of Web-customer satisfaction: An expectation and disconfirmation approach. *Information Systems Research, 13*(3), 296-315.

Morgan, R. M., & Hunt, S. D. (1994). The commitment-trust of relationship marketing. *Journal of Marketing, 58*, 20-38, July.

Napier, H. A., Judd, P. J., Rivers, O. N., & Wagner, S. W. (2001). Creating a winning e-business. Course Technology.

Narver, J. C., & Slater, S. F. (1990). The effect of a market orientation on business profitability. *Journal of Marketing, 54*(4), 20-35.

Ngai, E. W. T. (2005). Customer relationship management research (1992-2002): An academic literature review and classification. *Marketing Intelligence and Planning, 23*(6/7), 582-605.

Nordstrom, R. D., & Pinkerton, R. L. (1999). Taking advantage of internet sources to build a competitive intelligence system. *Competitive Intelligence Review, 10*(1), 54-61.

O'Reilly, T. (2005). *What is Web 2.0: Design patterns and business models for the next generation of software.* Retrieved from http://www.oreillynet.com/lpt/a/6228

Palmer, J. W., & Griffith, D. A. (1998). An emerging model of Web site design for marketing. *Communications of the ACM, 41*(3), 45-51.

Parvatiyar, A., & Sheth, J. N. (2001). Customer relationship management: Emerging practice, process, and discipline. *Journal of economic & Social Research, 3*(2), 1-34.

Porter, M. E. (2001). Strategy and the Internet. *Harvard Business Review, 79*(3), 63-78.

Raymond, L. (1987). Organizational characteristics and MIS success in the context of small business. *MIS Quarterly*, 37-52.

Reicheld, E. F., & Sasser, W. E. (1990). Zero-defection: Quality comes to services. *Harvard Business Review*, 105-111.

Romano, N. C., & Fjermestad, J. (2003). Electronic commerce customer relationship management: A research agenda. *Information Technology and Management, 4*(2-3), 233-258.

Ruekert, R.W. (1992). Developing a market orientation: An organizational strategy perspective. *International Journal of Research in Marketing, 9*(3), 225-246.

Sharma, S. (1996). *Applied multivariate techniques.* John Wiley & Sons.

Singh, S., & Ranchhod, A. (2004). Market orientation and customer satisfaction: Evidence from British machine tool industry. *Industrial Marketing Management, 33*(2), 135-144.

Shani, D., & Chalasani, S. (1992). Exploiting niches using relationship marketing. *The Journal of Consumer Marketing, 9*(3). 33-42.

Shankar, V., Smith, A. K., & Rangaswamy, A. (2003). Customer satisfaction and loyalty in online and offline environments. *International Journal of Research in Marketing, 20*(2), 153-175.

Shneider, G. P. (2002). Electronic commerce. Thomson-Course Technology.

Slater, S. F., & Narver, J. C. (1994). Market orientation, customer value, and superior performance. *Business Horizons, 37*(2), 22-29.

Stefanou, C., Sarmaniotis, C., & Stafyla, A. (2003). CRM and customer-centric knowledge management: an empirical research. *Business Process Management Journal, 9*(5), 617-634.

Susarla, A., Barua, A., & Whinston, A.B. (2003). Understanding the service component of application service provision: An empirical analysis of satisfaction with ASP services. *MIS Quarterly, 27*(1), 91-123.

Swift, R. S. (2001). *Accelerating customer relationships using CRM and relationship technologies.* Upper Saddle River, NJ: Prentice-Hall PTR.

Szymanski, D. M., & Hise, R. T. (2000). E-satisfaction: An initial examination. *Journal of Retailing, 76*(3), 309-322.

Turban, E., King, D., Lee, J., & Viehland, D. (2004). *Electronic commerce: A managerial perspective.* NJ: Prentice-Hall.

U. S. Census Bureau Quarterly Retail E-Commerce Sales. Retrieved from http://www.census.gov/mrts/www/ecomm.html.

Weerawardena, J., & O'Cass, A. (2004). Exploring the characteristics of the market-driven firms and antecedents to sustained competitive advantage. *Industrial Marketing Management, 33*(5), 419-427.

Winer, R. S. (2001). A framework for customer relationship management. *California Management Review, 43*(4), 89-105.

Wu, J. (2004). Influence of market orientation and strategy on travel industry performance: An empirical study of e-commerce in Taiwan. *Tourism Management, 25*, 357-365.

Zeithaml, V. A., Rust, R. T., & Lemon, K. N. (2001). The customer pyramid: Creating and serving profitable customers. *California Management Review, 43*(4), 118-142.

Chapter XV
The Formation of Online Trust

Anol Bhattacherjee
University of South Florida, USA

ABSTRACT

This chapter outlines three trust-building processes (relational, calculative, and institutional) that shape individual trust in online firms and describes how these processes change over time as users gain experience with the online firms. It hypothesizes three alternative belief structures resulting from the previous processes as determinants of trust, theorizes the temporal nature of their effects on trust as users observe and learn from the firm's actual behavior, and then empirically tests the hypothesized associations using data collected from a field survey of online banking users. The results indicate that relational, calculative, and institutional beliefs are indeed significant drivers of trust. However, calculative and institutional beliefs have stronger initial effects than relational beliefs for new consumers of online firms. The effect of calculative belief on trust decreases with time, while that of relational beliefs increases and that of institutional beliefs remains relatively unchanged. Research and practical implications of these findings are discussed.

INTRODUCTION

Trust is widely recognized as a key driver of online commerce (Keen, 1997). This is so because online commerce typically requires the exchange of sensitive personal or financial information such as e-mail address and credit card numbers among the transacting parties. Such information sharing opens up the trustor to the risks of undesirable consequences such as potential misuse of personal or financial data by the trustee. Some degree of trust is required to assure trustors that trustees will not take advantage of their vulnerability during or after the transaction. Trust reduces social uncertainty in exchange-based relationships, eliminates the need for bureaucratic control structures, and encourages long-term relationships, while lack of trust necessitates full disclosure of business rules, increases monitoring costs, and hence decreases business efficiencies (Luhmann, 1979).

Recent surveys report that only 29% of online consumers trust Web sites selling goods or services online, significantly lower than the 55-60% of consumers that trust traditional "brick-and-mortar" businesses (ConsumerWebWatch 2002). As an example, 65-year old retiree Starr Tolleson was hesitant to buy drugs online despite promised cost savings of over 20% for her $9600 annual prescription drug expense. "It is a little frightening to think that there is a possibility that the medicines that you order are not pure or not the ones you have ordered," (Parker-Pope 2001, p. B1). Growing incidences of Internet fraud, such as identity theft and fraudulent online businesses, has contributed to further erosion of trust.

Why is trust lacking in online commerce? In traditional "brick-and-mortar" commerce, trust is typically inspired by a firm's physical presence, its history of successful face-to-face transactions, and clear policies for customer satisfaction and dispute resolution. However, such trust is difficult to establish in online firms for at least four reasons (Kollock, 1999). First, these firms are often physically located in a different part of the country, making it difficult to take remedial actions if transactions do not meet expectations (e.g., returning merchandise). Second, many online firms are new upstarts with limited transactional history, and hence consumers have little prior basis to trust them. Third, the multiplicity of parties involved in online transactions (e.g., infrastructure providers, retailers, advertisers) makes it hard to identify who is to blame if things go wrong. Finally, legal policies related to improper conduct of online businesses are not well established or well understood, leading to consumers' lack of confidence in such firms.

In order to inspire consumer confidence and ensure their own survival, it is imperative that online firms consider proactive investing in trust building initiatives (Keen, 1997). However, doing so will require firms to understand the different mechanisms of trust formation, the relative efficacy of these mechanisms, and the stability of these effects over time. The notion of stability is important since trust is not static but builds or erodes over time (Luhmann, 1979; Rousseau, Sitkin, Burt, & Camerer, 1998), and hence strategies aimed at building initial trust among new customers may not be equally effective for retaining trust among more established customers.

Recent empirical research on trust has examined how online trust is formed based on Web site functionalities such as order fulfillment, privacy, navigation features (e.g., Bart, Shankar, Sultan, & Urban, 2005), online firm attributes such as reputation, structural assurance, and service quality (e.g., Kim, Xu, & Koh, 2005), or external influence such as peer or editorial recommendations (Smith, Menon, & Sivakumar, 2005). Walczuk and Lundgren (2005) summarized potential antecedents of trust into categories such as perception-based, personality-based, knowledge-based, and experience-based factors. Though these studies have provided some preliminary insights into how consumers can build initial trust in anonymous online firms, such insights have mostly been fragmented, situation-specific, and atheoretical. This study addresses this gap in trust research by theoretically postulating and empirically testing the relative and temporal effects of three generalized mechanisms of online trust formation using a field survey of online banking users. Specifically, the research questions of interest to this study are: (1) what are the key cognitive drivers of trust in online consumer-business relationships, (2) what are the relative effects of these drivers on consumers' initial trust in online firms, and (3) how do these effects change as consumers' relationship with online firms matures with time.

The rest of the chapter proceeds as follows. The second section outlines the theoretical bases of trust and their temporal effects on online relationships, and develops hypotheses for empirical testing. The third section describes the empirical study used for hypotheses testing. The fourth section describes the data analysis techniques and results. The final section discusses the implications of the findings for research and practice and the study's limitations.

THEORETICAL FOUNDATIONS

Conceptualizing Trust

Trust, as a research concept, has been examined in a wide range of disciplines including anthropology, psychology, economics, sociology, marketing, and organizational behavior. Such diverse disciplinary perspectives and research settings have led to multiplicity in the definitions of trust, its levels of analysis (i.e., individual, group, firm), its causal roles (i.e., trust as a cause, outcome, or moderator), its conceptualizations (i.e., trust as a personality trait, social structure, or economic choice), and its composition (e.g., fairness, competence, benevolence, honesty, predictability) (Lewicki & Bunker 1996; Mayer, Davis, & Schoorman, 1995; Rousseau et al. 1998). Synthesizing these diverse perspectives, Mayer et al. (1995) proposed an integrative definition of trust as "the willingness of a party to be vulnerable to the actions of another party based on the expectation that the other will perform a particular action important to the trustor, irrespective of the ability to monitor or control that other party" (p. 712).

The previous definition underscores two facets of trust: (1) willingness to be vulnerable (trust intention), and (2) expectations about the trustee behavior (trust beliefs). The distinction between trust beliefs and intention follow from Fishbein and Ajzen's (1975) theory of reasoned action (TRA), which specifies that one's intention to engage in a given behavior is influenced by her attitude toward that behavior, which in turn is based on her beliefs regarding the target behavior. An extension of this theory, the technology acceptance model (TAM) (Davis, Bagozzi, & Warshaw, 1989), has been employed to study trust formation in online settings (e.g., Gefen, 2000, McKnight, Cummings, & Chervany, 1998, Pavlou, 2003).

TRA includes subjective norm as an additional determinant of intention. However, this construct has been dropped from TAM as being less relevant and empirically non-significant (Davis et al., 1989). Recent trust research has also tended to drop the attitude construct in favor of a more parsimonious model linking beliefs directly to intentions (e.g., Gefen, 2000, McKnight et al., 1998, Pavlou, 2003), suggesting that technology usage is best understood in terms of specific beliefs rather than an overall attitude. Further, TAM explicates *perceived usefulness* (expected benefits from a given technology) and perceived ease of use (expected simplicity of learning and using a technology) as the two cognitive beliefs specifically relevant to technology usage, which have also been examined in trust research (e.g., Gefen, 2000, Pavlou, 2003).

While trust intention in any exchange-based relationship commonly refers to trustors' *willingness to transact* with the trustee, what are the salient trust beliefs in online settings? A multitude of such beliefs has been proposed in the trust literature, including competence, dependability, predictability, benevolence, loyalty, openness, discreetness, integrity, and honesty (cf. Mayer et al., 1995; McKnight, Choudhury, & Kacmar, 2002). Most classifications and typologies of trust tend to converge on three core beliefs: competence, benevolence, and integrity (Blau, 1964; Mayer et al., 1995; McKnight et al., 1998). These three beliefs suggest that consumers may trust an online firm (a) if they are reasonably confident in the firm's ability to handle their transactions accurately (competence), (b) if they expect that the firm will not take advantage of their vulnerability during or after the transaction (benevolence), and (c) if they perceive the firm as being generally honest (integrity). While some researchers have viewed these beliefs as independent predictors of trust, others (e.g., Bhattacherjee, 2002) have viewed them as trust dimensions and empirically observed no significant difference between first-order (as dimensions) and second order (as predictors) models of trust.

Prior research (Bart et al., 2005; Gefen et al., 2003; Mayer et al., 1995) suggests that higher levels of trust in an online firm can enhance consumers' willingness to engage in future transactions with that firm. This is so because most transactional or exchange-based relationships involve uncertainty regarding the firm's potentially opportunistic use of consumers' private financial or personal data (e.g., selling e-mail addresses or overcharging credit cards), and trust allows consumers to rule out or underemphasize undesirable behaviors on the part of the online firm. This expectation leads to the hypothesis:

H1: Consumers' trust in an online firm is positively related to their willingness to transact with that firm.

The technology usage literature suggests perceived usefulness (expected benefits) as the primary reason for technology users to use a new technology (Davis et al. 1989). Extending this expectation, perceived usefulness of transactions may also be an important reason for consumers to transact with online firms, rather than or in spite of their trust in that firm. Likewise, they may decide against online transactions if they perceive such transactions as being less useful or beneficial, despite having high levels of trust in that firm. Perceived usefulness may therefore confound the effect of trust on consumers' willingness to transact. To control for this rival explanation and to distinguish its potential effects from those of trust, perceived usefulness from online transaction is added to the hypothesized model as a control variable (see Figure 1). While other potential variables may also confound the association between trust and willingness to transact, such variables are not included here due to lack of theoretical significance.

Determinants of Trust

How is trust formed in online commerce? In a seminal study of traditional interpersonal relationships, Zucker (1986) described three mechanisms of trust production: (1) process-based trust—where trust is based on past or (expected) future exchanges between trustor and trustee, (2) characteristics-based (or identification-based) trust—where trust is based on the trustor's identification with characteristics of the trustee, and (3) institution-based (or transference-based) trust—where trust in known and trusted institutions are transferred to unknown trustees by virtue of their associations to trusted institutions.

Though identification-based trust appears to be salient in interpersonal contexts (e.g., we tend to trust people belonging to our same race,

Figure 1. A model of individual trust in online firms

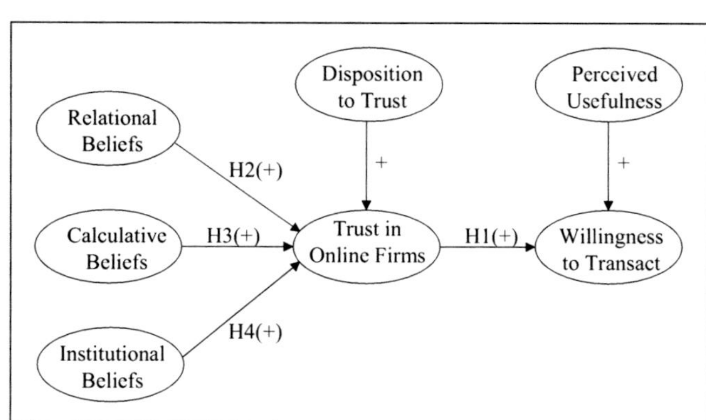

ethnic background, profession, social circle, etc.) or inter-organizational contexts (e.g., firms trust other firms belonging to the same industry), it is less relevant in consumer-firm relationships since consumers have very little in common with online firms to form a shared identity. Further, the zero-sum nature of firm-consumer relationship, given that consumers' goals from online transactions (e.g., lower prices) often contradict those of online firms (e.g., higher profits), makes it harder for consumers to establish identification-based trust. Hence, identification-based trust is excluded from this study as being less relevant in online firm-consumer relationships.

More recently, trust researchers have distinguished between two types of process-based trust—relational trust, based on prior exchanges, and calculative trust, based on expectations of future exchanges (Lewicki et al., 1996; McKnight et al., 1998). The former is backward looking, trustee-specific, and grounded in actual transaction history, while the latter is forward looking, generalized in nature, and based on transaction expectations rather than reality. McKnight et al. (1998) holds that these two modes of trust production may not coexist since trustors form calculative beliefs only when they lack prior experience to form relational beliefs, as is the case with first-time transactions. Hence, relational and calculative trust can be viewed as two alternate mechanisms of trust formation that are salient in different contexts.

In light of the previous arguments, consumer' trust in online firms is expected to be shaped by three trust-building mechanisms: relational, calculative, and institutional. The outcomes of these three mechanisms can be represented in the trustor's mind as relational, calculative, and institutional beliefs respectively, as described further below (see Figure 1).

Relational Belief

Relational belief is based on prior interactions or exchanges between the trusting parties, and is believed to be the most dominant, stable and potent mode of trust formation in any trust-based relationship (Luhmann, 1979; Zucker, 1986). This form of trust is based on observation and knowledge of the trustee's practices (e.g., billing, returns handling) and behaviors (e.g., shipping condition). Since such practices are generally learned over time, this type of trust is also called knowledge-based trust (Luhmann, 1979; Lewicki et al., 1996). Successful cycles of risk taking, exchange, and fulfillment help convey to the trustor the trustee's competence, benevolence, and integrity, thereby strengthening trust in the relationship (Rousseau et al., 1998). In contrast, failed transactions (e.g., delayed shipments, incorrect billing) adversely influence trustors' relational beliefs and trust in the trustee. Hence:

H2: Consumers' relational belief in an online firm is positively related to their trust in that firm.

Calculative Belief

In the absence of relational belief, trustors often rely on social cues such as the online firm's reputation or size of its customer base, for forming trust perceptions (Blau, 1964; Luhmann, 1979). The economics literature (e.g., Williamson, 1998) suggests that such cues help trustors subjectively estimate or "calculate" the trustee's potential economic rewards and costs of engaging in a trusted behavior; hence the term calculative belief. Reputed online firms such as Amazon, CitiBank, and Charles Schwab are generally expected to act in a trustworthy manner because of the large potential impact of untrustworthy behaviors on their reputation via negative publicity and customer base (Kollock, 1999). However, less known firms are not necessarily viewed as untrustworthy, if they can "signal" appropriate cues, such as number of customer accounts, number of items on sale, and number of transactions handled, to build calculative trust among their customer base. Note that calculative belief is forward-looking and does not require prior transaction history, and is particularly salient in the absence of relational belief. Hence, such belief may explain consumers' first-time decision to shop, exchange, or interact online (McKnight et al., 1998). Hence:

H3: Consumers' calculative belief in an online firm is positively related to their trust in that firm.

Institutional Belief

Economists hold that trust is an institutional attribute that can be transferred across organizational boundaries from established institutions or "trusted third parties" to less known or unknown entities by virtue of their associations with the trusted institutions (Lewicki et al., 1996; Zucker, 1986). Trusted third parties may include federal or state governmental agencies (e.g., Securities and Exchange Commission, Federal Deposit Insurance Corporation), reputed brands (e.g., Amazon, Wal-Mart), industry consortiums (e.g., Visa, Better Business Bureau), or organizations specifically designated to certify and communicate trustworthiness in businesses (e.g., TRUSTe, Verisign). Transferred trust is often viewed as an endorsement, certification, or guarantee by the trusted party that the trustee will likely not engage in behaviors that can potentially jeopardize its association with the trusted party.[1] Online firms have attempted to build institutional or transference-based trust by cobranding their site (e.g., via Web hosting) with popular online brands such as Yahoo or Amazon (e.g., Amazon zShops, Yahoo Stores) and by displaying Web assurance seals such as TRUSTe or BBBOnline Reliability or industry affiliations with FDIC or Visa on their Websites. For instance, 3000 firms obtained BBBOnline Reliability seals during 1997-99, while TRUSTe granted 675 seals during this time (Gogan, 1999). Hence:

H4: Consumers' institutional belief in an online firm is positively related to their trust in that firm.

Each of the previous beliefs represents a different cognitive base for consumers to form trust perceptions regarding an online firm. However, such trust may also result from consumers' general disposition to trust others. Disposition to trust is a generalized expectancy or belief that others are well meaning and honest, and in the absence of any reason otherwise, will likely behave appropriately across situational contexts (McKnight et al., 1998). Such trust typically is derived from one's inherent personal interpretive frame (e.g., worldview) and implicit assumptions about the world (e.g., faith in societal institutions), rather than in trustee attributes, affiliations, or behaviors. Though this construct's empirical effect on one's overall trust appears to be mixed, presumably due to its lack of domain specificity, McKnight et al. (1998) note that disposition to trust may be a significant driver of trust in ambiguous, novel, or unstructured situations or when other drivers of trust are lacking. Hence, this construct is included in our hypothesized research model as a control variable (see Figure 1). However, familiarity was excluded from this study, despite suggestions from the trust literature, because relational beliefs and familiarity are both based on the trustor's prior experience with the trustee and tend to exhibit strong positive correlation. Hence, including familiarity could have masked the true effect of relational beliefs due to multicollinearity. Studies that exclude relational beliefs as a variable of interest should however consider including familiarity as a control variable.

Temporal Effects on Trust

Despite a static depiction of trust in the previous section, trust is in fact a dynamic construct that evolves with time as the transacting parties become familiar with each other's behaviors (Luhman, 1979). For instance, Rousseau et al. (1998) suggest three temporal phases in trust-based relationships:

1. **Building:** When trust in the referent is formed or reformed,
2. **Stability:** When trust attains a steady-state equilibrium, and
3. **Dissolution:** When trust declines.

Why does trust change with time? The notion that one's beliefs may change with time comes from cognitive dissonance theory (CDT) (Festinger, 1957), which describes two causative mechanisms that may engender potential belief change: one's personal first-hand experience and information communicated from external sources. One's initial belief regarding others' behaviors is often based on information (e.g., social cues) communicated from external sources such as the trustor, its affiliates, or neutral third parties. Over time, as the person gains first-hand experience of other party's behaviors, he or she evaluates the extent of match (consonance) or mismatch (dissonance) between his or her initial belief and actual experience, and accordingly adjusts his or her beliefs to more accurately reflect the actual experience. Consonant experiences reinforce previously held beliefs, while dissonant experiences cause these beliefs to change. Experience-based beliefs tend to be more influential and stable than information-based beliefs, since the former is based on reality while the latter is based on expectations that may be biased, inaccurate, or unreliable (Fazio & Zanna, 1981). Over time, as one learns what to expect from another party's behavior, dissonance reduces and beliefs reach steady state.

Though CDT was not originally intended to explain trust formation, McKnight et al. (1998) used it to explain changes in trust beliefs. McKnight et al. noted that trust tends to be fragile or tentative during the initial stages of an exchange-based relationship, because it is based on assumptions or expectations (rather than reality) about the trustee's intentions, since the trustor lacks adequate information to assess the uncertainty associated with trustee behaviors. Initial trust is not based so much on evidence as on the lack of contrary evidence (Gambetta, 1998), which may create illusions of control that tend to dissipate with first-hand observed behaviors. As the trustor engages in and learns from repeated transactions with the trustee, over time, she may replace her assumptions and illusions with observed facts and experiences, and form a more informed and stable judgment regarding the trustee's intentions. Barring unfavorable experiences, the above process leads to the stabilization and possible increase in overall trust in the online trustee.[2]

However, not all of the three types of trust beliefs (relational, calculative, and institutional) change at the same rate or even in the same direction, because the belief structure driving initial fragile trust is qualitatively different from that related to the more stable later-stage trust. CDT suggests that during the initial stage of an exchange-based relationship, trust is based on externally acquired information, including social cues (e.g., brand name, reputational assets) and third party endorsements. This information corresponds respectively to calculative and institutional beliefs. Relational belief is weak or unstable at this time, given the lack of prior transactional experience with the online firm. However, as the trustor engages in repeated transactions with the trustee, her information-based beliefs are increasingly replaced with more stable experience-based beliefs. Hence, over time, relational belief assume dominance over calculative and institutional beliefs, as trust evolves from an arms-length transaction into a long-term strategic partnership characterized by mutual loyalty, faith, and reciprocated concerns (McAllister, 1995). Further, trust based on relational belief may be resilient to minor setbacks, particularly if the trustee takes proactive steps to restore good faith and fairness in the relationship (Rousseau et al., 1998). This expectation leads to the final three hypotheses:

H5: The effect of consumers' relational belief on trust in an online firm increases as they gain experience with that firm.

H6: The effect of consumers' calculative belief on trust in an online firm decreases as they gain experience with that firm.

H7: The effect of consumers' institutional belief on trust in an online firm decreases as they gain experience with that firm.

Hypotheses H5 through H7 represent the moderating effects of consumers' experience on the association between their trust belief and her trust intention. Further, note that though identification belief was not included in this study because of its lack of salience to consumer-based online commerce, such belief may be salient and should be considered in business-to-business (e.g., supply chain partnerships) or consumer-to-consumer (e.g., consumer auctions) online relationships. The next section describes the research methods employed to test the previous associations.

RESEARCH METHODS

Empirical Setting

The seven hypotheses discussed above were empirically tested the above research using field data collected from a survey of online retail banking customers. The banking context was chosen because it involves an exchange-based relationship, where trust between consumers (trustors) and the bank (trustee) is critical for the long-term success of the relationship. Survey respondents were customers of the online banking (OLB) division of one of the largest national banks in the United States. OLB offered its customers an integrated suite of online personal banking services including online checking and savings accounts, certificates of deposit, credit cards, home equity loans, home mortgage, insurance, investment services, portfolio management, and retirement planning services. OLB customers enjoyed higher yields on their accounts (compared to traditional off-line customers), greater flexibility and convenience (e.g., 24-hour integrated online access to all accounts), and sophisticated financial management tools such as online bill payment, online funds transfer, and customized reporting tools.

The sample consisted of 1,000 online customers randomly selected by OLB from its customer base of over 1 million users. Each customer received an electronic mail message from OLB soliciting their participation in a survey of online banking practices, appended to one of their regular monthly statements (also distributed via e-mail). The message outlined the purpose of the study, provided a hyperlink to an online survey form, and as an incentive, offered respondents the opportunity to register in a drawing of small cash prizes. The bank's privacy rules precluded it from making the customer list available to the researcher.

The online mode of data collection, though relatively novel in the context of scientific research, was appropriate since the subject of interest were online users, and Internet is the ideal way to reach such users. Ninety nine percent of the respondents indicated that they were comfortable with the process of filling out online surveys, and reasonably so since online banking itself involves completing online forms. Hence, the online data collection method did not introduce any novelty bias in subjects' responses.

Following a single round of data collection, 122 usable responses were obtained for a response rate of about 12%. The low response rate may be attributed to the fact that the solicitation message was attached to the end of customers' monthly statement, and therefore, may have been missed by some customers. Multiple rounds of data collection to improve response rate were not possible since the sponsor was unwilling to send follow-up requests to non-respondents to avoid being perceived as a "spammer."

Table 1. Scale items and statistics

Construct	Item	Mean	Standard Deviation	Factor Loading[a]
Willingness to transact	I intend to use OLB for some of my future banking transactions.	4.89	1.02	0.80
	I am likely to utilize the value-added services provided by OLB (e.g., online bill payment).	4.96	0.97	0.77
	I am inclined to purchase OLB's goods and services.	5.21	1.10	0.68
Trust	OLB has the skills/expertise to perform banking transactions in an expected manner.	4.56	1.12	0.78
	OLB is open and receptive to customer needs.	5.10	1.14	0.76
	OLB is fair in its conduct of customer transactions.	4.66	1.09	0.78
	Overall, OLB is trustworthy.	5.05	1.10	0.75
Perceived usefulness	Using OLB improves my performance in banking activities.	4.47	1.49	0.95
	Using OLB improves my productivity in banking activities.	4.34	1.37	0.93
	Using OLB improves my effectiveness in banking activities.	4.32	1.50	0.90
	I find OLB useful for much of my banking activities.	4.38	1.47	0.88
Relational belief	Based on previous transactions, I have confidence in OLB's handling of banking transactions.	4.09	1.40	0.92
	Based on previous transactions, I have confidence in OLB's handling of customer requests and complaints.	4.18	1.53	0.94
	OLB has always conducted my banking transactions in the way I expected them to be.	4.03	1.55	0.88
Calculative belief	OLB will probably not risk losing its customer base by performing banking transactions inappropriately.	3.19	1.20	0.85
	OLB will probably not risk losing its reputation by performing banking transactions inappropriately.	3.00	1.31	0.85
	It is in OLB's best interests to perform banking services appropriately.	3.07	1.25	0.89
Institutional belief	Federal agencies such as FDIC will ensure that OLB perform banking transactions appropriately.	3.91	1.41	0.90
	Online agencies such as TRUSTe affiliated to OLB will ensure that OLB perform banking transactions appropriately.	3.72	1.44	0.88
	Financial networks such as Visa or Mastercard affiliated to OLB will ensure that OLB perform banking transactions appropriately.	3.90	1.48	0.87
Disposition to trust	I generally trust others unless they give a reason to distrust them.	4.20	1.47	0.88
	I believe that people and firms are generally trustworthy.	4.16	1.43	0.92
	I am rarely suspicious of what others tell me.	4.13	1.43	0.92
Experience	Number of months I have been using OLB (fill-in item).	-	-	-

[a] Standardized factor loadings derived from CFA analysis. All loadings were significant at $p<0.001$
CFA model fit: $\chi^2/df=1.57$, RMSEA=0.07, NNFI=0.94, CFI=0.95, GFI=0.86, AGFI=0.81.

The respondent group ranged in age from 17 to 63 (mean of 33.7 years), were 62% male and 38% female, had annual incomes of $10,000 to $250,000 (mean of $75,000), subscribed to a wide range of professions (e.g., corporate employees, self-employed, academics, executives, retirees), and had diverse educational levels (from high-school graduates to doctoral degrees). At the time of the survey, respondents were using the OLB for 2 to 36 months (mean of 8.34 months) and had an online balance between $100 and $50,000 (mean of $7,000). Difference of means tests found that respondents did not differ significantly in age or income level from that of the target population (average customer demographics provided by OLB), alleviating concerns of potential non-response bias.

Instrument Construction

Eight variables were of interest to this study: willingness to transact, trust, relational belief, calculative belief, institutional belief, perceived usefulness, disposition to trust, and experience. Experience was measured using a single fill-in item, and the remaining variables were measured using multiple-item, seven-point Likert scales anchored between "strongly disagree" and "strongly agree." Most scale items were adapted from prior research, with slight rewording to adapt to the study's context. Given the lack of prior scales for measuring relational, calculative, and institutional beliefs at the time of this study, new scales were constructed for these constructs. Scale construction was based on Nunnally's (1978) "domain sampling" technique, starting with a conceptual definition of the construct of interest, explicating its domain of content, and selecting candidate items to best represent the entire domain. Individual scale items are listed in Table 1.

Willingness to trust was operationalized as subjects' intention to use OLB, based on Bhattacherjee's (2002) willingness to transact scale. This scale consisted of three items: two items tapping into two of the most frequent domains of OLB use, namely banking transactions (e.g., deposits, withdrawals) and value-added services (e.g., online bill payment), while the third item reflecting subjects' overall inclination to purchase OLB's goods and services.

The trust construct was operationalized in terms of its three component dimensions: ability, benevolence, and integrity, and measured using scale items adapted from Bhattacherjee (2002). Though the original scale had seven items (two items each for ability, benevolence, and integrity, plus one item measuring overall trust in OLB), dropping the item with the lower loading for each of the three trust dimensions did not result in a significant drop in scale reliability or validity. Hence, a parsimonious short-form four-item version of Bhattacherjee's (2002) scale was used to measure subjects' trust in OLB, by using one item for each of the three dimensions of trust and a fourth item measuring overall trust. The ability item examined whether subjects perceived OLB as having the necessary skills or expertise to perform banking transactions in an expected manner, the benevolence item examined perceived openness, and receptivity of OLB to subjects' needs, and the integrity item examined the perceived fairness of OLB in its banking transactions.

Relational belief was defined as trustor's confidence in the trustee based on past transactional experience. This construct was operationalized using two items that examined subjects' confidence in OLB's handling of banking transactions and in managing customer requests and complaints, based on their prior transaction history, plus a third item that examined the extent to which OLB's prior banking transactions met subjects' expectations.

Calculative belief referred to the extent to which trustors believed that the trustee would not jeopardize its reputation or customer base by engaging in opportunistic or inappropriate behaviors. This construct was measured using two items that examined subjects' perceptions on whether OLB would risk losing its reputation and customer base by performing inappropriate activities, plus a third item examining whether they believed that OLB would perform banking services appropriately, irrespective of their potential impacts on reputation or customer base.

Institutional belief related to the transference of trust from affiliated trusted third parties such as governmental agencies (e.g., FDIC), trust-building agencies (e.g., WebTrust, TRUSTe), or industry organizations (e.g., BBB, Visa) to the trustee. This construct was operationalized using three items were that examined the extent to which subjects trusted the bank's affiliation with federal agencies such as FDIC (since OLB's banking activities were regulated by this agency), trusted third parties such as TRUSTe (since OLB's privacy practices were certified by this organization), and credit card networks such as Mastercard or Visa (since OLB's credit operations utilized these financial networks).

Perceived usefulness, a control variable, was measured using Davis et al.'s (1989) perceived usefulness scale. This scale employed four items to examine perceptions of performance, productivity, efficiency, and overall usefulness of online banking use. Disposition to trust was measured using a three-item scale modified from Gefen (2000), which examined customers' general propensity to trust others (e.g., people, firms), without specifically referring to OLB as the trustee. Statistical validation of scales is described in the next section.

DATA ANALYSIS AND RESULTS

Instrument Validation

The measurement scales previously described were validated using the confirmatory factor analysis (CFA) approach. CFA combines ex ante theoretical expectations with empirical data for factor validation, and is therefore a stronger statistical technique than alternative approaches such as exploratory factor analysis. CFA was performed via the EQS procedure (Bentler, 1980), using a correlation matrix of individual items as input. Each scale item was linked to its hypothesized latent construct in a reflective manner and all constructs were allowed to covary freely. CFA requires a minimum sample size of 5-10 times the number of items; the current sample size of 122 observations (for 23 items) met this criterion.

The first step in scale validation was to examine the goodness-of-fit of the CFA model. This was assessed using a variety of fit metrics, including normed chi-square (χ^2/df), RMSEA (root mean square error of approximation), NNFI (non-normed fit index), CFI (comparative fit index), GFI (goodness of fit index), and AGFI (adjusted goodness of fit index). For the CFA model, χ^2/df was 1.57 (χ^2 = 328.23; df = 209), RMSEA was 0.07 (90% confidence interval between 0.05 and 0.08), NNFI was 0.94, CFI was 0.95, GFI was 0.86, and AGFI was 0.81 (see Table 1). Acceptance norms of these metrics are: model χ^2/df should be less than 3.0, RMSEA should be less than 0.8, NNFI and GFI should each exceed 0.9, and GFI and AGFI each exceeded 0.8 (Bentler & Bonnett 1980). Our CFI model met each of the previous criteria, hence demonstrating a good fit between the observed data and the hypothesized model.

Second, convergent validity was assessed using three criteria suggested by Fornell and Larcker (1981): (1) all indicator factor loadings (λ) should be significant and exceed 0.70 (such that the underlying scales explain more than 50% of item variances), (2) all construct reliabilities should exceed 0.80, and (3) average variance extracted (AVE) by each construct should exceed 0.50. As seen from Table 1, all but one λ-values in the CFA model exceeded 0.70 and were significant at p = .001. The lowest λ-value was 0.68 for the third willingness to transact item, which was close to the 0.70 threshold and therefore considered acceptable. Composite reliabilities (ρ_c) ranged between 0.80 and 0.95 for the seven scales (see Table 2), equaling or exceeding the required minimum of 0.80. AVE values ranged between 0.57 and 0.83, also exceeding the minimum 0.50 value (see Table 2). Hence, all three conditions for convergent validity were met.

Finally, for discriminant validity, the AVE for each construct should exceed the squared correlation between that and any other construct (Fornell et al., 1981). The factor correlation matrix in Table 2 indicates that the smallest AVE of 0.57 (for willingness to trust) was greater than the highest squared correlation between any pair of constructs (0.41 between willingness to trust and perceived usefulness). Hence, the discriminant validity condition was also met by all of our measured constructs.

Hypotheses Testing

The seven hypotheses specified earlier were tested in two phases. The first four hypotheses (H1-H4) were tested jointly using the structural equation modeling (SEM) approach, using EQS, while the remaining three hypotheses (H5-H7) were tested using moderated regression with aggregated scales. SEM is particularly appropriate for testing theoretically justified models (Bentler et al., 1980), as was the case in this study. Though our sample size of 122 subjects was adequate for testing the complete main effects model (with 24 measured items), it was not large enough to accommodate another nine interaction items; hence the moderated regression approach was used instead for H5-H7.

For purposes of SEM analysis, the measurement model was retained from the earlier CFA, while the structural model was modified to reflect the causalities indicated in Figure 1. The goodness-of-fit metrics for this model were as follows: χ^2/df of 1.72 (χ^2=373.29; df=217), RMSEA of 0.08, NNFI of 0.92, CFI of 0.93, GFI of 0.83, and AGFI of 0.78 (see Figure 2). Though the RMSEA and AGFI values were marginally outside of the desired range, the SEM model was considered acceptable in light of acceptable levels of the remaining fit metrics.

Next, standardized path coefficient, path significance, and variance explained (R^2 value) of each association (H1-H4) in the hypothesized model were examined. All four of our hypothesized effects and two control effects were significant at $p<0.05$. Perceived usefulness and trust jointly explained 49% of the variance in subjects' willingness to transact with the OLB. Most of this explanation

Table 2. Scale properties and correlations

Construct	Number of Items	Composite Reliability	AVE	Factor Correlations						
				WT	TR	PU	RL	CL	IN	DT
WT	3	0.80	0.57	1.00						
TR	4	0.85	0.59	.53[a]	1.00					
PU	4	0.95	0.83	.64[a]	.45[a]	1.00				
RB	3	0.93	0.83	.33[a]	.62[a]	.21[c]	1.00			
CB	3	0.89	0.74	.28[b]	.38[a]	.20[c]	.12[ns]	1.00		
IB	3	0.91	0.78	.33[a]	.41[a]	.27[b]	.10[ns]	.22[b]	1.00	
DT	3	0.93	0.82	.26[b]	.44[a]	.32[a]	.16[c]	.28[b]	.20[c]	1.00

Legend: WT: Willingness to trust; TR: Trust; PU: Perceived usefulness; RB: Relationship belief; CB: Calculative belief; IB: Institutional belief; DT: Disposition to trust.
[a] p<.001; [b] p<.01; [c] p<.05; [ns] p>.05.

Figure 2. SEM analysis of research model for initial-stage users

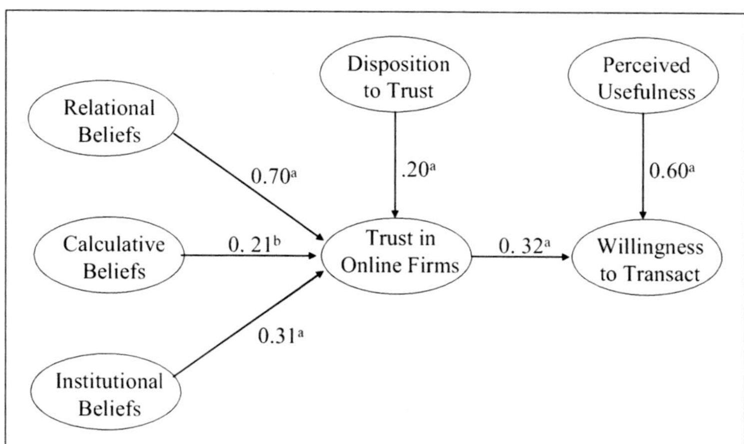

came from perceived usefulness (β=0.60; R^2=36%), as expected from prior research (e.g., Davis et al., 1989), while trust explained a relatively small proportion of the variance (β=0.32; R^2=10%). In turn, trust was predicted primarily by relational belief (β=0.70; R^2=49%), followed in decreasing order of explained variance by institutional belief (β=0.31; R^2=10%), calculative belief (β=0.21; R^2=4%), and disposition to trust (β=0.20; R^2=4%). Collectively, the four determinants explained 67% of the trust variance.

The previous effects demonstrate that subjects' trust in OLB was a significant predictor of their willingness to transact with the OLB (β=0.32), providing empirical support for hypothesis H1. However, this effect was smaller than that of the control variable perceived usefulness (β=0.60), suggesting that the primary reason for subjects to transact with OLB was not trust, but their expected benefits from such transactions. It is therefore possible that consumers may not transact with online firms unless they expect adequate benefits from such transaction, despite having high levels of trust in those firms. However, once transactional benefits are established, trust plays a significant role in motivating them to proceed with the transaction.

Relational, calculative, and institutional beliefs had significant positive effects on trust in OLB, providing support for hypotheses H2, H3, and H4 respectively. Relational belief had the strongest effect, (β=0.70), suggesting that consumers' trust in online relationships is driven primarily by relational considerations. Calculative belief had the smallest effect (β=0.21), but this could be an artifact of the subject sample in that respondents were already using OLB for at least two months at the time of the survey. It is possible that subjects were already experiencing a "wearing out" of their calculative trust and a build-up of relational trust, as expected of later-stage users. Institutional beliefs had a moderate effect (β=0.31), suggesting that third party institutions such as FDIC and Visa also play a significant role in influencing user trust towards online firms.

Hypotheses H5-H7 examined whether the effects of relational, calculative, and institutional beliefs on trust were moderated by subjects' experience with the online entity. These interaction effects were tested using moderated regression. Items in each scale were aggregated (averaged), the aggregated beliefs were multiplied with experience (a single item measure) to generate three interaction terms, and a univariate regression was run using aggregate trust score as the dependent variable, and eight independent variables: relational belief, calculative belief, institutional belief, disposition to trust (control variable), experience (covariate term), and interactions between experience and relational, calculative, and institutional beliefs. Results of the moderated regression analysis are presented in Table 3.

The moderated regression model was significant ($F=32.01$, $p<0.001$) and explained 69% of the variance (R^2) in the dependent variable (trust), attesting to the overall quality of the model. A nested F-test[3] comparing the above R^2 value (69%) with that of the standard regression model with interaction terms excluded (63%), found that the R^2 improvement in the moderated model was statistically significant at $p<0.001$. This provided evidence that the hypothesized moderating effects indeed provided a superior explanation of trust over and above that accorded by the main effects.

Two of the three hypothesized moderating effects (hypotheses H5 and H6) were significant in the moderated regression model with standardized effect sizes of 0.33 and -0.41 respectively, while H7 was not significant. Hence, the effects of relational and calculative beliefs on trust were moderated by users' experience with OLB, but that of institutional belief was not. The direction of moderating effects for H5 and H6 was also as expected (i.e., positive for relational belief and negative for calculative belief), suggesting that the effect of relational belief on trust increases as trustees gain first-hand experience with an online firm, while that of calculative belief decreases with experience. The results also suggested that the decrease in calculative trust over time is compensated by a corresponding increase in relational trust. However, contrary to expectations, the effect of institutional belief on trust was invariant with time, suggesting that the transference of trust for banking customers from established institutions

Table 3. Moderated regression results

Model Summary:					
	Sum of Squares	**df**	**F-statistic**	**Significance**	**R^2 (Adjusted R^2)**
Regression	215.71	8	32.01	0.000	0.69
Residual	95.20	113			(0.67)
Total	310.91	121			
Model Coefficients:					
Independent Variables	**Variable Mean**	**Standard Deviation**	**Standardized Beta**	**Standard Error**	**Significance**
EX	8.34	5.48	0.39	0.12	0.000
RB	3.96	1.47	0.48	0.09	0.000
CB	3.09	1.14	0.29	0.12	0.016
IB	3.84	1.34	0.15	0.10	0.112
DT	4.17	1.36	0.10	0.07	0.044
RB x EX	-	-	0.33	0.06	0.008
CB x EX	-	-	-0.41	0.04	0.001
IB x EX	-	-	-0.03	0.01	0.878

Legend: EX: Experience; RB: Relationship belief; CB: Calculative belief; IB: Institutional belief; DT: Disposition to trust.

such as FDIC and Visa may continue to occur even during later stages of online relationships.

DISCUSSION AND CONCLUSION

Key Findings and Implications

This study started with three research questions: (1) what are the key cognitive drivers of trust in online consumer-business relationships, (2) what are the relative effects of these drivers on consumers' trust in online firms, and (3) how do these effects change as the relationship matures over time. To answer these questions, three key drivers of online trust (relational, calculative, and institutional beliefs) were theorized based on the work of Zucker (1986) and others. These drivers were then linked to trust and willingness to transact by drawing on related research in technology use to create a model of online trust formation. Potential changes in the effects of the trust drivers over time were explored using Festinger's (1957) cognitive dissonance theory. Seven research hypotheses drawn from the previous analysis were then tested empirically using data collected from a field survey of online banking users. Data analysis supported our theoretical expectations that: (1) relational, calculative, and institutional beliefs regarding online firms are indeed key drivers of consumer trust in online firms, (2) relational belief had the strongest effect on trust, followed by institutional and calculative beliefs, and (3) the effect of relational belief increased with time as users gained experience with OLB, that of calculative belief decreased with time, and that of institutional belief remained invariant with time.

Several interesting findings were observed, some of which were related to our theorized hypotheses while others were not. First, though trust had a significant effect on consumers' willingness to engage in online transactions, the effect of trust was smaller than that of perceived usefulness (a control variable). This suggested that the primary driver of online transactions was not consumers' trust in the online entity, but their perceptions of usefulness or potential benefits from that transaction. It is therefore possible that a consumer having a high level of trust in an online firm may not transact with the firm if that transaction is not perceived to be adequately useful. Online firms should realize that trust only accounts for a small proportion of the variance in consumer behavior relative to perceived usefulness, and should attempt to create marketing programs that balance their trust-building strategies with educational strategies to inform potential users about the utility of their services. Further, as trust researchers examine the causes and effects of trust, they should control for salient non-trust constructs such as perceived usefulness, in order to derive more meaningful and accurate estimates of trust effects. It is possible that some of the mixed findings reported in the trust literature may be attributed to the lack of control for such non-trust constructs.

Second, customers' relational, calculative, and institutional beliefs regarding online firms influence their trust formation, and hence, indirectly influence their willingness to transact with these firms. This finding is important for business managers because it provides three policy levers that managers can utilize to build trust among their potential customers. Relational belief is based on prior transaction history, and hence, favors older firms with longer transactional histories over newer firms. While new firms can do little to build relational belief among potential customers, they can attempt to build calculative trust among potential customers by publicizing relevant information such as number of customers, transactions, and so forth on their Websites, or institutional trust by forming affiliations with trusted third parties such as reputed brands, industry associations, and regulatory agencies. However, the effectiveness of institutional trust may vary with customers' ability to recognize and appreciate the institutional affiliations, and hence, online firms should try to communicate the significance of their affiliations to unwary customers. Institutional belief-based trust will also be difficult to build in less-developed economies, where institutional mechanisms such as certification agencies and trusted third parties may not yet be available.

Given that we presented three alternative mechanisms for building consumer trust in online firms, which specific strategy should firms pursue to benefit most from their trust-building initiatives? Since relational belief was the most dominant driver of trust, online firms should focus on long-term customer relationships as a way of building trust. Despite the virtual nature of online relationships, newer techniques such as personalized marketing and customer relationship management may help online firms know their customers better, design better solutions for each customer, and thereby improve trust and retention. While building such relationships may take time, new online firms may attempt to build institutional and calculative beliefs to build an initial base of trust among their targeted customers. The larger effect of institutional belief on trust relative to calculative belief suggests that the former may be a more useful trust building strategy than the latter, especially for new customers.

Finally, this study also reported that as consumers gain first-hand experience with online firms over time, they rely more on relational belief, less on calculative belief, and about the same on institutional beliefs for building long-term trust. This suggests that different strategies may be required for building trust among long-term versus new customers with differential transaction histories. The focus of trust building initiatives for new customers should be on building institutional and calculative belief based trust, by noting the online firm's association with trusted third parties such as the BBB or FDIC (for institutional trust) and demonstrating metrics such as the size of customer base, average asset size per customer, and customer dropout rates (for calculative beliefs). However, long-term customers should be targeted with relational trust via marketing programs customized to their prior transactional experience, such as providing online bank customers with a greater array of tools to manage their money, a broader set of investment choices, and online access to related products such as year-end tax forms. Also, online firms should devise a transition path for shifting the focus of trust initiatives from institutional or calculative to relational beliefs for the same customer, as she gains experience with the firm's behavior.

Limitations of the Study

Like most other empirical studies, this study is not without limitations. The first limitation is potential non-response bias, given the low response rate in this study. It is possible that survey respondents may have differed systematically from the general population of OLB users. However, since sample demographics (specifically, age and income level) did not differ significantly from the average population demographics provided by OLB, it appears that the study's results was not significantly influenced by any non-response bias.

Second, sampling bias may be another concern, if the subject pool, which comprised entirely of current and continuing users of OLB, differed from discontinuers in their perceptions regarding the OLB. For instance, our hypotheses of the increasing effect of relational beliefs with time was contingent on subjects having a positive experience with the OLB, and this effect could have been *decreasing* if subjects' experience was negative. Studying OLB discontinuers to understand the drivers of trust dissolution would have been interesting research in its own right, however, given the study's focus on trust formation (rather than trust dissolution), the current sampling strategy was probably adequate.

Third, this organization where this study was conducted was not a pure online firm like

Amazon or NetBank, but a traditional "brick and mortar" bank that had been in operation for several decades and had gone online before the start of the study. It is possible that many of the study's respondents (OLB customers) formed their trust perceptions based on their prior experience with the brick and mortar division, and that the trust processes and consequent trust beliefs could have been different if this firm had no offline division. Hence, the findings of our study may have limited generalizability to the group of pure-play online firms or those that exist solely on the Internet.

Finally, the ideal empirical design for testing any temporal model of trust formation (as represented in hypotheses H5-H7) is a longitudinal study, capturing data from the same users at multiple points in time as they progress through the trusting relationship. Such a design was not possible in this study due to the sponsoring bank's concern for data privacy. While the temporal nature of the model was partially accounted using subjects' experience level with the OLB, future researchers are encouraged to employ a true longitudinal design to test the generalizability of our reported findings.

Despite the previous limitations, this study was possibly the first in the trust literature to (1) empirically examine the relative effects of different drivers of trust in online relationships, and (2) study how these effects vary with time as trust matures in such relationships. Not only does this study generate fresh insights into the causative and dynamic mechanisms of trust formation, but it also lays the foundation for a richer process model of trust, which in turn, may help inform future research in this area.

REFERENCES

Bart, Y., Shankar, V., Sultan, F., & Urban, G. L. (2005). Are the drivers and role of online trust the same for all Web sites and consumers? A large-scale exploratory empirical study. *Journal of Marketing, 69*(4), 133-152

Bentler, P. M. (1980). *EQS structural equations program manual.* Los Angeles: BMDP Statistical Software.

Bentler, P. M., & Bonnett, D. G. (1980). Significance tests and goodness of fit in the analysis of covariance structures. *Psychological Bulletin, 88*(3), 588-606.

Better Business Bureau. (2000). *Standards for BBBOnline reliability program participation.* Retrieved from http://www.bbbonline.org/businesses/reliability/standards.html

Bhattacherjee, A. (2002). Individual trust in online firms: Scale development and initial test. *Journal of Management Information Systems, 19*(1), 211-241.

Blau, P. M. (1964). *Exchange and power in social life.* New York: John Wiley & Sons.

ConsumerWebWatch. A Matter of Trust: What Consumers Want From Web Sites. April 16, 2002. www.consumerwebwatch.org.

Davis, F. D., Bagozzi, R. P., & Warshaw, P. R. (1989). User acceptance of computer technology: A comparison of two theoretical models. *Management Science. 35*(8), 982-1003.

Fazio, R. H., & Zanna, M. P. (1981). Direct experience and attitude-behavior consistency. In L. Berkowitz (Ed.), *Advances in experimental social psychology* (Vol. 6, pp. 161-202). New York: Academic Press.

Festinger, L. (1957). *A theory of cognitive dissonance.* Evanston, Ill.: Row and Peterson.

Fishbein, M., & Ajzen, I. (1975). *Belief, attitude, intention, and behavior: An introduction to theory and research.* Reading, MA: Addison-Wesley.

Fornell, C., & Larcker, D. F. (1981). Evaluating structural equations with unobservable variables and measurement error. *Journal of Marketing Research, 18*(2), 39-50.

Gambetta, D.G. (1988). *Trust.* New York: Basil Blackwell.

Gefen, D. (2000). E-commerce: The role of familiarity and trust. *Omega, 28*(6), 725-737.

Gefen, D., Karahanna, E., & Straub, D. W. (2003). Trust and TAM in online shopping: An integrated model. *MIS Quarterly. 27*(1), 51-91.

Gogan, J. (1999). Which site seals deliver? *Information Week. 738,* 146, June 14.

Jarvenpaa, S. L., Knoll, K., & Leidner, D. E. (1998). Is anybody out there? Antecedents of trust in global virtual teams. *Journal of Management Information Systems, 14*(4), 26-64.

Karahanna, E., Straub, D. W., & Chervany, N. L. (1999). Information technology adoption across time: A cross-sectional comparison of pre-adoption and post-adoption beliefs. *MIS Quarterly. 23*(2), 183-213.

Keen, P. G. W. (1997). Are you ready for the "trust" economy. *Computerworld, 31*(16), April 21, 80.

Kim, H. W., Xu, Y., & Koh, J. (2005). A comparison of online trust building factors between potential customers and repeat customers. *Journal of AIS, 5*(10), 392-340.

Kollock, P. (1999). The production of trust in online markets. In E. J. Lawler (Ed.), *Advances in group processes* (Vol. 16, pp. 99-123). Greenwich, CT: Jai Press.

Leimeister, J. M., Ebner, W., & Krcmar, H. (2005). Design, implementation, and evaluation of trust-supporting components in virtual communities for patients. *Journal of Management Information Systems, 21*(4), 101-135.

Lewicki, R. J., & Bunker, B. B. (1996). Developing and maintaining trust in work relationships. In R. M. Kramer & T. R. Tyler (Eds.), *Trust in Organizations.* Thousand Oaks, CA: Sage Publications.

Luhmann, N. (1979). *Trust and power.* London: John Wiley.

Mayer, R. C., Davis, J. H., & Schoorman, F. D. (1995). An integrative model of organizational trust. *Academy of Management Review, 20*(3), 709-734.

McAllister, D. J. (1995). Affect- and cognition-based trust as foundations of interpersonal cooperation in organizations. *Academy of Management Journal, 30,* 24-59.

McKnight, D. H., Choudhury, V., & Kacmar, C. (2002). Developing and validating trust measures for e-commerce: An integrative typology. *Information Systems Research. 13*(3), 334-359.

McKnight, D. H., Cummings, L. L., & Chervany, N. L. (1998). Initial trust formation in new organizational relationships. *Academy of Management Review, 23*(3), 473-490.

Nunnally, J. (1978). *Psychometric theory.* New York: McGraw Hill.

Parker-Pope, T. (2001). How to tell whether that online drugstore in really a good deal. *Wall Street Journal.* February 16, B1.

Pavlou, P. A. (2003). Consumer acceptance of electronic commerce: Integrating trust and risk with the technology acceptance model. *International Journal of Electronic commerce, 7*(3), 69-103.

Rousseau, D. M., Sitkin, R. S., Burt, R. S., & Camerer, C. (1998). Not so different after all: A cross-discipline view of trust. *Academy of Management Review, 23*(3), 393-404.

Smith, D., Menon, S., & Sivakumar, K. (2005). Online peer and editorial recommendations, trust, and choice in virtual markets. *Journal of Interactive Marketing, 19*(3), 15-37.

Stewart, K. (2003). Trust transfer on the World Wide Web. *Organization Science, 14*(1), 5-17.

TRUSTe (2000). How the TRUSTe program works. Retrieved from www.truste.org/webpublishers/pub_how.html

Venkatesh, V., Morris, M. G., Davis, G. B., & Davis, F. D. (2003). User acceptance of information technology: Toward a unified view. *MIS Quarterly, 27*(3), 425-478.

Walczuch, R., & Lundgren, H. (2004). Psychological antecedents of institution-based consumer trust in e-retailing. *Information & Management, 42*(1), 159-177.

Williamson, O. E. (1998). *The economic instutions of capitalism*. New York: Free Press.

Zucker, L. G. (1986). Production of trust: Institutional sources of economic structure, 1840-1920. In L. L. Cummings & B. M. Staw (Eds.), *Research in organizational behavior* (Vol. 8, pp. 53-111). Greenwich, CT: JAI Press.

ENDNOTES

1 Online firms displaying the BBBOnline Reliability seal are licensed by the Better Business Bureau (BBB) to be in business for at least one year, maintain a satisfactory complaint-handling record, respond promptly to customer complaints, agree to binding arbitration, and participate in BBB's self-regulation program (BBB 2000). Likewise, firms displaying the TRUSTe seal must post information disclosures, implement privacy policies, agree not to monitor personal communications, submit to periodical reviews by TRUSTe, and cooperate with all TRUSTe audits and reviews (TRUSTe 2000).

2 However, trust beliefs may be lowered with time if the trustor's experiences are unfavorable. In such cases, CDT suggests that trustors will revise their initial beliefs downward to eliminate the dissonance between their prior belief sets and actual transactional experience.

3 Computed as: $F = (R^2_{interaction} - R^2_{main}) / [(1 - R^2_{main})/df_{difference}]$

Chapter XVI
The Influence of Familiarity and Security on Decision Making Processes in E-Commerce:
The Role of User Experience

Fahim Akhter
Zayed University, UAE

Wendy Hui
Zayed University, UAE

ABSTRACT

E-commerce can enhance its acceptance among users through fostering online trust, which is vital for decision-making process. The perception and computation of trust is crucial for vendors and users for the success of e-commerce. The calculation and measurement of trust antecedent involves complex aspect such as presence of security controls and familiarity within the Web site. Most companies are acquiring "security technology" because everybody else is doing the same, but not because there has been a proper assessment of its association with trust. The purpose of this chapter is to analyze the role of trust antecedents such as security and familiarity when they are used collectively to do online transactions. Trust, in general, is an important factor in conducting e-transactions, which revolve around uncertainty and ambiguity. The fuzzy logic approach provides a means for coping with this uncertainty and vagueness that are present in e-commerce. Therefore, the fuzzy logic approach has been deployed to develop scales to measure the effects of users' familiarity and perception of security in an online business-to-consumer (B2C) context. This research provides guidelines to vendors on how they could ascertain the trust level of their business and ways of mitigate the negative impact on the trust level.

INTRODUCTION

E-commerce has already demonstrated its great benefits for both consumers and vendors. As time goes on, cheaper access to the Internet and the increasing involvement of mobile devices will yield more potential online customers. Online transactions in e-commerce can occur without any prior human contact or established interpersonal relationships. This lack of interpersonal trust creates a circumstance for a **security** risk. The responsibility is upon vendors to deploy appropriate use of technologies to reduce risk and foster trust, and to assist in improving customer awareness of genuine risks in order to increase their confidence in conducting online transactions.

Given that e-commerce is thriving, one may be tempted to assume that security aspects must have been addressed, and that the resulting environment is a trusted one. Unfortunately, however, the evidence suggests that as the use of e-commerce increases, so does the number of users who are encountering problems with it. Lacohee (2006) mentioned in their research that consumers repeatedly reported that they believe it is impossible to guarantee that electronic transactions or electronically held data can be secure against increasingly innovative forms of attack.

The Internet Fraud Complaints Center (2005) reported they received 231,493 complaint submissions in 2005 in respect of **e-commerce** fraud. This is an 11.6% increase over 2004 when 207,449 complaints were received. These filings were composed of fraudulent and non-fraudulent complaints primarily related to the Internet. These complaints were composed of many online activities such as auction fraud, non-delivery, and credit card fraud, as well as non-fraudulent complaints such as computer intrusions, spam/unsolicited e-mail, and child pornography (Figure 1). It is reported by IC3 that over 91.5% of all complaints were related to the Internet or online service.

The chart in Figure 1 has shown that fraud has found an opportunity to flourish within the Internet environment. In Figure 1, Internet auction fraud was by far the most reported offense, comprising 62.7% of referred fraud complaints. This represents an 11.9% decrease from the 2004 levels of auction fraud reported to Internet Crime Report (IC3). In addition, during 2005, the non-delivery of merchandise and/or payment represented 15.7% of complaints (down 0.1% from 2004), and credit and debit card fraud made up an additional 6.8% of complaints, which was up 25.9% from 2004 levels. Check fraud, investment fraud, and computer fraud complaints represented 5.4% of all remaining complaints. Other confidence fraud, identity theft, financial institutions fraud, and child pornography complaints together represented less than 2.5% of all complaints

The literature on **trust** can be quite confusing because the term is being used with a variety of meanings (Jøsang et al., 2007). According to them, trust can be interpreted as the reliability of something or somebody. Trust is the subjective probability by which an individual, A, expects

Figure 1. Top ten IC3 complaint categories

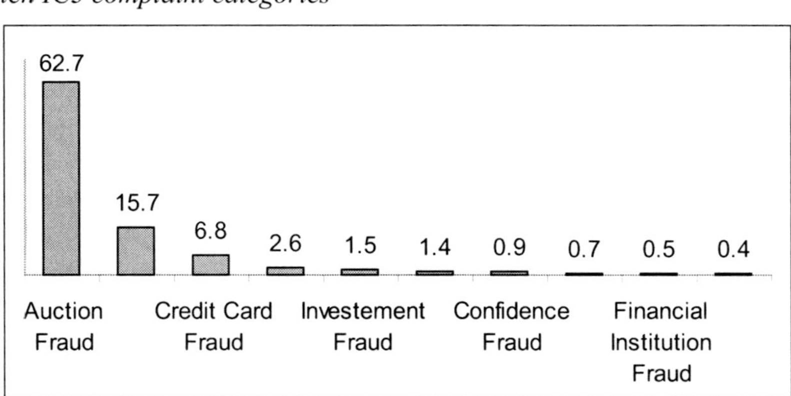

that another individual, B, performs a given action on which its welfare depends. Mayer et al. (1995) has defined trust as "the willingness of a party to be vulnerable to the actions of another party based on the expectation that the other will perform a particular action important to the trustor, irrespective of the ability to monitor or control that other party."

Gollmann (2006) concluded in his work that trust is a dangerous word to use as it has manifold and sometimes contradictory meanings. He had noticed that there is no immediate problem when trust is used in a specific research area to denote some concept of interest. However, complexity arise when interfacing between communities that employ this word differently, and with the general public which is unlikely to associate a word like trust with any specific technical definition adopted in a field of research.

Gefen (2000) described the **trust** in a broader sense. He believes trust is the confidence a person has in his or her favorable expectations of what other people will do, based, in many cases, on previous interactions. Although another party's previous behavior cannot guarantee that that party will behave as one expects, previous interactions in which that party behaved as expected increase trust that is the belief that the other will behave as one anticipates.

A major factor influencing the successful proliferation of e-commerce, identified by major corporations such as the U.S. Federal Administration and the Better Business Bureau, is people's trust in Internet vendors (Gefen, 2000). In fact, the major reason people do not buy online is their concern regarding online payments, lack of trust, security, and **familiarity**. Familiarity, according to Luhmann's (1979) theory, is a prerequisite of trust because it creates a framework and understanding of the environment and the trusted party within which the expectations of trust can be explicated.

Fuzzy logic provides a means for coping with the ambiguity and vagueness that are often present in e-commerce (Cox, 1994; Turban, 1995). Indeed, it was reported (Dahal, Hussain, & Hossain, 2005) that e-commerce is mainly a social activity featured by interaction among consumers, sellers, brokers etc. MATLAB was used because of the built-in support that assisted in understanding the intrinsic relationships between the driving parameters and their effects on the degree of online transactions in e-commerce. Researchers (Tseng & Chih-Hsiang, 2007) have proposed an intelligent management system to monitor the performance of Internet service systems. The management system is capable of detecting and resolving potential problems of Internet service systems, such that the stability and reliability of the system can be significantly improved. Cao and Yunfeng (2007) presented a fuzzy-based recommendation system for those less frequently purchased products, especially for consumer electronics.

LITERATURE REVIEW

Trust is one of the important factors in social interactions and most dominant factors for the success of **e-commerce**. Since e-commerce operates in a more complex environment than traditional business, a higher degree of trust is required between different stakeholders. In e-commerce, a trading party becomes vulnerable to the other party's behavior (Akhter, 2006). In other words, both vendors and consumers assume risks in a transaction, although they do not meet face-to-face. A consumer can see a picture of the product but not the product itself. Vendors can make promises of quality and delivery easily, but consumers do not know if these promises will be kept. To deal with these issues, consumers and vendors must expose a high degree of online trust.

Consumers' lack of trust has often been cited as a major obstacle to the adoption and widespread use of e-commerce (Karake-Shalhoub, 2002; Tassabehji, 2003). The stability of a business depends on the right balance of trust and distrust. Furthermore, people face information overload, increased uncertainty, and risk when they are engaged in e-commerce. As members of an e-commerce community, people cope with these obstacles and risk by relying on trust.

The rationale of choosing the **fuzzy** logic approach is based on the underlying reasoning process behind online transactions, which is based on human decision-making (Mohanty & Bhasker, 2005). Though many factors influence the decision process of online transactions such as **security** and **familiarity**, the perception of an influencing feature is more important than the actual level of the feature itself. For example, if the perceived security level is higher than its actual implementation, then it will contribute positively by the users.

METHODOLOGY

This study was based on the rationale that the actual level of any online transaction is based on two factors: level of trust of the given Web site and how competitive this site is for purchasing purposes. Therefore, any degree of online transaction will be based on the level of trust of the Web site. Hence, there is a need to develop an intelligent system that could simulate the human decision process. This intelligent system should include factors like security and **familiarity** as the trust **antecedents**.

FUZZY EXPERT SYSTEM: COMPLETE MODEL

In order to get a complete picture of the fuzzy expert system, an inference diagram can give a detailed explanation of the processes involved. Figure 2 illustrates the steps and processes involved. The process with the crisp inputs to the fuzzy expert system; for example, this might be the crisp input for **security**, and familiarity to get a value for the trust level.

Figure 2. Complete fuzzy expert system

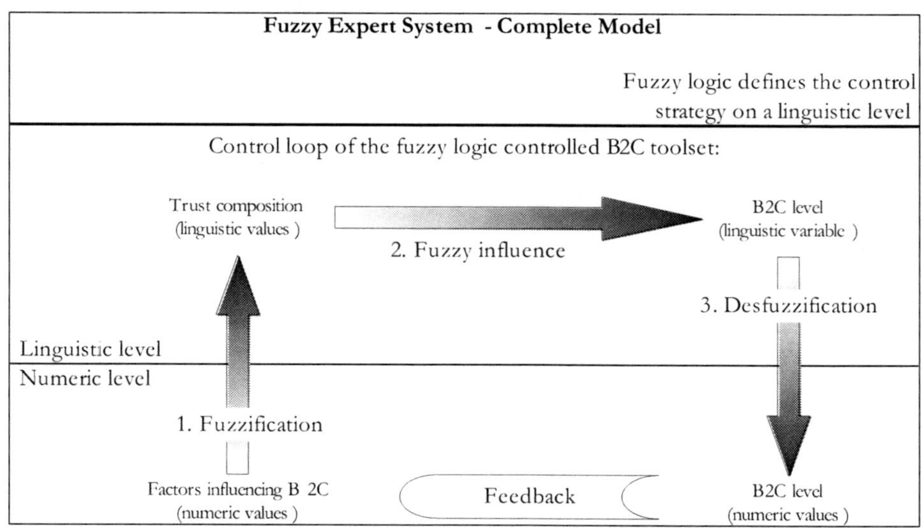

DATA COLLECTION AND ANALYSIS

This study used a Web-based survey because of its advantages such as convenience, viable, and effectiveness way to accessing difficult-to-reach respondents. On the other hand, a Web survey has some limitation such as unequal opportunity (David, 2000). Even though only respondents who have access to the Internet are able to participate in this survey, this condition is exactly what is desired for respondents of this study, which is why a Web-based survey was chosen.

A pilot test was conducted to test the instrument prior to collecting data. The purpose of the pilot test was to access whether the instruments were capturing the phenomena desired. The questionnaires were presented to undergraduate students who were enrolled in different disciplines. The pilot study was used to refine the survey tool used in the study and clarify the wording, contents, and the layout of the survey Web site. Participation in this study was voluntarily and extra credit was given to participants. A total of 150 participants took part in the survey.

FORMULATING SURVEY SITE

An internal Web site was designed to evaluate Amazon.com, Lastminute.com, and Uaemall.com. Once the Web site was published on the Intranet, the URL was provided to the participants. The respondents were asked to analyze the Web sites for purchasing an item of their choice using a credit card. The respondents were asked to go through the entire buying process of the three Web sites but told not to click the buy button to purchase the item. During this process, they had to respond to the questions under the categories (1) **security**, (2) familiarity, and (3) trust.

The three selected Web sites were well known for their brand recognition globally. Amazon.com is a popular American Web site that sells books, movies, stationeries, music, and electronic items on the Internet. Lastminute.com is a British Web site that assists consumers in the travel business. Uaemall.com is a popular Web site among Arab consumers who purchase electronic equipments, perfumes, branded cloths, and other luxury items.

PROCESSING OF DATA

Calculation of Security and Familiarity level

In the trust rules worksheet, a maximum of 27 unique rules can be identified from respondents input by sorting the security and familiarity columns in alphabetical order. This worksheet contains raw data straight from the survey and no interpretation is provided. In the *security* worksheet, a linguistic input has been assigned a numeric value such as 2, 1, or 0 to calculate the accumulated security level. The accumulated security level is the total sum of the four numeric values and the maximum is the percentage of the sum (x/8 multiplied by 100). This security level is then calculated as a percentage of a maximum value (usually 8) and from that the linguistic security level is drawn. It was decided to express the security level as one of three linguistic values, namely low, moderate, and high. The percentage of maximum is evenly distributed to establish linguistic security level such as low (0-33), moderate (34-66), and high (67-100). The familiarity worksheet follows the same pattern as that in the security worksheet. The rules describing the basis for a given trust level are based on the degrees of security and familiarity. These degrees are formulated in terms of their linguistic variables such as low, moderate and high. Trust ranges from very low to very high, in five distinct fuzzy sets.

ANALYSIS OF FACTORS INFLUENCING TRUST

In this section, we analyze all factors influencing **trust** as set up in this study. It views the factors from various angles in order to disclose any unexplored relations among them.

Trust vs. Security

In order to fully understand the contributions from various factors contributing to the trust level, it is required that we examine contributions from each factor separately. Figure 3 shows contributions to trust of a given Web site originating from the **security**. Therefore, the contribution from familiarity has been kept constant at three levels, namely: low, moderate, and high corresponding to numeric values (1, 4, and 7). Figure 3 shows that trust is monotonically increasing for increasing perceived security of a Web site for any given level of familiarity. However, when familiarity is "high" (numeric value of 7) the trust level is at its maximum at maximum security. The three curves have one common feature: they exhibit a "staircase shaped" curvature.

It is interesting to note that for "low" and "moderate" levels of familiarity the developed trust is almost identical up to a security level of about 5. Then, there is a sharp change on the trust level between "low" and "moderate" and the perceived trust for "moderate" familiarity is approaching that of "high." A general observation is that trust is positively related to security for any given value of familiarity. This observation is also plausible to the human mind. One feature that is disclosed from this figure is that for "high" levels of security the trust difference is less significant for "moderate" and "high" levels of familiarity. This result could not be anticipated from the outset.

Trust vs. Familiarity

Let us now examine how trust is contributed from familiarity (Figure 4) for constant values of security. The values for "low," "moderate," and "high"

Figure 3. Trust vs. security for constant familiarity

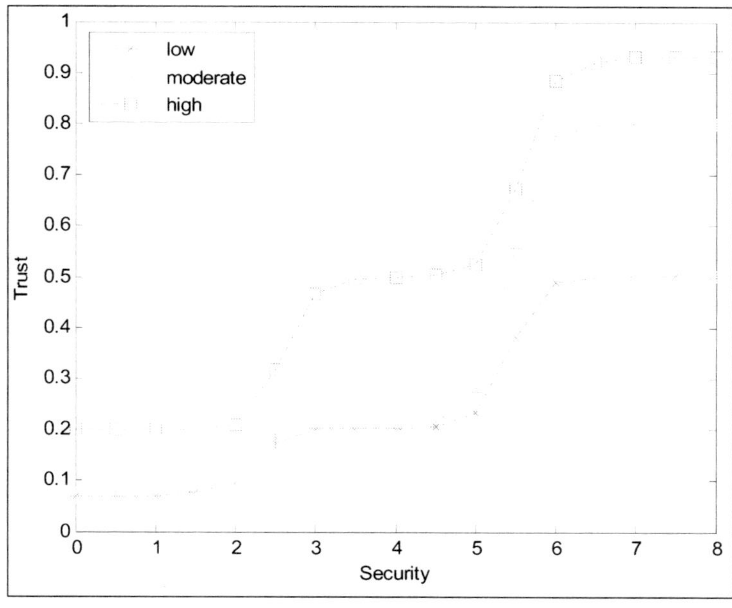

have the same interpretations as explained in the previous section. This figure is considerably different from the previous one. One stunning point to note is that trust levels remain low for any value of familiarity when security is low; when security is "moderate," trust level is only affected when the familiarity level is higher than 5 and exhibits a sudden sizeable jump only to flatten out after familiarity levels of 6 and higher.

When security is "high," trust remains high and is rather constant (at a value of about 0.8) with increasing familiarity. One peculiar feature is that the curve is somewhat concave for moderate familiarity and marginally convex for high familiarity. This suggests that trust is positively related to familiarity for "high" security, but exhibits a "ramp shaped" behavior at the familiarity level of about 3. In addition, trust is high for "high" security levels with increasing familiarity. One general point to note about the figure is that the hump is "softer" as security increases and familiarity decreases. This means that although increasing familiarity has a positive affect on trust, the relative increase is more visible for "moderate" values of security.

Trust as Function of Security and Familiarity

We now attempt to visualize trust levels as a continuous function of its input parameters. It should be noted that since the contribution of familiarity is identical, it suffices to view trust as a function of security and one other facto say familiarity. Figure 5 attempts to portray the variation of trust as encapsulated in the rules for trust.

Figure 5 shows that trust level is positively related to security and familiarity. That is, when familiarity and security are low then trust is also low. Furthermore, trust is at its maximum when the both security and familiarity are at their maximum. For low familiarity, trust is increasing in "steps" with increasing security, attaining its maximum at a level of about 0.5. Looking at Figure

Figure 4. Trust vs. familiarity for constant security

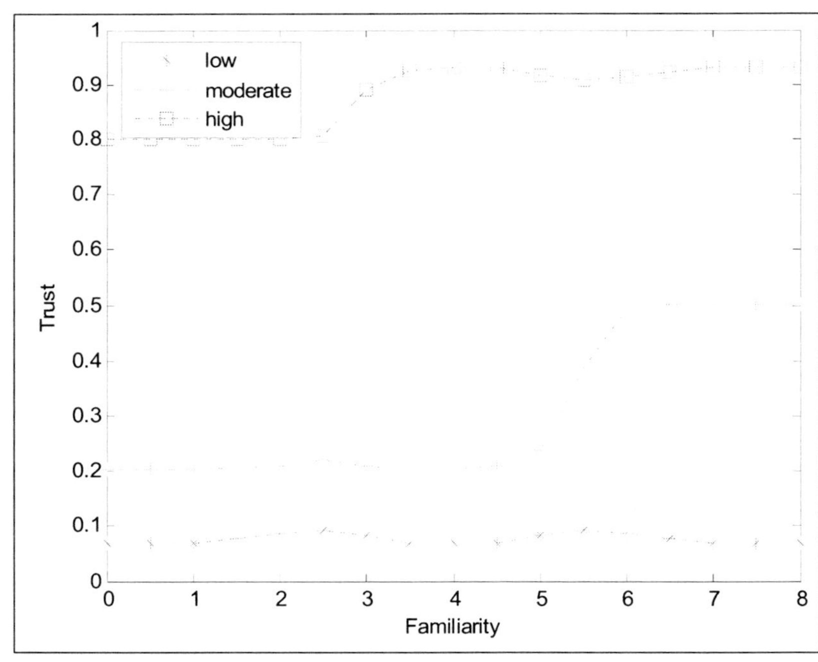

Figure 5. Trust level is positively related to levels of security and familiarity

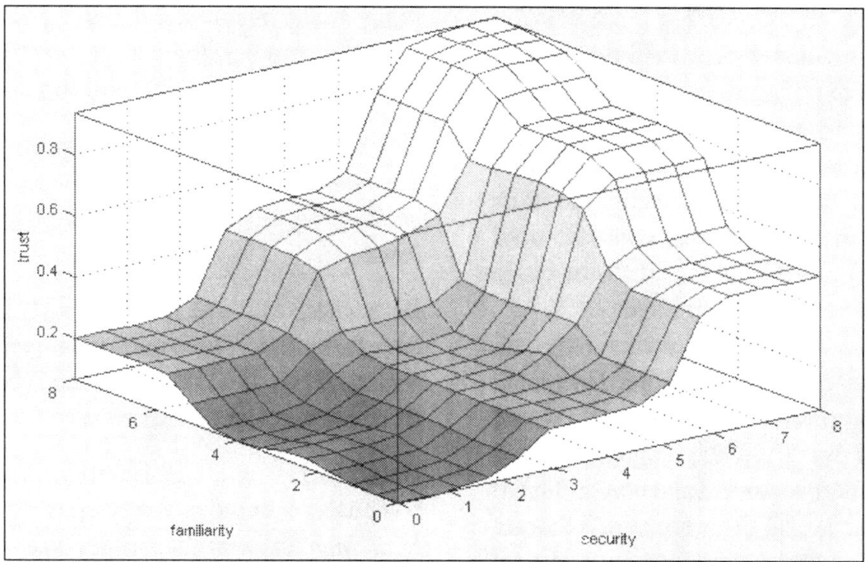

5 from its topmost point the gradient perpendicular to security is less than that which is perpendicular to familiarity axis. This suggests that lowering the security level has a greater detrimental affect on trust than that attained when decreasing familiarity levels of similar magnitude.

The highest gradient for trust is when familiarity is "moderate" and security is "moderate" to "high." This suggests that when people are somewhat familiar with a Web site then a small increase in security levels from between moderate to high security will boost their trust in a significant way. Looking at Figure 5 diagonally from low, low to high, high levels of security and familiarity one observes three plateaus where the last one is around 0.925, and remains at that level even when the input factors are increased further. This result is somehow unexpected and may be due to the fuzzy nature of the expert system where a "trust" or "truth" level of 100 % is unrealistic.

CONCLUSION

The consumers can broadly be categorized into two groups, namely those who are technically critical of a site and capable of measuring its security features and those who are not. Based on actual level of a feature, this survey can be used to decide the feature's contribution in a category. Hence the survey can make a buying decision more solid based on actual appearances of various features. An added advantage would be to feed this data to the fuzzy inference system (FIS) for trust and the user could compare his or her buying decision with that of others based on the outcome of the system.

The trust building procedure is completely different for technical and non-technical users (Bernecker, 2006). Whereas technical users may autonomously analyze facts and assess consequences on more or less theoretical grounds and in advance, the essential factors for non-technical users trust building are lack of negative news over a certain period of time, personal experience, and testimony by trusted sources. For those who are not necessarily technically inclined this survey can assist them in trying to gauge the presence of a feature, say security seals and attach to it a certain contribution (i.e., yes=2 no=0 and don't know=1). After all the requirements for trust are completed, the FIS for trust could be used to provide a perceived level that the user could compare with that of his or her own.

The vendor would benefit from the survey data that is aggregated over time and is used to amend or refine existing rule-sets. Since the data would be accumulated over time, the responses would be a blend from both technical and non-technical users. Hence, the actual occurrence of a feature would be replaced by its perceived equivalence. Since the existence of a feature is only relevant to the user if it can be acknowledged, and if it cannot, then the vendor must seriously reconsider inclusion of this aspect on the Web site.

In addition, the vendor can use the survey data to ascertain the trust level of the site as per user's perception and rectify it if needed. Lastly, as the usage of the survey procedure matures (possibly by providing incentives as discounts on a completed transaction) the FIS could be modified and adjusted where necessary. One limitation of the constructed FIS of this study is that all premises in the antecedent part of a rule have been connected with the AND operation where the OR operation could also be deployed. The implication and aggregation from the rule would then be significantly different.

REFERENCES

Akhter, F. (2006). The impact of foreign languages, customs, business policies, and infrastructure factors on the growth of B2C e-commerce. *IADIS International Conference E-Commerce*. December 9, Barcelona, Spain.

Cao, Y., & Yunfeng, L. (2007). An intelligent fuzzy-based recommendation system for consumer electronic products. *Expert Systems with Applications, 33*(1), 230-240, July.

Cox, E. (1994). *The fuzzy systems handbook: A practitioner's guide to building, using, and maintaining fuzzy systems*. Cambridge: Academic Press.

Bernecker, O. (2006). *Biometrics security: An end user perspective. Information security technical reports II* (pp. 111-118). Retrieved February 2007, from www.sciencedirect.com

Dahal, K., Hussain, Z., & Hossain, M. (2005). Loan risk analyzer based on fuzzy logic. *Proceeding of IEEE International Conference on E-Technology, E-Commerce and E-Services*, Hong Kong.

David, J. L. (2000). You've got surveys. *American Demographics, 22*(11), 42-44.

Gefen, D. (2000). E-commerce: The role of familiarity and trust. *Omega, 28*(6), 725-737, December 2000.

Gollmann, D. (2006). Why trust is bad for security *Electronic Notes in Theoretical Computer Science, 157*(3), 3-9, May 25, 2006.

Internet Fraud Compliant Center. (2005). IFCC 2002 Internet Fraud Report January 1, 2005-December 31, 2005. National White Collar Crime Center and the Federal Bureau of Investigation.

Johnson, C. et al. (2004). *2003 eCommerce: The year in review*. Forrester Research.

Jøsang, A. et al. (2007). A survey of trust and reputation systems for online service provision. Decision Support Systems, In Press, Corrected Proof, Available online 5 July.

Karake-Shalhoub, Z. (2002). *Trust and loyalty in electronic commerce: An agency theory perspective*. Westport, CT: Quorum Books.

Lacohee, H. (2006). Risk and restitution: Assessing how users establish online trust. *Computers & Security*, *25*(7), 486-493, October 2006.

Luhmann N. (1979). *Trust and power*. Chichester, UK: Wiley [translation from German].

Mayer R, et al. (1995). An integrative model of organizational trust. *Academy of Management Review, 20*(3), 709e34.

Mohanty, B. K., & Bhasker, B. (2005). Product classification in the Internet business—A fuzzy approach. *Journal of Decision Support Systems, 38,* 611-619.

Tassabehji, R. (2003). *Applying e-commerce in business*. Thousand Oaks, CA: SAGE publications Ltd.

Tseng, C. R., & Chih-Hsiang, W. (2007). An expert system approach to improving stability and reliability of Web service. *Expert Systems with Applications*, *33*(2), 379-388.

Turban, E. (1995). *Decision support and expert system: Management support systems*. Englewood Cliffs, NJ: Prentice Hall International.

Zadeh, L. (1973). Outline of a new approach to the analysis of complex system and decision processes. *IEEE Transactions on System, Man, and Cybernetics*, *SMC-3*(1), 28-44.

Zadeh, L. (1965). Fuzzy sets. *Information and Control*, *8*(3), 338-353.

Section V
Online Intermediaries

Chapter XVII
The Roles of Online Intermediaries in Collective Memory-Supported Electronic Negotiation

Nongkran Lertpittayapoom
Mahidol University, Thailand

Souren Paul
The College of Staten Island of CUNY—University of New York, USA

ABSTRACT

Following the emergence of the Internet, electronic negotiation has become an alternative to face-to-face negotiation. The rise of Web sites such as electronic marketplaces or electronic brokerages also fueled the popularity of electronic negotiation. The current forms of negotiation support systems (NSS) used to support many electronic negotiations offer very little support for historical negotiation data. In order to address this issue, the idea of a collective memory support in negotiations has been proposed in recent years. This chapter highlights the use of an online intermediary as an effective location from which collective memory support can be offered. The chapter proposes that an intermediary-based collective memory support will increase confidence in negotiation, reduce overall negotiation time, and strengthen trust between negotiators.

INTRODUCTION

The emergence of the Internet has welcomed thriving electronic commerce as evidenced by the rising trend of both the business-to-business (B2B) and business-to-customer (B2C) trade. Both B2B and B2C transactions were expected to be over $7 trillion annually by 2005 (Grover & Teng,

2001). By 2006, 75% of Fortune 1000 companies were expected to increase their investments in e-commerce to draw new customers and increase customer satisfaction rather than reduce the cost of sales (Sarner, 2004). This has convinced that the emergence of the Internet not only supports electronic transactions, but also acts as the platform through which services to businesses and customers are delivered (Kim, Jayaraman, & Rao, 2003). One of the emerging business enterprises to facilitate electronic transactions among parties is online intermediaries or e-marketplaces, which have become increasingly popular over the years as an alternative to traditional forms of commerce (Lee, 1998, Walczak, Gregg, & Berrenberg, 2006). Electronic brokerage, one form of online intermediary, accounted for more than 33% of the retail stock trades (Konana, Menon, & Balasubramanian, 2000). They were expected to generate 48% of online sales by 2005 (Forrester Research, 2001).

The emerging class of middlemen and intermediaries is expected to change the industry structures (Langdon & Shaw, 2002). As the World Wide Web has become the most popular information dissemination channel (Yang & Chung, 2003), the growth of the Internet has largely redefined the role of these intermediaries in the market. The emergence of online networks increases free flow of information and enables direct communication among buyers and suppliers, thereby reducing or replacing the role of the traditional intermediaries. The buyer-supplier interaction becomes easier and faster, and the transaction cost gets reduced (Grover & Ramanlal, 1999). However, the proliferation of the worldwide network enables the integration of multiple markets. As a result, the market becomes more consolidated as a whole, and the overall size of the market increases, thereby involving many participants or competitors (Grover et al., 1999) and expanding the amount of information available.

This increased amount of available information creates the problem of information overloading (Yang et al., 2003). This reveals the need for an online intermediary to organize the huge pool of information and facilitate the transactions among the parties. Moreover, the need for an online intermediary is enhanced in the B2B environment, where the interaction among businesses involves several steps before the business activity can be finalized in the form of a written agreement. An example is a contract such as outsourcing or partnership formation, which is the final outcome of the negotiation among business parties. The rising number of participants such as application service providers who offer a similar service in the electronic market, increases the customer's effort in searching for the provider who can offer the service that meets the customer's expectation the most (e.g., in terms of service reliability or price).

Although business agreements can be achieved through face-to-face interactions, electronic negotiation has emerged as an alternative following the widespread use of the Internet. This alternative not only encompasses the functionalities of traditional negotiation, but also reduces the inconvenience that may be experienced in the face-to-face negotiation. For example, with an asynchronous medium such as e-mail, a negotiator does not have to respond or propose a counteroffer immediately after receiving the proposal from the opponent (Maruca, 2000). As a result, the negotiator can evaluate the offer thoroughly, can negotiate with multiple partners simultaneously, and may achieve a better negotiation outcome within a shorter overall time period. The emergence of electronic negotiation in electronic commerce does not, however, lessen the need for an intermediary. The intermediary can facilitate the search for a prospective partner for negotiation, and mediate the negotiation activities. Although businesses may search for a possible candidate and initiate the negotiation by themselves, time and cost constraints may not allow the companies to find the best candidate or benefit the most from the negotiation. Furthermore, once the negotiation is initiated, both parties have to overcome the conflicting interests of the opponent in order to complete the negotiation successfully. This calls for the use of a negotiation support system (NSS) by the online intermediary so that the negotiation process can be coordinated and accelerated.

In addition to using the NSS, the concept of employing a collective memory for negotiation has been advocated in literature (Jamil & Paul, 2001; Maruca, 2000). The support from this collective memory, it is argued, provides more meaningful information or knowledge to the negotiators. Although the benefit of using collective memory has been elaborated in terms of increase in the positive negotiation outcome and improvement in negotiators' satisfaction, there has been no attempt to identify and hence explain the appropriate location of the collective memory. The growth of the online intermediary and its important role in electronic negotiation suggest its potential as an effective alternative for the location of the memory. In this study, we intend to explore the possibility of locating the negotiation memory with the online intermediary. The comparison between the memory support at the intermediary's location and at the individual negotiator's location is made, and the propositions regarding the expected outcome of these alternatives are presented.

NEGOTIATION, ELECTRONIC NEGOTIATION (E-NEGOTIATION), AND NEGOTIATION SUPPORT SYSTEMS (NSS)

Negotiation

Negotiation is a process in which two or more parties (individuals, groups, or organizations) attempt to resolve incompatible goals and arrive at agreeable outcome(s) (McGrath, 1984). Zartman (1978) viewed negotiation as an ongoing process that can be distinguished in three major dimensions, a learning process (Cross, 1977), a psychological process (Spector, 1977), and a joint decision-making process (Zartman, 1977). Each dimension relies on the assumption of individual rationality (Bartos, 1977). This means each negotiator is trying to maximize his or her own payoff (utility). Thus, an agreement is an equilibrium point in which the opposing interests are balanced.

A typical negotiation process involves three distinct phases—these are pre-negotiation analysis, conduct of negotiation, and post-settlement analysis (Kersten & Noranha, 1997).

The pre-negotiation phase involves activities necessary to initiate a negotiation such as the analysis of the situation, problem, opponent, and strategy. The conduct of negotiation phase primarily includes exchanges of messages and offers. The post-settlement analysis involves the evaluation of the negotiation outcomes and assessment of negotiators' satisfaction during and after the negotiation process.

The time needed for each phase of negotiation may vary depending upon the type of contract, merchandise involved in the negotiation, and characteristics and preferences of the negotiators. The more time spent in negotiating, the higher the cost incurred from the negotiation. In the pre-negotiation phase, a negotiator may want to search for suitable partners. As evinced in the Purchasing (2001) survey, they may prefer to deal with a small number of parties. However, as negotiators in the electronic market do not meet face-to-face and may be unknown to each other, the search for suitable partners may be extremely difficult and time consuming. Moreover, during the negotiation phase, considerable time may be spent in resolving the conflicts between parties that may arise as a result of opposite interests.

In order to overcome these difficulties, third parties may be involved to solve disputes and facilitate communication between parties. The third party, with a specialty in that particular area, may be able to find suitable partners who meet the requirements of a negotiator engaged in electronic negotiation. The involvement of the third party can facilitate and speed up the negotiation process. Third parties can also provide the supporting tools or locations to facilitate the communication between the negotiators, which is useful, particularly for small companies that do not own facilities.

Intermediary in Electronic Commerce

Lang and Whinston (1999) defined an intermediary as a middleman who facilitates transactions between potential traders. They further identified four ways that an intermediary can facilitate transactions, which are matching buyers with sellers, buying goods from sellers and selling them to buyers, buying goods and selling them after modifications, and selling transaction-related information only. Intermediaries in electronic commerce can perform the role of third parties in negotiations. Examples of each function are provided in Table 1.

The only form of intermediary that does not own the products during the transaction process is the first one, which is matching buyers and sellers. The three general tasks of an intermediary performing this type of transaction are determining the product offerings, searching out the potential buyers and sellers, and determining the prices (Bakos, 1998).

An intermediary creates a transaction value through the reduction of searching costs for the buyers and the reduction of inventory risks for the sellers (Schmitz, 2000). The sellers can be assured about the distributed destination of their products as well as the buyers' confidence in the products received. Additional services provided by an intermediary may include the logistic and settlement mechanisms. Logistic mechanisms involve the delivery of information, goods, or services to buyers. Settlement functions refer to the transfer of payment to sellers (Bakos, 1998). In an economic sense, intermediation is efficient as long as the marginal gains from an intermediary's service is higher than the marginal service cost plus the agency cost, which is the cost to prevent the intermediary's opportunistic behavior (Schmitz, 2000).

In electronic commerce, the role of middleman may appear in three conditions, disintermediation in which electronic markets enable direct buyer-seller transactions, reintermediation where tradi-

Table 1. Functions and examples of intermediaries in the market

Intermediary Function	Example	Example of Online intermediary
1. Match buyers and sellers	• Stock exchange • Commodity trading market • Auction market	• Ebay.com (auction market) • Ubid.com (auction market) • DealerNet (automotive intermediary)
2. Buy goods from sellers and sell them to buyers	• Retail stores	• Bestbuy.com (electronic product retailer) • Target.com (general merchandise retailer)
3. Buy goods and sell them after modification	• Retailer who offers a packaged good combining products from different producers	• CompUsa.com (computer distributor) • 1800Flowers.com (flowers delivery)
4. Sell transaction-related information only	• Online business information services • Financial cable networks	• Morningstar.com (financial service)

tional intermediaries reemerge in the electronic markets, and cybermediation or infomediation, which is the new form of online intermediary (Giaglis, Klein, & O'Keefe, 2002).

Some researchers (Scott, 2000; Wigand, 1996) propose that the emergence of the Internet and electronic commerce may potentially lead to disintermediation, which is the displacement or elimination of market or traditional intermediaries, enabling direct trade with buyers and consumers without agents. The use of IT and worldwide network allows suppliers to internalize activities that have been traditionally performed by intermediaries. This can cause traditional intermediaries to disappear as the transaction costs between the suppliers and the customers are less than that between both parties through intermediaries (Adelaar, 2000). As a result, direct transactions between companies enable the manufacturers or suppliers to retain a higher portion of profits that were once allocated to the intermediaries and exposes customers to a larger choice and lower prices (Sarkar, Butler, & Steinfield, 1995).

Nevertheless, the emergence of online intermediaries as a result of the Internet exposure is not likely to completely replace the functional roles of traditional intermediaries as long as the transactions involve tangible, not digitized products, do not have difficulty with geographical and time constraints, and do not require a special communication channel for specific supports such as broadcasting, personalization, and interaction (Peterson, Balasubramanian, & Bronnenburg, 1997). In some cases, the growing need for an intermediary to arrange electronic transactions forced traditional intermediaries to transform their business operations to be electronically compatible in order to survive the competition. Their existing business processes are enlarged to incorporate both traditional and electronic transactions. This type of transformation may be seen mostly with the second and third types of intermediaries in Table 1 where transactions are primarily involved with tangible products. Support for electronic transactions is viewed as an additional service provided by the traditional intermediary.

Unlike a traditional physical exchange through intermediaries, a transaction through an online intermediary is carried out primarily through information. Thus, the role of an online intermediary with its ability to facilitate electronic transactions is emphasized. While the need for traditional intermediaries is reduced according to a possible direct connection between a buyer and a seller through a worldwide network, the need for online intermediaries is created in order to handle online transactions more effectively. Berghel (2000) termed this activity as "symbiotic disintermediation." This refers to innovative distributors who create value by connecting suppliers to untapped online buyers who are beyond the commercial reach of the supplier. This activity also strengthens the marketing capability of the suppliers. For example, Amazon.com provides a useful service to customers. The service that was previously unavailable as a convenient, electronic platform for online book shopping. The transaction cost between the online intermediary and the customers is certainly lower than that between the traditional intermediary and the customers as seen in the reduced service charge. As a result, sellers or suppliers can find prospective buyers (that they would never find otherwise) through the search facilitation support provided by an online intermediary.

Intermediaries such as those in the first and fourth categories (in Table 1) are generally involved with information. In an electronic market, these intermediaries are sometimes called infomediaries, whose electronic support offered is generally combined from those of both intermediary categories. By definition, infomediaries leverage the Internet to unite buyers and suppliers in a single, virtual marketplace to facilitate a transaction (Grover et al., 2001) as well as information sharing and exchange (Singh, Iyer, & Salam, 2003). Infomediaries provide various kinds of informational services such as search services (search and guide clients regarding an informed choice), matching services (match a supplier and a buyer according to their needs), content services (provide information, such as a directory for alternative suppliers), community services (allow clients to share information with each other), and privacy protection services (protect a client's privacy) (Grover et al., 2001). Services provided by infomediaries are essentially relevant to electronic negotiation activities where only information is transferred among participants. Informediaries can, thus, support all three phases of a typical negotiation presented in the previous section. Infomediaries not only can support transaction and communication exchanges between negotiating parties, but can also speed up the negotiation process by the use of intelligent agents, which can assist parties to identify a prospective candidate for a negotiation and provide other forms of supports to the parties engaged in a negotiation. Examples of intelligent agents that support negotiations are Kasbah, AuctionBot, and T@T (Maes, Guttman, & Moukas, 1999). Finally, infomediaries can be developed to analyze the negotiation transactions and thus support in post-negotiation activities. The support of the infomediaries will be effective only when they are allowed to collect and store information regarding the negotiating parties and their communication exchanges.

Electronic Negotiation (E-Negotiation) and Negotiation Support Systems (NSS)

Apart from traditional negotiations, electronic negotiation emerged as a potential alternative to automate the negotiation process. While electronic negotiation is similar to traditional negotiation in terms of the negotiation process, it is different from traditional negotiation in terms of technological support. In both electronic and traditional negotiation settings, the negotiation process always starts with the search for a prospective candidate to accomplish a certain business purpose; continues with the communication between both parties during negotiating sessions; and ends the negotiation regardless of the outcome. Traditionally, both parties are required to meet face-to-face in order to exchange the offers. Later, the communication and exchanged transactions between parties can be accomplished electronically. Thus, for electronic negotiation, part or all of the entire negotiation process can be done through the Internet.

Electronic negotiation has gradually entered the market and become one of the critical electronic services available on the Internet (De Moor & Weigand, 2004; Kim et al., 2003). It can range from simple offer exchanges to complex extensive discussion regarding the products and services (Schoop, Jertila, & List, 2003). In this chapter, electronic negotiation is classified into two categories according to the complexity of the supporting technology. The first is electronic negotiation via e-mail; the second involves the use of negotiation support systems, especially Web-based negotiation support systems. Currently, electronic negotiations may be most widely conducted through e-mail. This involves the sharing of documents, such as offers, explanations of an offer, and so on. Electronic mail-based negotiations are simple and provide limited negotiation support. Additional form of negotiation support can be provided by negotiation support systems.

Negotiation support systems (NSSs) constitute a special category of group support systems (GSSs). They are designed to support the activities of two or more parties in a negotiation to reach an agreement (Perkins, Hershauer, Foroughi, & Delaney, 1996). The NSS is developed to support the computer-mediated negotiation (Croson, 1999). The core components of an NSS are an individual decision support system (DSS) for each party in the negotiation and an electronic communication channel between the parties (Perkins et al., 1996). The electronic communication channel is presented by Lim and Benbasat (1993) as the coordination system. This system not only controls access to the electronic blackboard but also coordinates the public and private displays, including the support for group decision processes. The systems are primarily developed to help negotiators prepare for negotiations, suggesting strategies and tactics to use during a negotiation, and occasionally proposing jointly beneficial solutions (Croson, 1999).

The latest development in negotiation support systems is the Web-based NSS. They range from those that are developed to support structured negotiations such as electronic auctions, artificial negotiation agents (e.g., eAgora (Chen, Vahidov, & Kersten, 2005)), or semantic Web (He & Jutla, 2006), to those that are developed to support complex or less structured negotiations such as WebNS, Inspire, Negoisst, and SmartSettle (Köhne, Schoop, & Staskiswicz, 2005). These systems enable communication between people from different locations and time zones as well as facilitate the negotiation related activities (e.g., electronic contracts (Jertila & Schoop, 2005)). As a result, Web-based negotiation support systems can overcome one of the limitations of traditional NSS, which is limited systems accessibility. Unlike the traditional NSSs, the Web-based systems can extend the support to a large group of negotiators who can be dispersed geographically in different parts of the globe.

Performance and Limitations of NSS and E-Negotiation

The computer-mediated negotiations or the negotiations through the NSS have been proven to provide a satisfactory result in terms of increasing the preferred negotiation outcomes, such as higher joint gains, more balanced contracts, and reduced negotiation time (Perkins et al., 1996).

Subsequent studies (Croson, 1999; Kersten et al., 1997) revealed similar results regarding negotiation outcome. Croson (1999) conducted an experimental study comparing face-to-face negotiations and electronic negotiation using e-mails as the medium between the negotiators. The results are consistent with previous studies. The outcomes are observed in terms of the efficiency and equality of agreements. In comparison with face-to-face negotiations, the electronic negotiations are more likely to arrive at integrative or joint agreements, which measure the gain each opponent achieves from the negotiation (Croson, 1999). Furthermore, the electronic negotiations also help the agreement to reach more equal divisions of the surplus than the face-to-face negotiations. Kersten et al. (1997) conducted another exploratory study using INSPIRE, a Web-based NSS. The study explored the effect of computer support in negotiation and the difference in decision-making among various cultures on the negotiation outcome. The result is consistent with the previous studies. Although the negotiator's satisfaction with the system differs among users from various countries, the overall satisfaction with the agreement is high or very high. Recently, an empirical study by Köhne et al. (2005) on the acceptance of electronic negotiation support system features also confirmed the positive results. The experiment, which focused on the communication support feature of the Negoisst system, revealed that the majority of the participants were willing to use the system in real negotiations as well as for the preparation and training purposes.

As seen from the aforementioned studies, electronic negotiations have increased positive negotiation outcomes in most cases. Nevertheless, there are some limitations associated with an electronic negotiation. In addition to the limitations in terms of information and communication technologies, users' computer literacy, model complexity, and psychological and sociological conditioning of negotiations (Chen et al., 2005), another primary limitation is the lack of information or knowledge sharing among negotiators (e.g., to develop shared cognition among negotiators (Swaab, Postmes, & Neijens, 2004)). The computer-mediated negotiation, both through e-mail and through the NSS, provides support for a particular negotiation process. However, the information or knowledge acquired from each negotiation cannot be shared or applied to benefit the other negotiations. In the case of data transferring through e-mails, the messages transferred may be kept for the record and then become the references for the next negotiation. However, as e-mails accumulate, the retrieval of specific negotiation information is likely to be problematic. The issue of storing information and/or knowledge acquired in a negotiation session and using it in subsequent similar negotiations has so far been a relatively less explored area of NSS research. We discuss this issue in the next section of this chapter.

Information and Knowledge Sharing in Negotiation

The lack of information or knowledge sharing helped establish the idea of providing a memory support in negotiations. The memory support can be provided in the form of collective memory or organizational memory, which is defined as "the means by which knowledge from the past, experience, and events influence present organizational activities" (Stein & Zwass, 1995). The collective memory for negotiation is a repository of tacit and explicit knowledge created from prior negotiation sessions. It enables knowledge sharing, which is the transfer and integration of prior knowledge with the current negotiation situation. As presented by Paul (2001), collective memory support can eliminate the limitation of the lack of knowledge sharing by maintaining the information regarding the prior negotiations. The information can be stored in the negotiation memory support system (NMSS). Once the stored information is accumulated in a meaningfully organized manner (Zach, 1999), it then becomes the knowledge, which can be used for other negotiations. This means the knowledge acquired from the previous negotiations can benefit the subsequent negotiations if it is properly shared. Although knowledge is often thought to be the property of individuals, a great deal of knowledge is both produced and held collectively (Brown & Duguid, 1998). This can be applied to the negotiation context. While the negotiators bargain to reach the most satisfactory outcomes during the negotiation process, they need to learn to adapt themselves or their offers to fit properly with the situation as a response to the other party's reaction. This is the learning process (Cross, 1977).

Furthermore, the negotiators are usually different in terms of their behavioral styles (Spector, 1977). Thus, one negotiation strategy that is successfully used with one opponent may not be applicable to the others. If all actions that take place in a negotiation can be stored, the knowledge created from one negotiation can reside not only in the negotiator's individual memory, but also within the system and can be learned by other negotiators. In addition, the memory support can also extend the negotiators' capabilities beyond their cognitive limits.

This memory concept for the negotiation fits well with the dynamic business environment where there is a high employee turnover among companies (Alavi & Leidner, 2001). The knowledge from the negotiations that is shared within a company will maintain the company's capability to continue the negotiation even if the particular negotiator leaves the company. Furthermore, the specific feature of each negotiation contract also supports the company in gaining knowledge about each negotiator (e.g., information about a supplier's dominant product or performance for a customer or information about a customer's preference for a supplier). The knowledge from the negotiations that is shared between companies will also facilitate other companies to learn more about each company's preference and to develop a more agreeable offer for both companies if the negotiation is expected to be successful.

As mentioned previously, information or knowledge gained from a situation such as a negotiation tends to be more episodic in nature, since the negotiation case varies from one to another. Nevertheless, some information may be general to all of the negotiations and can be seen in explicit form. This refers to semantic knowledge, which can be easily presented and acquired. For example, a NEDA/Texas AM survey presented top ten criteria that customers use when selecting distributors. They are on-time delivery, price, customer service, technical support, price protection, carrying local inventory, product-application support, cost efficiency, specific brand availability, and inventory management/support (Purchasing, 2001). Some of the information, such as on-time delivery, price protection, carrying local inventory, and specific brand availability are useful to almost all business organizations and hence can be maintained in a semantic form and shared by the organizations.

On the other hand, other information such as price, customer service, technical support, or product-application support, depends on the type and size of the contract and companies involved. These types of information, once accumulated, are likely to become situated or episodic knowledge that are relevant for a specific individual negotiation.

Although the knowledge can be created and shared, the issue that needs to be resolved is the location of the memory support systems. If a company does not have to negotiate with other companies (e.g., a supplier) on a regular basis, it may not be as efficient as it should be to maintain a separate facility and technical personnel only for this particular purpose. A support from the third party's location is a proposed alternative in this chapter, in addition to the memory implementation at the company's location. In the next section we discuss the architecture of both alternatives.

Architecture of Knowledge Shared E-Negotiation

The knowledge sharing capability can be achieved through the installation of a memory support system that can be external to a NSS (Jamil et al., 2001). Two potential architectures of the knowledge-shared e-negotiation are discussed in this section. These are: (1) The memory support installed at the third party's or the intermediary's location (Figure 1), and (2) The installation of the memory support at each negotiating party's (i.e., at each company's location (Figure 2)).

Figure 1. Knowledge shared e-negotiation architecture with NMSS at an intermediary's site

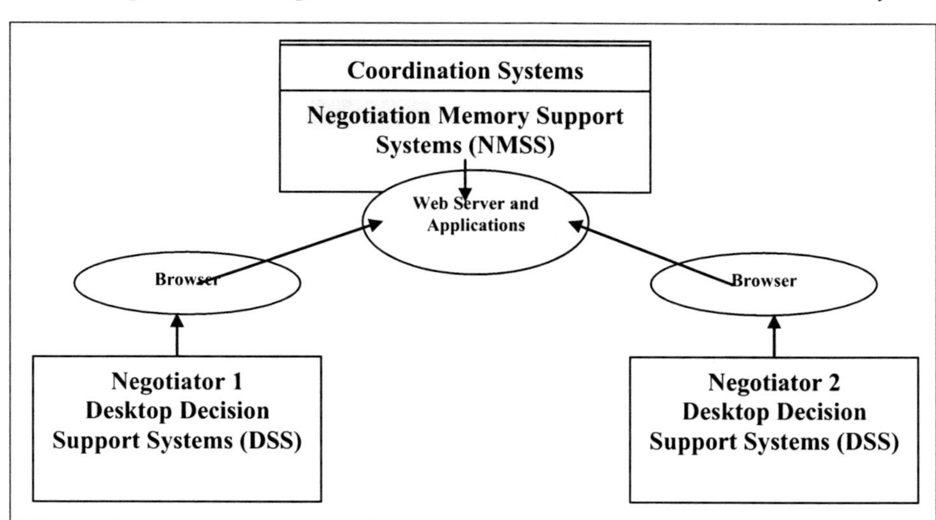

As seen from Figure 1, the communication between the two parties is accomplished through the client-server model, with the coordination system at an

intermediary's Web site. All companies using the intermediary will have to set up an account and provide some basic information (such as the company's address, type of business etc.) to the intermediary. Furthermore, the intermediary should be able to monitor and facilitate all activities of the negotiation, collect information from the negotiation process with permission from the negotiators, and hence build up a new instance or extend an existing instance of the negotiation in the collective memory.

Another possible architecture is the implementation of the NMSS at each negotiating party's location. In this, the intermediary will incorporate only the coordination role for both parties. The coordination system serves as a medium for both parties to communicate. Since the NMSS is implemented at the user's location, the information to support a negotiation is provided internally by each party's system. This information can be collected during the negotiation session. Once the negotiation is initiated, the negotiator can use the information provided by the negotiation memory to analyze and respond to the participating party during the negotiation process.

Although both architectures are able to support electronic negotiations, each architecture has its advantages and disadvantages, which are listed in Table 2.

RESEARCH QUESTIONS AND PROPOSITIONS

The knowledge-shared e-negotiation can, therefore, be implemented in two different architectures, one with the memory support installed at the company's location and the other with memory support at the intermediary's location. The question is which architecture is desirable in terms of satisfactory negotiation outcomes. One of the concerns associated with storing information at the intermediary's location is the security or privacy issue. While many negotiators may have reservations regarding the collection of individual preference patterns and other relevant information by the intermediary Web site, almost all of them will perhaps prefer to retrieve this information

Figure 2. Knowledge shared e-negotiation architecture with NMSS at the user's location

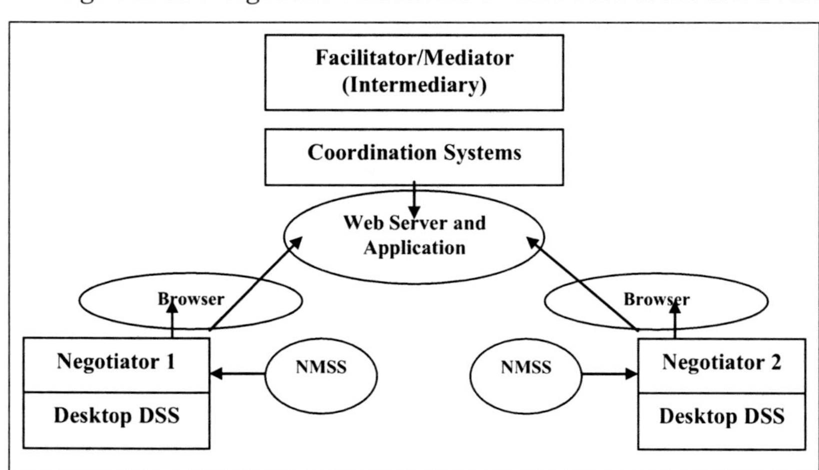

Table 2. Advantages and disadvantages of intermediary-based collective memory vs. local collective memory

Intermediary-Based Collective memory Support	Local Collective memory Support
Advantages: • More efficiently organized memory system can provide better and more useful knowledge for negotiation; • Large volume of negotiation information can be collected from multiple parties; • Memory development cost can be stretched out to a larger group of negotiators.	**Advantages:** • Each negotiating party has control over information collection; • Faster storage and retrieval of memory information.
Disadvantages: • Concern for security and privacy issues; • Increased time to store and retrieve memory information because the negotiator is in a remote location; • May not be an efficient alternative when interaction with the memory is frequent.	**Disadvantages:** • Development of a collective memory with all functionalities will be costly and may not be justifiable; • Limited set of memory information.

(especially about other negotiators) from the same Web site. This contradictory nature of negotiator behavior may make the intermediary-based memory support system dysfunctional.

Nonetheless, Culnan and Armstrong (1999) indicated that in general, individuals are less likely to perceive information collection procedures as privacy-invasive when (a) information is collected in the context of an existing relationship, (b) they perceive that they have the ability to control future use of the information, (c) the information collected or used is relevant to the transaction, and (d) they believe the information will be used to draw reliable and valid inferences about them. Their empirical evidence also confirmed their hypothesis that when customers are explicitly told that their information is treated fairly, there is no difference in terms of privacy concerns between customers who allow access to their personal information and those who do not.

We, therefore, argue that there may be no major difference between storing information either at the intermediary's or the user's location in terms of an individual negotiator's privacy concerns provided that each negotiator becomes aware of the advantages of using this memory information and perceives that the information collection can be controlled and that the information will be used to draw reliable and valid inferences. The literature highlights that the use of electronic support for negotiation process improves the negotiation outcome. Lim et al. (1993) proposed that computer support would improve the negotiation outcome such as the distance from the efficient frontier, the confidence with the solution, the settlement time, and the satisfaction. Delaney, Foroughi, and Perkins (1997) found that the use of NSS does not improve negotiation time but does improve the satisfaction of the negotiators. Later, Paul (2001) brought in the concept of having negotiation memory support for repetitive negotiations with multiple issues. Paul (2001) also proposed that the use of negotiation memory support would provide higher joint gain, less exploitation, shorter negotiation time, higher negotiator's confidence, and higher satisfaction.

Confidence in Negotiation Outcome

Negotiations involving the online intermediaries can be useful because win-win solutions can sometimes be discovered more easily through the support of the intermediaries who have full information and neutral motives (Segev & Beam, 1999). The advantage of having intermediary-based memory support is that the information is collected from each participant in a uniform structure. The negotiators can be assured that the same type of information is collected from all parties who have equal privilege to access the memory information. This is different from the situation where each party maintains its own memory and the possibility of having memory information asymmetry cannot be ruled out. This does not mean that each party is not able to maintain its own memory but it may not be cost efficient for companies that specialize in other business areas to maintain such memory only for the purpose of negotiation. Furthermore, if the negotiating parties are introduced by a trusted intermediary, the negotiators are likely to be confident that the other party has met certain requirements or preferences of the company that were specified to the intermediary by each individual negotiator during the pre-negotiation stage. Therefore, they may exchange documents or information without much reservation. In addition, the intermediary based collective memory is expected to store wide pool of knowledge that is derived from the transactions of a number of participants who access the intermediary network. Advancement in technology such as negotiation agents which are enabled to mine negotiation knowledge from previous negotiation sessions (Lau & Wong, 2007) will also enhance the intermediary's capability to assist the negotiations. On the contrary, individual negotiating parties interact with a limited number of participants. As such, the memory maintained locally by an individual party is likely to be narrow in scope. We, therefore, expect that users of intermediary based memory will be confident that the opponents engaged in negotiation have met the requirements specified in the pre-negotiation stage and the negotiation decision is based on a knowledge repository that is detailed in nature. Hence:

Proposition 1: Confidence in negotiation outcome will be higher with the support of negotiation memory from an intermediary than that from an individual negotiator.

Negotiation Time

Negotiation time is also critical to a negotiation. In businesses such as service-oriented software business where software is delivered by a vendor to a client based on the negotiated service level, negotiation between the two parties must be concluded in a very short time frame (Elfatatry & Layzell, 2004). As collective memory has been found to improve the speed of group decision making in a cognitive-conflict situation (Paul, Haseman, & Ramamurthy., 2004), it can produce similar results in negotiations by improving the speed of searching for partners, reaching negotiation settlement, and concluding the analysis. Locating the memory at the intermediary's may further improve the positive outcomes. While searching for partners, the negotiators can access the vast repository of information stored in the intermediary Web site on all negotiating parties, and by using appropriate queries, they can identify the parties who were engaged in similar negotiations in the past and also examine the outcome of those prior negotiations. This is expected to speed up their partner selection process. On the contrary, the collective memory maintained by an individual negotiator is likely to have limited information on other negotiators and may not be very useful in identifying the appropriate partner in negotiation.

Maglio and Barrett (2000) identified five basic functions of the intermediary, which are customizing (customize information for a particular user), filtering (remove information), annotating (add information), transcoding (change information to a different form), aggregating (combine information from multiple sources), and caching (store information for later use). These functions facilitate the data transformation between client and server for faster delivery and discovery. The functions are implemented through three types of operations, namely data generation, data editing, and data monitoring.

Once the source form of data is generated, the raw data can be edited and transcoded to personalize the information for a particular user. Moreover, the intermediary can track information as it passes through. Monitoring is used for caching Web resources for faster delivery, logging usage patterns, and building user models for Web-browsing activities (Maglio et al., 2000). Data can be updated periodically by the intermediary. Thus, a user can focus primarily on the content and issues of a negotiation. The pre-negotiation, which includes searching for partners, is not the only step that is accelerated; the negotiation and the post settlement stages can be faster as well. The useful knowledge provided by the intermediary can help the negotiators to have a better understanding of the opponent's negotiation style (e.g., the preference, the general acceptance region, etc.) and apply it to the current negotiation.

Once the negotiation is completed, the information transferred is already tracked by the intermediary and is ready for post-settlement viewing. Thus, it is expected that negotiators using intermediary-based negotiation memory support will be knowledgeable and will spend less overall time in different phases of negotiation, thereby lowering the negotiation time. As discussed earlier, the knowledge pool of collective memory maintained with individual parties are likely to be less detailed. As a consequence, the users relying on individual negotiator's collective memory may not be able to determine the pattern of negotiation preferred by the other party. This problem will be more acute when a negotiating party has no or very few transactions with the opponent in the past. Hence:

Proposition 2: Negotiation time will be shorter with the support of the negotiation memory from an intermediary than that from an individual negotiator.

Trust

A negotiation involves an expectation regarding the future cooperation between the negotiating parties as a result of the successful negotiation. Trust between the parties is another important determinant of the potential cooperation. Trust indicates willingness to accept vulnerability (trust intention) and expectations about the trustee behavior (trust belief) (Bhattacherjee, 2006). If the customer does not trust the supplier to be able to deliver products or services as promised, it could be one of the reasons that successful negotiation may not take place. In the physical world, customer trust is created through the physical presence, reputation, and accountability of a business (Barlow, Hess, & Seamons, 2001). While these attributes cannot be observed easily in a virtual world (i.e., in electronic negotiations), trust becomes increasingly important as markets progress from physical to virtual space (Palmer, Bailey, & Faraj, 2000). Trust in online firms was found to have an influence on consumers' willingness to transact or conduct online transactions (Bhattacherjee, 2006). Barlow et al. (2001) suggest that when a business is completely unfamiliar to a customer, trusted third parties could play a key role in engendering consumer trust, for example, in the form of a membership certificate. In addition to the progress in modern technology such as reliable encryption and authentication methods for electronic transactions, there is a need for the emergence of trusted intermediaries (Salam, Rao, & Pegels, 2003). Participants of Poultryfirst.com, a well-known focal point for online poultry auctions or FoodUSA.com, an online meat exchange, could be assured that the negotiating party that they meet through these sites could be trustworthy to a certain extent. Being a focal point of a large volume of business transactions, intermediaries can ensure valid transactions between business parties. This is because they achieve economies of scale in technological investment, thereby have lower risk of transaction failures (Adelaar, 2000) which may occur with direct transactions among business parties. In addition to trusting the third party to suggest a prospective candidate for consideration, a negotiator can also be ensured that the information collected during the negotiation is properly gathered and secured according to the agreement between the negotiator and the intermediary. Hence:

Proposition 3: Trust between negotiators will be strengthened more with the support of the negotiation memory from an intermediary than that from an individual negotiator.

CONCLUSION

Collective negotiation memory and knowledge sharing in electronic negotiation have been discussed. In this chapter, we discuss two possible architectures of implementing the negotiation memory support. These are intermediary-based memory support and local memory support (at the individual negotiator level). We also propose that the use of intermediary-based memory support can result in better negotiation outcomes.

The proposed model may be attractive and beneficial to small- to medium-sized companies that may not be negotiating too frequently and thus may not be able to maintain negotiation memory internally due to the lack of proper technical and/or financial support. The negotiation with an outsourcing contract, such as with an application service provider (ASP), may not take place as often as the purchasing contract between a customer and a supplier, so the memory may not need to be updated constantly. Therefore, the transferred responsibility of negotiation memory maintenance from a user to an intermediary may create more effective data management, support negotiations more efficiently, and thus produce a better negotiation outcome.

The proposed form of negotiation memory presented in this chapter can be extended to other research studies. There may be a difference among users from different cultures about the willingness to share the information and knowledge, an issue that happens even in the same organizational setting. For example, the effect of cultural difference on the negotiation has been extensively described (Avruch, Black, & Scimecca, 1998). It may become more complicated and even more challenging to include this construct in the model and investigate the relationship between cultural differences and the knowledge sharing issue of electronic negotiation.

Another research direction to extend the body of knowledge can be about the privacy issue of knowledge sharing among organizations. Although the privacy concern is assumed to be constant in this chapter, it can be a possible area of study regarding the type of information that organizations are willing to share. This leads in two possible directions. First, the architecture of the systems can be studied in depth in terms of the types of information attributes that can be stored with the intermediary. Second, the study can be extended in the context of the relationship between the level of shared knowledge received from the intermediary's repository and the joint gain as the result of a negotiation. The empirical results are crucial in this research direction, since feedback from the experiments is needed in order to further develop the functionality of the systems and the connection among system elements and users from different locations through the worldwide network.

REFERENCES

About. (2001). *Forrester research predicts that portals and affiliate programs will thrive*. Retrieved February 14, 2007, from http://retailindustry.about.com/library/bl/q2/bl_for040501.htm

Adelaar, T. (2000). Electronic commerce and the implications for market structure: the example of the art and antiques trade. *Journal of Computer-Mediated Communication, 5*(3). Retrieved September 28, 2005, from http://jcmc.indiana.edu/vol5/issue3/adelaar.htm

Alavi, M., & Leidner, D. E. (2001). Review: Knowledge management and knowledge management systems: Conceptual foundations and research issues. *MIS Quarterly, 25*(1), 107-136.

Avruch, K., Black, P. W., & Scimecca, J. A. (1998). *Conflict resolution: Cross-cultural perspectives.* CT: Praeger Publishers.

Bakos, Y. (1998). The emerging role of electronic marketplaces on the Internet. *Communication of the ACM, 41*(8), 35-42.

Barlow, T., Hess, A., & Seamons, K. E. (2001). Trust negotiation in electronic markets. *Proceeding of the 8th Research Symposium on Emerging Electronic Markets (RSEEM 01),* Maastricht, The Netherlands.

Bartos, O. J. (1977). Simple model of negotiation: A sociological point of view. In I. W. Zartman (Ed.), *The negotiation process: Theories and applications* (pp. 13-27). Beverly Hills, CA: Sage Publications.

Berghel, H. (2000). Predatory disintermediation. *Communications of the ACM, 43*(5), 23-29.

Bhattacherjee, A. (2006). Individual trust in online firms: The relative and temporal effects of antecedent beliefs. *International Journal of E-Business Research, 2*(4), 21-38.

Brown, J. S., & Duguid, P. (1998). Organizing knowledge. *California Management Review, 40*(3), 90-111.

Chen, E., Vahidov, R., & Kersten, G. E. (2005). Agent-supported negotiations in the e-marketplace. *International Journal of Electronic Business, 3*(1), 28-49.

Croson, R. T. A. (1999). Look at me when you say that: An electronic negotiation simulation. *Simulation and Gaming, 30*(1), 23-37.

Cross, J. G. (1977). Negotiation as a learning process. In I. W. Zartman (Ed.), *The negotiation process: Theories and applications.* (pp. 29-54). Beverly Hills, CA: Sage Publications.

Culnan, M. J., & Armstrong, P. K. (1999). Information privacy concerns, procedural fairness, and impersonal trust: An empirical investigation. *Organization Science, 10*(1), 104-115.

De Moor, A., & Weigand, H. (2004). Business negotiation support: Theory and practice. *International Negotiation, 9*(1), 31-58.

Delaney, M. M., Foroughi, A., & Perkins, W. C. (1997). An empirical study for the efficient of a computerized negotiation support system (NSS). *Decision Support Systems, 20*, 185-197.

Elfatatry, A., & Layzell, P. (2004). Negotiating in service-oriented environments. *Communications of the ACM, 47*(8), 103-108.

Giaglis, G. M., Klein, S., & O'Keefe, R. M. (2002). The role of intermediaries in electronic marketplaces: Developing a contingency model. *Information Systems Journal, 12*(3), 231-246.

Grover, V., & Ramanlal, P. (1999). Six myths of information and markets: Information technology networks, electronic commerce, and the battle for consumer surplus. *MIS Quarterly, 23*(4), 465-495.

Grover, V., & Teng, J. T. C. (2001). E-commerce and the information market. *Communications of the ACM, 44*(4), 79-86.

He, Y., & Jutla, D. N. (2006). Contextual e-negotiation for the handling of private data in ecommerce on a semantic Web. *Proceeding of the*

39th Hawaii International Conference on System Sciences, Kauai, HI.

Jamil, A., & Paul, S. (2001). Collective memory support for buyer-supplier negotiation on multiple issues: Design of a Web-based system. *Proceeding of the 7th Americas Conference on Information Systems,* Boston.

Jertila, A., & Schoop, M. (2005). Electronic contracts in negotiation support systems: Challenges, design, and implementation. *Proceeding of the 7th IEEE International Conference on E-Commerce Technology,* Munich, Germany.

Lang, K. R., & Whinston, A. B. (1999). A design of a DSS intermediary for electronic markets. *Decision Support Systems, 25*(3), 181-197.

Langdon, C. S., & Shaw, M. J. (2002). Emergent patterns of integration in electronic channel systems. *Communications of the ACM, 45*(12), 50-55.

Lau, R. Y. K., & Wong, O. (2007). Mining negotiation knowledge for adaptive negotiation agents in e-marketplaces. *Proceeding of the 40th Hawaii International Conference on System Sciences,* Big Island, HI.

Lee, H. G. (1998). Do electronic marketplaces lower the price of goods. *Communications of the ACM, 41*(1), 73-80.

Lim, L., & Benbasat, I. (1993). A theoretical perspective of negotiation support systems. *Journal of Management Information Systems, 9*(3), 27-44.

Kersten, G. E., & Noronha, S. J. (1997). Negotiation via the World Wide Web: A cross-cultural study of decision making. *InterNeg Research.* Retrieved September 28, 2005, from http://www.iiasa.ac.at/Research/DAS/interneg/research/misc/inc91.html

Kim, D. J., Agrawal, M., Jayaraman, B., & Rao, H. R. (2003). A comparison of B2B e-service solutions. *Communications of the ACM, 46*(12), 317-324.

Klein, S., & Selz, D. (2000). Cybermediation in auto distribution: Channel dynamics and conflicts. *Journal of Computer-Mediated Communication, 5*(3). Retrieved September 28, 2005, from http://jcmc.indiana.edu/vol5/issue3/kleinselz.htm

Köhne, F., Schoop, M., & Staskiewicz, D. (2005). An empirical investigation of the acceptance of electronic negotiation support system features. *Proceeding of the 13th European Conference on Information Systems,* Regensburg, Germany.

Konana, P., Menon, N. M., & Balasubramanian, S. (2000). The implication of online investing. *Communications of the ACM, 43*(1), 35-41.

Maes, P., Guttman, R. H., & Moukas, A. G. (1999). Agents that buy and sell. *Communications of the ACM, 42*(3), 81-91.

Maglio, P., & Barrett, R. (2000). Intermediaries personalize information streams. *Communications of the ACM, 43*(8), 96-101.

Maruca, R. F. (2000). The electronic negotiator. *Harvard Business Review,* 16-17, Jan-Feb.

McGrath, J. E. (1984). *Groups: Interaction and performance.* Englewood Cliffs, NJ: Prentice Hall.

Palmer, J. W., Bailey, J. P., & Faraj, S. (2000). The role of intermediaries in the development of trust on the WWW: The use and prominence of trusted third parties and privacy statements. *Journal of Computer-Mediated Communication, 5*(3). Retrieved September 28, 2005 from http://jcmc.indiana.edu/vol5/issue3/palmer.html

Paul, S. (2001). Collective memory support in negotiation: A theoretical framework. *Proceeding of the 34th Annual Hawaii International Conference on System Science,* Maui, HI.

Paul, S., Haseman, W. D., & Ramamurthy, K. (2004). Collective memory support and cognitive-conflict group decision-making: An experimental investigation. *Decision Support Systems, 36*, 261-281.

Perkins, W. C., Hershauer, J. C., Foroughi, A., & Delaney, M. M. (1996). Can a negotiation support system help a purchasing manager? *International Journal of Purchasing and Materials Management,* 37-45, spring.

Peterson, R. A., Balasubramanian, S., & Bronnenburg, B. J. (1997). Exploring the implications of the Internet for consumer marketing. *Journal of the Academy of Marketing Science, 25*(4), 329-346.

Purchasing, June 21, 2001, pp.40.

Salam, A. F., Rao, H. R., & Pegels, C. C. (2003). Consumer-perceived risk in e-commerce transactions. *Communications of the ACM, 46*(12ve), 325-331.

Sarkar, M. B., Butler, B., & Steinfield, C. (1995). Intermediaries and cybermediaries: A continuing role for mediating players in the electronic marketplace. *Journal of Computer-Mediated Communication, 1*(3). Retrieved September 28, 2005, from http://jcmc.indiana.edu/vol1/issue3/sarkar.html

Sarner, A. (2004). Prepare to reinvest in e-commerce for growth. Retrieved February 14, 2007, from http://www.gartner.com

Schmitz, S. W. (2000). The effects of electronic commerce on the structure of intermediation. *Journal of Computer-Mediated Communication, 5*(3). Retrieved Sep 28, 05 from http://jcmc.indiana.edu/vol5/issue3/schmitz.html

Schoop, M., Jertila, A., & List, T. (2003). <f>N</f>egoist: A negotiation support system for electronic business-to-business negotiations in e-commerce. *Data & Knowledge Engineering, 47*(3), 371-402.

Scott, J. (2000). Emerging patterns from the dynamic capabilities of Internet intermediaries. *Journal of Computer-Mediated Communication, 5*(3). Retrieved September 28, 2005, from http://jcmc.indiana.edu/vol5/issue3/scott.html

Segev, A., & Beam, C. (1999). Brokering strategies in electronic commerce markets. *Proceedings of the 1st ACM Conference on Electronic Commerce,* Denver, CO.

Singh, R., Iyer, L., & Salam, A. F. (2003). Web service for knowledge management in e-marketplaces. *e-Service Journal, 3*(1), 32-53.

Spector, B. I. (1977). Negotiation as a psychological process. In I. W. Zartman (Ed.), *The negotiation process: Theories and applications.* (pp. 55-66). Beverly Hills, CA: Sage Publications.

Stein, E. W., & Zwass, V. (1995). Actualizing organizational memory with information systems. *Information Systems Research, 6*(2), 85-117.

Swaab, R., Postmes, T., & Neijens, P. (2004). Negotiation support systems: Communication and information as antecedents of negotiation settlement. *International Negotiation, 9*(1), 59-79.

Walczak, S., Gregg, D. G., & Berrenberg, J. L. (2006). Market decision making for online auction seller: Profit maximization or socialization. *Journal of Electronic Commerce Research, 7*(4), 199-220.

Wigand, R. T. (1996). Electronic commerce: Definition, theory, and context. *The Information Society, 13*(1), 1-16.

Yang, C. C., & Chung, A. (2004). Intelligent infomediary for Web financial information. *Decision Support Systems, 38*(1), 65-80.

Zach, M. H. (1999). Managing codified knowledge. *Sloan Management Review,* 45-58, summer.

Zartman, I. W. (1978). *The negotiation process: Theories and applications.* Beverly Hills, CA: Sage Publications.

Zartman, I. W. (1977). Negotiation as a joint decision-making process. In I. W. Zartman (Ed.), *The negotiation process: Theories and applications.* (pp. 67-86). Beverly Hills, CA: Sage Publications.

Chapter XVIII
Morethailand.com:
Online Travel Intermediary

Pongsak Hoontrakul
Sasin of Chulalongkorn University, Thailand

Sunil Sahadev
University of Sheffield, UK

ABSTRACT

The case study showcases morethailand.com, an e-intermediary in the tourism industry. Based out of Thailand, the firm is in the process of finding a niche for itself through innovative online and off-line marketing strategies with the constraint of limited resources. The case study attempts to focus on the e-business challenges in the travel and tourism sector especially in a developing country like Thailand. It specifically highlights the clash between the traditional and modern form of intermediaries in the travel and tourism sector and how it is bound to evolve in the future. A comparison between different approaches to search engine marketing offers an interesting perspective to the literature pertaining to online e-commerce. An economic view on the case is also presented.

INTRODUCTION

It was a challenging task to grow by more than 10 times a year. That was the objective set by Mrs. Nontana Thanabatchai, the founder and managing director of morethailand.com for the coming two years. Morethailand.com was at a turning point in terms of its future performance. While the present increase in the visitor rate and enquiry conversion rate were quite creditable, to emerge as a dominant player in its field, a growth of over 10 times a year was absolutely important. Yet it was achievable if the latest efforts in improving, dynamic pricing, and searching engine optimization bear fruit. The opportunities were immense; the need was to implement a coherent set of strategies that would attract more customers and generate a high transaction rate.

Morethailand.com is an online travel intermediary based in Bangkok, Thailand. The company acts as an intermediary that helps customers around the world book rooms in Thailand hotels through the Internet. Morethailand.com was founded in the year 2002 after the need was felt for setting up a Thailand-based online travel intermediary. The company has a clutch of interconnected Web sites that together provide potential travelers a means for searching for and booking hotel rooms in Thailand. These Web sites also enable potential tourists to book tour packages as well as airline tickets. The Web site displays a list of hotels which are part of the network. A potential tourist can enquire about the availability of rooms as well as to book accommodation in the hotels listed in the Web sites. Provision for tour packages, airline booking, and travel related products are also available. The sites normally get around 5,000 hits a day. Attachment 1 gives a screenshot of the Web site.

Having established itself as a B2C (business-to-consumer) site, morethailand.com is looking forward to strengthening its position in its primary line of activity, that is, online travel intermediation. The primary area of focus was in increasing site traffic by attracting more and more potential tourists to its Web sites. The company was also keen to strengthen its supply side by forging partnerships with more and more independently owned and operated (IOO) hotels in Thailand. This would in turn enable morethailand.com to offer rooms to its customers at more competitive rates than the off-line travel agents who presently occupy the dominant position in the market. The biggest challenge in this endeavor was to compete with large travel wholesalers in gaining acceptance and support from the hotels. This was an extremely difficult task as most of the hotels in Thailand presently depend heavily on large travel

Attachment I. Morethailand.com, screenshot

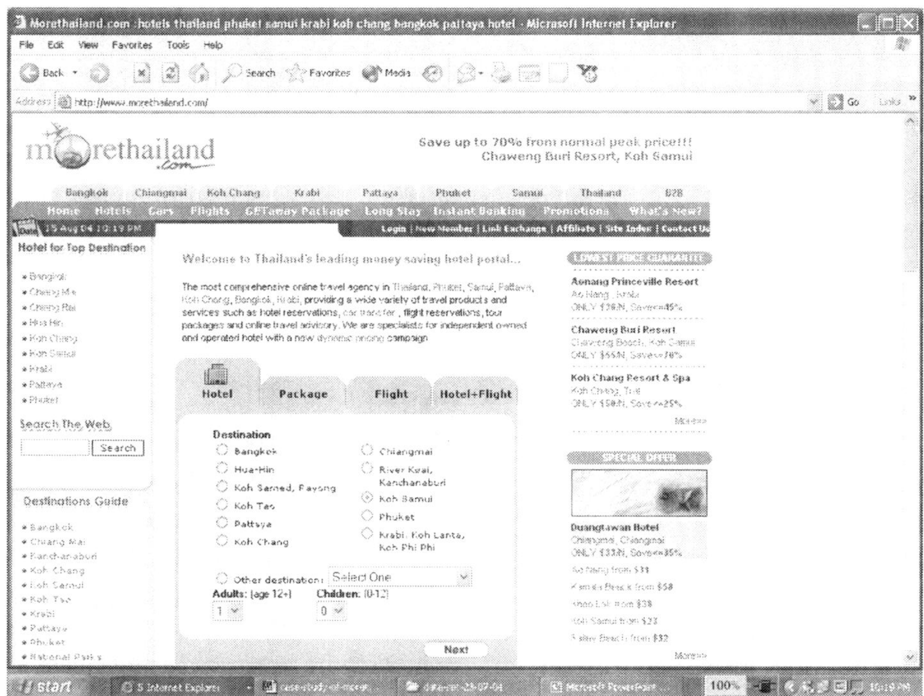

wholesalers or consolidators to sell their rooms in bulk. The off-line intermediaries, who are well entrenched in the market, ensure a steady cash flow for the hotels through bulk buying. The travel wholesalers in turn gain greater power and influence over the hotels who would not like to risk themselves by aligning with a relatively new player like morethailand.com. However, hotels that depend on travel wholesalers have to sell their rooms at a heavy discount to the wholesalers. It is estimated that many hotels sell their rooms to travel wholesalers at almost 30% of their walk-in price. The hotels are compelled to offer such heavy discounts since the travel wholesalers are in a position to ensure high occupancy rates for the hotels. Morethailand.com, on the other hand, demands considerably less discounts from the hotels, though it is presently not in a position to match the travel wholesalers in terms of the number of rooms sold. The critical success factor for morethailand.com is therefore about consistently ensuring higher occupancy rates to its partner hotels so as to gain their commitment and confidence. This in turn has to be achieved by attracting greater traffic to its Web sites and then converting these visitors to enquirers. The case study illustrates the operation of a small startup in the online travel industry and its efforts at capturing market share from much stronger and well entrenched off-line competitors through various e-commerce strategies. It is indeed a great challenge in the face of the turmoil that the Thai tourism industry is presently going through.

TECHNOLOGY ADOPTION FOR TRAVEL AND TOURISM MARKETING: A THEORETICAL PERSPECTIVE

The importance of information and communications technology in the travel and tourism sector has been well acknowledged. In fact, technology has become the main source of sustainable competitive advantage and a strategic weapon, especially in the tourism and hospitality industries owing to the pivotal role information plays in the description, promotion, distribution, amalgamation, organization, and delivery of tourism products (Poon, 1993; Sheldon, 1997). Within the larger ICT adoption, the adoption of Internet and e-commerce in the travel and tourism industry has led to wide ranging transformations both in the industry structure and basic processes. UNCTAD (2000) in its e-commerce and development report states: "The tourism industry is learning fast that the Internet can satisfy the acute need for information at all stages of the tourism product life cycle far better than any other existing technology." The extent of adoption of the Internet as a medium for transaction in the travel and tourism sector is testified by the fact that in the year 2001 almost half of America booked either airfare, hotel reservations, or car rentals online (UNCTAD, 2000). Since 2001, it has increased even further. It is a well-known fact that small or remote destinations and products with well-developed and innovative Web sites can now have equal Internet access. However, the usage of the Internet as a viable medium for promotion and transaction of travel and tourism related services have not been so widespread in the developing countries. The rate of adoption has been hampered by several factors, economic and historical. There has been very little research trying to look at the adoption of e-commerce in the travel and tourism sector in the developing countries. The case study of morethailand.com attempts to contribute to this stream of research. It brings out the main challenges and the unique contextual factors that hamper this adoption in the hotel industry in Thailand, a country that finds a prominent place in the tourism map of any traveler.

TOURISM INDUSTRY IN THAILAND

Tourism is one of the most important sectors in Thailand with about 6% of its GDP contributed by the tourism sector alone (TAT, 2003). In 2003 the Tourism Authority of Thailand (TAT), the nodal agency for tourism promotion in the country, estimated that about 9.31 million people had visited Thailand. The tourist arrivals in Thailand are expected to increase to 12 million in 2004 and are ultimately posed to reach 20 million by 2007 (TAT, 2003). Figure 1 shows the trend in tourism arrival over the past several years.

As Figure 2 indicates, most of the tourists who come to Thailand stay for an average of eight days. This implies that a greater proportion of tourists who arrive in Thailand are holiday makers, with the proportion of business travelers comparatively less.

THE TRAVEL INTERMEDIARY SECTOR IN THAILAND

The intermediaries in the travel and tourism sector exist mainly because of the lack of expertise

Figure 1. Tourist arrivals in Thailand over the past five years (TAT, 2003)

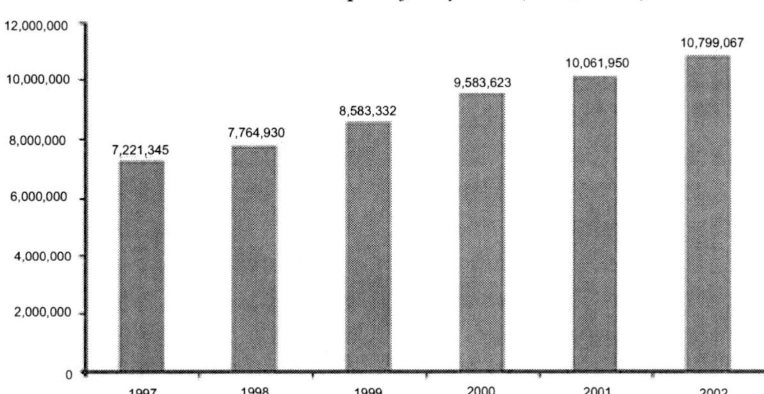

Figure 2. Average length of stay in Thailand

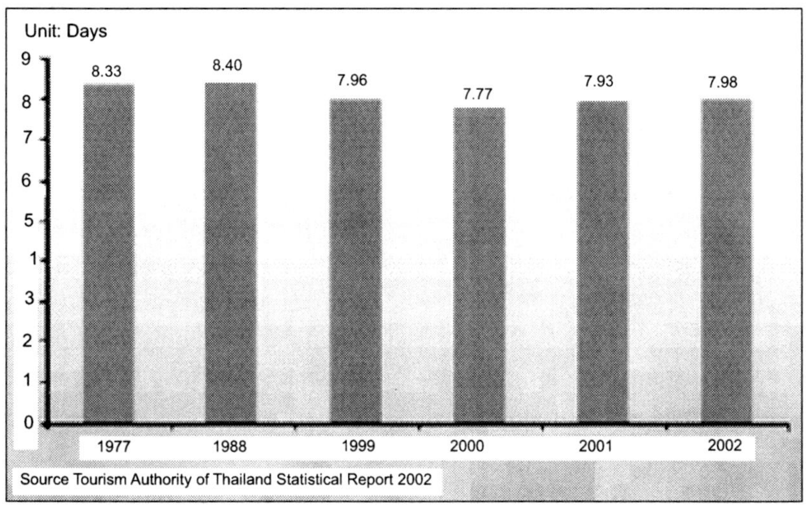

and inclination of the eventual service providers to indulge in direct sales. Being primarily service providers, hotels generally consider it difficult to attract customers on their own. They are therefore quite happy to stick to their area of expertise and thus do not have the inclination or resources to shoulder the responsibility of selling rooms directly. On the other hand, without expending adequate selling effort, it is quite difficult to achieve high occupancy rates in large hotels with more than 200 rooms because word-of-mouth as a means of promotion is very limited in scope. Further, in the travel and tourism sector the customers and service providers are normally separated by large geographical distances. This makes the position of the intermediary at close contact with the customer absolutely indispensable. It is for this reason that most hotels rely heavily on travel agencies or tour operators to market their properties. The travel agencies perform the task of managing the inventory of the hotels, especially for new hotels and new destinations. The hotels in turn offer rooms to these intermediaries at a heavy discount which serves as the operating margin for the travel agent. Figure 3 shows the different types of distribution channels in the travel and tourism industry that sell hotel rooms on behalf of the hotels to the travelers.

The basic inability and disinclination of hotels to market their products directly to its customers can be attributed to certain fundamental economic reasons. If hotels attempt to promote their properties on their own, they will be (1) unable to achieve economies of scale and (2) unable to achieve economies of scope. The inability to achieve economies of scale is due to the highly dispersed customer base spread across all the continents that in turn necessitates that any marketing effort has to be truly global in nature. Further, the atomized nature of demand necessitates the presence of an extremely large sales network for a hotel that is to be in a position to achieve sales targets consistently. Consequently, the promotional expenditure associated with selling tourism products on a global scale will be very high. Since a large sales and marketing network is economically feasible only when large numbers of rooms (maybe tens of thousands of room nights) are sold through it, a single hotel or even a relatively large hotel will not be in a position to achieve any economies of scale if it attempts to market directly without the help of intermediaries.

The potential customer, on the other hand, will be more interested if a whole host of choices are provided like a beach resort, a golf holiday, a river cruise, and so forth, at the point of sale so

Figure 3.

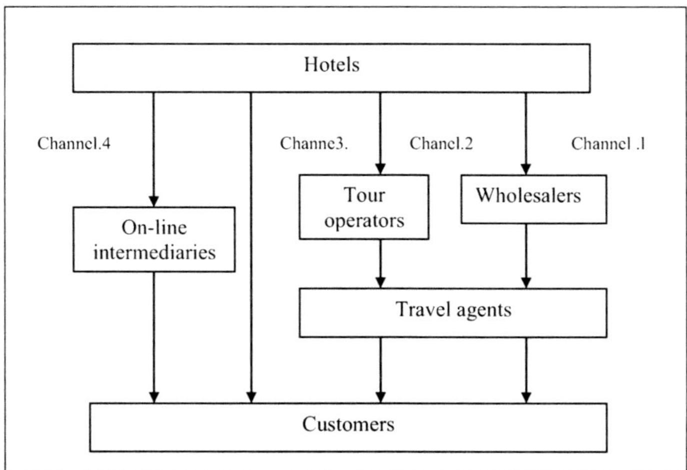

that the customer can choose a particular hotel or destination according to preference. When a single hotel offers its products on an individual basis, the choice set presented to the potential customer will naturally be very limited and thereby reduces the potential customer's motivation to search and select. Therefore it becomes absolutely essential to rely on intermediaries who can achieve both economies of scale and scope in distribution by bundling an attractive choice set for the customers.

The preeminence of intermediaries can also be justified on the basis of the unique features of the tourism product. At the point of sale, tourism is little more than an information product since the customer decides about consuming a product mostly based on the information about the product from various sources. Further, during the period leading up to the time when the product is actually consumed, consumers must be confident that the experience purchased will materialize and satisfy their expectations. Tourism is also thus considered a credence good as discussed by Hoontrakul (2004). This is because experience attributes predominate in a tourism product (Cooper et al., 1998). While a potential customer can see photos and get a very general feel of the destination the customer is going to visit, it is extremely important that the customer is made to imagine the experience of visiting a destination. This is probably possible on a large scale only with the help of intermediaries who could explain and give a credible idea about what the visitor can expect. Intermediaries therefore are required to reduce the high level of information asymmetry that exists between the potential customer and the service provider. During the transaction phase, it is hence important that the customer is fed with the right information which the customer can feel confident about. This fact puts the established intermediary located at the customer's end in a position of great advantage.

As can be seen from Figure 3, there are four possible ways through which a customer can book an accommodation in a hotel. Of the four, the first channel which involves the wholesaler and the travel agent is the most established and popular one. The wholesalers are large intermediaries with links to several hotels and several travel agents. The wholesalers demand huge discounts from the hotels as they deal with big volumes. The discounts normally are in the range of 50 to 60% (sometimes even 70%) of the room rent eventually charged by the hotel from the guest. A part of this discount is passed on to the travel agent who is in direct contact with the customer. The other part becomes the operating revenue for the wholesaler. Due to the huge volume handled, the wholesalers are very powerful in the market. It is estimated that about 70% of the hotels are highly reliant on the wholesalers for their marketing effort. The wholesalers are typically based in Europe from where most of the tourists originate. It is widely acknowledged that the large tourism wholesalers have been instrumental in developing the Thai tourism market. When most of the destinations were relatively unknown, the wholesalers had marketed it quite enthusiastically, especially in the developed countries. This rapidly led to the development of these destinations. The travel wholesalers like LTU, TUI, and Thomas Cook with monopsony-like market power thus enjoyed the first mover advantage in dealing with most of the hotels, especially in gaining access to a large inventory of rooms at a relatively bargain price.

The second channel comprised of the travel wholesaler, tour operator, and the travel agent is the second most popular channel. Tour operators package the tour for the customer and sell these packages through the travel agent. The customer in fact may not even know which hotel the customer will be staying in while booking for the tour. The third channel via the direct channel or walk-ins are not very practicable to depend upon especially for large hotels with more than 200 rooms. This is because intense competition among the hoteliers has made it impossible to sell their rooms entirely on the support of word-of-mouth. Further, since there is a huge geographical barrier between the tourist and the hotel, creating awareness about the hotel itself is a stupendous task. However some rooms (less than 10%) get sold directly.

The online channel is the latest and emerging channel, which was expected at one time to revolutionize the sector. However, the utility of the channel for a hotel still remains quite limited, as the business generated by this channel for an average hotel is still not significant. The online channel is comprised of different routes. For instance, a hotel can be a member of a large Web site like expedia.com or rely on an emerging online intermediary like morethailand.com.

THE ONLINE TRAVEL AND TOURISM CHANNEL

With increasing Internet penetration, the online travel industry has seen phenomenal growth over the years (Marcussen, 2004). The online travel industry consists of large global distribution systems (GDS), online travel agents who operate on a global basis as well as online travel agents with a regional presence. The GDS like SABRE, Amadeus, World Span, Galileo, and so forth, have been in existence since the late 1970s. These systems span the entire world and enable travel agencies to book airline tickets or hotel rooms anywhere in the world. Of these systems, only World Span is available through the Internet.

Large global intermediaries like expedia.com, orbitz.com, travelocity.com, and so forth, have a worldwide presence. They enable customers anywhere in the world to search for and book rooms in any part of the world. These Web sites often cater to large hotels or hotel chains that have a well-known brand. Another type of online travel intermediary is the global marketing representatives like utell.com, Best Western, Concorde, and so forth. These companies cater to independent owned hotels which are not large enough to invest in being a part of the GDS. These companies provide an interface between the hotels and the travel agencies (O'Conner, 1999).

The latest entrants in this field are e-intermediaries that operate exclusively through the Internet. While they are similar to large e-intermediaries like expedia.com or orbitz.com, the new intermediaries normally concentrate on particular regions and cater to small or independent hotels. Some of the main players in this field in Thailand, apart from morethailand.com, are asiatravel.com, sawadee.com, phuket.com, and hotels-thailand.com. However, except morethailand.com, most of the other e-intermediaries are nothing more than electronic directories since they operate mostly on a commission basis. These intermediaries basically provide a much cheaper and easier way for hotels to sell their rooms through cyberspace. The business model for these intermediaries is quite simple. They enter into a contract with hotels in a destination and include their names on their Web site. Customers who visit the Web sites of these companies can search and book a room matching their requirements through the Web site. The e-intermediary receives a commission/profit for each room booked through their Web site. The main cost for the e-intermediaries is to maintain staff for the back office activities and promotion of their Web sites. The back office activities include receiving and answering to the enquiries from the customers, contacting the hotels for availability of rooms, and finalizing the transactions. The marketing activities include search engine optimization, e-mail marketing, and other means of off-line promotion. Hotels which find it costlier to have electronic interfaces can easily make themselves available to a global audience through the Internet by contracting with these e-intermediaries. Customers are also benefited since it makes it easier for them to search and book rooms at affordable rates.

The emergence of e-intermediaries as a strong contender against off-line travel wholesalers and consolidators can be attributed to several technological and market-related factors (Buhalis & Licata, 2002). With the rapid expansion of the

Internet in the developed countries, the prime market for Thailand, the advantage enjoyed by the travel wholesalers due to their proximity to the customers has been blunted to a substantial extent. With the "death of distance," the information delivery through the Internet satisfies most of the customers quite well. Further, e-intermediaries were in a position to operate with considerably less operating costs than the large travel wholesalers located in some of the most expensive cities with a large employee contingent. This enabled the e-intermediaries to match the travel wholesalers in terms of the discounts charged from hotels. In fact e-intermediaries often are able to offer more attractive benefits to the hotels than large travel wholesalers.

Table 1. The number of hotels (accommodation establishments) in the important destinations in Thailand

		Bangkok	Krabi	Pattaya	Phuket	Samui
Source:	www2.tat.or.th/stat					
Year	2003					
Supply						
Number of Accom. Estab.		259	290	250	549	357
Grade 1		78	53	12	178	33
Grade 2		46	192	14	304	30
Grade 3		35	45	25	3	23
Grade 4		69	-	84	10	70
Grade 5		31	-	116	54	200
Number of Rooms Available		54,904	9,088	25,349	31,302	10,913
Grade 1		30,247	2,036	4,599	13,712	2,599
Grade 2		9,108	5,577	2,888	13,786	1,635
Grade 3		5,688	1,475	4,899	367	969
Grade 4		7,361	-	7,752	525	1,975
Grade 5		2,500	-	5,211	2,912	3,735

Note:	
Classification	Room rate (Baht)
Grade 1	>2500
Grade 2	1501 - 2500
Grade 3	1001 - 1500
Grade 4/5	<1000

THE HOTEL INDUSTRY IN THAILAND

Hotels in Thailand are typically classified into tier-I and tier-II. Table 1 gives the number of hotels in each category at the most favorite destinations in Thailand. The tier-I hotels are typically large hotels and generally form part of a hotel chain. These hotels are mostly associated with a global hotel chain like Group Accor or Holiday Inn. They are often professionally managed and use a global distribution system like SABRE, AMADEUS, and so forth, or are attached to a global Web site like expedia.com or travelocity.com. The potential customers book rooms in these hotels when they use any of these intermediary networks. Out of the estimated 10,000 hotel properties in Thailand, not more than 10% are considered as belonging to tier-I. Almost all international hotel chains like Group Accor, Marriott, Holiday Inn, Hilton, and so forth, are present in Thailand apart from Thailand-based chains like Dusit Thani, Central, and so forth.

The tier-II hotels are normally known as IOO. Many of these hotels are small with less than 200 rooms, though a few large IOO hotels also exist. However, most of the IOO hotels are stand-alone hotels. These lodges were normally owned by a local landlord and the management structure in these hotels presents a typical principal-agent problem in the Jensen and Meckling (1976) sense. These properties would typically have an owner, a general manager, and a sales director. The owner would often be a local landowner, not quite competent to run the affairs of the hotel and is only interested in the profits generated. Normally these landlords had constructed the hotel in their land by managing to secure funds from different sources. Once the property is built, they expect a steady stream of profits. The general manager and the sales directors are professionals but often have conflicting interests with the owners. The owner is more interested in the amount of profit and cash flow generated from operations and thus not too keen to give huge discounts to the travel wholesalers. The sales director in turn is more interested in incentive payout from the total sale, while the general manager would like to improve occupancy rates and hotel food and beverage sales. Thus, they would not be wary of teaming up with travel wholesalers who would often demand high levels of discounts in return for ensuring a steady occupancy rate. This agency problem leads to high turnover of executives in many of these IOOs. It is estimated that a sales director's average tenure in an IOO is not more than two years. These conflicting interests and the differences in perceptions make it difficult for the e-intermediaries to enter into contracts with these hotels. While the management teams will often be pro-travel wholesalers, the owner may be more appreciative of the efforts of the e-intermediary. Since the level of discounts provided by the hotel to the e-intermediary as well as the commitment of rooms during high season are two major issues that determine viability of e-intermediaries, such internal problems within hotel organizations often prove to be very difficult to tackle. It is hence conjectured that online intermediaries would have a much easier time with the IOO hotels, when managed by the owner.

The IOOs do not have any major presence on the World Wide Web though they may have their own Web sites. Very few transactions take place directly between the customers and the hotels through their Web sites. This is because it is very unlikely for a potential customer to come and visit the Web site without any promotion of the Web site on the part of the hotel.

The IOOs find e-intermediaries like morethailand.com an attractive proposition to collaborate with since they do not have the manpower or expertise to manage the inventory transactions if they become part of a GDS or other centralized reservation systems. Only chain hotels can afford to become part of a GDS since they require a well developed and constantly updated electronic database to be a part of the GDS. Further, it is estimated that even in those hotels which are linked to the GDS hardly 10% of the rooms are booked through that route. This is mainly because of the fact that a GDS is only a network that enables online reservation on a global scale and does not indulge in any kind of promotion activities with regard to the hotels. On the other hand, the e-intermediaries through their promotional campaigns market themselves as well as the hotels that are part of it.

Attachment 2.

Northern Region	
Location	no. of hotels
Chiang Mai	32
Ghiang Rai	8
Pitsanulok	7
Rest	16
Total	**63**
Central /Eastern /Western	
Location	no. of hotels
Bangkok	62
Pattaya	47
Huahin	21
Koh Chang	12
Koh Samet	13
Kanchanaburi	14
Rest	23
Total	**192**
North Eastern	
Location	no. of hotels
Nakhon Ratchsima	6
Rest	10
Total	**16**
Southern	
Location	no. of hotels
Phuket	76
Krabi	59
Samui	56
Phang Nga	18
Rest	2
Total **211**	

Morethailand.com offers the hotels that are part of their network (1) flexibility in managing their inventory and (2) support by means of Internet marketing and other types of promotional activities. Hotels can also promote themselves through the morethailand.com Web site by renting out a preferred area in the site which could catch the attention of the Web surfers when they open the Web page. For the hotels, morethailand.com is of course only one of the avenues for selling rooms. Usually hotels will form linkages with several intermediaries like travel agents, tour operators, e-intermediaries, and so forth.

CONTRACTUAL AGREEMENTS WITH HOTELS

Morethailand.com has contractual arrangements with around 500 hotels located all over Thailand. The number of hotels having linkages with morethailand.com from the different regions of Thailand is given in Attachment 2. For morethailand.com to make available rooms of a particular hotel to be booked through its Web site, the company has to enter into contractual agreements with the concerned hotels. These agreements cover aspects like commission sharing, clauses on cancellation of rooms, procedures for payment, and so forth. Hotels usually sell rooms to intermediaries in three ways: (1) the commission rate, (2) the contractual rate, and (3) the merchant system. In the commission rate system, the hotels decide the eventual selling price and give a commission to the intermediary as per the contract while in the contractual rate system the hotels sell rooms to the intermediary at a particular rate and the intermediary in turn has the freedom to sell the rooms at whatever rate it deems fit. In both the systems, however, there is no commitment from the intermediary side to sell a certain number of rooms. In the merchant model followed by a few large online intermediaries like expedia.com, the intermediary actually buys rooms at a very low rate from the hotel and then resells them to the travelers. In this system the intermediary loses money if it is not capable of selling the rooms to the customers. In the case of morethailand.com, about 20% of its contracts are at commission rates while 70% are in contract rates.

Each of the contracts will be valid for a year. It takes at least a week to more than a month to get a contract signed from a hotel. On average, the commission (either in the form of commission or discounts) given to morethailand.com will be in the range of around 30%. The contract with the hotel also mentions the policy with regard to cancellations. Almost 70% of the hotels in the list charge an average room rent of Thai baht 3000 to 5000 per night. It is estimated that about 50% of the hotels in the list do not get any enquiries at all while most of the bookings are for about 20% of the hotels. Morethailand.com is very selective in inducting hotels into its network for cost-effectiveness. Only hotels of a particular standard are included in the network. The main reason is that the firm wants to ensure a certain standard in the service provided by the hotels to its customers who book rooms through morethailand.com. Subsequently, the partner hotels would be visited for inspection at least once in a year by the staff from morethailand.com. Accommodations which give poor service constantly, as reported by the customers, are deleted or suspended from the list by morethailand.com.

Morethailand.com has just started with the merchant system with a few hotels. In the merchant model, morethailand.com purchases room inventories prepaid at a cheaper rate for a specific period of time and promotes through its Web site. The potential customers are offered these rooms at a competitive rate as morethailand.com is able to pass on the benefits of the heavy discounts to the customers. In addition, morethailand.com is experimenting with the dynamic pricing model by varying prices offered to the customers on the basis of their time of booking. Customers who book in advance are offered rooms at a cheaper rate than those who book later.

MORETHAILAND.COM VISITOR STATISTICS

Presently there are 12 Web sites for the company and each Web site contributes directly and indirectly to the traffic. Maintaining 12 Web sites is part of a well thought out strategy. Other than morethailand.com, all the other Web sites are mainly meant to provide information. For instance a Web site like www.moresamui.com is primarily meant

Table 2. Hits and unique visitors for the major Web sites in the morethailand.com stable

Web site	Hit/week	Avg./Day	Unique Visitors	Avg./Day
morethailand	4,429,170	142,876	64,250	2,073
morebangkok	484,810	15,639	20,866	673
morekrabi	238,436	7,691	6,316	204
morephuket	241,337	7,785	6,432	207
moresamui	344,760	11,121	9,395	303
morepattaya	92,957	2,999	2,288	74
morethilandmap	398,344	12,850	4,927	159
thaiparks123	1,309,091	42,229	15,311	494
total	7,538,905	243,190	129,785	4,187

to provide information about hotels in a destination called Samui. Morethailand.com on the other hand is primarily meant to be a transaction site. Though a customer could do transactions through an allied site like www.moresamui.com, transaction is not the primary purpose behind maintenance of the Web site. Most of these allied Web sites serve the purpose of increasing the company's visibility when potential customers search using destinations as keywords in search engines. This is because travelers familiar with Thailand often search using destination-specific keywords like Sumui, Phuket, or Krabi and having a Web site with the keyword as a part of its URL increases the possibility of achieving a higher rank in the Web site listings of search engines.

Together, all the 12 Web sites generate around 22,000 hits and 5,000 unique visitors per day. Table 2 gives the number of hits and number of unique visitors to morethailand.com and its associated sites during the month of October 2004. Analysis of the traffic shows that most of the competitors are generating more hits than this figure. Sawadee.com, which is the closest competitor for morethailand.com is estimated to generate four times more hits than morethailand.com. As Table 2 indicates, the number of hits received by the Web sites allied to morethailand.com also varies

Table 3. Details about traffic to morethailand.com

Overview	% Change	19-25 Jun.04		12-18 Jun.04	
		Visitor	Avg.	Visitor	Avg.
Unique Visitor (Web trend)	-4.56%	17228	2461	18051	2579
Adword	1.16%	2098	300	2074	296
Adword (Destination)	2.27%	1487	212	1454	208
Adword (Nationalities)	-1.45%	611	87	620	89
Search Engine	5.03%	3154	451	3003	429
Search Engine (Google)	9.39%	1561	223	1427	204
Search Engine (Yahoo)	-11.97%	618	88	702	100
Referring Domain	-6.45%	20862	2980	22301	3186
Our Storefronts	14.01%	6421	917	5632	805
Direct	-19.85%	5378	768	6710	959
No Referer	-9.17%	6450	921	7101	1014
Top Spiders	-26.46%	2527	361	3436	491
Googlebot	12.19%	451	64	402	57
Yahoobot	-32.13%	1992	285	2935	419
Unique Visitor (Truehits)	3.21%	3957	565	3834	548

considerably. Table 3 gives details for the total hits and the break up of the sources through which these hits originated. It is estimated that about 300 hits are generated per day from google.com while yahoo.com generates 100 hits and msn.com generates another 100 hits.

THE CUSTOMER PROFILE

It is worth noting that most of the visitors to the morethailand.com Web sites are repeat travelers having traveled in Thailand before. Nearly all Web site visitors are well educated and have good knowledge of the destinations they are about to choose. About 70% of the customers are from Europe and the rest are from other parts of the world including the U.S. In terms of volume of transactions, around 80% are for leisure travel while the rest are for business travel. This skewed ratio for leisure travel is explained by the fact that most of the hotels listed on the Web sites are located in destinations better known for leisure travel. Business travelers usually visit just Bangkok and since morethailand.com has less than 100 hotels listed in Bangkok, it is quite natural that the Web site caters mostly to the leisure traveler.

The customers generally progress through three stages before they indulge in a transaction. In the initial stage the customers just visit the site. Once they are serious about traveling to Thailand, the visitors post an enquiry about the rooms and the price at which these rooms are available. This is considered the enquiry phase. It is estimated that just 4 to 5% of the visitors end up enquiring about the product displayed on the Web site. Out of the enquirers about 35 to 40% eventually end up transacting with the company during the

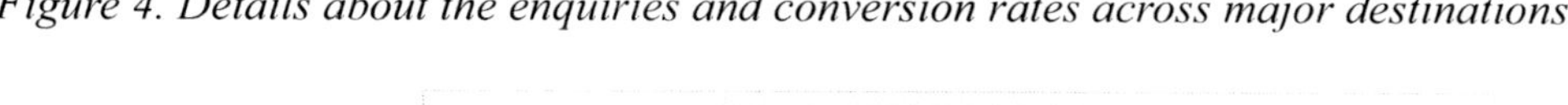
Figure 4. Details about the enquiries and conversion rates across major destinations

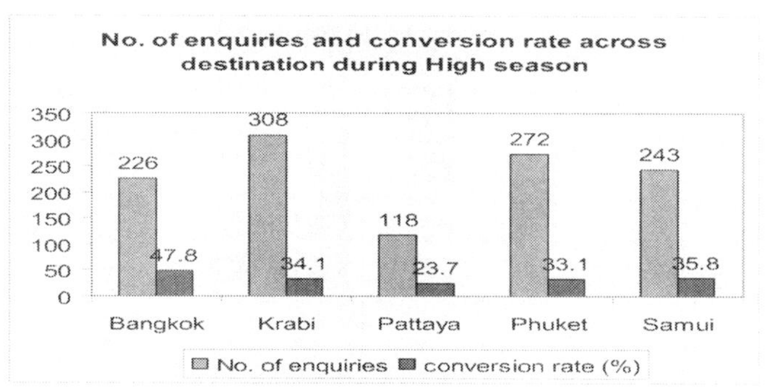

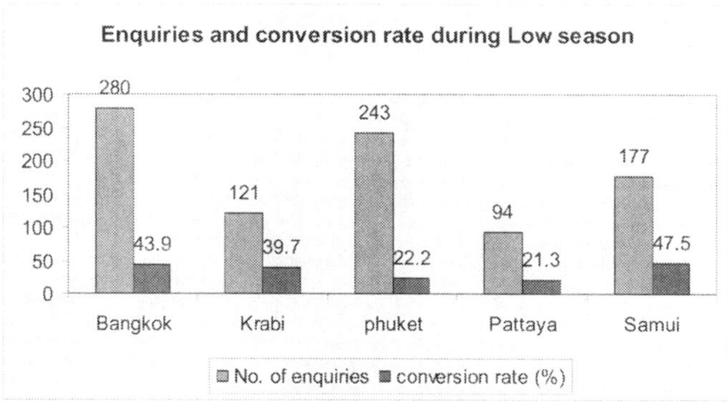

normal season. The transaction rate for the five main destinations focused by morethailand.com is shown in Figure 4.

High season in Thailand would mean the months of November to March of every year. It is estimated that about 70% of the tourists visit Thailand during these five months (TAT, 2004). As indicated in Figure 4, the enquiry conversion rates vary from one location to another and also from one season to another. Except in Bangkok where there is little impact of seasonal demand, in all other destinations, the number of enquiries is considerably less in low season than in high season. The conversion rate does not seem to be determined by the seasonal fluctuation since it is seen to be varying unevenly across different seasons across different destinations.

It has also been observed that 80% of the bookings are for rooms with rents ranging between 1500 to 3000 Thai bahts. Enquiries are classified on the basis of the price of the rooms and the actual sales are classified on the price of the rooms, shown in Figure 5.

Before the enquiry culminates into a transaction, the potential customer may require more information about the destination, the hotel to stay, even about the possibility of reducing the price. The entire process normally takes about a week. Hence the sales cycle is about five to seven days. Once the visitor transforms to an enquirer, it is assumed that the enquirer is in touch with other Web sites offering similar products to compare the price. The communication normally progresses through e-mail during this phase. Once the enquirer is convinced about the right hotel and the right price, the enquirer transacts with morethailand.com. Once the transaction is complete with the amount paid, either through

Figure 5 . Type of enquiries and sales classified in terms of the price per room

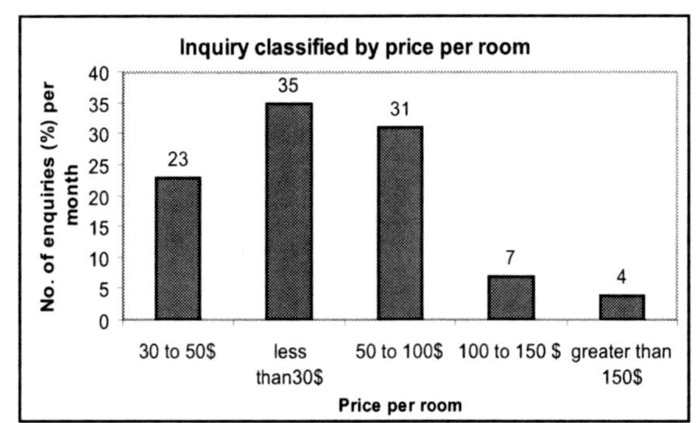

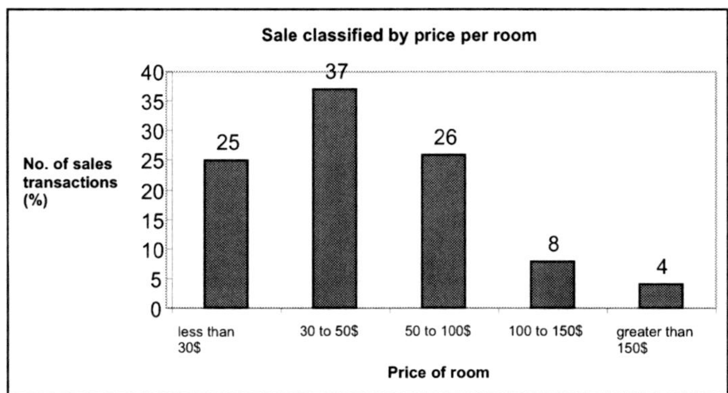

credit card or through bank transfer, the amount net its commission is passed on to the respective hotel at least three days before the customer checks in.

While this is the normal process of transaction with the customer through morethailand.com, two types of transactions are actually possible. The normal transactions explained previously are not instant and have a sales cycle of about five to seven days. In the second type, called instant transactions, the traveler gets instant confirmation for a room booked through the Web site. However, such instant transactions are normally less than 10% of the total transactions. Moreover the instant booking facility will not be available with all the hotels listed in the Web site. For making available the instant booking facility, morethailand.com has to enter into a special contract with the hotel so that some rooms are kept apart for morethailand.com for a particular period of time.

Since the site also offers lucrative tour packages, almost one new package is introduced every week. At a time, there can be about 60 such packages. Among the variety of packages offered, the long stay packages in turn are very popular since the price at which they are offered is very low compared to the normal rates. It is in fact estimated that about 50% of the customers who book through morethailand.com opt for long stay packages.

It is difficult to list factors that lead to greater conversion from the enquiry. The room rent quoted by the hotels in the list is considered to be a main reason. Other factors include the service provided by the Web site in terms of the variety of packages, confidence of the traveler with the service providers listed in the site, and so forth. Since it is difficult to understand the real factors that lead to greater conversion, it is also difficult to either differentiate or position the services. The average duration of stay of a traveler who books through morethailand.com is estimated to be about three to seven days. It is of course clear that most of the travelers who transact through morethailand.com are price-sensitive customers, as they have a definite threshold as far as the price of a room is concerned. Since the Web site also offers, but is not focused on, an airline booking facility, a small percentage (about 10%) of the travelers also use morethailand.com for composite booking of their stay and travel. For packages, the main attraction seems to be the price reduction offered through the long stay packages as well as the pick up and transfer arrangements. Another trend that has been noticed is the increase in customer traffic caused due to the popularity of certain hotels. Certain properties end up becoming very attractive with the travelers either due to the superior service that they provide or because of the scenic beauty of their location, and thus attract customers to the Web site. The positive word of mouth about the hotel also contributes to the increase in traffic.

ONLINE MARKETING EFFORT OF THE MORETHAILAND.COM

The main marketing activities of the company are comprised of search engine optimization (SEO) and search engine marketing (SEM) carried out on some of the most popular search engines like google.com, yahoo.com, and msn.com. SEO relates to altering the content of the Web site in order to make it easier for the search engines to find and understanding the content's essence. A search engine's mission is to deliver the most relevant results to searchers; therefore, the search engine rank that a Web site will enjoy is dependent on the content and linking strategy. This is a constant process and involves the full time attention of about four staff members. It has been found that increasing the traffic to the site is a major way of increasing the transaction levels. SEO aims to keep the company's Web sites in the first 10 positions in the list that emerges when the customer types the most popular keywords in the three search engines. This is ensured through positioning specific keywords in strategic positions on the Web pages, trying for achieving links from other sites to morethailand.com, and so forth. Reputation management, online PR, and content freshness based on seasonal search behavior, as well as trend adjustments, are on-going processes that will enhance a search engine friendly site.

Apart from SEO, the company also conducts SEM whereby it advertises on google.com to obtain sponsored links for certain keywords. These sponsored links appear on the right side of the screen when certain keywords are used for searching through google.com. In order that a Web site URL appears as a sponsored link in the first screen for a keyword, google.com charges a certain amount per click-through. This click-through rate varies from one keyword to another based on its popularity. This is because, for each keyword, there will be more than one claimant for the first few spaces in the sponsored link. In order to be in the first three positions in the sponsored link space, each of the sites have to bid for the keyword. The bidding is for the click-through rate.

Table 4. Outcome of the destination specific campaign carried out between November 24-30, 2005

Campaign	Impression	Clicks	Clicks Last Week	Cost	Conversions	Cost / Conv.	CTR	Avg CPC	Avg Position	Avg Position Last Week
Samui	13,287	124	140	$42.47	1	$42.47	0.90%	$0.34	4.6	3.8
Bangkok	4,169	83	61	$26.43	5	$5.29	2.00%	$0.32	6.6	7.4
Phuket	14,554	305	271	$102.79	7	$14.68	2.10%	$0.34	5.5	5.7
Krabi	20,115	289	285	$51.00	4	$12.75	1.40%	$0.18	3.6	3.4
Pattaya	7,133	103	111	$43.14	4	$10.78	1.40%	$0.42	5.4	5.4
Koh Chang	10,463	249	285	$35.84	4	$8.96	2.40%	$0.14	2.9	3
Chiang Mai	8,597	126	125	$34.13	3	$11.38	1.50%	$0.27	4.2	2.6
Chiang Rai	24,742	172	11	$27.15	0	$0.00	0.70%	$0.16	na	na
Phitsanulok	1,144	23	16	$2.07	0	$0.00	2.00%	$0.09	1.7	1.7
Sukhothai	0	0	43	$0.00	0	$0.00	0.00%	$0.00	3.5	3
Koh Tao	6,976	160	12	$27.14	0	$0.00	2.30%	$0.17	4.4	4.7
Trang	778	12	12	$1.15	0	$0.00	1.50%	$0.10	na	na
Hua Hin	8,642	83	95	$23.88	3	$7.96	1.00%	$0.29	na	na
Kanchanaburi	2,088	32	39	$2.38	0	$0.00	1.50%	$0.07	na	na
Ayuthaya	2,636	21	26	$3.02	0	$0.00	0.80%	$0.14	na	na
Khon Kaen	2,506	39	44	$2.75	0	$0.00	1.60%	$0.07	2.1	1.8
Ubon Ratchathani	1,000	25	32	$1.25	0	$0.00	2.50%	$0.05	2.3	1.9
Udon Thani	2,467	70	45	$4.77	0	$0.00	2.80%	$0.07	5.8	3.8
Nakhon Ratchasima	1,157	26	16	$1.89	0	$0.00	2.20%	$0.07	2.4	1.9
Overall	177,971	2,277	2,076	$475.80	31	$15.35	1.30%	$0.21		

If a company bids the highest for a keyword like "Phuket," then when the customer searches using the keyword "Phuket" in google.com, the link to a relevant site will appear as the first among three or four sites in the sponsored link portion of the screen. It is always important to be in the first three; otherwise a Web site may not appear on the first page of the keyword results. As a consequence, the sponsored link will be of little use. The most crucial part in SEM is therefore to identify the most popular keywords and successfully bid for them. This is because there are thousands of keywords that are used by the customers to search in google.com and it is virtually impossible to get sponsored links for each of these keywords. The paid campaigns through google.com are classified into (1) nationality specific campaigns in which Google sites of specific countries are considered and (2) destination specific campaigns where the sponsored links for destinations are sought and paid for.

Table 5. Results of a nationality-based campaign carried out during November 24-30, 2005

Campaign	Clicks	Clicks Last Week	Cost	Conversions	Conversion %	Cost / Conv.	Impressions	CTR	Avg CPC	Avg Position	Avg Position Last Week
Australia	20	17	$7.98	0	0.00%	0	1751	1.10%	$0.40	6.6	6.6
Canada	1	0	$0.20	0	0.00%	$0.00	171	0.60%	$0.20	5.6	6.2
China	8	7	$1.20	0	0.00%	$0.00	925	0.90%	$0.15	3.7	4.1
Denmark	63	68	$25.17	0	0.00%	0	4783	1.30%	$0.40	4	5
England	57	63	$17.60	0	0.00%	0	5709	1.00%	$0.31	5.9	6
Finland	24	17	$8.47	1	4.20%	$8.47	4179	0.60%	$0.35	4.8	5
Hong Kong & Taiwan	10	7	$1.81	0	0.00%	$0.00	403	2.50%	$0.18	5.6	5.2
India	14	11	$2.25	0	0.00%	$0.00	576	2.40%	$0.16	4.6	4.3
Japan	15	15	$8.41	0	0.00%	0	1068	1.40%	$0.56	4.3	4.6
Netherland	16	34	$4.86	0	0.00%	$0.00	2907	0.60%	$0.30	6	5.6
Norway	29	42	$10.38	0	0.00%	0	7835	0.40%	$0.36	3.9	3.9
Promotion_ big saving	2	14	$0.22	0	0.00%	$0.00	1072	0.20%	$0.11	5.5	2.9
Russia	0	0	$0.00	0	0.00%	0	2	0.00%	$0.00	5	5.5
Singapore.	10	6	$2.85	0	0.00%	$0.00	929	1.10%	$0.28	6.1	7
Sweden	171	211	$68.67	2	1.20%	$34.34	23153	0.70%	$0.40	3.3	3
Switzerland	5	15	$0.72	1	20.00%	$0.72	621	0.80%	$0.14	5.2	5.3
U.S.A	43	37	$55.43	0	0.00%	0	9959	0.40%	$1.29	4.7	4.7
Overall	927	1076	$306.16	6	0.60%	$51.03	137953	0.70%	$0.33	4.7	4.6

COMPARISON BETWEEN DESTINATION- AND NATIONALITY-BASED CAMPAIGNS THROUGH GOOGLE.COM

The destination-specific campaigns and nationality-specific campaigns use two different approaches. In destination-based campaigns, keywords associated with specific destinations like Bangkok, Samui, Krabi, and so forth, are booked in google.com so that when Web searchers type any of these destination-based keywords, a link to morethailand.com or any other associated Web site appears in the search screen on the right side. Morethailand.com has to pay a specific click-through amount for obtaining a specific position on the screen. Table 4 shows a report of the outcome of a destination campaign through google.com. Overall, during the week when this report was taken, morethailand.com paid about US$475.00 for 2,277 clicks and 31 enquiries. The summary table (Table 6) shows the total transactions that directly resulted from the 31 enquiries and the volume of the transactions from these enquiries. A total of 15 enquiries were converted to orders with a value of US$4730.57. With an order processing cost of roughly about US$7 per order and a margin of roughly 15%, this works out to an ROI of about 10%.

For nationality specific campaigns, morethailand.com pays for sponsored links in nationality specific google.com sites; for instance, to cater to the Italian audience, morethailand.com pays for sponsored links in the Italian version of google.com via google.co.it. The details of the outcome of the nationality specific campaign for a particular week in November 2005 are given in Table 5. The nationality campaign is much less profitable, but more targeted oriented to achieve other marketing objectives (e.g., strategic coverage, visibility, branding, etc.). The total amount spent was about US$306 which generated 927 clicks and 6 direct conversions. The campaign during the week considered generated to confirmed orders with a total volume of about US$1787.00. This turns out to a ROI of about -20% after considering the order processing cost.

However, it is not always vital to look at specific conversions; the click-through that has been achieved is an immense advantage in terms of promotion of the Web site, especially in terms of achieving greater visibility and patronage in the long run. Further the conversions registered in the calculations are just the direct registrations. In reality there will be several customers who might click and browse the Web on a particular occasion and transact much later. The ROI calculation mentioned previously does not capture such transactions which are the indirect effects of the google-based promotion campaigns. Overall, it can be said that campaigns which are essentially based on click through rates are much less profit-

Table 6. Total enquiries and sales due to the search engine marketing activities during the time period November 24-30, 2005, for morethailand.com and associated sites

	Enquiry		Sale		
	total number	Volume (US$)	total number	Volume (US$)	
Total Inquiry	93	29,762.63	44	12,739.69	43%
Adword Track Inquiry	37	15,550.18	17	6,517.95	42%
- Destination	31	11,826.43	15	4,730.57	40%
- Nationality	6	3,723.75	2	1,787.38	48%

able in the short run. Their major contribution is in the long run. For a firm like morethailand.com, it is more profitable to have organic enquiries which are attracted through word of mouth or through repeat customers. The search engine-based marketing campaigns only serve the purpose of attracting first time customers and developing a brand image in the market for the firm.

OFF-LINE MARKETING

About the off-line marketing effort and public relations (PR) of the company, Mr. Tri Pramoj, nonexecutive director to morethailand.com on off-line marketing said:

The off-line marketing efforts and public relation campaign of the company mainly focuses on building relationships for branding and brand awareness with the supply side of the tourism service delivery chain. It is increasingly being realized that only through developing stronger relationships with hotels can the company expect more favorable prices and thus be able to offer rooms at competitive process to its customers.

During high season, good relationships with hotels assume a strategic importance since often it is only through such good relationships that rooms are made available in the most attractive hotels. The main activities in relationship building include conducting seminars for hoteliers, participating in tourism fares and public relation campaign to make hoteliers understand the significance of e-intermediaries. The idea is to position morethailand.com as a knowledge-based intermediary that does not limit itself to mere room booking activities. The company conducts around one seminar every three months where hoteliers are invited to attend a series of talks for half a day by the founder and top executives of the company. This also serves as an occasion for the executives of the company to interact with the hoteliers and develop relationships with them. Since the e-intermediary concept is relatively new and the hoteliers are yet to get substantial bookings through this channel, it is felt that these efforts are required to get greater cooperation from the hoteliers. Another activity promoted by the company is a PR campaign through a professional PR agency. The PR campaign aims to improve the visibility of the company among the trade. The campaign involves publishing articles about the Web site, general articles about the tourism industry and the role of the intermediaries as well as publishing interviews with the founder and the CEO of the company in various media like the national television network and major newspapers. These activities attempt to improve the stature of the company among the travel and tourism industry so that it becomes possible for the company to get the support of the hoteliers in its endeavor.

ORGANIZATIONAL STRUCTURE

Morethailand.com has a small organization comprising of mostly young professionals. Presently there are 30 employees in the company. This is in line with the company's philosophy of being technology driven and purposeful in all its endeavors. However, the employees of the company are presented with a good learning opportunity. The operations of the company are divided into five departments:

1. **Reservation department:** Headed by a manager with sufficient experience in the travel industry, the department looks after the communication with the customers. The department is the actual direct interface with the customer for the company. Apart from the manager, the department has three staff members. The department is also responsible for developing the products like designing special packages, negotiating with hotels, and so forth.

2. **Online marketing and SEM sStaff:** The online marketing staff is responsible mainly for search engine optimization. The department has apart from a manager, four staff members. They undertake all the search engine promotional activities of the organization including SEM and content writing. This activity is of prime importance in attracting customers.
3. **Web master and SEO department:** This department is responsible for updating the Web site, ensuring the overall attractiveness of the Web site and SEO. Apart from a manager there are four other staff members working in this department. They prepare a site traffic report every Wednesday for analysis by the company.
4. **IT-department:** This department looks after the hardware and software aspects of the Web site. In this department there are three programmers and one systems engineer apart from the manger who heads it.
5. **Key-in department:** The main task of this department is to look after the main paper work including the responsibility of up-keeping the contracts with the hotels and other service providers. There are two staff members in this department. The key-in department reports to the reservation department.
6. **Finance and accounting department:** The finance and accounts department consists of three staff members.

Each of the departments also has an external advisor who provides a strategic vision for the functioning of the departments. The employees are given performance-based incentives.

It is estimated that about 70% of the company's costs are incurred as salaries and about 20% on advertisements in google.com. The company also incurs expenditure on off-line promotion like participating in travel and tour fairs, conducting seminars for hoteliers, and so forth. It is estimated that to process each order, the company has to spend about 40 Thai bahts (almost equivalent to US$1.00).

CONCLUSION AND DISCUSSION

As is evident from the case study, a startup morethailand.com is trying to establish itself in an industry that is itself in its infancy. The future of this industry is as yet quite uncertain. The main challenge the industry has to face is the market power dominance of the conventional off-line travel wholesalers who are moving online in the market. The hotels are often not in a position to come out of the clutches of the travel wholesalers and help the online intermediaries wholeheartedly. On the other hand, only if the hotels give adequate support by allotting sufficient rooms to the e-intermediaries can the intermediaries give a stiff competition to travel wholesalers. In addition, the customers will adopt e-intermediaries in a big way only when the e-intermediaries are able to sell hotel rooms at rates comparable to that offered by travel agents. The industry therefore is in a transition phase with the e-intermediaries trying their level best to break the stranglehold of the travel wholesalers. Though at present the market power of off-line the travel wholesaler is declining, it still has a long way to go before online travel intermediary may emerge significantly. From an e-commerce perspective this provides an interesting scenario as it illustrates how e-commerce and IT can change the relative power structure in an industry. It is an instance where the traditional loyalties and economies of scale enjoyed by conventional intermediaries are challenged by the cost efficiencies of the new age Internet-based companies. In the developed countries the transition to a predominantly Internet-based intermediation has already happened in the hotel industry. It is in the developing economies like Thailand with a significantly big tourism industry that the new wave of e-commerce-based intermediation is taking root. Morethailand.com as a representative of this new wave of companies is traversing through a path which is abounding in opportunities and challenges. Morethailand.com considers itself a bridge between the independently owned and operated hotels and the worldwide tourism market. The IOOs hitherto had very little direct access to the international tourist market. Morethailand.com believes that through linking IOOs in Thailand to the worldwide tourism market, it is actually opening up more choice and more possibilities to the global tourist, an activity that it feels is quite sustainable.

On the supply side, the IOOs continue to face an agency problem between the owners and management. This may be a major obstacle to ICT adaptation and e-commerce usage since the management is very keen to keep existing off-line channels and their networks for their own benefit. On the other hand, in the long run, due to increasing competition and the consequent reduction in margins, if the owner can not resolve this agency problem, IOOs would end up being part of a large hotel chain or sold outright.

The biggest challenge for morethailand.com however is to promote its offer on the World Wide Web with its limited resources. Morethailand.com has selected search engine optimization (SEO) and search engine marketing (SEM) as the two main means of increasing its presence in the B2C space. The business model selected by morethailand.com, though very promising, is not totally unique. Moreover, in Thailand there are numerous e-intermediaries that follow similar business models. The main differentiating factor between morethailand.com and many of its competitors is its high reliance on IOOs and its adoption of the merchant model. By featuring a large number of hotels on the Web site, morethailand.com hopes to improve the choice for its visitors. For those who want to explore new areas and visit hitherto unknown destinations, they will find morethailand.com would be a better option to search. Further, through the merchant model, morethailand.com intends to offer rooms at a cheaper rate to the customers than most of its competitors including the travel wholesalers. Morethailand.com has to grapple with the challenges posed by two domains. At the supply side, the company has to contact and negotiate with hotels to get them listed in their Web sites and once an enquiry is received from a potential customer, to get the rooms allotted during the dates required for the customer. On the demand side, the company has to market its Web site to its customers. The demand side activity requires such responsibilities as developing the content of the Web site and search engine optimization so that potential customers could access the site when they search for any information on hotels in Thailand or other associated subjects. The company has to deal with both online competitors as well as off-line competitors on the supply as well as the demand side.

REFERENCES

Buhalis, D., & Licata, C. M. (2002). The future of eTourism intermediaries. *Tourism Management, 23*, 207-220.

Cooper, C., Fletcher, J., Gilbert, D., & Wanhill, S. (1998). *Tourism principles and practice.* Essex: Pearson.

Hoontrakul, P. (2004). *Value revelation in differentiated goods for travel industry* (Discussion Paper). Bangkok: Sasin of Chulalongkorn University.

Jensen, M. C., & Meckling, W. H. (1976). Theory of the firm: Managerial behavior, agency costs and ownership structure. *Journal of Financial Economics, 3*, 303-360.

Marcussen, C. H. (2004). *Trends in European Internet distribution of travel and tourism ser-*

vices. Retrieved May 29, 2006, from http://www.rcb.dk/uk/staff/chm/trends.htm accessed on 3/December/2004

O'Conner, P. (1999). *Electronic information distribution tourism and hospitality.* Cambridge: CABI Publishing.

Poon, A. (1993). *Tourism, technology and competitive strategies.* Oxford: CAB International.

Ryan, P., & Hoontrakul, P. (2003). An economic analysis of the tourism industry: Implications for online intermediary. *Chulalongkorn Journal of Economics, 15*(3), 205-235.

Sheldon, P. (1997). *Tourism information technology.* Oxford: CAB.

TAT. (2003). *Tourism Authority of Thailand statistical report 2003.* Bangkok: Tourism Authority of Thailand.

TAT. (2004). *Tourism Authority of Thailand statistical report 2004.* Bangkok: Tourism Authority of Thailand.

UNCTAD. (2000). Electronic commerce and tourism new perspectives and challenges for developing countries. In *Proceedings of the United Nations Conference on Trade and Development.* Retrieved May 29, 2006, from http://www.Pongsak.Hoontrakul.com

This work was previously published in the International Journal of E-Business Research, Vol. 2, Issue 4, edited by I. Lee, pp. 94-114, copyright 2006 by Idea Group Publishing (an imprint of IGI Global).

Compilation of References

Aberer, K., & Despotovic, Z.(2001). Managing trust in a peer-2-peer information system. *Proceedings of the Conference on Information and Knowledge Management* (pp. 310-317). CIKM01. (Nov. 5-10, 2001). Atlanta, Georgia.

About. (2001). *Forrester research predicts that portals and affiliate programs will thrive*. Retrieved February 14, 2007, from http://retailindustry.about.com/library/bl/q2/bl_for040501.htm

ABS. (2002). *Yearbook Australia, 2002*. Retrieved November 10, 2004, from http://www.abs.gov.au/ausstats/abs%40.nsf/94713ad445ff1425ca25682000192af2/1647509ef7e25faaca2568a900154b63? OpenDocument

Acuna, C. J., & Carlos, R. J. (2006). Modeling semantic Web services: A case study. *Proceedings of the 6th International Conference on Web Engineering* (pp. 32-39), Palo Alto, California.

Adams, H., Gisolfi, D., Snell, J., & Varadan, R. (2002). *Best practices for Web services: Back to the basics, Part 2*: IBM Developer Works.

Adelaar, T. (2000). Electronic commerce and the implications for market structure: the example of the art and antiques trade. *Journal of Computer-Mediated Communication, 5*(3). Retrieved September 28, 2005, from http://jcmc.indiana.edu/vol5/issue3/adelaar.htm

Afuah, A., & Tucci, C. (2003). *Internet business models and strategies: Text and cases*. Boston: McGraw-Hill.

Agarwal, V., Dasgupta, K., Karnik, N., Kumar, A., Kundu, A., Mittal, S., & Srivastava, B. (2005). A service creation environment based on end to end composition of Web services. *Proceedings of the 14th International Conference on World Wide Web* (pp. 128-137), Chiba, Japan.

Agarwal, V., Karnik, N., & Kumar, A. (2002, April). *Architectural issues for metering and accounting of grid services*. IBM Research Report No. RI02010. Retrieved from http://domino.watson.ibm.com/library/cyberdig.nsf/Home

Agarwal, V., Karnik, N., & Kumar, A. (2003). Metering and accounting for composite e-services. *Proceedings of the 2003 IEEE International Conference on Electronic Commerce (CEC 2003)* (pp. 35-39), Newport Beach, California.

Agarwal, V., Karnik, N., & Kumar, A. (2004). An information model for metering and accounting. *Proceedings of the IEEE/IFIP Network Operations and Management Symposium (NOMS 2004)* (pp. 541-554), Seoul, Korea.

Agency, X. N. (2005). Competition on China's e-commerce market intensifies. *Business CustomWire*.

Aichholzer, G., & Schmutzer, R. (2000). Organisational, technological, and regulatory challenges for realising electronic government. In *Proceedings of the 8th European Conference on Information Systems*, Vienna, Austria.

Aissi, S., & Malu, P., & Srinivasan, K. (2002). E-business process modeling: The next big step. *IEEE Computer, 35*(5), 55-62.

Akel, M. (2001). The Internet advantage: A process for integrating electronic commerce into economic development strategy. *Economic Development Review, 17*(3), 13-19.

Akhter, F. (2006). The impact of foreign languages, customs, business policies, and infrastructure factors on the growth of B2C e-commerce. *IADIS International Conference E-Commerce.* December 9, Barcelona, Spain.

Alavi, M., & Leidner, D. E. (2001). Review: Knowledge management and knowledge management systems: Conceptual foundations and research issues. *MIS Quarterly, 25*(1), 107-136.

Albaugh, V., & Madduri, H. (2004). The utility metering service of the universal management infrastructure. *IBM Systems Journal, 43*(1), 179-189.

Al-Ghailani, H. H., & Moor, W. C. (1995). Technology transfer to developing countries. *International Journal of Technology Management, 10*(7, 8), 687-703.

Allcock, S. P. A., Webber, S., & Yeates, R. (1999). Business information and the Internet: Use of the Internet as an information resource for SME. British Library Research and Information Report. (136).

Allen, D. K., Colligan, D., Finnie, A., & Kern, T. (2000). Trust, power and interorganisational information systems: The case of the electronic trading community TransLease. *Journal of Information Systems, 10*, 21–40.

Alonso, G., Casati, F., Kuno, H., & Machiraju, V. (2004). *Web services—Concepts, architectures, and applications.* Berlin Heidelberg: Springer-Verlag.

Anderson, J. C., & Narus, J. A. (1990). A model of distributor firm and manufacturer firm working partnerships. *Journal of Marketing*, (54), 42-58, January.

Andreescu, F. (2006). Organisational challenges of implementing e-business in the public services: The case of Britain's National Mapping Agency. *International Journal of E-Business Research, 2*(4), 39-60.

Angeles, R. (2000). Revisiting the role of Internet-EDI in the current electronic commerce scene. *Logistics Information Management, 13*(1), 45-57.

Anglano, C., Barale, S., Gaido, L., Guarise, A., Lusso, S., & Werbrouck, A. (2002, March). *An accounting system for the DataGrid Project.* Retrieved January 2007, from http://www.to.infn.it/grid/accounting/techrep/DataGrid-01-TED-0115-3_0.pdf

Anzböck, R. & Dustdar, S. (2005, September 5-7). Semi-automatic generation of Web services and BPEL processes—A model-driven approach (extended version). *Lecture Notes in Computer Science* (vol. 3649, pp. 64-79).

Apigian, C. H., Ragu-Nathan, B. S., Ragu-Nathan, T. S., & Kunnathur, A. (2005). Internet technology: The strategic imperative. *Journal of Electronic Commerce Research, 6*(2), 123-145.

Arkin, A., Askary, S., Fordin, S., Jekeli, W., Kawaguchi, K., Orchard, D., Pogliani, S., Riemer, K., Struble, S., Takacsi-Nagy, P., Trickovic, I., & Zimek, S. (2002). *Web service choreography interface (WSCI) 1.0. W3C Note*, August 2002. Retrieved January, 2005, from http://www.w3.org/TR/wsci

ARM. (2004). *Application response measurement (ARM).* Open Group Technical Standard. Retrieved January 2007, from http://www.opengroup.org/management/arm

Armstrong, J. S., & Overton, T. S. (1977). Estimating non-response bias in mail surveys. *Journal of Marketing Research*, (14), 396-402.

Arpinar, B., Aleman-Meza, B., Zhang, R., & Maduko, A. (2004). Ontology-driven Web services composition platform. *Proceedings of the IEEE International Conference on E-Commerce Technology*, IEEE.

Arsanjani, A., Hailpern, B., Martin, J., & Tarr, P. (2003). Web services: Promises and compromises. *ACM Queue, 1*(1), 48-58.

Arunachalam, S. (1999). Information technology: What does it mean for scientists and scholars in the developing world? *American Society for Information Science, 25*(4), 21-24.

Aschmoneit, P., & Lenz, M. (2001). The role of trust in business-to-business electronic commerce. In *Proceedings of the Seventh Americas Conference on Information Systems*, Boston (pp. 1–9).

Ashrafi, N., & Kuilboer, J. P. (2005). Privacy protection via technology: Platform for privacy preferences (P3P). *International Journal of E-Business Research, 1*(2), 56-69.

Aspden, R. (2006). The Bangalore Effect. *New Statesman, 135*(4777), 26-27.

Auger, P., & Gallaugher, J. M. (1997). Factors affecting adoption of an Internet-based sales presence for small businesses. *The Information Society*. 13(1), 55-74.

Avruch, K., Black, P. W., & Scimecca, J. A. (1998). *Conflict resolution: Cross-cultural perspectives*. CT: Praeger Publishers.

Ba, S., Whinston, A., & Zang, H. (1999, December 13-15). Building trust in the electronic market using an economic incentive mechanism. In P. De, & J. I. DeGross (Eds.), *Proceedings of the International Conference on Information Systems 1999*, Charlotte, NC (pp. 218–212).

Baake, P., & Boom, A. (2001). Vertical product differentiation, network externalities, and compatibility decisions. *International Journal of Industrial Organization, 19*(1,2), 267-284.

Babbie, E. R. (2002). *The basics of social research*. Belmont, CA: Wadsworth/Thomson Learning.

Baets, W. (1992). Aligning information systems with business strategy. *Journal of Strategic Information Systems, 1*(4), 205-213.

Bagchi, K., Hart, P., & Peterson, M. (2004). National culture and information technology product adoption. *Journal of Global Information Technology Management, 7*(4).

Baida, Z., Gordijn, J., Akkermans, H., Saele, H., & Morch, A. (2005). Finding e-service offerings by computer-supported customer need reasoning. *International Journal of e-business Research, 1*(2), 91-112.

Baïna, K., Benali, K., & Godart, C. (2003). Dynamic interconnection of heterogeneous workflow processes through services. The *11th International Conference on Cooperative Information Systems* (CoopIS'03), In *Confederated International Conferences* (DOA/CoopIS/ODBASE'03), (LNCS) 2888, Catania, Sicily, Italy, November 3-7, 2003. Springer-Verlag.

Bakos, J. Y., & Brynjolfsson, E. (1993). Information technology, incentives, and the optimal number of suppliers. *Journal of Management Information Systems, 10*(2), 37-53.

Bakos, Y. (1998). The emerging role of electronic marketplaces on the Internet. *Communication of the ACM, 41*(8), 35-42.

Balogun, J., Gleadle, P., Hope Hailey, V., & Willmott, H. (2005). Managing change across boundaries: Boundary-shaking practices. *British Journal of Management, 16*, 261-278.

Bambauer, D., Diebert, R. J., Palfrey, J. G., Jr., Rohoziniski, R., Villeneuve, N., & Zittrain, J. (2005). Internet filtering in China 2004-2005: A country study. *Berkman Center for Internet & Society at Harvard Law School, Research Publication No. 2005-10.*

Barlow, T., Hess, A., & Seamons, K. E. (2001). Trust negotiation in electronic markets. *Proceeding of the 8th Research Symposium on Emerging Electronic Markets (RSEEM 01)*, Maastricht, The Netherlands.

Barmouta, A., & Buyya, R. (2003). GridBank: A grid accounting services architecture (GASA) for distributed systems sharing and integration. *Proceedings of the 17th Annual International Parallel & Distributed Processing Symposium (IPDPS 2003) Workshop on Internet Computing and E-Commerce* (pp. 245-252), Nice, France.

Barnes, D., Hinton, M., & Mieczkowska, S. (2004). Managing the transition from bricks-and-mortar to clicks-and-mortar: A business process perspective. *Knowledge and Process Management, 11*(3), 199-209.

Barnes, D., Hinton, M., & Mieczkowska, S. (2005). Enhancing customer service operations in e-business: The emotional dimension. *Journal of Electronic Commerce in Organizations, 3*(2), 17-32.

Barnes, S., & Hunt, B. (2001). *E-commerce and e-business: Business models for global success*. Oxford: Butterworth Heinemann.

Barnett, R. R., & Mackness, J. R. (1983). An action research study of small firm management. *Journal of Applied Systems, 10*, 63-83.

Barret, M. I. (1999). Challenges of EDI adoption for electronic trading in the London insurance market. *European Journal of Information Systems, 8*(1), 1–15.

Barry, H., & Milner, B. (2002). SME's and electronic commerce: A departure from the traditional prioritization of training? *Journal of European Industrial Training.* 25(7), 316-326.

Bart, Y., Shankar, V., Sultan, F., & Urban, G. L. (2005). Are the drivers and role of online trust the same for all Web sites and consumers? A large-scale exploratory empirical study. *Journal of Marketing, 69*(4), 133-152

Bartos, O. J. (1977). Simple model of negotiation: A sociological point of view. In I. W. Zartman (Ed.), *The negotiation process: Theories and applications* (pp. 13-27). Beverly Hills, CA: Sage Publications.

Bastos, R. M. & Ruiz, D. D. A. (2002). Extending UML activity for workflow modelling in production systems. In *Proceedings of the 35th Hawaii International Conference on Systems Sciences* (pp. 3786-3795).

Becker, J., Rosemann, M., & Von Uthmann, C. (2000). Guidelines of business process modeling. In W. van derAalst, J. Sedel, & A. Oberweis (Eds.), *Business process management: Models techniques and empirical studies* (pp. 30-49). Berlin: Springer-Verlag.

Becker, S., & Berkemeyer, A. (2004). A case study on a security maturity assessment of a business-to-business electronic commerce organization. *Journal of Electronic Commerce in Organizations, 2*(4), 1-19.

Beckinsale, M., Levy, M. & Powell, P. (2006). Exploring Internet adoption drivers in SMEs. *Electronic Markets, 16*(4), 361-370.

Begin, L., & Boisvert, H. (2002). E-commerce: Evaluating the external business environment. *CMA Management, 76*(2), 16–21.

Benatallah, B., Casati, F., & Toumani, F. (2004). Web service conversation modeling: A cornerstone for e-business automation. *IEEE Internet Computing, 8*(1), 46-54.

Benatallah, B., Sheng, Q. Z., & Dumas, M. (2003). The self-serv environment for Web services composition. *IEEE Internet Computing, 7*(1), 40-48.

Benbasat, I., Goldstein, D., & Mead, M. (1987, September). The case research strategy in studies of information systems. *MIS Quarterly*, 369–384.

Benjamin, R., & Levinson, E. (1993). A framework for managing IT-enabled change. *Sloan Management Review, 34*(4), 23-33.

Benoy, J., Cook, R., & Javalgi, R. (2001). Marketing on the Web: How executives feel, what businesses do. *Business Horizons, 44*(4), 32-40.

Bensaid, B., & Lesne, J. P. (1996). Dynamic monopoly pricing with network externalities. *International Journal of Industrial Organization, 14*(6), 837-855.

Bensaou, M. (1997). Interorganizational cooperation: The role of information technology (an empirical comparison of US and Japanese supplier relations). *Information Systems Research 8*(2), 107-124.

Bensaou, M., & Venkatraman, N. (1995). Configurations of interorganizational relationships: A comparison between US and Japanese automakers. *Management Science 41*(9), 1471-92.

Bentler, P. M. (1980). *EQS structural equations program manual.* Los Angeles: BMDP Statistical Software.

Bentler, P. M. (1990), Comparative fit indexes in structural models. *Psychological Bulletin*, (107), 238-246.

Bentler, P. M., & Bonnett, D. G. (1980). Significance tests and goodness of fit in the analysis of covariance structures. *Psychological Bulletin, 88*(3), 588-606.

Berghel, H. (2000). Predatory disintermediation. *Communications of the ACM, 43*(5), 23-29.

Berman, B., & Thelen, S. (2004). A guide to developing and managing a well-integrated multi-channel retail strategy. *International Journal of Retail and Distribution Management, 32*(2/3), 147-156.

Bernecker, O. (2006). *Biometrics security: An end user perspective. Information security technical reports 11* (pp. 111-118). Retrieved February 2007, from www.sciencedirect.com

Berry, L. L. (1995). Relationship marketing of services: Growing interest, emerging perspectives. *Journal of the Academy of Marketing Science, 23*, 236-245.

Better Business Bureau. (2000). *Standards for BBBOnline reliability program participation.* Retrieved from http://www.bbbonline.org/businesses/reliability/standards.html

Bhaskar, R. (2004). A customer relationship management system to target customers at Cisco. *Journal of Electronic Commerce in Organizations, 2*(4), 1-19.

Bhattacherjee, A. (2002). Individual trust in online firms: Scale development and initial test. *Journal of Management Information Systems, 19*(1), 211-241.

Bhattacherjee, A. (2006). Individual trust in online firms: The relative and temporal effects of antecedent beliefs. *International Journal of E-Business Research, 2*(4), 21-38.

Bianchini, D., De Antonellis, V., Pernici, B., & Plebani, P. (2006). Ontology-based methodology for e-service discovery. *Information Systems, 31*(4-5), 361-380.

Bibby, A., & Brea, C. (2003). Business process reengineering through Web services: A user-experience perspective. *Web services Journal.*

Bichier, M., & Lin, K. J. (2006). Service-oriented computing. *IEEE Computer, 39*(3), 99-101.

Bieber, G., & Carpenter, J. (2001). *Introduction to service-oriented programming* (Rev 2.1). Retrieved January 2005, from http://www.openwings.org/download/specs/ServiceOrientedIntroduction.pdf

Bielski, L. (2003). Web services goes live: One deployment at a time. *American Bankers Association. ABA Banking Journal, 95*(7), 49-58.

Birkhofer, B., Schoegel, M., & Tomczak, T. (2000). Transaction- and trust-based strategies in e-commerce—A conceptual approach. *Electronic Markets, 10*(3). Retrieved August 26, 2004, from http://www.electronicmarkets.org/modules/pub/view.php/electronicmarkets-221

Blau, P. M. (1964). *Exchange and power in social life.* New York: John Wiley & Sons.

Boar, B. (1994). Information technology and business alignment: a strategic assessment. In B. Voss, & D. Willey (Eds.), *Handbook of Business Strategy* (pp. 173-188). New York: Faulkner & Gray.

Boddy, D., & Macbeth, D. (2000). Prescriptions for managing change: a survey of their effects in projects to implement collaborative working between organisations. *International Journal of Project Management, 18*, 297-306.

Bollen, K. A. (1989). *Structural equations with latent variables.* New York: Wiley.

Boone, C., De Brabander, B., & Hellemans, J. (2000). Research note: CEO locus of control and small firm performance. *Organization Studies, 21*(3). 641-646.

Bowen, D. E., & Schneider, A. (1988). Services marketing and management: Implications for organizational behavior. *Research in Organizational Behavior, 10*, 43-80.

Boyne, G. (2002). Public and private management: What's the difference. *Journal of Management Studies, 39*(1), 97-122.

Boyne, G. (2004). A 3Rs strategy for public service turnaround: Retrenchment, repositioning, and reorganisation. *Public Money and Management, April*, 97-103.

Boyne, G., & Walker, R. (2004). Strategy content and public service organizations. *Journal of Public Administration Research and Theory, 14*(2), 231-252.

BPMI.org, Business Process Management Initiative. (n.d.). Retrieved January, 2005, from http://www.bpmi.org/

BPMI.org. (2002). *BPML/BPEL4WS—A convergence path toward a standard BPM stack.* BPMI.org Position

Paper. Retrieved January 2005, from http://www.bpmi.org/

Brandenburger, A. M., & Nalebuff, B. J. (1996). Inside Intel. *Harvard Business Review, 74*(6), 168-175, November-December.

Brown, J. S., & Duguid, P. (1998). Organizing knowledge. *California Management Review, 40*(3), 90-111.

Brown, S. L., & Eisenhardt, K. M. (1997). The art of continuous change: Linking complexity theory and time-paced evolution in relentlessly shifting organisation. *Administrative Science Quarterly, 42*, 1-34.

Brownlee, N., & Blount, A. (2000, September). *Accounting attributes and record formats.* IETF working group on authentication, authorization, and accounting. Retrieved July 2003, from http://www.ietf.org/rfc/rfc2924.txt

Buhalis, D., & Licata, C. M. (2002). The future of eTourism intermediaries. *Tourism Management, 23*, 207-220.

Buinessline. (2004). Tele-density, Net connectivity low: Policy thrust on spectrum, broadband must. *Businessline Chennai*, 1.

Burdett, D. (2003). *The business Web services scorecard: Using Web services for business—The present and the future.* Commerce One Operations Inc.

Burk, R., & Horvath, D. B. (1997). *Unix unleashed: System administrator's edition.* Sams.

Burn, J. M., & Robbins, G. (2001). *Strategic planning for e-government: A customer value based model. Proceedings of the 7th Americas Conference on Information Systems* (pp. 1578-1583), Boston, USA.

Burt, R. S., & Knez, M. (1996). Trust and third-party gossip. In R. M. Kramer, & T. R. Tyler (Eds.), Trust in organisations: *Frontiers of theory and research* (pp. 68–89). Thousand Oaks, CA: Sage Publications.

Buyya, R., Abramson, D., & Giddy, J. (2001). A case for economy grid architecture for service oriented grid computing. *Proceedings of the 10th IEEE International Heterogeneous Computing Workshop (HCW 2001)* (pp. 776-790).

Cachon, G., & Fisher, M. (2000). Supply chain inventory management and the value of shared information. *Management Science, 46*(8), 936–953.

Cao, Y., & Yunfeng, L. (2007). An intelligent fuzzy-based recommendation system for consumer electronic products. *Expert Systems with Applications, 33*(1), 230-240, July.

Cappiello, C., Missier, P., Pernici, B., Plebani, P., & Batini, C. (2004). QoS in multichannel IS: The MAIS approach. *Proceedings of the International Workshop on Web Quality (WQ'04) in conjunction with the ICWE 2004*, Munich, Germany.

Cardoso, J., Bostrom, R. P., & Sheth, A. (2004). Workflow management systems and ERP systems: Difference, commonalities, and applications. *Information Technology and Management, 5*, 319-338, Kluwer Academic Publishers.

Carlton, D. W. (2001). Free riding and sales strategies for the Internet. *The Journal of Industrial Economics, 49*(4), 521-540.

Carmichael, C., Turgoose, C., Older Gary, M., & Todd, C. (2000). Innovation and SMEs. *Journal of Industry and Higher Education*, 244-248.

Carmines, E. G., & McIver, J. P. (1981). Analyzing models with observed variables. In G.. W. Bohrnstedt & E. F. Borgatta (Eds.), *Social measurement: Current issues.* Beverly Hills: Sage.

Casati, F., Shan, E., Dayal, U., & Shan, M. (2003). Business-oriented management of Web services. *Communications of the ACM, 46*(10), 55-61.

Cash, J. I., & Konsynski, B. R. (1985). IS redraws competitive boundaries. *Harvard Business Review, 64*(2), 134–142.

Castelfranchi, C., Falcone, R., & Pezzulo, G. (2003). Integrating trustfulness and decision using fuzzy cognitive maps. *Trust Management 2003, LNCS 2692* (pp. 195-210).

CCID. (2005). Report on the Status of EC in the World—April 2004. *Chinese Center for Information Industry.*

Chafle, G., Dasgupta, K., Kumar, A., Mittal, S., & Srivastava, B. (2006). Adaptation in Web service composition and execution. *Proceedings of the IEEE International Conference on Web services (ICWS 2006)*, Chicago, USA (pp. 549-557).

Chakravarty, S., Dogan, K., & Tomlinson, N. (2006). A hedonic study of network effects in the market for word processing software. *Decision Support Systems, 41*(4), 747-763.

Chan, C., & Swatman, P. M. C. (2000). From EDI to Internet commerce: The BHP Steel experience. *Internet Research: Electronic Networking Applications and Policy, 10*(1), 72-82.

Chan, K. (2005). China tightens censorship of foreign broadcasters. *The Christian Post.*

Chappell, D. (2004). *Understanding BPM servers*. Chappell & Associates. Retrieved December 2004, from http://www.microsoft.com/biztalk/techinfo/default.asp

Chaston, I. (2001). The Internet and e-commerce: An opportunity to examine organisational learning in progress in small manufacturing firms. *International Small Business Journal, 19*(2), 13-30.

Chavez, R., Leiter, M., & Kiely, T. (2000). Should you spin off your Internet business? *Business Strategy Review, 11*(2), 19-31.

Chen, E., Vahidov, R., & Kersten, G. E. (2005). Agent-supported negotiations in the e-marketplace. *International Journal of Electronic Business, 3*(1), 28-49.

Chen, L., Haney, S., Pandzik, A., Spigarelli, J., & Jesseman, C. (2003). Small business Internet commerce: A case study. *Information Resources Management Journal, 16*(3), 17-42.

Chen, M. (2003). Factors affecting the adoption and diffusion of XML and Web services standards for e-business systems. *International Journal of Human—Computer Studies [H.W. Wilson - AST], 58*(3), 259.

Chen, M. (2005). An analysis of the driving forces for Web services adoption. *Information Systems and eBusiness Management, 3*(3), 265-279.

Chen, M., Chen, A., & Shao, B. (2003). The implications and impacts of Web services to electronic commerce research and practices. *Journal of Electronic Commerce Research, 4*(4), 128-139.

Chen, S., & Leteney, F. (2000). Get real! Managing the next stage of Internet retail. *European Management Journal, 18*(5), 519-528.

Chen, X. (2003). *Comparison of Internet development between China and Korea*. Retrieved from http://news.cinhuanet.com/newsmedia/2003-02/09/content_720249.htm

Chen, Y. S., Chen, G., & Wu, S. (2005). Issues and opportunities in e-business research: A Simonian perspective. *International Journal of E-business Research, 1*(1), 37-53.

Chesse, J. P. (2001). Distribution: It's more than moving the goods.

Cheung, E. (2001a, January 4). *Profiling Indian Internet users: Part 1*. eMarketer. Retrieved from www.mail-archive.com/gkd@phoenix.edc.org/msg00368.html

Cheung, E. (2001b). *Profiling Indian Internet users: Part 2*. Retrieved August 21, 2004, from www.mail-archive.com/gkd@phoenix.edc.org/msg00368.html

Chiang, D. M., & Teng, C. I. (2001). Pricing strategies with network externalities between two groups of customers. *NTU Management Review, 12*(1), 1-36.

Chiang, D. M., & Teng, C. I. (2003). Installed base collapsing strategies with network externalities. *Journal of Management, 20*(5), 829-857.

Chiang, D. M., & Teng, C. I. (2005). Consumption externalities: Review and future research opportunities. *Electronic Commerce Studies, 3*(1), 15-38.

Chien, A., & Salem, E. (2001, Nov 5). *Building an e-business strategy for Mainland China*. Retrieved May 29, 2004, from http:// www.cio.com/research/ec/edit/110501_China.html

Choi, J. P. (1994). Network externalities, compatibility choice, and planned obsolescence. *Journal of Industrial Economics, 42*(2), 167-182.

Choi, S. Y., Stahl, D. O., & Whinston, A. B. (1997). Is Microsoft a Monopolist? *Brazilian Electronic Journal of Economics, 1*, 0 (December 10).

Chong, S. (2001). *Electronic commerce adoption by small-medium sized enterprises in Australia and Singapore.* Working Paper, School of Information Systems, Curtin University of Technology, Perth, Western Australia.

Chou, C. F., & Shy, O. (1990). Network effects without network externalities. *International Journal of Industrial Organization, 8*(2), 259-270.

Chou, D.C., Yen, D.C., Lin, B., & Cheng, P.H.-L. (1999). Cyberspace security management. *Industrial Management & Data Systems, 99*(8), 353-361.

Choudhury, V., Hartzel, K. S., Konsynski, B. R. (1998). Uses and consequences of electronic markets: An empirical investigation in the aircraft parts industry. *MIS Quarterly, 22*(4), 471-507

Christiansen, S. (2002, December 8-13 2002). *The business case for XML Web services.* Paper presented at the XML Conference 2002, Baltimore.

Chung, J., Lin, K., & Mathieu, R. G. (2003). Web services computing: Advancing software interoperability. *IEEE Computer, 36*(10), 35-37.

Church, J., & Gandal, N. (1993). Complementary network externalities and technological adoption. *International Journal of Industrial Organization, 11*(2), 239-260.

CIA. (2006). *World Fact Book.* Retrieved from https://www.cia.gov/cia/publications/factbook/geos/ch.html

CII. (2000). CHINA E-Commerce Index Report. Retrieved May 29, 2004, from http://tech.sina.com.cn/Internet/China/2000-08-08/33014.shtml

CIM. (2005). *Common information model.* Distributed management task force. Retrieved May 10, 2005, from http://www.dmtf.org/standards/cim

Clark, T. H., & Stoddard, D. B. (1996). Interorganizational business process redesign: Merging technological and process innovation. *Journal of Management Information Systems, 13*(2), 9-28.

Clarke, I., & Flaherty, T. B. (2004). Challenges of transforming a traditional brick-and-mortar store into a bricks-and-clicks model: A small business case study. *Journal of Electronic Commerce in Organizations, 2*(4), 74-87.

Clay, K. (2001). Prices and price dispersion on the Web: Evidence from the online book industry. *The Journal of Industrial Economics, 49*(4), 441-462.

Clegg, C. W., Chu, C., Smithson, S., Henney, A., et al. (2002). *E-business prospects: Findings from an expert panel.* London: Department of Trade and Industry.

Clegg, C., Chu, C., Smithson, S., Henney, A., et al. (2005). Sociotechnical study of e-business: Grappling with an octopus. *Journal of Electronic Commerce in Organizations, 3*(1), 53-71.

Clemons, E. K., & Row, M. C. (1992). Information technology and industrial cooperation: The changing economics of coordination and ownership. *Journal of Management Information Systems, 9*(2), 9-28.

Clemons, E. K., & Row, M. C. (1993). Limits to interfirm coordination through information technology: Results of a field study in consumer packaged goods distribution. *Journal of Management Information Systems, 10*(1), 73-95.

Clemons, E. K., Reddi, S. P., & Row, M. C. (1993). The impact of information technology on the organization of economic activity: The "move to the middle" hypothesis. *Journal of Management Information Systems, 10*(2), 9-35.

CNNIC. (2006, July). *185th Statistical Survey Report on the Internet Development in China.* China Internet Network Information Center Retrieved January 21, 2007, from http://www.cnnic.net.cn/en/index/0O/02/index.htm

Colaco, S. (2003). *Internet potential in India.* Retrieved August 21, 2004, from http://www.stylusinc.com/Internet_potential_India.htm

Colombo, M. G. (2001). Technology-based entrepreneurs: does internet make a difference? *Small Business Economics, 16*(3), 177-190.

Coltman, T., Devinney, T. M., Latukefu, A., & Midgley, D. F. (2001), E-business: Revolution, evolution, or hype? *California Management Review, 44*(1), 57-78.

Communications, M. (2006). China's Web users increase 18% in 2005. *Telcomworldwide*, 1.

Computer Industry Almanac, Inc. (2002). Internet users will top one billion in 2005. Retrieved November 10, 2004, from http://www.c-i-a.com/pr032102.htm

Confalonieri, R., Domingue, J., & Motta, E. (2004). Orchestration of semantic Web services in IRS-III. In *Proceedings of the 1st AKT Workshop on Semantic Web Services* (AKT-SWS04) KMi, The Open University, Milton Keynes, UK, December 8, 2004.

Conner, K. R. (1995). Obtaining strategic advantage from being imitated: When can encouraging "clones" pay? *Management Science, 41*(2), 209-225.

Conner, K. R., & Rumelt, R. P. (1991). Software piracy: An analysis of protection strategies. *Management Science, 37*(2), 125-139.

ConsumerWebWatch. A Matter of Trust: What Consumers Want From Web Sites. April 16, 2002. www.consumerwebwatch.org.

Cooper, C., Fletcher, J., Gilbert, D., & Wanhill, S. (1998). *Tourism principles and practice.* Essex: Pearson.

Corp., I. D. (2003). India's Internet subscriber base to grow 27%. *World IT Report*, N.

Costello, S. (2001). *Study: Companies slow to adopt B2B.* Retrieved September 28, 2002, from http://www.computerworld.com/managementtopics/ebusiness/story/0,10801,58375,00.html

Cote, L., Sabourin, V., & Vezina, M. (2004). *Electronic business models—A study on the adoption of electronic business by small and medium-sized Canadian enterprises.* Retrieved from http://www.cefrio.qc.ca

Country Profile, C. (2006). Transport, communications, and the Internet. *Economist Intelligence Unit*, 26-29.

Cox, E. (1994). *The fuzzy systems handbook: A practitioner's guide to building, using, and maintaining fuzzy systems.* Cambridge: Academic Press.

Creswell, J. W. (1994). *Research design: Qualitative and quantitative approaches.* Thousand Oaks, CA: Sage Publications.

Croson, R. T. A. (1999). Look at me when you say that: An electronic negotiation simulation. *Simulation and Gaming, 30*(1), 23-37.

Cross, J. G. (1977). Negotiation as a learning process. In I. W. Zartman (Ed.), *The negotiation process: Theories and applications.* (pp. 29-54). Beverly Hills, CA: Sage Publications.

Culnan, M. J., & Armstrong, P. K. (1999). Information privacy concerns, procedural fairness, and impersonal trust: An empirical investigation. *Organization Science, 10*(1), 104-115.

Cummings, J., & Bromily, P. (1996). The organisational trust inventory (OTI): Development and validation. In R. M. Kramer, & T. R. Tyler (Eds.), *Trust in organisations: Frontiers of theory and research* (pp. 302–330). Thousand Oaks, CA: Sage Publications.

Curbera, F., Khalaf, R., Mukhi, N., Tai, S., & Weerawarana, S. (2003). The next step in Web services. *Communications of the ACM, 46*(10), 29-34.

Curtis, B., Keller, M. I., & Over, J. (1992). Process modeling. *Communications of ACM, 35*(9), September.

Cyert, R. M., & March, J. G. (1992). *A behavioural theory of the firm* (2nd ed.). Oxford: Blackwell.

Dadam, P., Reichert, M., & Kuhn, K. (1997, November). Clinical workflows—The killer application for process-oriented information systems? Ulmr Informatik Berichte. Nr 97-16. Fakultat fur Informatik. Universitat Ulm.

Dahal, K., Hussain, Z., & Hossain, M. (2005). Loan risk analyzer based on fuzzy logic. *Proceeding of IEEE*

International Conference on E-Technology, E-Commerce and E-Services, Hong Kong.

Daly, S. P., & Cui, L. X. (2003). E-logistics in China: Basic problems, manageable concerns, and intractable solutions. *Industrial Marketing Management, 32*, 235-242.

Daniel, E. M., White, A., & Ward, J. M. (2004). Exploring the role of third parties in inter-organizational Web service adoption. *Journal of Enterprise Information Management, 17*(5), 351-360.

Daniel, E., & Grimshaw, D. J. (2002b). An exploratory comparison of electronic commerce adoption in large and small enterprises. *Journal of Information Technology, 17*(3), 133-147.

Daniel, E., Wilson, H., & Myers, A. (2002). Adoption of e-commerce by SMEs in the UK: Toward a stage model. *International Small Business Journal, 20*(3), 253-270.

Daniel, E., Wilson, H., & Myers, A. (2002a). Adoption of e-commerce by SMEs in the UK. *International Small Business Journal, 20*(3), 253-270.

Daniel, F., & Pernici, B. (2006). Insights into Web service orchestration and choreography. *International Journal of E-Business Research, 2*(1), 58-77, Idea Group Publishing, January-March 2006.

Das, S. R., Zahra, S. A., & Warkentin, M. E. (1991). Integrating the content and process of strategic MIS planning with competitive strategy. *Decision Sciences, 22*(1), 953-984.

Dasgupta, S., Agarwal, D., Ionnidis, A., & Gopalakrishnan, S. (1999). Determinants of information technology adoption: An extension of existing models to firms in a developing country. *Journal of Global Information Management, 7*(3), 30-40.

David, J. L. (2000). You've got surveys. *American Demographics, 22*(11), 42-44.

Davis, F. D., Bagozzi, R. P., & Warshaw, P. R. (1989). User acceptance of computer technology: A comparison of two theoretical models. *Management Science. 35*(8), 982-1003.

Davis, G. B., & Olson, M. H. (1985). *Management information systems: Conceptual foundations, structure, and development.* New York: McGraw-Hill.

Davis, R. (2001). *Business process modelling with ARIS: A practical guide.* London: Springer.

Day, G. S. (1994). The capabilities of market-driven organization. *Journal of Marketing, 58*, 37-52, October.

Day, G., & Schoemaker, P. (2000). Avoiding the pitfalls of emerging technologies. *California Management Review, 42*(2), 8-33.

De Antonellis, V., Melchiori, M., De Santis, L., Mecella, M., Mussi, E., Pernici, B., & Plebani, P. (2006). A layered architecture for flexible e-service invocation. *Software Practice & Experience, 36*(2), 191-223.

De Moor, A., & Weigand, H. (2004). Business negotiation support: Theory and practice. *International Negotiation, 9*(1), 31-58.

Delaney, M. M., Foroughi, A., & Perkins, W. C. (1997). An empirical study for the efficient of a computerized negotiation support system (NSS). *Decision Support Systems, 20*, 185-197.

DeSanctis, G., & Gallupe, R. B. (1987). A foundation for the study of group decision support systems. *Management Science, 33*(5), 589-609.

Deshpade, R. (1999). Developing a market orientation. Sage Publications, Inc.

Di Benedetto, C. A., Calantone, R. J., & Zhang, C. (2003). International technology transfer. *International Marketing Review, 20*(4), 446-462.

Dixon, T., Thompson, B., & McAllister, P. (2002). *The value of ICT for SMEs in the UK: A critical review of literature.* Report for the Small Business Service Research Programme.

Dobson, G., Lock, R., & Sommerville, I. (2005). QoSOnt: An ontology for QoS in service centric systems. *Proceedings of the eScience All Hands Meeting*, Nottingham, September 2005.

Doll, W. J., Xia, W., & Torkzadeh, G. (1994). A confirmatory factor of the end-user computing satisfaction instrument. *MIS Quarterly 18*(4), 453-461.

Dollar, D. (1992). Outward-oriented developing economies really do grow more rapidly: Evidence from 95 LDCs, 1976-1985. *Economic Development and Cultural Change, 40*(3), 523-544.

Doney, P., & Cannon, J. (1997). An examination of the nature of trust in buyer-seller relationships. *Journal of Marketing, 61*, 35–51.

Drew, S. (2003). Strategic use of e-commerce by SMEs in the East of England. *European Management Journal, 21*(1), 79-88.

DTI. (2001) *Business in the information age—International Benchmarking Study 2000.* (UK Department of Trade and Industry). Retrieved from www.ukonlineforbusiness.gov.uk

Duan, Y. (2004). E-commerce training for SMEs. In M. Khosrow-Pour (Ed.), *Encyclopedia of information science and technology* (pp. 962-965). Hershey, PA: Idea Group Publishing.

Dustdar, S., & Schreiner, W. (2004). A survey on Web services composition. Distributed Systems Group, Technical University of Vienna.

Dutta, S., & Segev, A. (1999). Business transformation on the Internet. *European Management Journal, 17*(5), 466-476.

Dyer, J. H., Cho, D. S., & Chu, W. (1998). Strategic supplier segmentation: The next "best practice" in supply chain management. *California Management Review, 40*(2), 57-77.

EBPG. (2002). eEurope go digital: Benchmarking national and regional e-business policies for SMEs. Final report of the EBusiness Policy Group, 28 June 2002.

ebXML Business Process Team. (2002, April 2002). *Business process and business document modeling worksheets and guidelines.* Retrieved January 6, 2003, from http://www.collaborativedomain.com/standards/documents/bpWS-1.05-2%20DRAFT%20(May%2016).doc

E-commerce. (2005a). Country commerce: China. In *Country Commerce 2005* (pp. 123-134).

E-commerce. (2005b). Country commerce: India. In *Country Commerce 2005* (pp. 93-99): Economist Intelligence Unit Limited.

Economides, N. (1996). The economics of networks. *International Journal of Industrial Organization, 14*(6), 673-699.

Economist. (2005). India vs. China. *Business China*, 4-5.

Economist. (2006). Exporting success. *Economist, 378*(8463), 69.

Ehrhardt, M. (2004). Network effects: Standardization and competitive strategy: How companies influence the emergence of dominant designs. *International Journal of Technology Management, 27*(2,3), 272.

Eibach, W., & Kuebler, D. (2001, July). *Metering and accounting for Web services.* IBM DeveloperWorks. Retrieved July 2000, from http://www-106.ibm.com/developerworks/Webservices/library/ws-maws/?dwzone=Webservices

Eisenberg, B., & Nickull, D. (2001). *ebXML technical architecture specification v1.04.* Retrieved January 2005, from http://www.ebxml.org/specs/index.htm

Eisenhardt, K. (1989). Building theories from case study research. *Academy of Management Review, 14*(4), 532-550.

EIU. (2006). The 2006 e-readiness rankings. *The Economist Intelligence Unit*, 1-27. Retrieved 12/30/06 from http://a330.g.akamai.net/7/330/2540/20060424215053/graphics.eiu.com/files/ad_pdfs/2006Ereadiness_Ranking_WP.pdf

Elfatatry, A., & Layzell, P. (2004). Negotiating in service-oriented environments. *Communications of the ACM, 47*(8), 103-108.

Elgin, B. (2006, February 15). The Web and China: Not so simple. *Business Week Online.*

eMarketer. (2006). Indian Internet users to reach 100 million. *eMarketer.com.*

Emmerich, W., Butchart, B., Chen, L., Wassermann, B., & Price, S. L. (2006). Grid service orchestration using the business process execution language (BPEL). *Journal of Grid Computing, 3*(3-4), 283-304.

EMPG. (2002). eEurope go digital: Benchmarking national and regional e-business policies for SMEs. Final Report of the E-business Policy Group, 28 June.

Ende, J., & Wijnberg, N. (2003). The organization of innovation and market dynamics: Managing increasing returns in software firms. *IEEE Transactions on Engineering Management, 50*(3), 374.

Enzmann, M., & Schneider, M. (2004). A privacy-friendly loyalty system for electronic marketplaces. *Proceedings of the 2004 IEEE International Conference on e-Technology, e-Commerce, and e-Service* (EEE04), Taiwan.

Enzmann, M., & Schneider, M. (2005). Improving customer retention in e-commerce through a secure and privacy-enhanced loyalty system (Forthcoming). *Information Systems Frontiers, 7*(4-5), 359-370, December 2005.

Erl, T. (2005). *Service-oriented architecture (SOA): Concepts, technology, and design.* Prentice Hall PTR.

Eschenbacher, D. (2006). Insider's view China. *Campaign* (32), 15.

Estrem, W. A. (2003). An evaluation framework for deploying Web services in the next generation manufacturing enterprise. *Robotics and Computer-Integrated Manufacturing, In Press, Corrected Proof.*

Evans, J. R., & King, V. E. (1999). Business-to-business marketing and the World Wide Web. *Industrial Marketing Management, 28*(4), 343-358.

Fahey, A., Srivastava, R., Sharon, J. S., & Smith, D. E. (2001). Linking e-business and operating processes: The role of knowledge management. *IBM Systems Journal, 40*(4), 889-907.

Fariselli, P., Oughton, C., Picory, C., & Sugden, R. (1999). Electronic commerce and the future for SMEs in a global market place: Networking and public policies. *Small Business Economics, 12*(3), 261-275.

Farrel, M. A. (2000). Developing a market-oriented learning organization. *Australian Journal of Management, 25*(2), 201-222.

Farrell, J., & Lausen, H. (2006). *Semantic annotations for WSDL.* W3C Working Draft, September 2006. Retrieved January 2007, from http://www.w3.org/TR/sawsdl/

Farrell, J., & Saloner, G. (1986). Installed base and compatibility: Innovation, product pre-announcements, and predation. *American Economic Review, 76*, 940-955.

Farrell, J., & Saloner, G. (1992). Converters, compatibility, and control of interfaces. *Journal of Industrial Economics, 40*(1), 9-35.

Fazio, R. H., & Zanna, M. P. (1981). Direct experience and attitude-behavior consistency. In L. Berkowitz (Ed.), *Advances in experimental social psychology* (Vol. 6, pp. 161-202). New York: Academic Press.

Fensel, D., & Bussler, C. (2002). The Web service modeling framework WSMF. *Electronic Commerce: Research and Applications, 1*(2002), 113-137.

Fensel, D., & Bussler, C. (2002). The Web service modeling framework WSMF. *Electronic Commerce: Research and Applications, 1*(2002), 113-137.

Festinger, L. (1957). *A theory of cognitive dissonance.* Evanston, Ill.: Row and Peterson.

Fillis, I., Johannson, U., & Wagner, B. (2004). Factors impacting on adoption and development in the smaller firm. *International Journal of Enterpreneurial Behaviour & Research, 10*(3), 178-191.

Fishbein, M., & Ajzen, I. (1975). *Belief, attitude, intention, and behavior: An introduction to theory and research.* Reading, MA: Addison-Wesley.

Fontana, J. (2004). Service-oriented hype to meet hard realities. *Network World, 21*, 68-69.

Fornell, C., & Larcker, D. F. (1981). Evaluating structural equations of market orientation with unobservable variables and measurement error. *Journal of Marketing Research, 18*, 39-50, February.

Foster, I., Kesselman, C., & Tuecke, S. (2001). The anatomy of the grid: Enabling scalable virtual organizations. *International Journal of High Performance Computing Applications, 15*(3), 200–222.

Foster, I., Kesselman, C., Nick, J. M., & Tuecke, S. (2002). Grid services for distributed system integration. *IEEE Computer, 35*(6), 37-46.

Fowler, M. (2003). *Patterns of enterprise application architecture*. Boston: Addison-Wesley.

Fox, G., & Gannon, D. (2006). Workflow in grid systems. *Concurrency and Computation: Practice & Experience, 18*(10), 1009-1019, August 2006.

Friedman, T. L. (2005). The world is flat: A brief history of the twenty-first century. In. New York: Farrar, Strauss and Giroux.

Fukuyama, F. (1995). *The virtual handshake: E-commerce and the challenge of trust*. Merrill Lynch. Retrieved from http://www.ml.com/

Gallaugher, J. M., & Wang, Y. M. (2002). Understanding network effects in software markets: Evidence from Web server pricing. *MIS Quarterly, 26*(4), 303-327.

Gambetta, D.G. (1988). *Trust*. New York: Basil Blackwell.

Gant, J. P., & Gant, D. B. (2001). Web portals and their role in e-government. *Proceedings of the 7th American Conference on Information Systems* (pp. 1616-1623), Boston, USA.

Gao, J. (2005). E-commerce issues in Australian manufacturing: A newspaper medium perspective. *Journal of Electronic Commerce in Organizations, 3*(4), 20-41.

Gardner, T. (2003, May). Mapping from UML to BPEL4WS. In *OMG MDA Implementers' Workshop*, Orlando, FL).

Garicano, L. (2001). The effects of business-to-business e-commerce on transaction costs. *The Journal of Industrial Economics, 49*(4), 463-486.

Gary, C. (2003). A stage model of ICT adoption in small firms. Workshop in Rimini—Firms and Consumers Facing E-Commerce: Strategies to Increase Its Adoption and Usage". Open University Business School, UK

Gavirneni, S., Kapuscinski, R., & Tayur, S. (1999). Value of information in capacitated supply chains. *Management Science, 45*, 16–24.

Gebert, H., Geib, M., Kolbe, L., & Brenner, W. (2003). Knowledge-enabled customer relationship management: integrating customer relationship management and knowledge management concepts. *Journal of Knowledge Management, 7*(5), 107-123.

Gefen, D. (2000). E-commerce: The role of familiarity and trust. *Omega, 28*(6), 725-737.

Gefen, D. (2002). Reflections on the dimensons of trust and trustworthiness among online consumers. *DATA BASE for Advances in Information Systems, 33*(3), 38–46.

Gefen, D., Karahanna, E., & Straub, D. W. (2003). Trust and TAM in online shopping: An integrated model. *MIS Quarterly. 27*(1), 51-91.

General Practice Computing Group. (2000). *The general practice data model*. Retrieved from http://www.gpcg.org/publications/docs/GPCG_standards_activity.PDF

Geng, X., Gopal, R. D., Ramesh, R., & Whinston, A. B. (2003). Scaling Web services with capacity provision networks. *IEEE Computer, 36*(11), 64-72.

Giaglis, G. M., Klein, S., & O'Keefe, R. M. (2002). The role of intermediaries in electronic marketplaces: Developing a contingency model. *Information Systems Journal*, (12), 231-246, July.

Gibbs, J., Kraemer, K. L., & Dedrick, J. (2003). Environment and policy factors shaping global e-commerce diffusion: A cross-country comparison. *Information Society, 19*(1), 5-20.

Gisolfi, D. (2001, April). *Web services Architect Part 2: Models for dynamic e-business*. Retrieved July 2002, from http://www-106.ibm.com/developerworks/Webservices/library/ws-arc2.html

Glushko, R. J., & McGrath, T. (2002). *Document engineering for e-business*. Paper presented at the Document Engineering 2002, McLean, Virginia, USA.

Gogan, J. (1999). Which site seals deliver? *Information Week. 738,* 146, June 14.

Golbeck, J., Parsia, B., & Hendler, J. (2003). Trust networks on the semantic Web. *Proceedings of Cooperative Intelligent Agents 2003.*

Gollmann, D. (2006). Why trust is bad for security *Electronic Notes in Theoretical Computer Science*, *157*(3), 3-9, May 25, 2006.

Gong, L. (2001). JXTA: A network programming environment. *IEEE Internet Computing*, *5*(3), 88-95.

Gonsalves, A. (2002). GE unit adds Web services. *Information Week*. 30 April.

Goode, S. (2002). Management attitudes toward the World Wide Web in Australian small business. *Information Systems Management*, 45-48.

Graafland-Essers, I., & Ettedgui, E. (2003). *Benchmarking e-government in Europe and the US*. RAND.

Grefen, P., Pernici, B., & Sanchez, G. (1999); Database support for workflow management—The WIDE Project. Kluwer.

Gregorio, D. D., Kassicieh, S. K., & de Gouvea Neto, R. (2005). Drivers of k-business activity in developed and emerging markets. *IEEE Transactions on Engineering Management, 52*(2), 155-166.

Groenfeldt, T. (1997). Who's in the driver's seat? *Journal of Business Strategy, 18*(1), 36-41.

Grover, V., & Ramanlal, P. (1999). Six myths of information and markets: Information technology networks, electronic commerce, and the battle for consumer surplus. *MIS Quarterly, 23*(4), 465-495.

Grover, V., & Teng, J. T. C. (2001). E-commerce and the information market. *Communications of the ACM, 44*(4), 79-86.

Grunberg, D. B. (1999). Internet: Friend or foe? *Franchising World, 31*(5), 39.

Gupta, M., Judge, P., & Ammar, M. (2003). A reputation system for peer-to-peer networks. *NOSSDAV'03* (pp. 144-152). (Jun. 1-3, 2003).

Gupta, S., Jain, D. C., & Sawhney, M. S. (1999). Modeling the evolution of markets with indirect network externalities: An application to digital television. *Marketing Science, 18*(3), 396-416.

Gurguis, S. A., & Zeid, A. (2005). Towards autonomic Web services: Achieving self-healing using Web services. *Proceedings of the Workshop on Design and Evolution of Autonomic Application Software* (pp. 1-5), St. Louis, Missouri.

Gutierrez, C., Fernandez-Medina, E., & Piattini, M. (2005). Web services enterprise security architecture: A case study. *Proceedings of the 2005 Workshop on Secure Web services* (pp. 10-19).

Hachigian, N. (2001). China's cyber strategy. *Foreign Affairs*, 118-133.

Hagel III, J. (2002). *Out of box: Strategies for achieving profits today and growth through Web services*. Boston: Harvard Business School Press.

Hagel III, J., & Brown, J. S. (2002). *Orchestrating business processes—Harnessing the value of Web services technology*. Retrieved January 6, 2003, from http://www.johnhagel.com/paper_orchestratingWebservices.pdf

Hagel III, J., Brown, J. S., & Layton-Rodin, D. (2002). *The secret to creating value from Web services today: Start simply*. Retrieved January 6, 2003, from http://www.johnhagel.com/paper_startsimply.pdf

Hair, J. F., Anderson, R. E., Tatam, R. L., & Black, W. C. (1998). *Multivariate data analysis* (5th ed.). NJ: Prentice-Hall.

Hakimpour, F., Domingue, J., Motta, E., Cabral, L., & Lei, Y. (2004). Integration of OWL-S into IRS-III. *Proceedings of the 1st AKT Workshop on Semantic Web Services (AKT-SWS04)*; KMi, The Open University, Milton Keynes, UK.

Haller, A., Cimpian, E., Mocan, A., Oren, E., & Bussler, C. (2005). WSMX—A semantic service-oriented architecture. *Proceedings of the International Conference on Web Service* (ICWS 2005). Orlando, Florida, 2005.

Hammer, M., & Champy, J. (1993). *Reengieneering the corporation. A manifesto for reengineering*. New York: Harper Business.

Hammer, M., & Champy, J. (1993). *Reengineering the corporation: A manifesto for business revolution*. New York: Harper Business.

Han, J. K., Kim, N., & Srivastava, R. K. (1998). Market orientation and organizational performance: Is innovation a missing link? *Journal of Marketing, 62*, 30-45.

Hansen, M. (2000). Networked incubators: Hothouses of the new economy. *Harvard Business Review, 78*(5), 74-84.

Harden, L., Heyman, B., & Bruner, R. (2000). *Net results.2: Best practices for Web marketing*. Indianapolis, IN: New Riders.

Hardy, C., Phillips, N., & Lawrence, T (1996). Forms and facades of trust. In R. M. Kramer, & T. R. Tyler (Eds.), *Trust in organisations: Frontiers of theory and research* (pp. 65–85). Thousand Oaks, CA: Sage Publications.

Harmsen, H., & Hensen, B. (2004). Identifying the determinants of value creation in the market: A competence-based approach. *Journal of Business Research, 57*(5), 533-541.

Harrison, A. (1996). Openness and growth: A time-series, cross-country analysis for developing countries. *Journal of Development Economics, 48*(2), 419-447.

Hart, P., & Saunders, C. (1997). Power and trust: Critical factors in the adoption and use of electronic data interchange. *Organisation Science, 8*(1), 23–42.

Hart, P., & Saunders, C. (1998). Emerging electronic partnerships: Antecedents and dimensions of EDI use from the supplier's perspective. *Journal of Management Information Systems, 14*(4), 87-111.

Hatcher, L. (1994). *Step-by-step approach to using the SAS system for factor analysis and structural equation modeling*. Cary, NC: SAS Institute Inc.

He, Y., & Jutla, D. N. (2006). Contextual e-negotiation for the handling of private data in ecommerce on a semantic Web. *Proceeding of the 39th Hawaii International Conference on System Sciences*, Kauai, HI.

Heeks, R. (2001). *Building e-government for development: A framework for national and donor action*. Manchester: Institute for Development Policy and Management.

Heeks, R. (2002). *Information systems for public sector management*. Manchester: Institute for Development Policy and Management.

Henderson, J., & Venkatraman, N. (1993). Strategic alignment: Leveraging information technology for transforming organizations. *IBM Systems Journal, 32*(1), 4-16.

Hertzum, M., Andersen, H., Andersen, V., & Hansen, C. (2002). Trust in information sources: Seeking information from people, documents, and virtual agents. *Interacting with Computers, 14*(5), 575-599.

Hess, C. M., & Kemerer, C. F. (1994). Computerized loan origination systems: An industry case study of the electronic markets hypothesis. *MIS Quarterly, 18*(3), 251-275.

Hewitt, P. (2005). Taking the lead in global digital excellence. *Computer Weekly, 16*.

Hewlett-Packard Company. (2002). *Web services conversation language (WSCL) 1.0. W3C Note*, March 2002. Retrieved December, 2004, from http://www.w3.org/TR/wscl10/

Hibbard, J. D., Kumar, N., & Stern, L. W. (2001). Examining the impact of destructive acts in marketing channel relationships. *Journal of Marketing Research*, (38), 45-61, February.

Hoffman, D. L., Novak, T. P., & Peralta, M. A. (1999). Building consumer trust online. *Communications of the ACM, 42*(4), 80-85.

Holcombe, R. G., & Sobel, R. S. (2000). Consumption externalities and economic welfare. *Eastern Economic Journal, 26*(2), 157-170.

Holland, C. P., & Lockett, G. (1997). Mixed mode network structures: The strategic use of electronic communication by organizations. *Organization Science, 8*(5), 475-488.

Holland, C., Lockett, G., & Blackman, I. (1992). Planning for electronic data interchange. *Strategic Management Journal, 13*(7), 539-550.

Hoontrakul, P. (2004). *Value revelation in differentiated goods for travel industry* (Discussion Paper). Bangkok: Sasin of Chulalongkorn University.

Hopkins, J. (2006, December 20). EBay shuts down China site, teams with Beijing partner. *USA Today*, p. 03b.

Hoy, M.G. & Phelps, J. (2003). Consumer privacy and security protection on church Web sites: Reasons for concern. *Journal of Public Policy and Marketing, 22*(1), 58-70.

Hsiao, R. (2001, December 16-19). Technology fears: Barriers to the adoption of business-to-business electronic commerce. In V. Storey, S. Sakar, & J. I. DeGross (Eds.), *Proceedings of the International Conference on Information Systems 2001*, New Orleans, LA (pp. 181–192).

Hsu, P., Kraemer, K. L., & Dunkle, D. (2006). Determinants of e-business use in U.S. firms. *International Journal of Electronic Commerce, 10*(4), 9-45, summer.

Hu, J., & Lin, H. (2005). The online auction Web site that beats eBay in China. *Business Weekly*, (921), July 18-24, 2005 (in Chinese).

Huang, Z., & Janz, B. D. (2002, August 9-11). Internet EDI adoption: Trust in technology and application knowledge. In *Proceedings of the Eighth Americas Conference on Information Systems*, Dallas, TX (pp. 2222–2227).

Hull, R., & Su, J. (2005). Tools for composite Web services: A short overview. *ACM SIGMOD Record, 43*(2), 86-95.

Hurley, R., & Hult, T. M. (1998). Innovation, market orientation, and organizational learning: An integration and empirical examination. *Journal of Marketing, 62*(3), 42-54.

Hwang Y. C., & Yuan S. T. (2006). *Exploring collective wisdom in ambient e-service environment: Implementation method and evaluations.* Technical report. National Cheng-Chi University, Taiwan.

Hwang Y. C., & Yuan S. T. (2007). A roadmap for ambient e-service: Applications and embracing model. *International Journal of E-Business Research, 13*(1), 51-73.

Hwang, Y. C., & Yuan, S. T. (2005). Ambient e-service embracing model. *Proceedings of the 7th IEEE International Conference on E-Commerce Technology* (pp. 535-538). (CEC2005) Germany.

Iacovou, C. L., Benbasat, I., Dexter, & A. S. (1995). Electronic data interchange and small organizations: Adoption and impact of technology. *MIS Quarterly, 19*(4), 465-485.

IBM. (2003). *IBM patterns for e-business.* Retrieved January 9, 2003, from http://www-106.ibm.com/developerworks/patterns/

IDS Scheer AG. (2002). ARIS methods (for Version 6).

Intelligence, B. I. (2006). Up and down the ladder. *Business India Intelligence, 13*(9), 3-4.

Internet Fraud Compliant Center. (2005). IFCC 2002 Internet Fraud Report January 1, 2005-December 31, 2005. National White Collar Crime Center and the Federal Bureau of Investigation.

IPDR. (2002, October). *Network data management—Usage (NDM-U) For IP-based services version 3.1.1.* Retrieved January 2003, from http://www.ipdr.org/download-docs/index.html

iWatch. (2005). Wake up call for India.

Iyengar, S. (2004, March 18-19). Business process integration: Using UML and BPEL4WS. In *SI-SE 2004 10th Anniversary Symposium*, University of Zurich.

Jabisetti, N., & Lee, Y. (2005). OWL-S-based autonomic services for grid computing. *Proceedings of the IEEE International Conference on Web services* (pp. 825-826), July 11-15, 2005.

James, D. (2002). Dark clouds should part for international market. *Marketing News, 36*(1), 9, 13.

James, J. (2003). Sustainable Internet access for the rural poor? Elements of an emerging Indian model. *Futures, 35*, 461-472.

James, L. R., Mulaik, S. A., & Brett, J. M. (1982). *Causal analysis: Assumptions, models, and data*. Beverly Hills: Sage.

Jamil, A., & Paul, S. (2001). Collective memory support for buyer-supplier negotiation on multiple issues: Design of a Web-based system. *Proceeding of the 7th Americas Conference on Information Systems*, Boston, MA.

Jarvenpaa, S. L., & Tractinsky, N. (1999). Consumer trust in an Internet store. *Journal of Computer-Mediated Communication, 5*(2), 1–33.

Jarvenpaa, S. L., Knoll, K., & Leidner, D. E. (1998). Is anybody out there? Antecedents of trust in global virtual teams. *Journal of Management Information Systems, 14*(4), 26-64.

Jaworski, B. J., & Kohli, A. K. (1993). Market orientation, antecedent, and consequences. *Journal of Marketing, 57*, 53-70, July.

Jeffcoate, J., Chappell, C., & Feindt, S. (2002). Best practice in SME adoption of e-commerce. *Benchmarking: An International Journal, 9*(2), 122-132.

Jensen, M. C., & Meckling, W. H. (1976). Theory of the firm: Managerial behavior, agency costs and ownership structure. *Journal of Financial Economics, 3*, 303-360.

Jertila, A., & Schoop, M. (2005). Electronic contracts in negotiation support systems: Challenges, design, and implementation. *Proceeding of the 7th IEEE International Conference on E-Commerce Technology*, Munich, Germany.

Jih, W. J. (2002). Effects of electronic commerce implementations in Taiwan. *Journal of Computer Information Systems, XXXXII*(3), 68-76.

Jih, W. J. (2003). Simulating real world experience using accumulative system development projects. *Journal of Information Systems Education, 14*(2), 181-192.

Jih, W. J., & Lee, S. F. (2004). Exploring relationships between motivating factors and life styles of cellular phone users. *Journal of Computer Information Systems, XLIV*(2), 65-73.

Johnson, C. et al. (2004). *2003 eCommerce: The year in review*. Forrester Research.

Johnston, H., & Vitale, M. (1988). Creating competitive advantage with interorganisational systems. *MIS Quarterly, 6*, 153–65.

Johnston, R. B., & Mak, H. C. (2000). An emerging vision of Internet-enabled supply-chain electronic commerce. *International Journal of Electronic Commerce, 4*(4), 43-59.

Jones, C., Hecker, R., & Holland, P. (2003). Small firm Internet adoption: Opportunities forgone, a journey not begun. *Journal of Small Business and Enterprise Development, 10*(3), 287-297.

Jones, S. (2005). *Enterprise SOA adoption strategies*. InfoQ Mini-Book Series, 2006. Retrieved January 21, 2007, from http://www.infoq.com/minibooks/enterprise-soa

Jøsang, A. et al. (2007). A survey of trust and reputation systems for online service provision. Decision Support Systems, In Press, Corrected Proof, Available online 5 July.

Joshi, P., Singh, H., & Phippen, A. D. (2004). Web services: Measuring practitioner attitude. *14*(5), 366-371.

Jost, W., & Wagner, K. (2002). The ARIS toolset. In A. W. Scheer, F. Abolhassan, W. Jost, & M. Kirchmer (Eds.), *Business process excellence: ARIS in practice* (pp. 16-31). Berlin Heidelberg New York: Springer.

Jung, J., Hur, W., Kang, S., & Kim, H. (2004). Business process choreography for B2B collaboration. *IEEE Internet Computing, 8*(1), 37-45, Jan-Feb 2004.

Kalakota, R., & Whinston, A. B. (1999). *Electronic commerce: A managers guide*. Reading, MA: Addison-Wesley.

Kambil, A., Nunes, P. F., & Wilson, D. (1999). Transforming the marketspace with all-in-one markets. *International Journal of Electronic Commerce, 3*(4), 11-28.

Kannabiran, G., & Narayan, P. C. (2005). Deploying Internet banking and e-commerce—Case study of a private-sector bank in India. *Information Technology for Development, 11*(4), 363-379.

Kaplan, S., & Sawhney, M. (2000). E-hubs: The new B2B marketplaces. *Harvard Business Review*, 97-103, May-June.

Karahanna, E., Straub, D. W., & Chervany, N. L. (1999). Information technology adoption across time: A cross-sectional comparison of pre-adoption and post-adoption beliefs. *MIS Quarterly. 23*(2), 183-213.

Karahannas, M., & Jones, M. (1999, December 13-15). Interorganisational systems and trust in strategic alliances. In P. De, & J. I. DeGross (Eds.), *Proceedings of the International Conference on Information Systems 1999*, Charlotte, NC (pp. 346–357).

Karake-Shalhoub, Z. (2002). *Trust and loyalty in electronic commerce: An agency theory perspective*. Westport, CT: Quorum Books.

Katz, M. L., & Shapiro, C. (1985). Network externalities, competition, and compatibility. *American Economic Review, 75*, 424-440.

Katz, M. L., & Shapiro, C. (1986). Technology adoption in the presence of network externalities. *Journal of Political Economy, 94*, 822-841.

Kavantzas, N., Burdett, D., Ritzinger, G., Fletcher, T., Lafon, Y., & Barret, C. (2005). *Web services choreography description language version 1.0*. W3C Candidate Recommendation, 9 November 2005. Retrieved January 2007, from http://www.w3.org/TR/ws-cdl-10/

Keating, G., Ramussen, S., Raven, M., Tso, E., Cocq, J., & Dotson, P. (2001). *Use of Web-based consensus building and confllCT clarification process for the Navajo Nation governmental efficiency evaluation*. Unpublished manuscript.

Keen, P. (2002). *Electronic commerce and the concept of trust*. Retrieved February 22, 2003, from http://www.peterkeen.com/ecr1.htm

Keen, P. G. W. (1993). Information technology and the management difference: A fusion map. *IBM Systems Journal, 32*(1), 17-39.

Keen, P. G. W. (1997). Are you ready for the "trust" economy. *Computerworld, 31*(16), April 21, 80.

Keeney, R., & Raiffa, H. (1993). *Decisions with multiple objectives: Preferences and value trade-offs*. Cambridge University Press.

Keller, A., Kreger, H., & Schopmeyer, K. (2001). Towards a CIM schema for runtime application management. *Proceedings of the 12th IFIP/IEEE International Workshop on Distributed Systems: Operations & Management (DSOM)*, Nancy, France. Retrieved January 2007, from http://www.loria.fr/~festor/DSOM2001//proceedings/S7-2.pdf

Kennedy, M. (2005). *Oracle BPEL process manager quick start guide, 10g (10.1.2)*; Beta Draft, April, 2005. Retrieved May 2005, from http://download-uk.oracle.com/otndocs/products/bpel/quickstart.pdf

Kenyon, C., & Cheliotis, G. (2002). Architecture requirements for commercializing grid resources. *Proceedings of the 11th IEEE International Symposium on High Performance Distributed Computing HPDC-11 (HPDC'02)*, Edinburgh, Scotland (pp. 215-224).

Kersten, G. E., & Noronha, S. J. (1997). Negotiation via the World Wide Web: A cross-cultural study of decision making. *InterNeg Research.* Retrieved September 28, 2005, from http://www.iiasa.ac.at/Research/DAS/interneg/research/misc/inc91.html

Khalaf, R. (2002). Enterprise services. *Communications of the ACM, 45*(10), 77-82.

Khalaf, R., & Nagy, W. A. (2003). *Business process with BPEL4WS: Understanding BPEL4WS, Part 7, Adding correlation and fault handling to a process.* Research report, IBM developerWorks, April 2003. Retrieved January 2005, from http://www-106.ibm.com/developerworks/webservices/ library/ws-bpelcol7/

Khalifa, M., & Liu, V. (2004). The state of research on information system satisfaction. *Journal of Information Technology Theory and Application, 5*(4), 37-49.

Kiggen, E. (2001, January 8). Study: High-tech scores low in India. Retrieved February 2, 2002, from www.newsfactor.com/

Kiiski, S., & Pohjola, M. (2002). Cross-country diffusion of the Internet. *Information Economics and Policy, 14*(2), 297-310.

Kim, D. J., Agrawal, M., Jayaraman, B., & Rao, H. R. (2003). A comparison of B2B e-service solutions. *Communications of the ACM, 46*(12), 317-324.

Kim, E. (2001, August 3-5). A model of sustainable trust in B2C e-markets. In *Proceedings of the Americas Conference on Information Systems*, Boston, MA (pp. 804–809).

Kim, H. W., Xu, Y., & Koh, J. (2005). A comparison of online trust building factors between potential customers and repeat customers. *Journal of AIS, 5*(10), 392-340.

Kim, S., Shaw, T., & Schneider, H. (2003). Web site design benchmarking within industry groups. *Internet Research, 13*(1), 17-26.

Kinateder, M., & Rothermel, K. (2003). Architecture and algorithms for a distributed reputation system. *Trust Management 2003, LNCS 2692* (pp. 1-16).

Kincaid, J. W. (2003). *Customer relationship management: Getting it right!* Upper Saddle River, NJ: Prentice-Hall PTR.

Kleijen, S., & Raju, S. (2003). An open Web services architecture. *ACM Queue, 1*(1), 38-47.

Klein, S., & Selz, D. (2000). Cybermediation in auto distribution: Channel dynamics and conflicts. *Journal of Computer-Mediated Communication, 5*(3). Retrieved September 28, 2005, from http://jcmc.indiana.edu/vol5/issue3/kleinselz.htm

Knape, T., Hederman, L., Wade, V.P., Gargan, M., Harris, C., & Rahman, Y. (2003). A UML approach to process modelling of clinical practice guidelines for enactment. In R. Baud (Ed.), *The new navigators.* IOS Press.

Knol, W. H. C., & Stroken, J. M. H. (2001). The diffusion and adoption of information technology in small and medium sized enterprises through IT scenarios. *Technology Analysis & Strategic Management, 13*(2), 227-246.

Kohli, A. K., & Jaworski, B. J. (1990). Market orientation: The construct, research propositions, and managerial implications. *Journal of Marketing, 54*(2), 1-18.

Köhne, F., Schoop, M., & Staskiewicz, D. (2005). An empirical investigation of the acceptance of electronic negotiation support system features. *Proceeding of the 13th European Conference on Information Systems,* Regensburg, Germany.

Koller, M. (2001). Grocer builds net traffic—Albertson's expands in Seattle, pushes online/storefront strategy. *InternetWeek*, (872), 13-14.

Kollock, P. (1999). The production of trust in online markets. In E. J. Lawler (Ed.), *Advances in group processes* (Vol. 16, pp. 99-123). Greenwich, CT: Jai Press.

Konana, P., Menon, N. M., & Balasubramanian, S. (2000). The implication of online investing. *Communications of the ACM, 43*(1), 35-41.

Koo, C. M., Koh, C. E., & Nam, K. (2004). An examination of Porter's competitive strategies in electronic virtual markets: A comparison of two online business models. *International Journal of Electronic Commerce, 9*(1), 163-179.

Kornish, L. J. (2006). Technology choice and timing with positive network effects. *European Journal of Operational Research, 173*(1), 268-282.

Kotha, S., Rajgopal, S., & Rindova, V. (2001). Reputation building and performance: An empirical analysis of the top-50 pure Internet firms. *European Management Journal, 19*(6), 571-586.

Kotler, P. (2000). *Marketing management* (10th ed.). NJ: Prentice Hall.

Kotler, P. (2003). *Marketing Management.* Prentice Hall.

Koziol, M. (2006). Advice for e-mail marketing to China. *B to B, 91*(15), 19.

Kramer, R. (1994). The sinister attribution error: Paranoid cognition and collective distrust in organisations. *Motivations and Emotions, 18*, 199–230.

Kreger, H. (2003). Fulfilling the Web services promise. *Communications of the ACM, 46*(6), 29-34.

Kristiansen, E. G. (1998). R&D in the presence of network externalities: Timing and compatibility. *Rand Journal of Economics, 29*(3), 531-547.

Kshetri, N. (2005). What determines Internet Diffusion Loci in developing countries: Evidence from China and India. *Pacific Telecommunications Review, 23*(3), 25-34.

Kula, V., & Tatoglu, E. (2003). An exploratory study of Internet adoption by SMEs in an emerging market economy. *European Business Review, 15*(5), 324-333.

Kulviwat, S., Thaku, R., & Guo, C. (2006). An exploratory study of consumer adoption of online shopping: Mediating effect of online purchase intention. *International Journal of E-Business Research, 2*(2), 68-82.

Kumar, A., & Agarwal, V. (2006). A customizable engine for metrics collection, aggregation, and composition. *Proceedings of the 10th IEEE/IFIP Network Operations and Management Symposium (NOMS 2006)*, Vancouver, Canada (pp. 162-173).

Kumar, N., Stern, L. W., & Anderson, J. C. (1993). Conducting interorganisational research using key informants. *Academy of Management Journal, 36*(6), 1633.

Kwok, R., Lee, M., & Turban, E. (2001). On inter-organisational EC collaboration—The impact of inter-cultural communication apprehension. In *Proceedings of the 34th Hawaiian Information Conference on Systems Sciences, Vol. 1* (pp. 1011–1019). IEEE Publishing.

Kwon, I. G., & Suh, T. (2004). Factors affecting the level of trust and commitment in supply chain relationships. *The Journal of Supply Chain Management*, 4-14.

Labour Government. (1999). *Modernising Government White Paper*, March 1999.

Labour Government. (2001). *E-government strategic framework*, April 2001.

Lacohee, H. (2006). Risk and restitution: Assessing how users establish online trust. *Computers & Security, 25*(7), 486-493, October 2006.

Lang, K. R., & Whinston, A. B. (1999). A design of a DSS intermediary for electronic markets. *Decision Support Systems, 25*(3), 181-197.

Langdon, C. S. (2003). The state of Web services. *IEEE Computer, 36*(7), 93-94.

Langdon, C. S., & Shaw, M. J. (2002). Emergent patterns of integration in electronic channel systems. *Communications of the ACM, 45*(12), 50-55.

Langdon, C. S. (2003). The state of Web services. *IEEE Computer, 6*(7), 93-94.

Lanjouw, J. O., & Mody, A. (1996). Innovation and the international diffusion of environmentally responsive technology. *Research Policy, 25*(4), 549-571.

Lau, R. Y. K., & Wong, O. (2007). Mining negotiation knowledge for adaptive negotiation agents in e-marketplaces. *Proceeding of the 40th Hawaii International Conference on System Sciences,* Big Island, HI.

Lavie, D. (2002). The competitive advantage of interconnected firms: An extension of the resource-based view. *Academy of Management Proceedings*, C1-6.

Lawrence, K. (2002). Factors inhibiting the collaborative adoption of electronic-commerce among Australia SMEs. In S. Burgess (Ed.), Managing information technology in small business: Challenges & solutions (pp. 178-192). Hershey, PA: Idea Group Publishing. Lawson, R., Alcock, C., Cooper, J., & Burgess, L. (2003). Factors affecting adoption of electronic commerce technologies by SMEs: An Australian study. *Journal of Small Business and Enterprise Development, 10*(3), 265-276.

Leavitt, N. (2004). Are Web services finally ready to deliver? *IEEE Computer, 37*(11), 14-18, Nov. 2004.

Lee, C. S., & Shu, W. (2005). Four models of Internet-enabled distribution structures. *Information Systems Management, 22*(3), 14-22.

Lee, H. G. (1998). Do electronic marketplaces lower the price of goods. *Communications of the ACM, 41*(1), 73-80.

Lee, H. L., & Whang, S. (2000). Information sharing in a supply chain. *International Journal of Technology Management, 20*, 373–387.

Lee, H. L., Padmanabhan, V., & Whang, S. (1997). Information distortion in a supply chain: The bullwhip effect. *Management Science*, *43*(4), 546-558.

Lee, H., & Wang, S. (2001). Winning the last mile of e-commerce. *Sloan Management Review, 42*(4), 54-62.

Lee, J., & Runge, J. (2001). Adoption of information technology in small business: Testing drivers of adoption for entrepreneurs. *Journal of Computer Information Systems, 42*(1), 44-57.

Lee, S. M., & Cata, T. (2005). Critical success factors of Web-based e-service. *International Journal of E-Business Research, 1*(3), 21-40.

Lee, S., Jih, W., & Fang, S. (2006). Investigating the impact of customer relationship management practices of e-commerce on online customer's Web site satisfaction: A model-building approach. *International Journal of E-Business Research, 2*(4), 61-77.

Lee, Y., & O'Connor, G. C. (2003). New product launch strategy for network effect products. *Journal of the Academy of Marketing Science, 31*(3), 241-255.

Lee-Kelley, L., Gilbert, D., & Mannicom, R. (2003). How e-CRM can enhance customer loyalty. *Marketing Intelligence & Planning, 21*(4/5), 239-248.

Leimeister, J. M., Ebner, W., & Krcmar, H. (2005). Design, implementation, and evaluation of trust-supporting components in virtual communities for patients. *Journal of Management Information Systems, 21*(4), 101-135.

Lemon, S. (2005). Chinese official calls for expanding IT use. *Computerworld, 39*(47), 12.

Levinson, N. S. (2004). Developing nations. In H. Bidgoli (Ed.), *The Internet Encyclopedia* (Vol. 1, pp. 434-443). Hoboken, NJ: John Wiley & Sons.

Levy, M., & Powell, P. (2002). SME transformation: Modelling progressions. In S. Wrycza (Ed.), *Information systems and the future of the digital economy, Proceedings of the 10th European Conference on Information Systems*, Gdansk, Poland, June 2002.

Levy, M., Powell, P., & Yetton, P. (2002). The dynamics of SME information systems. *Small Business Economics, 19*(4), 341-354.

Lewicki, R. J., & Bunker, B. B. (1996). Developing and maintaining trust in work relationships. In R. M. Kramer, & T. R. Tyler (Eds.), *Trust in organisations: Frontiers of theory and research* (pp. 114–139). Thousand Oaks, CA: Sage Publications.

Lewicki, R. J., & Bunker, B. B. (1996). Developing and maintaining trust in work relationships. In R. M. Kramer & T. R. Tyler (Eds.), *Trust in Organizations.* Thousand Oaks, CA: Sage Publications.

Li, F. (2003). Implementing e-government strategy in Scotland: Current situation and emerging issues. *Journal of E-Commerce in Organizations, 1*(2), 44-65.

Li, F. (2005). Social aspects of e-business. *Journal of E-Commerce in Organizations, Special issue 3*(2), i-iv.

Li, F. (2007). *What is e-business? How the Internet transforms organizations.* Oxford: Blackwell Publishing.

Li, L. (2002). Information sharing in a supply chain with horizontal competition. *Management Science, 48*(9), 1196–1212.

Liaw, S-T., Morrison, I., Lewis, B., & Deveny, E. (2004). Modelling the clinical processes of prescribing (MCPOP)—Information, clinical workflow, and processes. In K. Walduck & B. Cesnik (Eds.), *HIC 2004: Twelfth National Health Informatics Conference* (pp. 194-199). Brunswick East, Vic.: Health Informatics Society of Australia.

Liikanen, E. (2001). *eEurope and the role of SMEs*. Paper presented at the European Commission Go Digital Meeting, 6 April.

Lim, E., & Saiu, K. (2003). *Advances in mobile commerce technologies.* Hershey, PA: Idea Group Publishing.

Lim, L., & Benbasat, I. (1993). A theoretical perspective of negotiation support systems. *Journal of Management Information Systems, 9*(3), 27-44.

Lin, K. J., Ho, J., & Zhang, L. J. (2004). First wave of Web services adoption in research. *International Journal of Web services Research, 1*(4), 1-4.

Lin, K., Lu, H., & Yu, T. (2004). A distributed trust and reputation management framework for e-services. *IEEE International Conference on Services Computing*, Shanghai, China.

Lin, L., & Kulatilaka, N. (2006). Network effects and technology licensing with fixed fee, royalty, and hybrid contracts. *Journal of Management Information Systems, 23*(2), 91-118.

Lings, I. N. (2004). Internal market orientation construct and consequences. *Journal of Business Research, 57*, 405-413.

Linthicum, D. S. (2002, Jan 17). *An application integration value-add? expoQ's David Linthicum on Web services in EAI.* Retrieved August 18, 2003, from http://searchWebservices.techtarget.com/originalContent/0,289142,sid26_gci788646,00.html

Litan, R. E., & Rivlin, A. M. (2001). Projecting the economic impact of the internet. *The American Economic Review, 91*(2), 313-317.

Lu, W., Du, J., Zhang, J., Feicheng, M., & Le, T. (2002). Internet development in China. *Journal of Information Science, 28*(3), 207-223.

Luftman, J., & McLean, E. R. (2004). Key issues for IT executive. *MIS Quarterly Executive, 3*(3), June, 89-104.

Luhmann, N. (1979). *Trust and power.* London: John Wiley.

Luo, J. C. (2006). *The 2006 report on current conditions and future trends of e-commerce businesses in Taiwan.* Institute of Information Industry Research Report Series. Retrieved from http://gcis.nat.gov.tw/ec/knowledge/topics/detail.asp?DocID=1028&picName=basic

Lymer, A., Nayak, A., Johnson, R., & Spaul, B. (1998). *UK business and the information superhighway: The impact of the Internet on SMEs.* ACCA Occasional Research Paper, No. 23: The Association of Chartered Certified Accountants.

Maamar, Z., Mostefaoui, S. K., & Yahyaoui, H. (2005). Toward an agent-based and context-oriented approach for Web services composition. *IEEE Transactions on Knowledge and Data Engineering, 17*(5), 686-697, May 2005.

MacMillan, D. (2006). Nations that censor the net. *Business Week Online* (pp. 8).

Madlberger, M., & Kotzab, H. (2001). Adapting the Internet as distribution channel for stationary retailers: The Austrian case. *Electronic Markets, 11*(1). Retrieved August 26, 2004, from http://www.electronicmarkets.org/modules/pub/view.php/electronicmarkets-118

Maes, P., Guttman, R. H., & Moukas, A. G. (1999). Agents that buy and sell. *Communications of the ACM, 42*(3), 81-91.

Maglio, P., & Barrett, R. (2000). Intermediaries personalize information streams. *Communications of the ACM, 43*(8), 96-101.

Mahadevan, B. (2000). Business models for Internet-based e-commerce: An anatomy. *California Management Review, 42*(4), 55-69.

Mahajan, V., Shrinivasan, R., & Wind, J. (2002). The dot.com retail failures of 2000: Were there any winners? *Journal of the Academy of Marketing Science, 30*(4), 474-486.

Mahrer, H., & Brandtweiner, R. (2004). Success factors for implementing e-government services: The case of the Austrian e-government service portal. *International Journal of Information Technology and Management, 3*(2/3/4), 235-245.

MAIS. (n.d.). *MAIS project home page.* Retrieved January 2005, from http://www.mais-project.it

Malloy, B. A., Kraft, N. A., Hallstrom, J. O., & Voas, J. M. (2006). Improving the predictable assembly of service-oriented architectures. *IEEE Software, 23*(2), 12-15.

Malone, T. W., Yates, J., & Benjamin R. I. (1987). Electronic markets and electronic hierarchies. *Communications of the ACM,* 30(6), 484-497.

Manes, A. T. (2003). *Web services: A manager's guide.* Boston: Addison Wesley.

Marchetti, C., Pernici, B., & Plebani, P. (2004). A quality model for multichannel adaptive information. *WWW (Alternate Track Papers & Posters) 2004,* New York City, NY, pp.48-54.

Marcussen, C. H. (2004). Trends in European Internet distribution of travel and tourism services. Retrieved May 29, 2006, from http://www.rcb.dk/uk/staff/chm/trends.htm accessed on 3/December/2004

Martin L. M., & Matlay, H. (2001). Innovative use of the Internet in established small firms: The impact of knowledge management and organisational learning in accessing new opportunities. *Qualitative Market Research: An International Journal, 6*(1), 18-26

Martin, D. (2003). *The OWL services coalition. OWL-S: Semantic markup for Web services.* White Paper. Retrieved December 2004, from http://www.daml.org/services/owl-s/1.0/owl-s.html

Maruca, R. F. (2000). The electronic negotiator. *Harvard Business Review,* 16-17, Jan-Feb.

Maruyama, H. (2002). New trends in e-business: From B2B to Web services. *New Generation Computing, 20,* 125-139.

Massetti, B., & Zmud, R. W. (1996). Measuring the extent of EDI usage in complex organizations: Strategies and illustrative examples. *MIS Quarterly,* 20(3), 331-345.

Matlay, H., & Addis, M. (2003). Adoption of ICTs and e-commerce in small business: An HEI-based consultancy perspective. *Journal of Small Business and Enterprise Development, 10*(3), 321-335.

Matsuno, K., Mentzer, J. T. (2000). The effects of strategy type on the market orientation-performance relationship. *Journal of Marketing, 64*(4), 1-16.

Maurer, R. (1996). *Beyond walls of resistance.* Bard Press.

Maurino, A., Modafferi, S., Mussi, E., & Pernici, B. (2004). A framework for provisioning of complex e-services. *IEEE International Conference on Services Computing (SCC 2004),* Shanghai.

Mayer R, et al. (1995). An integrative model of organizational trust. *Academy of Management Review, 20*(3), 709e34.

Mayer, R. C., Davis, J. H., & Schoorman, F. D. (1995). An integrative model of organizational trust. *Academy of Management Review, 20*(3), 709-734.

McAllister, D. J. (1995). Affect- and cognition-based trust as foundations of interpersonal cooperation in organizations. *Academy of Management Journal, 30,* 24-59.

McCarthy, T. (2000). China's Internet gold rush. *Time, 155*(8), 50-51.

McDonagh, P., & Prothero, A. (2000). Euroclicking and the Irish SME: Prepared for e-commerce and the single currency. *Irish Marketing Review, 13*(1), 21-33

McGrath, J. E. (1984). *Groups: Interaction and performance.* Englewood Cliffs, NJ: Prentice Hall.

McIlraith, S., Son, T. C., & Zeng, H. (2001). Semantic Web services. *IEEE Intelligent Systems.* Special issue on semantic Web, *16*(2), 46-53.

McKay, J., Prananto, A., & Marshall, P. (2000). *E-business maturity: The SOGe model.* Paper presented at the proceedings of the 11th Australasian Conference on Information Systems (ACIS), 6-8 Dec, Queensland University of Technology, Brisbane, Australia.

Mckinney, V., Yoon, K., & Zahedi, F. W. (2002). The measurement of Web-customer satisfaction: An expectation and disconfirmation approach. *Information Systems Research, 13*(3), 296-315.

McKnight, D. H., & Chervany, N. L. (2000). What is trust? A conceptual analysis and an interdisciplinary model. In *Proceedings of the Americas Conference on Information Systems 2000*, Long Beach, CA (pp. 877–883).

McKnight, D. H., Choudhury, V., & Kacmar, C. (2002). Developing and validating trust measures for e-commerce: An integrative typology. *Information Systems Research. 13*(3), 334-359.

McKnight, D. H., Cummings, L. L., & Chervany, N. L. (1998). Initial trust formation in new organisational relationships. *The Academy of Management Review, 23*(3), 473–490.

Meall, L. (2002). Eastern promise. *Accountancy*, 60-61.

Mehrtens, J., Cragg, P. B., & Mills, A. M. (2001). A model of Internet adoption by SMEs. *Information & Management, 39*(3), 165-176.

Mehrtens, J., Cragg, P. B., & Mills, A. M. (2001). A model of Internet adoption by SMEs. *Information and Management, 39*, 165-176.

Mentzas, G. (1997). Implementing an IS strategy—A team approach. *Long Range Planning, 10*(1), 84-95.

Metrics. (2003, June). *Common information model (CIM) metrics model, Version 2.7.* Distributed management task force. Retrieved July 2003, from http://www.dmtf.org/standards/documents/CIM/DSP0141.pdf

MetricsSchema. (2003, March). *CIM metrics schema, Version 2.7.* Distributed management task force, Retrieved January 2007, from http://www.dmtf.org/standards/documents/CIM/CIM_Schema27/CIM_Metrics27-Final.pdf

Microsoft Corporation. (n.d.). *Microsoft BizTalk Server.* Retrieved January 2005, from http://www.microsoft.com/biztalk/

Milanovic, N., & Malek, M. (2004). Current solutions for Web service composition. *IEEE Internet Computing, 8*(6), 51-59 Nov.-Dec. 2004.

Miles, M. B., & Huberman, A. M. (1989). *Qualitative data analysis: A sourcebook of new methods.* Thousand Oaks, CA: Sage Publications.

Miller, R. R. (2001). Leapfrogging? India's information technology industry and the Internet. Retrieved May 10, 2002, from http://www.ifc.org/economics/pubs/dp42/dp42.pdf

Min, S., & Wolfinbarger, M. (2005). Market share, profit margin, and marketing efficiency of early movers, bricks and clicks, and specialists in e-commerce. *Journal of Business Research*, (58), 1030-1039.

Min, S., Song, S., & Keebler, J. S. (2002). An Internet-mediated market orientation (IMO): Building a theory. *Journal of Marketing Theory and Practice, 10*(2), 1-11.

Mintzberg, H. (1971). Managerial work: Analysis from observation. *Management Science, 18*(3), B97–B112.

Mir, R., & Mir, A. (2005). Catalysis, not leapfrog: An institutionalist argument for a limited role of ICTs in India's Development. *Asian Business & Management, 4*(4), 411-429.

Mirchandani, D. A., & Motwani, J. (2001). Understanding small business electronic commerce adoption: An empirical analysis. *Journal of Computer Information Systems, 41*(3), 70-73.

Mishra, A. K. (1996). Organisational responses to crisis — The centrality of trust. In R. M. Kramer, & T. R. Tyler (Eds.), *Trust in organisations: Frontiers of theory and research* (pp. 261–287). Thousand Oaks, CA: Sage Publications.

Mohanty, B. K., & Bhasker, B. (2005). Product classification in the Internet business—A fuzzy approach. *Journal of Decision Support Systems, 38,* 611-619.

Molla, A., Heeks, R., & Balcells, I. (2006). Adding clicks to bricks: A case study of e-commerce adoption by a Catalan small retailer. *European Journal of Information Systems, 15*(4), 424-438.

Morgan, D. L. (1988). *Focus groups as qualitative research* (Vol. 16). Newbury Park, CA: SAGE Publications.

Morgan, R. M., & Hunt, S. D. (1994). The commitment-trust of relationship marketing. *Journal of Marketing, 58*, 20-38, July.

Morris, I. (2006). China's broadband boom. *Telecommunications—International Edition, 40*(11), 16-18.

Motta, E., Domingue, J., Cabral, L., Gaspari, M. (2003). IRS-II: A framework and infrastructure for semantic Web services. In D. Fensel, K. Sycara, & J. Mylopoulos (Eds.), *The semantic Web—ISWC 2003. Lecture Notes in Computer Science* (Vol. 2870, pp. 306-318). Heidelberg: Springer-Verlag.

Mui, L., Halberstadt, A., & Mohtashemi, M. (2003). Evaluating reputation in multi-agents systems. In R. Falcone, S. Barber, L. Korba, & M. Singh (Eds.), *Trust, reputation, and security: Theories and practice* (pp. 123-137). Springer-Verlag, Berlin.

Mukhopadhyay, T., & Kekre, S. (2002). Strategic and operational benefits of electronic integration in B2B procurement processes. *Management Science, 48*(10), 1301-1313.

Mullaney, T. J. (1999). Needed: The human touch: Online retailers are beginning to discover the importance of customer-service reps who can talk and thank. *BusinessWeek*, (3659), EB 52.

Muller-Lankenau, C., Wehmeyer, K., & Klein, S. (2006). Multi-channel strategies: Capturing and exploring diversity in the European retail grocery industry. *International Journal of Electronic Commerce, 10*(2), 85-122, winter.

Myers, M. D. (1997). *Qualitative research in information systems.* Retrieved April 3, 2002, from http://www.qual.auckland.ac.nz/

Nadherny, C. C. (1998). Technology and direct marketing leadership. *Direct Marketing, 61*(7), 42-45, November.

Nannery, M. (2000). HMV's Cooler Britannia. *Chain Store Age, 76*(8), 84-85.

Napier, H. A., Judd, P. J., Rivers, O. N., & Wagner, S. W. (2001). Creating a winning e-business. Course Technology.

Narver, J. C., & Slater, S. F. (1990). The effect of a market orientation on business profitability. *Journal of Marketing, 54*(4), 20-35.

National Health Supply Chain Taskforce Interoperability Working Group. (2002). *Electronically connecting trading partners: A proposed interoperability standard.* National Health Supply Chain Taskforce Interoperability Working Group.

Ndede-Amadi, A. A. (2004). What strategic alignment, process redesign, enterprise resource planning, and e-commerce have in common: Enterprise-wide computing. *Business Process Management Journal, 10*(2), 184-199.

Neuman, W. L. (2000). *Social research methods: Qualitative and quantitative approaches* (4th ed.). Sydney: Allyn and Bacon.

New Mexico State University—College of Agriculture and Home Economics (1999-2003). *Evaluation handbook.* Retrieved January 6, 2003, from http://www.cahe.nmsu.edu/grants/evaluation/eval_section2.html#focus

News, B. (2004, July 7). *Women lead rural India's Internet rush.* BBC News Retrieved August 21, 2004, from http://newsvote.bbc.co.uk/mpapps/pagetools/print/news.bbc.co.uk /2/hi/south_asia/3871529.stm

Ngai, E. W. T. (2005). Customer relationship management research (1992-2002): An academic literature review and classification. *Marketing Intelligence and Planning, 23*(6/7), 582-605.

Nicholls, A., & Watson, A. (2005). Implementing e-value strategies in UK retailing. *International Journal of Retail and Distribution Management, 33*(6/7), 426-443.

Nielson, J. F., Host, V., & Mols, N. P. (2005). Adoption of Internet-based marketing channels by small-and-medium-sized manufacturers. *International Journal of E-Business Research, 1*(2), 1-23.

Nordas, H. K. (2002). Patterns of foreign direct investment in poor countries. *Journal of International Trade & Economic Development, 11*(3), 247-266.

Nordstrom, R. D., & Pinkerton, R. L. (1999). Taking advantage of internet sources to build a competitive intelligence system. *Competitive Intelligence Review, 10*(1), 54-61.

Norris, P. (2000, Aug 1-6). *The global divide: Information poverty and Internet access worldwide.* Paper presented at the International Political Science World Congress, Quebec City.

Nunnally, J. (1978). *Psychometric theory.* New York: McGraw Hill.

O'Conner, P. (1999). *Electronic information distribution tourism and hospitality.* Cambridge: CABI Publishing.

O'Reilly, T. (2005). *What is Web 2.0: Design patterns and business models for the next generation of software.* Retrieved from http://www.oreillynet.com/lpt/a/6228

Odlyzko, A. (2003). Privacy, economics, and price discrimination on the Internet. *The 5th International Conference on Electronic Commerce* (ICEC 2003). ACM Press.

Orchard, D. (2002). *Web services pitfalls.* Retrieved from http://www.xml.com/pub/a/2002/02/06/Webservices.html

Orlikowski, W. J., & Baroudi, J. J. (1991). Studying information technology in organisations: Research approaches and assumptions. *Information Systems Research, 2*(1), 1-28.

Osborne, D., & Gaebler, T. (1997). *Reinventing government.* London: Signum.

Osterwalder, A. (2004). *The business model ontology: A proposition in a design science approach.* PhD Thesis, Ecole Des Hautes Etudes Commerciales (EHEC), University of Lausanne, Lausanne.

Osterwalder, A., & Pigneur, T. (2002). *An e-business model ontology for modelling e-business.* Paper presented at the 15th Electronic Commerce Conference—E-Reality: Constructing the E-Economy, Bled, Slovenia, 17-19 June.

Ouvry, A. S. (2002). Workflow analysis and modeling in medical it projects. *Medicamundi, 46*(2), 47.

OWL-S Coalition. (2004). *OWL-S 1.0 Release.* Retrieved from http://www.daml.org/services/owl-s/1.1/

Oyclaran-Oyeyinka, B., & Lal, K. (2004). Determinants of e-business adoption: Evidence from firms in India, Nigeria, Uganda. *INTECH Discussion Paper Series* (2004-14).

Padmanabhan, V., Rajiv, S., & Srinivasan, K. (1997). New products, upgrades, and new releases: A rationale for sequential product introduction. *Journal of Marketing Research, 34*(4), 456-472.

Palmer, J. W., & Griffith, D. A. (1998). An emerging model of Web site design for marketing. *Communications of the ACM, 41*(3), 45-51.

Palmer, J. W., Bailey, J. P., & Faraj, S. (2000). The role of intermediaries in the development of trust on the WWW: The use and prominence of trusted third parties and privacy statements. *Journal of Computer-Mediated Communication, 5*(3). Retrieved September 28, 2005 from http://jcmc.indiana.edu/vol5/issue3/palmer.html

Panlogic. (2006). *Connecting with China*: Panlogic.

Papadopoulou, P., Kanellis, P., & Martakos, D. (2001). Investigating trust in e-commerce: A literature review and a model for its formation in customer relationships. In *Proceedings of the Seventh Americas Conference on Information Systems*, Boston, MA (pp. 791–798).

Papazoglou, M. P. (2003). Web services and business transactions. *World Wide Web: Internet and Web Information Systems, 6*, 49-91.

Papazoglou, M. P., & Georgakopoulos, D. (2003). Service-oriented computing. *Communications of the ACM, 46*(10), 25-28.

Parish, A., Kibblewhite, G., Woodley, M., & Richardson, J. (2002). *The UK electronics industry e-commerce initiative—A study of the adoption of e-commerce*. Retrieved from www.intellectuk.org/publications/reports

Parker, G. G., & van Alstyne, M. W. (2005). Two-sided network effects: A theory of information product design. *Management Science, 51*(10), 1494-1504.

Parker-Pope, T. (2001). How to tell whether that online drugstore in really a good deal. *Wall Street Journal*. February 16, B1.

Parvatiyar, A., & Sheth, J. N. (2001). Customer relationship management: Emerging practice, process, and discipline. *Journal of economic & Social Research, 3*(2), 1-34.

Paternò, F. (2003). Understanding interaction with mobile devices. *Interacting with Computers, 15*(4), 473-478.

Patricia Seybold Group. (2002). *An executive's guide to Web services*. Patricia Seybold Group.

Paul, S. (2001). Collective memory support in negotiation: A theoretical framework. *Proceeding of the 34th Annual Hawaii International Conference on System Science*, Maui, HI.

Paul, S., Haseman, W. D., & Ramamurthy, K. (2004). Collective memory support and cognitive-conflict group decision-making: An experimental investigation. *Decision Support Systems, 36*, 261-281.

Paulson, L. D. (2002). Choreographing Web services. *IEEE Computer, 35*(11), 25-25, Nov. 2002.

Pavlou, P. A. (2003). Consumer acceptance of electronic commerce: Integrating trust and risk with the technology acceptance model. *International Journal of Electronic commerce, 7*(3), 69-103.

Pavlou, P., Tan, Y., & Gefen, D. (2003). The transitional role of institutional trust in online interorganisational relationships. In *Proceedings of the 36th Hawaii International Conference on Systems Sciences — Track 7, 2003* (p. 215a). IEEE Publishing.

Peleg, M., Boxwala, A.A., Tu, S., Greenes, R.A., Shortliffe, E.H., & Patel, V.L. (2001). Handling expressiveness and comprehensibility requirements in GLIF3. In V. Patel et al. (Eds.), *Medinfo 2001*. Amsterdam. IOS Press.

Peleg, M., Tu, S., Bury, J., Ciccarese, P., Fox, J., Greenes, R.A., et al. (2003). *Comparing models of decision and action for guideline-based decision support: A case study approach*. Stanford University Report, No: SMI-2002-0922.

Peltz, C. (2003). Web services orchestration and choreography. *IEEE Computer, 36*(10), 46-53.

Peltz, C. (2003). Web services orchestration and choreography. *IEEE Computer, 36*(10), 46-52, Oct. 2003.

Peltz, C. (2003). Web services orchestration—A review of emerging technologies, tools, and standards. Hewlett-Packard Company, 2003.

Pennington, R., Wilcox, H. D., & Grover, V. (2004). The role of system trust in business-to-consumer transactions. *Journal of Management Information Systems, 20*(3), 197-226.

Perkins, W. C., Hershauer, J. C., Foroughi, A., & Delaney, M. M. (1996). Can a negotiation support system help a purchasing manager? *International Journal of Purchasing and Materials Management*, 37-45, spring.

Peterson, R. A., Balasubramanian, S., & Bronnenburg, B. J. (1997). Exploring the implications of the Internet for consumer marketing. *Journal of the Academy of Marketing Science, 25*(4), 329-346.

Petre, P. (1985). How to keep customers happy captives. *Fortune, 112*(5), 42-46, September 2.

Pettigrew, A. (1985). *The awakening giant: Continuity and change in ICI.* Oxford: Basil Blackwell.

Pettigrew, A. (1990). Longitudinal field research on change. Theory and practice. *Organization Science, 1,* 267-292.

Pitta, D. A. (2002). Internet currency. *The Journal of Consumer Marketing, 19*(1), 86-87.

Podsakoff, P. M., & Organ, D. M. (1986). Self-reports in organizational research: Problems and prospects. *Journal of Management, 12*(4), 531-543.

Polleres, A., & Lara, R. (2005). *D4.1v0.1 A conceptual comparison between WSMO and OWL-S.* WSMO Working Draft, January 2005. Retrieved January 2005, from http://www.wsmo.org/2004/d4/d4.1/v0.1/20050106/

Poon, A. (1993). *Tourism, technology and competitive strategies.* Oxford: CAB International.

Poon, S. (2000). Business environment and Internet commerce benefits—A small business perspective. *European Journal of Information Systems, 9,* 72-81.

Poon, S., & Swatman, P. (1999). An exploratory study of small business Internet commerce issues. *Information and Management, 35,* 9-18.

Poon, S., & Swatman, P. M. C. (1999). An exploratory study of small business Internet commerce, *Information & Management, 35*(1), 9-18.

Porter, M. E. (2001). Strategy and the Internet. *Harvard Business Review, 79*(3), 63-78.

Powell, T. C., & Dent-Micallef, A. (1997). Information technology as competitive advantage: The role of human, business, and technology resources. *Strategic Management Journal, 18*(5), 375-405.

Prakash, G. (2005). Leapfrogging into the knowledge era: Use of ICT for development. *IIMB Management Review, 17*(3), 47-56.

Prananto, A., McKay, J. A., & Marshall, P. (2003). A study of the progression of e-business maturity in Australian SMEs: Some evidence of the applicability of the stages of growth for e-business model. *Proceedings of the 7th Pacific Asia Conference on Information Systems (PACIS),* July 10-13.

Premkumar, G., & Ramamurthy, K. (1995). The role of interorganizational and organizational factors on the decision mode for adoption of interorganizational systems. *Decision Sciences, 26*(3), 303-336.

Prencipe, L. W., & McCarthy, J. (2002). Battle of the shopping carts. *InfoWorld, 24*(40), 46-47.

Press, L., Foster, W., & Goodman, S. (1999). *The Internet in India and China.* Retrieved from http://www.isoc.org/inet99/proceedings/3a/3a_3.htm

Press, L., Foster, W., Wolcott, P., & McHenry, W. (2002). The Internet in India and China. *First Monday, 7*(10).

Purchasing, June 21, 2001, pp.40.

Qiaoqiao, Z. (2004). *Xinhuanet.com.* Retrieved January 18, 2007, from http://news.xinhuanet.com/it/2004-08/04/content_1708666.htm

Quayle, M. (2003). E-business in a turbulent world: Usage in European small and medium size enterprises. *International Journal of Electronic Business, 1*(1), 41-52.

Quibria, M. G., Tschang, T., & Reyes-Macasaquit, M. L. (2002). New information and communication technologies and poverty: Some evidence from developing Asia. *Journal of the Asia Pacific Economy, 7*(3), 285-310.

Rabin, S. (2001). Providing a high-performance commerce site. *Information Systems Management, 18*(4), 40-51.

Ramsey, E., Ibbotson, P., Bell, J., & Gary, B. (2003). E-opportunities of service sector SMEs: An Irish cross-boarder study. *Journal of Small Business and Enterprise Development. 10*(3), 250-264.

Rao, M. (2002a, Jan 25). *E-government services to create billion-dollar market in India.* Kotak Street Retrieved

April 11, 2002, from http://kotakstreet.com/webapp/kotak/MarketMonitor/KotakByLanesID.jsp?id=63

Rao, M. (2002b, Apr 18). New report highlights entrepreneurial drive in India, calls for better infrastructural and educational support. Retrieved April 22, 2002, from www.Indiainfoline.com/nevi/inwi/

Rao, M. (2002c, Feb 25). Rural community networks: growing social capital via interactive technologies. Retrieved May 2, 2002, from www.Indiainfonline.com

Rao, S. S., Metts, G., & Monge, C. A. M. (2003). Electronic development in small- and medium-sized enterprises: A stage model and its implications. *Business Process Management Journal, 9*(1), 11-32.

Ratnasingham, P., & Kumar, K. (2000). Trading partner trust in e-commerce participation. In *Proceedings of the 21st International Conference in Information Systems*, Brisbane (pp. 544–552).

Raymond, L. (1987). Organizational characteristics and MIS success in the context of small business. *MIS Quarterly*, 37-52.

Rayport, J. (1999). The truth about internet business models. *Strategy and Business,* Third Quarter.

Rayport, J. F., & Jaworski, B. J. (2002). *Introduction to e-commerce.* Boston, MA: McGraw-Hill/Irwin.

Redmond, C., & Wade, V. (1998). Towards flexible metering and charging for information services. *Proceedings of the ICCC/IFIP Conference on Electronic Publishing*, Budapest, Hungary. Retrieved January 2007, from http://citeseer.ist.psu.edu/630476.html

Redmond, C., & Wade, V. (2002). Service level accounting in telecommunications. *Proceedings of the 8th IFIP/IEEE Network Operations and Management Symposium (NOMS)* (pp. 283-296), Florence, Italy.

Reicheld, E. F., & Sasser, W. E. (1990). Zero-defection: Quality comes to services. *Harvard Business Review*, 105-111.

Reijers, H., & Jansen-Vullers, M. J. (2005). Better processes = better e-commerce. *Quality Progress, 38*(3), 57-63.

Reinhardt, G., & Levesque, M. (2004). A new entrant's decision on virtual versus bricks-and-mortar retailing. *Journal of Electronic Commerce Research 5*(3), 136-152.

Remenyi, D., Money, A., Sherwood-Smith, M., & Irani, Z. (2000). *Effective measurement and management of IT costs and benefits* (2nd ed.). Butterworth-Heinemann.

Resnick, P., Zeckhauser, R., Friedman, E., & Kuwabara, K. (2000). Reputation systems: Facilitating trust in Internet interactions. *Communications of the ACM, 43*(12), 45-48.

Robins, B., Sleeper, B., & McTiernan, C. (2003). *Web services rules: Real-world lessons from early adopters.* The Stencil Group.

Roehm, H. A., & Roehm, M. L. (2005). The hybrid split ad technique and onsite rewards. *Journal of Consumer Behaviour, 4*(3), 173-184.

Roman, D., & Scicluna, J. (2006). *Ontology-based choreography of WSMO services.* WSMO Final Draft, May 2006. Retrieved January 2007, from http://www.wsmo.org/TR/d14/v0.3/

Roman, D., Lausen, H., & Keller, U. (2004). *D2v1.0. Web service modeling ontology (WSMO).* WSMO Working Draft; September 2004. Retrieved January 2005, from http://www.wsmo.org/2004/d2/v1.0/20040920/

Romano, N. C., & Fjermestad, J. (2003). Electronic commerce customer relationship management: A research agenda. *Information Technology and Management, 4*(2-3), 233-258.

RosettaNet. (2006). Retrieved December 2006, from http://www.rosettanet.org

Ross-Talbot, S., & Fletcher, T. (2006). *Web services choreography description language: Primer.* W3C Working Draft, June 2006. Retrieved January 2007, from http://www.w3.org/TR/ws-cdl-10-primer/

Rousseau, D. M., Sitkin, R. S., Burt, R. S., & Camerer, C. (1998). Not so different after all: A cross-discipline view of trust. *Academy of Management Review, 23*(3), 393-404.

Roussos, G., Peterson, D., & Patel, U. (2003). Mobile identity management: An enacted view. *International Journal of E-Commerce, 8*(1). 81-100.

Ruekert, R.W. (1992). Developing a market orientation: An organizational strategy perspective. *International Journal of Research in Marketing, 9*(3), 225-246.

RUS. (2003). *Resource usage service working group, global grid forum*. Retrieved November 2004, from http://forge.gridforum.org/projects/rus-wg/

Russell, C. (1989). Kiss and tell. *American Demographics, 11*(12), 2.

Rust, T. R., & Kannan, P. K. (2003). E-service: A new paradigm for business in the electronic environment. *Communications of the ACM, 46*(6), 36-42.

Ryan, P., & Hoontrakul, P. (2003). An economic analysis of the tourism industry: Implications for online intermediary. *Chulalongkorn Journal of Economics, 15*(3), 205-235.

Sabater, J., & Sierra, C. (2002). Reputation and social network analysis in multi-agent systems. *The 1st International Joint Conference on Autonomous Agents & Multiagent Systems* (pp. 475-482). AAMAS'02, July 15-19, 2002, Bologna, Italy.

Sahai, A., Ouyang, J., & Machiraju, V. (2001). End-to-end transaction management for Web based services. *Proceedings of the 3rd International Workshop on Advanced issues of E-Commerce and Web based Information Systems (WECWIS)* (pp. 128-135).

Saini, A., & Johnson, J. L. (2005). Organizational capabilities in e-commerce: An empirical investigation of e-brokerage service providers. *Journal of the Academy of Marketing Science, 33*(3), 360-375.

Salam, A. F., Rao, H. R., & Pegels, C. C. (2003). Consumer-perceived risk in e-commerce transactions. *Communications of the ACM, 46*(12ve), 325-331.

Salleh, N. A. M., Rohde, F., & Green, P. (2006). The effect of enacted capabilities on adoption of a government electronic procurement system by Malaysian SMEs. *Electronic Markets, 16*(4), 292-311.

Samtani, G., & Sadhwani, D. (2002). ROI and Web services. In *Web service Business Strategies and Architectures*: Expert Press.

Santos-Paulino, A. (2005). Trade liberalisation and economic performance: Theory and evidence for developing countries. *World Economy, 28*(6), 783-821.

Sarkar, M. B., Butler, B., & Steinfield, C. (1995). Intermediaries and cybermediaries: A continuing role for mediating players in the electronic marketplace. *Journal of Computer-Mediated Communication, 1*(3). Retrieved September 28, 2005, from http://jcmc.indiana.edu/vol1/issue3/sarkar.html

Sarkar, M. E., & El Sawy, O. A. (2003). The four tigers of global e-business infrastructure: Strategies and implications for emerging economies. *Communications of the Association for Information Systems, 12*, 1-22.

Sarner, A. (2004). Prepare to reinvest in e-commerce for growth. Retrieved February 14, 2007, from http://www.gartner.com

Saulnier, C. F. (2000). Groups as data collection method and data analysis technique: Multiple perspectives on urban social work education. *Small Group Research, 31*(5), 607-627.

Saunders, A., & Cook, S. (2002). E25 after the deluge. *Management Today*, 40-45.

Sawhney, M. (2002). Fields of online dreams; e-commerce can flourish anywhere if you build the right business model. *CIO*, 128-130.

Scheer, A. W. (1998a). *ARIS—Business process frameworks*. Berlin et al: Springer.

Scheer, A. W. (1998b). *ARIS—Business process modelling*. Berlin et al: Springer.

Scheer, A. W., Abolhassan, F., Jost, W., & Kirchmer, M. (2002). *Business process excellence: ARIS in practice*. Berlin, Heidelberg, New York: Springer.

Schilit, B., Adams, N., & Want, R. (1994). Context-aware computing applications. *Proceedings of the 1st International Workshop on Mobile Computing Systems and Applications* (pp. 85-90).

Schmelzer, R., & Bloomberg, J. (2002, June 18). *Want to service-enable your enterprise? Model first!* Retrieved January 6, 2003, from http://searchWebservices.techtarget.com/tip/1,289483,sid26_gci833705,00.html

Schmidt, R. (2003). Web services-based architectures to support dynamic inter-organizational business processes. In M. Jeckle, & L. J. Zhang (Eds.), *International Conference on Web services, ICWS-Europe 2003, LNCS 2853* (pp. 123-136), Berlin.

Schmitz, S. W. (2000). The effects of electronic commerce on the structure of intermediation. *Journal of Computer-Mediated Communication, 5*(3). Retrieved Sep 28, 05 from http://jcmc.indiana.edu/vol5/issue3/schmitz.html

Scholler, D. (2003, 07/04/2003). *Web services Architecture: Part 1 - Service Development Excellence*. Retrieved 01/06/2003, from http://www.ge-bac.com/article.php?story=20030407225246949

Schoop, M., Jertila, A., & List, T. (2003). <f>N</f>egoist: A negotiation support system for electronic business-to-business negotiations in e-commerce. *Data & Knowledge Engineering, 47*(3), 371-402.

Scott Morton, F. (2001). Internet car retailing. *The Journal of Industrial Economics, 49*(4), 501-520.

Scott, J. (2000). Emerging patterns from the dynamic capabilities of Internet intermediaries. *Journal of Computer-Mediated Communication, 5*(3). Retrieved September 28, 2005, from http://jcmc.indiana.edu/vol5/issue3/scott.html

Scott, J. (2000). Facilitating interorganisational learning with information technology. *Journal of Management Information Systems, 17*(2), 81–113.

Scupola, A. (2002). Adoption issues of business-to-business Internet commerce in European SMEs. *Proceedings of the 35th Hawaii International Conference on System Sciences* (Vol. 7), Hawaii, USA.

Segev, A., & Beam, C. (1999). Brokering strategies in electronic commerce markets. *Proceedings of the 1st ACM Conference on Electronic Commerce,* Denver, CO.

Shand, B., Dimmonck, N., & Bacon, J. (2003). Trust for ubiquitous, transparent collaboration. *Proceedings of the 1st IEEE International Conference on Pervasive Computing and Communications* (PerCom'03).

Shani, D., & Chalasani, S. (1992). Exploiting niches using relationship marketing. *The Journal of Consumer Marketing, 9*(3). 33-42.

Shankar, V., Smith, A. K., & Rangaswamy, A. (2003). Customer satisfaction and loyalty in online and offline environments. *International Journal of Research in Marketing, 20*(2), 153-175.

Shapiro, C., & Varian, H. R. (1998). *Information rules*. HBS Press.

Shapiro, C., & Varian, H. R. (1999). The art of standard wars. *California Management Review, 41*(2), 8-32.

Shapiro, D. L., Sheppard, B. H., & Cheraskin, L. (1992, October). Business on a handshake. *The Negotiation Journal*, 365–378.

Sharma, S. (1996). *Applied multivariate techniques*. John Wiley & Sons.

Sheldon, P. (1997). *Tourism information technology*. Oxford: CAB.

Sheppard, B. H., & Tuchinsky, M. (1996). Micro-OB and the network organisation. In R. M. Kramer, & T. R. Tyler (Eds.), *Trust in organisations: Frontiers of theory and research* (pp. 140–165). Sage Publications.

Shneider, G. P. (2002). Electronic commerce. Thomson-Course Technology.

Shoib, G., & Nandhakumar, J. (2003). Cross-cultural IS adoption in multinational corporations. *Information Technology for Development, 10*(4), 249-261.

Sina. (2006). *Tech Sina*. Retrieved January 22, 2007, from http://tech.sina.com.cn/it/2006-09-29/07251165444.shtml

Singh, M. P., Huhns, M. N. (2005). *Service-oriented computing: Semantics, processes, agents*. John Wiley & Sons.

Singh, R., Iyer, L., & Salam, A. F. (2003). Web service for knowledge management in e-marketplaces. *e-Service Journal, 3*(1), 32-53.

Singh, S., & Ranchhod, A. (2004). Market orientation and customer satisfaction: Evidence from British machine tool industry. *Industrial Marketing Management, 33*(2), 135-144.

Sirin, E., Parsia, B., & Hendler, J. (2004). Filtering and selecting semantic Web services with interactive composition techniques. *IEEE Intelligent Systems, 19*(4), 42-49.

Sivashanmugam, K., Miller, J., Sheth, A., & Verma, K. (2004). Framework for semantic Web process composition. *Special Issue of the International Journal of Electronic Commerce (IJEC)*, Eds: Christoph Bussler, Dieter Fensel, Norman Sadeh, Feb 2004.

Slater, S. F., & Narver, J. C. (1994). Market orientation, customer value, and superior performance. *Business Horizons, 37*(2), 22-29.

Smeltzer, L. R. (1997, Winter). The meaning and origin of trust in buyer-supplier relationships. *International Journal of Purchasing and Materials Management*, 40–48.

SMF. (2002, March). *z/OS MVS system management facilities (SMF)*. Retrieved July 2002, from http://publibz.boulder.ibm.com/epubs/pdf/iea2g230.pdf

Smith, D., Menon, S., & Sivakumar, K. (2005). Online peer and editorial recommendations, trust, and choice in virtual markets. *Journal of Interactive Marketing, 19*(3), 15-37.

Smith, M. D. (2001). Consumer decision-making at an Internet shopbot: Brand still matters. *The Journal of Industrial Economics, 49*(4), 541-559.

Smith, M. K., Welty, C., & McGuinness, D. L. (2004). *OWL Web ontology language guide*. W3C Recommendation, February 2004. Retrieved January 2005, from http://www.w3.org/TR/2004/REC-owl-guide-20040210/

Smyth, M., & Ibbotson, P. G. (2001). *Internet connectivity in Ireland*. Retrieved from www.bankofireland.co.uk

So, W.C. & Sculli, D. (2002). The role of trust, quality, value and risk in conducting e-business. *Industrial Management and Data Systems, 102*(9), 503-512.

Soderstrom, E., et al. (2002). Towards a framework for comparing process modeling languages. In A. Banks Pidduck et al. (Ed.s), *Proceedings of CAiSE 2002* (pp. 600-611). Heidelberg Berlin: Springer.

Sofaer, S., Kreling, B., Kenney, E., Swift, E. K., & Dewart, T. (2001). Family members and friends who help beneficiaries make health decisions. *Health Care Financing Review; Washington, 23*(1), 16.

Song, J., & Zahedi, F. (2002, August 9-11). A theoretical framework for the use of Web infomediaries. In *Proceedings of the Americas Conference on Information Systems*, Dallas, TX (pp. 2250–2256).

Spector, B. I. (1977). Negotiation as a psychological process. In I. W. Zartman (Ed.), *The negotiation process: Theories and applications*. (pp. 55-66). Beverly Hills, CA: Sage Publications.

Spencer, J. (2003). "I ordered that?' Web retailers make it easier to return goods. *The Wall Street Journal*, (Eastern Edition), D. 1.

Srinivasan, K., Kekre, S., & Mukhopadhyay, T. (1994). Impact of electronic data interchange technology on JIT shipments. *Management Science, 40*(10), 1291-1304.

Stal, M. (2002). Web services: Beyond component-based computing. *Communications of the ACM, 45*(10), 71-76.

Stats, I. W. (2007). *Internet usage in Asia*. Retrieved January 9, 2007, from http://www.Internetworldstats.com/stats3.htm

Stefanou, C., Sarmaniotis, C., & Stafyla, A. (2003). CRM and customer-centric knowledge management: an empirical research. *Business Process Management Journal, 9*(5), 617-634.

Stein, E. W., & Zwass, V. (1995). Actualizing organizational memory with information systems. *Information Systems Research, 6*(2), 85-117.

Stewart, K. (2003). Trust transfer on the World Wide Web. *Organization Science, 14*(1), 5-17.

Stock, G. N., Greis, N. P., & Kasarda, J. D. (2000). Enterprise logistics and supply chain structure: The role of fit. *Journal of Operations Management*, (18), 531-547.

Stockdale, R., & Standing, C. (2004). Benefits and barriers of electronic marketplace participation: An SME perspective. *The Journal of Enterprise Information Management, 17*(4), 301-311.

Stone, M. (2003). SME e-business and supplier-customer relations. Journal *of Small Business and Enterprise Development, 10*(3), 345-353.

Strauss, A. (1987). *Qualitative analysis for social scientists.* New York: Cambridge University Press.

Strauss, J., El-Ansary, A., & Frost, R. (2006). *E-marketing* (4th ed.). Upper Saddle River, NJ: Pearson/Prentice Hall.

Suarez, F. F. (2005). Network effects revisited: The role of strong ties in technology selection. *Academy of Management Journal, 48*(4), 710-720.

Sun, B., Xie, J., & Cao, H. H. (2004). Product strategy for innovators in markets with network effects. *Marketing Science*, *23*(2), 243.

Susarla, A., Barua, A., & Whinston, A.B. (2003). Understanding the service component of application service provision: An empirical analysis of satisfaction with ASP services. *MIS Quarterly, 27*(1), 91-123.

Swaab, R., Postmes, T., & Neijens, P. (2004). Negotiation support systems: Communication and information as antecedents of negotiation settlement. *International Negotiation, 9*(1), 59-79.

Swift, R. S. (2001). *Accelerating customer relationships using CRM and relationship technologies.* Upper Saddle River, NJ: Prentice-Hall PTR.

Sydow, J. (1998). Understanding the institution of interorganisational trust. In C. Lane, & R. Bachmann (Eds.), *Trust within and between organisations* (pp. 31–63). New York: Oxford University Press.

Szymanski, D. M., & Hise, R. T. (2000). E-satisfaction: An initial examination. *Journal of Retailing, 76*(3), 309-322.

Talib, M. A., Yang, Z., & Ilyas, Q. M. (2005). A framework towards Web services composition modeling and execution. *Proceedings of the IEEE EEE05 International Workshop on Business Services Networks* (pp. 4-10), Hong Kong.

Tan, F. B., Lin, H. J., & Urguhart, C. (2006). An exploratory study of the design preferences of U.S. and Chinese virtual communities. *International Journal of E-Business Research, 2*(3), 46-70.

Tan, Z. A., & Ouyang, W. (2004). Diffusion and impacts of the Internet and e-commerce in China. *Electronic Markets, 14*(1), 25-35.

Tassabehji, R. (2003). *Applying e-commerce in business.* Thousand Oaks, CA: SAGE publications Ltd.

TAT. (2003). *Tourism Authority of Thailand statistical report 2003.* Bangkok: Tourism Authority of Thailand.

TAT. (2004). *Tourism Authority of Thailand statistical report 2004.* Bangkok: Tourism Authority of Thailand.

Teng, C. I., & Chiang, D. M. (2006). Triggering the chain reaction: Customer targeting strategies in markets with network effects. *Electronic Commerce Studies, 4*(1), 23-36.

Teng, C. I., Tseng, F. C., & Chiang, D. M. (2006). Customer-capturing strategies: The way to replace existing technology characterized by network effects. *Technovation, 26*(12), 1384-1389.

Tetteh, E., & Burn, J. (2001). Global strategies for SME-business: Applying the SMALL framework. *Logistics Information Management, 14*(1-2), 171-180.

The Java Rule Engine API. (n.d.). JSR000094. Retrieved November 1, 2005, from http://www.jcp.org/aboutJava/communityprocess/final/jsr094/

The Stencil Group. (2002). *The laws of evolution: A pragmatic analysis of the emerging Web services market*: The Stencil Group.

Thiagarajan, K. (2002, March 31). China: The hidden dragon. *Businessline,* 1.

Tilley, S., Gerdes, J., Hamilton, T., Huang, S., Miller, H., Smith, D., & Wong, K. (2004). On business value and technical challenges of adopting Web services. *Journal of Software Maintenance and Evolution: Research and Practice, 16*, 31-50.

Timmers, P. (1998). Business models for the electronic markets. *Electronic Markets, 8*(2), 3-8.

Timmers, P. (2003). *Electronic commerce* (2nd ed.). Chichester: John Wiley.

Tosic, V., Pagurek, B, Patel, K., Esfandiari, B, & Ma, W. (2003). Management applications of the Web service offerings language (WSOL). *CAiSE 2003,* 468-484.

Travica, B. (2002). Diffusion of electronic commerce in developing countries: The case of Costa Rica. *Journal of Global Information Technology Management, 5*(1), 4-24.

Truman, G. E. (2000). Integration in electronic exchange environments. *Journal of Management Information Systems, 17*(1), 209-244, Summer.

TRUSTe (2000). How the TRUSTe program works. Retrieved from www.truste.org/webpublishers/pub_how.html

Tseng, C. R., & Chih-Hsiang, W. (2007). An expert system approach to improving stability and reliability of Web service. *Expert Systems with Applications, 33*(2), 379-388.

Tseng, F. C, Teng, C. I., & Chiang, D. M. (2005). Competing on utility thresholds: The way to capture markets characterized by network effects. *Proceedings of the International Conference on Business and Information,* Hong Kong, July, 2005.

Tseng, F. C., Teng, C. I., & Chiang, D. M. (2007). Delivering superior customer perceived value in the context of network effects. *International Journal of E-business Research, 3*(1), 40-49.

Tu, S. W., Campbell, J. et al. (2003). The structure of guideline recommendations: A synthesis. *American Medical Informatics Association Symposium* (pp. 679-83).

Tuecke, S., Czajkowski, K., Foster, I., Frey, J., Graham, S., Kesselman, C., Maguire, T., Sandholm, T., Vanderbilt, P., & Snelling, D. (2003). *Open grid services infrastructure (OGSI) Version 1.0.* Global grid forum draft recommendation. Retrieved January 2007, from http://www.globus.org/alliance/publications/papers/Final_OGSI_Specification_V1.0.pdf

Turban, E. (1995). *Decision support and expert system: Management support systems.* Englewood Cliffs, NJ: Prentice Hall International.

Turban, E., King, D., Lee, J., & Viehland, D. (2004). *Electronic commerce: A managerial perspective.* NJ: Prentice-Hall.

Turban, E., King, D., Viehland, D., & Lee, J. (2006). *Electronic commerce—A managerial perspective*. Upper Saddle River, NJ: Prentice Hall.

Turban, E., Lee, J., King, D., & Chung, H. M. (2000). *Electronic commerce: A managerial perspective.* New Jersey: Prentice Hall.

Twigg, A. (2003). A subjective approach to routing in P2P and ad hoc networks. *Trust Management 2003* (pp. 225-238), LNCS 2692.

U. S. Census Bureau Quarterly Retail E-Commerce Sales, Retrieved from http://www.census.gov/mrts/www/ecomm.html.

UNCTAD. (2000). Electronic commerce and tourism new perspectives and challenges for developing countries. In *Proceedings of the United Nations Conference on Trade and Development*. Retrieved May 29, 2006, from http://www.Pongsak.Hoontrakul.com

University, B. (2004). B2B e-commerce: Is Chinese enterprise getting ready? Retrieved May 29, 2004, from http://www.Chinabyte.com/20010904/1416727.shtml

UR. (2003). *Usage record working group, global grid forum*. Retrieved November 2004, from http://forge.gridforum.org/projects/ur-wg/

Van der Aalst, W. M. P., ter Hofstede, A. H. M., Kiepuszewski, B., & Barros, A. P. (2003). Workflow patterns. *Distributed and Parallel Databases*, *14*(3), 5-51, July 2003.

Van der Wiele, T., Williams, R., Van Iwaarder, J., Wilson, M., & Dale, B. (2002). The e-business research network: Summary of the results of the Dutch pilot survey. In *Proceedings of the British Academy of Management*, September 2002, UK.

Venkatesh, V., Morris, M. G., Davis, G. B., & Davis, F. D. (2003). User acceptance of information technology: Toward a unified view. *MIS Quarterly*, *27*(3), 425-478.

Venkatraman, N., & Zaheer, A. (1990). Electronic integration and strategic advantage: A quasi-experimental study in the insurance industry. *Information Systems Research*, 1(4), 377-93.

Vinoski, S. (2004). WS-nonexistent standards. *IEEE Internet Computing*, *8*(6), 94-96, Nov.-Dec. 2004.

Vogels, W. (2003). Web services are not distributed objects: Common misconceptions about the fundamentals of Web service technology. *IEEE Internet Computing*, *7*(6), 59-66.

W3C - World Wide Web Consortium (n.d.). Retrieved January, 2007, from http://www.w3.org

W3C. (2001). *Web services description language (WSDL) 1.1*. *W3C Note*, March 2001, http://www.w3.org/TR/wsdl

Walczak, S., Gregg, D. G., & Berrenberg, J. L. (2006). Market decision making for online auction seller: Profit maximization or socialization. *Journal of Electronic Commerce Research*, *7*(4), 199-220.

Walczuch, R., & Lundgren, H. (2004). Psychological antecedents of institution-based consumer trust in e-retailing. *Information & Management*, *42*(1), 159-177.

Walsh, J. K. (2004). India. *Global Markets Update*.

Wang, G. A. (2002). On obstacles to e-business development in Mainland China. *Quarterly Journal of Electronic Commerce*, *3*(4), 417-427.

Wang, X. P. (2005). Yahoo! invests in alibaba.com. *Commercial Times*, Aug. 12, 2005 (in Chinese).

Weerawarana, S., & Curbera, F. (2002). *Business process with BPEL4WS: Understanding BPEL4WS, Part 1, Concepts in business processes*. Research report, IBM developerWorks, Aug. 2002. Retrieved January 2005, from http://www-106.ibm.com/developerworks/webservices/library/ws-bpelcol1/

Weerawardena, J., & O'Cass, A. (2004). Exploring the characteristics of the market-driven firms and antecedents to sustained competitive advantage. *Industrial Marketing Management*, *33*(5), 419-427.

WEF. (2004). WEF Report: Developing Countries lead in ICT Access. *Economic Bureau of the World Economic Forum*.

Weitzel, T., Beimborn, D., & König, W. (2006). A unified economic model of standard diffusion: The impact of standardization cost, network effects, and network topology. *MIS Quarterly*, *30*(special issue), 489-514.

Westland, J. C. (1992). Congestion and network externalities in the short run pricing of information system services. *Management Science*, *38*(7), 992-1009.

Westley, F., & Vredenburg, H. (1997). Organizational collaboration and the preservation of global biodiversity. *Organization Science*, *8*(4), 381–403.

WfMC - Workflow Management Coalition (n.d.). Retrieved January, 2007, from http://www.wfmc.org

Whiteley, R. (1992). *The customer driven company*. Reading, MA: Addison-Wesley.

Wigand, R. T. (1996). Electronic commerce: Definition, theory, and context. *The Information Society, 13*(1), 1-16.

Wilhelm, U. G., Staamann, S. M., & Buttyan, L. (2000). A pessimistic approach to trust in mobile agent platforms. *IEEE Internet Computing* (pp. 40-48), September-October.

Wilkov, R. (2002). *How to get real value fro Web services... Today.* Retrieved January 6, 2003, from http://www.ebizq.net/topics/dev_tools/features/1567.html

Williamson, O. E. (1975). *Markets and hierarchies: Analysis and antitrust implications.* New York: Free Press.

Williamson, O. E. (1985). *The economic institutions of capitalism: Firms, markets, relational contracting.* New York: Free Press.

Williamson, O. E. (1998). *The economic instutions of capitalism.* New York: Free Press.

Willmott, D. (2000). The top 100 Web sites and the technologies that make them work. *PC Magazine, 19*(2), 144-159.

Winer, R. S. (2001). A framework for customer relationship management. *California Management Review, 43*(4), 89-105.

Witt, U. (1997). "Lock-in" vs. "critical masses"—industrial change under network externalities. *International Journal of Industrial Organization, 15*(6), 753-773.

Wohed, P., van der Aalst, W. M. P. Dumas, M., & ter Hofstede, A. H. M. (2003, October). Analysis of Web services composition languages: The case of BPEL4WS. In *Proceedings of the 22nd International Conference on Conceptual Modeling (ER'2003)*, Chicago (pp. 200-215).

Wolcott, P., & Goodman, S. (2003). Global diffusion of the Internet I: India: Is the elephant learning to dance? *Communications of the Association for Information Systems, 11*, 560-646.

Wright, D. (2002). *Beyond the hype: How to make Web services work for your organization, Part 2—How to begin to use Web services in your business.* Retrieved January 6, 2003, from http://www.lightshipinc.com/lightship/download/download.aspx?Title=BeyondHypePart2

WSRF. (2006). *Web services resource framework (WSRF)—Primer v1.2.* OASIS Web services resource framework (WSRF) TC. Retrieved January 2007, from http://docs.oasis-open.org/wsrf/wsrf-primer-1.2-primer-cd-02.pdf

Wu, C. (2004). A readiness model for adopting Web services. *Journal of Enterprise Information Management, 17*(5), 361-371.

Wu, J. (2004). Influence of market orientation and strategy on travel industry performance: An empirical study of e-commerce in Taiwan. *Tourism Management, 25*, 357-365.

xCBL.org. (2006). *XML common business library.* Retrieved December, 2006, from http://www.xcbl.org

Xie, J., & Sirbu, M. (1995). Price competition and compatibility in the presence of positive demand externalities. *Management Science, 41*(5), 909-926.

Xu, S., Zhu, K., & Gibbs, J. (2004). Global technology, local adoption: A cross-country investigation of Internet adoption by companies in the United States and China. *Electronic Markets, 14*(1), 13-25.

Yang, C. C., & Chung, A. (2004). Intelligent informediary for Web financial information. *Decision Support Systems, 38*(1), 65-80.

Yao, S. (2006). On economic growth, FDI and exports in China. *Applied Economics, 38*(3), 339-351.

Yaoping, J. (2005, Sept. 6). *ChinaIRN.com.* Retrieved January 21, 2007, from http://www.Chinairn.com/doc/4080/40189.html/

Yin, R. (1994). *Case study research* (2nd ed.). Thousand Oaks, CA: Sage Publications.

Yin, R. (1994). *Case study research: Design and methods* (2nd ed.). London: Sage

Yoder, R. A., Borkholder, P. L., & Friesen, B. D. (1991). Privatization and development: The empirical evidence. *The Journal of Developing Areas, 25*, 425-434.

Young, S., Huang, C. H., & McDermott, M. (1996). Internationalization and competitive catch-up processes: Case study evidence on Chinese multinational enterprises. *Management International Review, 36*(4), 295-314.

Zach, M. H. (1999). Managing codified knowledge. *Sloan Management Review,* 45-58, summer.

Zadeh, L. (1965). Fuzzy sets. *Information and Control, 8*(3), 338-353.

Zadeh, L. (1973). Outline of a new approach to the analysis of complex system and decision processes. *IEEE Transactions on System, Man, and Cybernetics, SMC-3*(1), 28-44.

Zand, D. E. (1972). Trust and managerial problem solving. *Administrative Science Quarterly, 17*, 229-239.

Zartman, I. W. (1977). Negotiation as a joint decision-making process. In I. W. Zartman (Ed.), *The negotiation process: Theories and applications.* (pp. 67-86). Beverly Hills, CA: Sage Publications.

Zartman, I. W. (1978). *The negotiation process: Theories and applications.* Beverly Hills, CA: Sage Publications.

Zeithaml, V. A., Rust, R. T., & Lemon, K. N. (2001). The customer pyramid: Creating and serving profitable customers. *California Management Review, 43*(4), 118-142.

Zhang, D. (2005). Web services composition for process management in e-business. *The Journal of Computer Information Systems, 45*(2), 83-91.

Zhou, C., Chia, L. T., & Lee, B. S. (2005). Semantics in service discovery and QoS measurement. *IT Professional, 7*(2), 29-34.

Zhu, K., Kraemer, K., Gurbaxani, V., & Xu, S. X. (2006). Migration to open-standard interorganizational systems: Network effects, switching costs, and path dependency. *MIS Quarterly, 30*(special issue), 515-539.

Zimmermann, O., et al. (2004). *Elements of service-oriented analysis and design: An interdisciplinary modeling approach for SOA projects*, IBM. Retrieved January 21, 2007, from http://www-128.ibm.com/developerworks/Webservices/library/ws-soad1/

Zucker, L. G. (1986). Production of trust: Institutional sources of economic structure, 1840-1920. In L. L. Cummings & B. M. Staw (Eds.), *Research in organizational behavior* (Vol. 8, pp. 53-111). Greenwich, CT: JAI Press.

About the Contributors

In Lee is an associate professor in the Department of Information Management and Decision Sciences in the College of Business and Technology at Western Illinois University. He received his MBA from the University of Texas at Austin and PhD from University of Illinois at Urbana-Champaign. He is a founding editor-in-chief of the *International Journal of E-Business Research*, the primary objective of which is to provide an international forum for researchers and practitioners to advance the knowledge and practice of all facets of electronic business. He has published his research in *Communications of the ACM, IEEE Transactions on Engineering Management, IEEE Transactions on Systems, Man, and Cybernetics, International Journal of Production Research, Computers and Operations Research, Computers and Industrial Engineering, Knowledge and Process Management, Business Process Management Journal, Journal of E-Commerce in Organizations*, and others. His current research interests include e-commerce technology development and management, agent-oriented enterprise modeling, and intelligent simulation systems.

* * * * *

Vikas Agarwal is a research staff member in IBM Research at India Research Lab since May 2000. He received his BE in computer science and engineering from Gorakpur University (India) (1998), and his MTech in computer science and engineering from Indian Institute of Technology Kanpur (2000) where his thesis dealt with remote process execution in heterogeneous Unix environments. He subsequently joined IBM's India Research Lab in New Delhi where he worked on e-commerce, grid computing, Web services, and semantic Web technologies. His research interests include distributed systems, Web/grid services, and object-oriented systems.

Praveen Aggarwal is associate professor of marketing at the University of Minnesota Duluth. He received his PhD from Syracuse University. His research interests include consumer choice behavior, assisted decision-making, and price promotion strategies. His research has been published in a number of journals including the *Journal of Consumer Marketing, Managerial, & Decision Economics, Journal of Marketing Management, Journal of Business Research, Journal of Consumer Behavior, Marketing Management Journal, Journal of Small Business Studies,* and *Journal of Product and Brand Management*, as well as in the proceedings of several national and international marketing conferences.

Fahim Akhter received his BSc in management information systems from the University of Missouri—St. Louis (USA), MBA from the Lindenwood University (USA), and PhD in informatics from the University of Bradford (England). He has more than 10 years of academic experience in lecturing, curriculum design, and research at the Colgate University of New York and Baruch College at City University of New York. Akhter's research activities are in the areas of e-commerce, trust, security, and user-interface design. He has written numerous papers in the areas of information technology and e-commerce, which have been published in international journals and proceedings such as *Information & Software Technology—Elsevier, International Journal of E-Business Research, IEEE*, and *ACM*. He has served in different program committees, advisory boards, and editorial review boards for various international journals and conferences.

Francesca Andreescu is lecturer in organisational behaviour and human resource management and member of the work and employment research unit (WERU) in the Business School at the University of Greenwich. After completing her first degree in business and management (1996) and an MSc in human resource management (1997). She moved on to working in the financial services for five years before she decided to go back to university to do her PhD. She is currently finalising her doctorate dissertation, which is near completion on the role of the human resource function in strategy formulation and implementation at the University of Southampton, UK. Her research interests span the areas of strategic human resource management, change management and the impact of e-business on management practices in British commercialised public sector organisations.

Anol Bhattacherjee is an associate professor of information systems at University of South Florida. He received PhD and MBA degrees from the University of Houston and prior BS and MS degrees from Indian Institute of Technology (India). His research interests include information technology adoption and post-adoption, medical informatics, and virtual communities. His prior research has been published in *MIS Quarterly, Information Systems Research, Journal of Management Information Systems, Decision Sciences, Decision Support Systems, IEEE Transactions on Systems, Man, and Cybernetics, Data Base*, and *Information & Management*, among other refereed journals. The author also serves on the current editorial board of *MIS Quarterly*.

Ranjit Bose is a professor of management information systems and holder of Albert and Mary Jane Black endowed professorship at the Anderson School of Management of the University of New Mexico. He has received his BTech and MTech from Indian School of Mines, India and his PhD from the University of Texas at Austin. His primary research emphasis is on the design and development of intelligent decision support and e-business systems. His research has appeared in several computer science and MIS journals.

Amanda Diggles Cassidy is a project officer, Patient Administration System (PAS) Project, Information Services, Acute Health Systems, CASE Program. Cassidy earned her BIS, Honours (first class) at the University of Tasmania, Australia. She previously presented her research on trust in online B2B relationships at the Pacific-Asia Conference on Information Systems.

Taihoon Cha is associate professor of marketing in the Department of Management at Hankuk University of Foreign Studies, Seoul, Korea. His PhD in marketing is from Syracuse University. He has published several articles in academic journals such as the *Journal of Consumer Marketing* and *Journal of Product and Brand Management*. He has also presented his research work at major marketing conferences such as AMA, AMS, and ACR. His research work is in the areas of marketing strategy formulation and consumer behavior in online environments.

David M. Chiang is professor of operations management and logistics in the Department of Business Administration at The National Taiwan University, Taipei, Taiwan. He earned his PhD in management science from The University of Iowa (1992). Chiang's research interests include supply chain management, logistics management, and inventory management. He has published in *Annals of Operations Research, Journal of Management and System, BJU International, Journal of Management,* and *International Journal of Production Research.*

Florian Daniel is a PhD candidate in the Information Technology Department at Politecnico di Milano. His main research interests include conceptual modeling techniques for Web applications and Web services, active/reactive Web applications, and workflow management systems. His current research activities focus on the modeling of multi-channel and context-aware Web applications within the conceptual framework provided by WebML (Web modeling language) and on the component-based development of composite applications at the presentation layer. He has participated in the Italian research project FIRB MAIS (multichannel adaptive information systems) and is currently participating in the European research project COOPER. He graduated with full marks (cum laude) in computer science engineering at Politecnico di Milano in 2003. In 2004, he won a three-year grant for his PhD studies by the Italian Department of Education (MIUR).

Yanqing Duan is a reader in information systems at The University of Bedfordshire Business School. Her principal research interest is how the emerging information and communication technologies (ICT) can be effectively used in, and their impact on, supporting decision making, facilitating knowledge transfer, and improving skills development. This research focus is reflected in the context of ICT based knowledge management and transfer, use of intelligent systems in supporting organizational and individual decision making, small to medium enterprises (SMEs) adoption of e-commerce/e-business, and Web-based training systems for SMEs. She has coordinated many European Commission funded research projects and published about 90 papers in journals, books, and international conference proceedings.

Marlon Dumas is associate professor at the Faculty of IT, Queensland University of Technology, Brisbane, Australia. His research interests fall in the area of BPM and service-oriented architectures (SOA). He is co-author of more than 80 publications in these and related areas, and co-editor of a book on process-aware information systems. He is an active consultant in the area of BPM and SOA and chief investigator in a number of research projects co-sponsored by industry partners, including SAP.

Shyh-Rong Fang currently is a professor in the Department of Business Administration at the National Chung-Hsing University, Taichung Taiwan R.O.C. He obtained his doctoral degree in business management from National Taiwan University (1993). He has published extensively in the marketing and management fields. His current research focuses on relationship marketing, services marketing, and marketing management.

Pongsak Hoontrakul is distinctively known for both scholar and practitioner worlds. Academically he is a senior research fellow at Sasin of Chulalongkorn University, Thailand. Capital market, derivative products, banking, and financial economics are among his recent studies. His current researches are in information economics, travel industry, and new economy. Internationally, he is a member of International Advisory Council of Schulich School of Business, York University, Toronto, a board member of Asia Finance Association, Singapore, and a past member of World Economic Forum, Geneva. Commercially, Dr. Pongsak serves as a Chairman of Audit Committee and independent director of United Overseas Bank (Thai) Pcl a subsidiary of United Overseas Bank Group, Singapore As a founder of www.A2Z-protravel.com, he has pioneered an online travel intermediary for Thailand. In the political areas, his past positions included the advisor to Deputy Prime Minister (for ICT) and the advisor to the Parliament Committee for Economic Affair and Human Rights. Currently, he is an advisor to the Senate Committee for Fiscal, Banking, and Financial Institution

Xiaoqing Huang is currently a senior engineer and chief supervisor of general engineer office at Guangxi Institute of Supervising and Testing on Product Quality. He received his MA from Wuhan University of Technology in 1991. He was a visiting scholar of the Albers School of Business and Economics of Seattle University in 2003.

Wendy Hui holds a BE in electrical and electronics engineering from the University of Canterbury, New Zealand, an MBA from the Chinese University of Hong Kong, and a PhD in information systems from the Hong Kong University of Science and Technology. Her research interests include information security and e-learning. Her works have been published in the *Communications of the AIS, Journal of Information Technology Theory and Applications*, and a number of peer-reviewed conference proceedings. She is currently teaching information security at the Abu Dhabi campus.

Yuan-Chu Hwang is a PhD candidate for information management in National Chengchi University, Taiwan. He received the BS degree in computer science & engineering from Yuan-Ze University (1997) and the MS degree in information management from National Chungcheng University (1999). His research interests include mobile/ubiquitous commerce and privacy/trust issues for social mobile applications.

Wen-Jnag (Kenny) Jih currently is a professor of computer information systems at the Jennings A. Jones College of Business of the Middle Tennessee State University. He previously taught at Longwood University (Virginia), University of Tennessee at Chattanooga, Auburn University (Alabama), Da-Yeh University (Taiwan), and Chung-Yuan Christian University. He also served as the dean of School of Management at Da-Yeh University from 1997 to 2001. His recent research interests include e-commerce, m-commerce, knowledge management, e-CRM, strategic impact of information technologies, network design and management, and innovative instruction methods in information systems.

Neeran Karnik is a product architect with the Data Center Management Group at Symantec Corp. He obtained his BE degree in computer engineering from Mumbai University (1991), and his PhD in computer science from the University of Minnesota (1998). His areas of interest include systems management, autonomic computing, service-oriented architecture, and security.

Ben Kim is Genevieve Albers professor in the Department of Management and also director of the Center for Electronic Commerce and Information Systems at Seattle University. Before joining Seattle

University, he taught at the University of Nebraska - Lincoln for 10 years. He holds PhD, MBA, and BA degrees from the University of Minnesota, University of Washington, and Seoul National University, respectively. His teaching and research interests include corporate information strategy and management, e-commerce, and information/communication technology of East Asia. He has conducted seminars on information systems and corporate strategies for government agencies and businesses of the United States, Korea, and Eastern European countries.

Seunghan Kim is a principal consultant of SCM business group in Samsung SDS, which is the SI (system integration) affiliate of the Samsung conglomerate. He holds a PhD from Seoul National University, Seoul, Korea. His research interests focus on electronic commerce, supply chain management, and logistics. He has many years of consulting experience with various companies from a variety of industries including CPG, retail, healthcare, electronics, and high-tech

Arun Kumar is a research staff member at the New Delhi facility of IBM Research since 1999. He has contributed to various distributed systems projects specifically in the areas of Web services, semantic Web, grid computing, eUtilities, access control, and Web server farms. Prior to that, he worked briefly as a software engineer with Hughes Software Systems, India. His current research interests include Web services, semantic Web technologies, systems management, data modeling, and object-oriented programming. Kumar received a master of Technology in computer science and engineering from Indian Institute of Technology Madras, India (1999), a master of computer science from DAVV Indore, India (1997), and a bachelor of computer science from University of Delhi, India (1995). He is in the program committee for ACM SAC 2007—Semantic Web and Applications Track and has been a reviewer for several conferences.

Marcello La Rosa is a PhD candidate within the business process management group of the Faculty of IT, Queensland University of Technology, Brisbane, Australia. He graduated in computer engineering at Politecnico di Torino, Italy (2005). Since then La Rosa has been conducting research in the areas of service-oriented architectures and BPM, with a focus on business process models configuration.

Albert L. Lederer is a professor of information systems in the Gatton College of Business and Economics of the University of Kentucky. He earned his PhD in industrial and systems engineering, his MS in computer and information science from the Ohio State University, and his BA in psychology from the University of Cincinnati. His research has appeared in *MIS Quarterly, Communications of the ACM, Journal of MIS, Information Systems Research, Decision Sciences Journal*, and elsewhere. His major research area is information systems planning.

Su-Fang Lee teaches marketing and business statistics in the Department of Business Administration at the Overseas Chinese Institute in Taiwan. She obtained her doctorate degree in business management from the DaYeh University. She has two master degrees, one in statistics and another one in agricultural marketing. Her research interest centers around applications of Internet technologies in marketing and consumer behavior.

Wonyoung Lee is a director of a consulting firm, Marketing Lab. He holds a PhD in business administration from the Hankuk University of Foreign Studies, Seoul, Korea. His research interests are in the areas of electronic commerce, mobile commerce, and supply chain management.

Nongkran Lertpittayapoom is a lecturer at Information and Communication Technology (ICT) Program at Mahidol University, Thailand. She has recently graduated from Southern Illinois University Carbondale. Her major is management of information systems. She holds her Bachelor's degree in economics from Kasetsart University, Thailand, and a master's degree in business administration from Southern Illinois University Carbondale. She has presented her research at International Conference on Information Systems (ICIS), Hawaii International Conference on System Sciences (HICSS), Americas Conference on Information Systems (AMCIS), and Annual Meeting of the Decision Sciences Institute (DSI). Her research interests include knowledge management, interorganizational knowledge sharing, organizational learning, virtual collaborations, and electronic commerce.

Bryn Lewis is a computer scientist with a research background in artificial intelligence, machine learning, digital libraries, and classification systems. Recent projects have included development of SISMO (single input source multiple output), a knowledge and content management system that is able to be integrated with clinical systems to enable decision support. Lewis is currently working for the National Prescribing Service and engaged in a number of projects including electronic decision support.

Iain Morrison is professor of information systems at The University of Melbourne. His areas of expertise include IT strategic planning and policy development, information systems design and development, intellectual property and its management, IT contracts, business continuity planning, telecommunications; advanced technologies (XML, PKI, Web Services), and their application. Current research interests include the architecture, design, and deployment of distributed systems used for e-commerce including automated process flow.

Sony Nugrahanto received his bachelor's degree in computer science from the Sepuluh Nopember Institute of Technology (ITS), Indonesia (1998) and his masters degree in information systems from La Trobe University, Australia (2003). Before coming to Australia, he worked as a senior developer for BaliCamp, a software development company in Indonesia. Nugrahanto is currently a Doctor of Philosophy student at Melbourne University. His research investigates the use of workflow technology to develop guideline-based decision support systems.

Souren Paul is an associate professor of management information systems at the School of Business and Economics at North Carolina A&T State University. He holds bachelor's and master's degrees in electronics and tele-communications engineering from Jadavpur University, India, and a PhD in management information systems from the University of Wisconsin Milwaukee. He has published research articles in *Journal of Management Information Systems, Decision Support Systems, Information & Management,* and *Journal of Information Systems Education.* His current research interests are in the areas of cognition and knowledge sharing in collaborative technology supported group work, virtual teams, and organizational knowledge management systems.

Barbara Pernici is full professor of computer engineering at Politecnico di Milano. Her research interests include cooperative information systems, workflow management systems, information systems modeling and design, temporal databases, and applications of database technology. She holds a Dr. Eng. from Politecnico di Milano and a master's of science in computer science from Stanford University. She has published 35 papers in international journals, including *IEEE* and *ACM Transactions*, co-edited 10 books, and published about 130 papers at the international level. She is an editor of the *Requirements Engineering Journal*. She has participated in several ESPRIT/IST projects (TODOS, Equator, ITHACA, F3, WIDE, Chorochronos). She was chief scientist of the Italian FIRB MAIS (multichannel adaptive information systems), 2002-2005. She is chair of Working Group 8.1 Design and Evaluation of Information Systems of IFIP (International Federation for Information Processing).

Carol Pollard is associate professor of information systems. Her research interests include decision support systems, impact of emerging technologies, and technology transfer. Her current research focuses on the healthcare sector and small to medium-sized firms. Carol has published her research in *MIS Quarterly, Journal of Management Information Systems and Information and Management,* and has presented at numerous national and international conferences. Carol is currently research director, Center for Applied Research on Emerging Technologies (CARET) at Appalachian State University; Vice President, International of GITMA; Chair, ACIS Executive Committee and an Advisory Board member of Teradata University Network.

Peter Raven is an associate professor of marketing and director of International Business Programs at Seattle University. He has published in a number of international scholarly journals, including the *Journal of Services Marketing, Transportation Journal, Asian Case Research Journal, Internet Encyclopedia, Journal of International Marketing, Journal of Consumer Marketing, Journal of Marketing Channels, Franchising Research: An International Journal, Journal of Global Marketing, Journal of Consumer Satisfaction, Dissatisfaction and Complaining Behavior, Journal of Advertising Research*, and others.

Ravni Rohatgi is an e-business graduate from University of Portsmouth. She works for a leading financial investment bank and is developing her research interest in e-business application in organisations.

Michael Rosemann is a professor for information systems and co-leader of the Business Process Management (BPM) Group at Queensland University of Technology, Brisbane, Australia. Michael is Chief Investigator of a number of research projects funded by the Australian Research Council (ARC) and industry partners such as SAP. He is the author/editor of five books, more than 130 refereed papers, and editorial board member of seven international journals. His book *Process Management* has been translated into German, Russian, and Chinese. Rosemann has extensive consulting experience in BPM across various industries including telecommunications, banking, insurance, utility, logistics, and media.

Sunil Sahadev is a PhD from the Indian Institute of Technology Chennai, India and a post doctoral fellow from the Asian Institute of technology Bangkok. He is presently working as a lecturer at the school of management, University of Sheffield, UK. His research interests include distribution channel management, marketing of high technology products and tourism management. He has published papers in such reputed journals like *European Journal of Marketing* and *Industrial Marketing Management.*

Jan-Hendrik Sewing is a senior consultant with Siemens Management Consulting, the international Top-Management Consultancy of Siemens AG, one of the world's largest electrical engineering and electronics companies. He has extensive consulting experience in the area of strategy and organization across various industries including telecommunications, automotive, plant automation, and utilities. Jan graduated in industrial engineering & management science at University of Karlsruhe, Germany, in 2003. During his studies, Sewing was invited to spend 6 months as visiting research assistant with the Business Process Management Group of the Faculty of IT, Queensland University of Technology, Brisbane, Australia.

Hyonkil Shin is a professor of business administration at the Hankuk University of Foreign Studies, Seoul, Korea. He holds a PhD in industrial engineering from the University of Texas at Arlington. His research interests are in the areas of electronic commerce and supply chain management.

Vijayan Sugumaran is an associate professor of management information systems in the Department of Decision and Information Sciences at Oakland University, Rochester, Michigan, USA. His research interests are in the areas of ontologies and semantic Web, intelligent agent and multi-agent systems, component based software development, knowledge-based systems, and data & information modeling. His most recent publications have appeared in *Communications of the ACM, Healthcare Management Science, Data and Knowledge Engineering, The DATABASE for Advances in Information Systems, Information Systems Journal, Journal of Information Systems and E-Business Management, Expert Systems with Applications,* and *Logistics Information Management.* Sugumaran is the editor-in-chief of the *International Journal of Intelligent Information Technologies* and also serves on the editorial board of seven other journals. He is the chair of Intelligent Information Systems track for the Information Resources Management Association International Conference (IRMA 2001, 2002, 2005, 2006) and the Intelligent Agent and Multi-Agent Systems in Business mini-track for Americas Conference on Information Systems (AMCIS 1999-2005). He also served as the chair of E-Commerce track for Decision Science Institute's Annual Conference, 2004.

Ching-I Teng is an Assistant Professor in the Graduate Institute of Business Administration, Chang Gung University, Taiwan. He received his PhD in management from National Taiwan University in 2002. His research interests include network effects, electronic commerce, and consumer psychology and behavior in cyberspace. He has papers published in (or accepted by) *CyberPsychology & Behavior, Technovation, The Service Industries Journal, and Electronic Commerce Studies,* and other 10 academic journals.

Yuan-Cheng Tsai received his BS of mechanical engineering degree from Chung Cheng Institute of Technology, MS of mechanical engineering, and the doctorate degree in business management from Da-Yeh University. He is the manager of Integrated Logistic Support in the Aeronautical Systems Research Division, Chung-Shan Institute of Science and Technology (CSIST) and serves as the deputy secretary general of the National Defense Association of Sino. His research interests include marketing, new product development management, human factor engineering, logistic management, and e-business.

Fan-Chen Tseng is an associate professor in the Department of Information and Electronic Commerce at Kainan University (KNU), Taiwan R.O.C. He received his BSEE and MSEE degrees from the department of electrical engineering at Taiwan University in 1984 and 1986, respectively. After that, he was with the Swire Group (Taiwan), United Microelectronics Corporation (UMC), and National Yi-Lan University. He received his PhD degree in information engineering at Taiwan University (2002). His current research and teaching interests are in the area of data mining and information retrieval. Recently, his interests also cover the area of electronic commerce management and Internet marketing.

Mark Xu has a PhD in MIS and is currently a principal lecturer and course leader in e-business at University of Portsmouth. Mark's specialist interests are in e-business strategy and implementation, executive information systems with a focus on environment information scanning. He has published more than 40 research papers in international journals and conferences. He co-authored two official study books for CIMA, and edited a book: managing strategic intelligence—techniques and technologies. He serves as a editorial board member and reviewer for a number of UK and US Journals.

Soe-Tsyr Yuan received her PhD from the Computer Science Department of Oregon State University in USA. Currently, she is a professor of information management in College of Commerce of National Chengchi University in Taiwan. Her contemporary research areas include mobile/ubiquitous commerce, intelligent agents and data mining, service-oriented computing, and service science.

Youlong Zhuang is an assistant professor of information systems at Columbia College. He received his PhD in decision sciences and information systems from the Gatton College of Business and Economics at the University of Kentucky. His research has appeared in *Decision Support Systems, International Journal of E-Business Research, International Journal of Electronic Business, Information and Management, International Journal of Electronic Commerce, Journal of Electronic Commerce Research, Electronic Commerce Research,* and *Database for Advances in Information Systems.* His major research area is electronic commerce.

Index

T

U

V

W

CPSIA information can be obtained at www.ICGtesting.com
Printed in the USA
LVOW021657011211

257420LV00004B/1/P

9 781599 048314